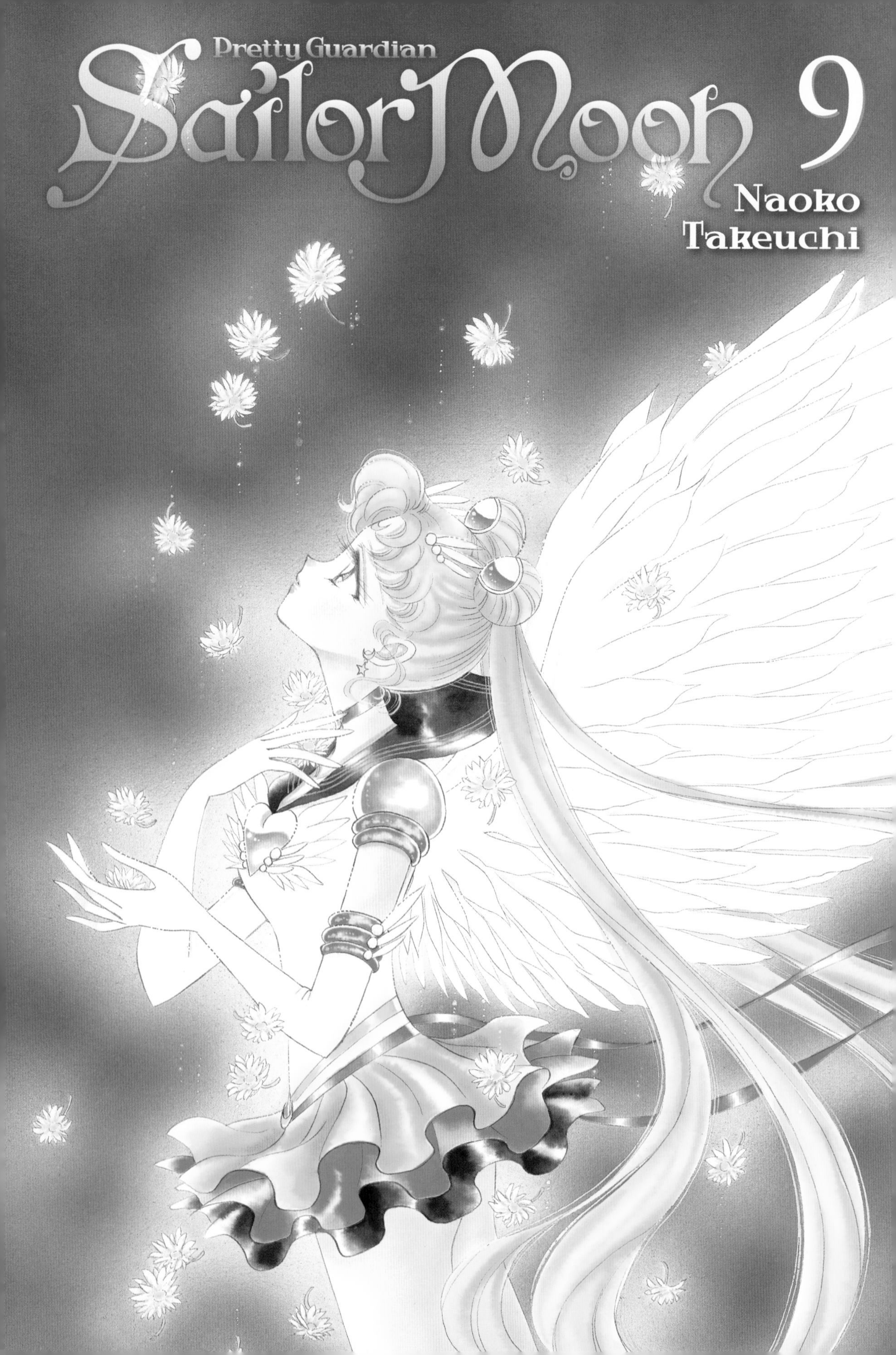
Pretty Guardian
Sailor Moon 9
Naoko
Takeuchi

CONTENTS

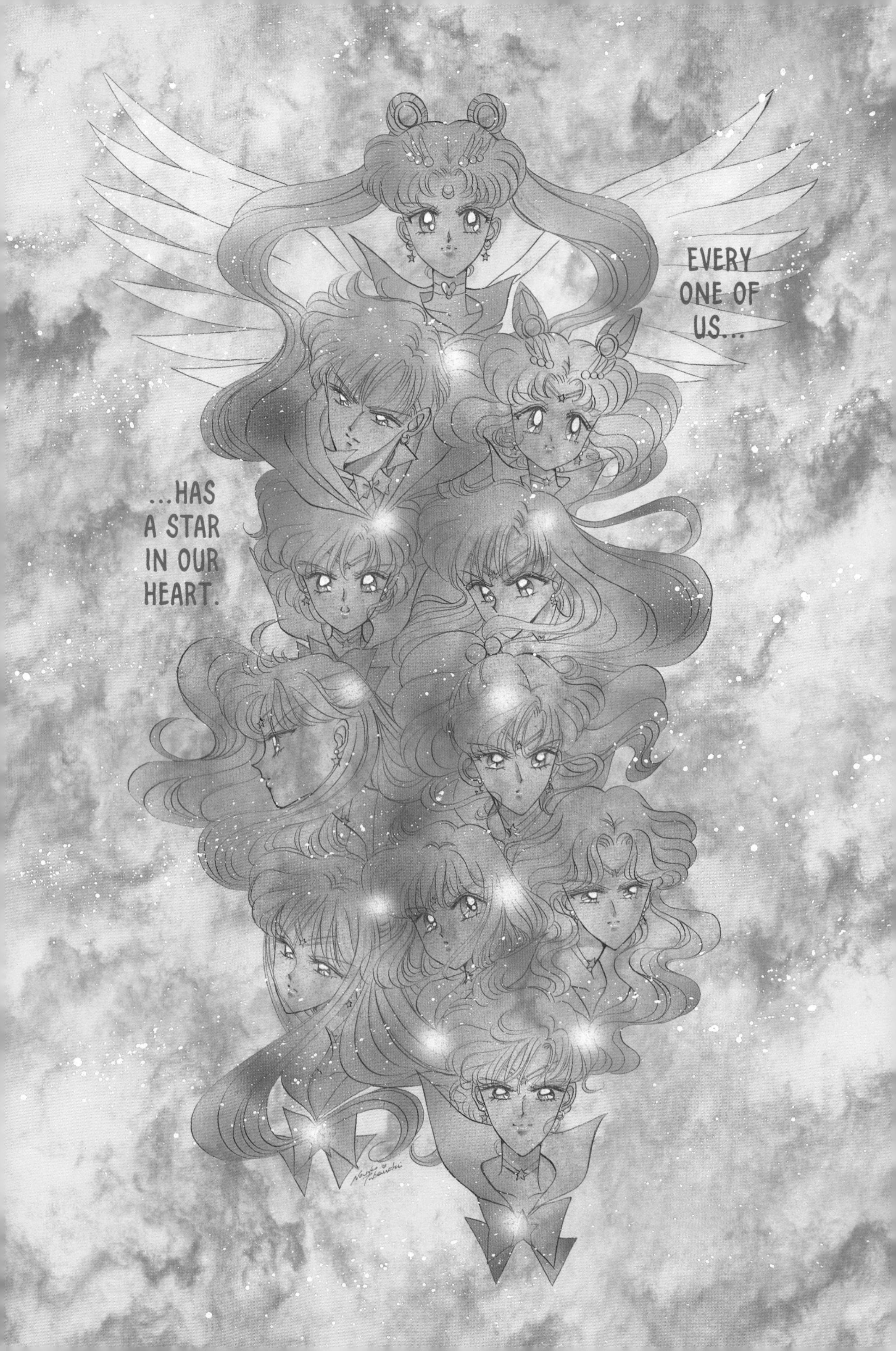
EVERY ONE OF US...
...HAS A STAR IN OUR HEART.

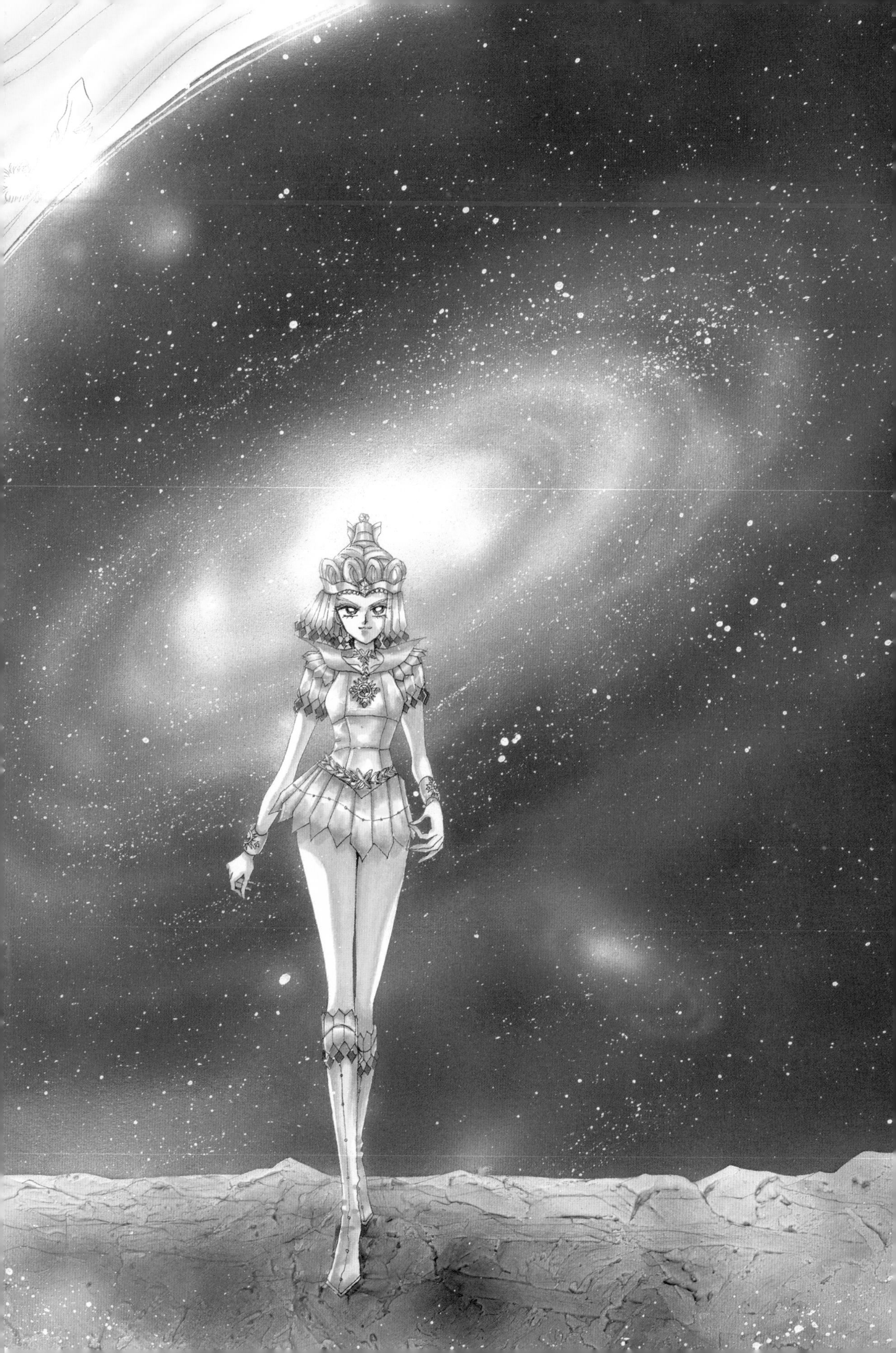

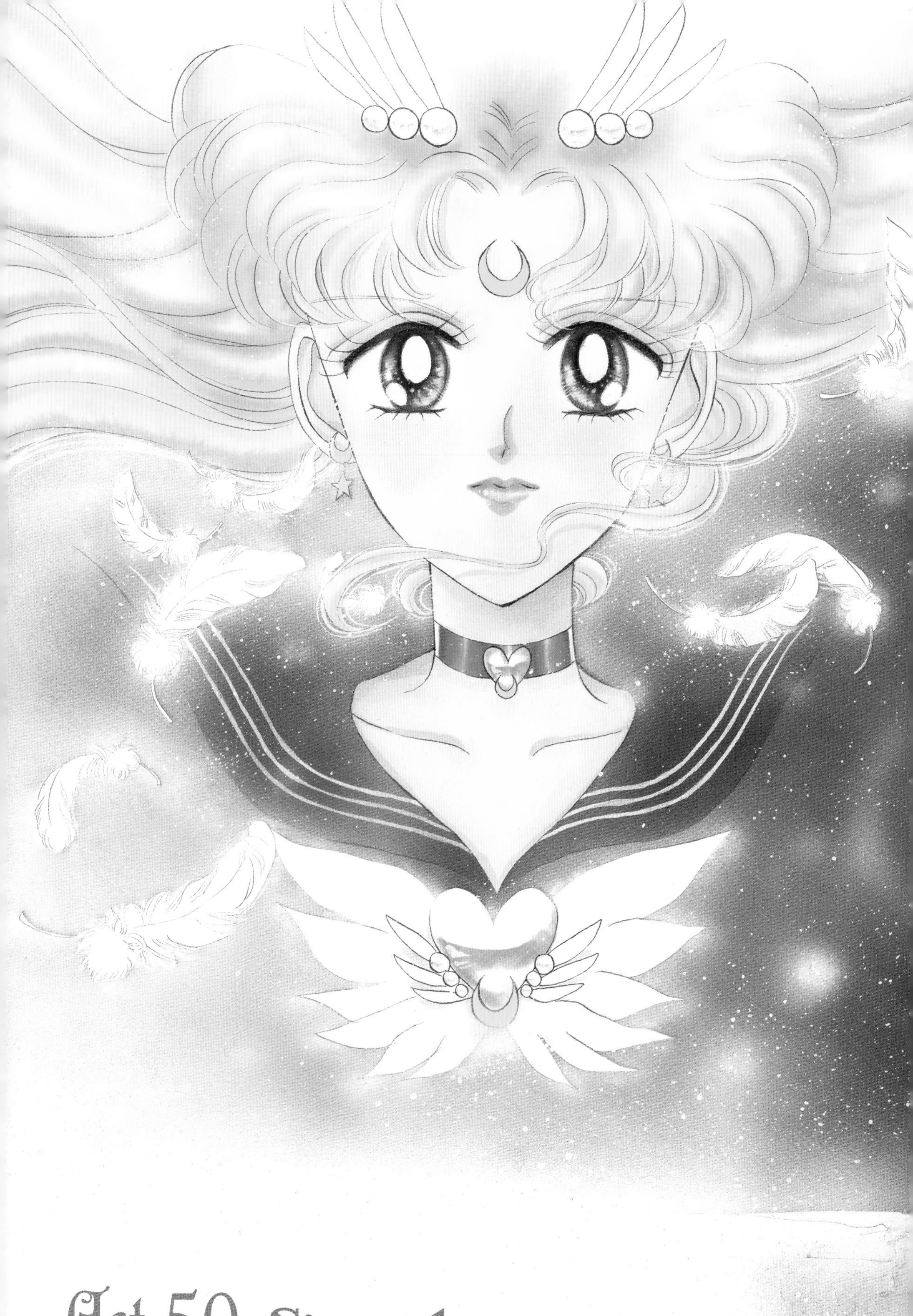

Act. 50 Stars 1

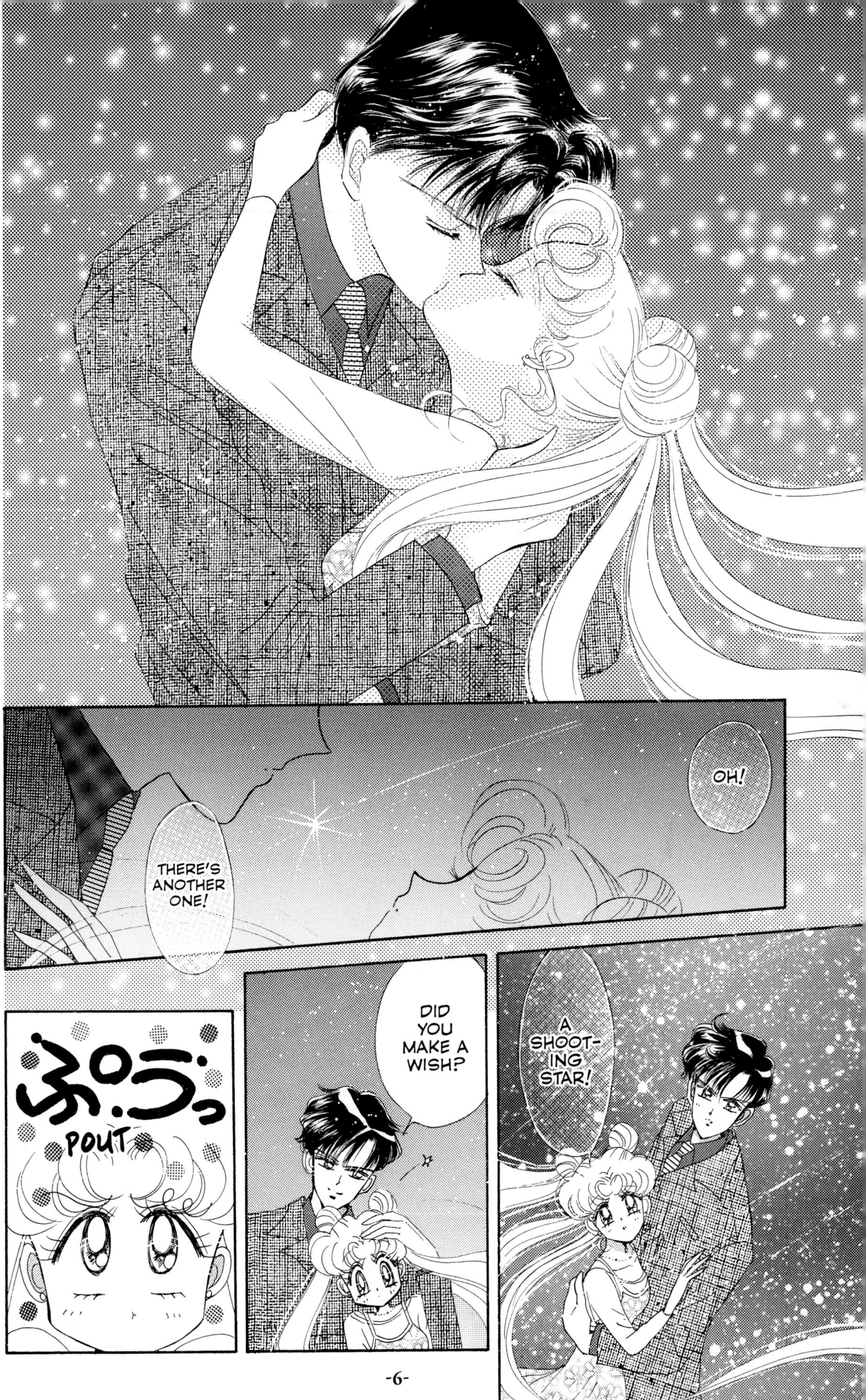
OH!
THERE'S ANOTHER ONE!
A SHOOT-ING STAR!
DID YOU MAKE A WISH?
ぷうっ
POUT

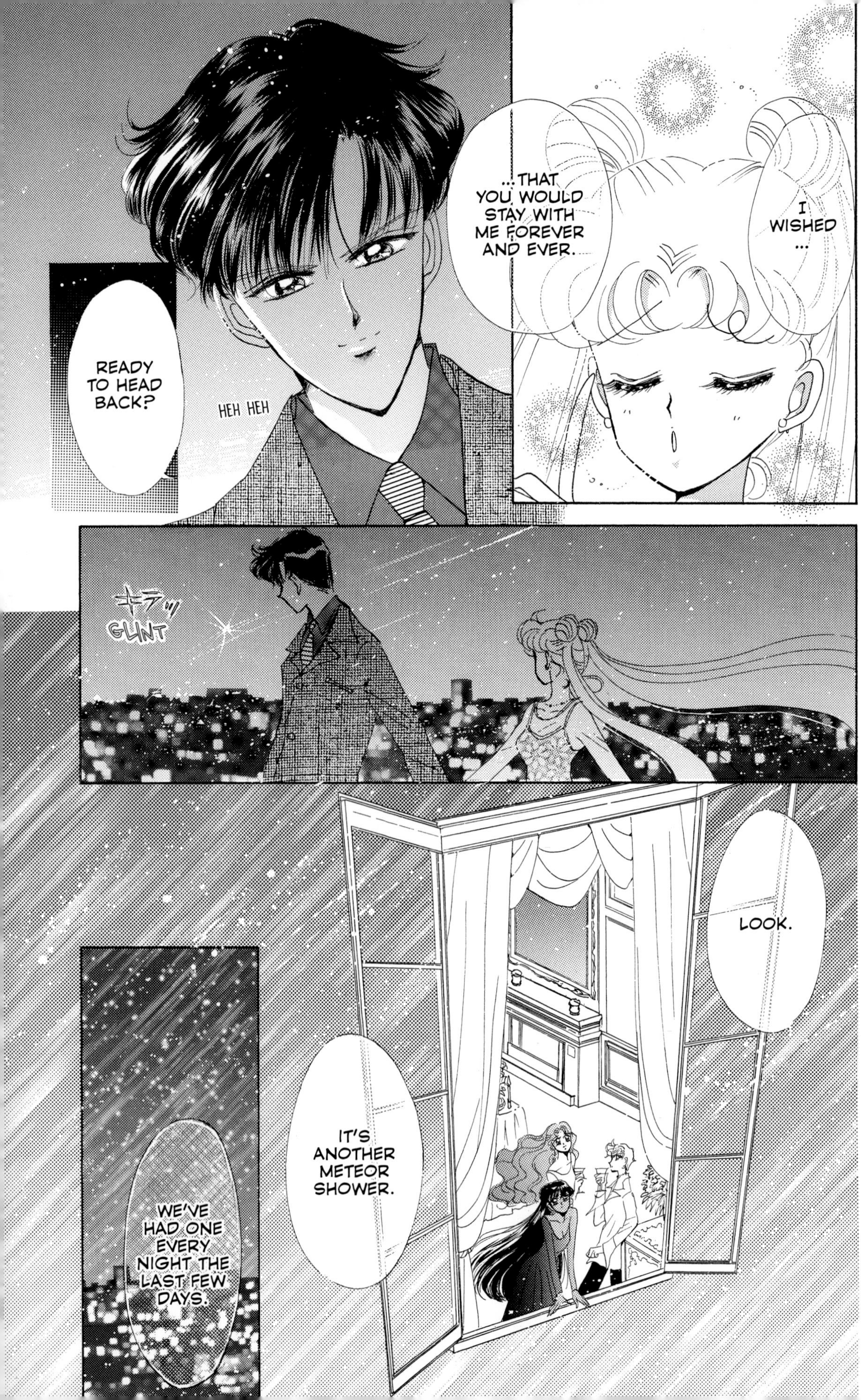
I WISHED ...
...THAT YOU WOULD STAY WITH ME FOREVER AND EVER.
HEH HEH
READY TO HEAD BACK?
キラッ
GLINT
LOOK.
IT'S ANOTHER METEOR SHOWER.
WE'VE HAD ONE EVERY NIGHT THE LAST FEW DAYS.

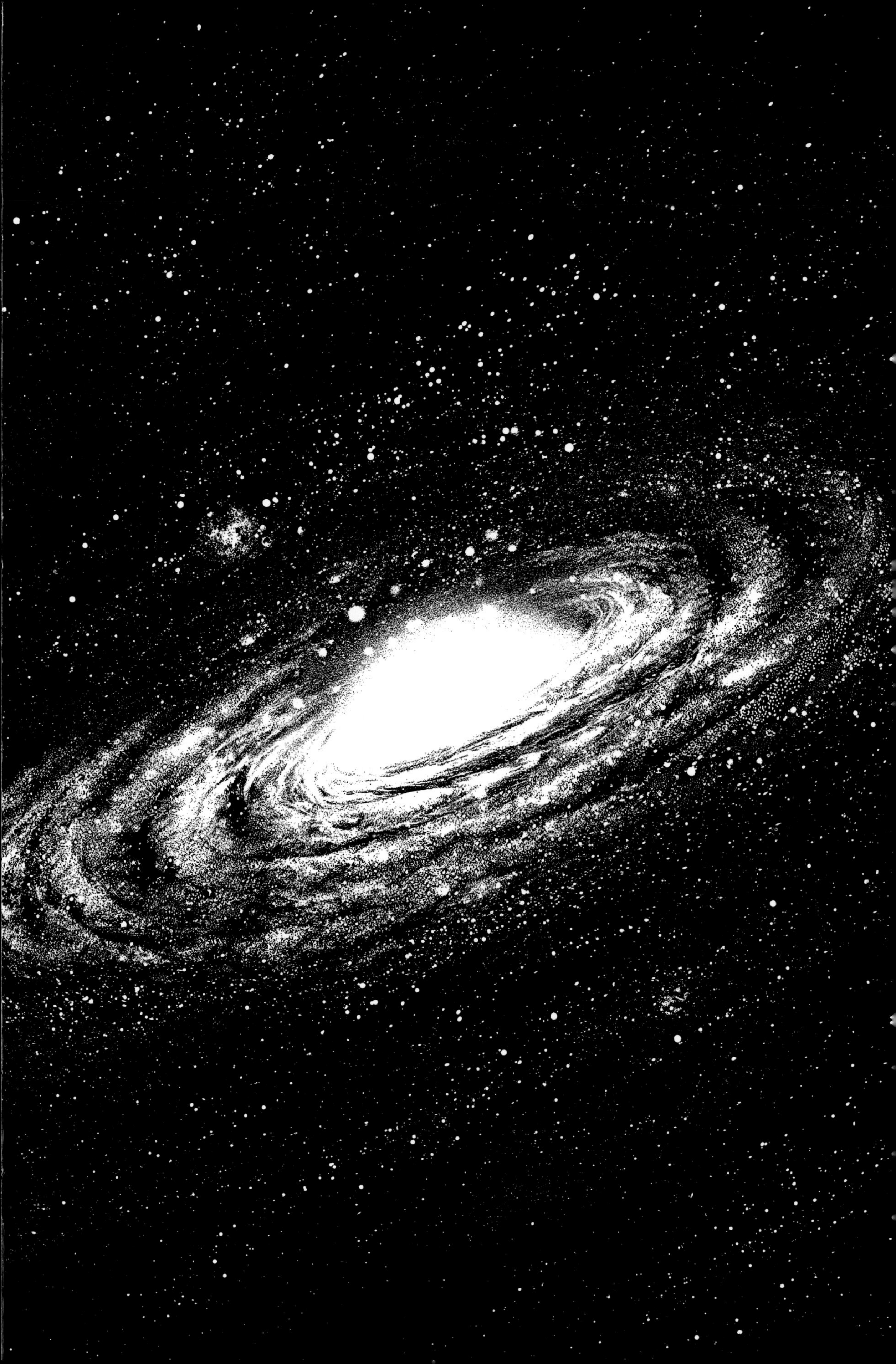

BEEEAM

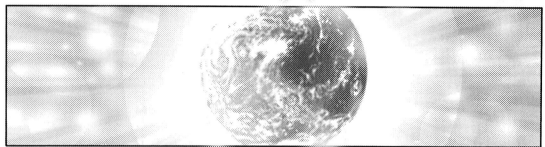

SUCH A BEAUTIFUL SHINE...

SO *THIS* IS THE LIGHT THAT COMES FROM THE SILVER MOON CRYSTAL AND THE GOLDEN CRYSTAL.

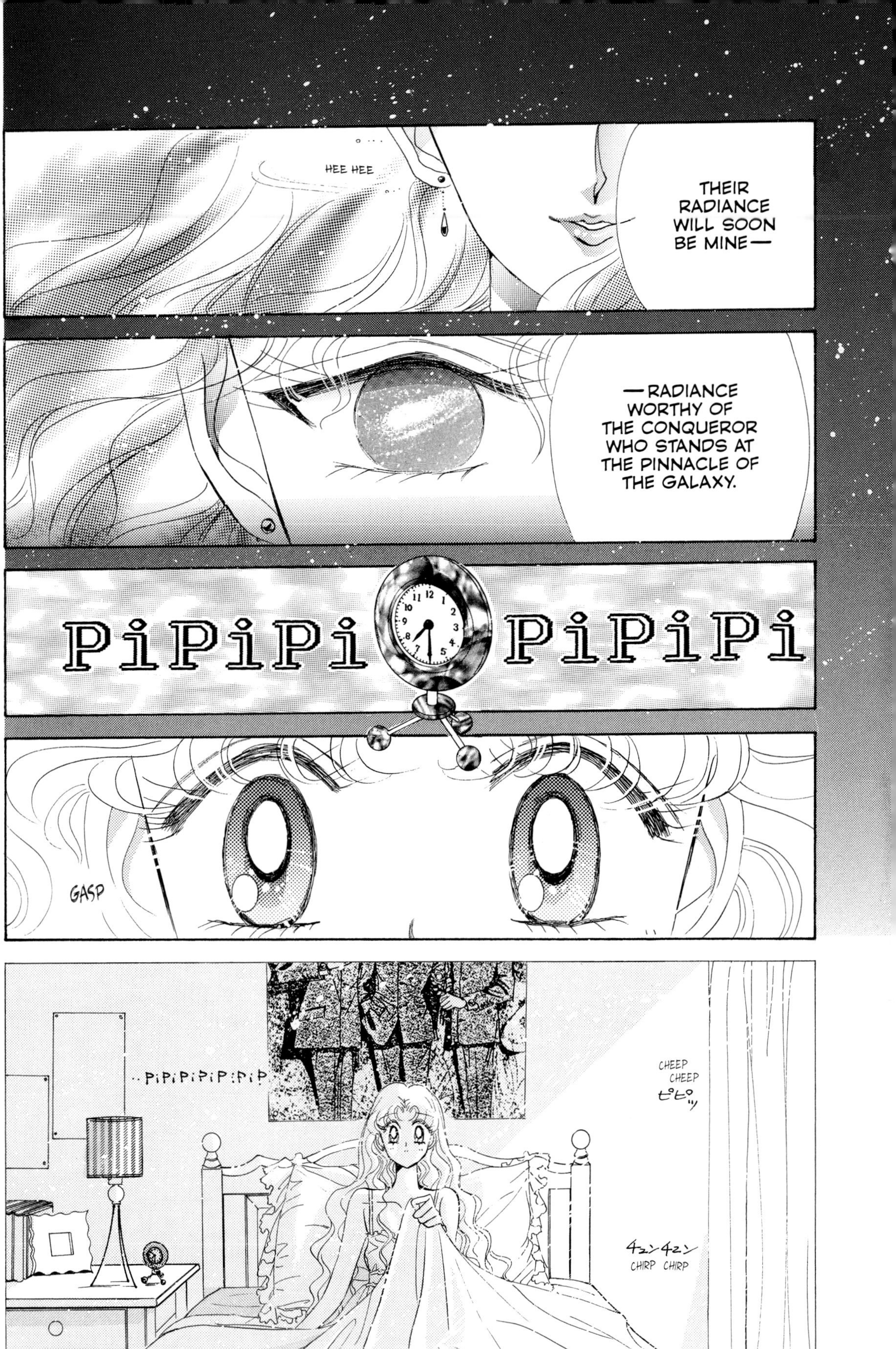
HEE HEE
THEIR RADIANCE WILL SOON BE MINE—
—RADIANCE WORTHY OF THE CONQUEROR WHO STANDS AT THE PINNACLE OF THE GALAXY.
PiPiPi PiPiPi
GASP
CHEEP CHEEP
ピピッ
チュンチュン
CHIRP CHIRP
..PiPiPiPiP:PiP

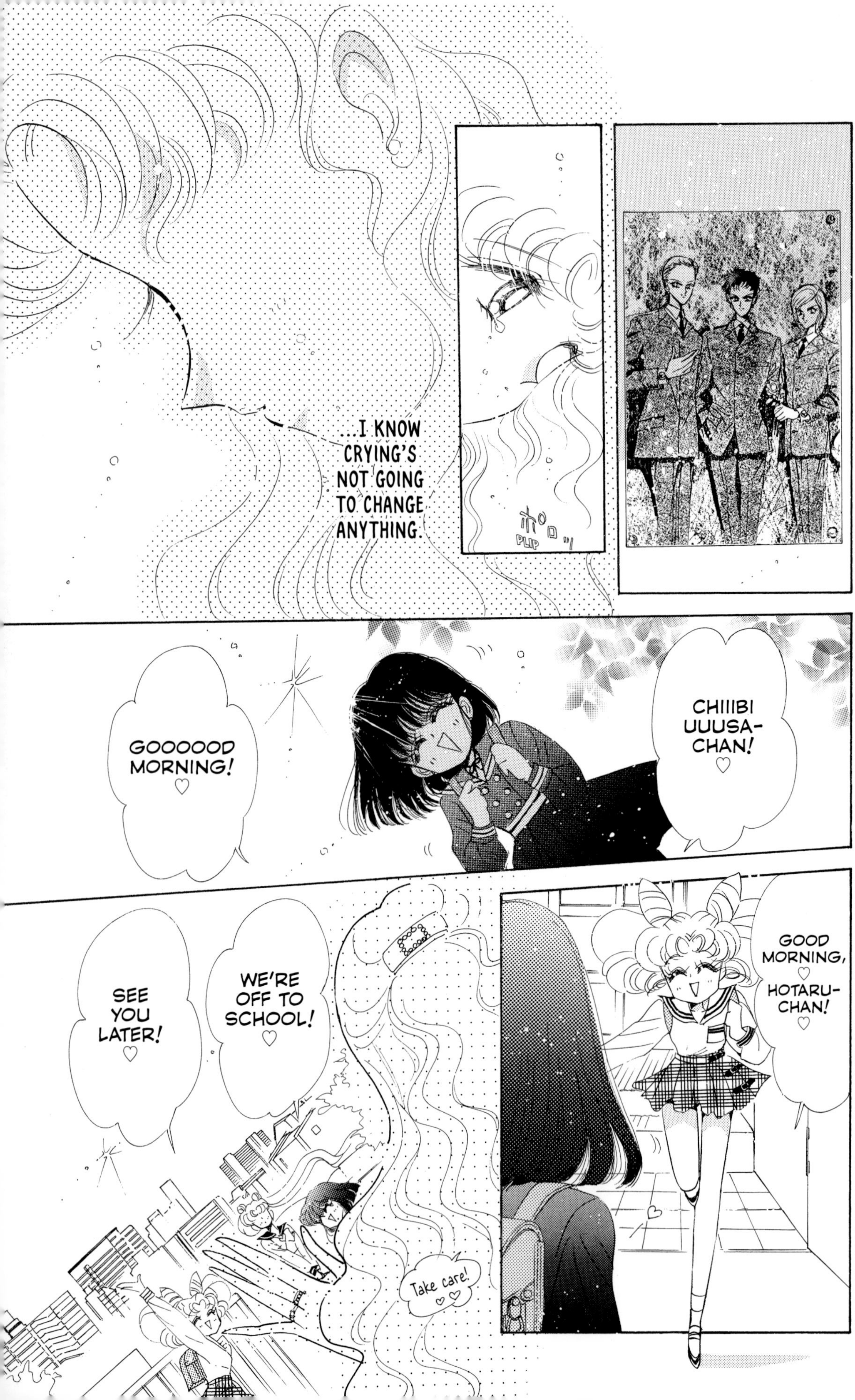
ホロッ
PLIP
...I KNOW CRYING'S NOT GOING TO CHANGE ANYTHING.
CHIIIBI UUUSA-CHAN! ♡
GOOOOOD MORNING! ♡
GOOD MORNING, ♡ HOTARU-CHAN! ♡
WE'RE OFF TO SCHOOL! ♡
SEE YOU LATER! ♡
Take care! ♡♡

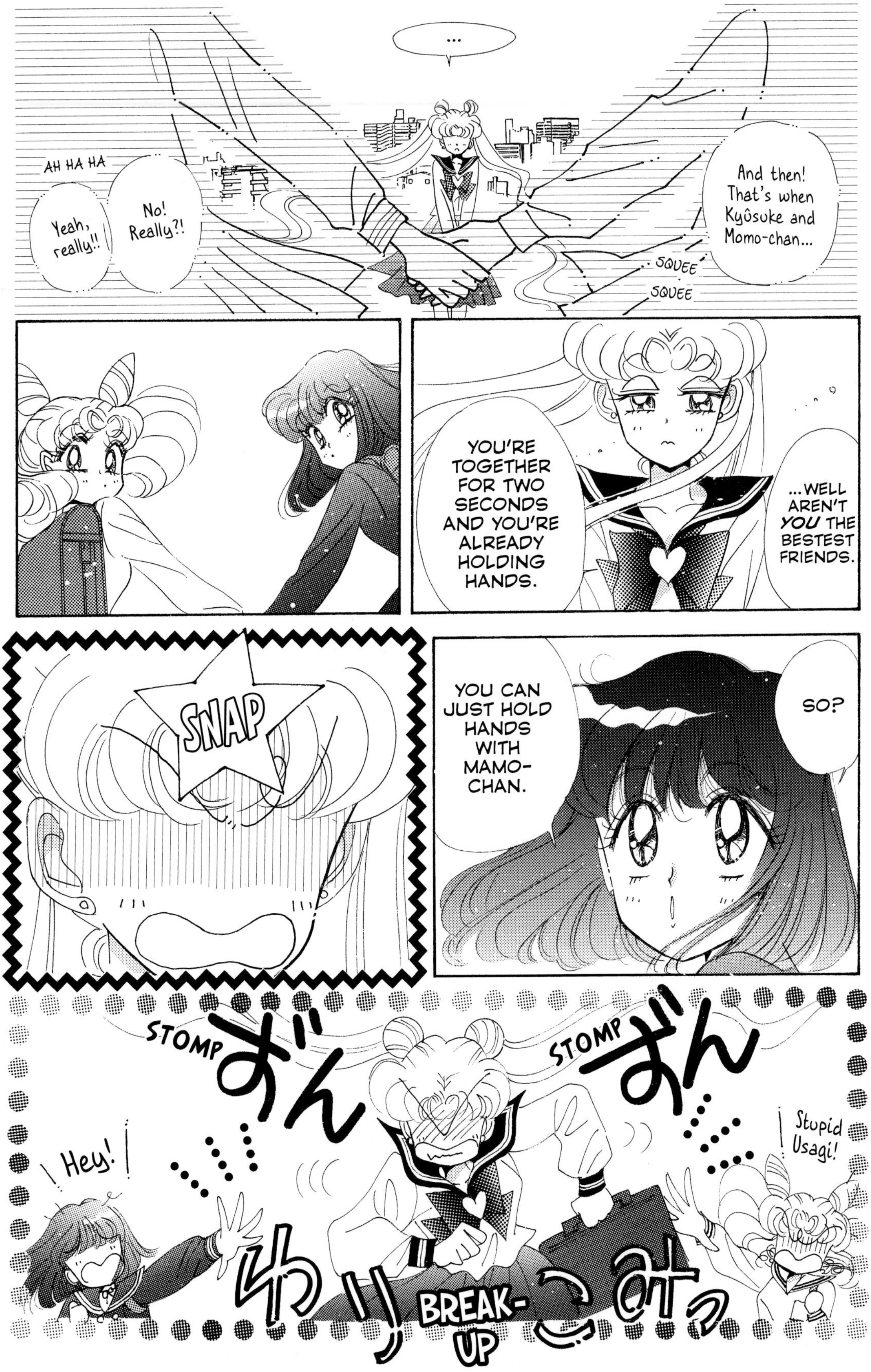
...
And then! That's when Kyûsuke and Momo-chan...
SQUEE
SQUEE
No! Really?!
AH HA HA
Yeah, really!!
...WELL AREN'T *YOU* THE BESTEST FRIENDS.
YOU'RE TOGETHER FOR TWO SECONDS AND YOU'RE ALREADY HOLDING HANDS.
SO?
YOU CAN JUST HOLD HANDS WITH MAMO-CHAN.
SNAP
STOMP ずん
STOMP ずん
Stupid Usagi!
Hey!
わりこみっ
BREAK-UP

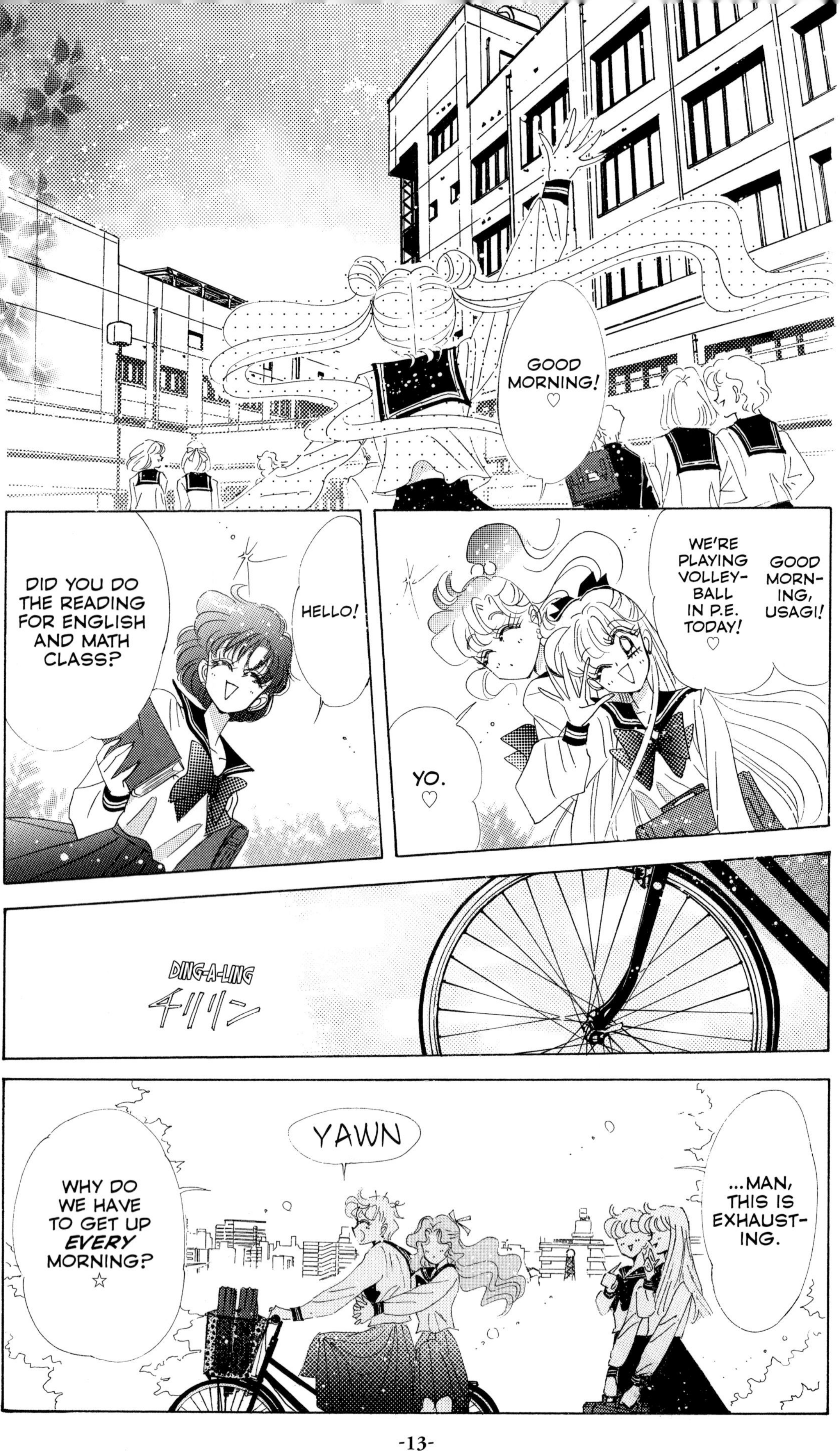
GOOD MORNING! ♡
GOOD MORN-ING, USAGI!
WE'RE PLAYING VOLLEY-BALL IN P.E. TODAY! ♡
YO. ♡
HELLO!
DID YOU DO THE READING FOR ENGLISH AND MATH CLASS?
DING-A-LING
チリリン
...MAN, THIS IS EXHAUST-ING.
YAWN
WHY DO WE HAVE TO GET UP *EVERY* MORNING? ☆

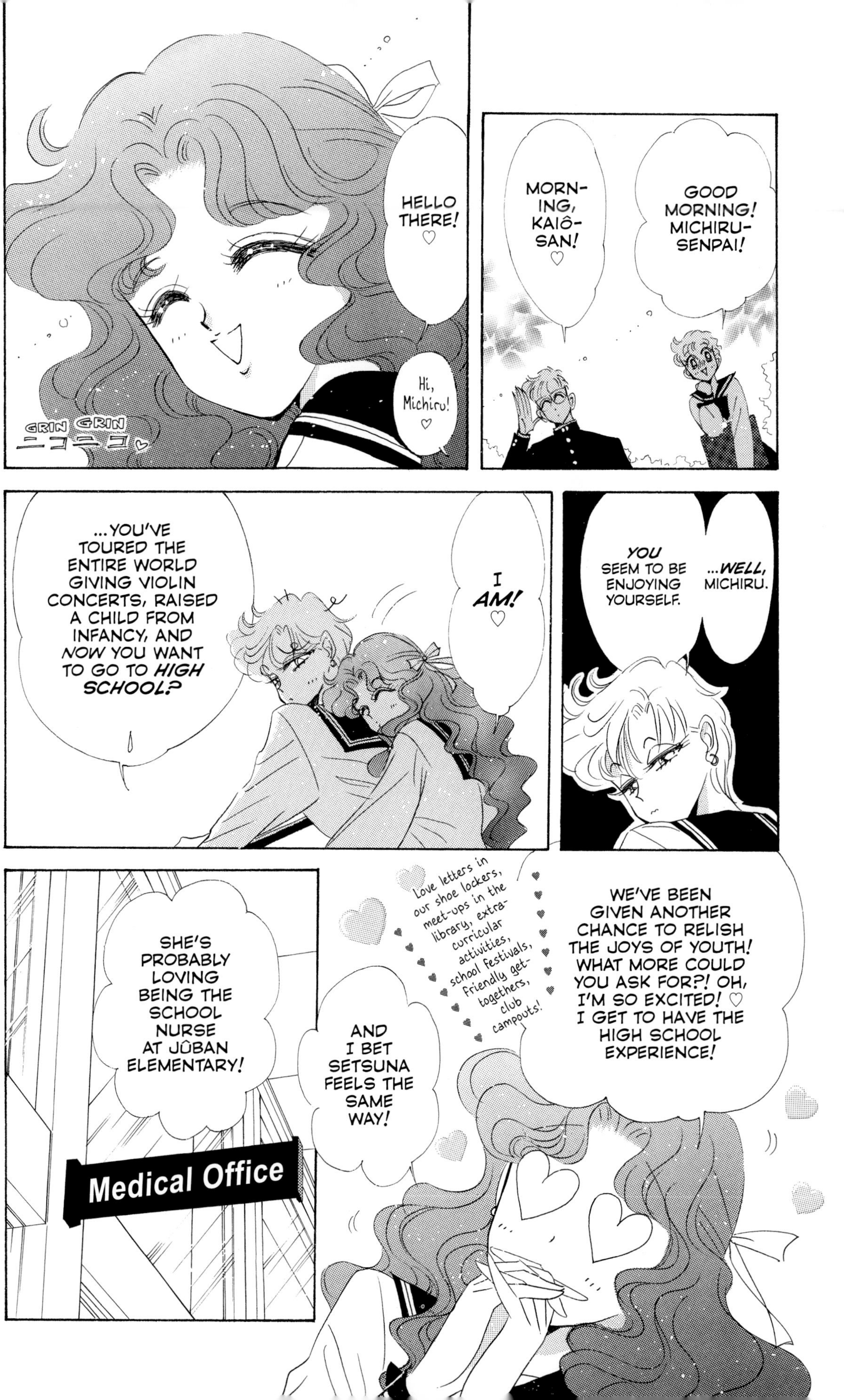
GOOD MORNING! MICHIRU-SENPAI!
MORNING, KAIÔ-SAN! ♡
HELLO THERE! ♡
Hi, Michiru! ♡
GRIN GRIN
ニコニコ♡
...WELL, MICHIRU.
YOU SEEM TO BE ENJOYING YOURSELF.
I AM! ♡
...YOU'VE TOURED THE ENTIRE WORLD GIVING VIOLIN CONCERTS, RAISED A CHILD FROM INFANCY, AND NOW YOU WANT TO GO TO HIGH SCHOOL?
WE'VE BEEN GIVEN ANOTHER CHANCE TO RELISH THE JOYS OF YOUTH! WHAT MORE COULD YOU ASK FOR?! OH, I'M SO EXCITED! ♡ I GET TO HAVE THE HIGH SCHOOL EXPERIENCE!
Love letters in our shoe lockers, meet-ups in the library, extra-curricular activities, school festivals, friendly get-togethers, club campouts!
AND I BET SETSUNA FEELS THE SAME WAY!
SHE'S PROBABLY LOVING BEING THE SCHOOL NURSE AT JÛBAN ELEMENTARY!
Medical Office

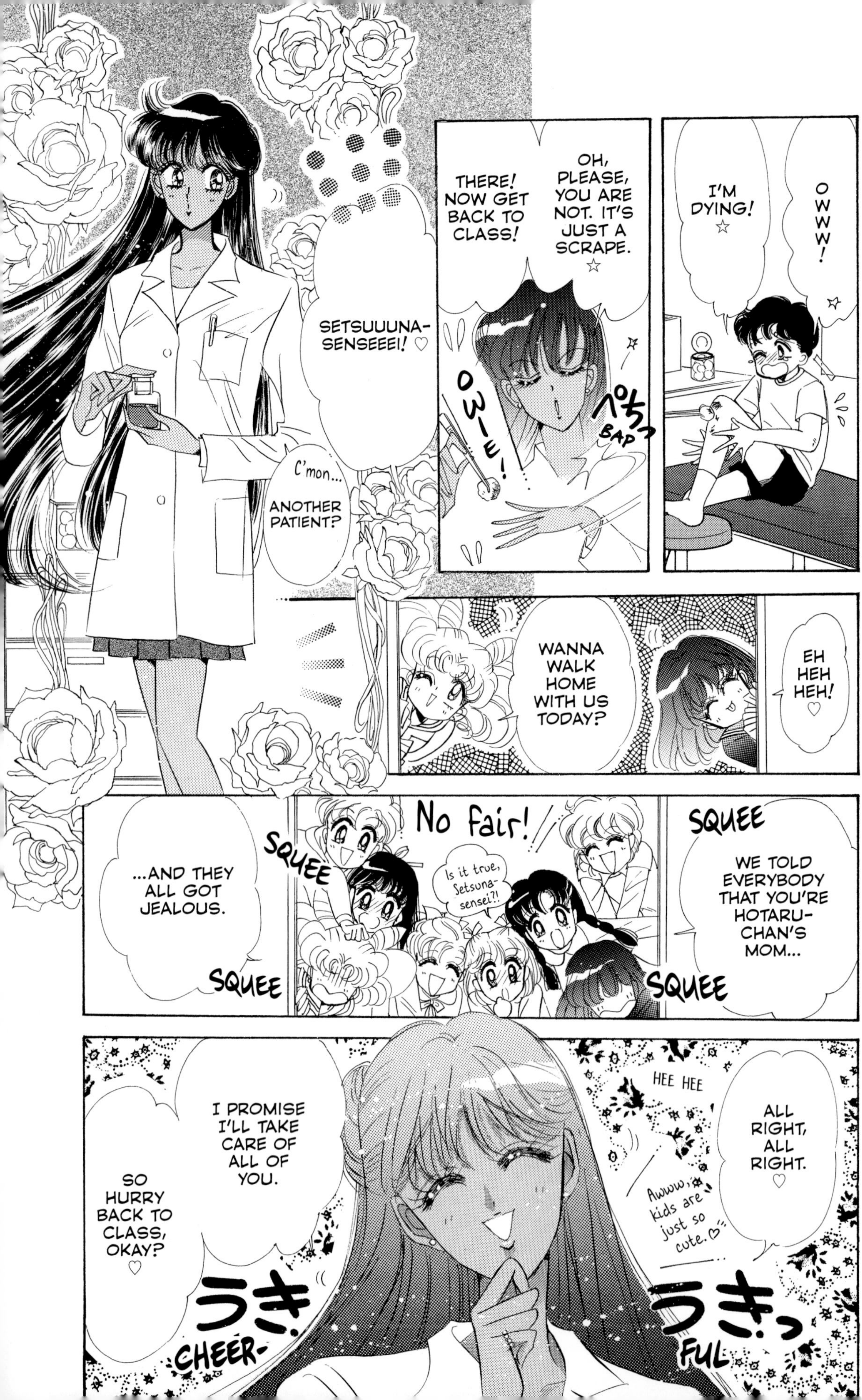
OWWW!
I'M DYING! ☆
OH, PLEASE, YOU ARE NOT. IT'S JUST A SCRAPE. ☆
THERE! NOW GET BACK TO CLASS!
ぺちっ
BAP
OWIE!
EH HEH HEH! ♡
WANNA WALK HOME WITH US TODAY?
SETSUUUNA-SENSEEI! ♡
C'mon...
ANOTHER PATIENT?
SQUEE
WE TOLD EVERYBODY THAT YOU'RE HOTARU-CHAN'S MOM...
SQUEE
No fair!
Is it true, Setsuna-sensei?!
SQUEE
SQUEE
...AND THEY ALL GOT JEALOUS.
ALL RIGHT, ALL RIGHT. ♡
HEE HEE
Awww, kids are just so cute. ♡
I PROMISE I'LL TAKE CARE OF ALL OF YOU.
SO HURRY BACK TO CLASS, OKAY? ♡
うきっ
FUL
うき
CHEER-

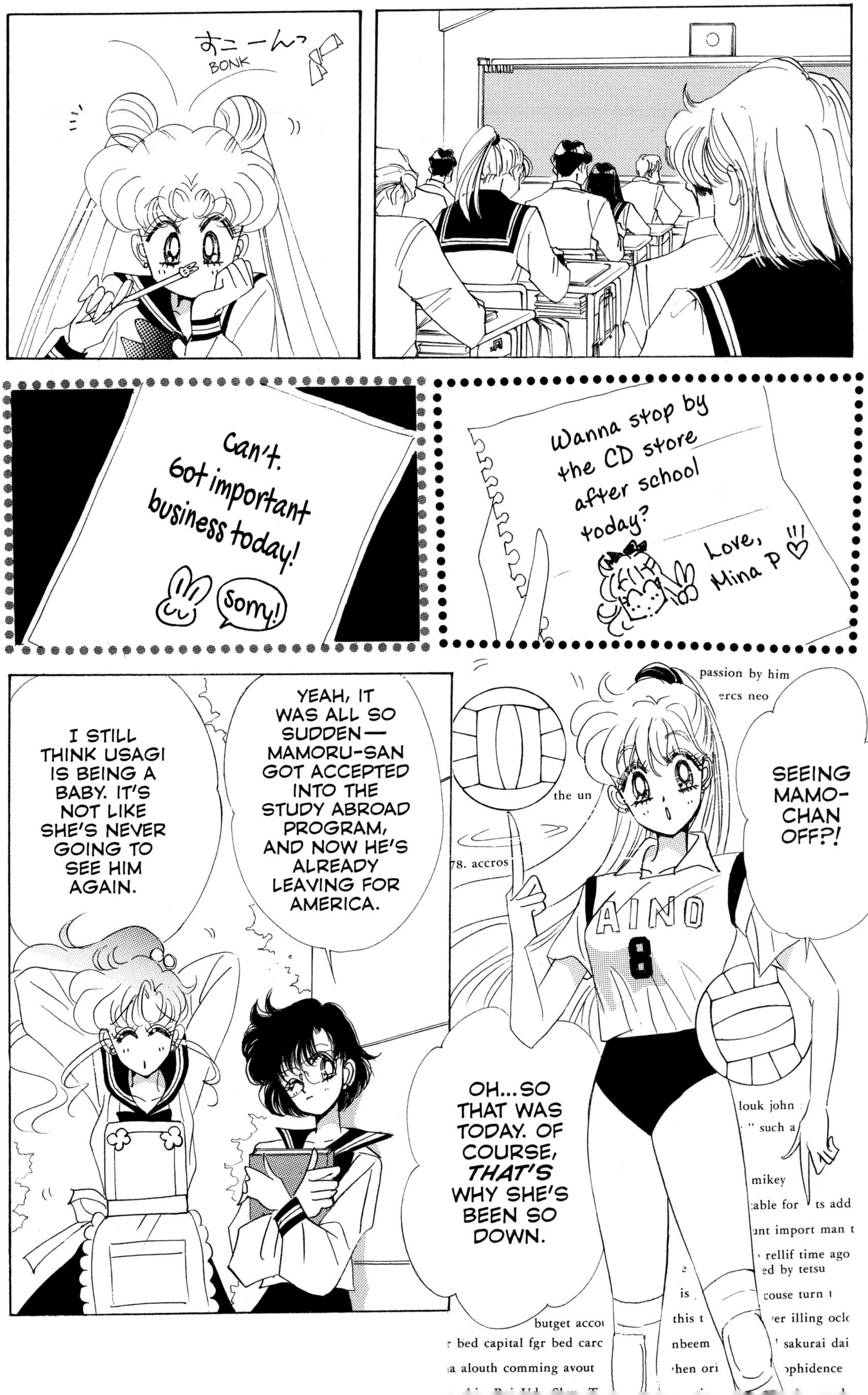
すこーんっ
BONK
Wanna stop by the CD store after school today?
Love, Mina P
Can't. Got important business today!
Sorry!
SEEING MAMO-CHAN OFF?!
OH...SO THAT WAS TODAY. OF COURSE, *THAT'S* WHY SHE'S BEEN SO DOWN.
YEAH, IT WAS ALL SO SUDDEN—MAMORU-SAN GOT ACCEPTED INTO THE STUDY ABROAD PROGRAM, AND NOW HE'S ALREADY LEAVING FOR AMERICA.
I STILL THINK USAGI IS BEING A BABY. IT'S NOT LIKE SHE'S NEVER GOING TO SEE HIM AGAIN.
AINO
8

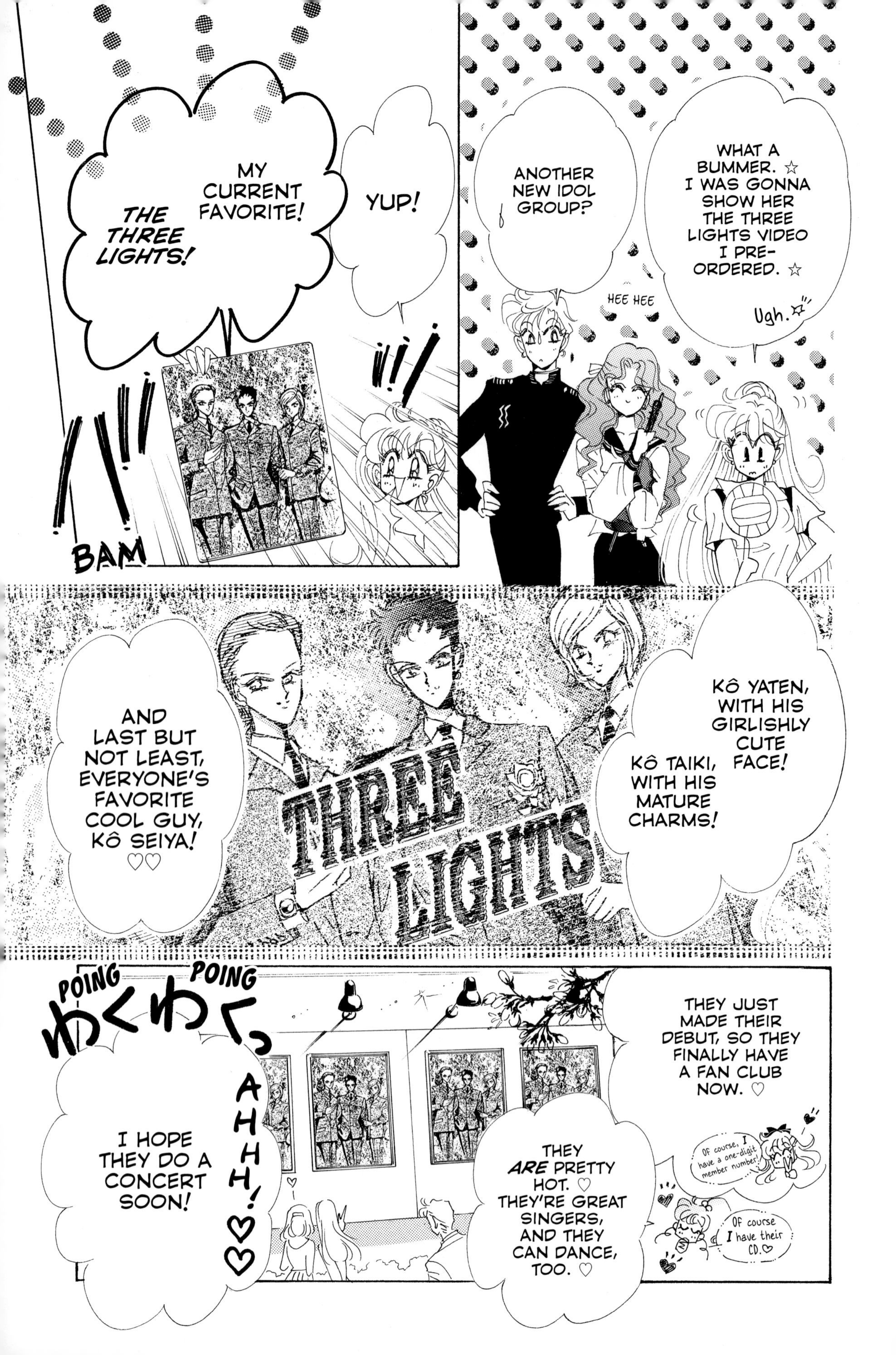
WHAT A BUMMER. ☆ I WAS GONNA SHOW HER THE THREE LIGHTS VIDEO I PRE-ORDERED. ☆
Ugh.☆
ANOTHER NEW IDOL GROUP?
HEE HEE
YUP!
MY CURRENT FAVORITE!
THE THREE LIGHTS!
BAM
KÔ YATEN, WITH HIS GIRLISHLY CUTE FACE!
KÔ TAIKI, WITH HIS MATURE CHARMS!
THREE LIGHTS
AND LAST BUT NOT LEAST, EVERYONE'S FAVORITE COOL GUY, KÔ SEIYA! ♡♡
THEY JUST MADE THEIR DEBUT, SO THEY FINALLY HAVE A FAN CLUB NOW. ♡
Of course, I have a one-digit member number!
Of course I have their CD.♡
THEY ARE PRETTY HOT. ♡ THEY'RE GREAT SINGERS, AND THEY CAN DANCE, TOO. ♡
AHHH!♡♡
I HOPE THEY DO A CONCERT SOON!
POING POING
わくわく

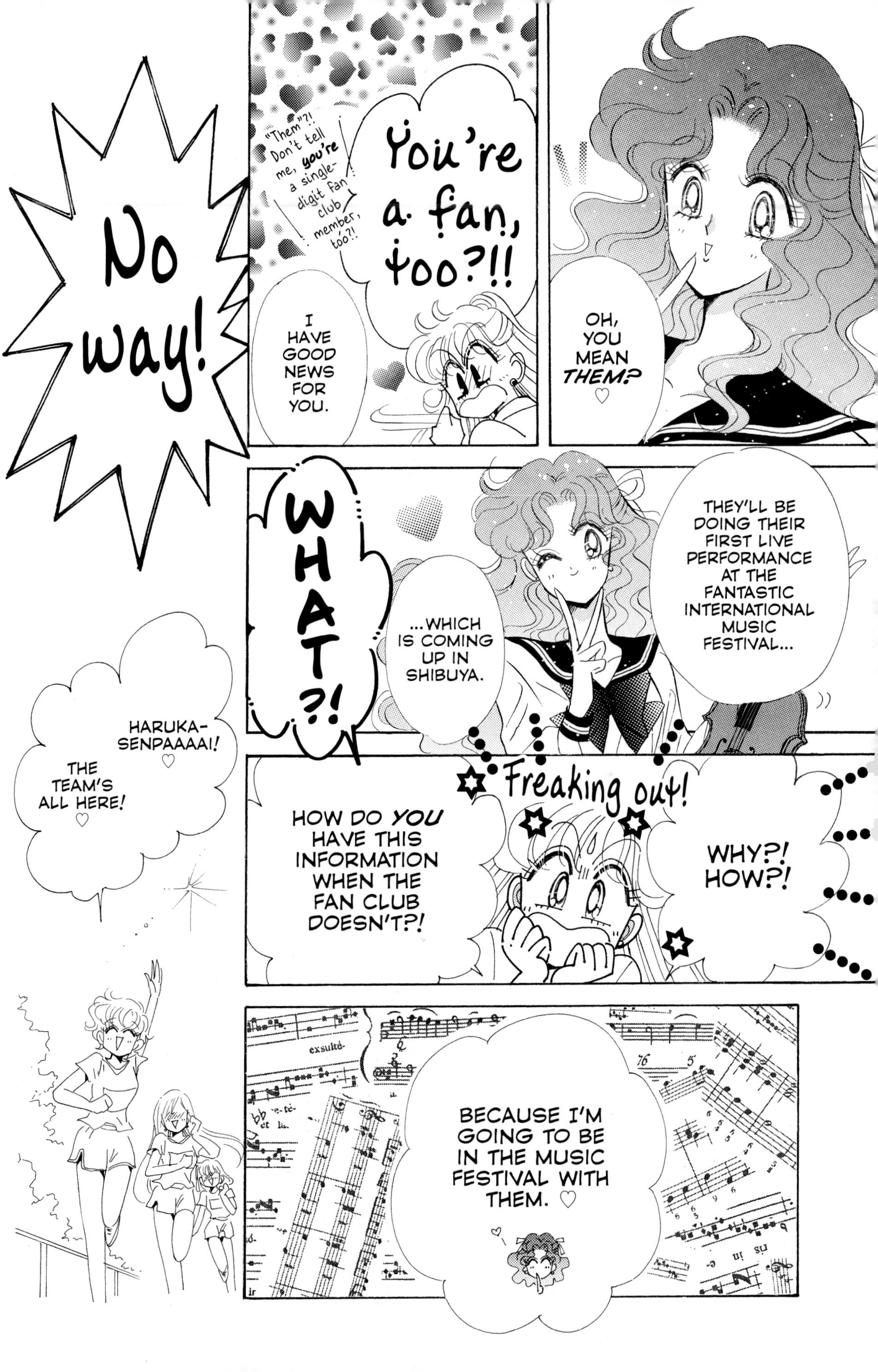

OH, YOU MEAN *THEM?* ♡
I HAVE GOOD NEWS FOR YOU.
You're a fan, too?!!
"Them"?! Don't tell me, **you're** a single-digit fan club member, too?!
No way!
THEY'LL BE DOING THEIR FIRST LIVE PERFORMANCE AT THE FANTASTIC INTERNATIONAL MUSIC FESTIVAL...
...WHICH IS COMING UP IN SHIBUYA.
WHAT?!
Freaking out!
WHY?! HOW?!
HOW DO *YOU* HAVE THIS INFORMATION WHEN THE FAN CLUB DOESN'T?!
BECAUSE I'M GOING TO BE IN THE MUSIC FESTIVAL WITH THEM. ♡
HARUKA-SENPAAAAI! ♡
THE TEAM'S ALL HERE! ♡

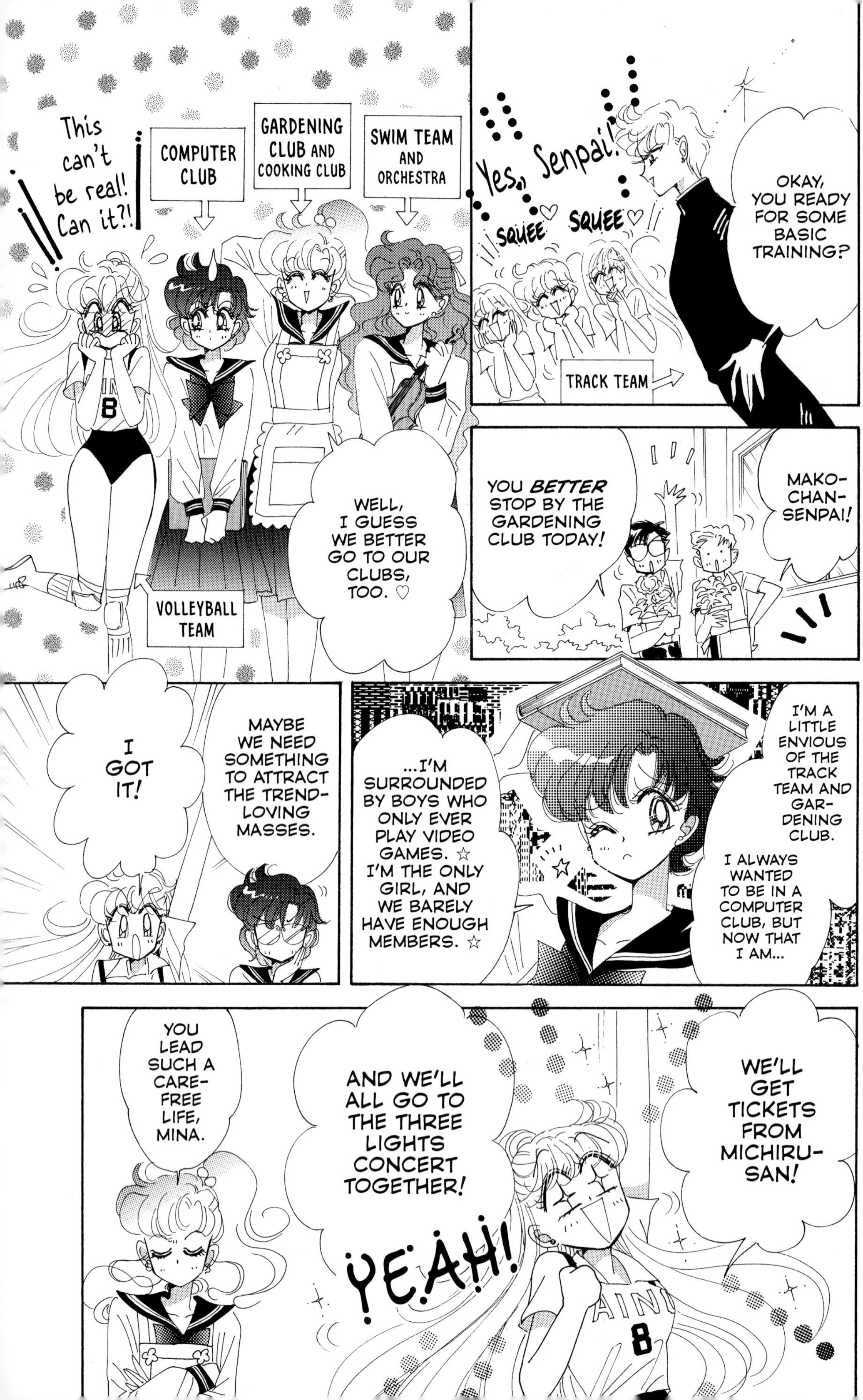
OKAY, YOU READY FOR SOME BASIC TRAINING?
Yes, Senpai!!
SQUEE♡
SQUEE♡
TRACK TEAM
MAKO-CHAN-SENPAI!
YOU *BETTER* STOP BY THE GARDENING CLUB TODAY!
SWIM TEAM AND ORCHESTRA
GARDENING CLUB AND COOKING CLUB
COMPUTER CLUB
This can't be real! Can it?!
WELL, I GUESS WE BETTER GO TO OUR CLUBS, TOO. ♡
VOLLEYBALL TEAM
I'M A LITTLE ENVIOUS OF THE TRACK TEAM AND GAR-DENING CLUB.
I ALWAYS WANTED TO BE IN A COMPUTER CLUB, BUT NOW THAT I AM...
...I'M SURROUNDED BY BOYS WHO ONLY EVER PLAY VIDEO GAMES. ☆ I'M THE ONLY GIRL, AND WE BARELY HAVE ENOUGH MEMBERS. ☆
MAYBE WE NEED SOMETHING TO ATTRACT THE TREND-LOVING MASSES.
I GOT IT!
WE'LL GET TICKETS FROM MICHIRU-SAN!
AND WE'LL ALL GO TO THE THREE LIGHTS CONCERT TOGETHER!
YEAH!
YOU LEAD SUCH A CARE-FREE LIFE, MINA.

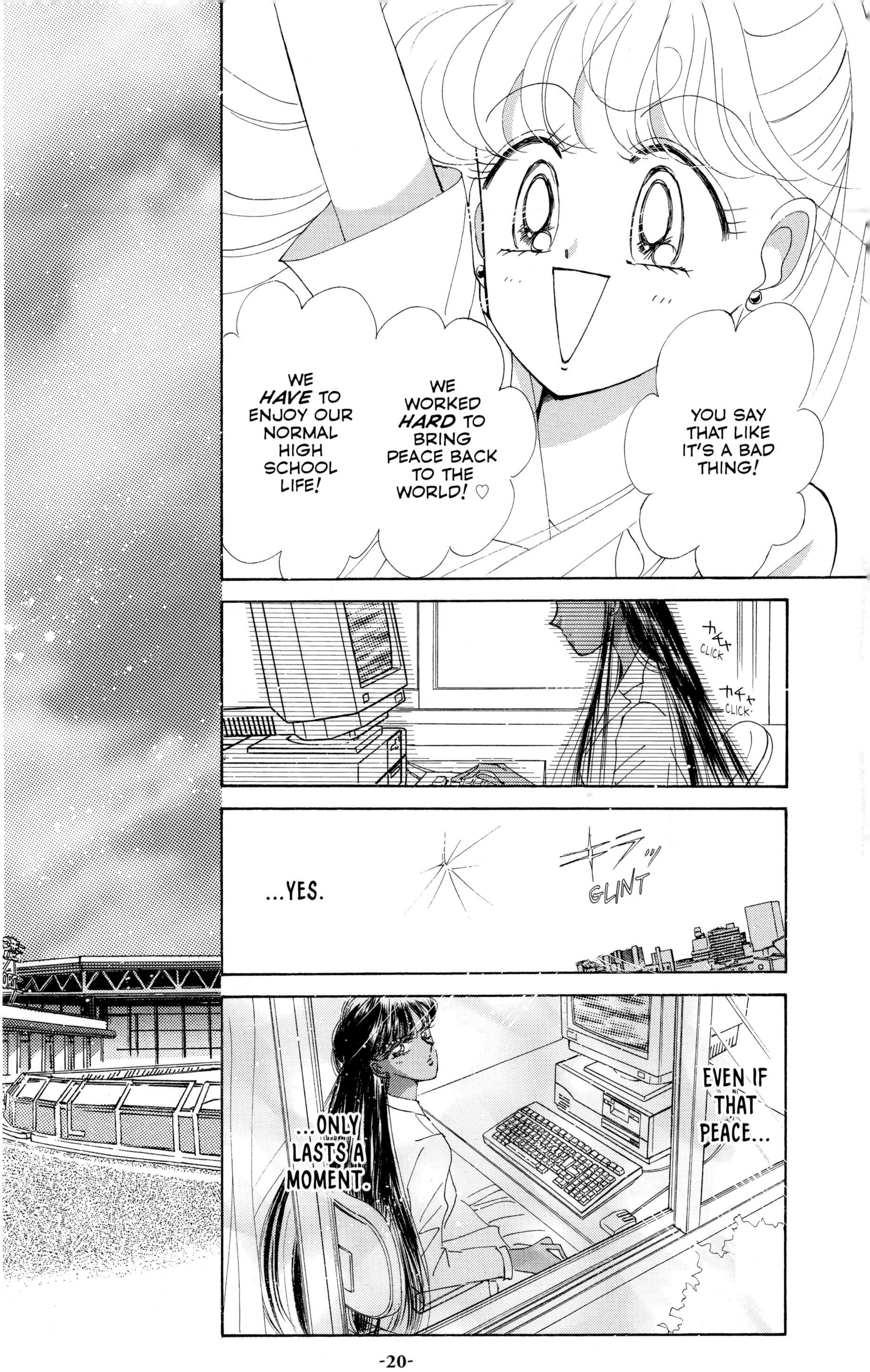
YOU SAY THAT LIKE IT'S A BAD THING!
WE WORKED HARD TO BRING PEACE BACK TO THE WORLD! ♡
WE HAVE TO ENJOY OUR NORMAL HIGH SCHOOL LIFE!
CLICK
CLICK
GLINT
...YES.
EVEN IF THAT PEACE...
...ONLY LASTS A MOMENT.

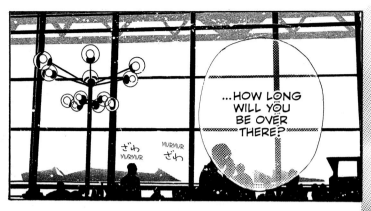

...HOW LONG WILL YOU BE OVER THERE?
MURMUR ざわ
ざわ MURMUR
ABOUT A YEAR...
...BUT IT MIGHT END UP BEING A LITTLE LONGER.
...OH.
...A YEAR, HUH?
MURMUR ざわ
ざわ MURMUR
NEW TOKYO INTERNATIONAL
WELL, YOU'VE ALWAYS WANTED TO GO TO HARVARD.
AND THEY CHOSE YOUR RESEARCH PAPER, SO NOW YOU FINALLY CAN.
YOU REALLY ARE AMAZING, MAMO-CHAN... I SHOULD BE HAPPIER FOR YOU.

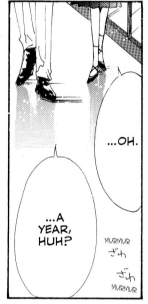

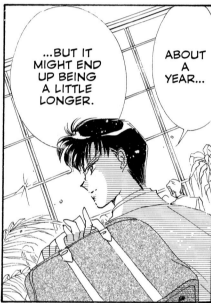

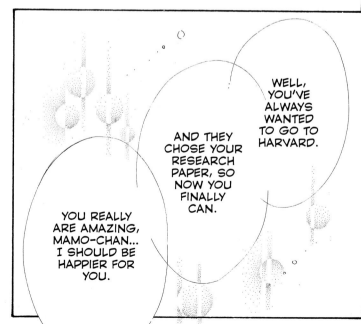

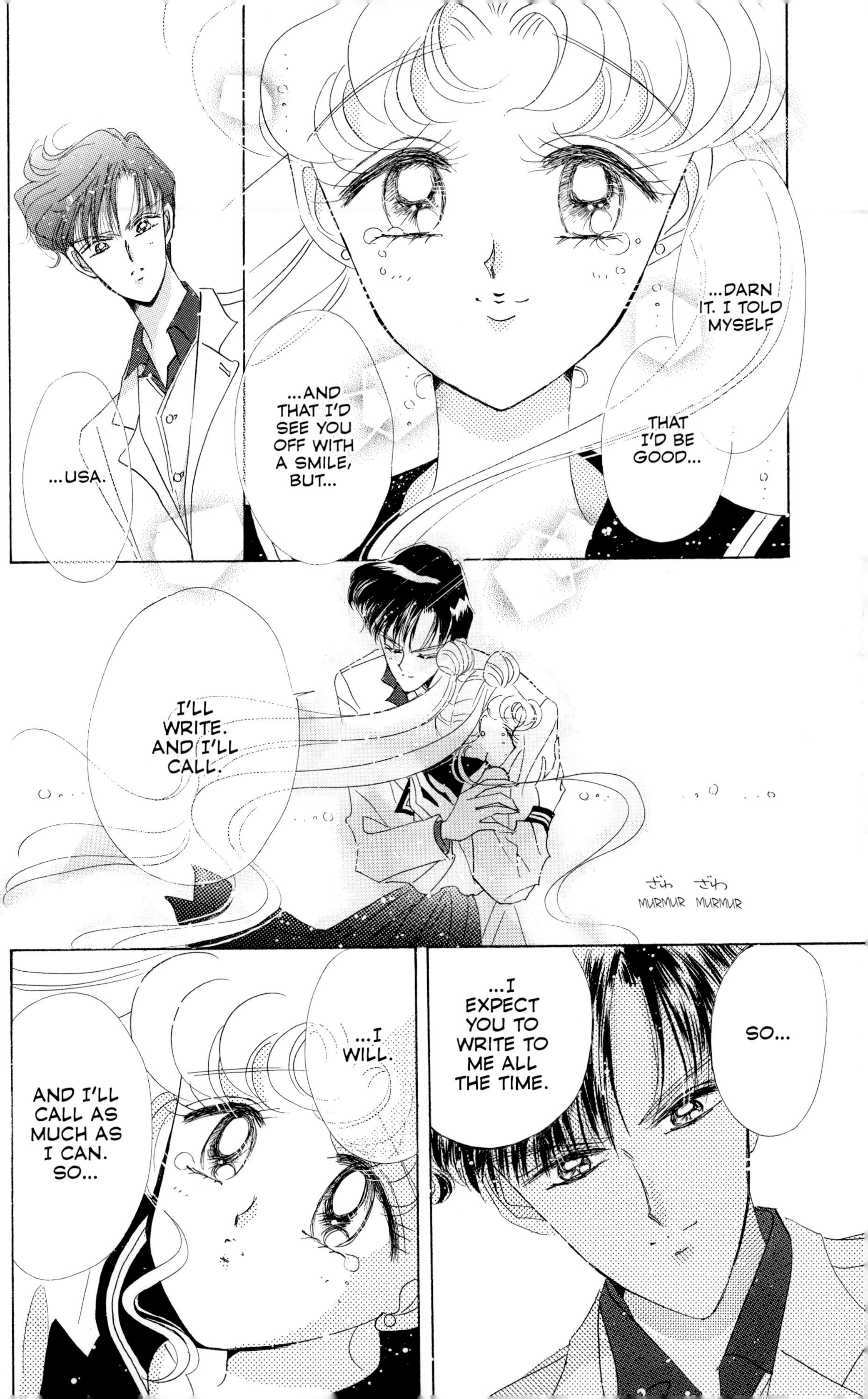
...DARN IT. I TOLD MYSELF
THAT I'D BE GOOD...
...AND THAT I'D SEE YOU OFF WITH A SMILE, BUT...
...USA.
I'LL WRITE. AND I'LL CALL.
ざわ ざわ
MURMUR MURMUR
SO...
...I EXPECT YOU TO WRITE TO ME ALL THE TIME.
...I WILL.
AND I'LL CALL AS MUCH AS I CAN. SO...

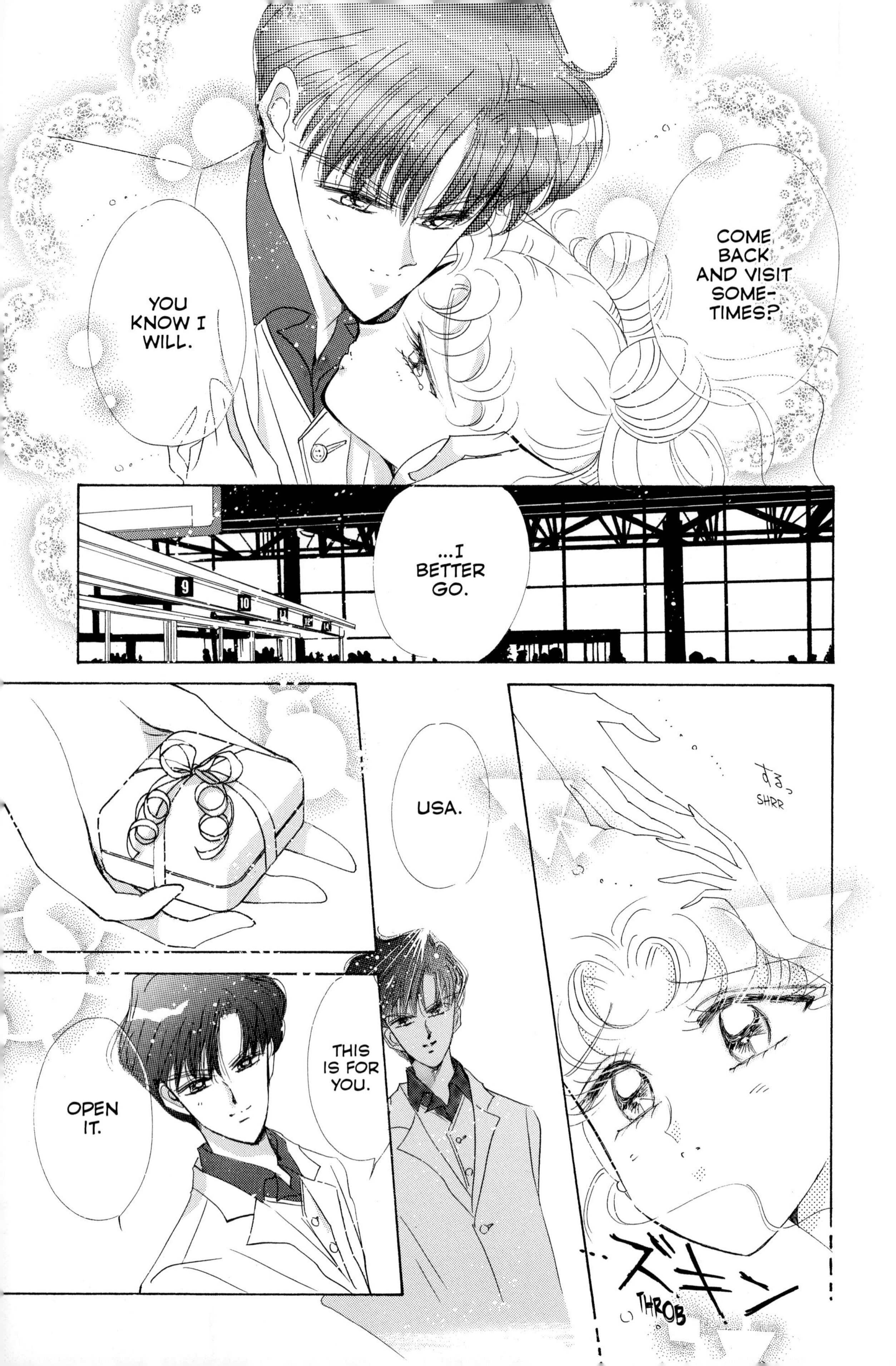
COME BACK AND VISIT SOME-TIMES?
YOU KNOW I WILL.
...I BETTER GO.
USA.
するっ
SHRR
ズキン
THROB
THIS IS FOR YOU.
OPEN IT.

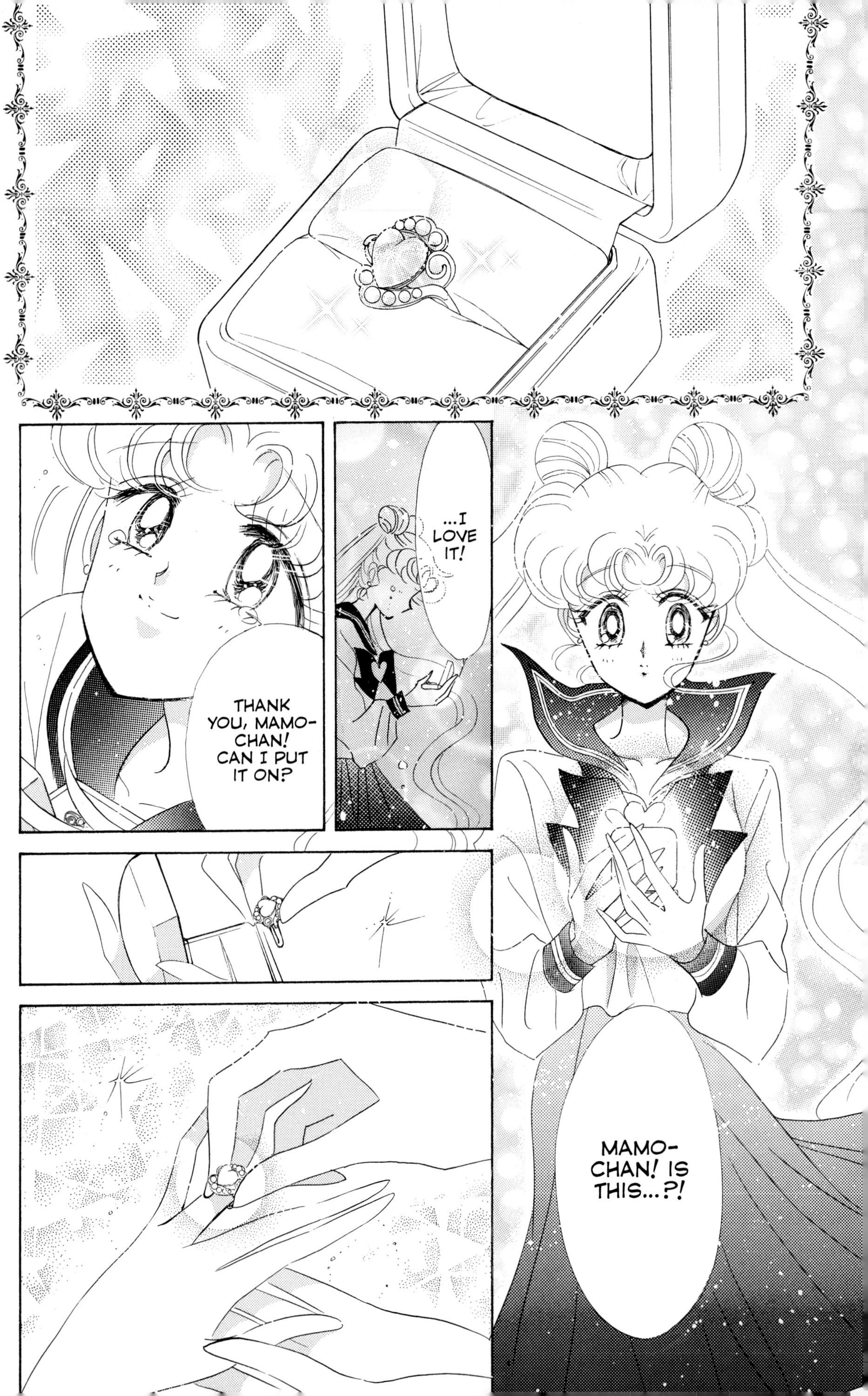
MAMO-CHAN! IS THIS...?!
...I LOVE IT!
THANK YOU, MAMO-CHAN! CAN I PUT IT ON?

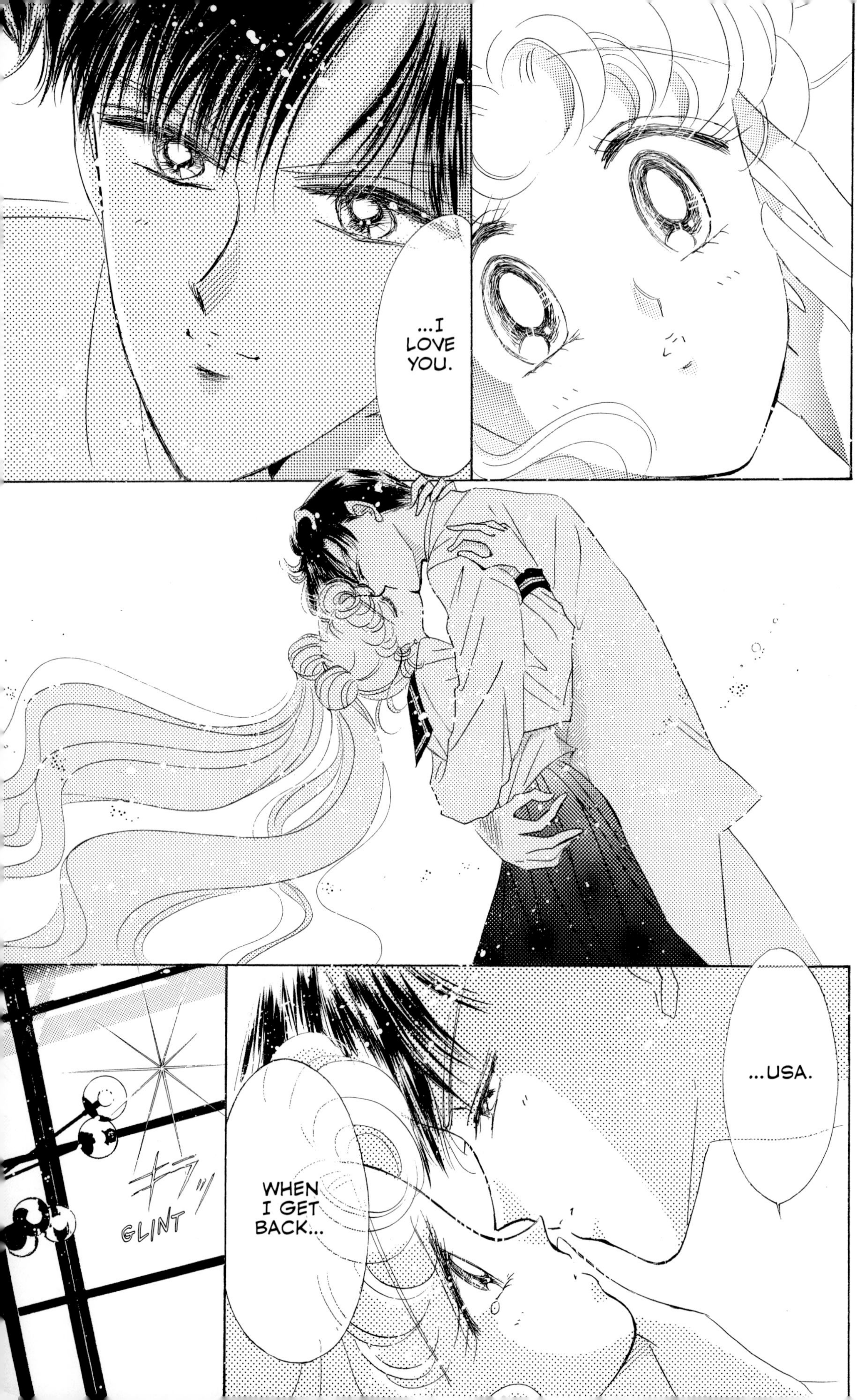
...I LOVE YOU.
...USA.
WHEN I GET BACK...
キラッ
GLINT

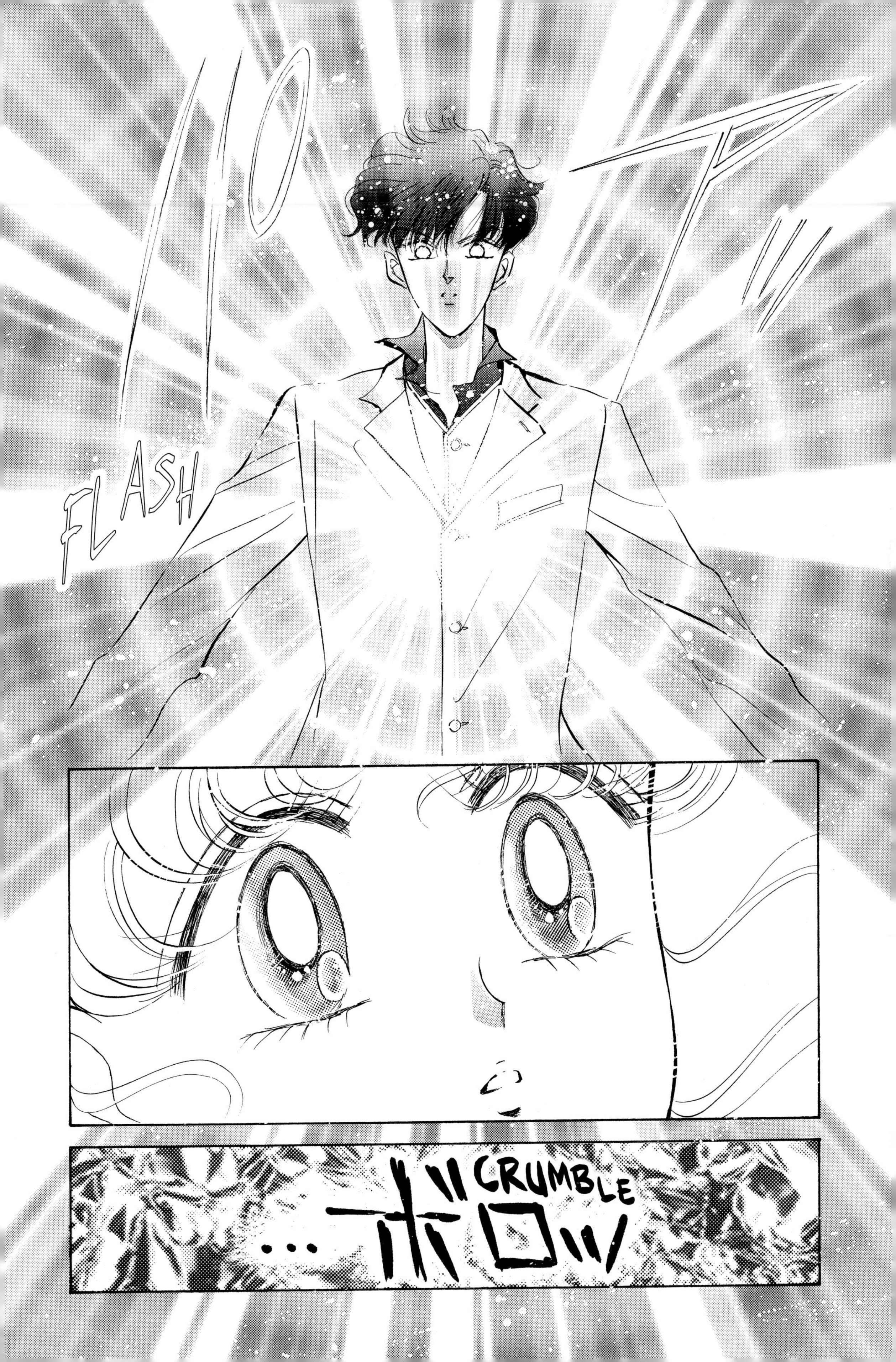
パアッ
FLASH
…ボロッ
CRUMBLE

CRUMBLE

CRUMBLE

CRUMBLE

FLAAASH

NYOO

SWOO

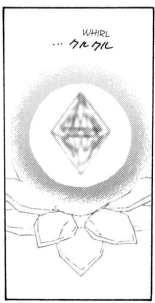

WHIRL

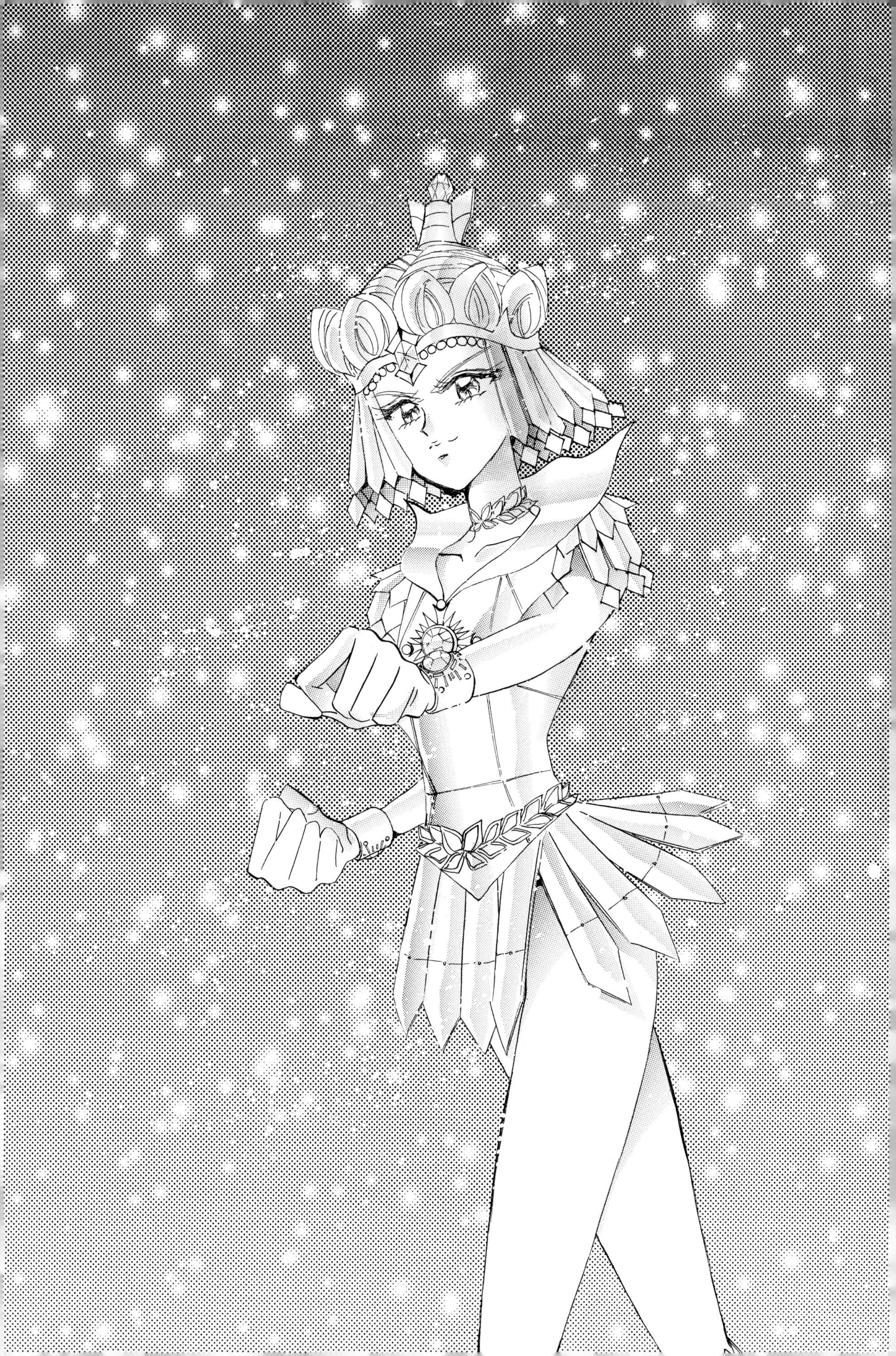

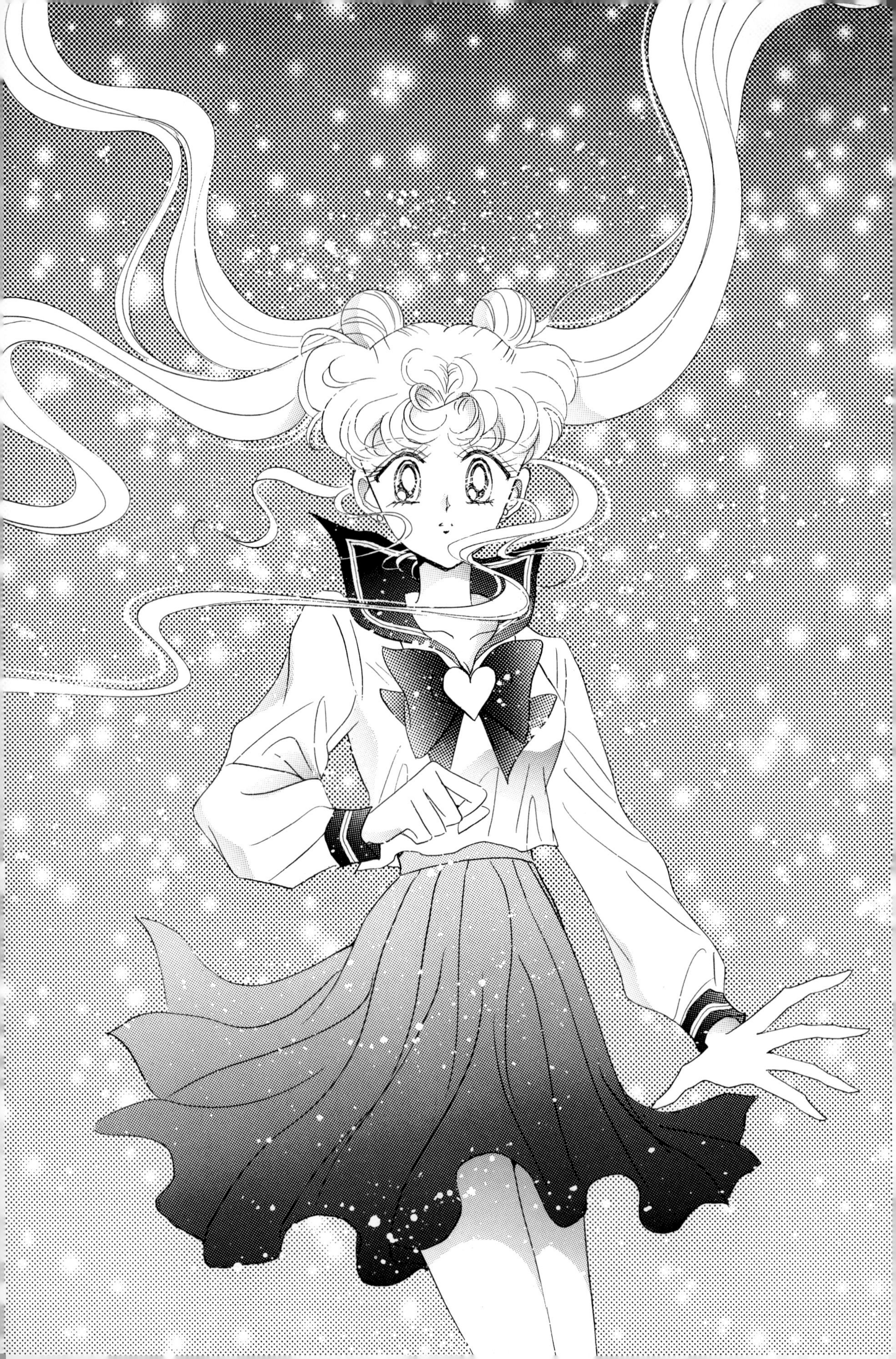

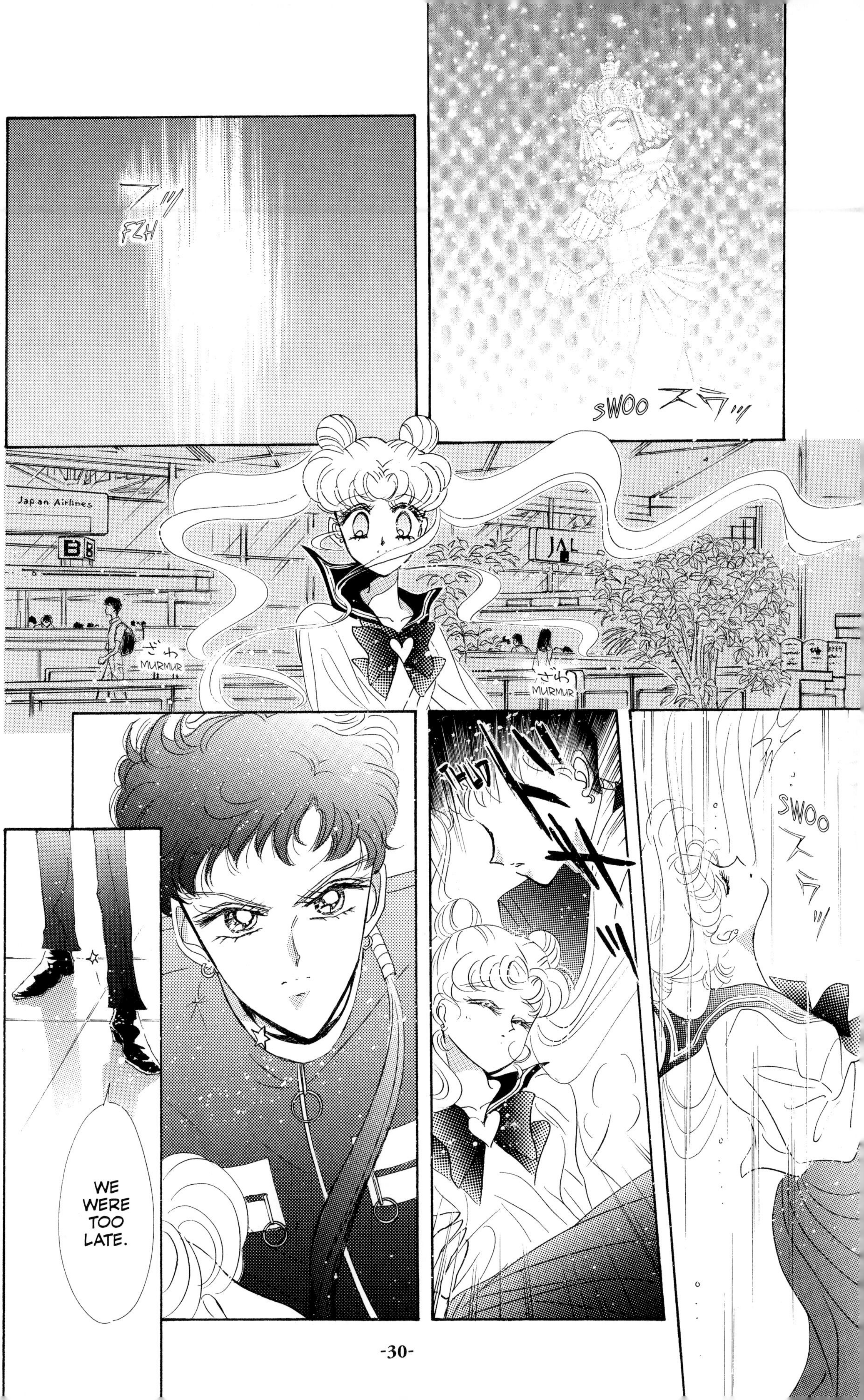
SWOO スラッ
フッ
FZH
ざわ
MURMUR
ざわ
MURMUR
SWOO
スラッ
THUD
WE WERE TOO LATE.

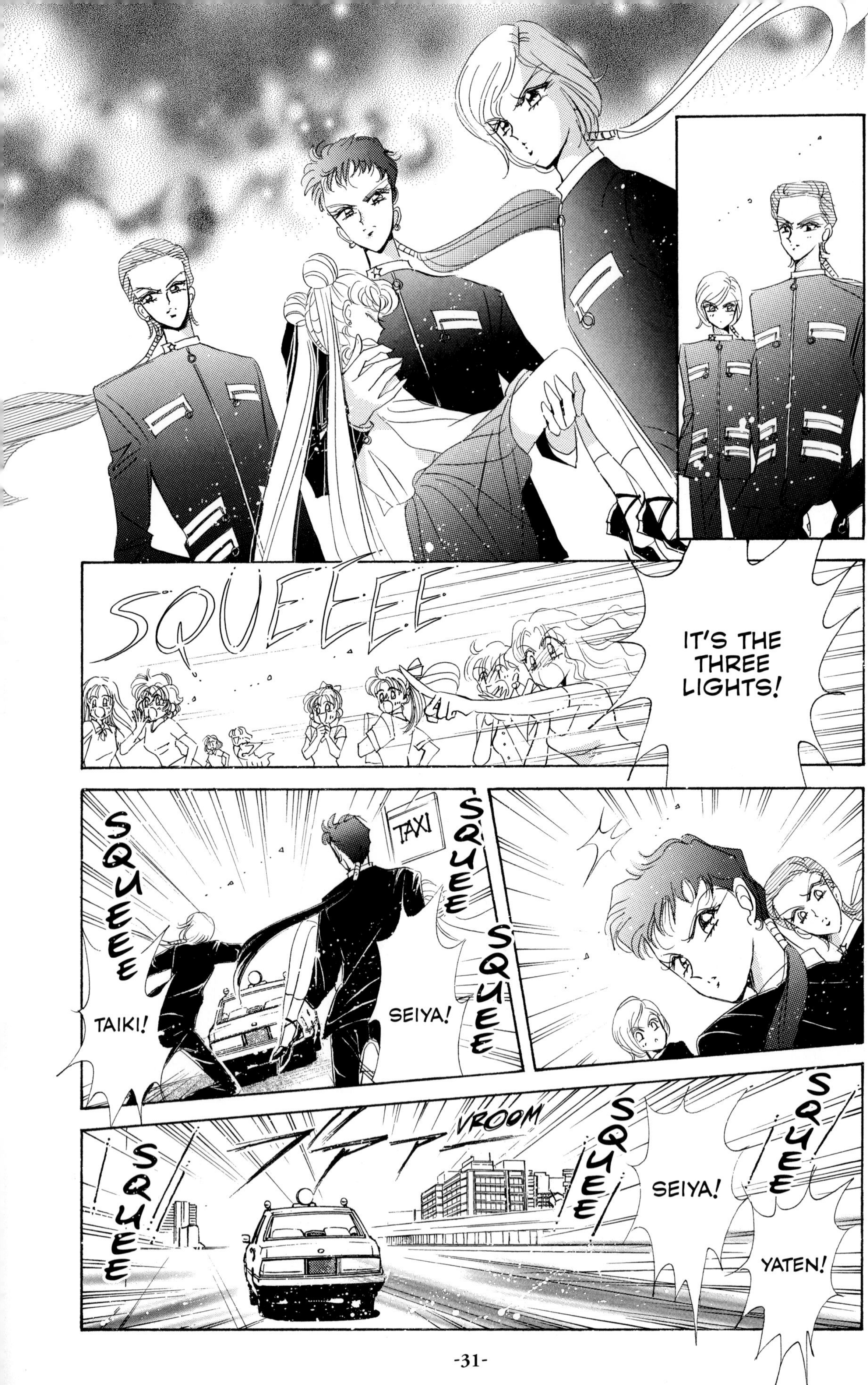
IT'S THE THREE LIGHTS!
SQUEEEE
SQUEEE
SQUEEE
SEIYA!
SQUEEEE
TAIKI!
SQUEEE
SQUEEE
SEIYA!
YATEN!
VROOM
SQUEEE

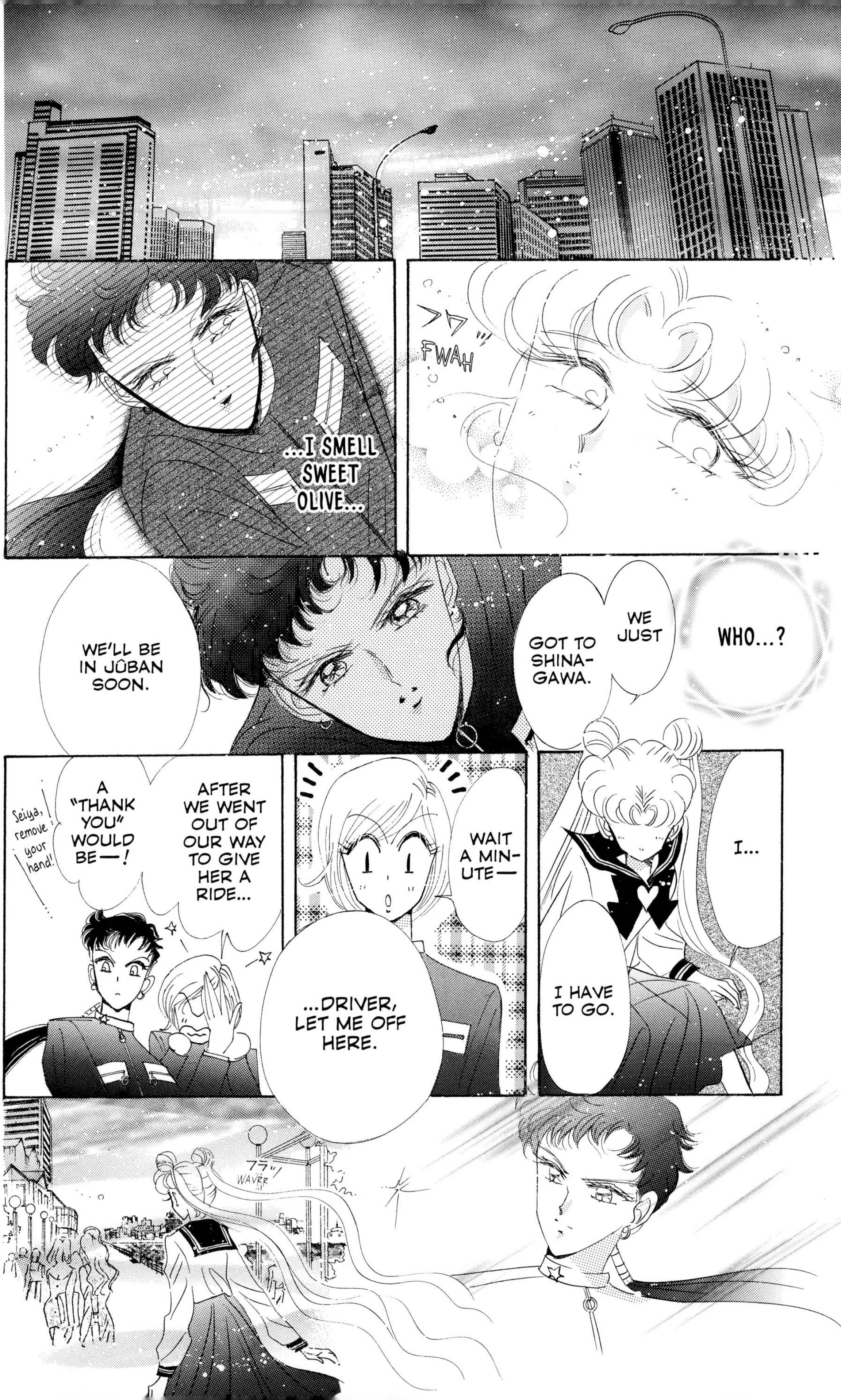
FWAH
...I SMELL SWEET OLIVE...
WHO...?
WE JUST GOT TO SHINAGAWA.
WE'LL BE IN JÛBAN SOON.
I...
I HAVE TO GO.
WAIT A MIN-UTE—
...DRIVER, LET ME OFF HERE.
AFTER WE WENT OUT OF OUR WAY TO GIVE HER A RIDE...
A "THANK YOU" WOULD BE—!
Seiya, remove your hand!
WAVRR

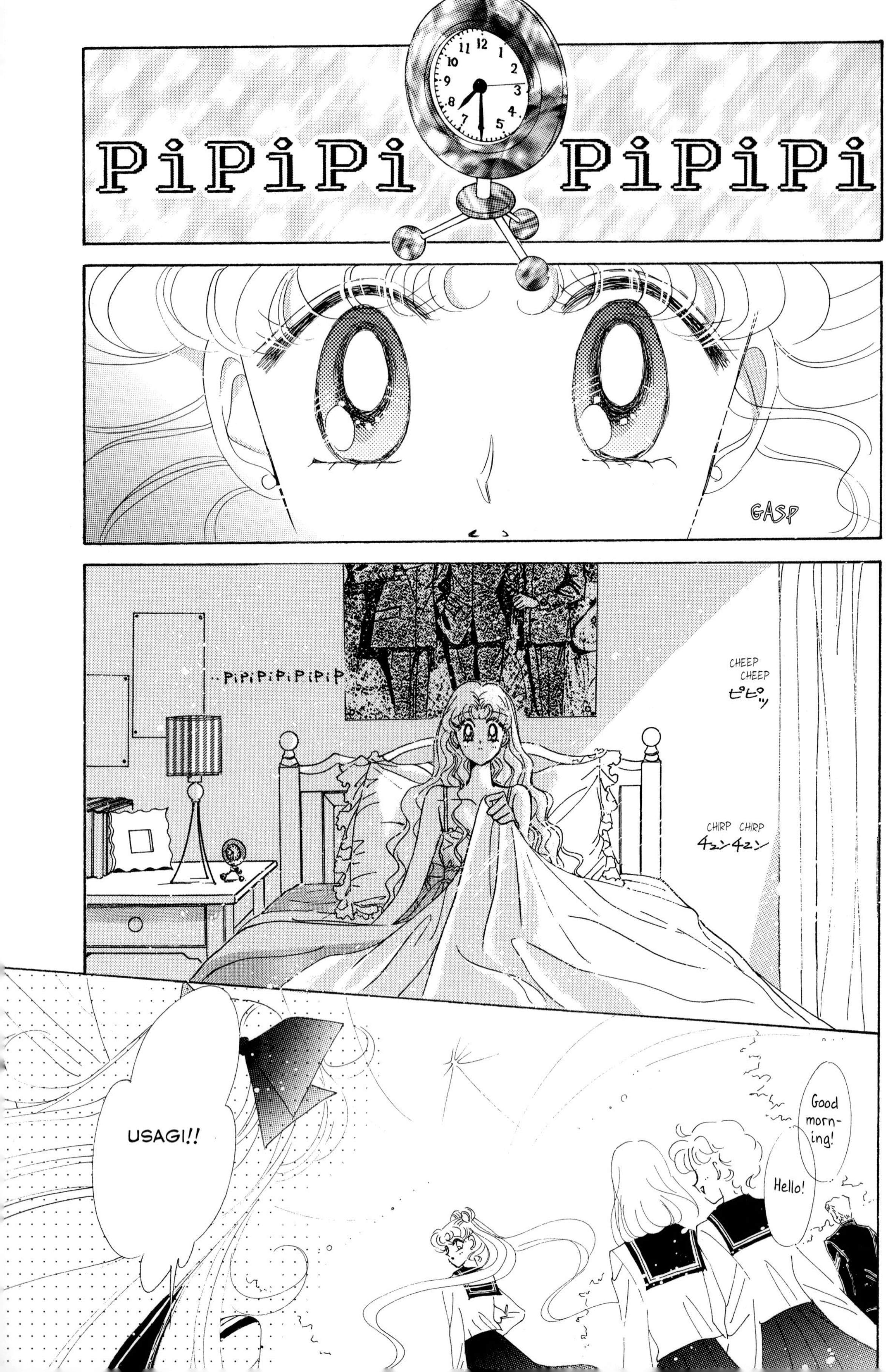
PiPiPi PiPiPi
GASP
CHEEP CHEEP
ピピッ
CHIRP CHIRP
チュンチュン
..PiPiPiPiPiPiP
Good morning!
Hello!
USAGI!!

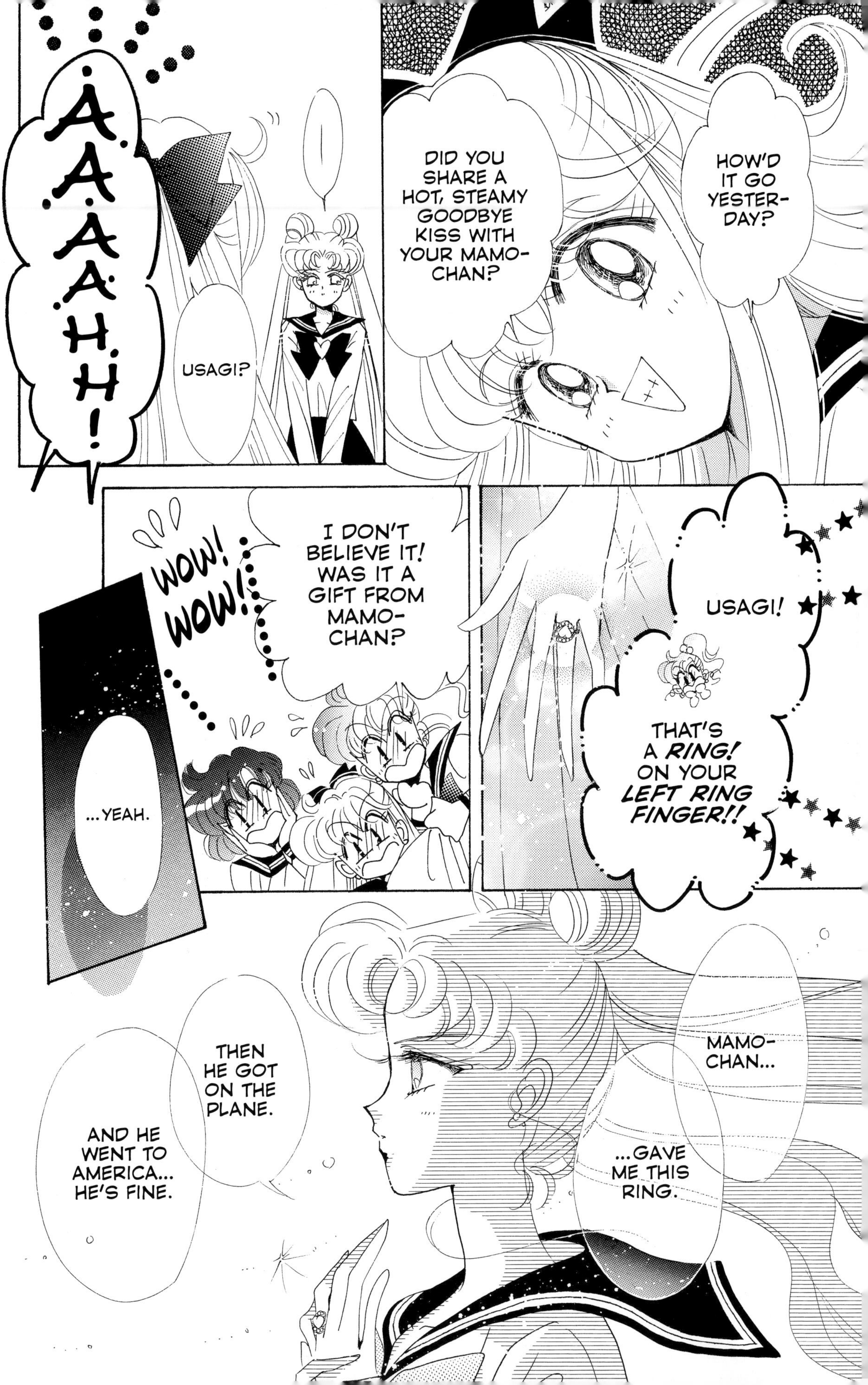
HOW'D IT GO YESTER-DAY?
DID YOU SHARE A HOT, STEAMY GOODBYE KISS WITH YOUR MAMO-CHAN?
!
USAGI?
AAAAHH!
USAGI!
THAT'S A RING! ON YOUR LEFT RING FINGER!!
I DON'T BELIEVE IT! WAS IT A GIFT FROM MAMO-CHAN?
WOW! WOW!
...YEAH.
MAMO-CHAN...
...GAVE ME THIS RING.
THEN HE GOT ON THE PLANE.
AND HE WENT TO AMERICA... HE'S FINE.

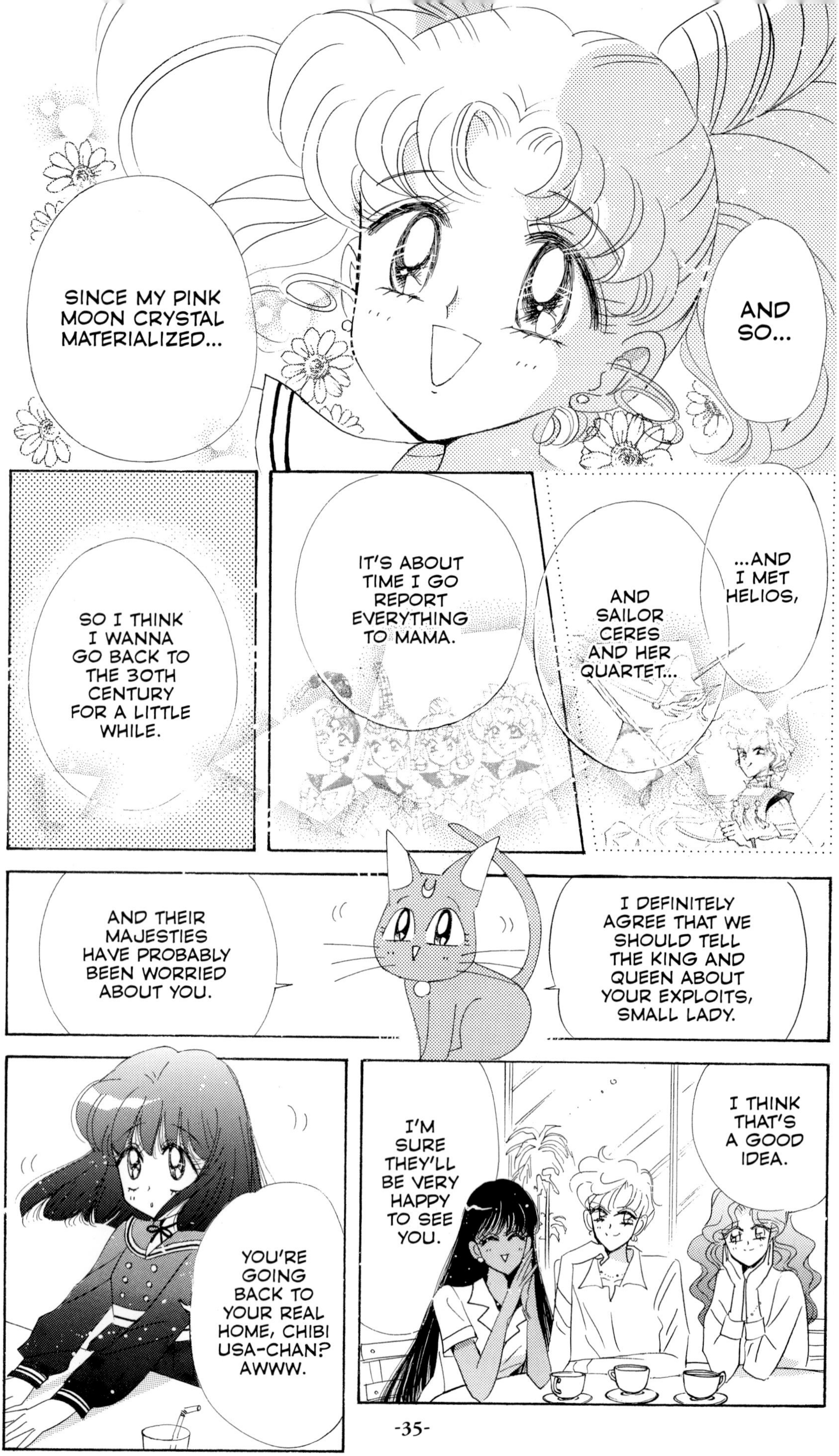
AND SO...
SINCE MY PINK MOON CRYSTAL MATERIALIZED...
...AND I MET HELIOS,
AND SAILOR CERES AND HER QUARTET...
IT'S ABOUT TIME I GO REPORT EVERYTHING TO MAMA.
SO I THINK I WANNA GO BACK TO THE 30TH CENTURY FOR A LITTLE WHILE.
I DEFINITELY AGREE THAT WE SHOULD TELL THE KING AND QUEEN ABOUT YOUR EXPLOITS, SMALL LADY.
AND THEIR MAJESTIES HAVE PROBABLY BEEN WORRIED ABOUT YOU.
I THINK THAT'S A GOOD IDEA.
I'M SURE THEY'LL BE VERY HAPPY TO SEE YOU.
YOU'RE GOING BACK TO YOUR REAL HOME, CHIBI USA-CHAN? AWWW.

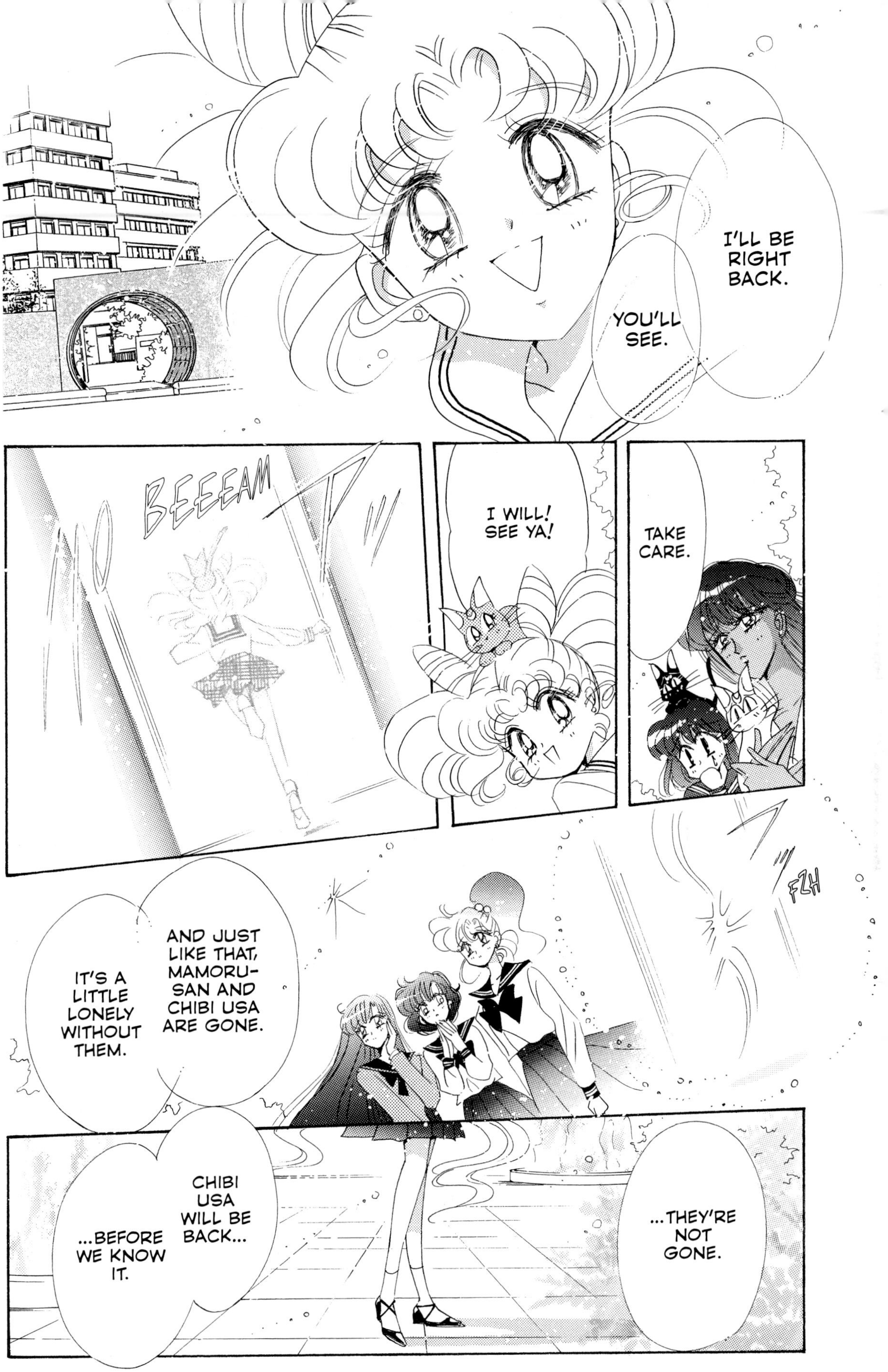
I'LL BE RIGHT BACK.
YOU'LL SEE.
TAKE CARE.
I WILL! SEE YA!
BEEEAM
FZH
AND JUST LIKE THAT, MAMORU-SAN AND CHIBI USA ARE GONE.
IT'S A LITTLE LONELY WITHOUT THEM.
...THEY'RE NOT GONE.
CHIBI USA WILL BE BACK...
...BEFORE WE KNOW IT.

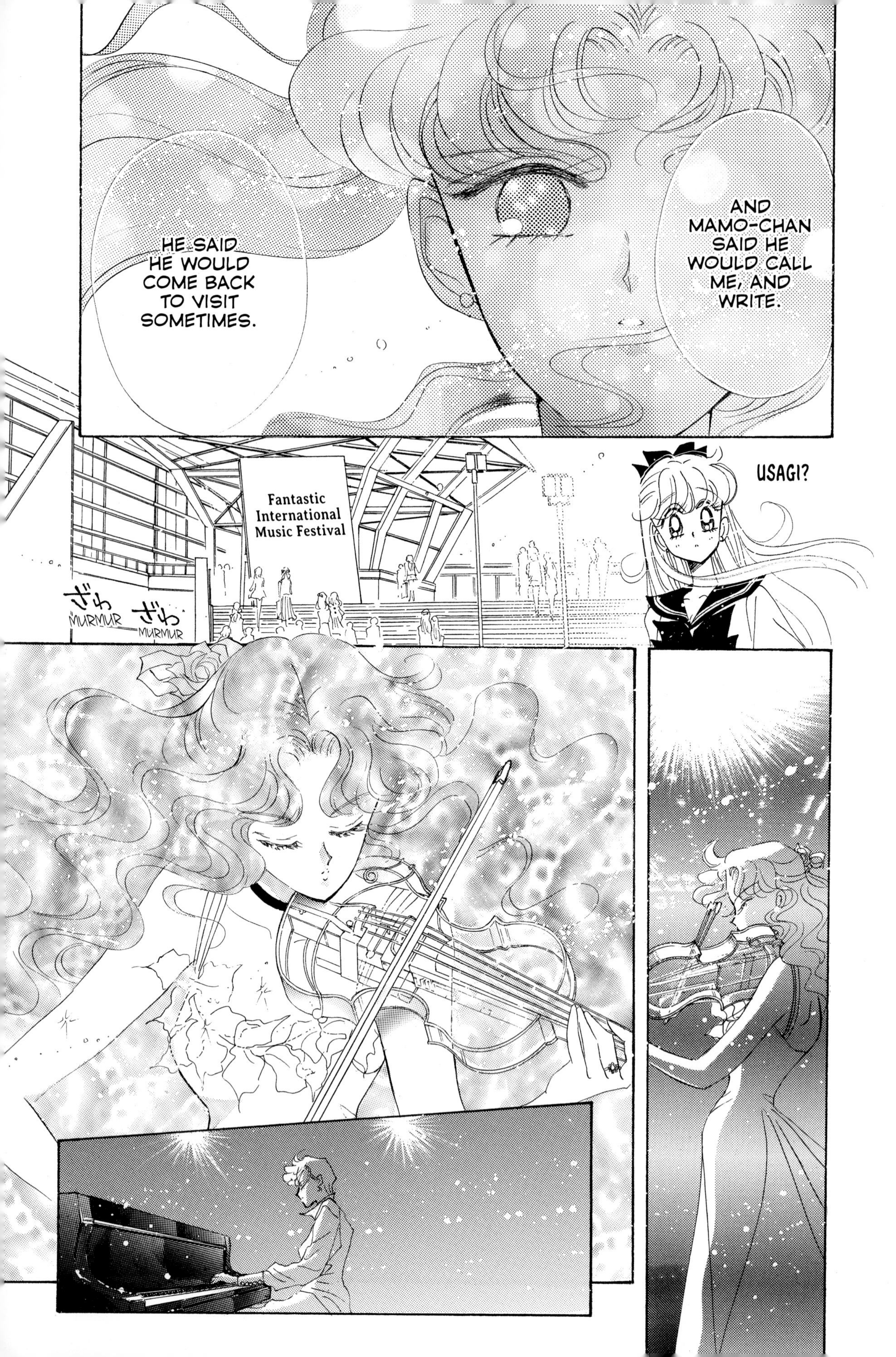
AND MAMO-CHAN SAID HE WOULD CALL ME, AND WRITE.
HE SAID HE WOULD COME BACK TO VISIT SOMETIMES.
USAGI?
Fantastic International Music Festival
ざわ MURMUR
ざわ MURMUR

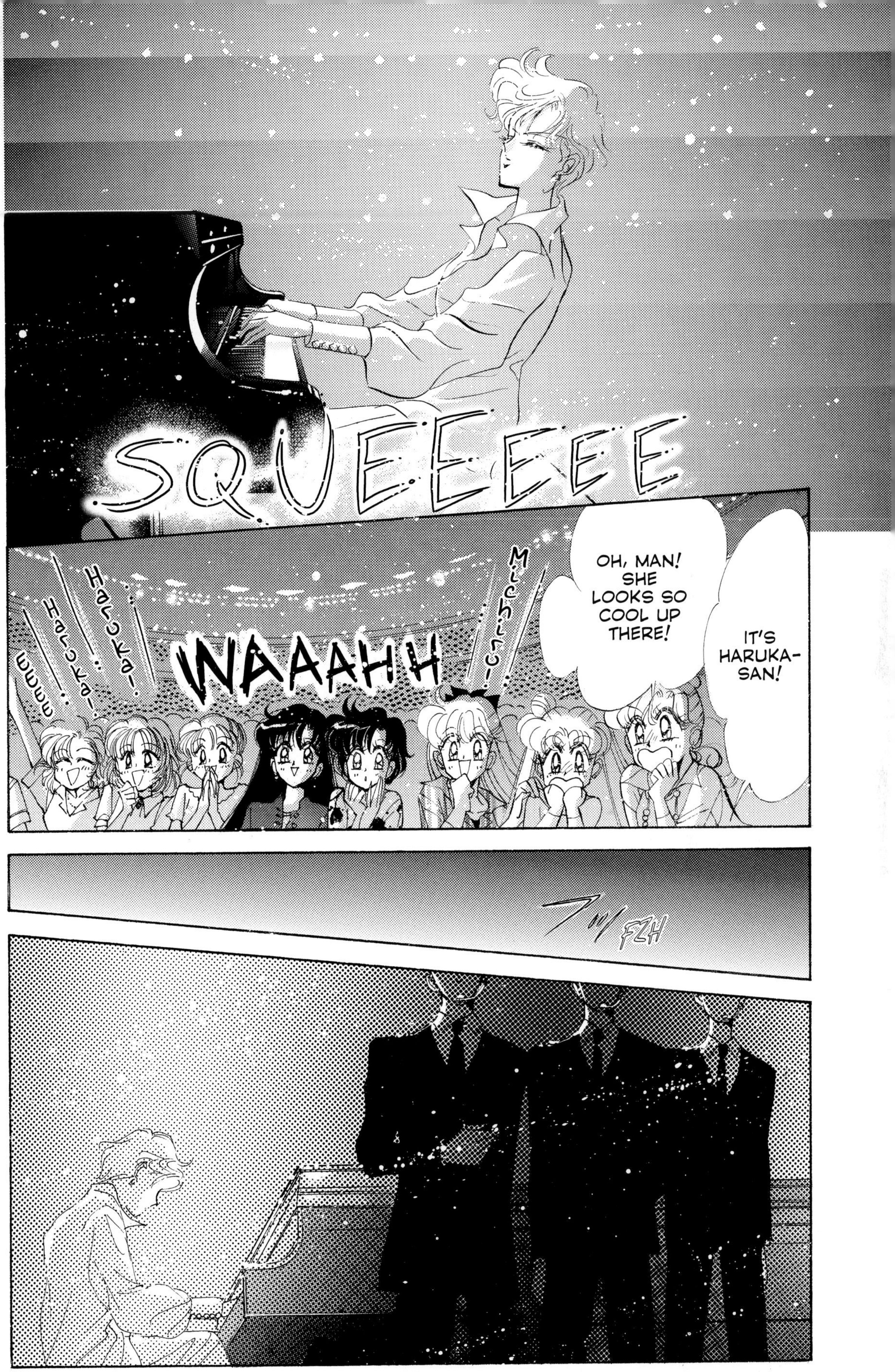
SQUEEEEE
IT'S HARUKA-SAN!
OH, MAN! SHE LOOKS SO COOL UP THERE!
Michiru-!
WAAAHH
Haruka-!
Haruka-!
EEE
FZH

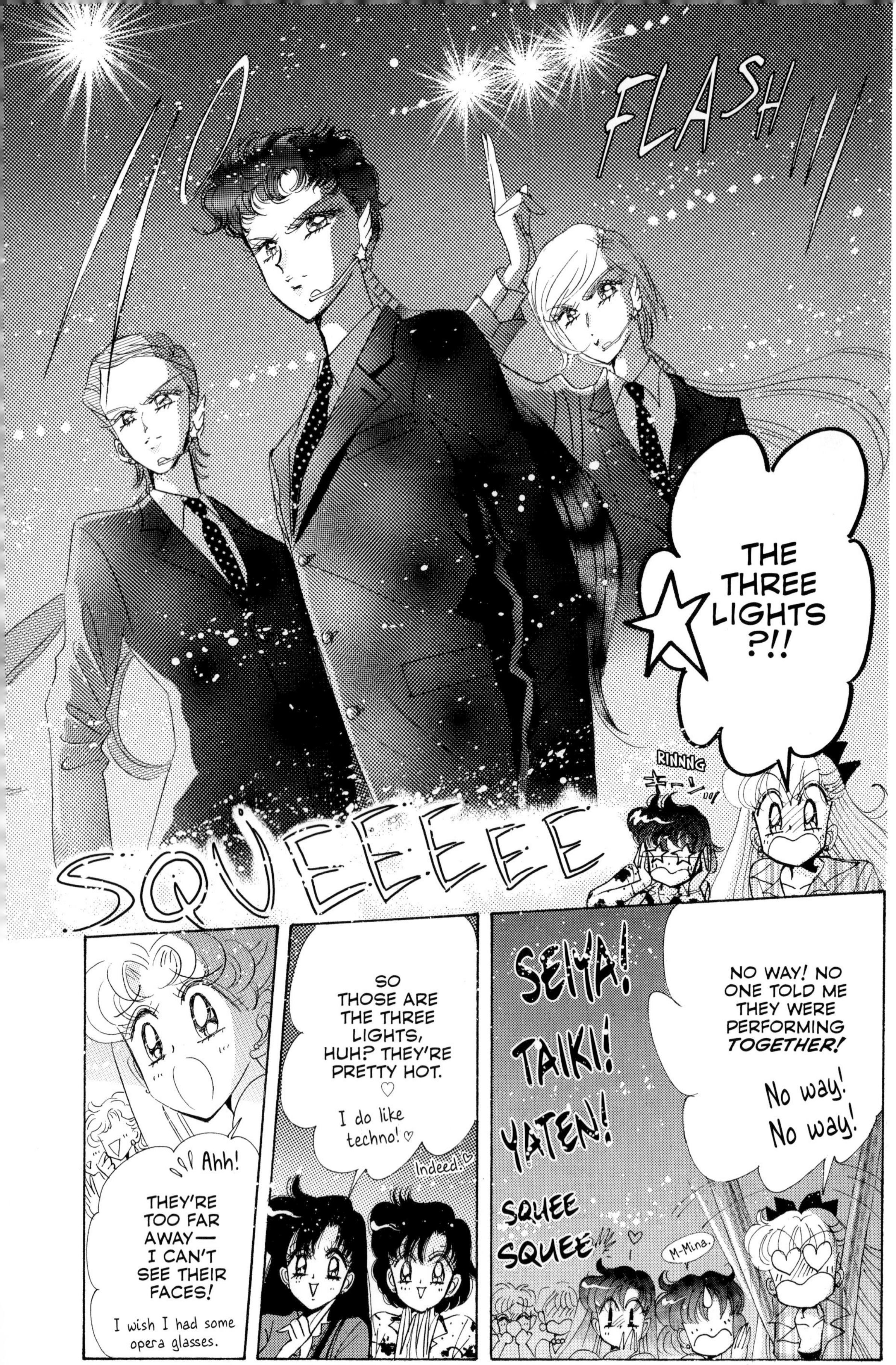
FLASH
THE THREE LIGHTS ?!!
RINNNG
SQUEEEEEE
NO WAY! NO ONE TOLD ME THEY WERE PERFORMING *TOGETHER!*
No way! No way!
SEIYA! TAIKI! YATEN!
SQUEE SQUEE
M-Mina.
SO THOSE ARE THE THREE LIGHTS, HUH? THEY'RE PRETTY HOT. ♡
I do like techno! ♡
Indeed! ♡
Ahh!
THEY'RE TOO FAR AWAY— I CAN'T SEE THEIR FACES!
I wish I had some opera glasses.

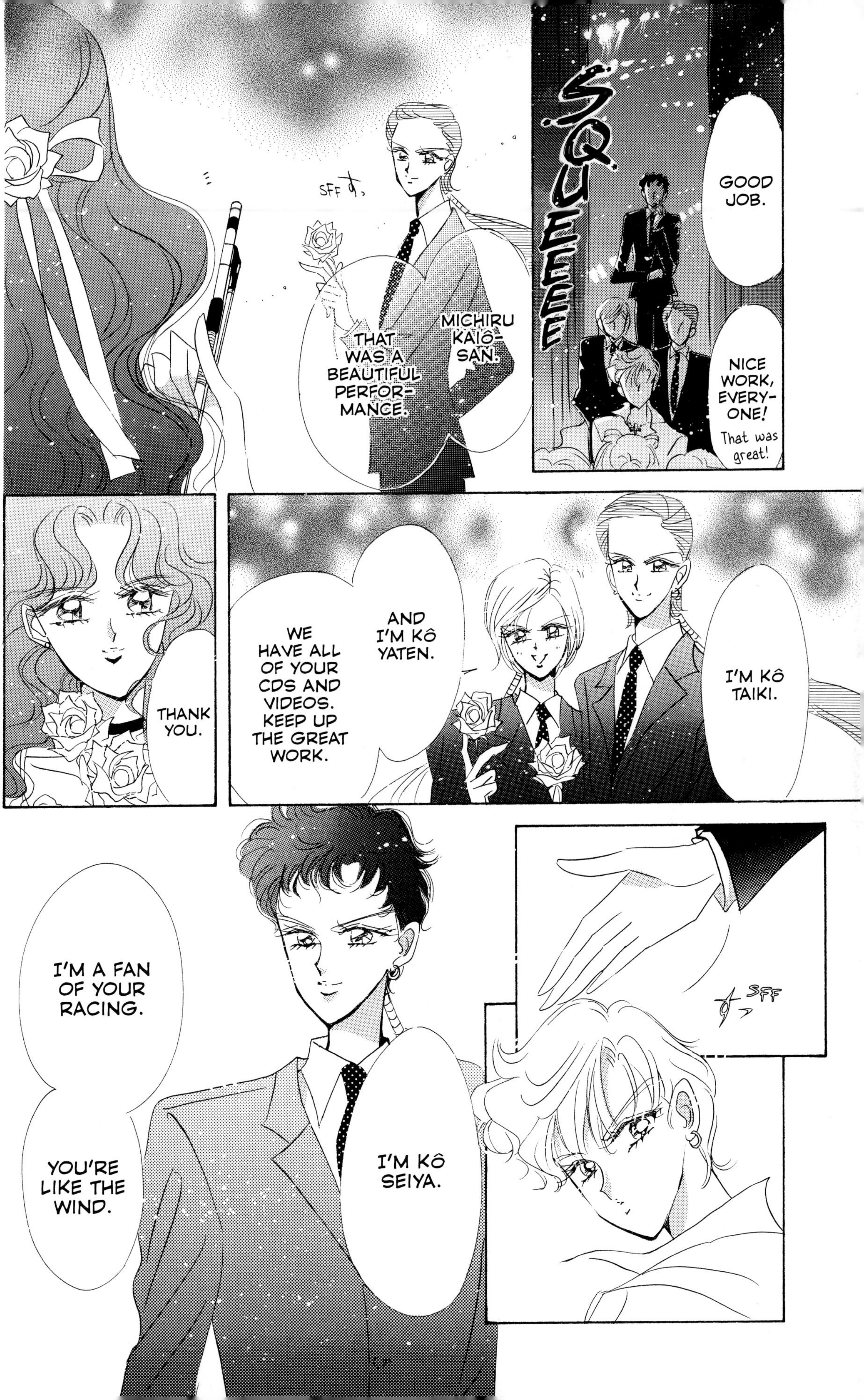
SQUEEEEE
GOOD JOB.
NICE WORK, EVERYONE!
That was great!
SFF
MICHIRU KAIÔ-SAN.
THAT WAS A BEAUTIFUL PERFORMANCE.
I'M KÔ TAIKI.
AND I'M KÔ YATEN.
WE HAVE ALL OF YOUR CDS AND VIDEOS. KEEP UP THE GREAT WORK.
THANK YOU.
SFF
I'M KÔ SEIYA.
I'M A FAN OF YOUR RACING.
YOU'RE LIKE THE WIND.

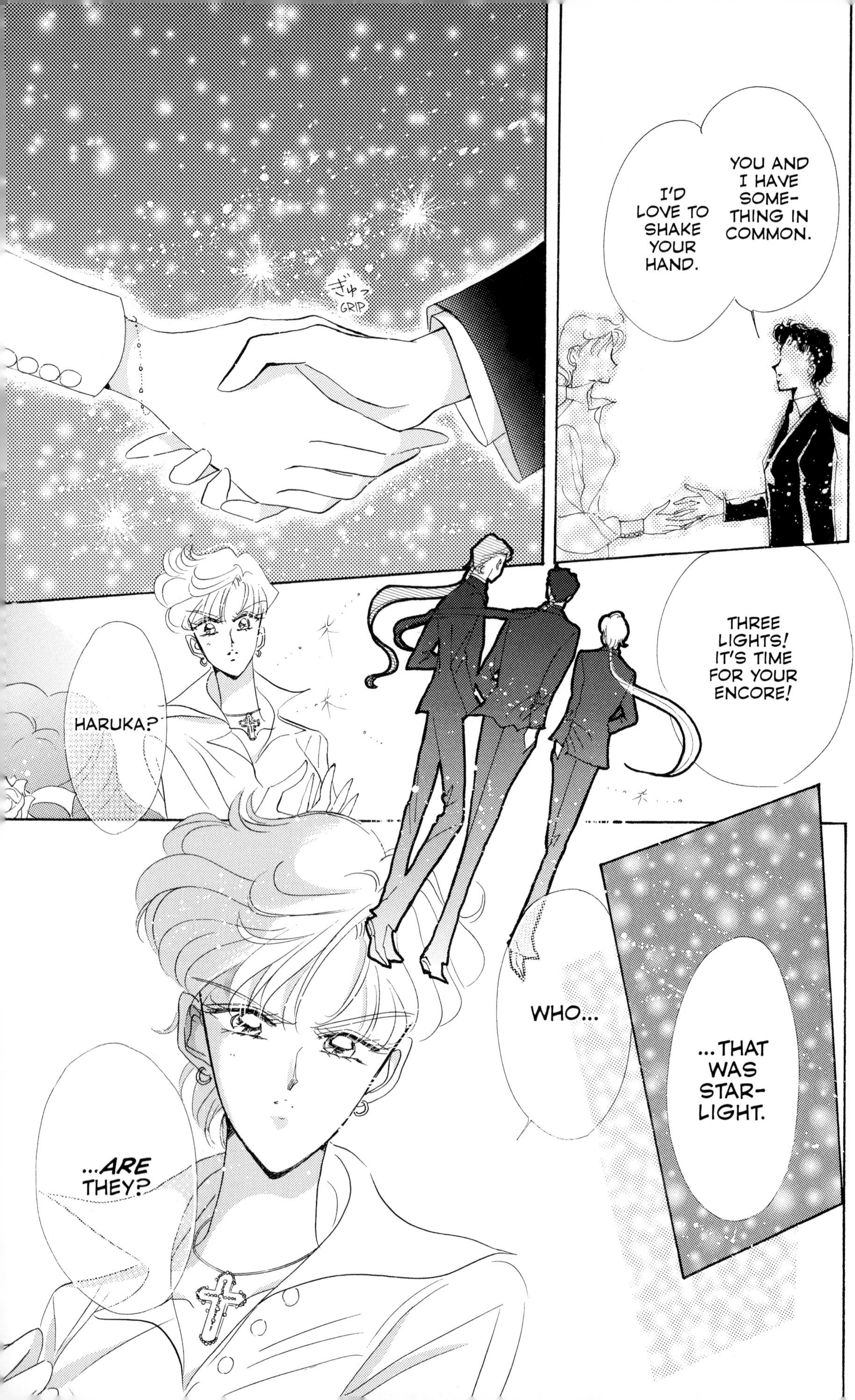
YOU AND I HAVE SOME-THING IN COMMON.
I'D LOVE TO SHAKE YOUR HAND.
ぎゅっ GRIP
THREE LIGHTS! IT'S TIME FOR YOUR ENCORE!
HARUKA?
...THAT WAS STAR-LIGHT.
WHO...
...*ARE* THEY?

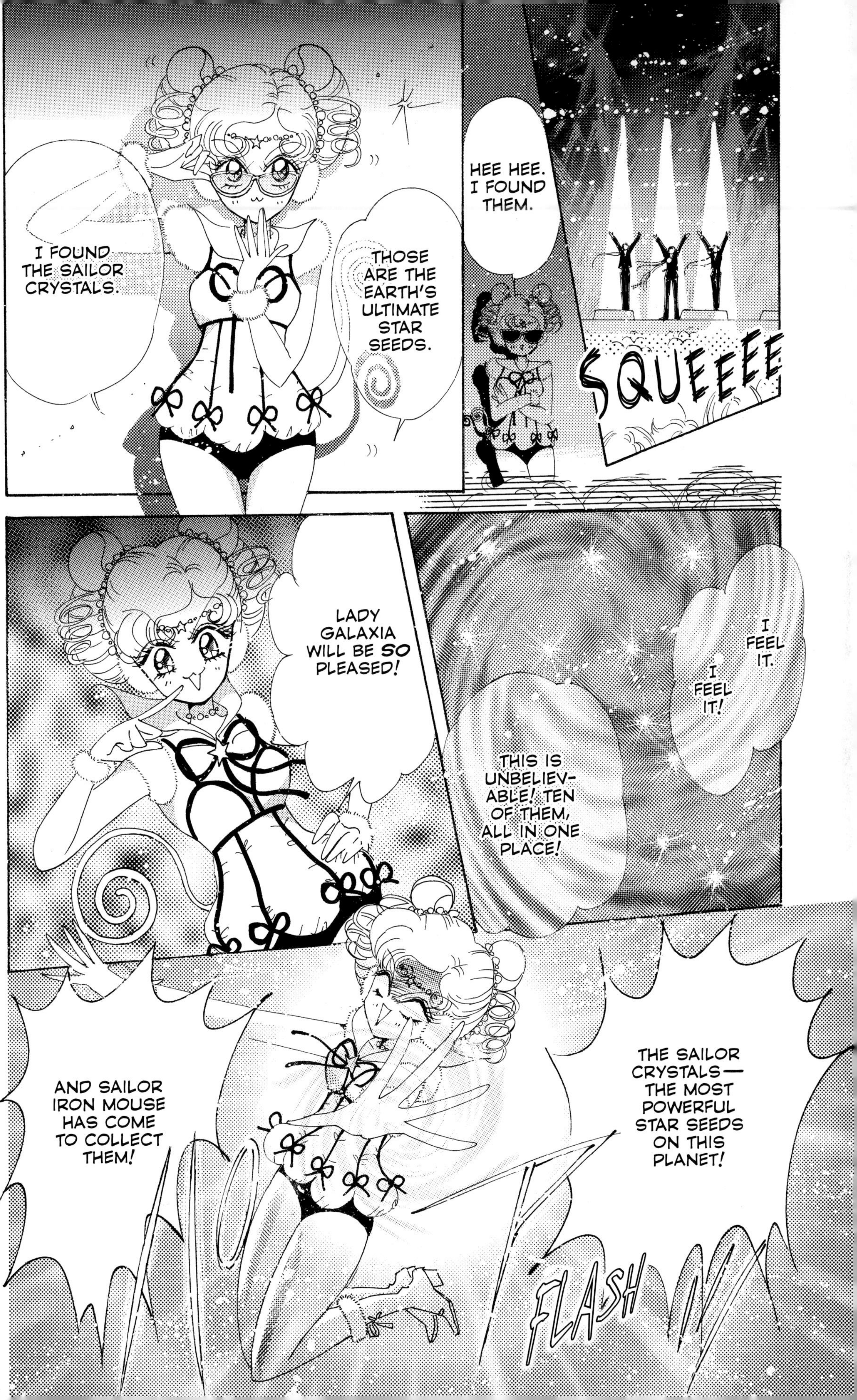
HEE HEE. I FOUND THEM.
SQUEEEEE
I FOUND THE SAILOR CRYSTALS.
THOSE ARE THE EARTH'S ULTIMATE STAR SEEDS.
I FEEL IT.
I FEEL IT!
THIS IS UNBELIEV-ABLE! TEN OF THEM, ALL IN ONE PLACE!
LADY GALAXIA WILL BE SO PLEASED!
THE SAILOR CRYSTALS—THE MOST POWERFUL STAR SEEDS ON THIS PLANET!
AND SAILOR IRON MOUSE HAS COME TO COLLECT THEM!
FLASH

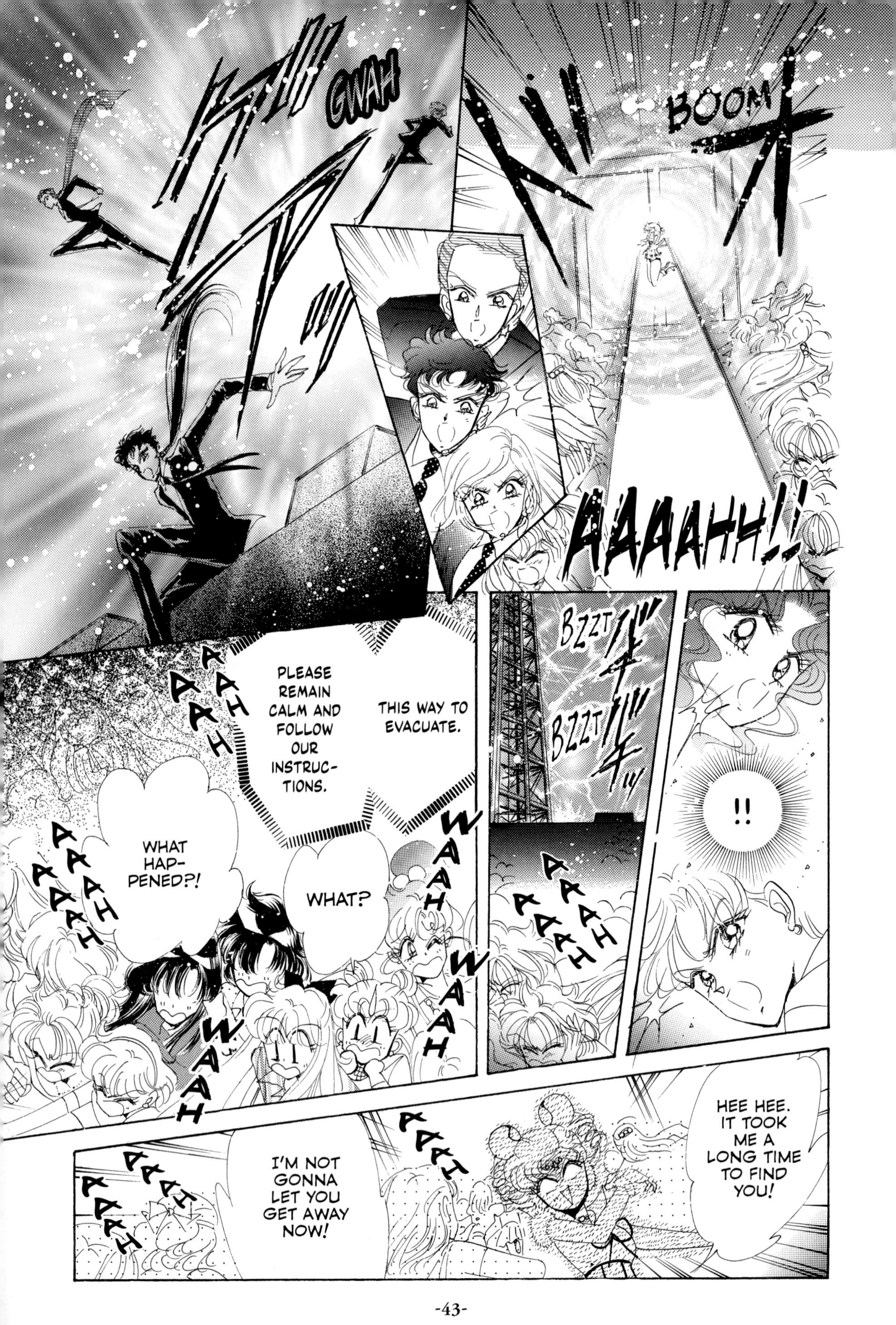
BOOM
GWAH
AAAAHH!!
!!
BZZT
BZZT
AAAAH
THIS WAY TO EVACUATE.
PLEASE REMAIN CALM AND FOLLOW OUR INSTRUCTIONS.
AAAH
WAAAH
WHAT?
WHAT HAPPENED?!
AAAAH
WAAAH
HEE HEE. IT TOOK ME A LONG TIME TO FIND YOU!
AAAH
I'M NOT GONNA LET YOU GET AWAY NOW!
AAAAH

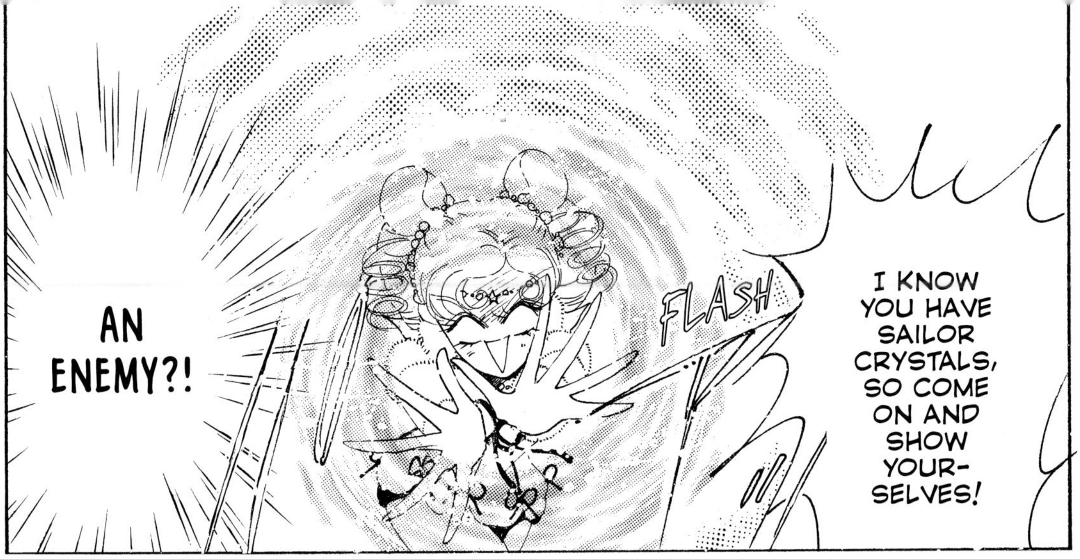
I KNOW YOU HAVE SAILOR CRYSTALS, SO COME ON AND SHOW YOUR-SELVES!
FLASH
AN ENEMY?!

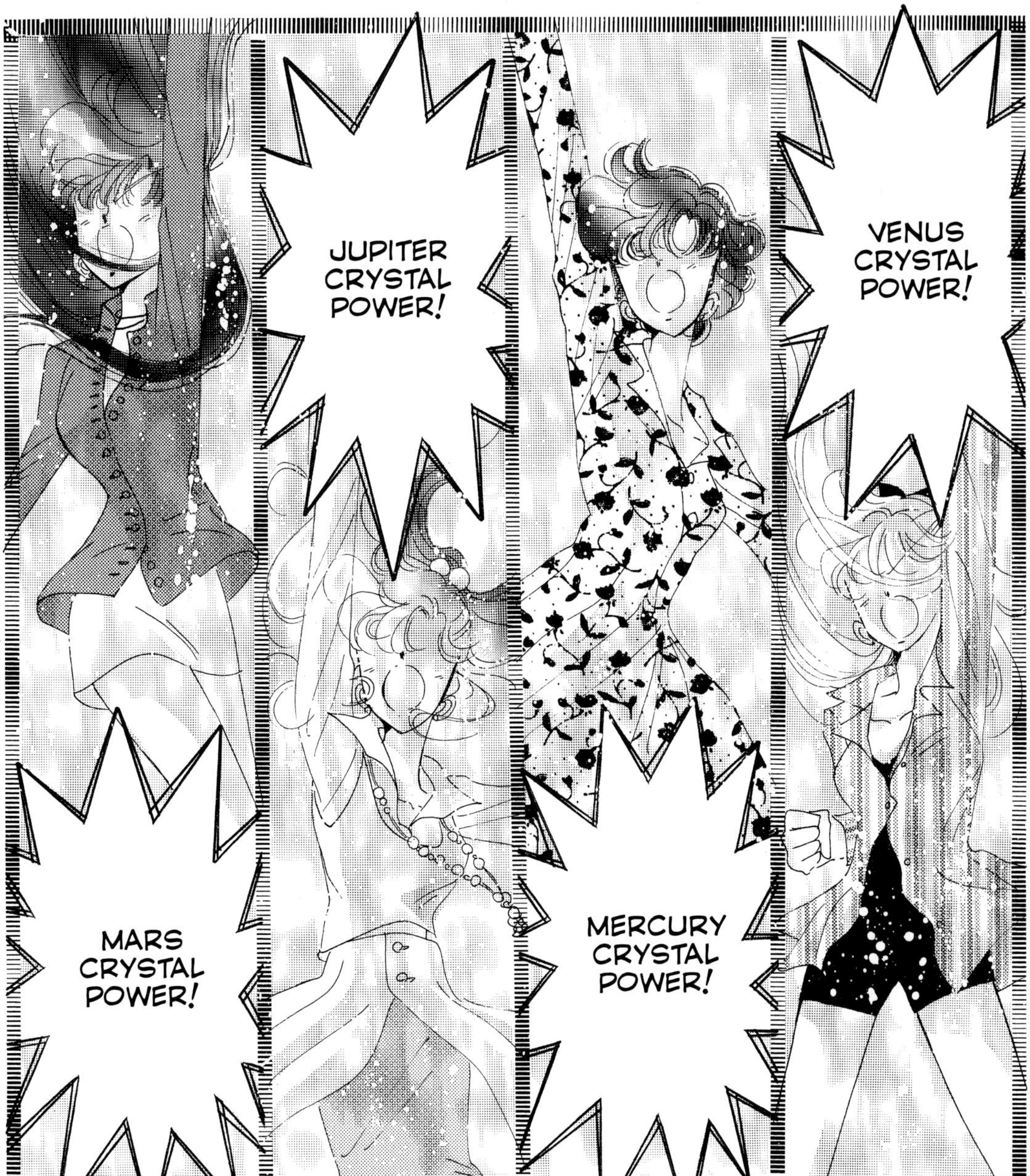
VENUS CRYSTAL POWER!
MERCURY CRYSTAL POWER!
JUPITER CRYSTAL POWER!
MARS CRYSTAL POWER!

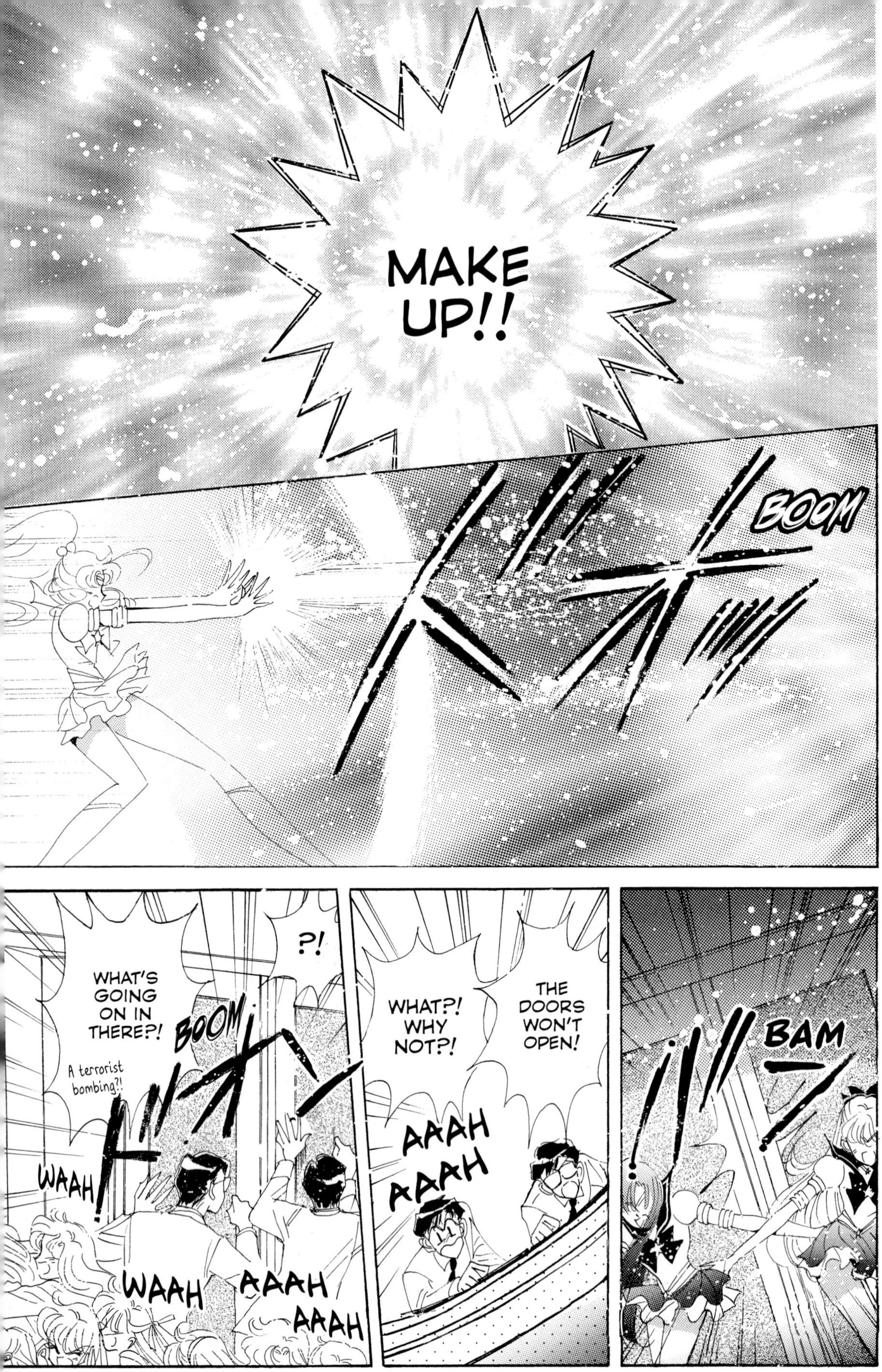
MAKE UP!!
BOOM
BAM
THE DOORS WON'T OPEN!
WHAT?! WHY NOT?!
AAAH AAAH
?!
WHAT'S GOING ON IN THERE?!
BOOM
A terrorist bombing?!
WAAH
WAAH
AAAH AAAH

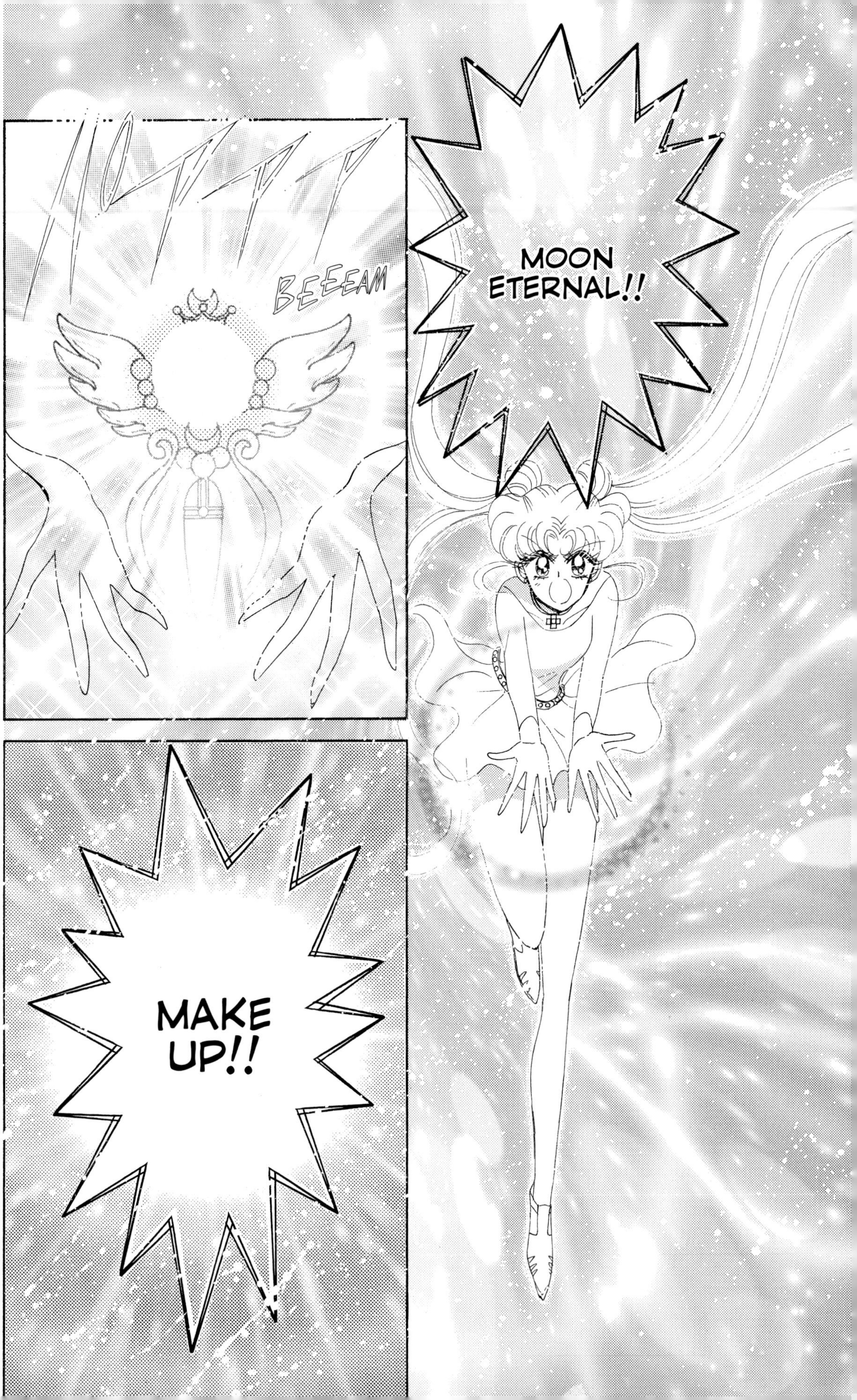
MOON ETERNAL!!
BEEEAM
MAKE UP!!

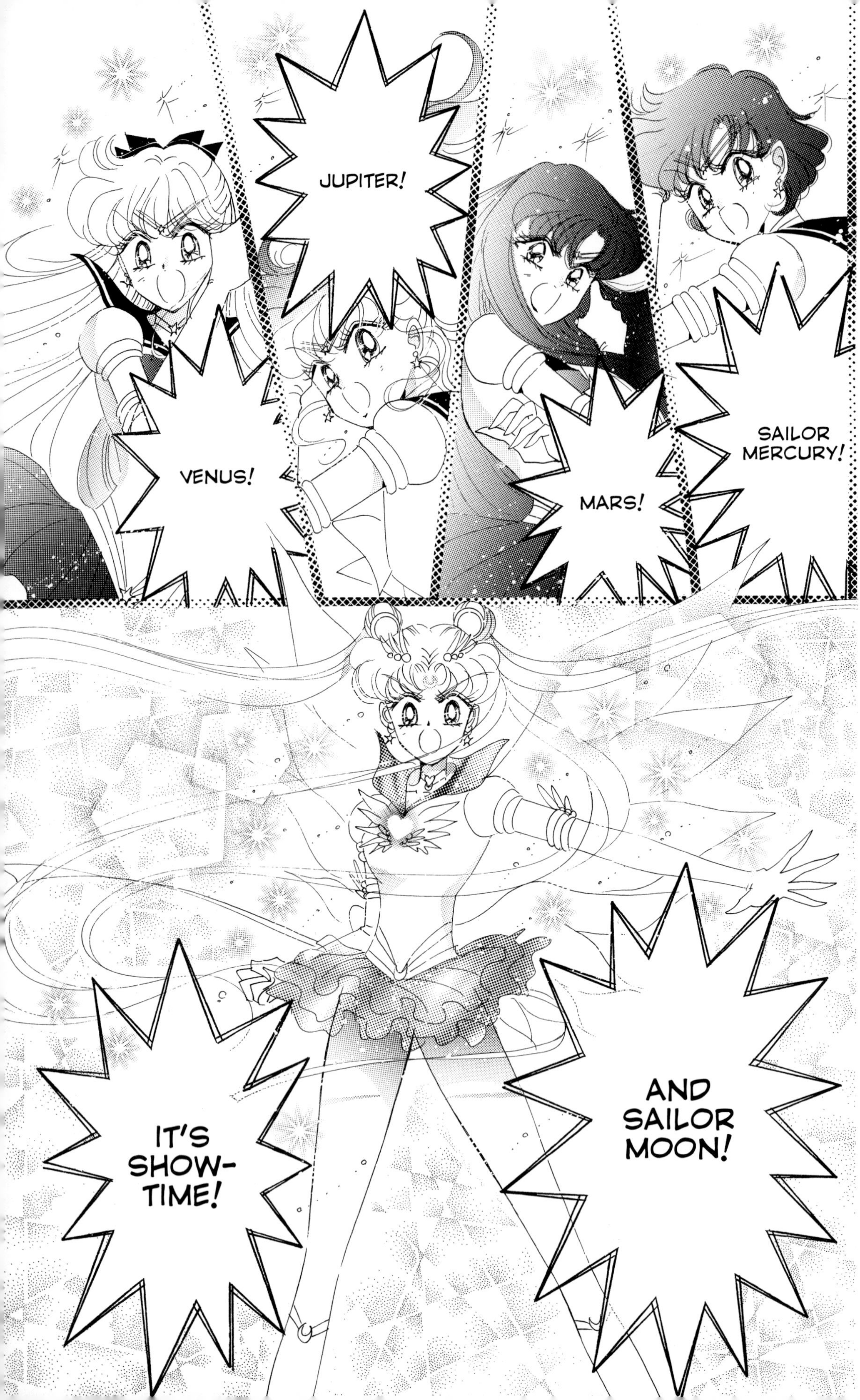
SAILOR MERCURY!
MARS!
JUPITER!
VENUS!
AND SAILOR MOON!
IT'S SHOW-TIME!

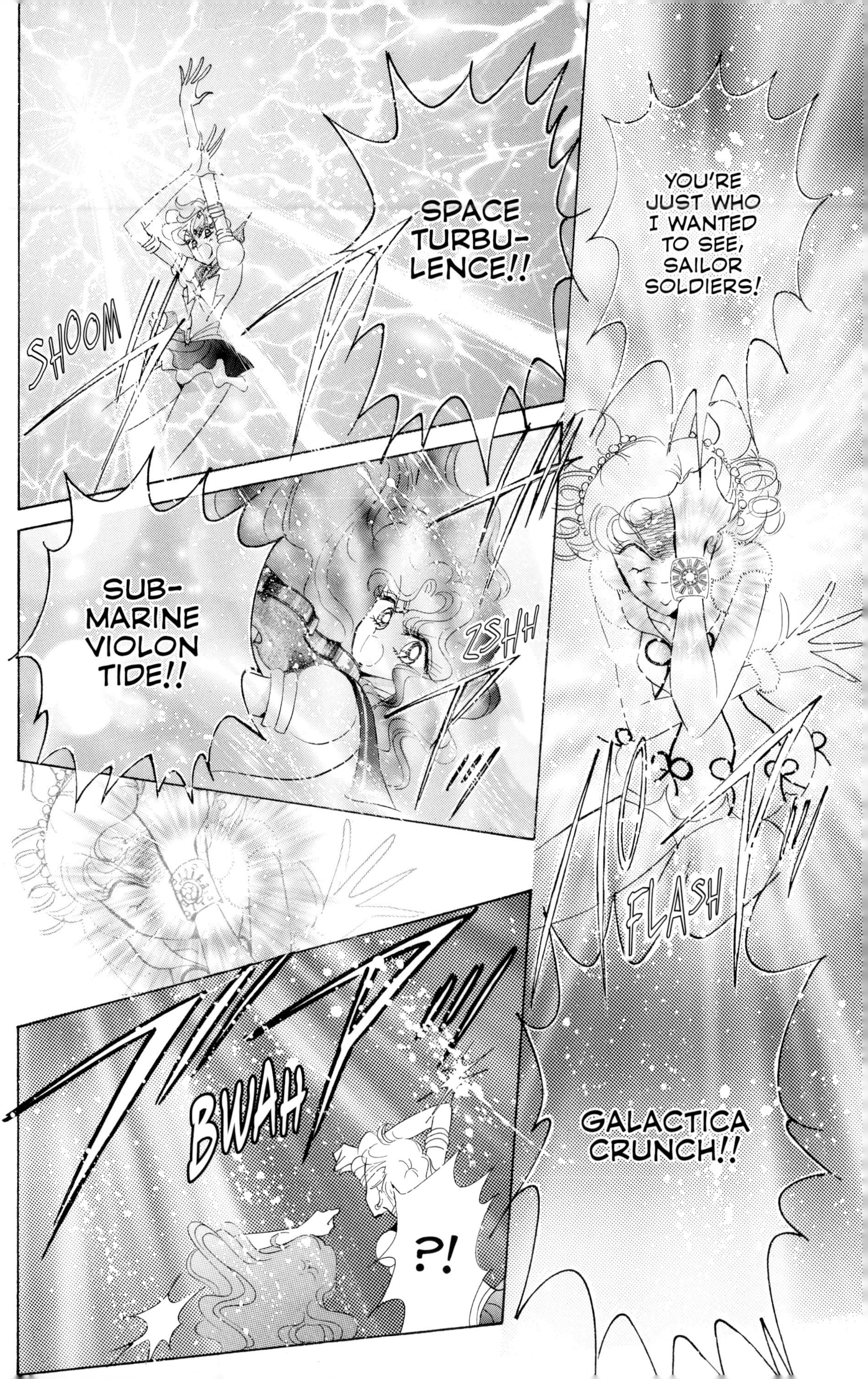
YOU'RE JUST WHO I WANTED TO SEE, SAILOR SOLDIERS!
FLASH
GALACTICA CRUNCH!!
SPACE TURBULENCE!!
SHOOM
SUBMARINE VIOLON TIDE!!
ZSHH
BWAH
?!

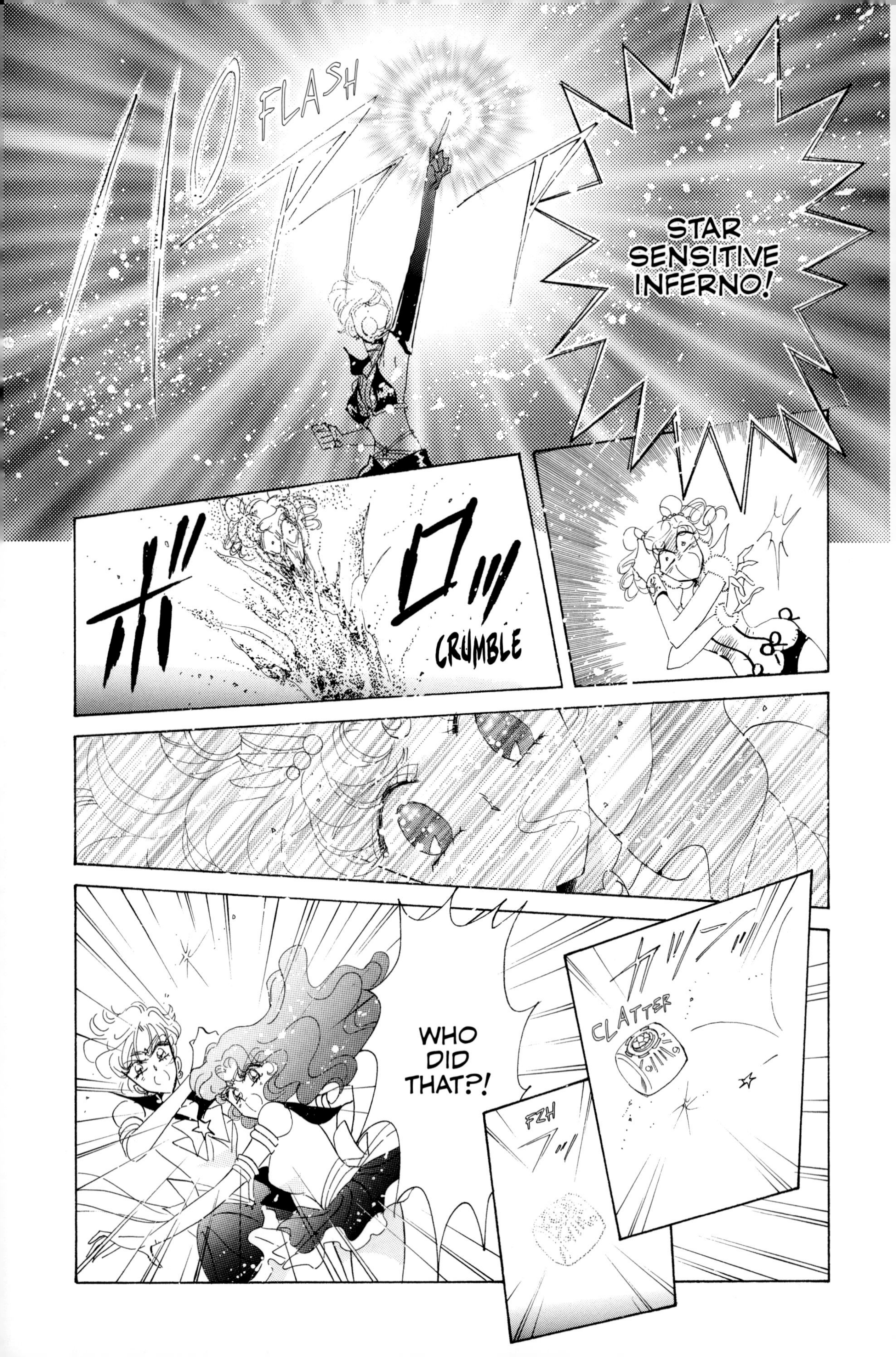
FLASH
STAR SENSITIVE INFERNO!
CRUMBLE
CLATTER
FZH
WHO DID THAT?!

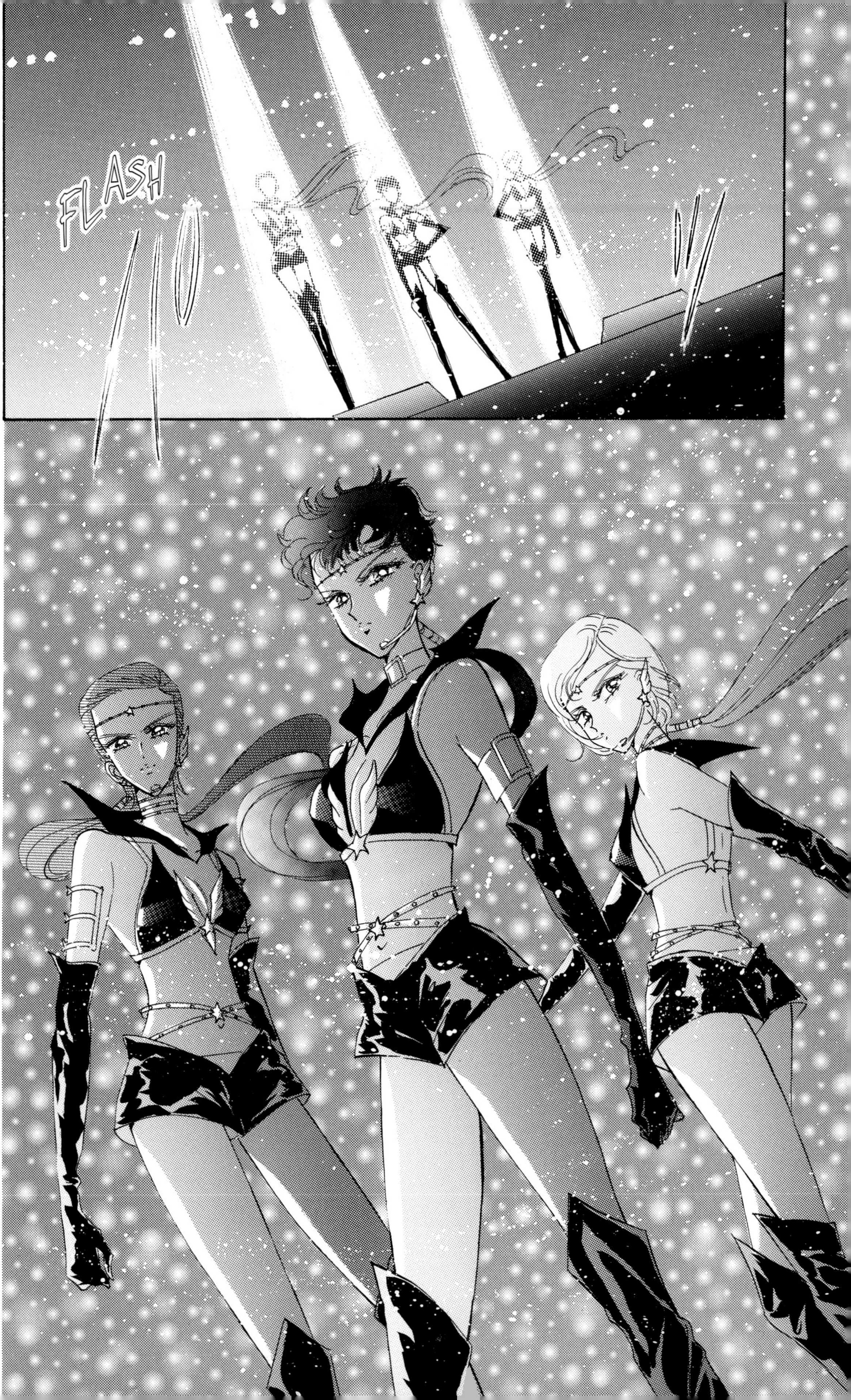
FLASH

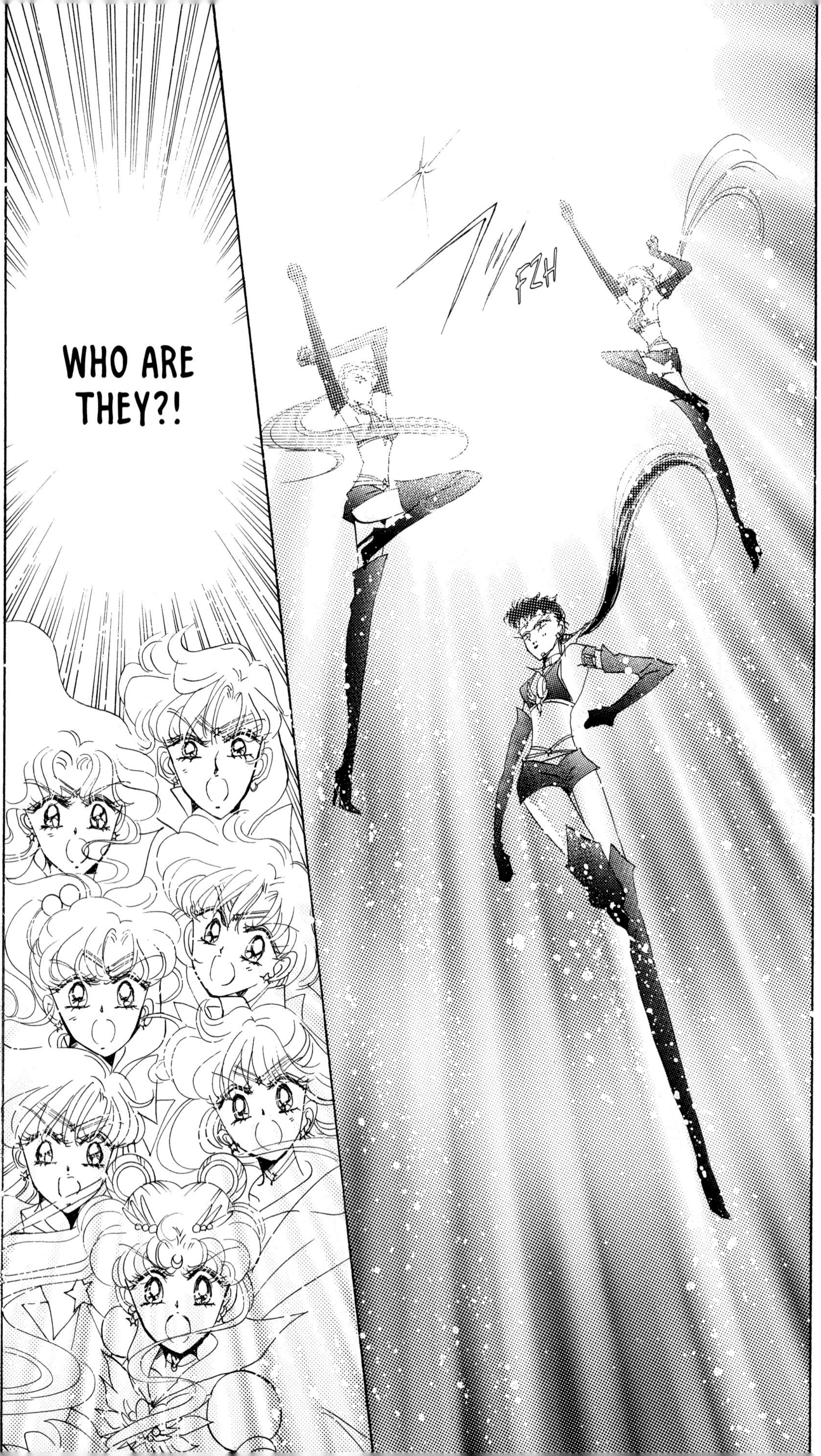
FZH
WHO ARE THEY?!

Pretty Guardian

Sailor Moon

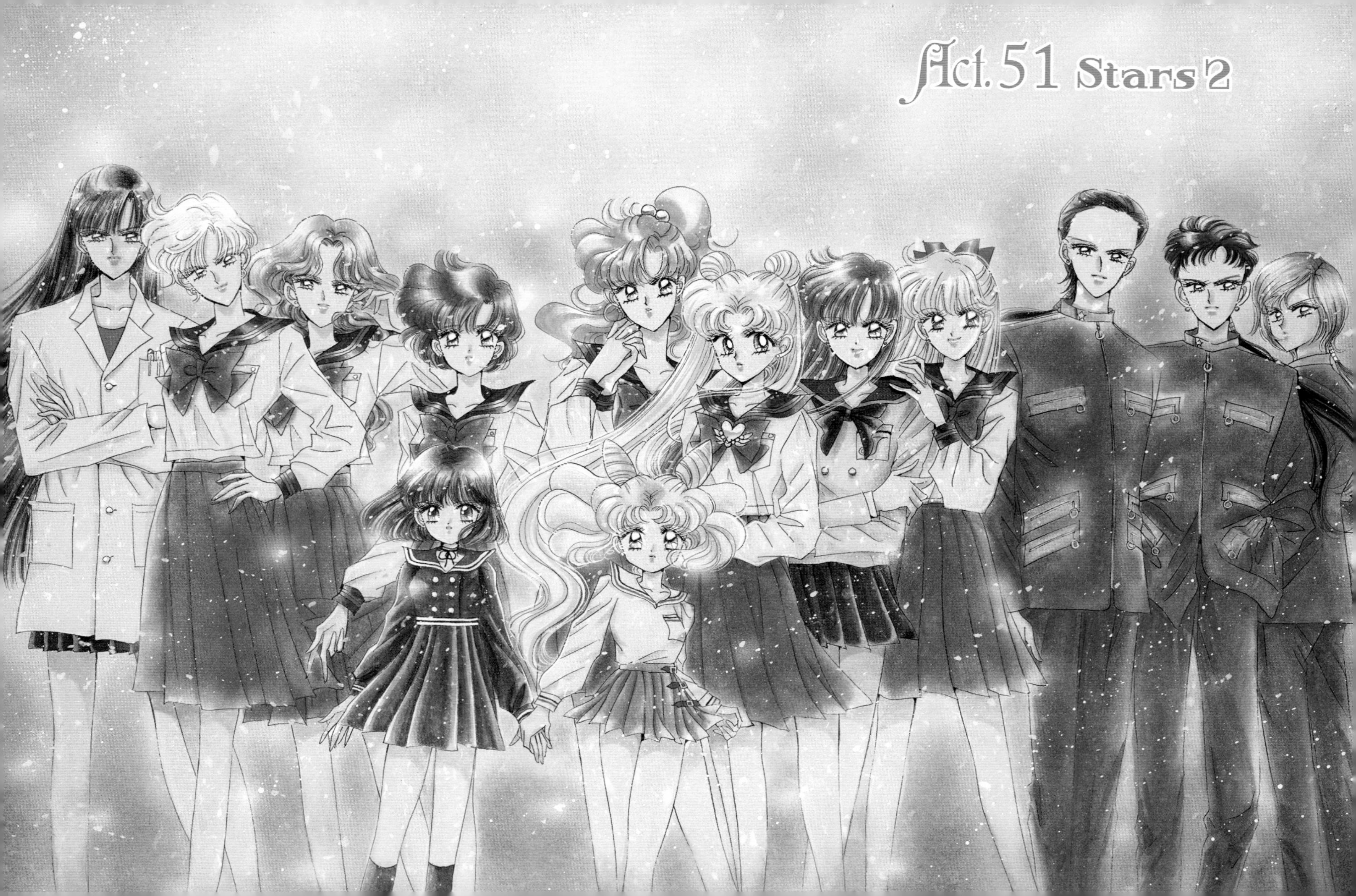
Act.51 Stars 2

Pretty Guardian

Sailor Moon

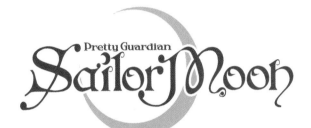

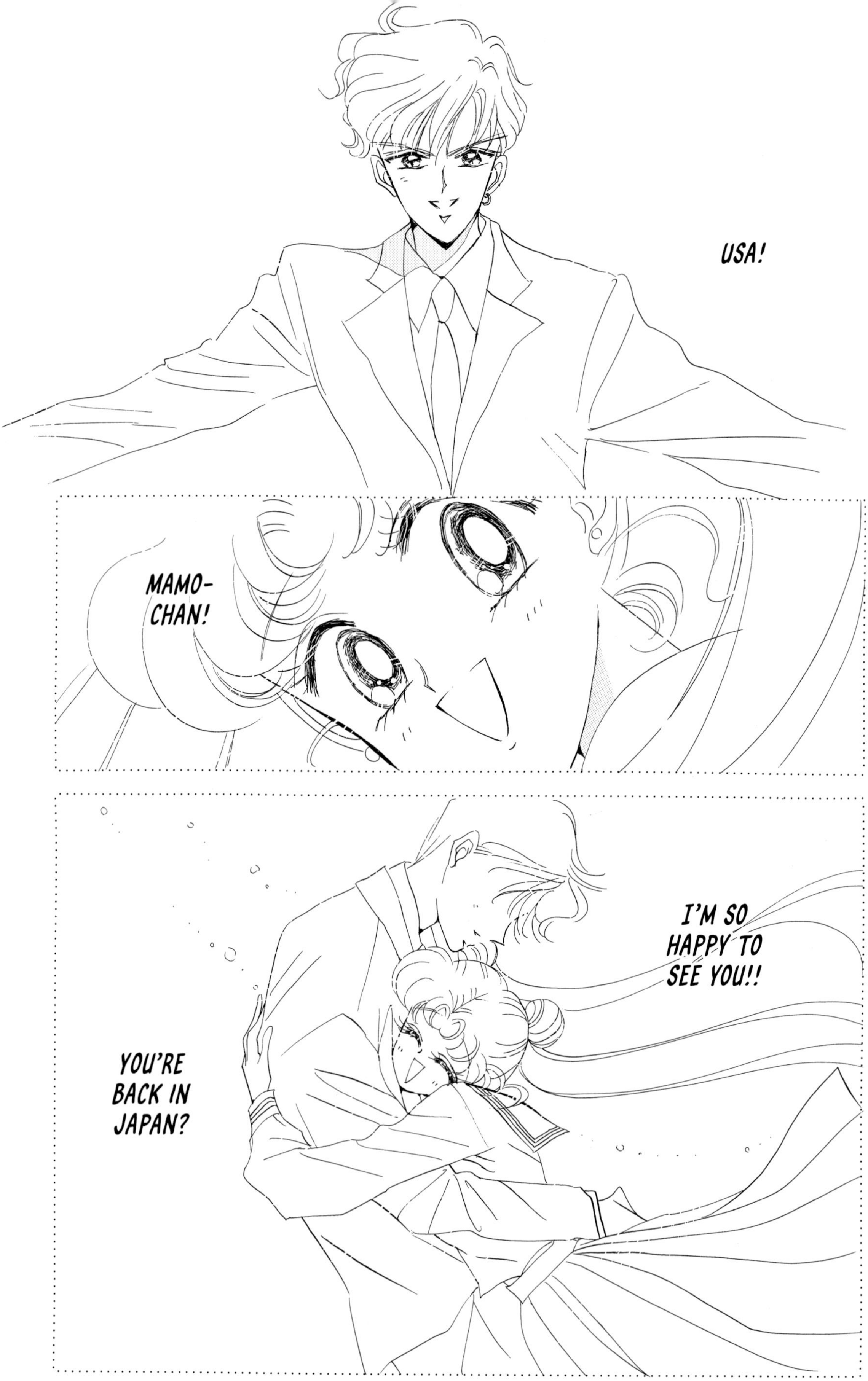
USA!
MAMO-CHAN!
I'M SO HAPPY TO SEE YOU!!
YOU'RE BACK IN JAPAN?

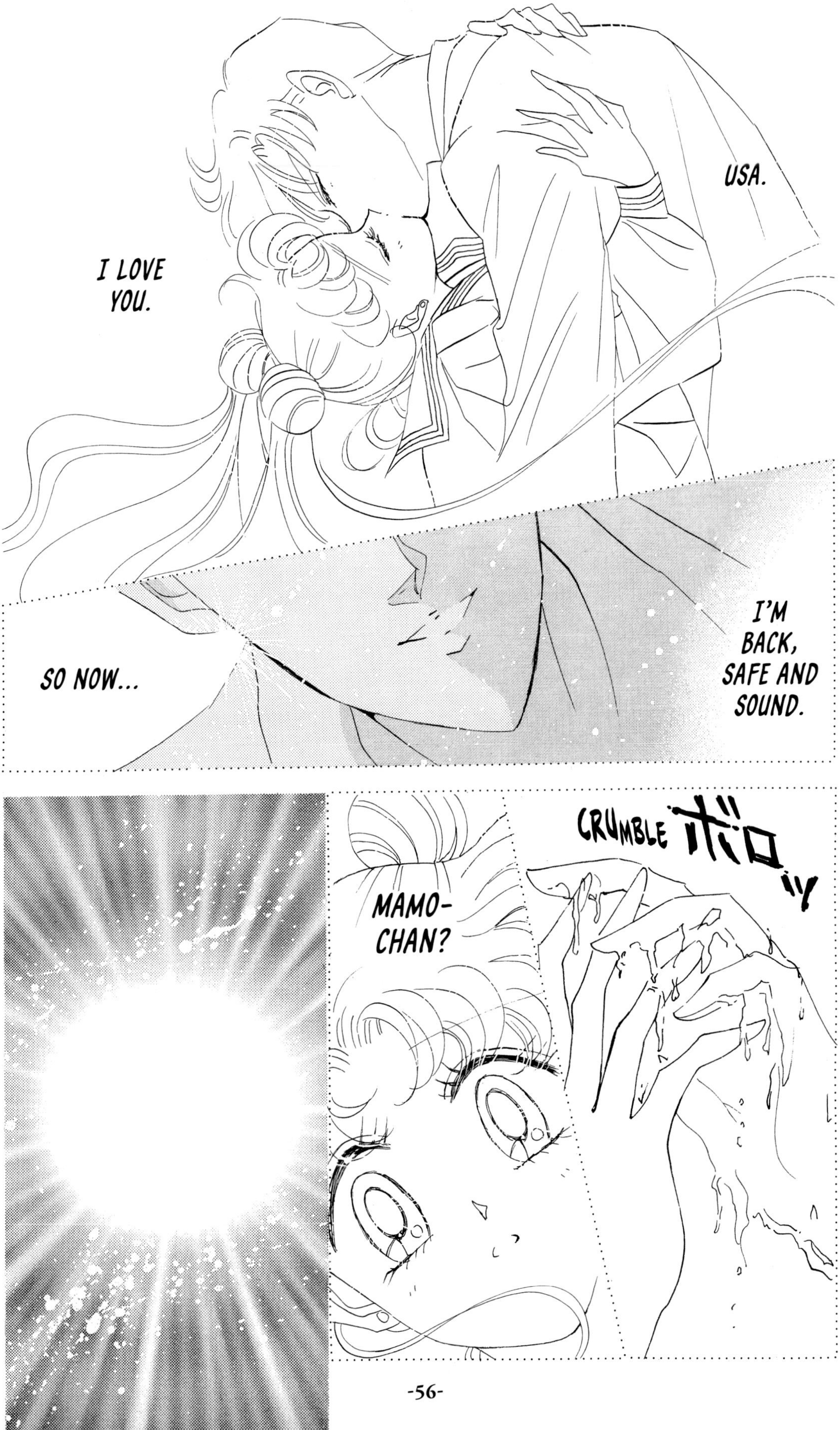
USA.
I LOVE YOU.
I'M BACK, SAFE AND SOUND.
SO NOW...
CRUMBLE ボロッ
MAMO-CHAN?

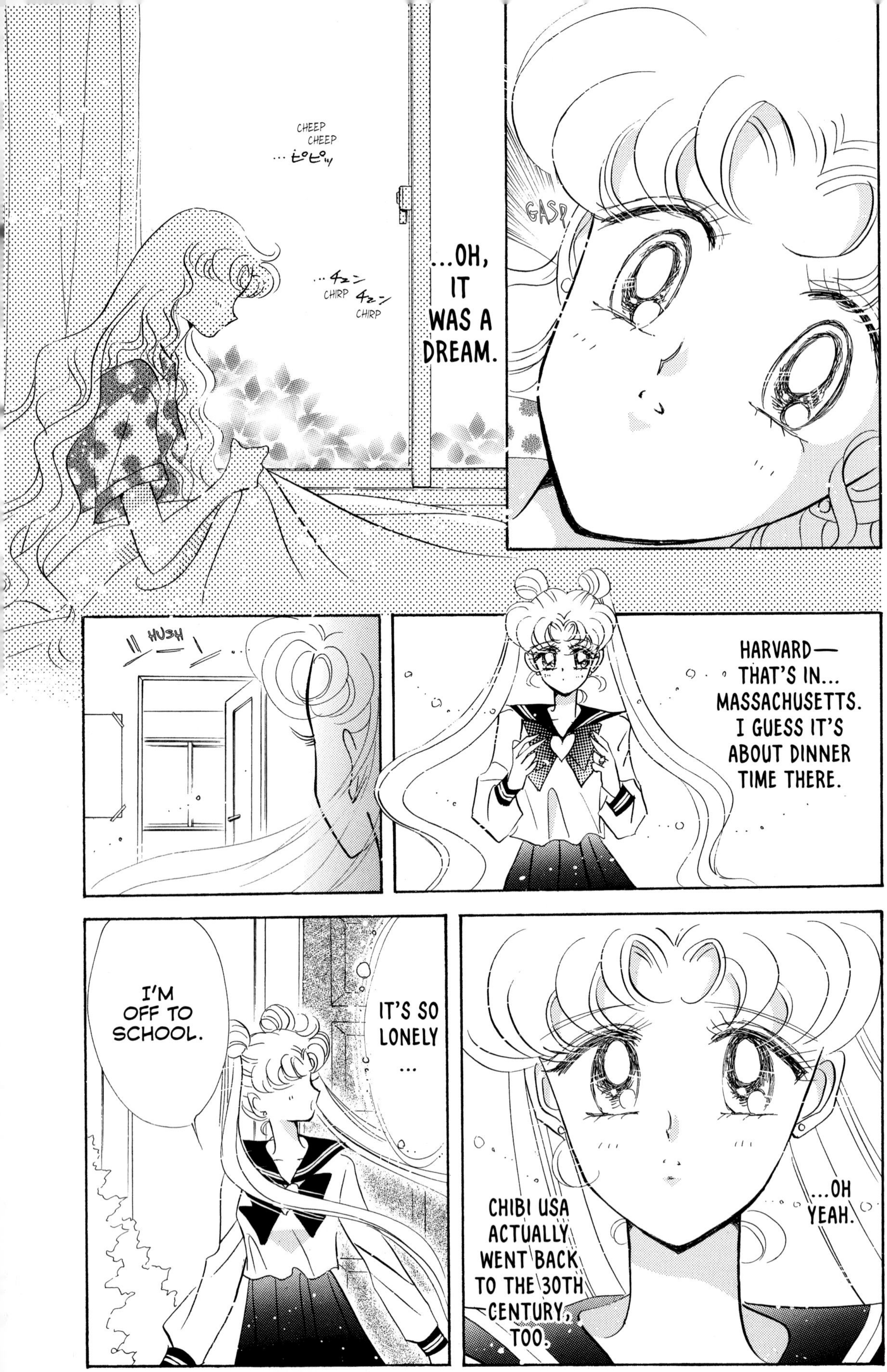
GASP
CHEEP CHEEP
...ピピッ
...チュン CHIRP
チュン CHIRP
...OH, IT WAS A DREAM.
HARVARD—THAT'S IN... MASSACHUSETTS. I GUESS IT'S ABOUT DINNER TIME THERE.
HUSH
...OH YEAH.
CHIBI USA ACTUALLY WENT BACK TO THE 30TH CENTURY, TOO.
IT'S SO LONELY ...
I'M OFF TO SCHOOL.

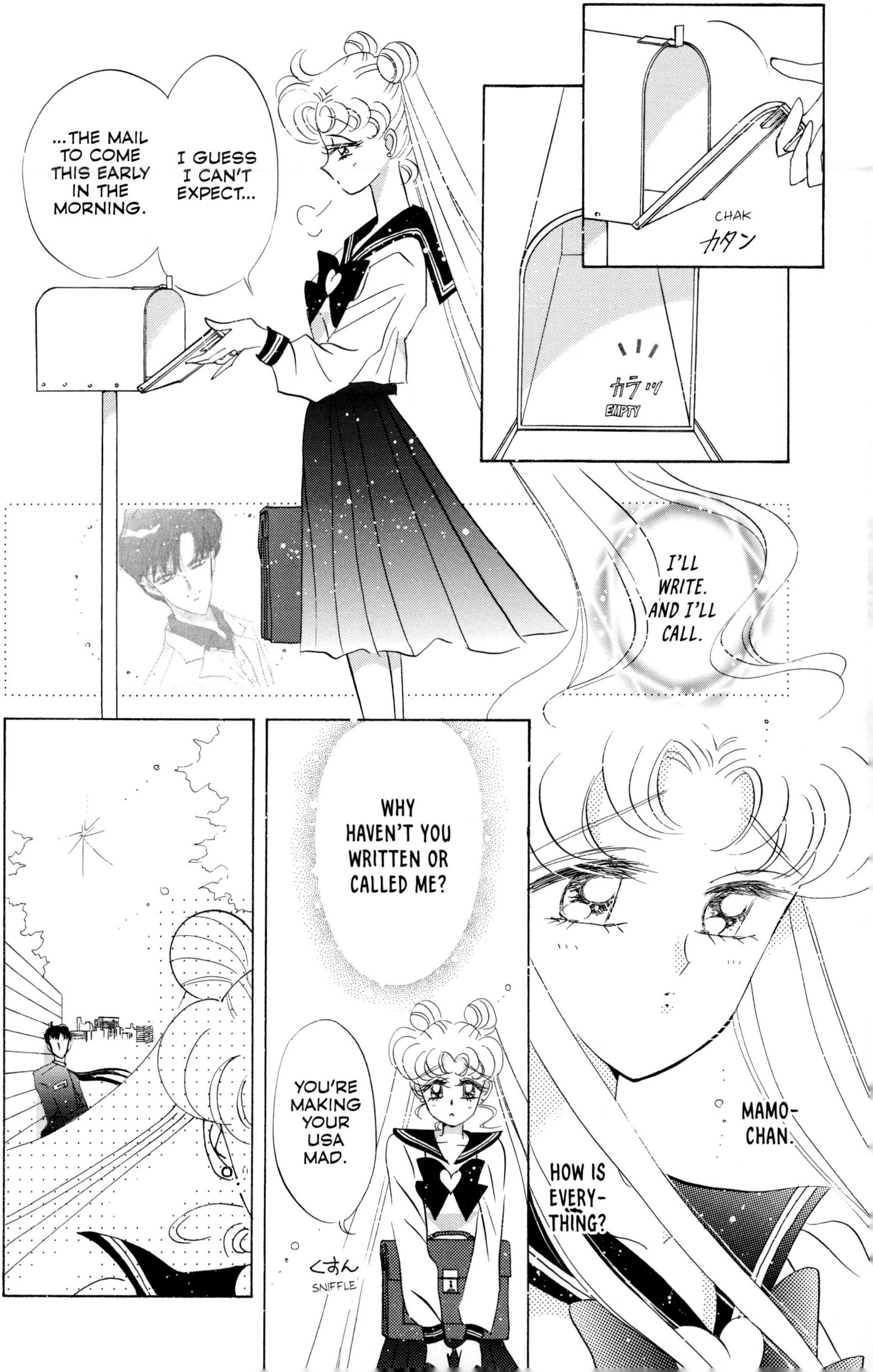
CHAK
カタン
カラッ
EMPTY
I GUESS I CAN'T EXPECT...
...THE MAIL TO COME THIS EARLY IN THE MORNING.
I'LL WRITE. AND I'LL CALL.
MAMO-CHAN.
HOW IS EVERY-THING?
WHY HAVEN'T YOU WRITTEN OR CALLED ME?
YOU'RE MAKING YOUR USA MAD.
くすん
SNIFFLE

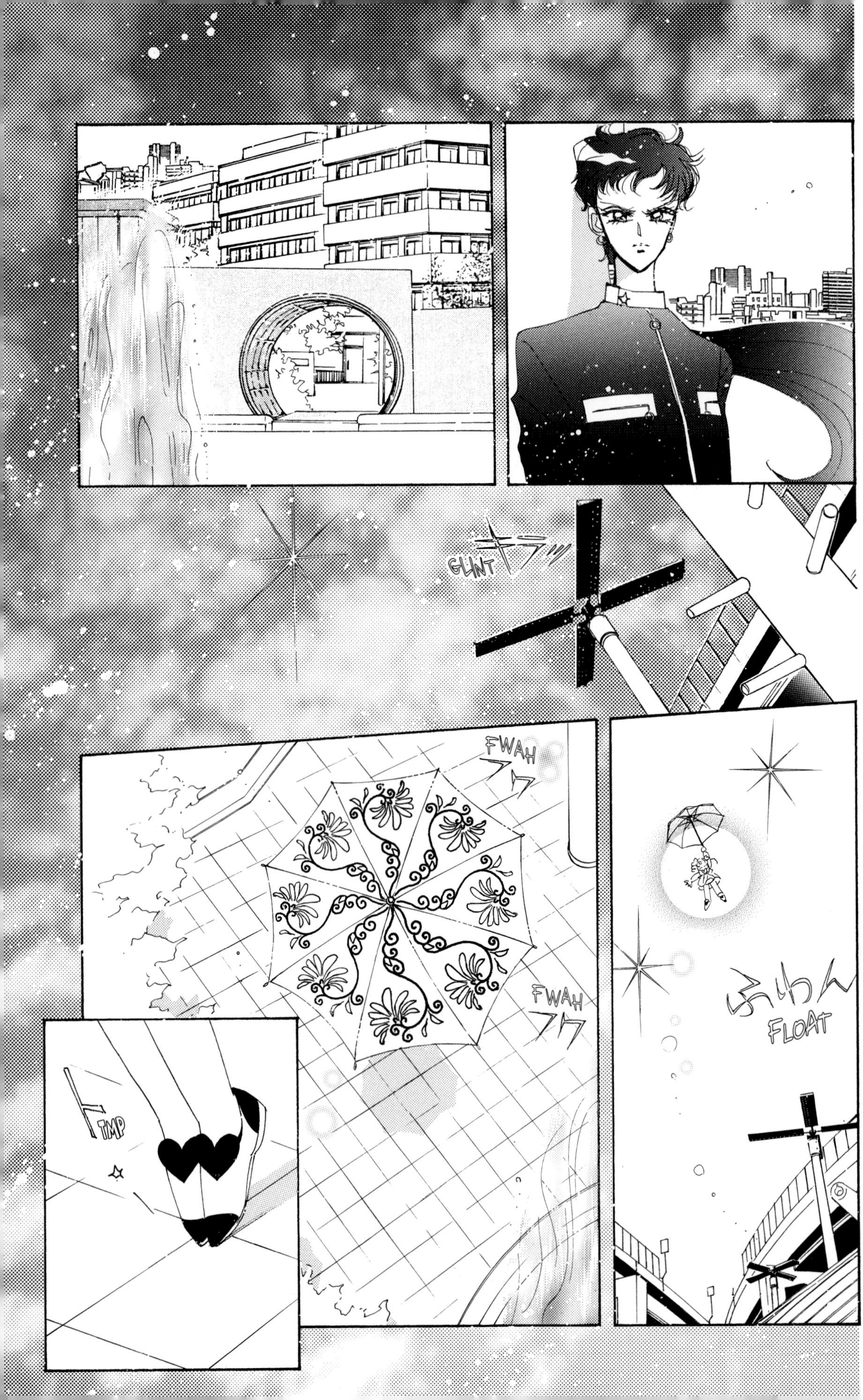
GLINT
キラッ
ふわん
FLOAT
FWAH
フワ
FWAH
フワ
TMP

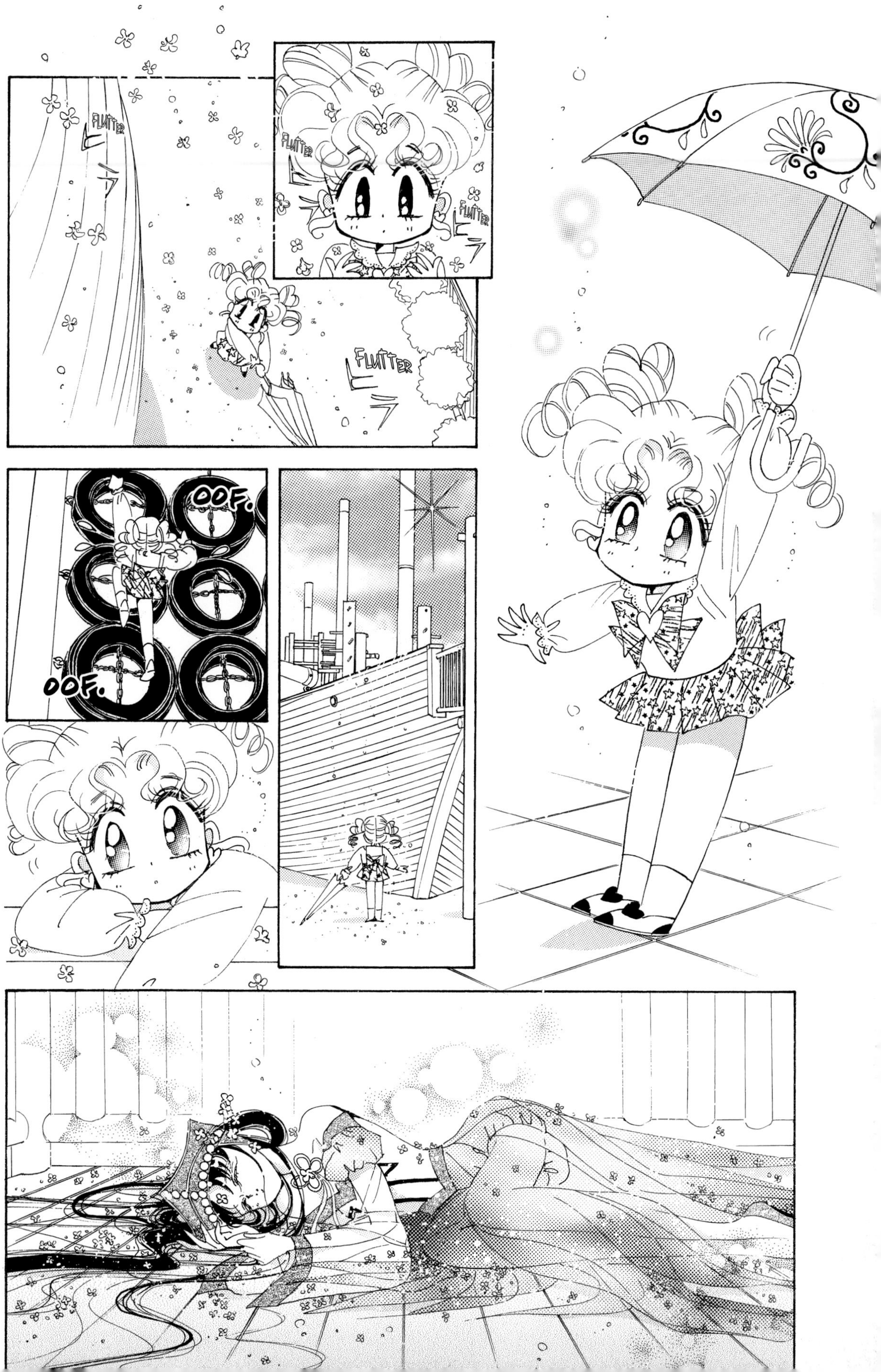
FLUTTER
ヒラ
FLUTTER
ヒラ
FLUTTER
ヒラ
FLUTTER
ヒラ
OOF.
OOF.

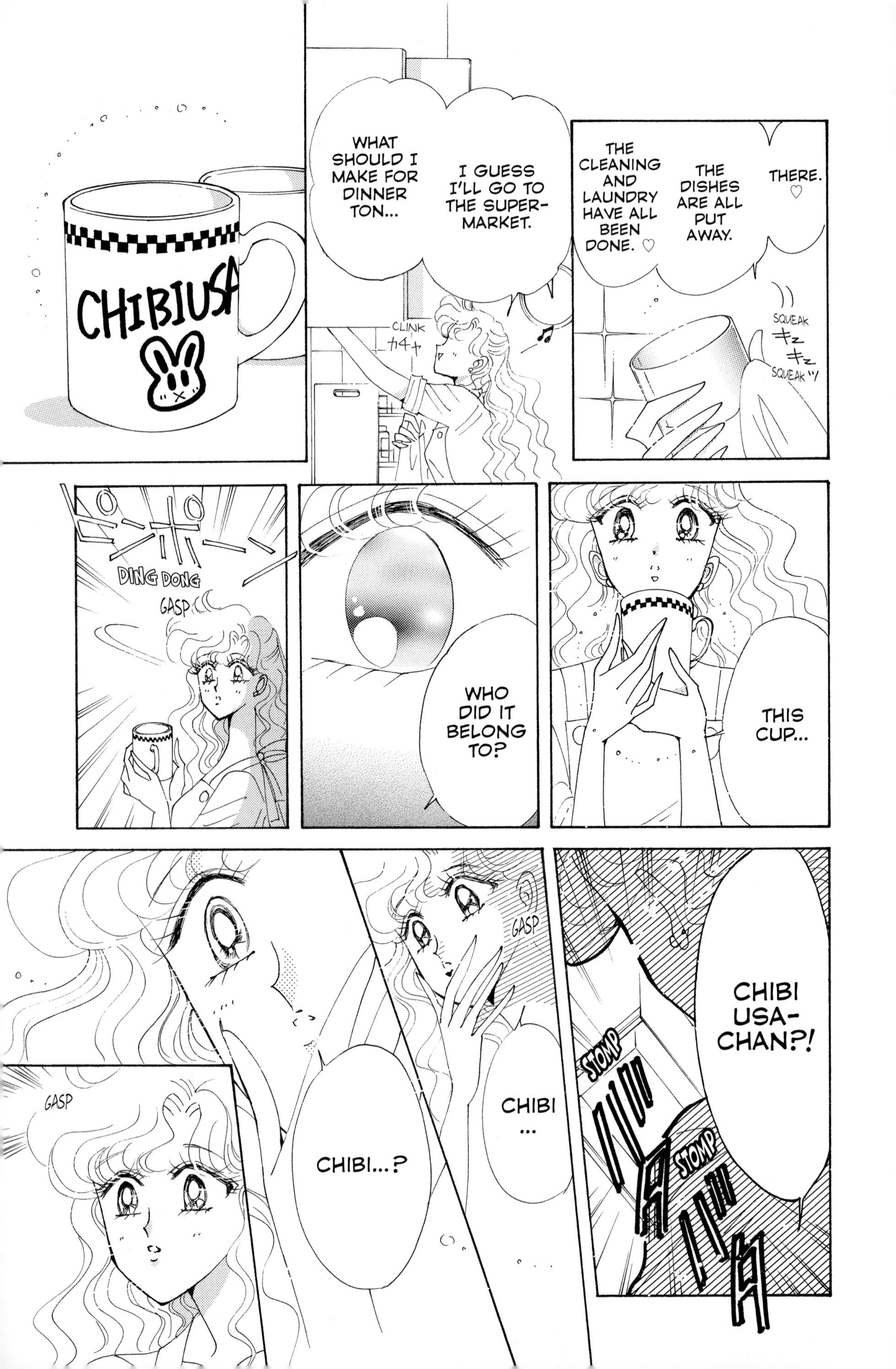
THERE. ♡
THE DISHES ARE ALL PUT AWAY.
THE CLEANING AND LAUNDRY HAVE ALL BEEN DONE. ♡
SQUEAK キュ
キュッ SQUEAK
I GUESS I'LL GO TO THE SUPER-MARKET.
WHAT SHOULD I MAKE FOR DINNER TON...
CLINK カチャ
CHIBIUSA
THIS CUP...
WHO DID IT BELONG TO?
ピンポーン
DING DONG
GASP
CHIBI USA-CHAN?!
STOMP
STOMP
GASP
CHIBI ...
CHIBI...?
GASP

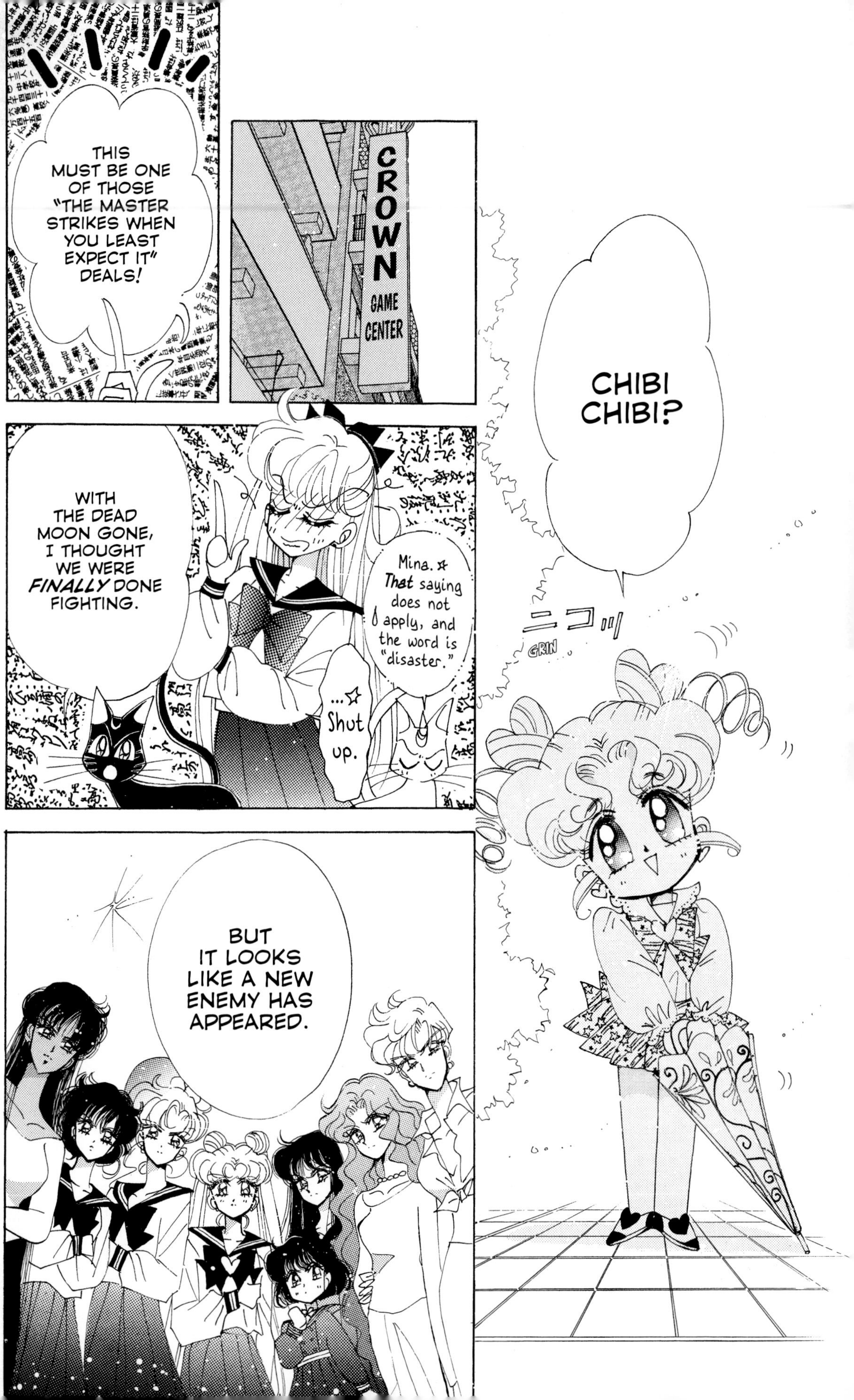
CROWN
GAME CENTER
THIS MUST BE ONE OF THOSE "THE MASTER STRIKES WHEN YOU LEAST EXPECT IT" DEALS!
CHIBI CHIBI?
ニコッ
GRIN
WITH THE DEAD MOON GONE, I THOUGHT WE WERE FINALLY DONE FIGHTING.
Mina. ☆ That saying does not apply, and the word is "disaster."
...☆ Shut up.
BUT IT LOOKS LIKE A NEW ENEMY HAS APPEARED.

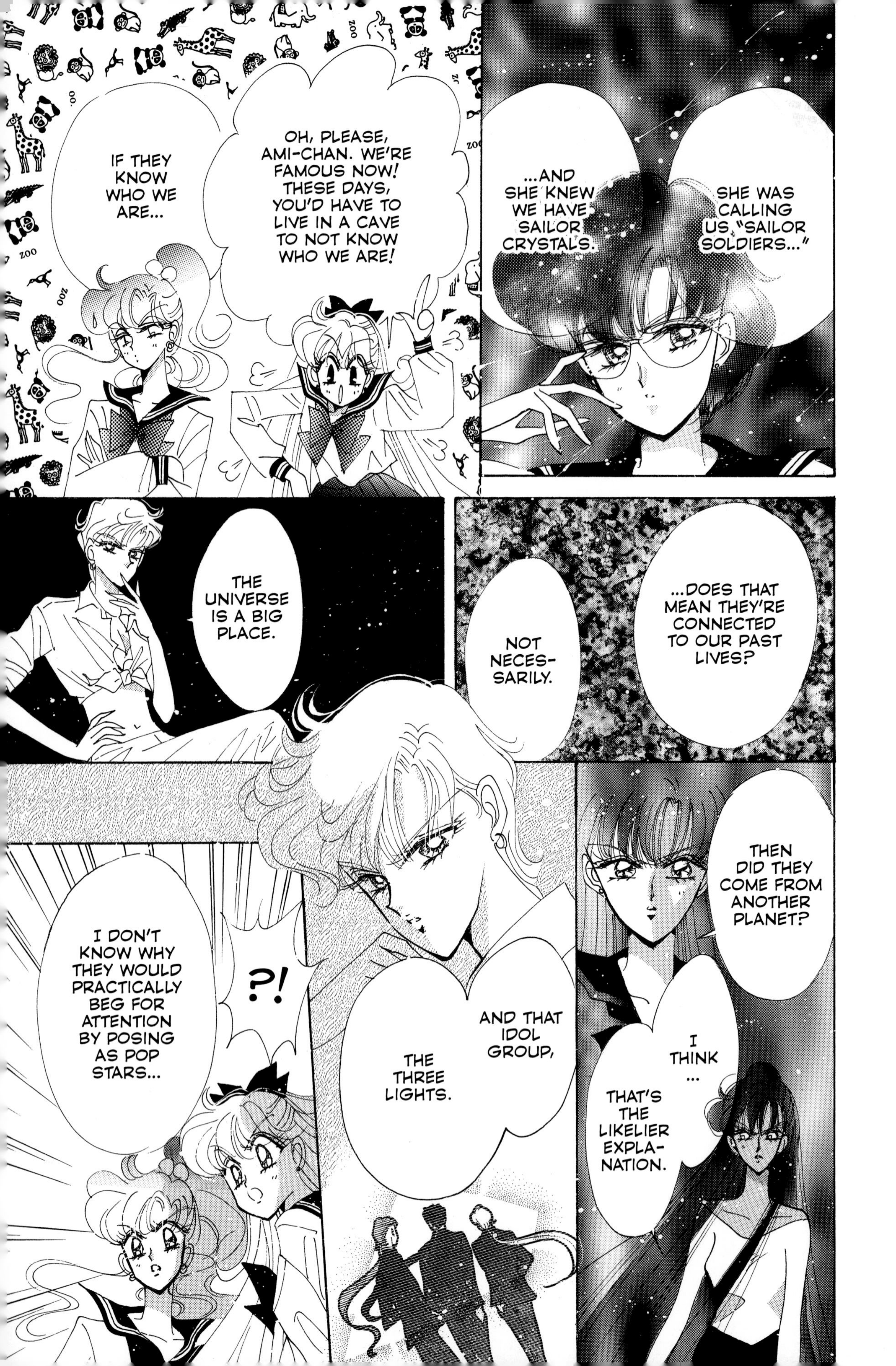
SHE WAS CALLING US "SAILOR SOLDIERS..."
...AND SHE KNEW WE HAVE SAILOR CRYSTALS.
IF THEY KNOW WHO WE ARE...
OH, PLEASE, AMI-CHAN. WE'RE FAMOUS NOW! THESE DAYS, YOU'D HAVE TO LIVE IN A CAVE TO NOT KNOW WHO WE ARE!
...DOES THAT MEAN THEY'RE CONNECTED TO OUR PAST LIVES?
NOT NECES-SARILY.
THE UNIVERSE IS A BIG PLACE.
THEN DID THEY COME FROM ANOTHER PLANET?
I THINK...
THAT'S THE LIKELIER EXPLA-NATION.
AND THAT IDOL GROUP,
THE THREE LIGHTS.
I DON'T KNOW WHY THEY WOULD PRACTICALLY BEG FOR ATTENTION BY POSING AS POP STARS...
?!

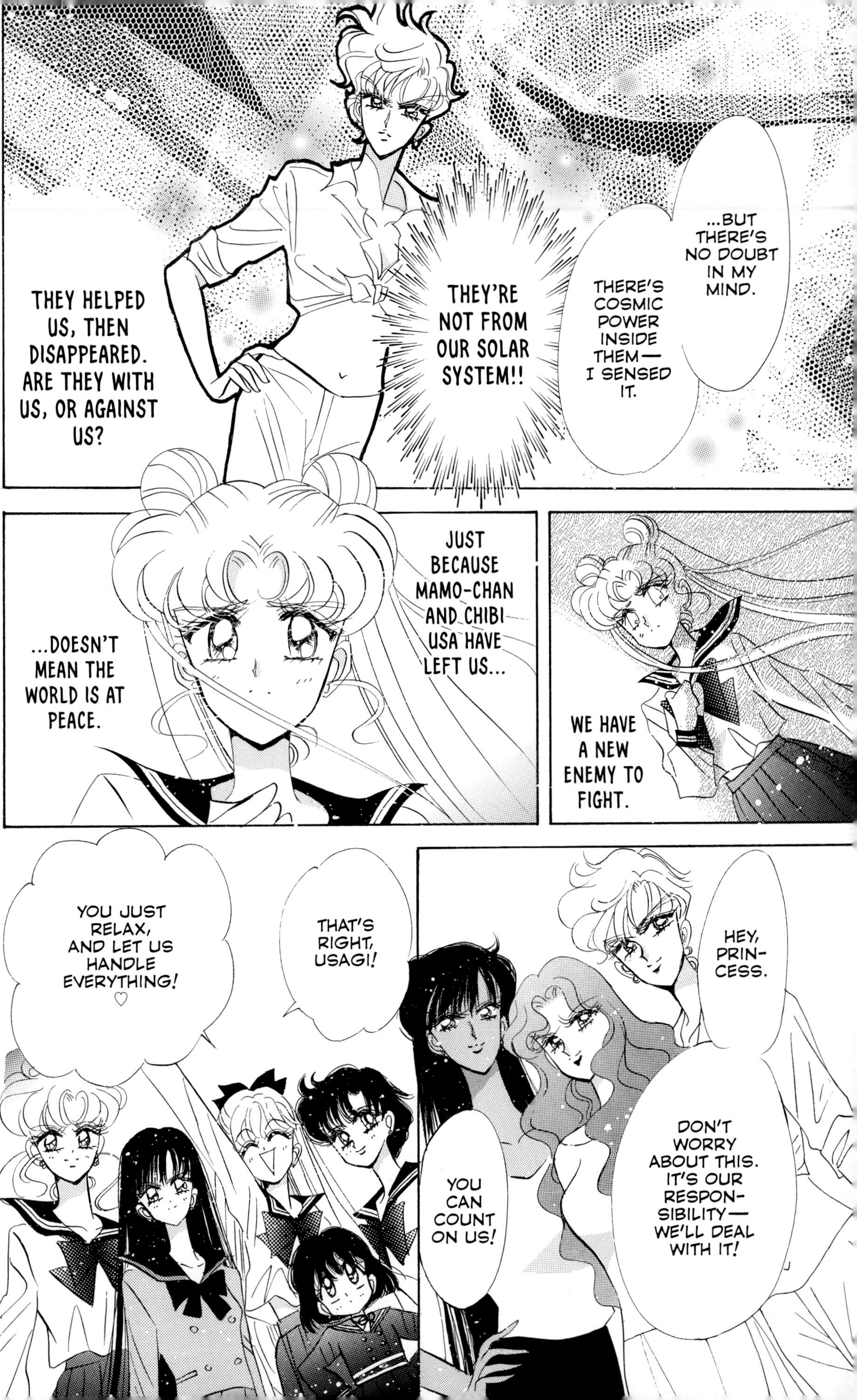

...BUT THERE'S NO DOUBT IN MY MIND.
THERE'S COSMIC POWER INSIDE THEM— I SENSED IT.
THEY'RE NOT FROM OUR SOLAR SYSTEM!!
THEY HELPED US, THEN DISAPPEARED. ARE THEY WITH US, OR AGAINST US?
WE HAVE A NEW ENEMY TO FIGHT.
JUST BECAUSE MAMO-CHAN AND CHIBI USA HAVE LEFT US...
...DOESN'T MEAN THE WORLD IS AT PEACE.
HEY, PRINCESS.
DON'T WORRY ABOUT THIS. IT'S OUR RESPONSIBILITY— WE'LL DEAL WITH IT!
YOU CAN COUNT ON US!
THAT'S RIGHT, USAGI!
YOU JUST RELAX, AND LET US HANDLE EVERYTHING! ♡

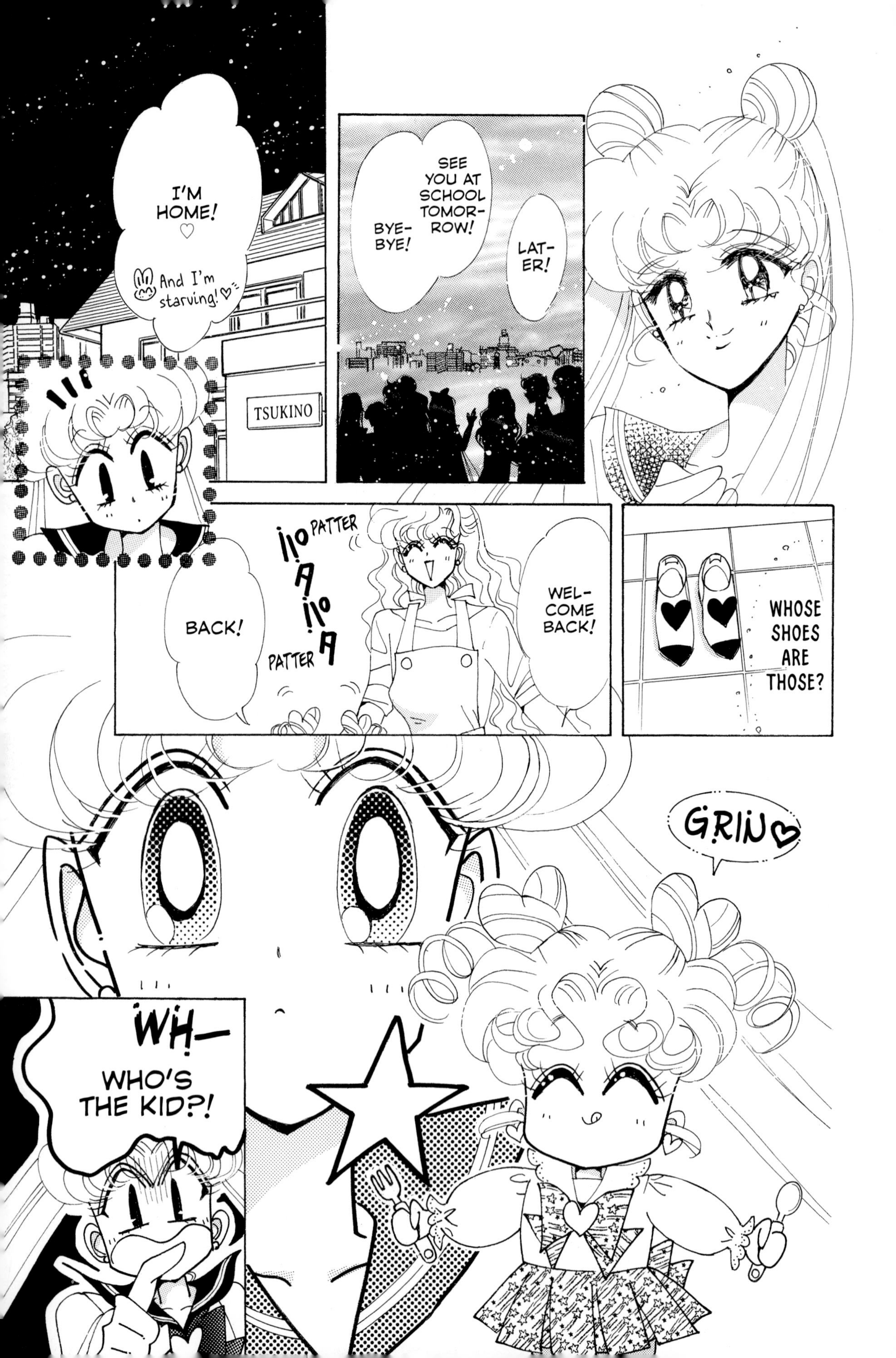
LATER!
SEE YOU AT SCHOOL TOMORROW!
BYE-BYE!
I'M HOME! ♡
And I'm starving! ♡
TSUKINO
WHOSE SHOES ARE THOSE?
WELCOME BACK!
PATTER
PATTER
BACK!
GRIN ♡
WH— WHO'S THE KID?!

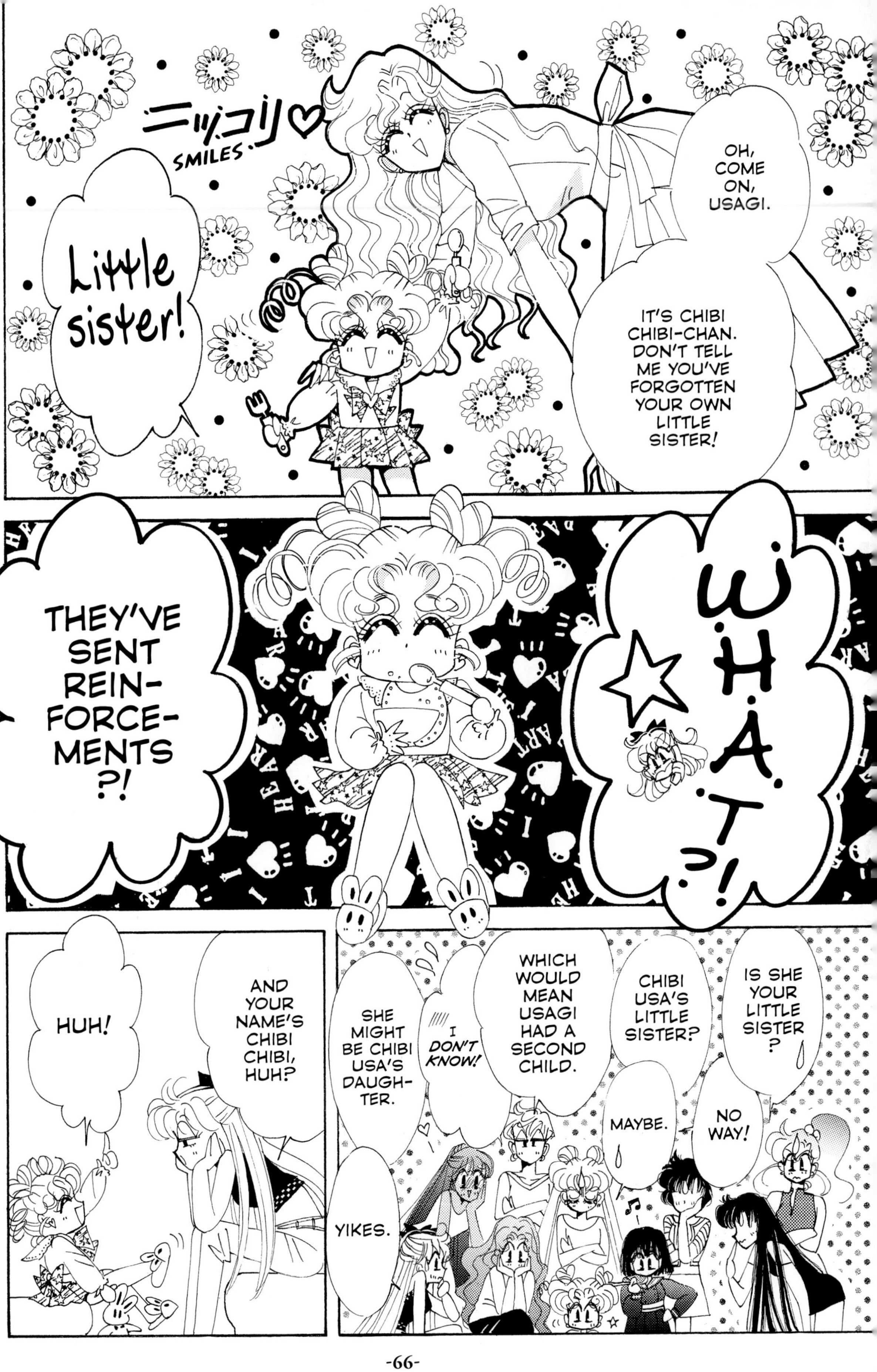
OH, COME ON, USAGI.
IT'S CHIBI CHIBI-CHAN. DON'T TELL ME YOU'VE FORGOTTEN YOUR OWN LITTLE SISTER!
ニッコリ♡
SMILES.
Little sister!
W.H.A.T?!
THEY'VE SENT REIN-FORCE-MENTS?!
IS SHE YOUR LITTLE SISTER?
NO WAY!
CHIBI USA'S LITTLE SISTER?
MAYBE.
WHICH WOULD MEAN USAGI HAD A SECOND CHILD.
I DON'T KNOW!
SHE MIGHT BE CHIBI USA'S DAUGH-TER.
YIKES.
AND YOUR NAME'S CHIBI CHIBI, HUH?
HUH!

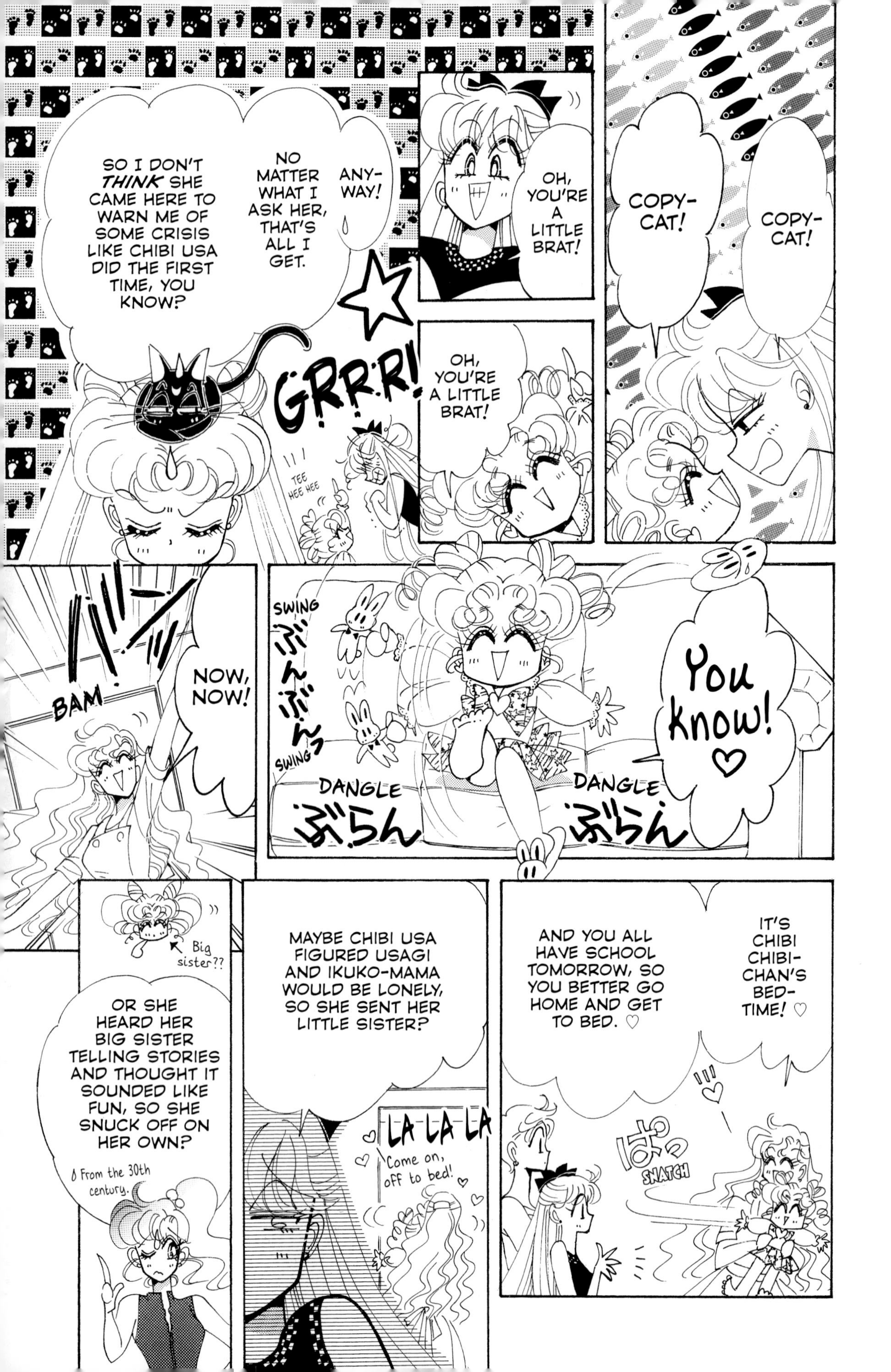
COPY-CAT!
COPY-CAT!
OH, YOU'RE A LITTLE BRAT!
OH, YOU'RE A LITTLE BRAT!
ANY-WAY!
NO MATTER WHAT I ASK HER, THAT'S ALL I GET.
SO I DON'T *THINK* SHE CAME HERE TO WARN ME OF SOME CRISIS LIKE CHIBI USA DID THE FIRST TIME, YOU KNOW?
GRRR!
TEE HEE HEE
You know! ♡
SWING
ぶんぶん
SWING
DANGLE
ぶらん
DANGLE
ぶらん
NOW, NOW!
BAM
IT'S CHIBI CHIBI-CHAN'S BED-TIME! ♡
AND YOU ALL HAVE SCHOOL TOMORROW, SO YOU BETTER GO HOME AND GET TO BED. ♡
ぱっ
SNATCH
MAYBE CHIBI USA FIGURED USAGI AND IKUKO-MAMA WOULD BE LONELY, SO SHE SENT HER LITTLE SISTER?
LA LA LA
Come on, off to bed!
Big sister??
OR SHE HEARD HER BIG SISTER TELLING STORIES AND THOUGHT IT SOUNDED LIKE FUN, SO SHE SNUCK OFF ON HER OWN?
From the 30th century.

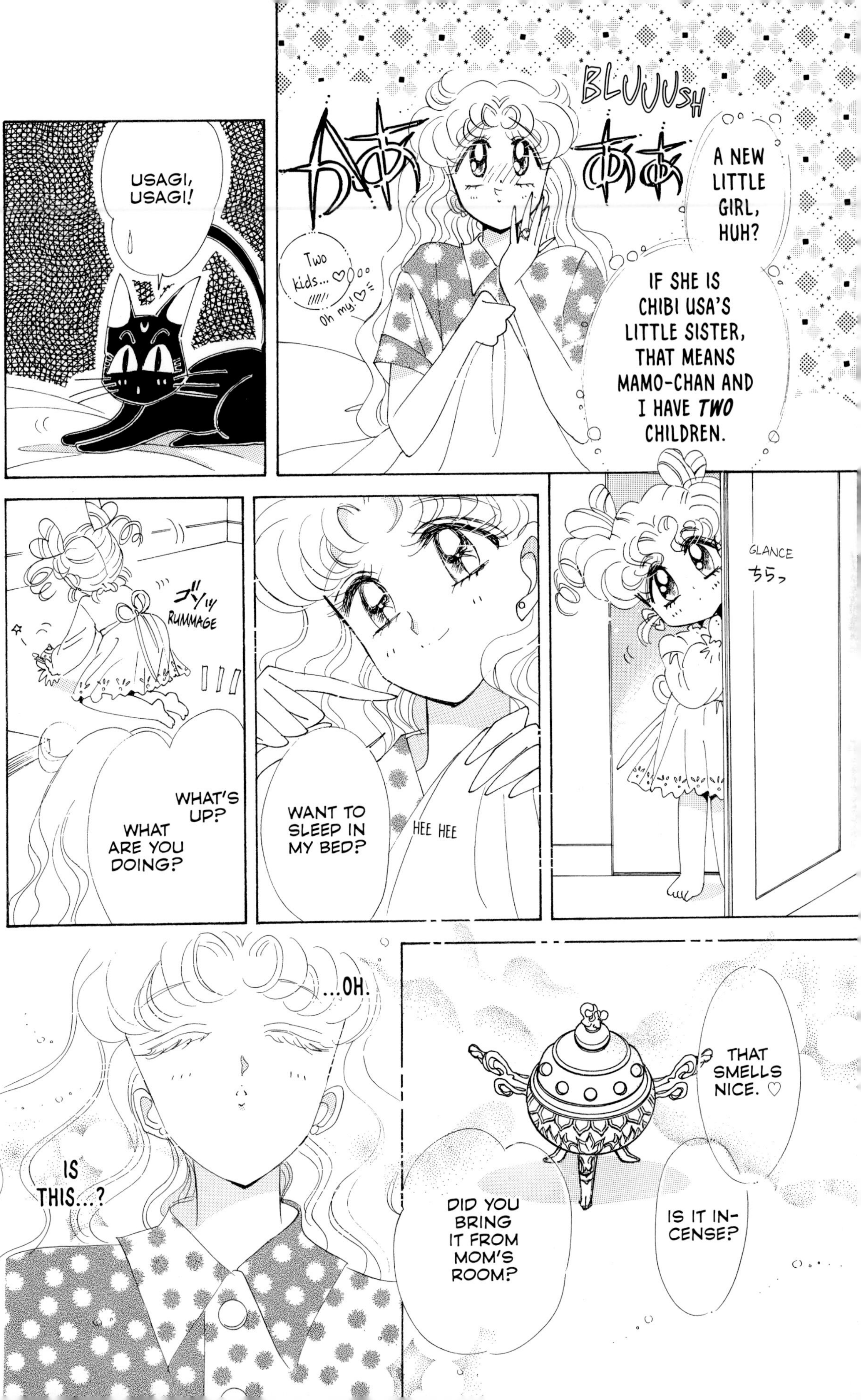
BLUUUSH
A NEW LITTLE GIRL, HUH?
IF SHE IS CHIBI USA'S LITTLE SISTER, THAT MEANS MAMO-CHAN AND I HAVE *TWO* CHILDREN.
Two kids... ♡
Oh my! ♡
USAGI, USAGI!
GLANCE
ちらっ
HEE HEE
WANT TO SLEEP IN MY BED?
ゴソッ
RUMMAGE
WHAT'S UP?
WHAT ARE YOU DOING?
THAT SMELLS NICE. ♡
IS IT IN-CENSE?
DID YOU BRING IT FROM MOM'S ROOM?
...OH.
IS THIS...?

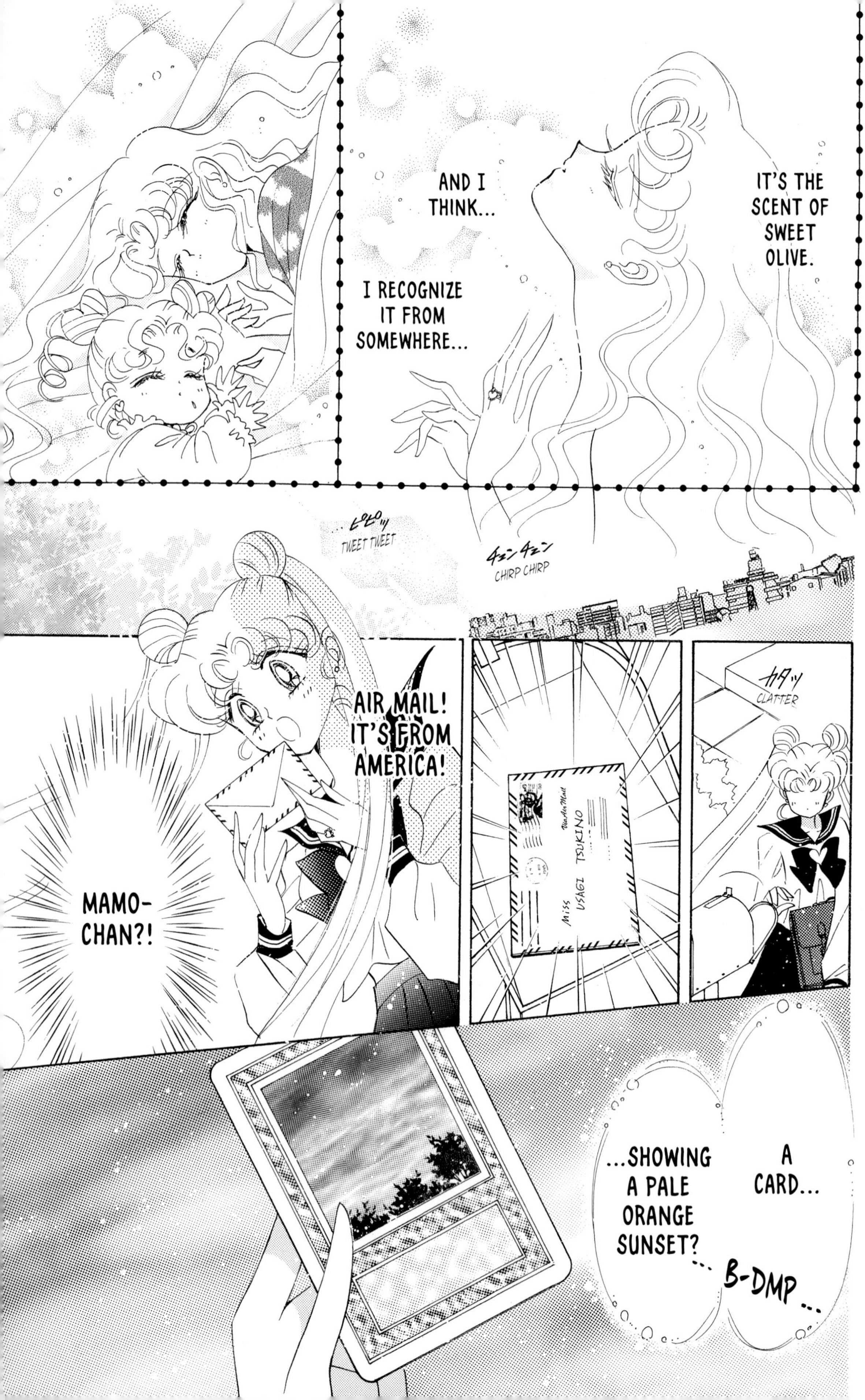
IT'S THE SCENT OF SWEET OLIVE.
AND I THINK...
I RECOGNIZE IT FROM SOMEWHERE...
チュンチュン
CHIRP CHIRP
ピロロッ
TWEET TWEET
カタッ
CLATTER
Via Air Mail
Miss USAGI TSUKINO
AIR MAIL! IT'S FROM AMERICA!
MAMO-CHAN?!
A CARD...
...SHOWING A PALE ORANGE SUNSET?
B-DMP...

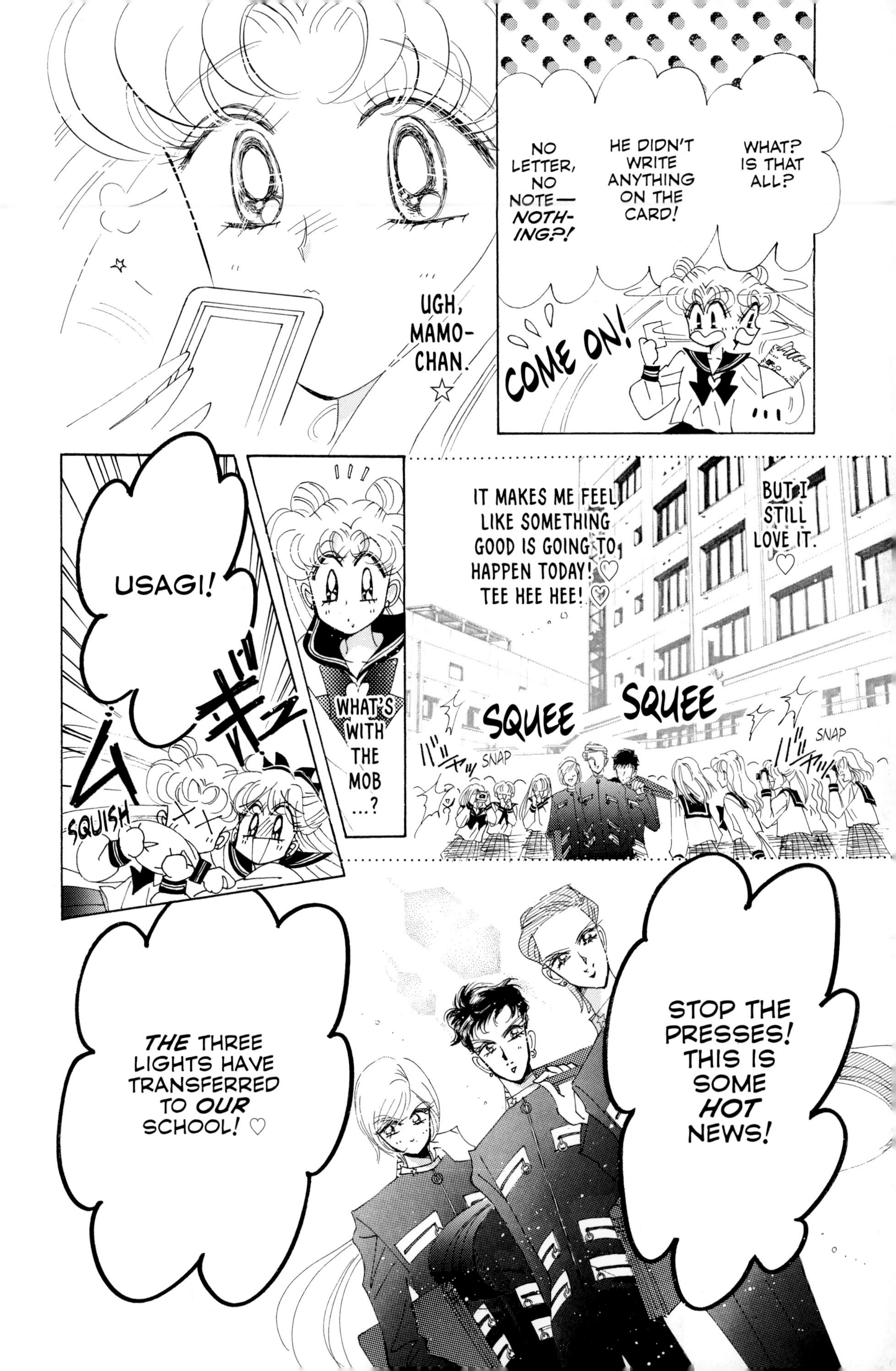
WHAT? IS THAT ALL?
HE DIDN'T WRITE ANYTHING ON THE CARD!
NO LETTER, NO NOTE—NOTHING?!
COME ON!
UGH, MAMO-CHAN. ☆
BUT I STILL LOVE IT. ♡
IT MAKES ME FEEL LIKE SOMETHING GOOD IS GOING TO HAPPEN TODAY! ♡ TEE HEE HEE! ♡
SQUEE
SQUEE
SNAP
SNAP
WHAT'S WITH THE MOB ...?
USAGI!
SQUISH
STOP THE PRESSES! THIS IS SOME HOT NEWS!
THE THREE LIGHTS HAVE TRANSFERRED TO OUR SCHOOL! ♡

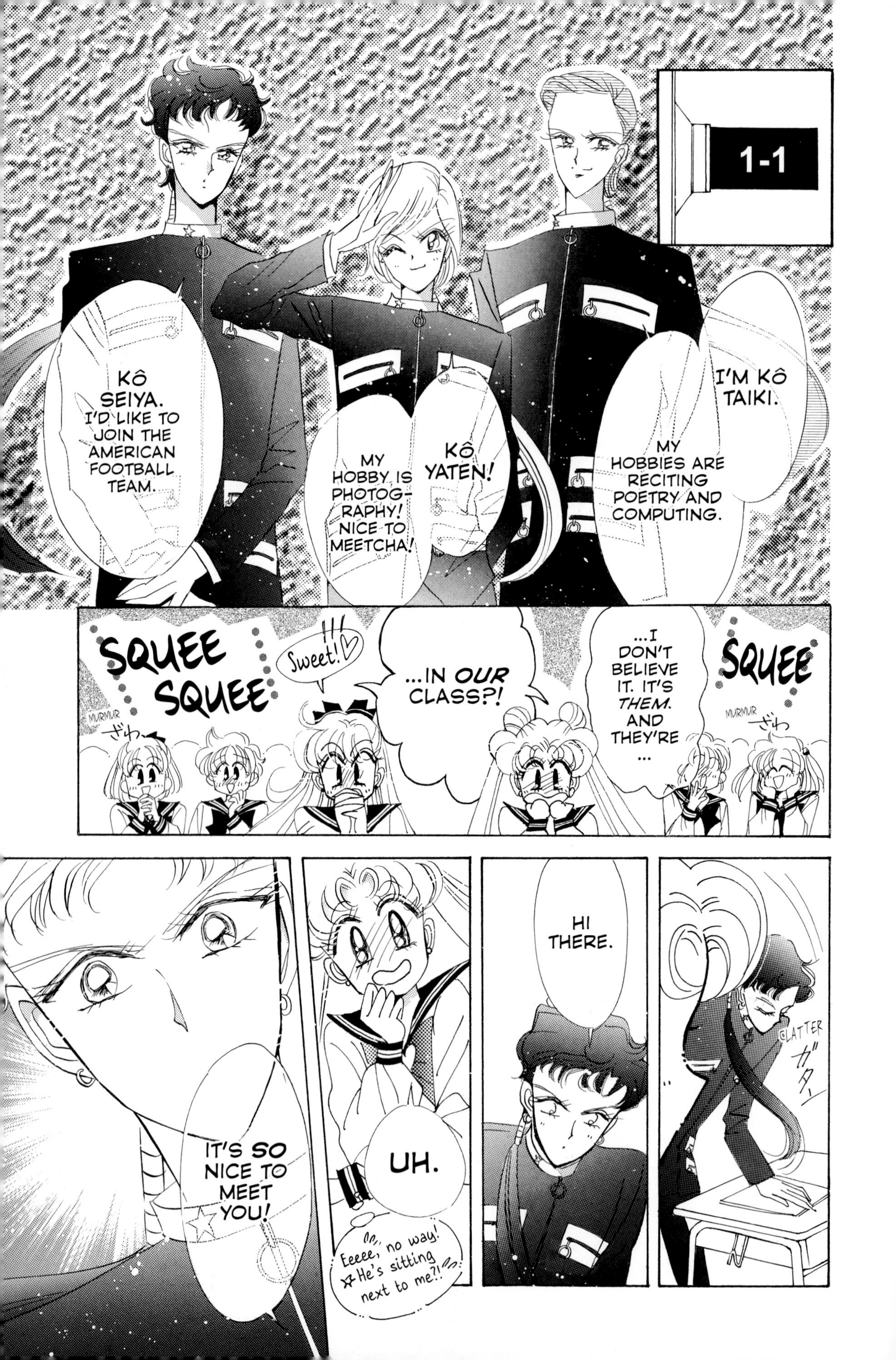
1-1
I'M KÔ TAIKI.
MY HOBBIES ARE RECITING POETRY AND COMPUTING.
KÔ YATEN!
MY HOBBY IS PHOTOG-RAPHY! NICE TO MEETCHA!
KÔ SEIYA. I'D LIKE TO JOIN THE AMERICAN FOOTBALL TEAM.
SQUEE
MURMUR ざわ
...I DON'T BELIEVE IT. IT'S *THEM*. AND THEY'RE ...
...IN *OUR* CLASS?!
Sweet!!!!
SQUEE SQUEE
MURMUR ざわ
CLATTER ガタ
HI THERE.
UH.
Eeeee, no way! He's sitting next to me?!
IT'S SO NICE TO MEET YOU!

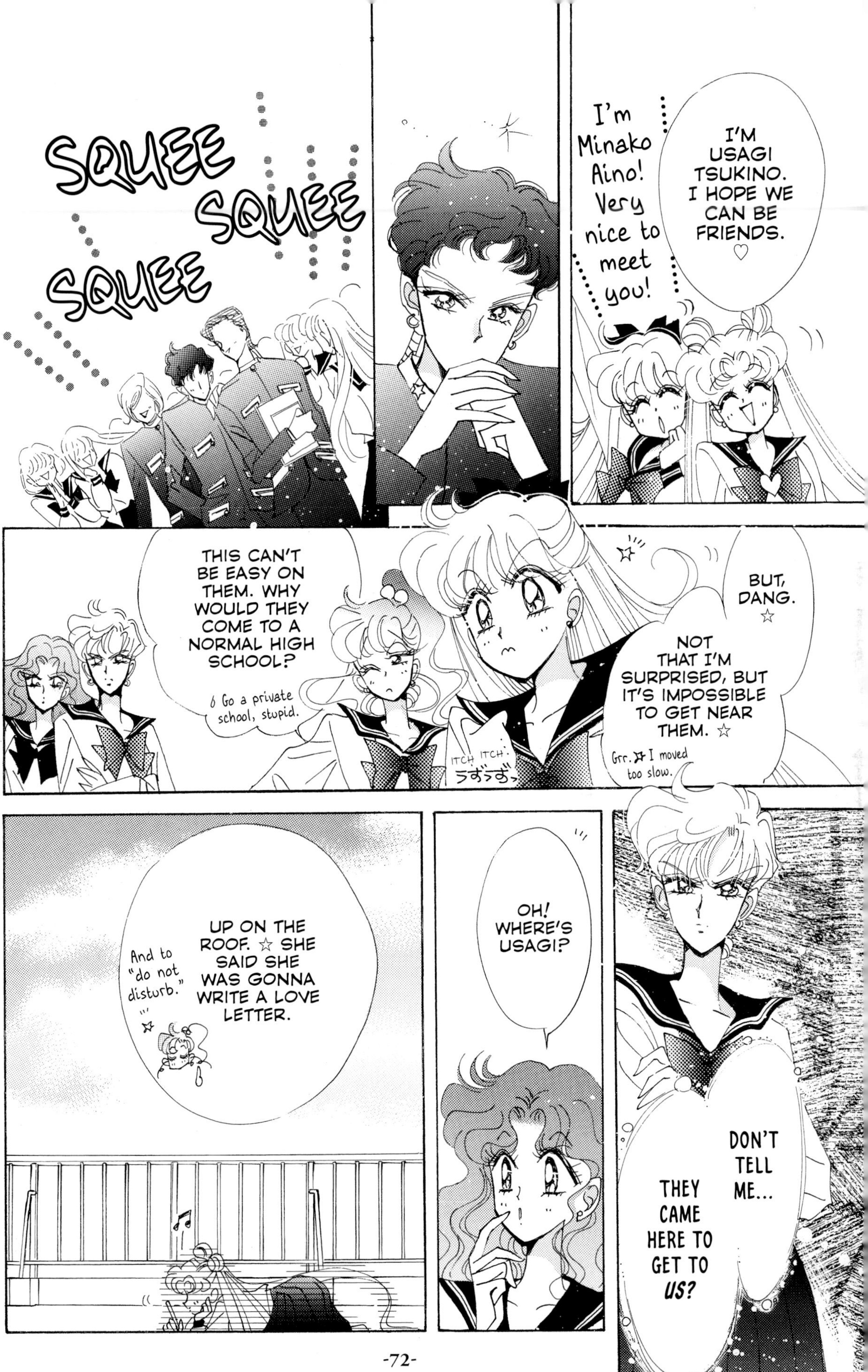
I'M USAGI TSUKINO. I HOPE WE CAN BE FRIENDS. ♡
I'm Minako Aino! Very nice to meet you!
SQUEE
SQUEE
SQUEE
BUT, DANG. ☆
NOT THAT I'M SURPRISED, BUT IT'S IMPOSSIBLE TO GET NEAR THEM. ☆
Grr. ☆ I moved too slow.
ITCH ITCH
うずうず
THIS CAN'T BE EASY ON THEM. WHY WOULD THEY COME TO A NORMAL HIGH SCHOOL?
Go a private school, stupid.
DON'T TELL ME...
THEY CAME HERE TO GET TO *US?*
OH! WHERE'S USAGI?
UP ON THE ROOF. ☆ SHE SAID SHE WAS GONNA WRITE A LOVE LETTER.
And to "do not disturb."

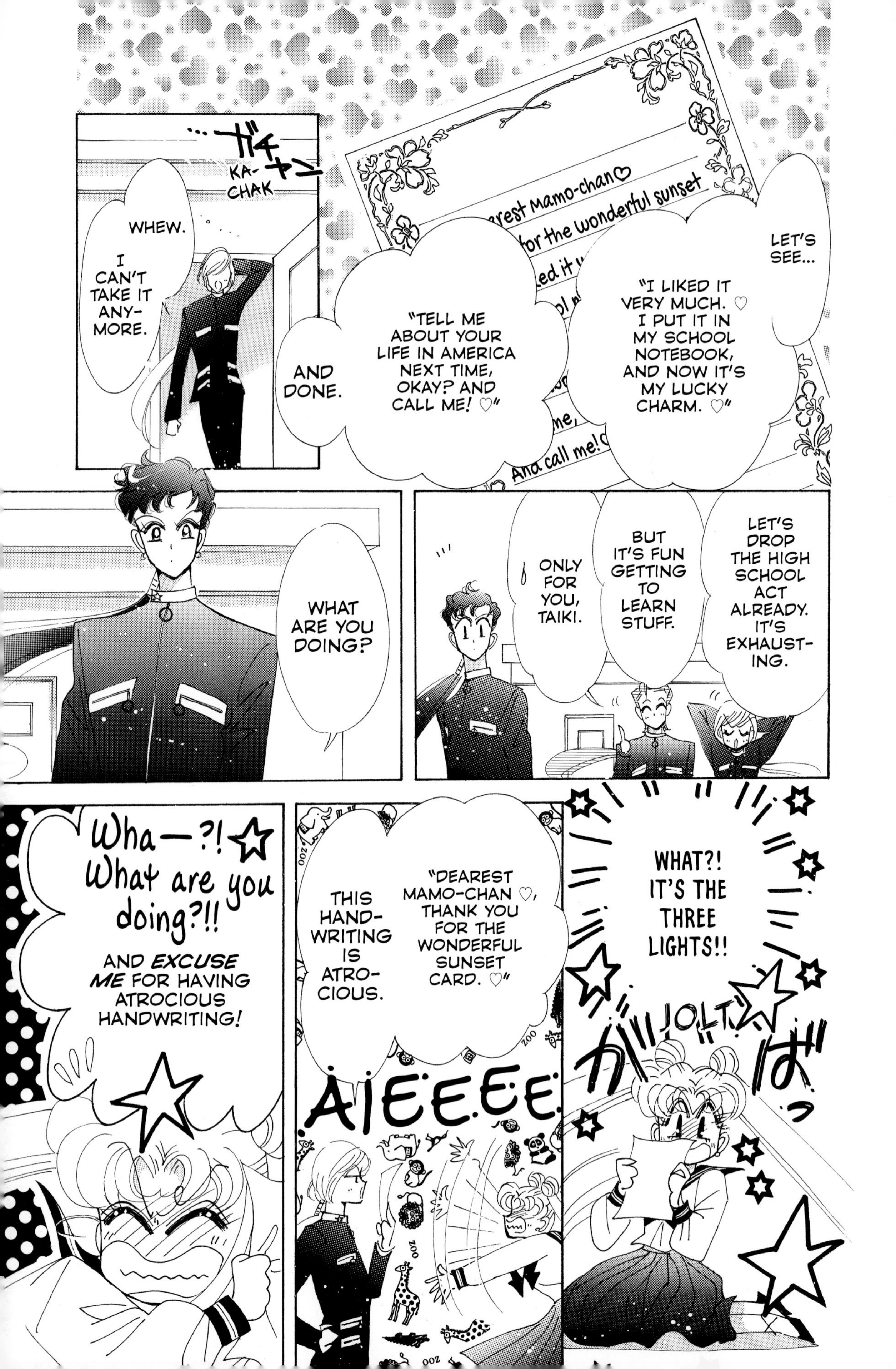
for the wonderful sunset
And call me!
LET'S SEE...
"I LIKED IT VERY MUCH. ♡ I PUT IT IN MY SCHOOL NOTEBOOK, AND NOW IT'S MY LUCKY CHARM. ♡"
"TELL ME ABOUT YOUR LIFE IN AMERICA NEXT TIME, OKAY? AND CALL ME! ♡"
AND DONE.
KA-CHAK
WHEW.
I CAN'T TAKE IT ANY-MORE.
LET'S DROP THE HIGH SCHOOL ACT ALREADY. IT'S EXHAUST-ING.
BUT IT'S FUN GETTING TO LEARN STUFF.
ONLY FOR YOU, TAIKI.
WHAT ARE YOU DOING?
WHAT?! IT'S THE THREE LIGHTS!!
JOLT
"DEAREST MAMO-CHAN ♡, THANK YOU FOR THE WONDERFUL SUNSET CARD. ♡"
THIS HAND-WRITING IS ATRO-CIOUS.
AIEEEE
Wha—?! What are you doing?!!
AND *EXCUSE ME* FOR HAVING ATROCIOUS HANDWRITING!

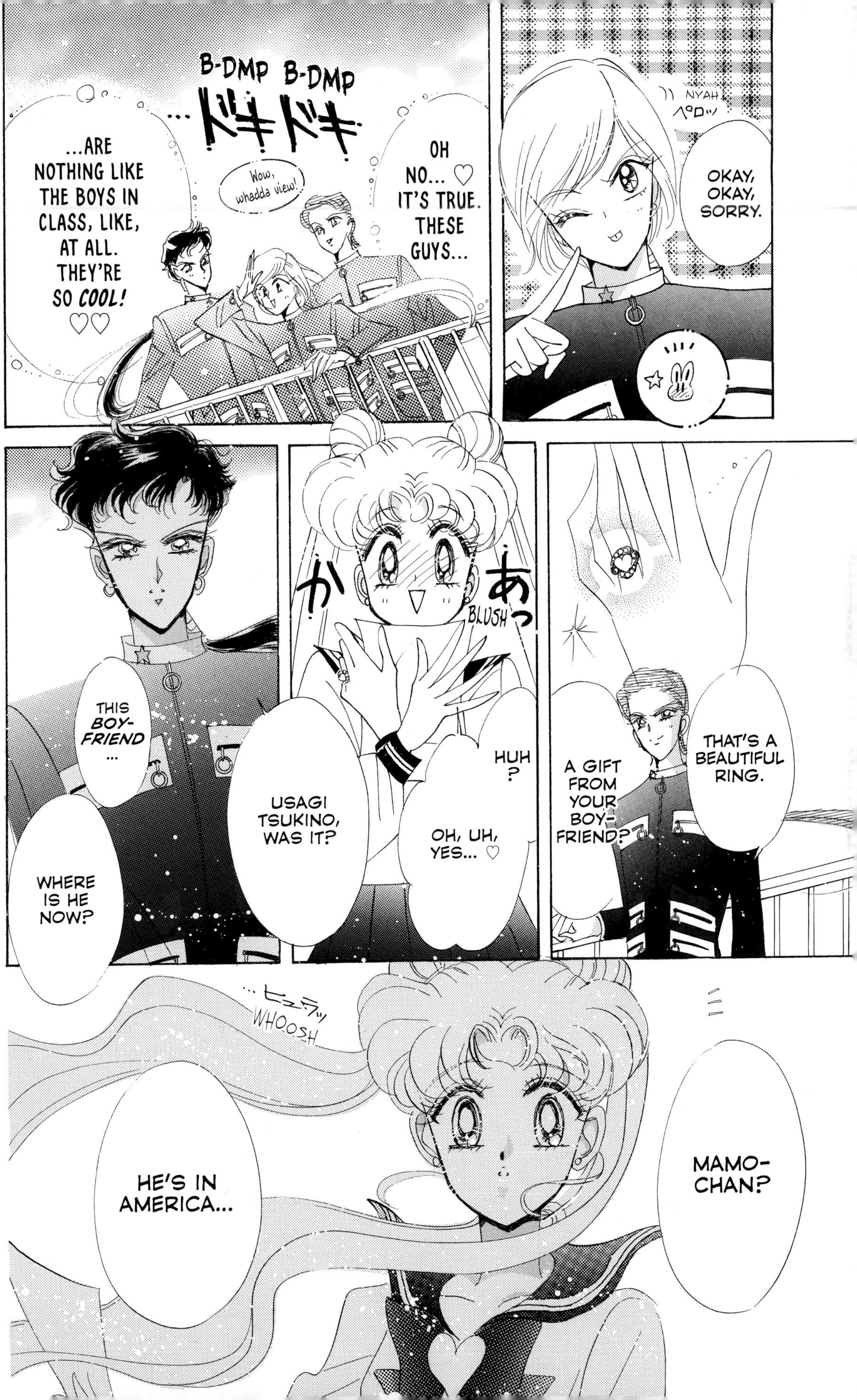
NYAH ペロッ
OKAY, OKAY, SORRY.
OH NO... ♡ IT'S TRUE. THESE GUYS...
B-DMP B-DMP ...ドキドキ
...ARE NOTHING LIKE THE BOYS IN CLASS, LIKE, AT ALL. THEY'RE SO *COOL!* ♡♡
Wow, whadda view!
THAT'S A BEAUTIFUL RING.
A GIFT FROM YOUR BOY-FRIEND?
かあっ BLUSH
HUH?
OH, UH, YES... ♡
USAGI TSUKINO, WAS IT?
THIS *BOY-FRIEND*...
WHERE IS HE NOW?
MAMO-CHAN?
...ヒュラッ WHOOSH
HE'S IN AMERICA...

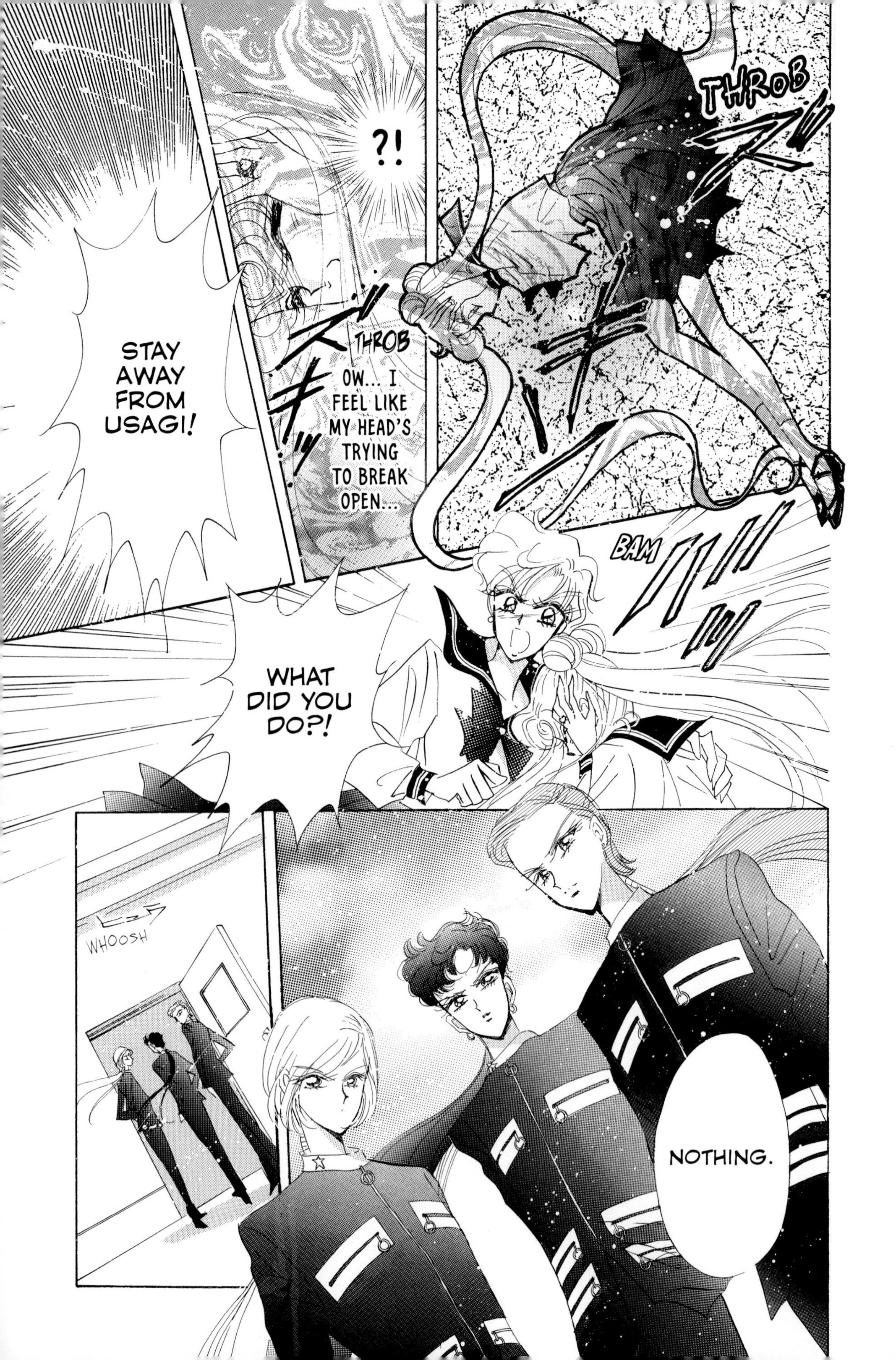
THROB
?!
THROB
OW... I FEEL LIKE MY HEAD'S TRYING TO BREAK OPEN...
STAY AWAY FROM USAGI!
BAM
WHAT DID YOU DO?!
NOTHING.
WHOOSH

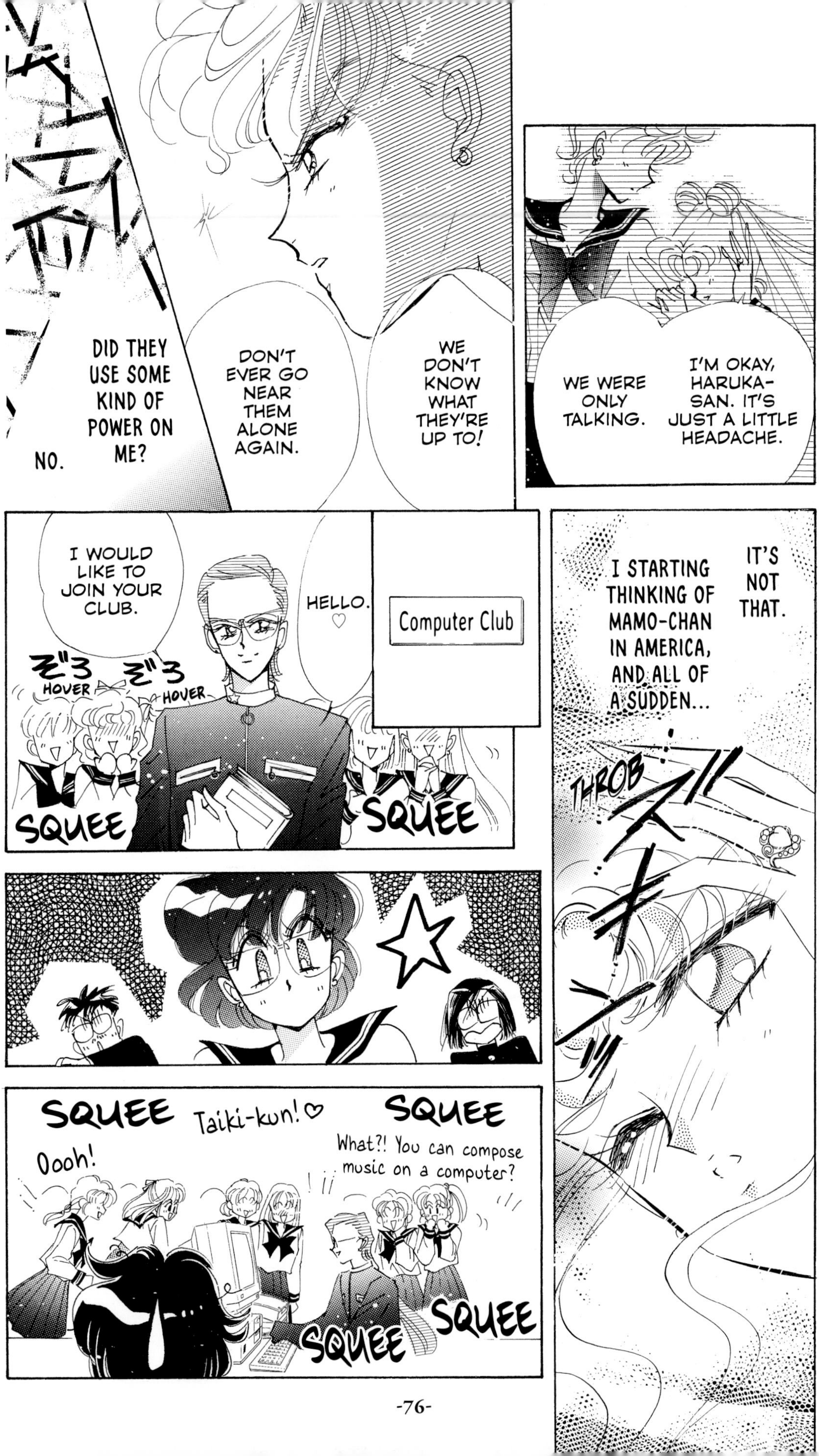
I'M OKAY, HARUKA-SAN. IT'S JUST A LITTLE HEADACHE.
WE WERE ONLY TALKING.
WE DON'T KNOW WHAT THEY'RE UP TO!
DON'T EVER GO NEAR THEM ALONE AGAIN.
DID THEY USE SOME KIND OF POWER ON ME?
NO.
IT'S NOT THAT.
I STARTING THINKING OF MAMO-CHAN IN AMERICA, AND ALL OF A SUDDEN...
THROB
Computer Club
HELLO. ♡
I WOULD LIKE TO JOIN YOUR CLUB.
ぞろ HOVER
ぞろ HOVER
SQUEE
SQUEE
SQUEE
Taiki-kun! ♡
SQUEE
What?! You can compose music on a computer?
Oooh!
SQUEE
SQUEE

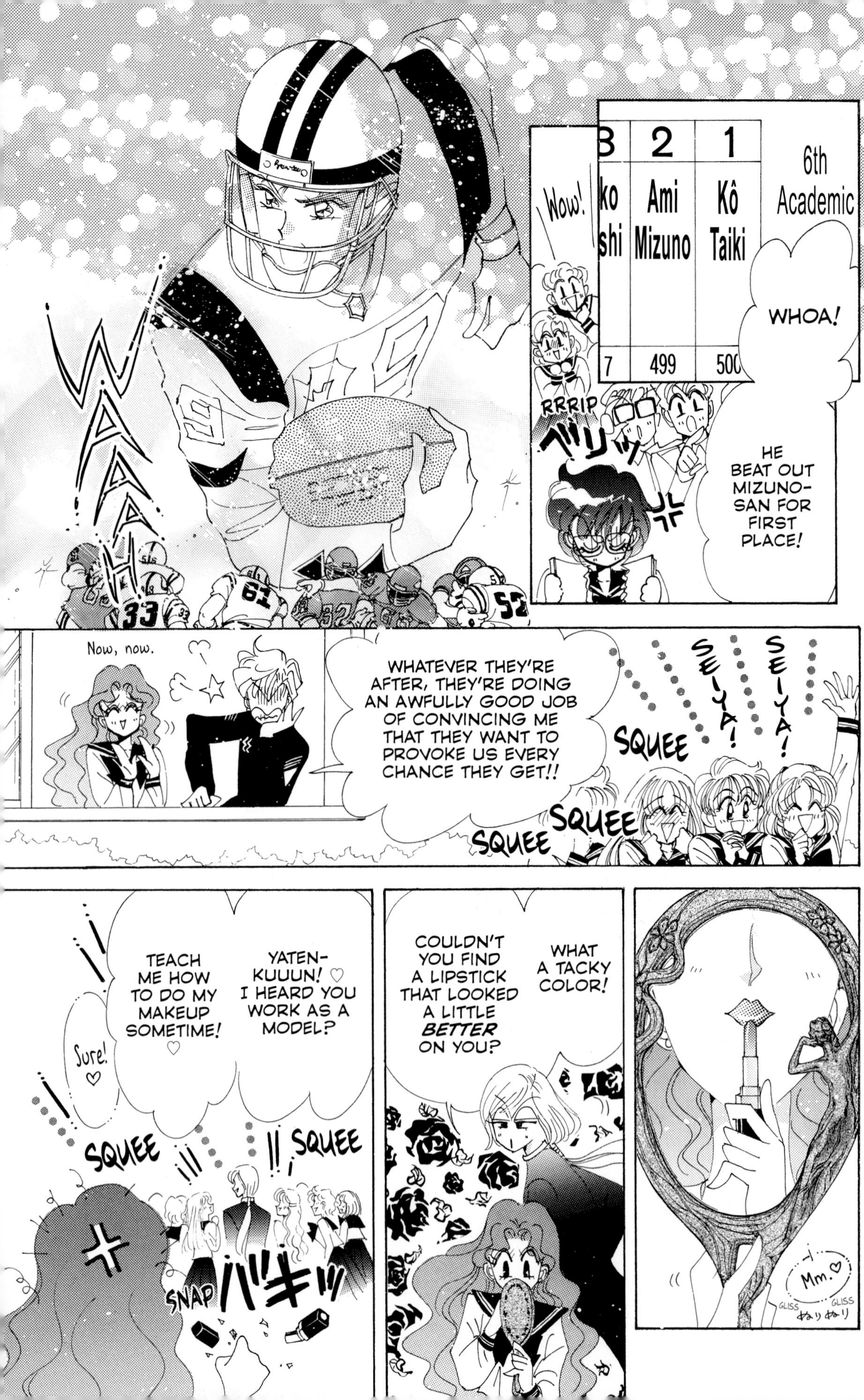
6th Academic
1 Kô Taiki 500
2 Ami Mizuno 499
WHOA!
Wow!
RRRIP
ベリッ
HE BEAT OUT MIZUNO-SAN FOR FIRST PLACE!
WAAAAH
SEIYA! SEIYA!
SQUEE
SQUEE
SQUEE
WHATEVER THEY'RE AFTER, THEY'RE DOING AN AWFULLY GOOD JOB OF CONVINCING ME THAT THEY WANT TO PROVOKE US EVERY CHANCE THEY GET!!
Now, now.
Mm.♡
GLISS GLISS ぬりぬり
WHAT A TACKY COLOR!
COULDN'T YOU FIND A LIPSTICK THAT LOOKED A LITTLE *BETTER* ON YOU?
YATEN-KUUUN! ♡ I HEARD YOU WORK AS A MODEL?
TEACH ME HOW TO DO MY MAKEUP SOMETIME! ♡
Sure! ♡
SQUEE
SQUEE
SNAP バキッ

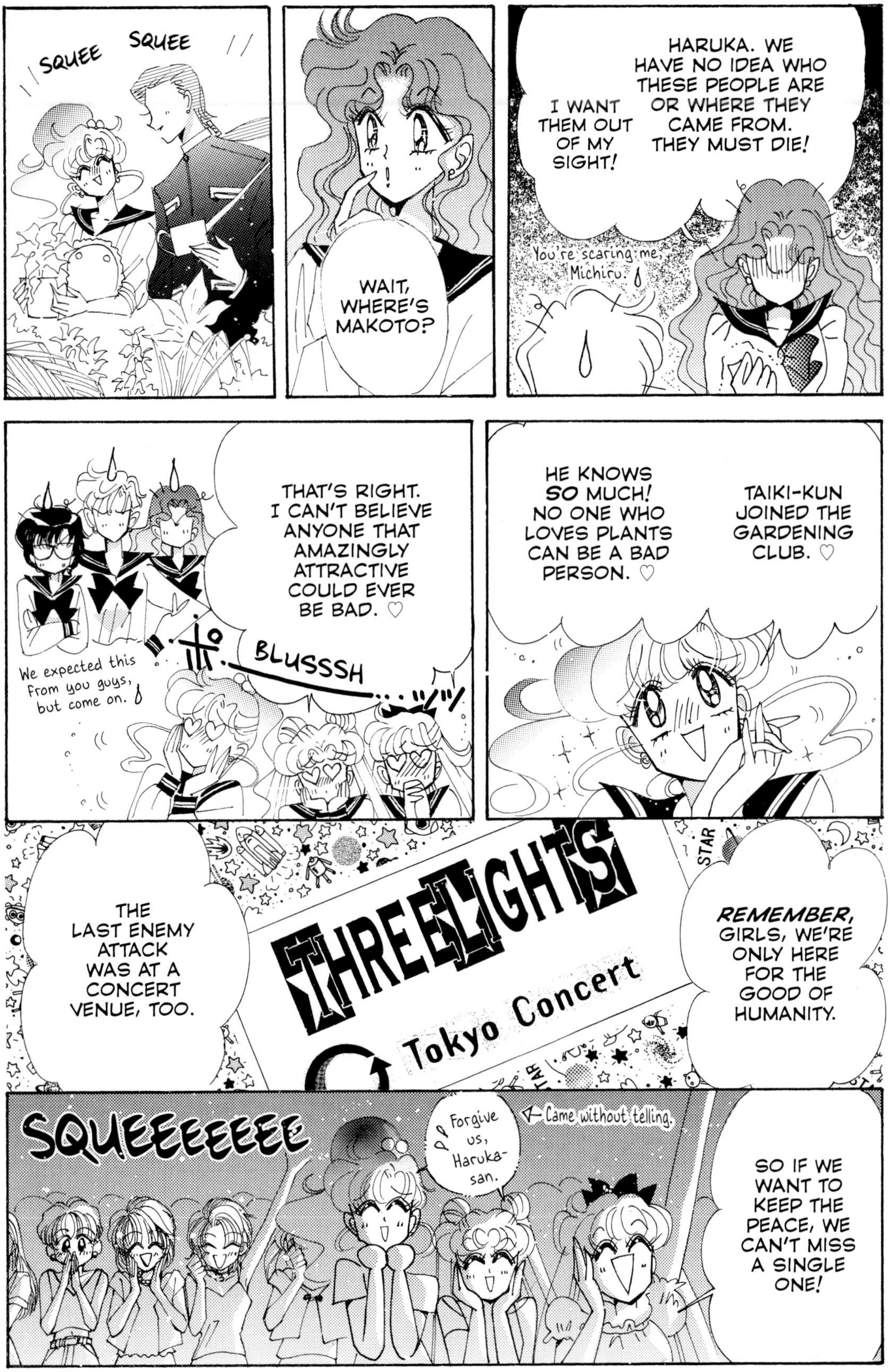
HARUKA. WE HAVE NO IDEA WHO THESE PEOPLE ARE OR WHERE THEY CAME FROM. THEY MUST DIE!
I WANT THEM OUT OF MY SIGHT!
You're scaring me, Michiru.
WAIT, WHERE'S MAKOTO?
SQUEE
SQUEE
TAIKI-KUN JOINED THE GARDENING CLUB. ♡
HE KNOWS SO MUCH! NO ONE WHO LOVES PLANTS CAN BE A BAD PERSON. ♡
THAT'S RIGHT. I CAN'T BELIEVE ANYONE THAT AMAZINGLY ATTRACTIVE COULD EVER BE BAD. ♡
BLUSSSH
We expected this from you guys, but come on.
REMEMBER, GIRLS, WE'RE ONLY HERE FOR THE GOOD OF HUMANITY.
THREELIGHTS
Tokyo Concert
STAR
THE LAST ENEMY ATTACK WAS AT A CONCERT VENUE, TOO.
SO IF WE WANT TO KEEP THE PEACE, WE CAN'T MISS A SINGLE ONE!
Came without telling.
Forgive us, Haruka-san.
SQUEEEEEEEE

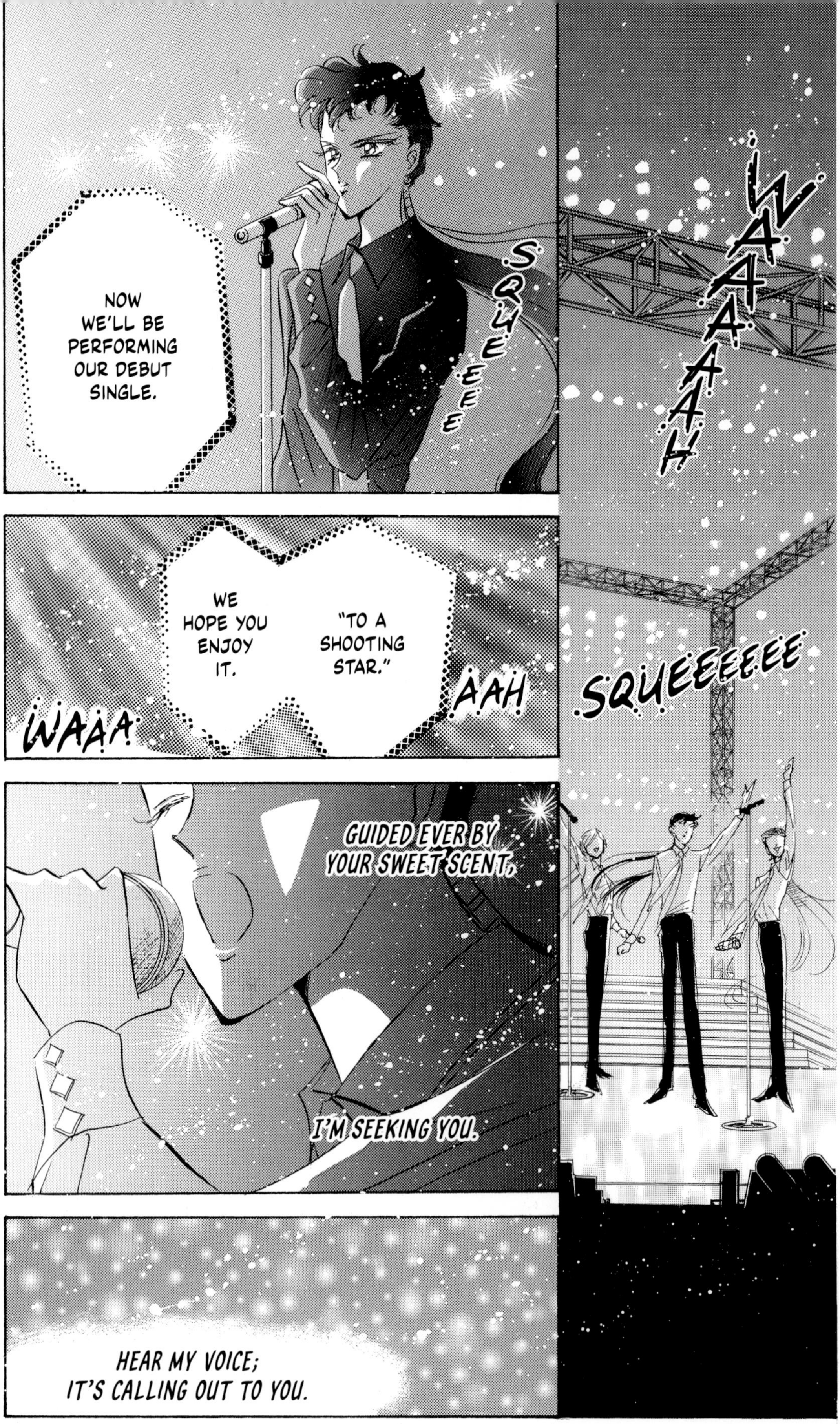
WAAAAAAH
SQUEEEEEEE
SQUEEEEE
NOW WE'LL BE PERFORMING OUR DEBUT SINGLE.
AAH
"TO A SHOOTING STAR."
WE HOPE YOU ENJOY IT.
WAAA
GUIDED EVER BY YOUR SWEET SCENT,
I'M SEEKING YOU.
HEAR MY VOICE; IT'S CALLING OUT TO YOU.

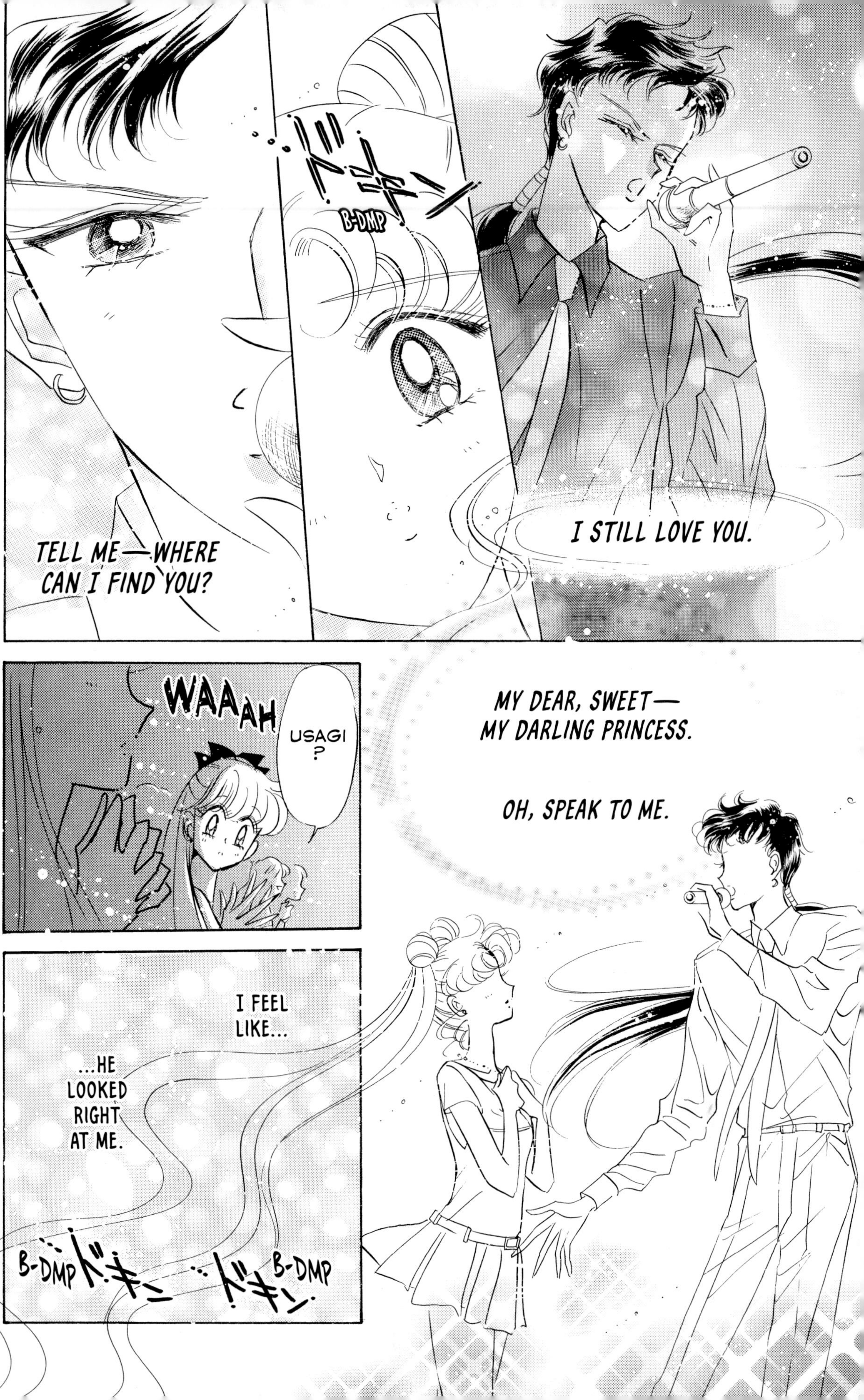

I STILL LOVE YOU.
B-DMP
TELL ME—WHERE CAN I FIND YOU?
MY DEAR, SWEET— MY DARLING PRINCESS.
OH, SPEAK TO ME.
WAAAH
USAGI?
I FEEL LIKE...
...HE LOOKED RIGHT AT ME.
B-DMP
B-DMP

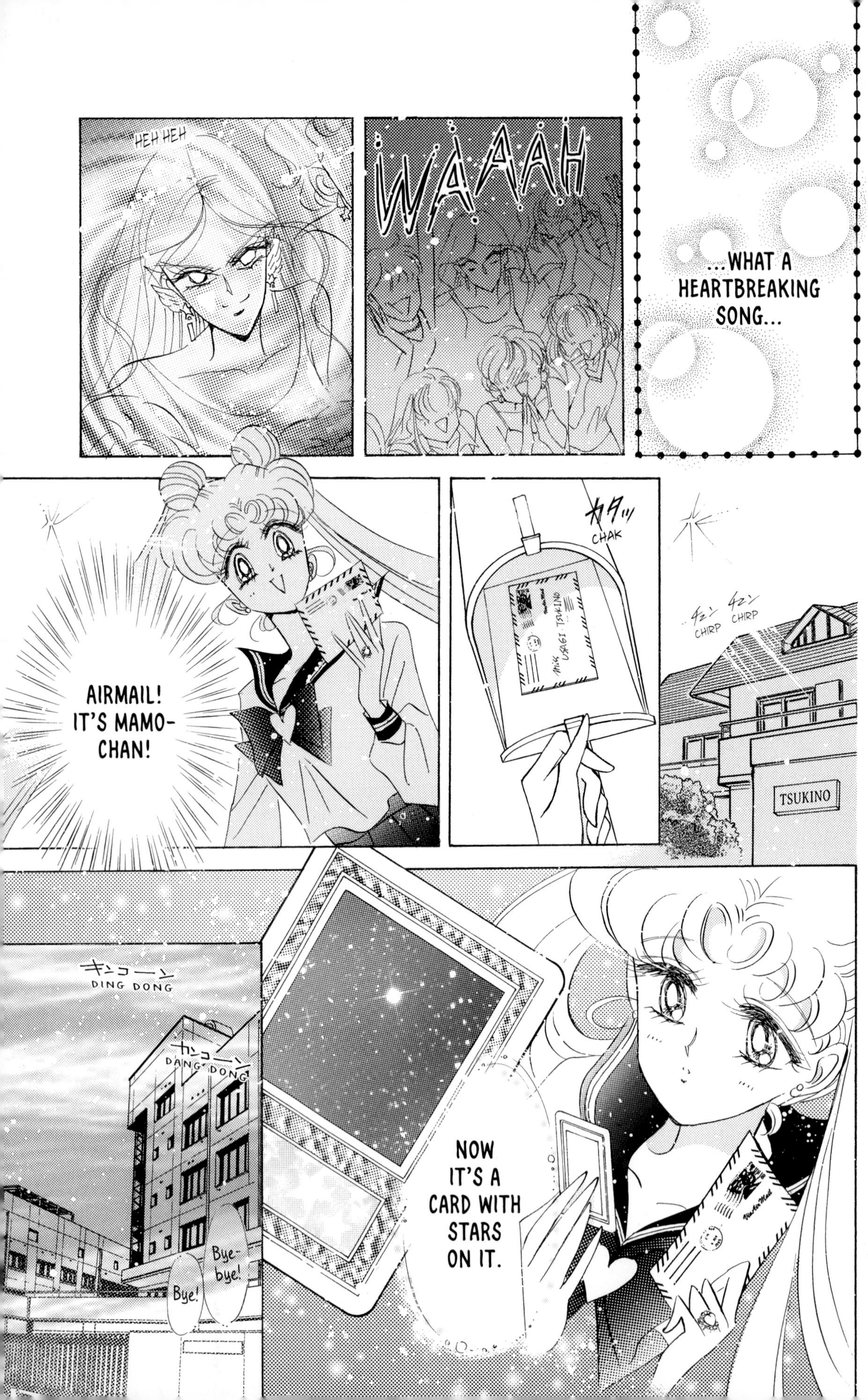
...WHAT A HEARTBREAKING SONG...
WAAAH
HEH HEH
チュン チュン
CHIRP CHIRP
TSUKINO
カタッ
CHAK
MISS USAGI TSUKINO
AIRMAIL! IT'S MAMO-CHAN!
NOW IT'S A CARD WITH STARS ON IT.
キンコーン
DING DONG
カンコーン
DANG DONG
Bye-bye!
Bye!

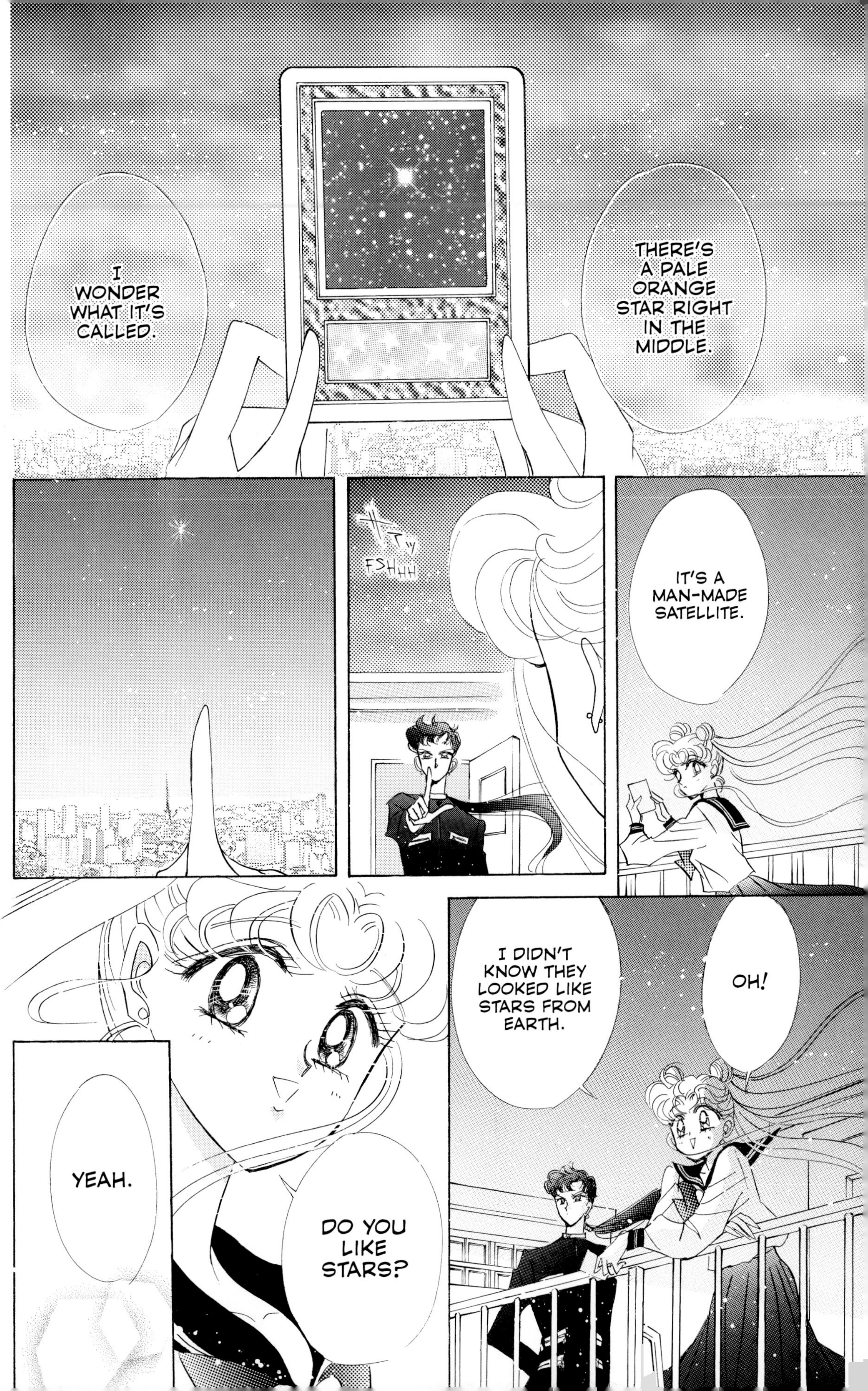
THERE'S A PALE ORANGE STAR RIGHT IN THE MIDDLE.
I WONDER WHAT IT'S CALLED.
IT'S A MAN-MADE SATELLITE.
FSHHH
OH!
I DIDN'T KNOW THEY LOOKED LIKE STARS FROM EARTH.
DO YOU LIKE STARS?
YEAH.

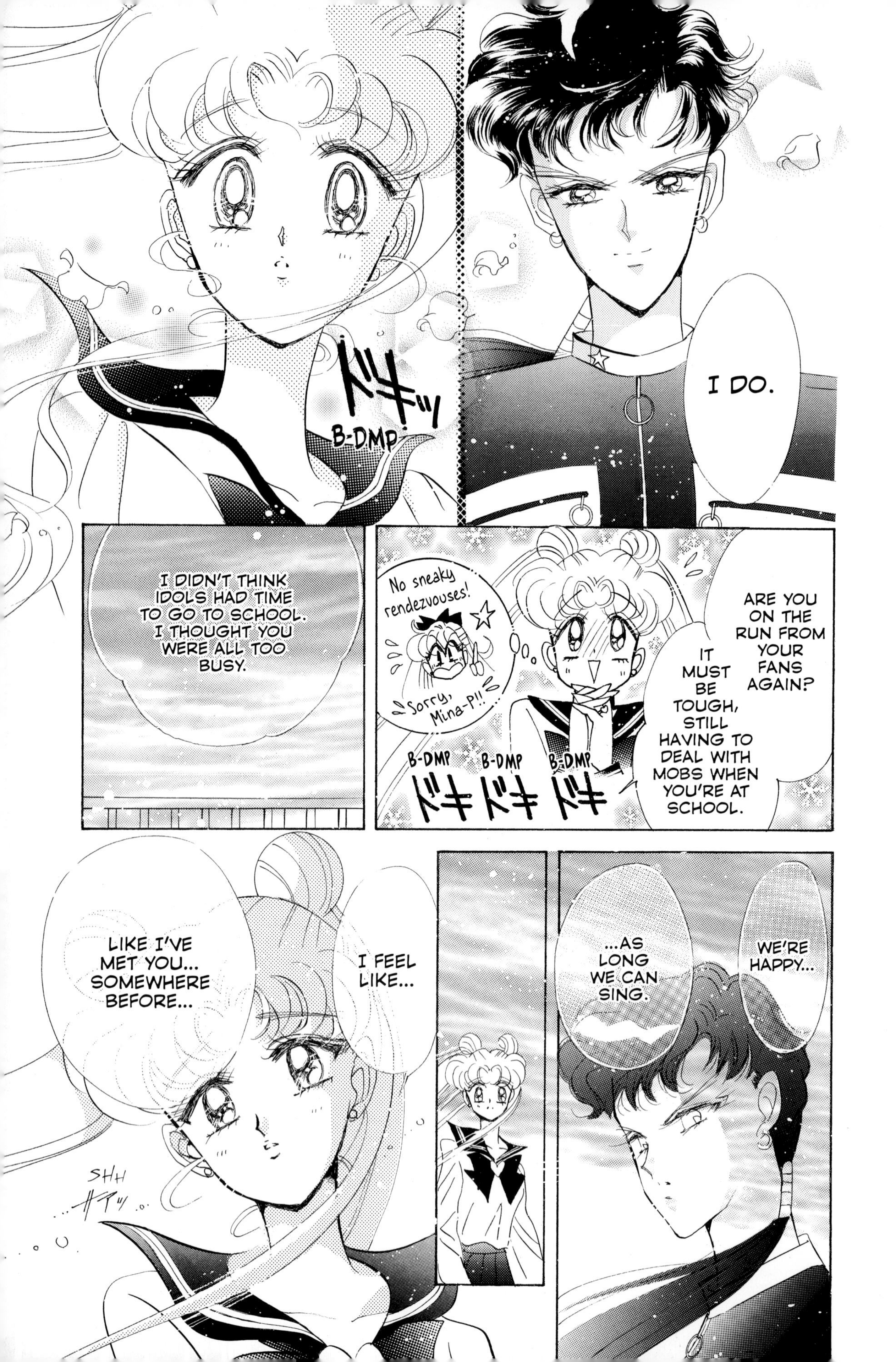
I DO.
B-DMP
ドキッ
ARE YOU ON THE RUN FROM YOUR FANS AGAIN?
IT MUST BE TOUGH, STILL HAVING TO DEAL WITH MOBS WHEN YOU'RE AT SCHOOL.
No sneaky rendezvouses!
Sorry, Mina-P!!
B-DMP B-DMP B-DMP
ドキドキドキ
I DIDN'T THINK IDOLS HAD TIME TO GO TO SCHOOL. I THOUGHT YOU WERE ALL TOO BUSY.
WE'RE HAPPY...
...AS LONG WE CAN SING.
I FEEL LIKE...
LIKE I'VE MET YOU... SOMEWHERE BEFORE...
SHH
ザアッ

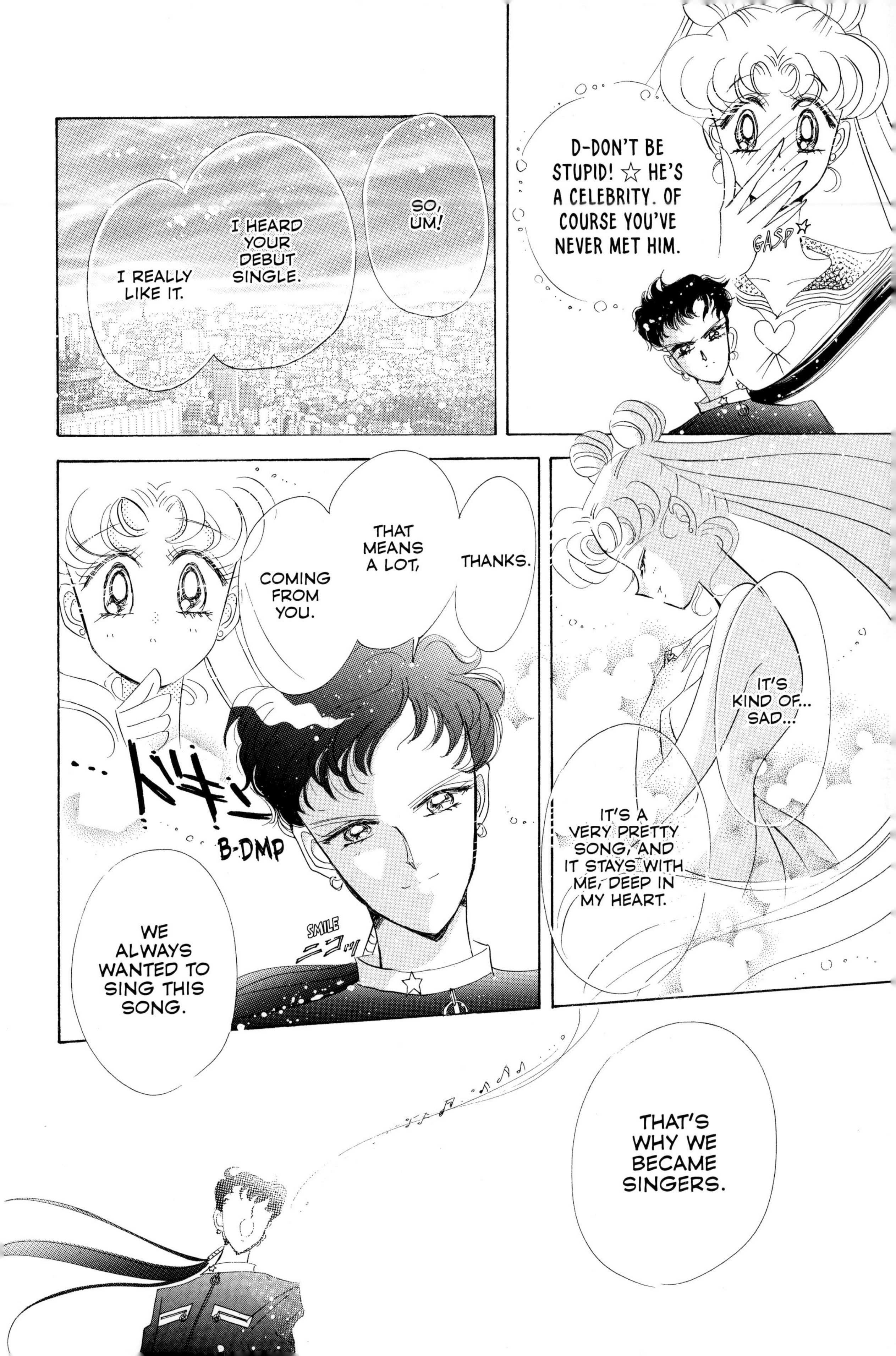
D-DON'T BE STUPID! ☆ HE'S A CELEBRITY. OF COURSE YOU'VE NEVER MET HIM.
GASP☆
SO, UM!
I HEARD YOUR DEBUT SINGLE.
I REALLY LIKE IT.
IT'S KIND OF... SAD...
IT'S A VERY PRETTY SONG, AND IT STAYS WITH ME, DEEP IN MY HEART.
THANKS.
THAT MEANS A LOT,
COMING FROM YOU.
B-DMP
SMILE
WE ALWAYS WANTED TO SING THIS SONG.
THAT'S WHY WE BECAME SINGERS.

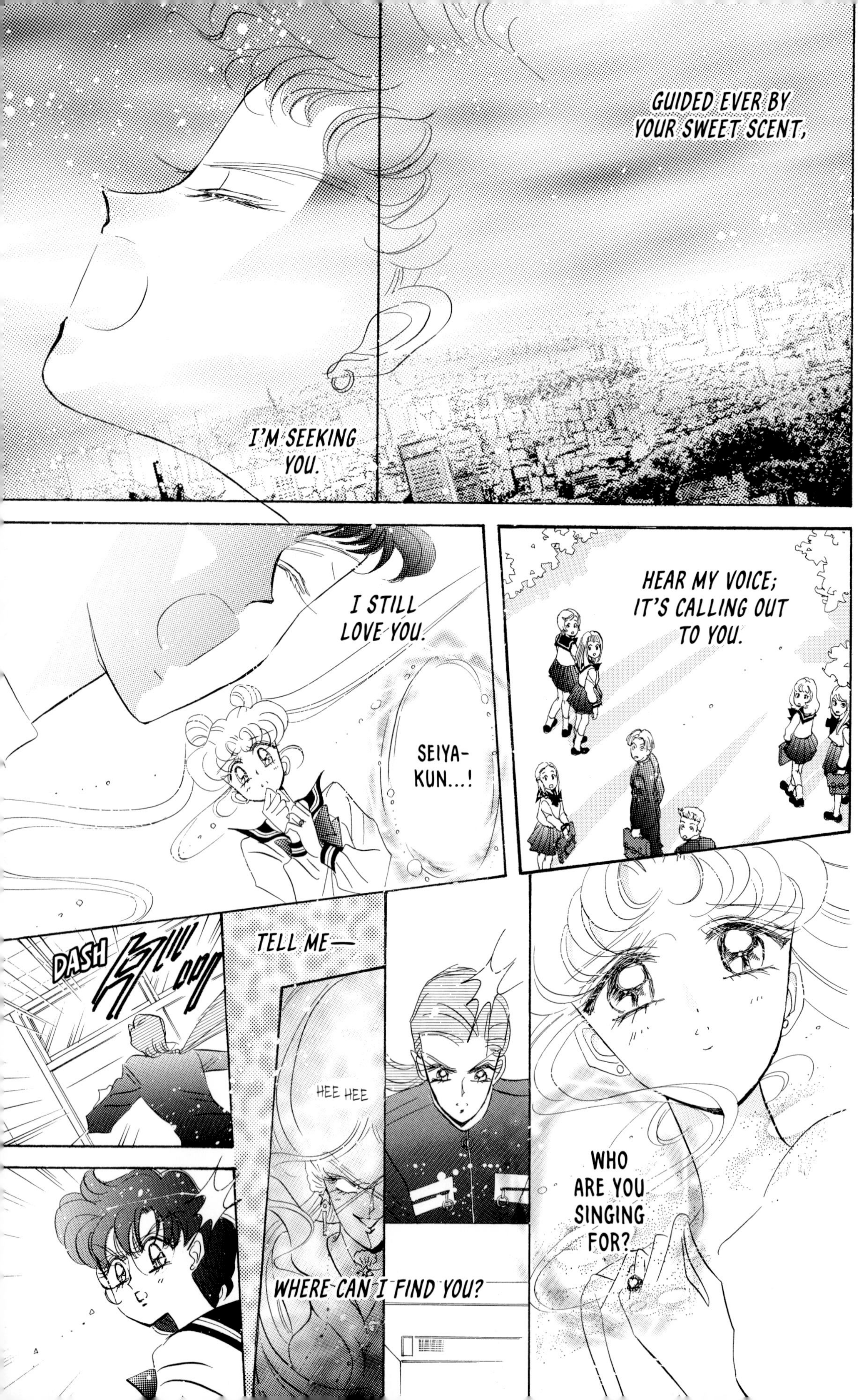
GUIDED EVER BY YOUR SWEET SCENT,
I'M SEEKING YOU.
HEAR MY VOICE; IT'S CALLING OUT TO YOU.
I STILL LOVE YOU.
SEIYA-KUN...!
WHO ARE YOU SINGING FOR?
TELL ME—
HEE HEE
WHERE CAN I FIND YOU?
DASH

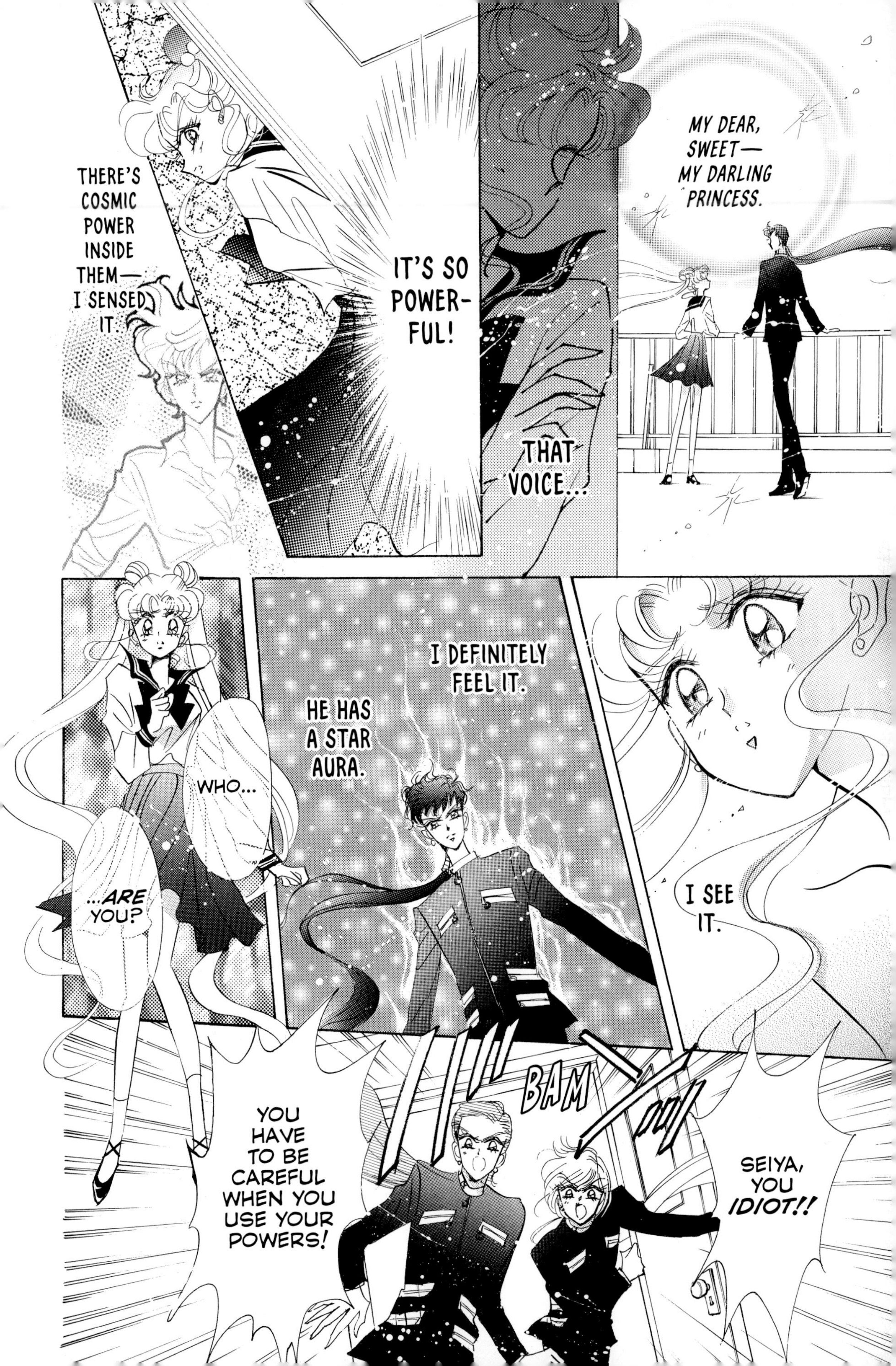
MY DEAR, SWEET— MY DARLING PRINCESS.
THAT VOICE...
IT'S SO POWERFUL!
THERE'S COSMIC POWER INSIDE THEM— I SENSED IT.
I SEE IT.
I DEFINITELY FEEL IT.
HE HAS A STAR AURA.
WHO...
...*ARE* YOU?
BAM
SEIYA, YOU *IDIOT!!*
YOU HAVE TO BE CAREFUL WHEN YOU USE YOUR POWERS!

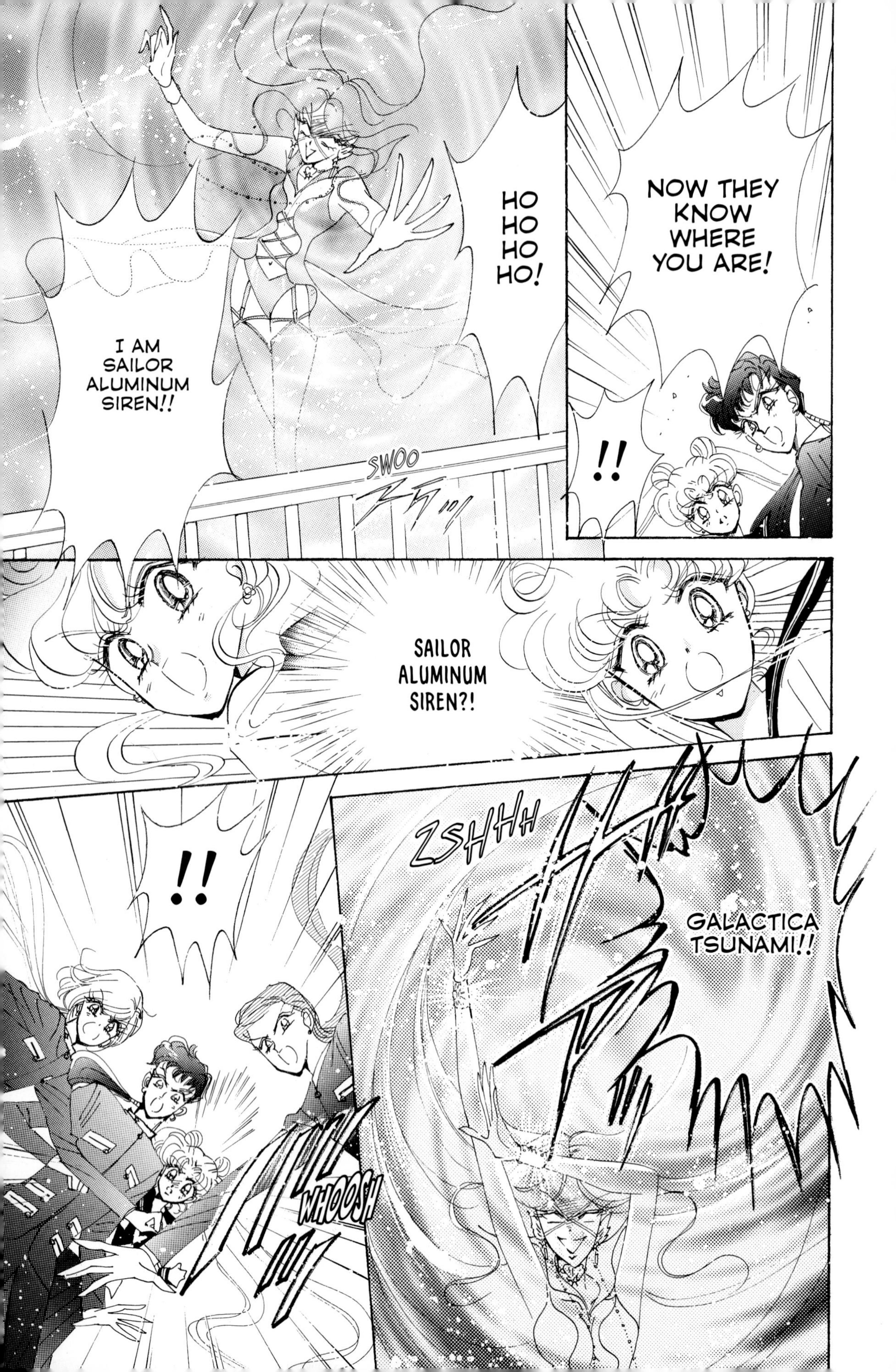
NOW THEY KNOW WHERE YOU ARE!
!!
HO HO HO HO!
I AM SAILOR ALUMINUM SIREN!!
SWOO
SAILOR ALUMINUM SIREN?!
ZSHHH
GALACTICA TSUNAMI!!
!!
WHOOSH

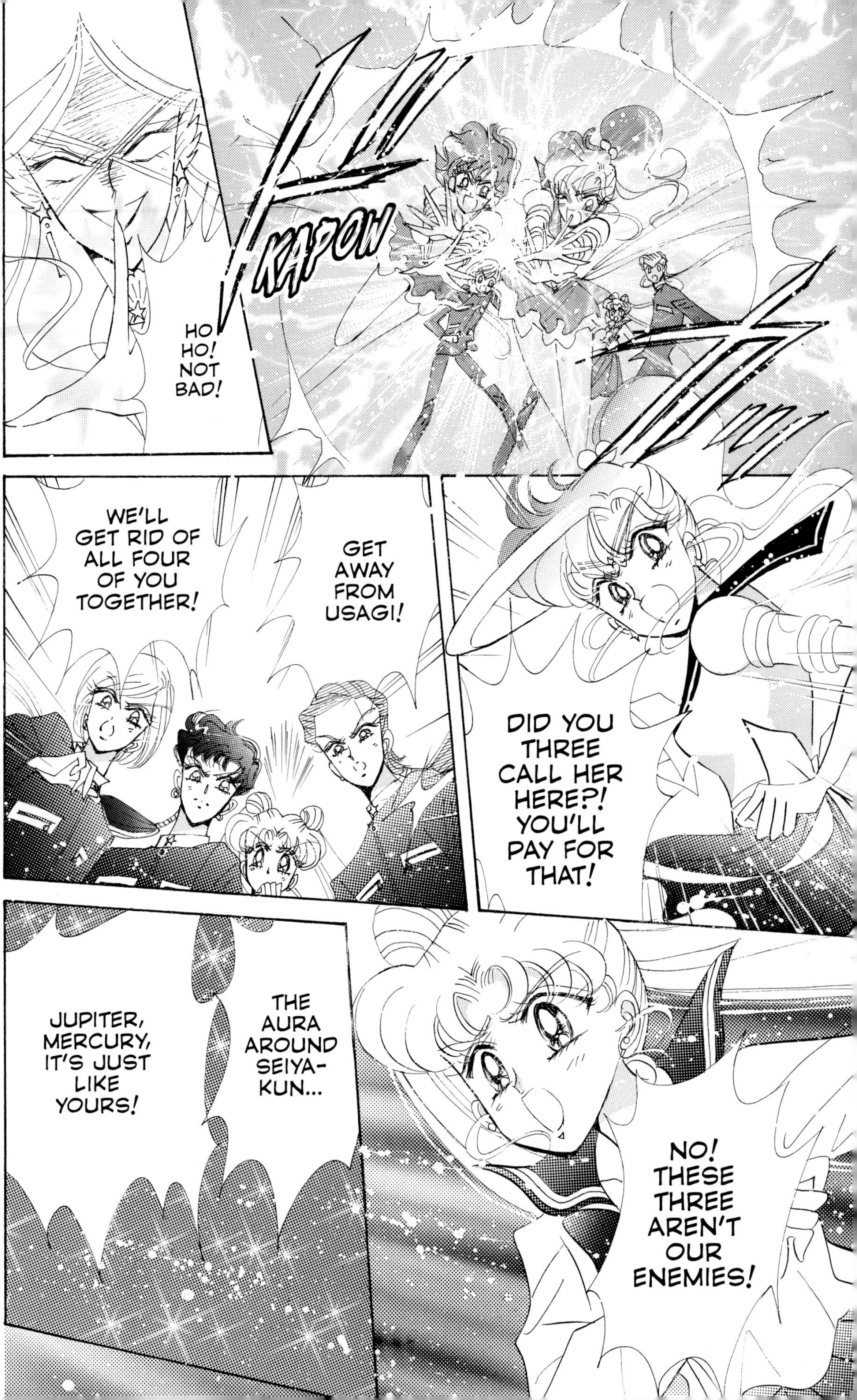
KAPOW
HO HO! NOT BAD!
DID YOU THREE CALL HER HERE?! YOU'LL PAY FOR THAT!
GET AWAY FROM USAGI!
WE'LL GET RID OF ALL FOUR OF YOU TOGETHER!
NO! THESE THREE AREN'T OUR ENEMIES!
THE AURA AROUND SEIYA-KUN...
JUPITER, MERCURY, IT'S JUST LIKE YOURS!

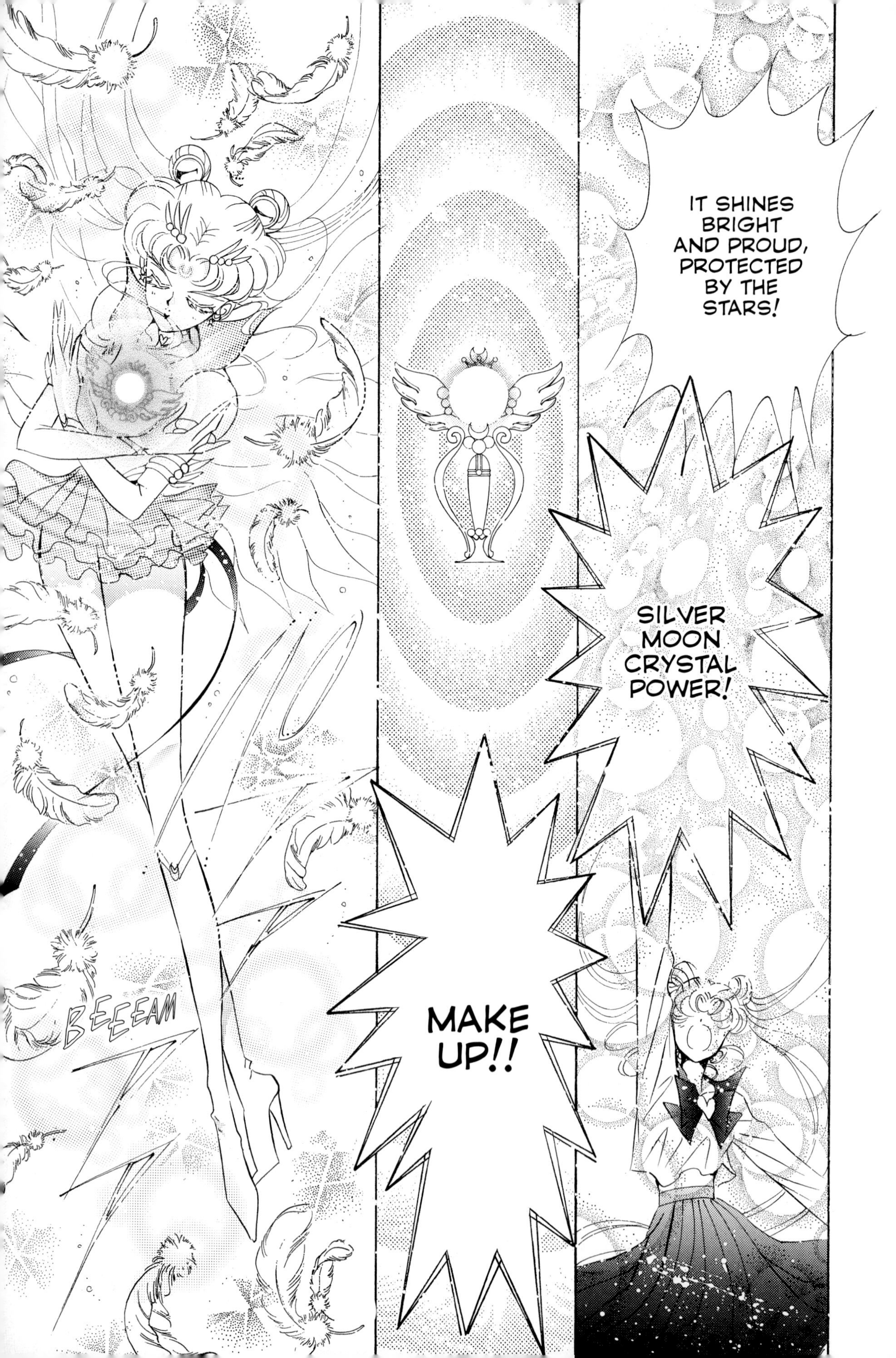
IT SHINES BRIGHT AND PROUD, PROTECTED BY THE STARS!
SILVER MOON CRYSTAL POWER!
MAKE UP!!
BEEEEAM

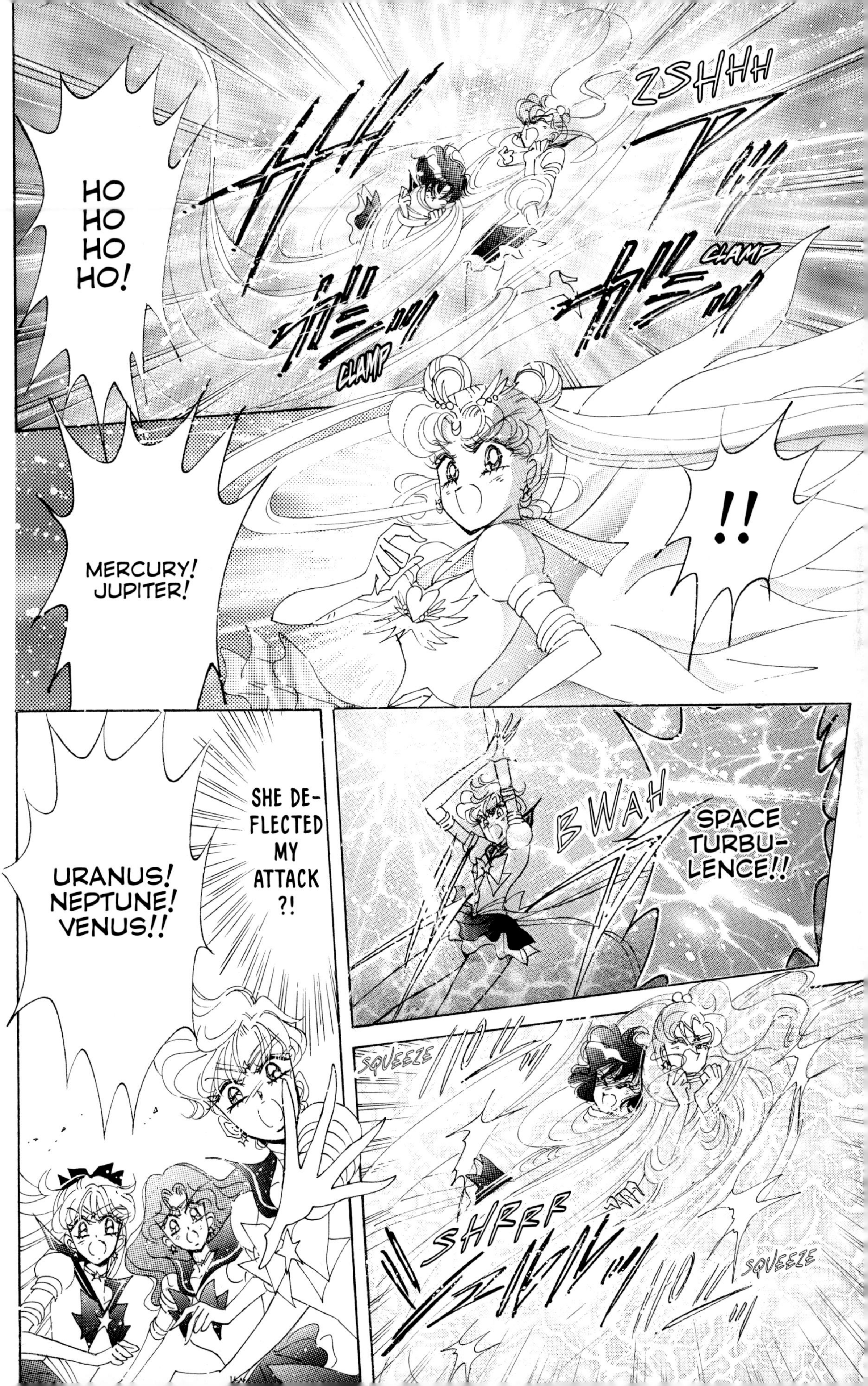

ZSHHH
CLAMP
CLAMP
HO HO HO HO!
!!
MERCURY! JUPITER!
SPACE TURBU-LENCE!!
BWAH
SQUEEZE
SQUEEZE
SHRRR
SHE DE-FLECTED MY ATTACK ?!
URANUS! NEPTUNE! VENUS!!

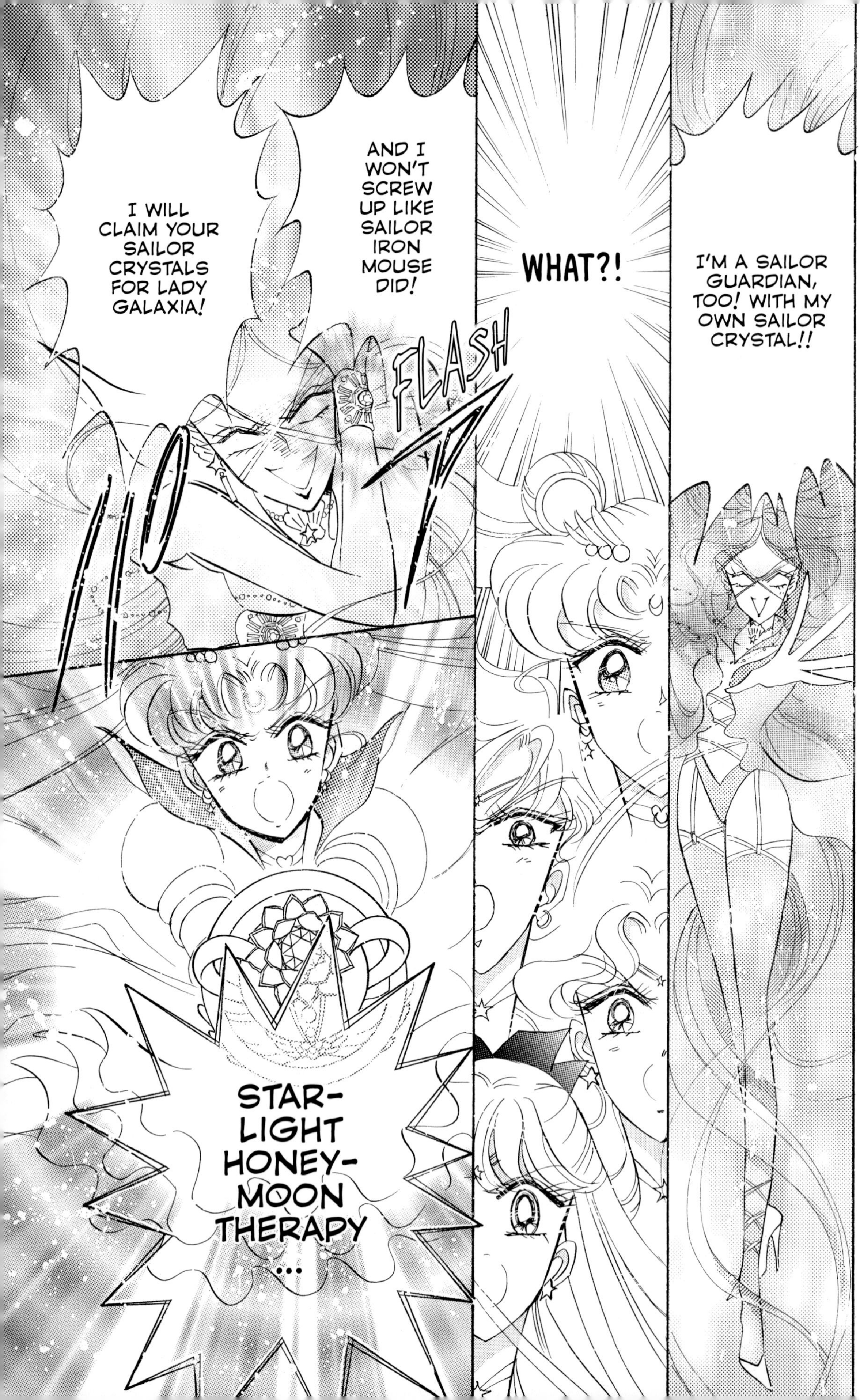
I'M A SAILOR GUARDIAN, TOO! WITH MY OWN SAILOR CRYSTAL!!
WHAT?!
I WILL CLAIM YOUR SAILOR CRYSTALS FOR LADY GALAXIA!
AND I WON'T SCREW UP LIKE SAILOR IRON MOUSE DID!
FLASH
STAR-LIGHT HONEY-MOON THERAPY ...

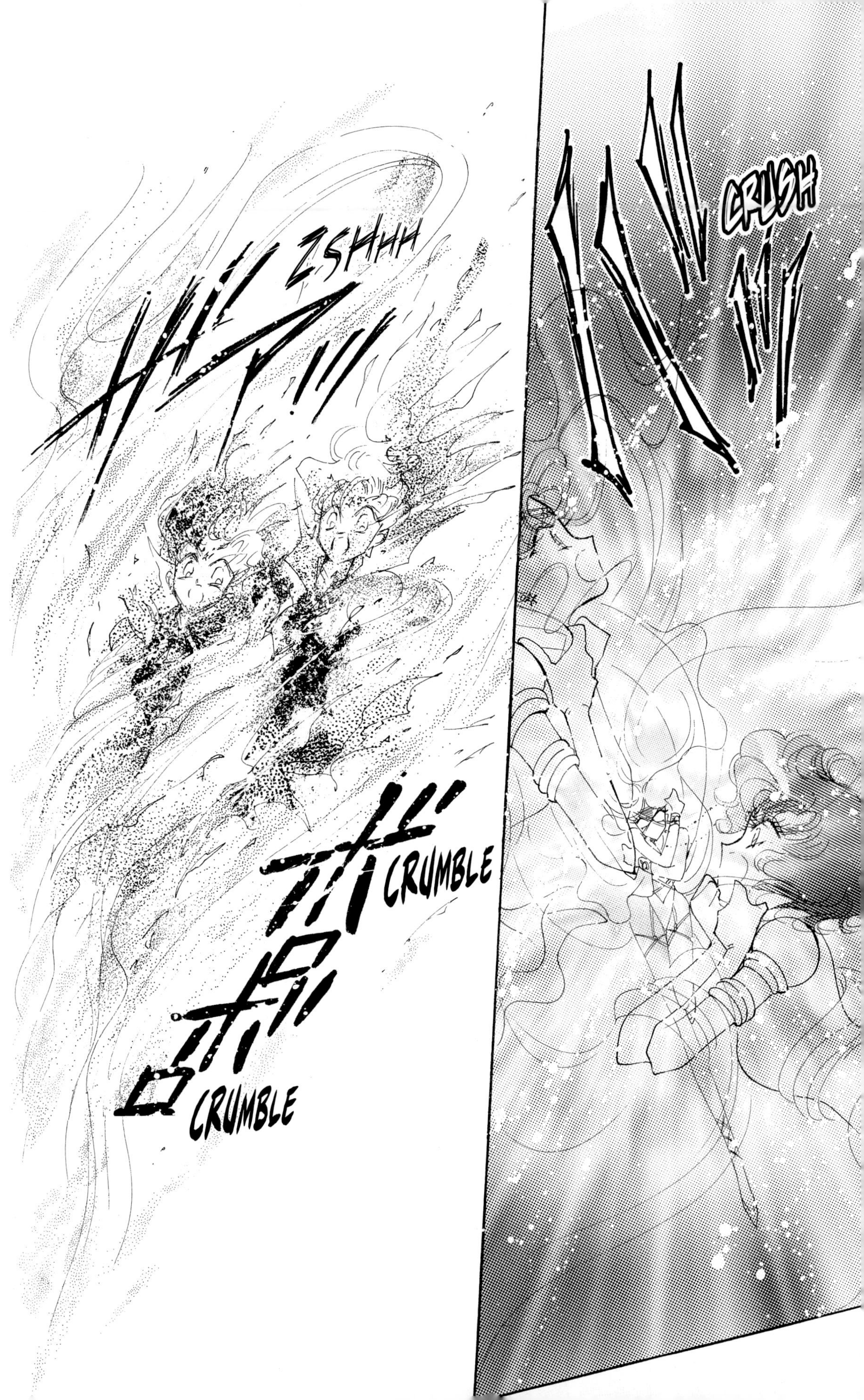
CRUSH
ZSHHH
CRUMBLE
CRUMBLE

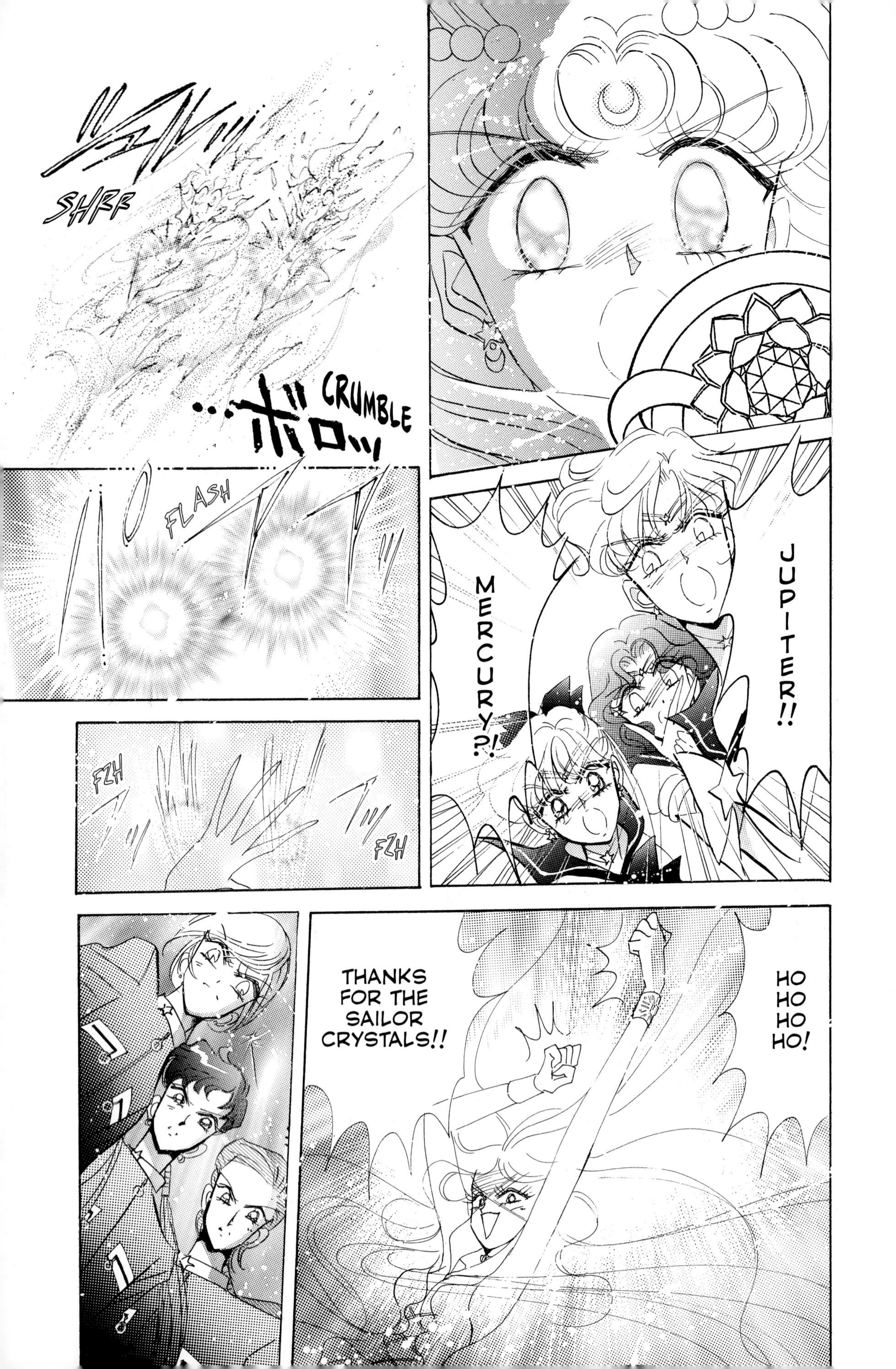
SHRR
…ボロッ
CRUMBLE
JUPITER!!
MERCURY?!
FLASH
FZH
FZH
HO HO HO HO!
THANKS FOR THE SAILOR CRYSTALS!!

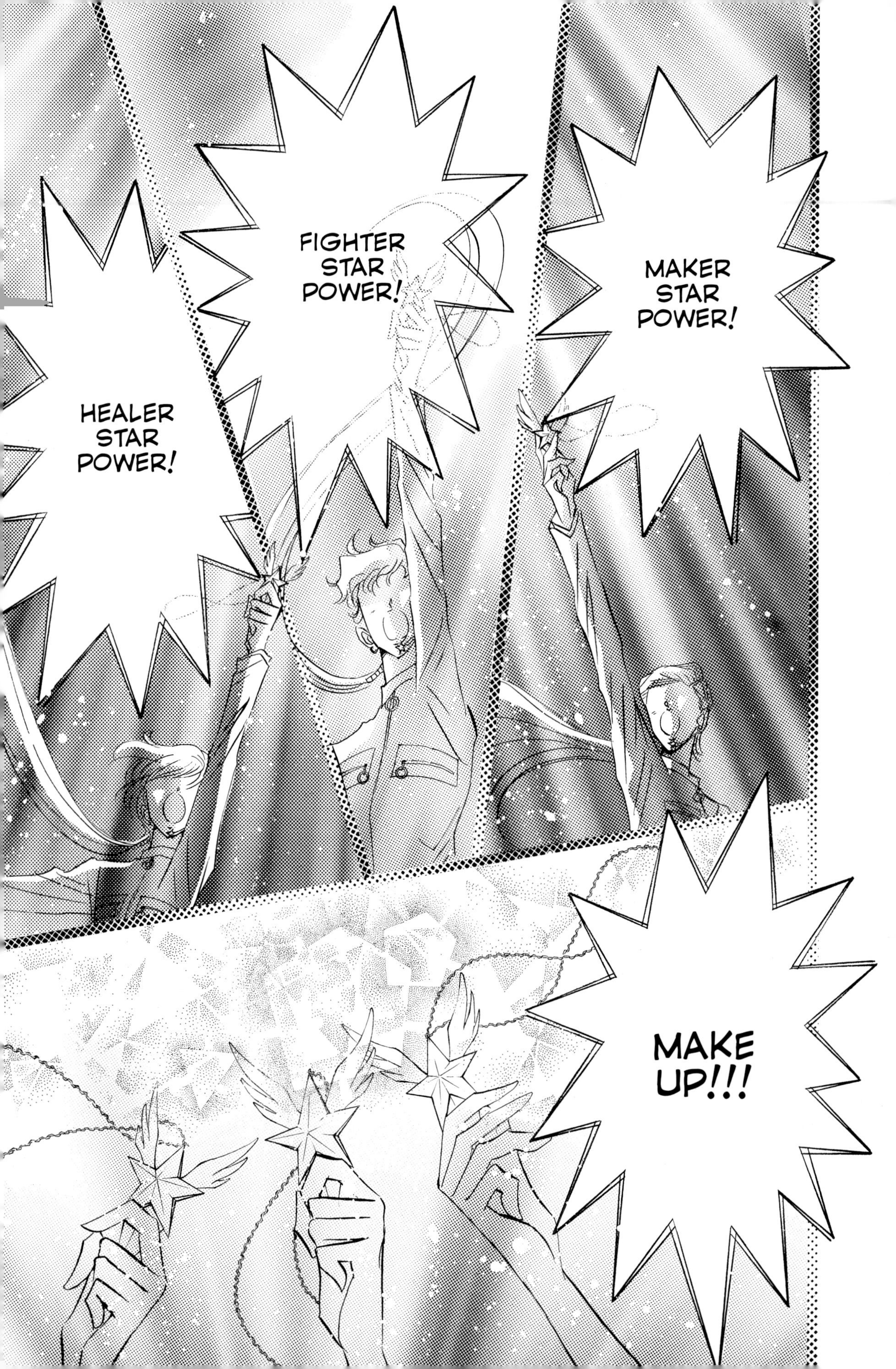
MAKER STAR POWER!
FIGHTER STAR POWER!
HEALER STAR POWER!
MAKE UP!!!

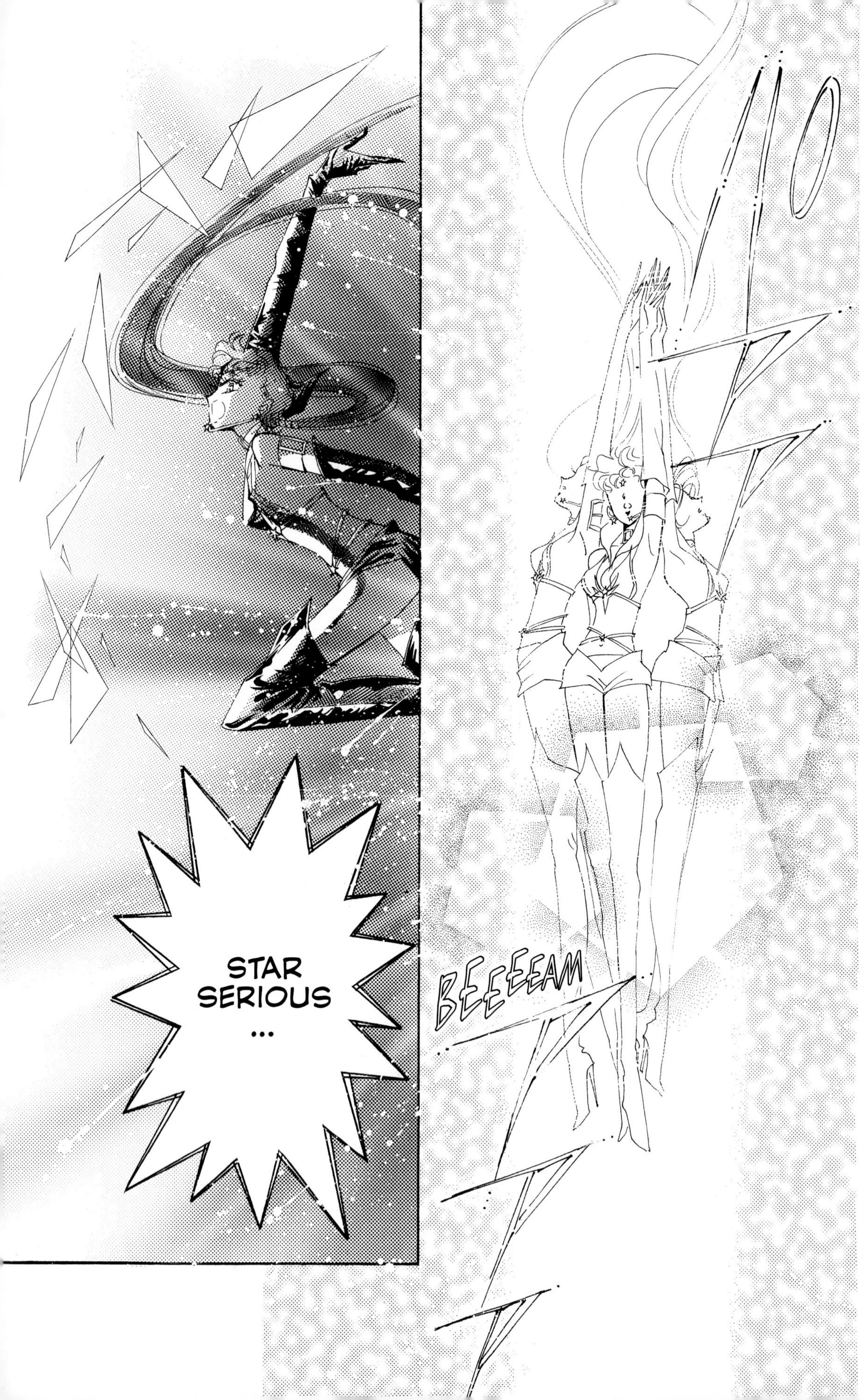
BEEEEAM
STAR SERIOUS ...

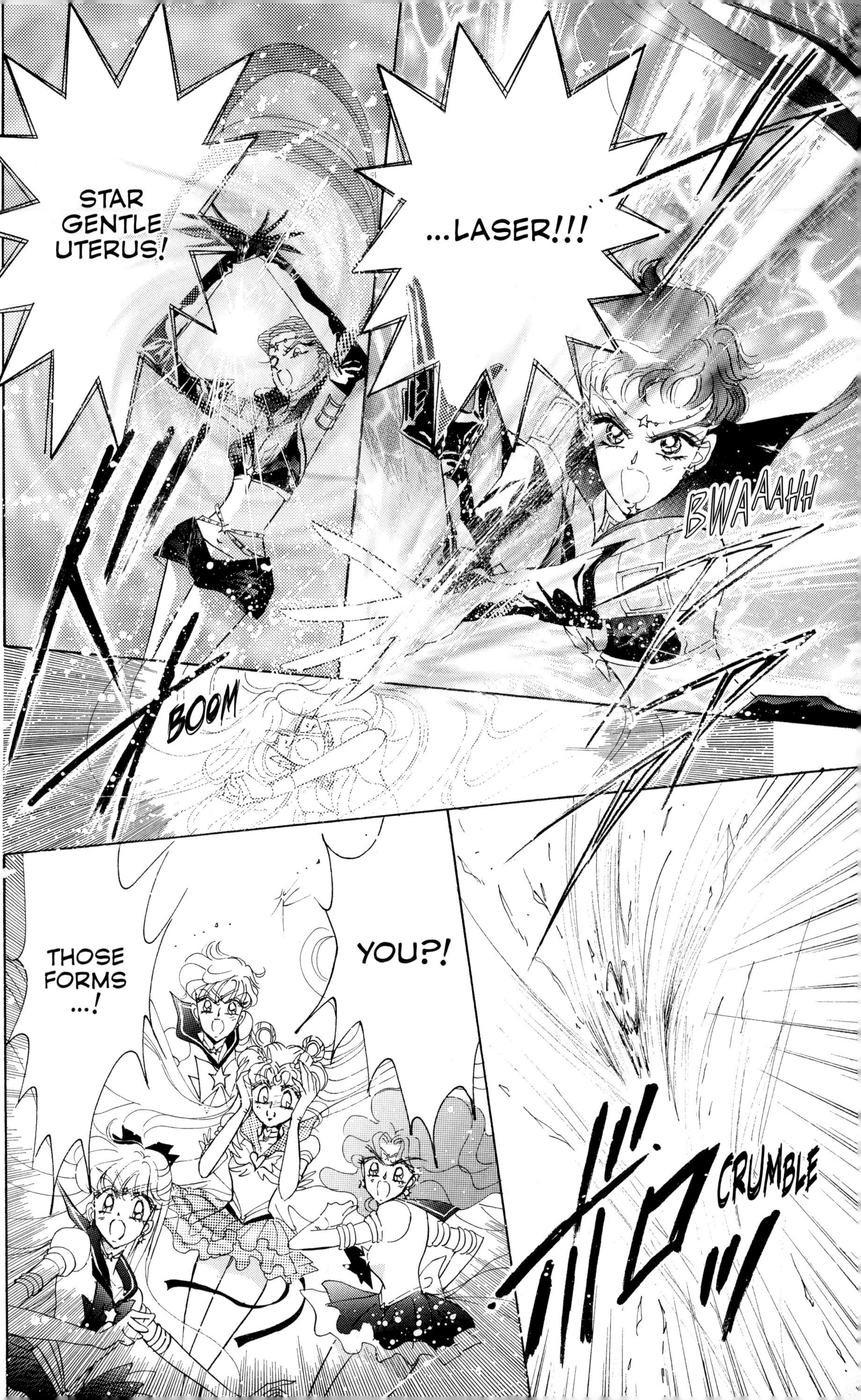
...LASER!!!
STAR GENTLE UTERUS!
BWAAAHH
BOOM
CRUMBLE
YOU?!
THOSE FORMS ...!

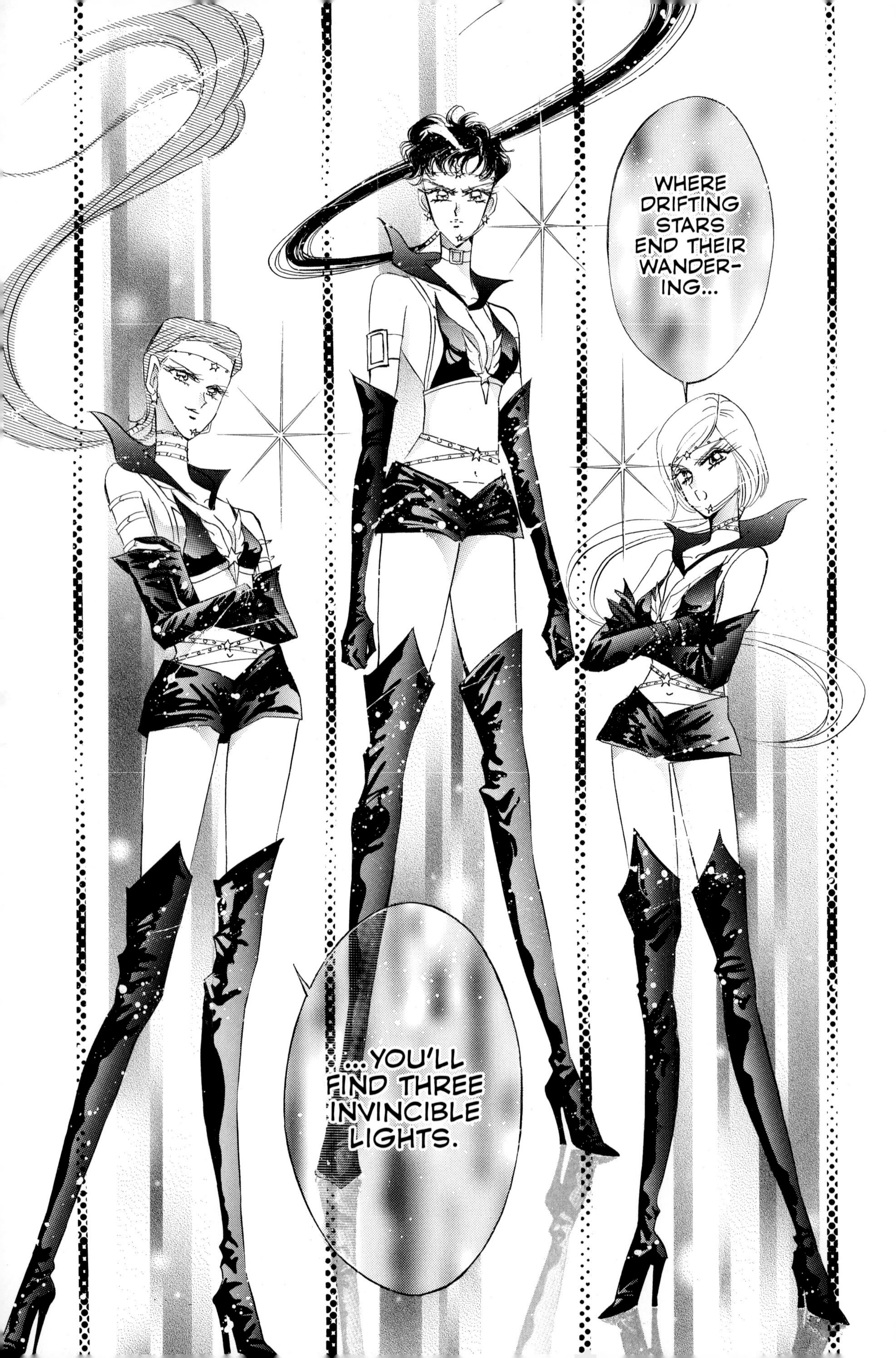
WHERE DRIFTING STARS END THEIR WANDER-ING...
...YOU'LL FIND THREE INVINCIBLE LIGHTS.

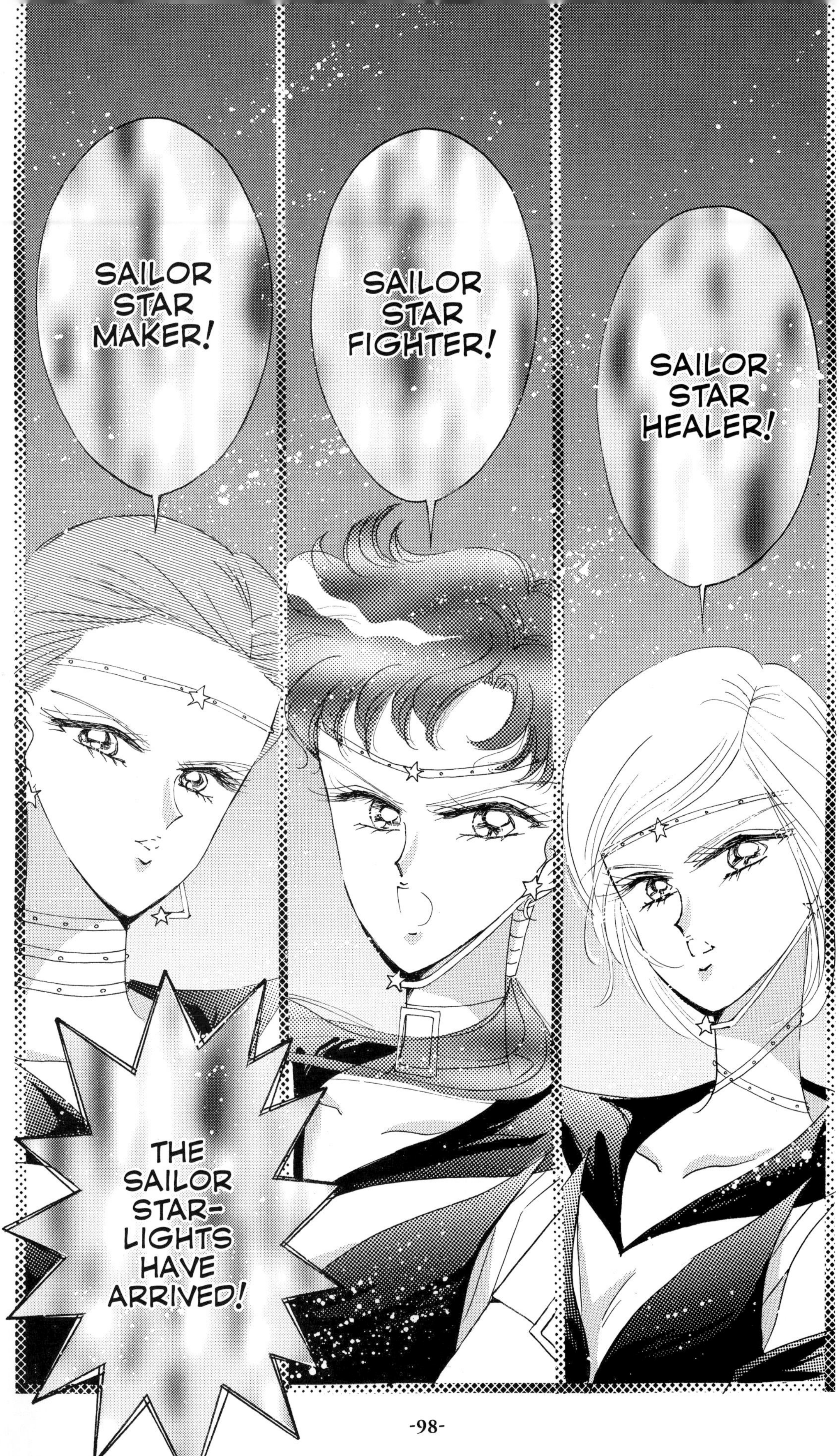
SAILOR STAR HEALER!
SAILOR STAR FIGHTER!
SAILOR STAR MAKER!
THE SAILOR STAR-LIGHTS HAVE ARRIVED!

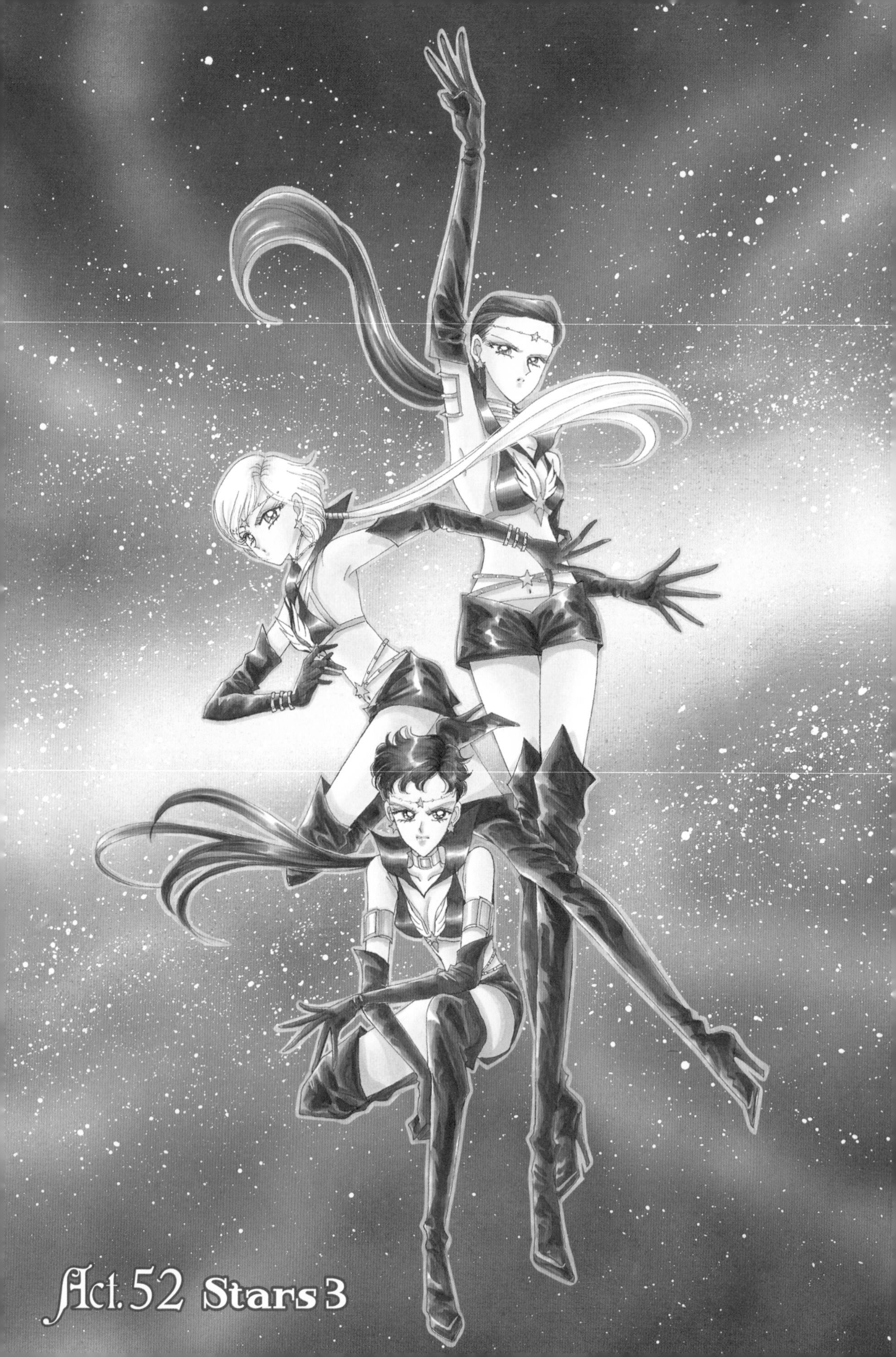

Act. 52 Stars 3

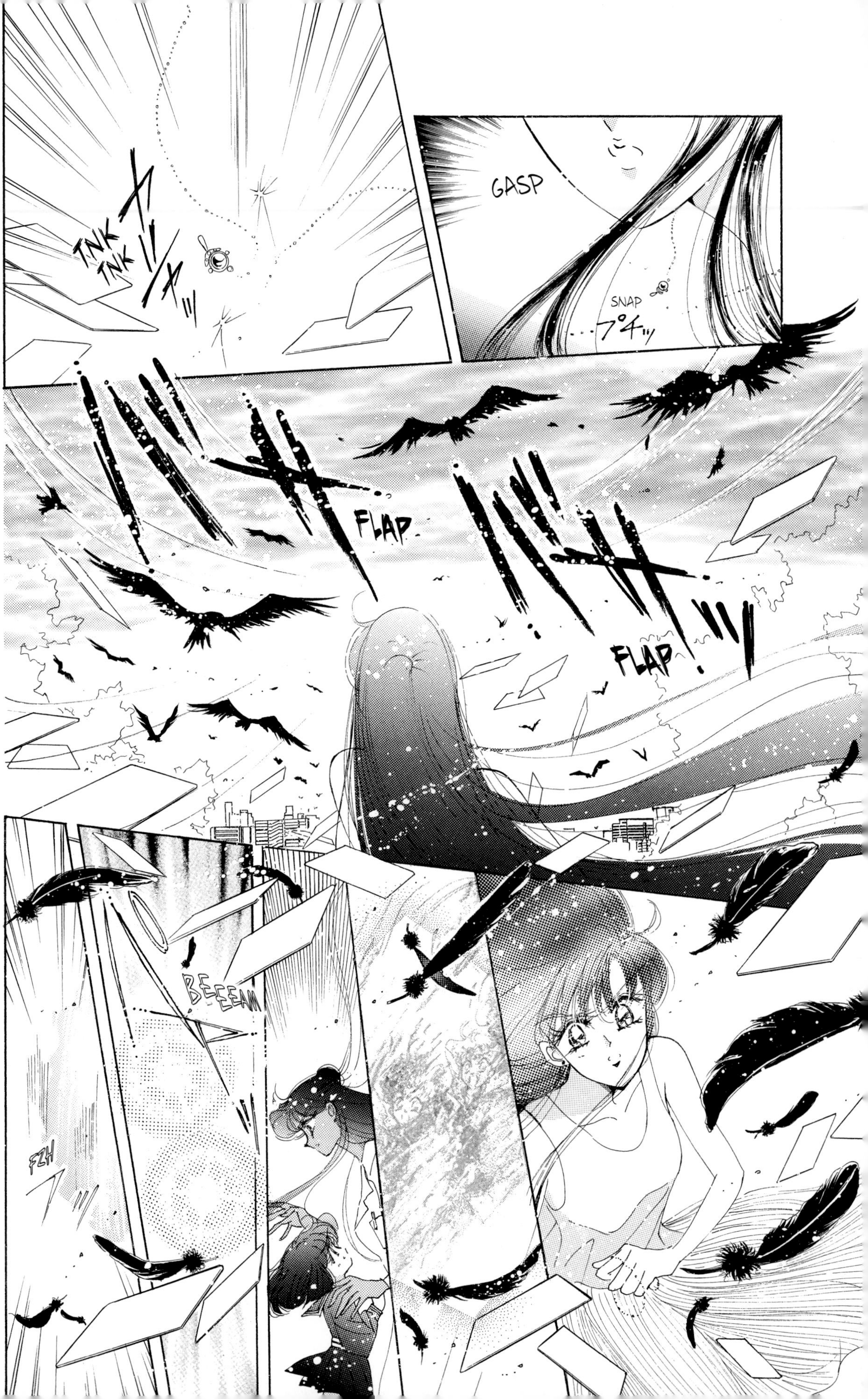
GASP
SNAP
プチッ
TNK TNK
FLAP
FLAP
BEEEAM
FZH

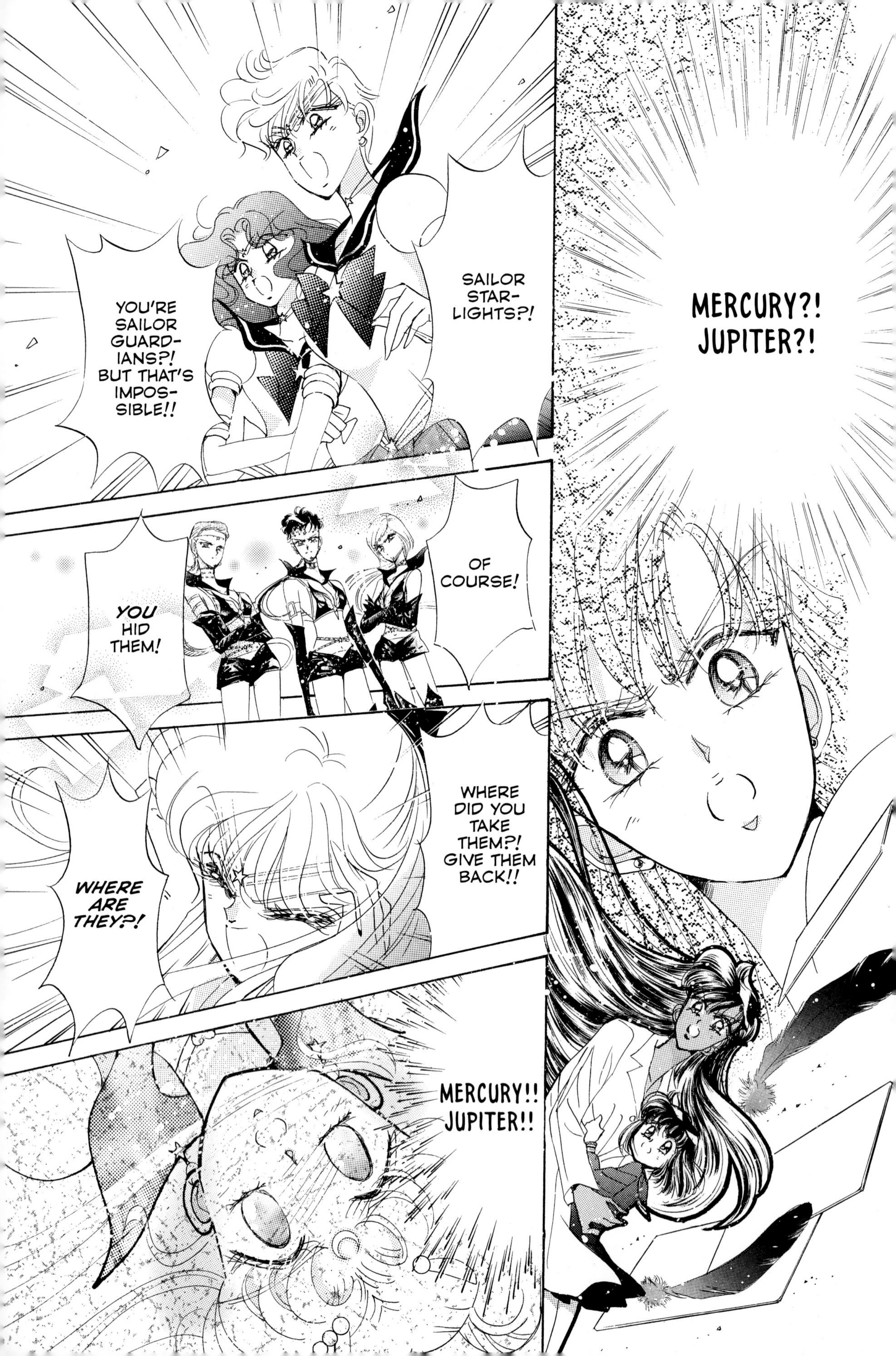
MERCURY?! JUPITER?!
SAILOR STARLIGHTS?!
YOU'RE SAILOR GUARDIANS?! BUT THAT'S IMPOSSIBLE!!
OF COURSE!
YOU HID THEM!
WHERE DID YOU TAKE THEM?! GIVE THEM BACK!!
WHERE ARE THEY?!
MERCURY!! JUPITER!!

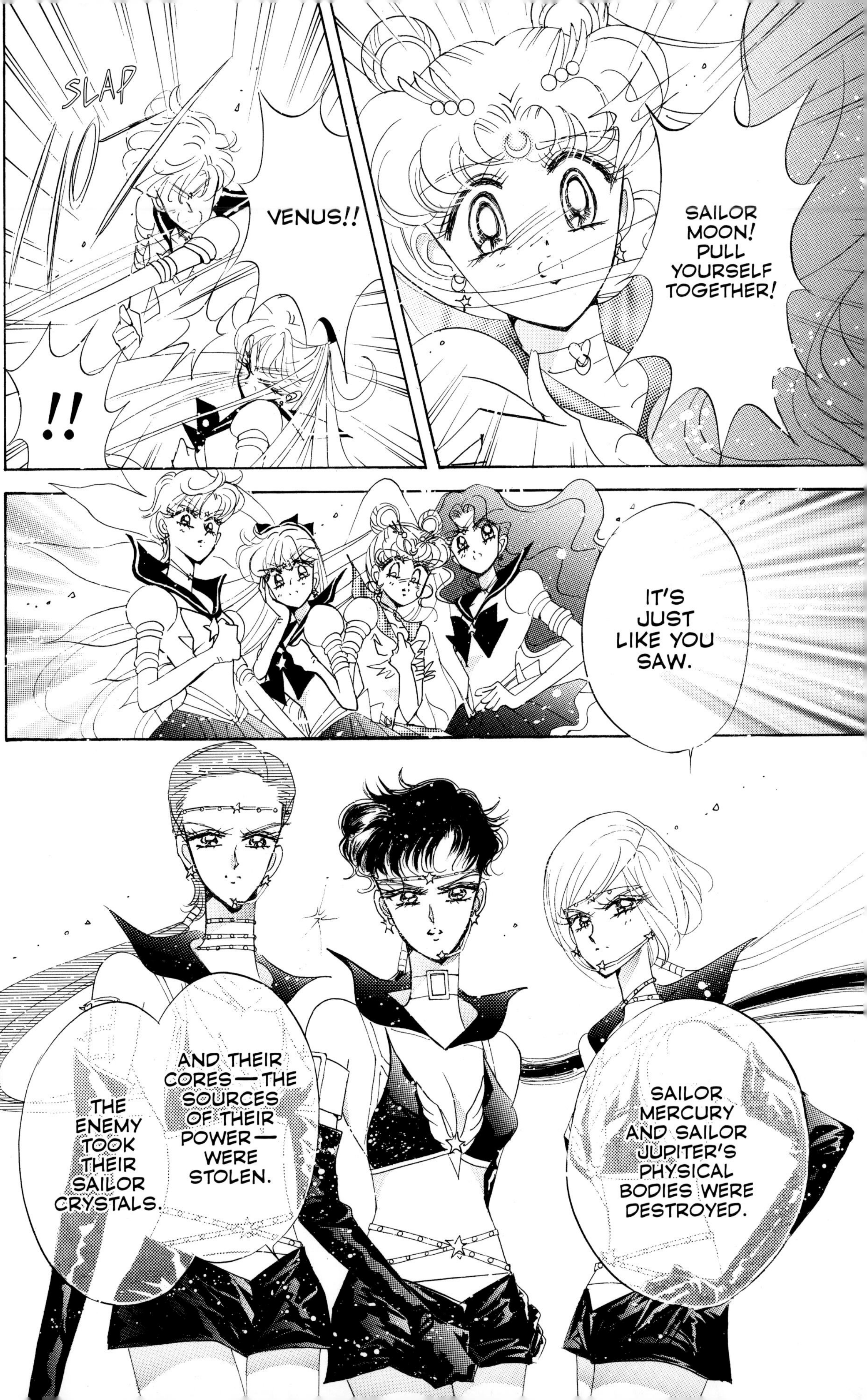
SAILOR MOON! PULL YOURSELF TOGETHER!
SLAP
VENUS!!
!!
IT'S JUST LIKE YOU SAW.
SAILOR MERCURY AND SAILOR JUPITER'S PHYSICAL BODIES WERE DESTROYED.
THE ENEMY TOOK THEIR SAILOR CRYSTALS.
AND THEIR CORES—THE SOURCES OF THEIR POWER—WERE STOLEN.

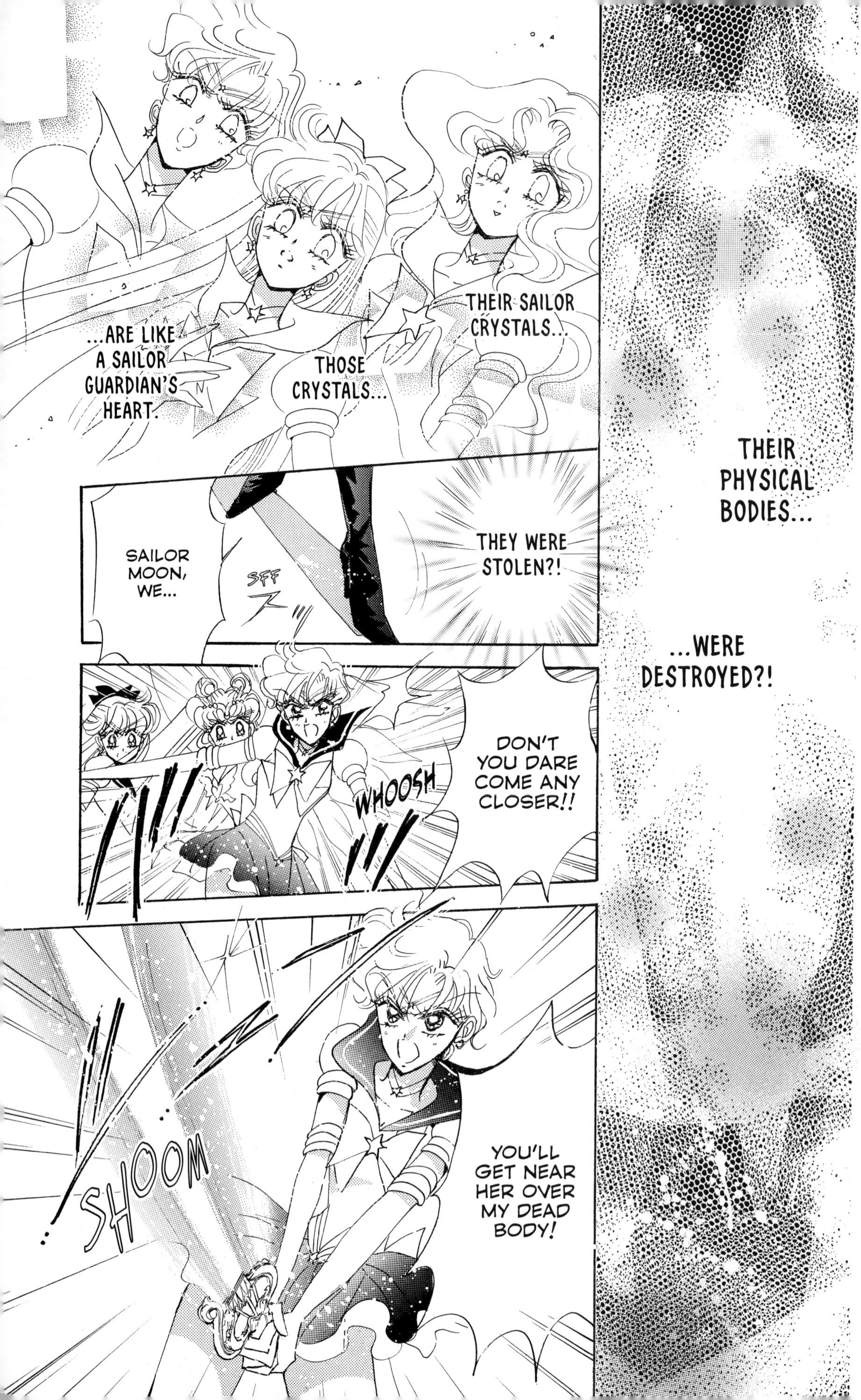
THEIR PHYSICAL BODIES...
...WERE DESTROYED?!
THEIR SAILOR CRYSTALS...
THOSE CRYSTALS...
...ARE LIKE A SAILOR GUARDIAN'S HEART.
THEY WERE STOLEN?!
SFF
SAILOR MOON, WE...
DON'T YOU DARE COME ANY CLOSER!!
WHOOSH
YOU'LL GET NEAR HER OVER MY DEAD BODY!
SHOOM

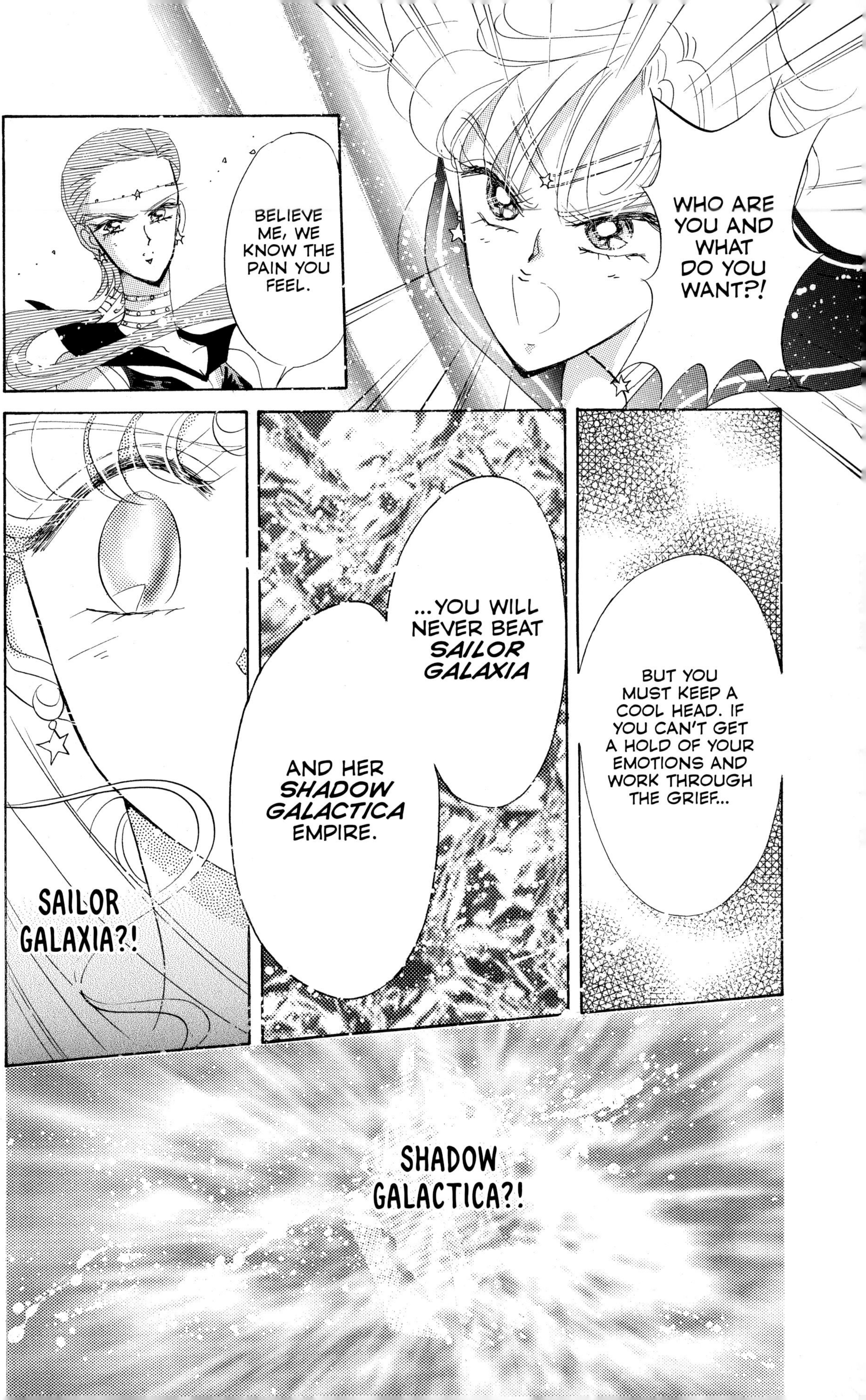
WHO ARE YOU AND WHAT DO YOU WANT?!
BELIEVE ME, WE KNOW THE PAIN YOU FEEL.
BUT YOU MUST KEEP A COOL HEAD. IF YOU CAN'T GET A HOLD OF YOUR EMOTIONS AND WORK THROUGH THE GRIEF...
...YOU WILL NEVER BEAT SAILOR GALAXIA
AND HER SHADOW GALACTICA EMPIRE.
SAILOR GALAXIA?!
SHADOW GALACTICA?!

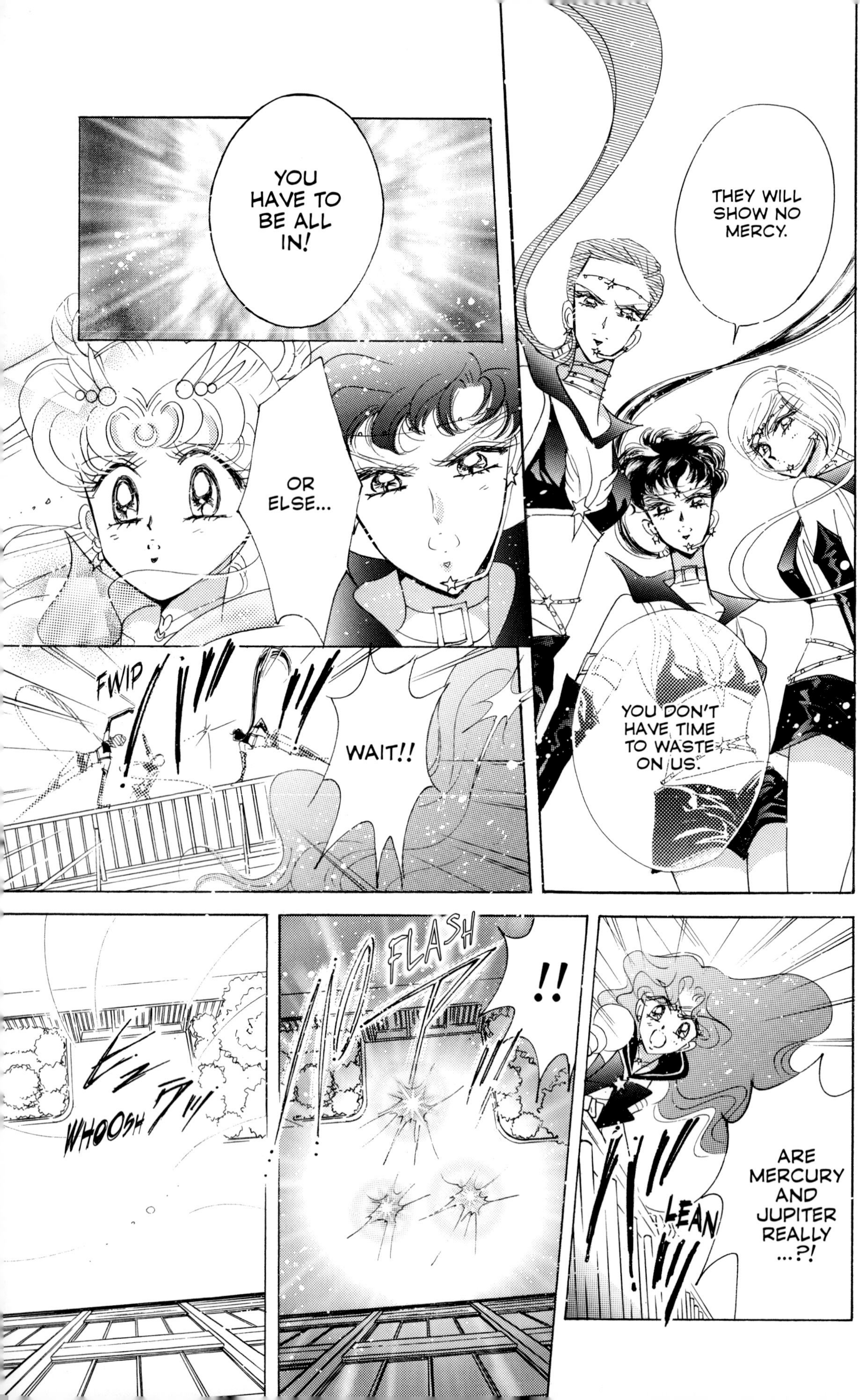
THEY WILL SHOW NO MERCY.
YOU DON'T HAVE TIME TO WASTE ON US.
YOU HAVE TO BE ALL IN!
OR ELSE...
WAIT!!
FWIP
ARE MERCURY AND JUPITER REALLY ...?!
LEAN
!!
FLASH
WHOOSH

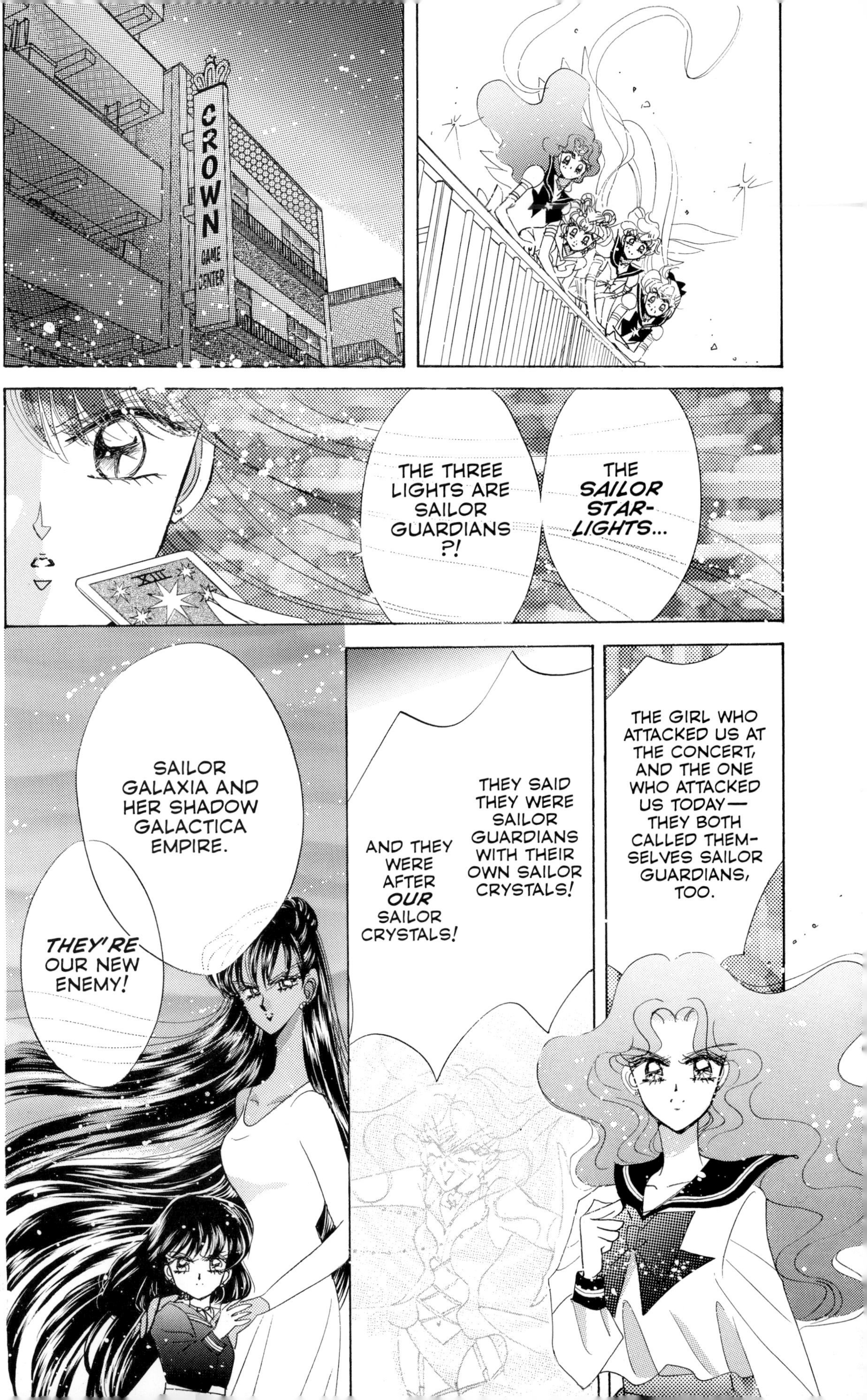
CROWN GAME CENTER
THE SAILOR STAR-LIGHTS...
THE THREE LIGHTS ARE SAILOR GUARDIANS?!
THE GIRL WHO ATTACKED US AT THE CONCERT, AND THE ONE WHO ATTACKED US TODAY— THEY BOTH CALLED THEM-SELVES SAILOR GUARDIANS, TOO.
THEY SAID THEY WERE SAILOR GUARDIANS WITH THEIR OWN SAILOR CRYSTALS!
AND THEY WERE AFTER *OUR* SAILOR CRYSTALS!
SAILOR GALAXIA AND HER SHADOW GALACTICA EMPIRE.
THEY'RE OUR NEW ENEMY!

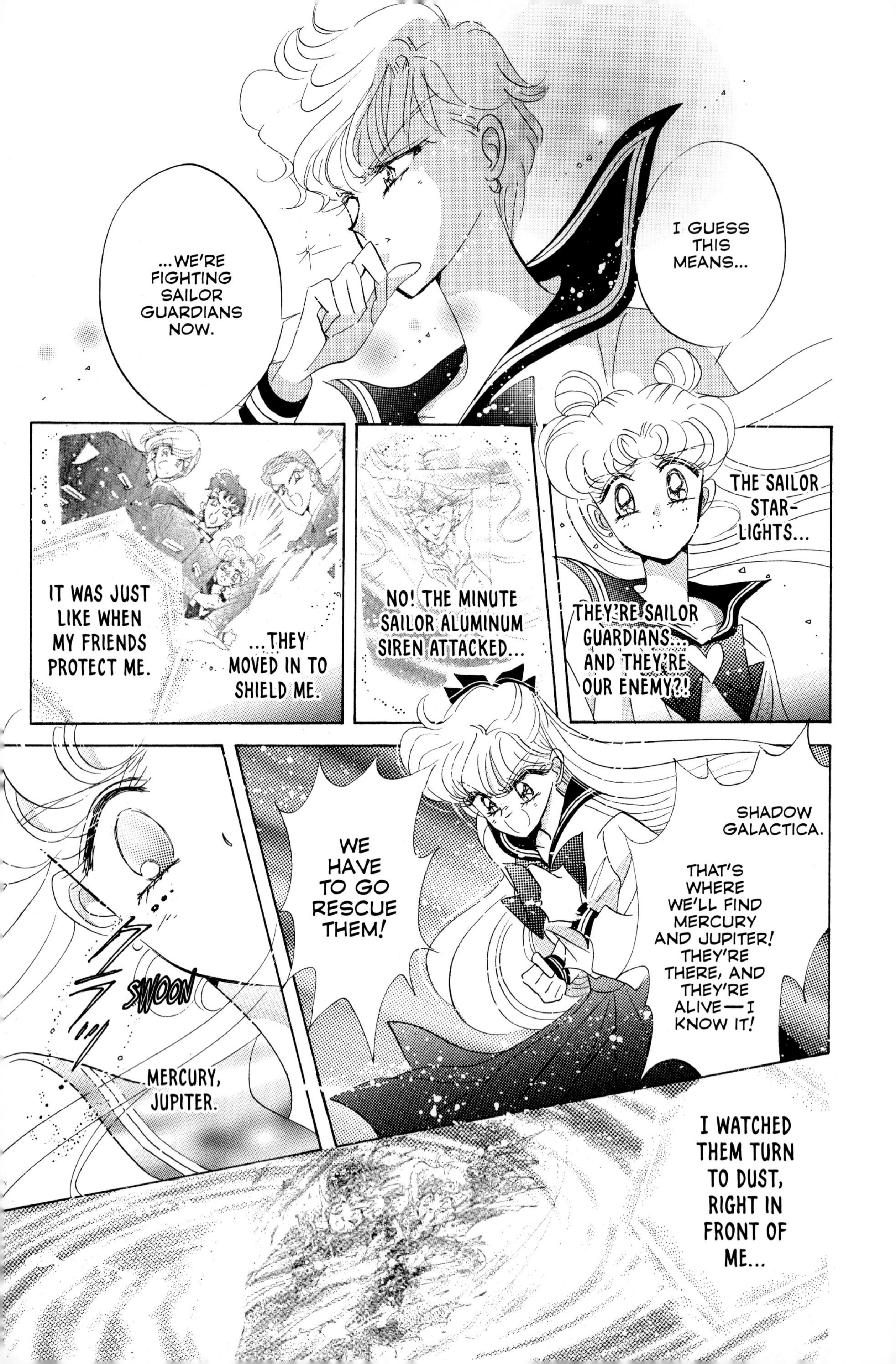
I GUESS THIS MEANS...
...WE'RE FIGHTING SAILOR GUARDIANS NOW.
THE SAILOR STAR-LIGHTS...
THEY'RE SAILOR GUARDIANS... AND THEY'RE OUR ENEMY?!
NO! THE MINUTE SAILOR ALUMINUM SIREN ATTACKED...
...THEY MOVED IN TO SHIELD ME.
IT WAS JUST LIKE WHEN MY FRIENDS PROTECT ME.
SHADOW GALACTICA.
THAT'S WHERE WE'LL FIND MERCURY AND JUPITER! THEY'RE THERE, AND THEY'RE ALIVE—I KNOW IT!
WE HAVE TO GO RESCUE THEM!
SWOON
MERCURY, JUPITER.
I WATCHED THEM TURN TO DUST, RIGHT IN FRONT OF ME...

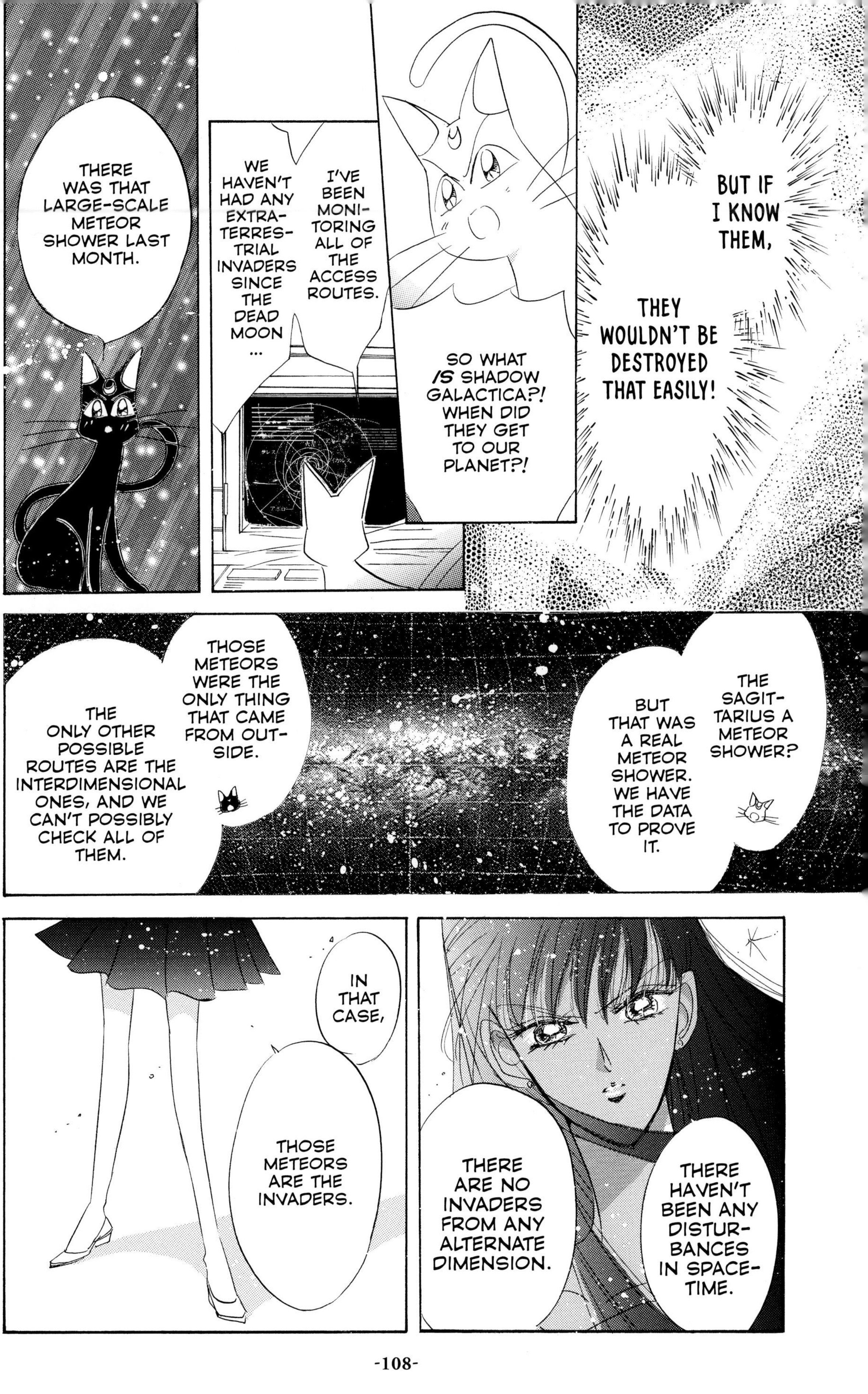

BUT IF I KNOW THEM,
THEY WOULDN'T BE DESTROYED THAT EASILY!
SO WHAT *IS* SHADOW GALACTICA?! WHEN DID THEY GET TO OUR PLANET?!
I'VE BEEN MONITORING ALL OF THE ACCESS ROUTES.
WE HAVEN'T HAD ANY EXTRATERRESTRIAL INVADERS SINCE THE DEAD MOON ...
THERE WAS THAT LARGE-SCALE METEOR SHOWER LAST MONTH.
THE SAGITTARIUS A METEOR SHOWER?
BUT THAT WAS A REAL METEOR SHOWER. WE HAVE THE DATA TO PROVE IT.
THOSE METEORS WERE THE ONLY THING THAT CAME FROM OUTSIDE.
THE ONLY OTHER POSSIBLE ROUTES ARE THE INTERDIMENSIONAL ONES, AND WE CAN'T POSSIBLY CHECK ALL OF THEM.
THERE HAVEN'T BEEN ANY DISTURBANCES IN SPACE-TIME.
THERE ARE NO INVADERS FROM ANY ALTERNATE DIMENSION.
IN THAT CASE,
THOSE METEORS ARE THE INVADERS.

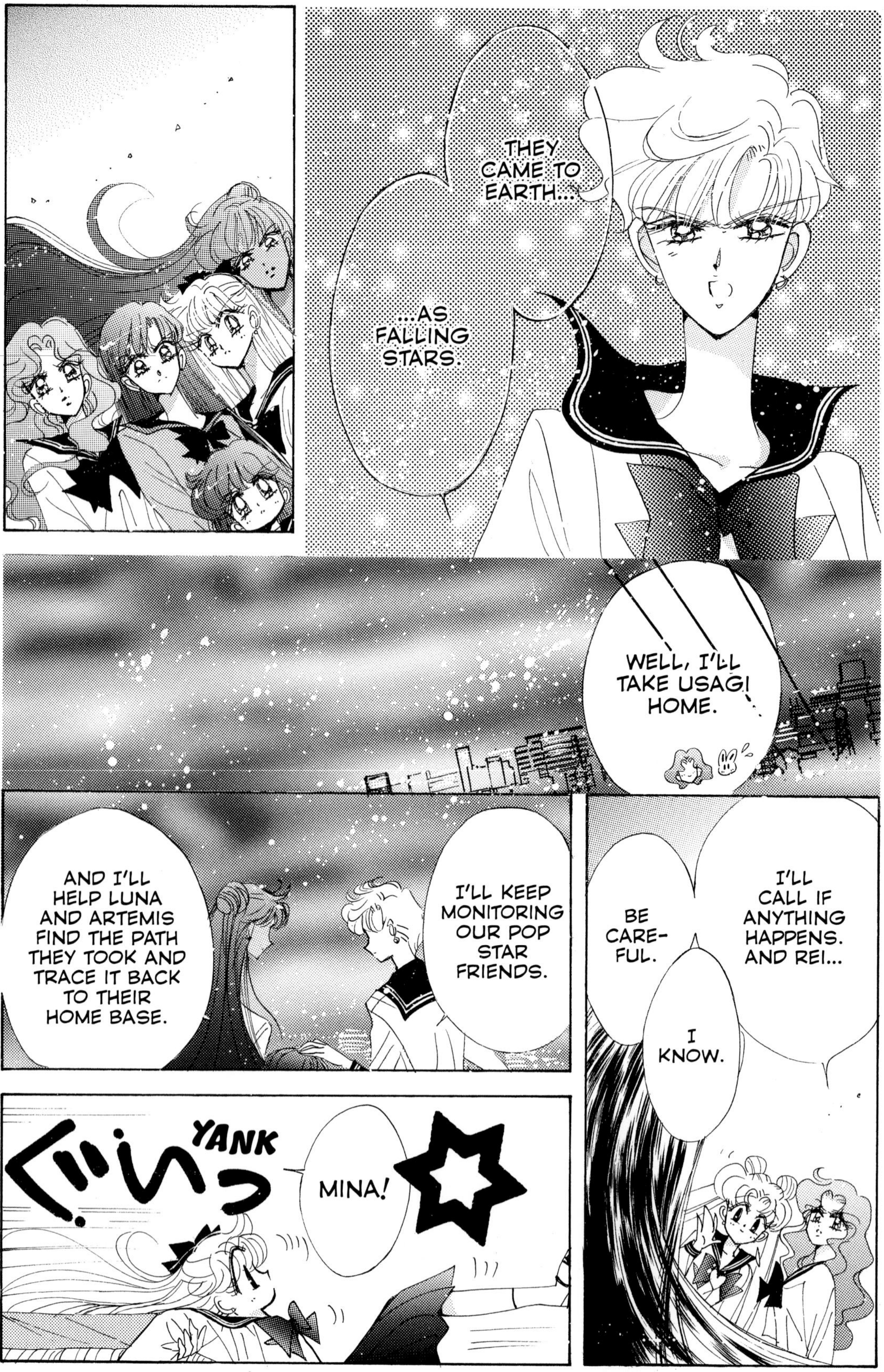
THEY CAME TO EARTH...
...AS FALLING STARS.
WELL, I'LL TAKE USAGI HOME.
I'LL CALL IF ANYTHING HAPPENS. AND REI...
BE CARE-FUL.
I KNOW.
I'LL KEEP MONITORING OUR POP STAR FRIENDS.
AND I'LL HELP LUNA AND ARTEMIS FIND THE PATH THEY TOOK AND TRACE IT BACK TO THEIR HOME BASE.
MINA!
YANK

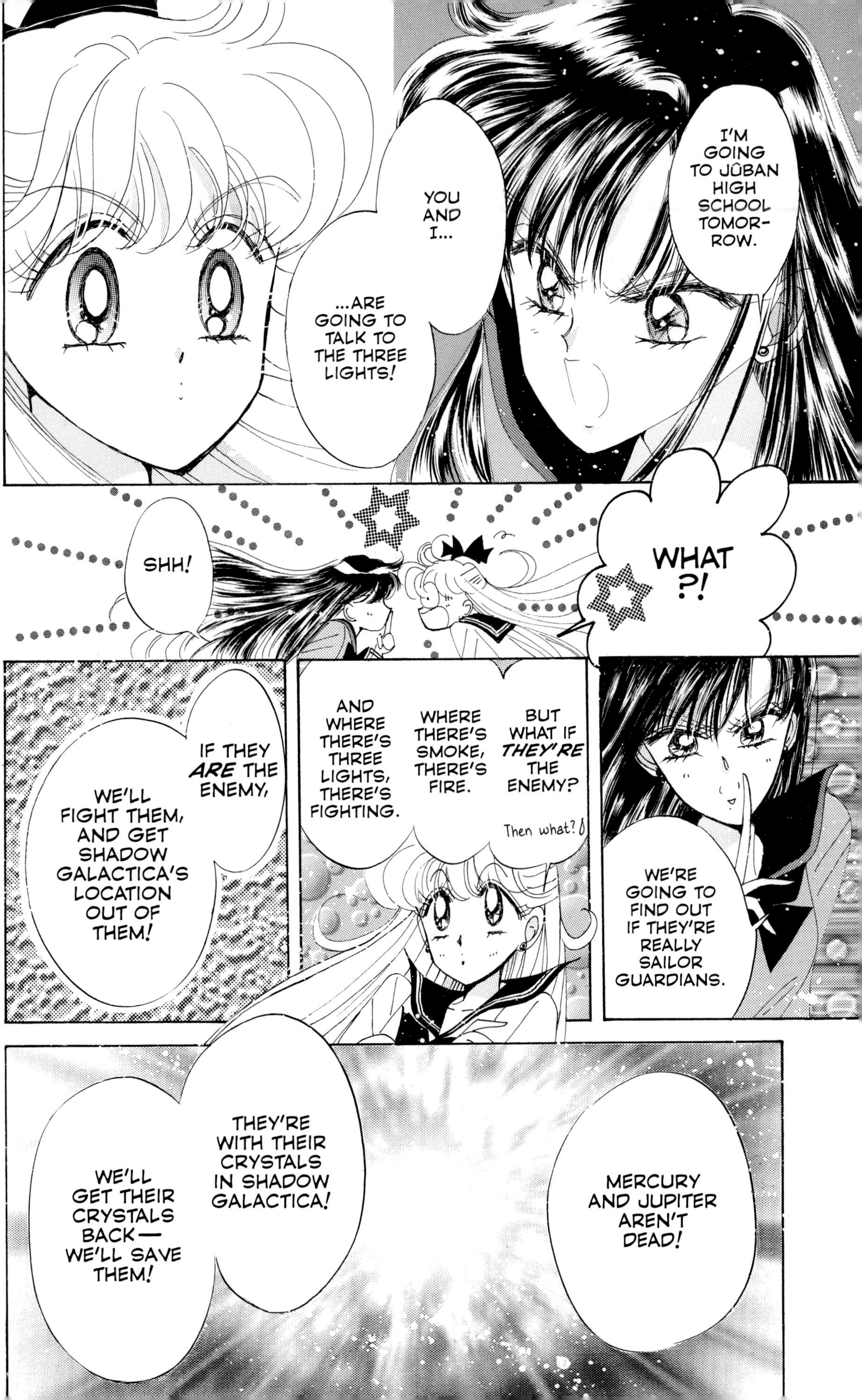
I'M GOING TO JÛBAN HIGH SCHOOL TOMORROW.
YOU AND I...
...ARE GOING TO TALK TO THE THREE LIGHTS!
WHAT?!
SHH!
WE'RE GOING TO FIND OUT IF THEY'RE REALLY SAILOR GUARDIANS.
BUT WHAT IF THEY'RE THE ENEMY?
Then what?
WHERE THERE'S SMOKE, THERE'S FIRE.
AND WHERE THERE'S THREE LIGHTS, THERE'S FIGHTING.
IF THEY ARE THE ENEMY,
WE'LL FIGHT THEM, AND GET SHADOW GALACTICA'S LOCATION OUT OF THEM!
MERCURY AND JUPITER AREN'T DEAD!
THEY'RE WITH THEIR CRYSTALS IN SHADOW GALACTICA!
WE'LL GET THEIR CRYSTALS BACK—WE'LL SAVE THEM!

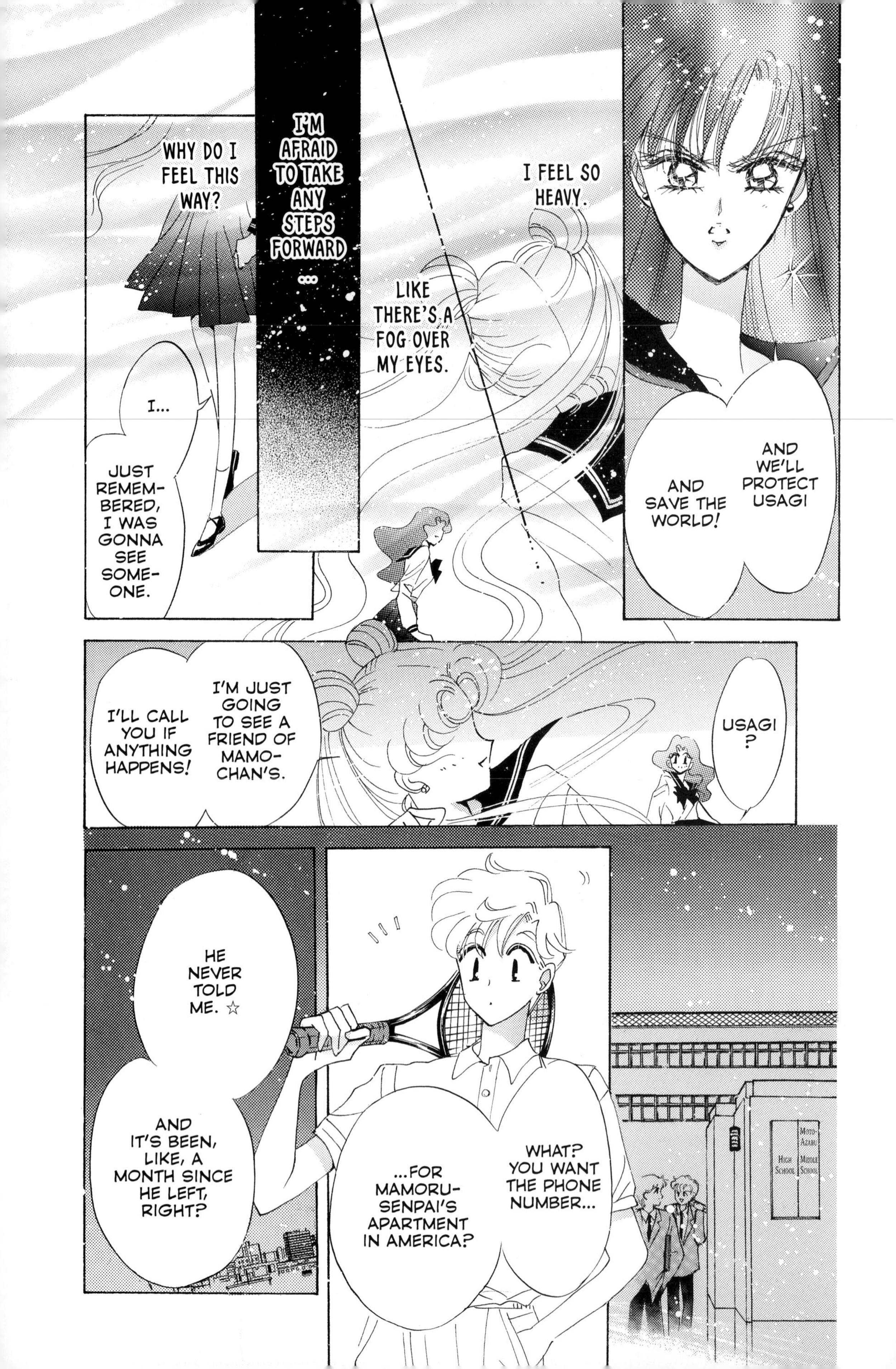
AND WE'LL PROTECT USAGI
AND SAVE THE WORLD!
I FEEL SO HEAVY.
LIKE THERE'S A FOG OVER MY EYES.
I'M AFRAID TO TAKE ANY STEPS FORWARD ...
WHY DO I FEEL THIS WAY?
I...
JUST REMEMBERED, I WAS GONNA SEE SOMEONE.
USAGI?
I'M JUST GOING TO SEE A FRIEND OF MAMO-CHAN'S.
I'LL CALL YOU IF ANYTHING HAPPENS!
MOTO-AZABU
HIGH SCHOOL
MIDDLE SCHOOL
WHAT? YOU WANT THE PHONE NUMBER...
...FOR MAMORU-SENPAI'S APARTMENT IN AMERICA?
HE NEVER TOLD ME. ☆
AND IT'S BEEN, LIKE, A MONTH SINCE HE LEFT, RIGHT?

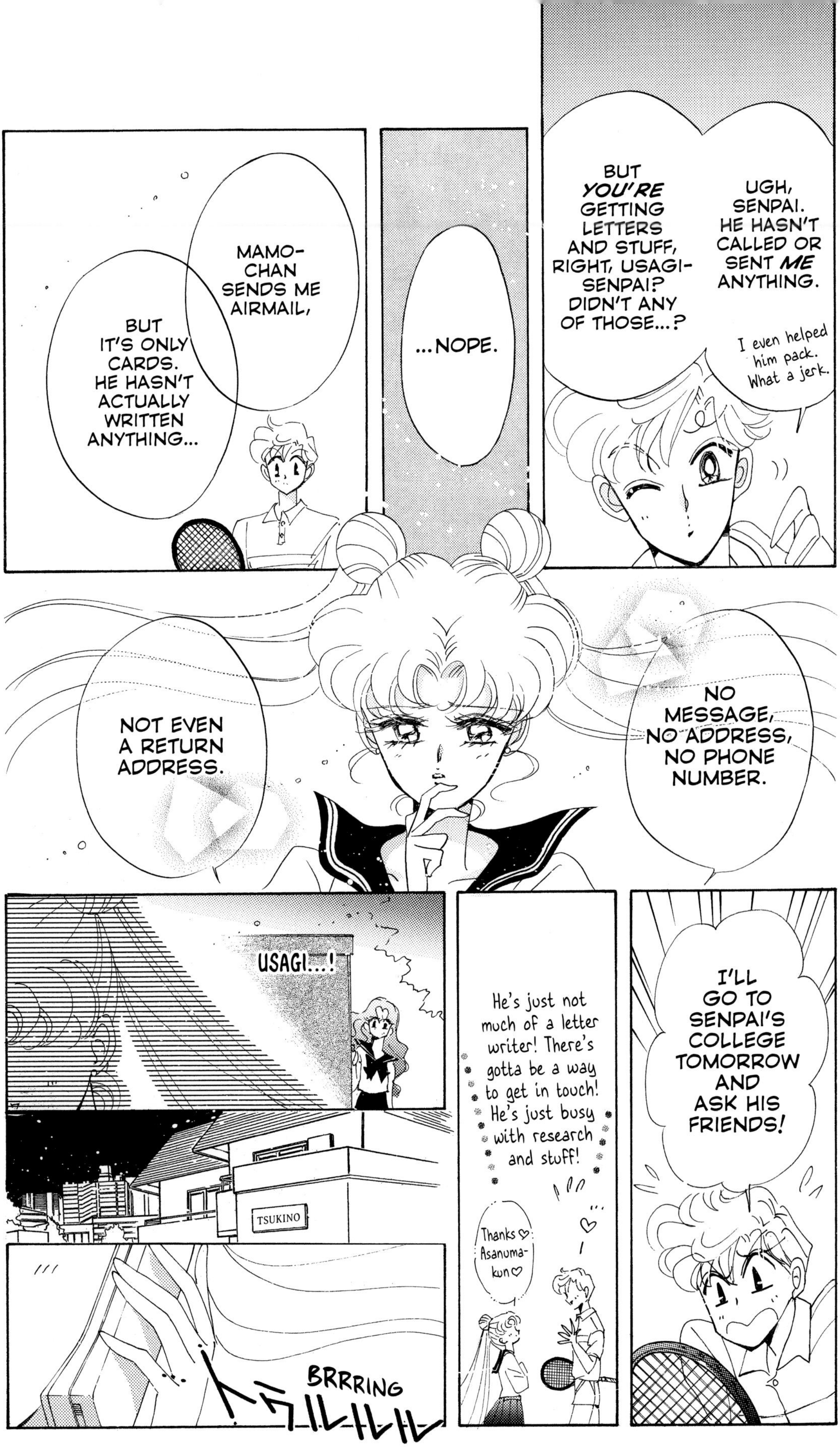

UGH, SENPAI. HE HASN'T CALLED OR SENT *ME* ANYTHING.
BUT *YOU'RE* GETTING LETTERS AND STUFF, RIGHT, USAGI-SENPAI? DIDN'T ANY OF THOSE...?
I even helped him pack. What a jerk.
...NOPE.
MAMO-CHAN SENDS ME AIRMAIL,
BUT IT'S ONLY CARDS. HE HASN'T ACTUALLY WRITTEN ANYTHING...
NO MESSAGE, NO ADDRESS, NO PHONE NUMBER.
NOT EVEN A RETURN ADDRESS.
I'LL GO TO SENPAI'S COLLEGE TOMORROW AND ASK HIS FRIENDS!
He's just not much of a letter writer! There's gotta be a way to get in touch! He's just busy with research and stuff!
Thanks♡ Asanuma-kun♡
USAGI...!
TSUKINO
BRRRING

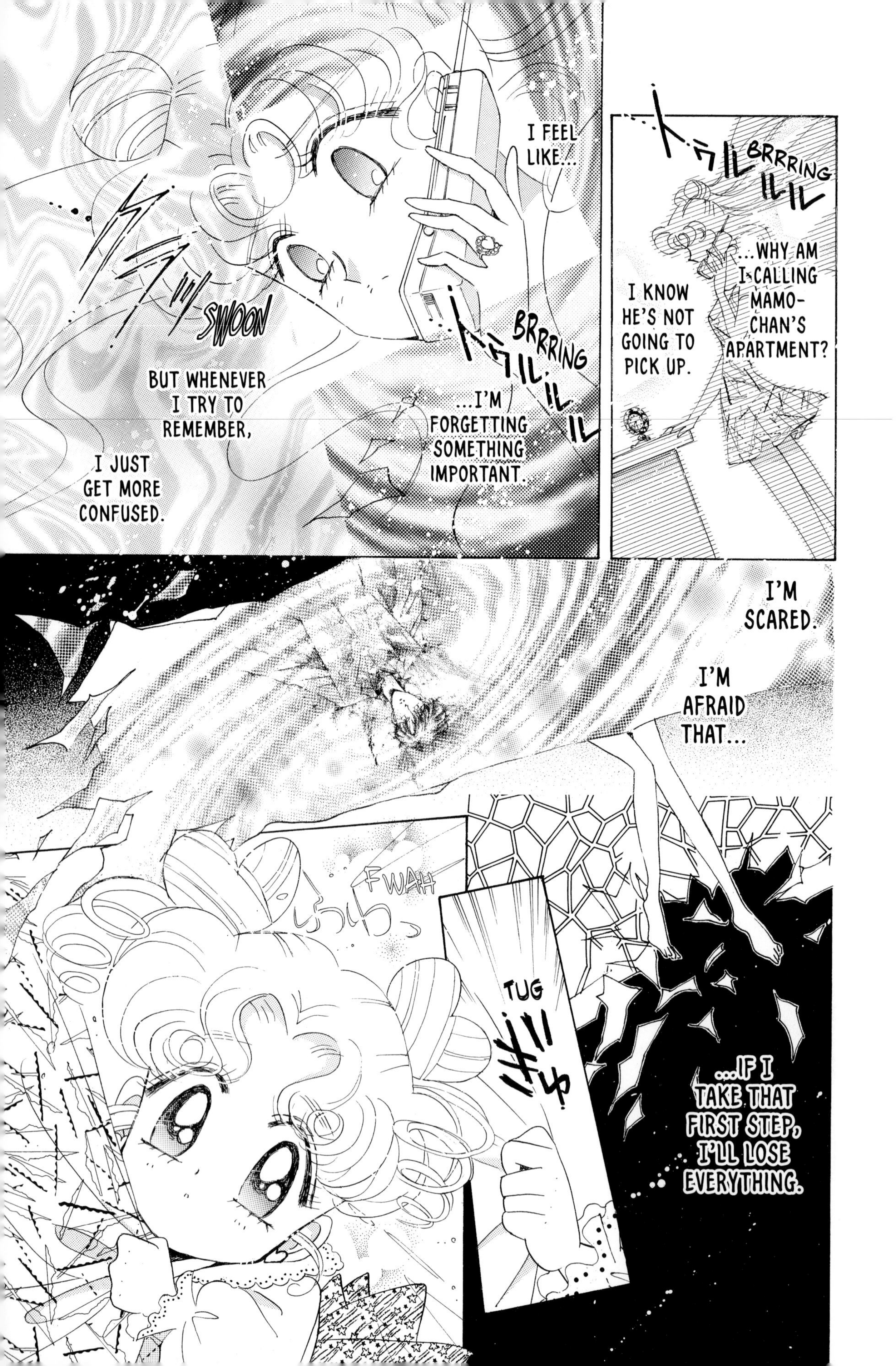
BRRRING
...WHY AM I CALLING MAMO-CHAN'S APARTMENT?
I KNOW HE'S NOT GOING TO PICK UP.
I FEEL LIKE...
BRRRING
...I'M FORGETTING SOMETHING IMPORTANT.
SWOON
BUT WHENEVER I TRY TO REMEMBER,
I JUST GET MORE CONFUSED.
I'M SCARED.
I'M AFRAID THAT...
...IF I TAKE THAT FIRST STEP, I'LL LOSE EVERYTHING.
TUG
FWAH

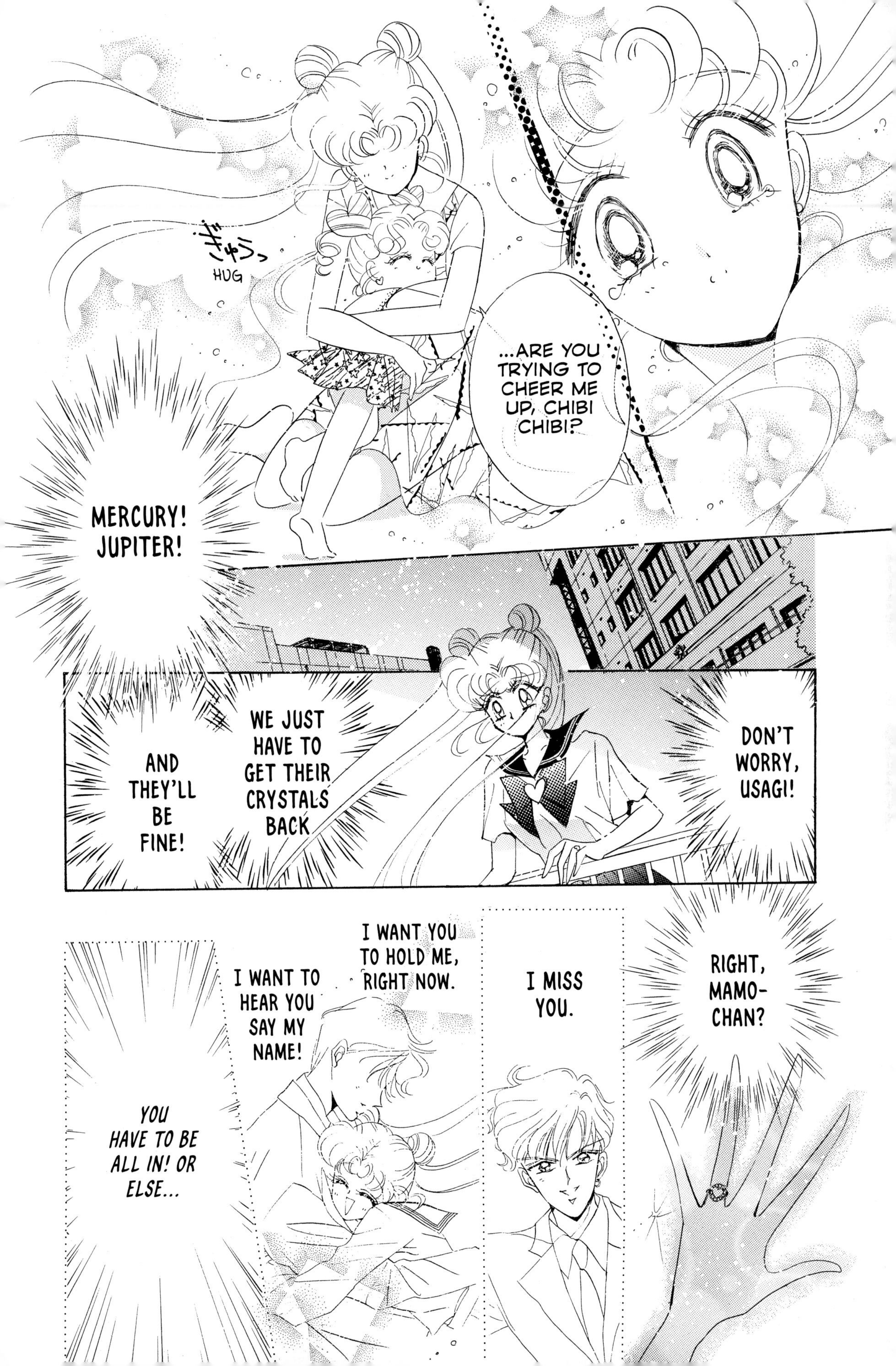
...ARE YOU TRYING TO CHEER ME UP, CHIBI CHIBI?
ぎゅうっ
HUG
MERCURY! JUPITER!
DON'T WORRY, USAGI!
WE JUST HAVE TO GET THEIR CRYSTALS BACK
AND THEY'LL BE FINE!
RIGHT, MAMO-CHAN?
I MISS YOU.
I WANT YOU TO HOLD ME, RIGHT NOW.
I WANT TO HEAR YOU SAY MY NAME!
YOU HAVE TO BE ALL IN! OR ELSE...

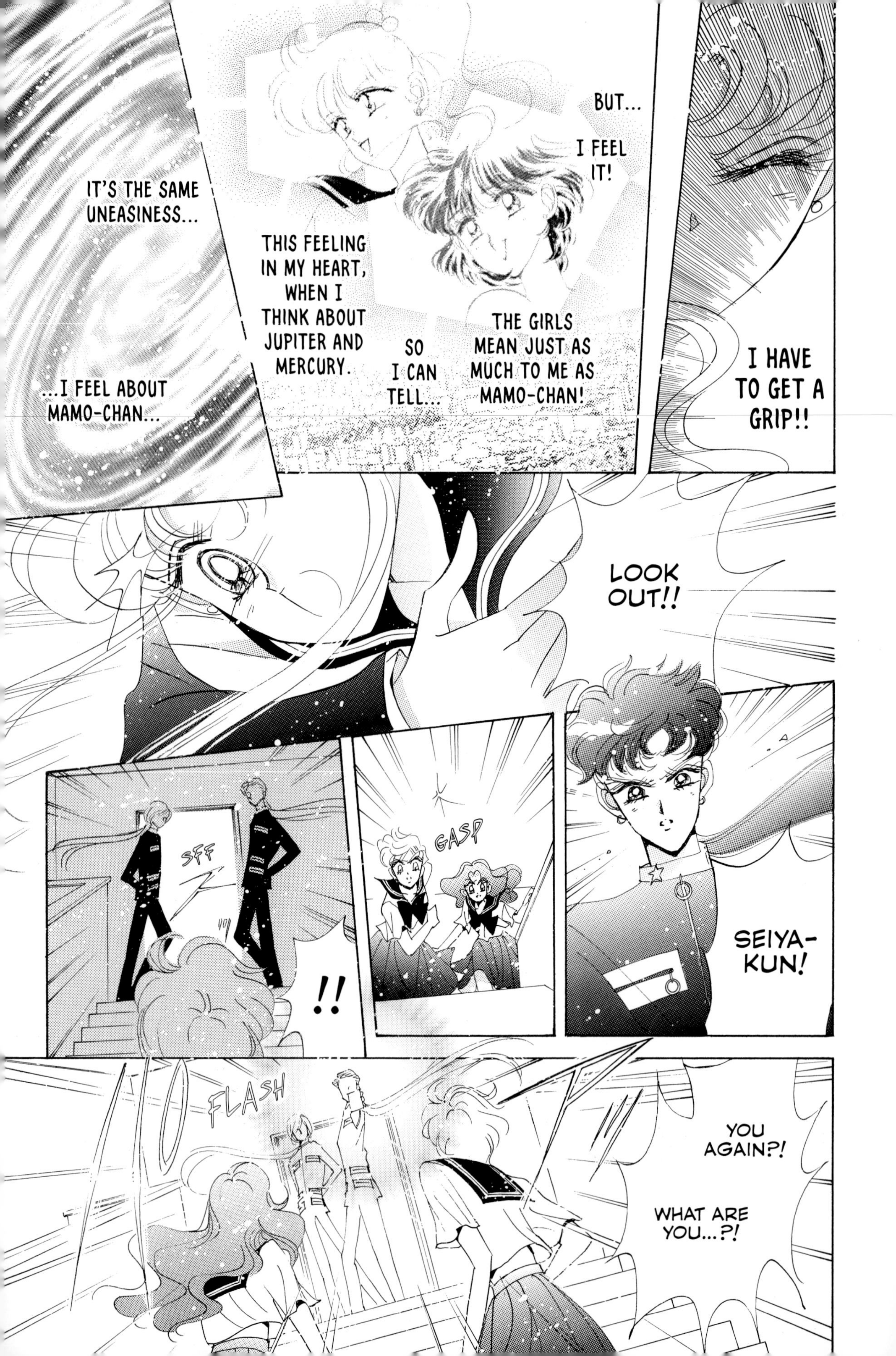
I HAVE TO GET A GRIP!!
BUT...
I FEEL IT!
THE GIRLS MEAN JUST AS MUCH TO ME AS MAMO-CHAN!
SO I CAN TELL...
THIS FEELING IN MY HEART, WHEN I THINK ABOUT JUPITER AND MERCURY.
IT'S THE SAME UNEASINESS...
...I FEEL ABOUT MAMO-CHAN...
LOOK OUT!!
SEIYA-KUN!
GASP
SFF
!!
YOU AGAIN?!
WHAT ARE YOU...?!
FLASH

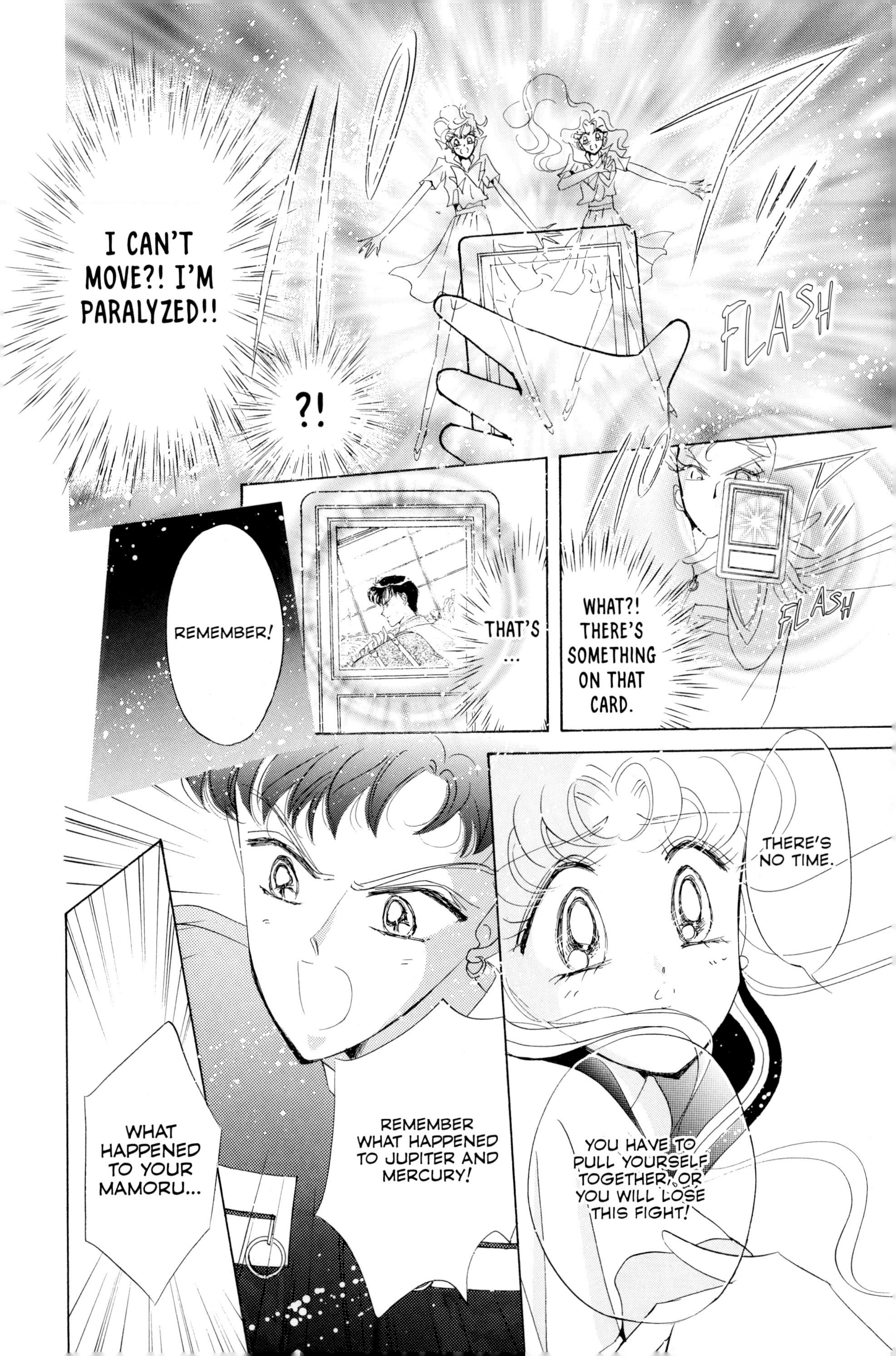
FLASH
I CAN'T MOVE?! I'M PARALYZED!!
?!
FLASH
WHAT?! THERE'S SOMETHING ON THAT CARD.
THAT'S ...
REMEMBER!
THERE'S NO TIME.
YOU HAVE TO PULL YOURSELF TOGETHER, OR YOU WILL LOSE THIS FIGHT!
REMEMBER WHAT HAPPENED TO JUPITER AND MERCURY!
WHAT HAPPENED TO YOUR MAMORU...

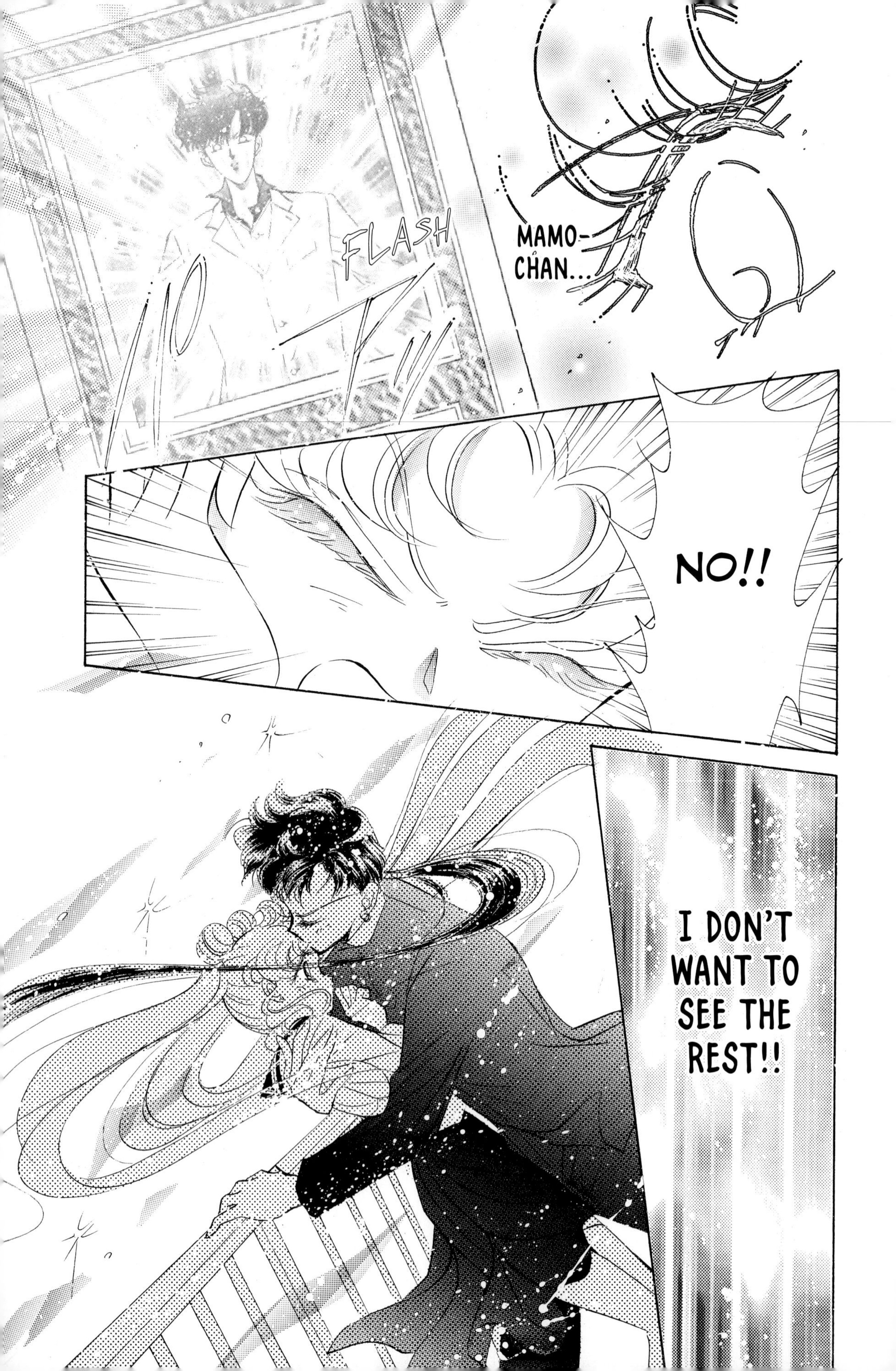
MAMO-CHAN...
FLASH
NO!!
I DON'T WANT TO SEE THE REST!!

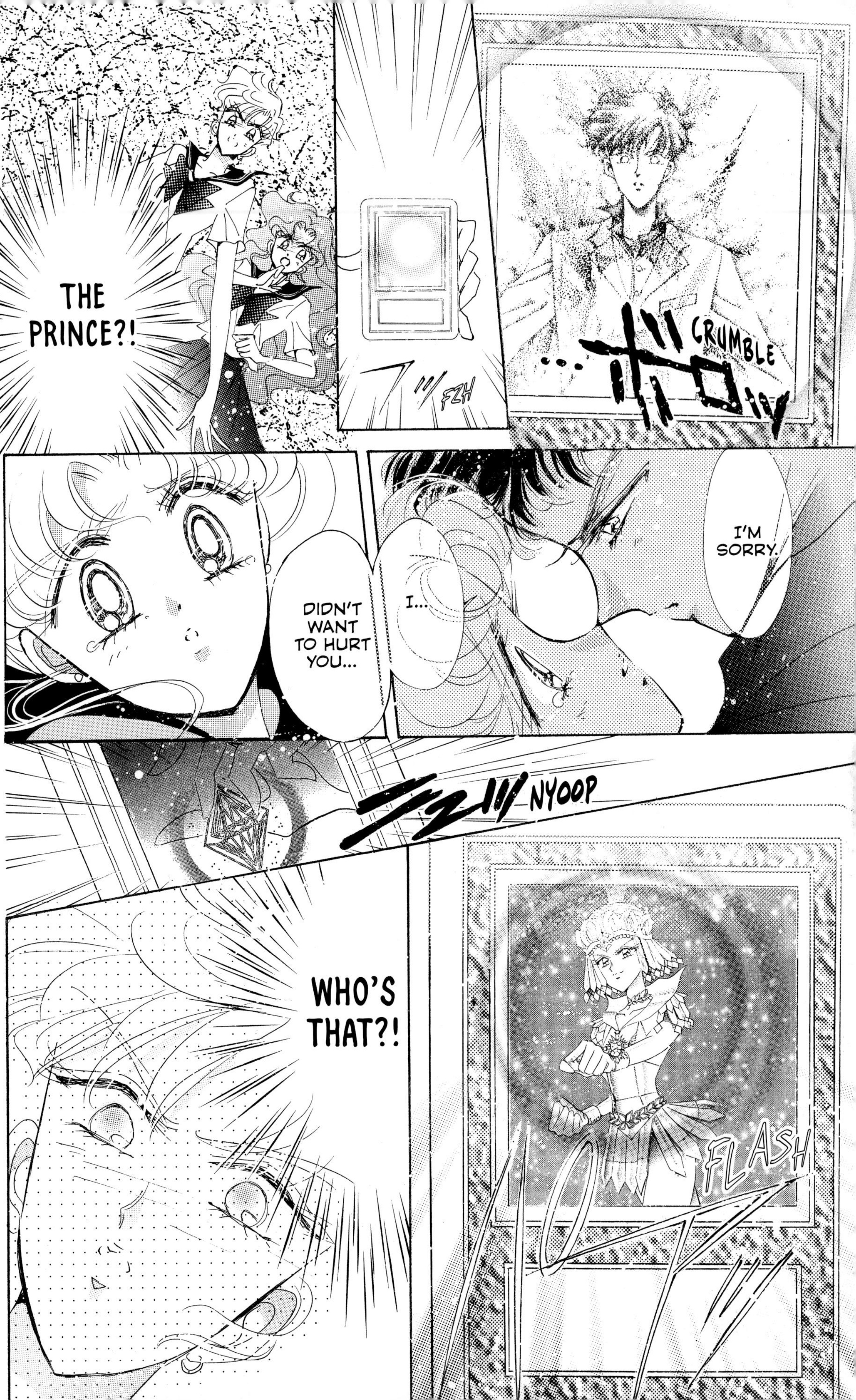
CRUMBLE
FZH
THE PRINCE?!
I'M SORRY.
I...
DIDN'T WANT TO HURT YOU...
NYOOP
FLASH
WHO'S THAT?!

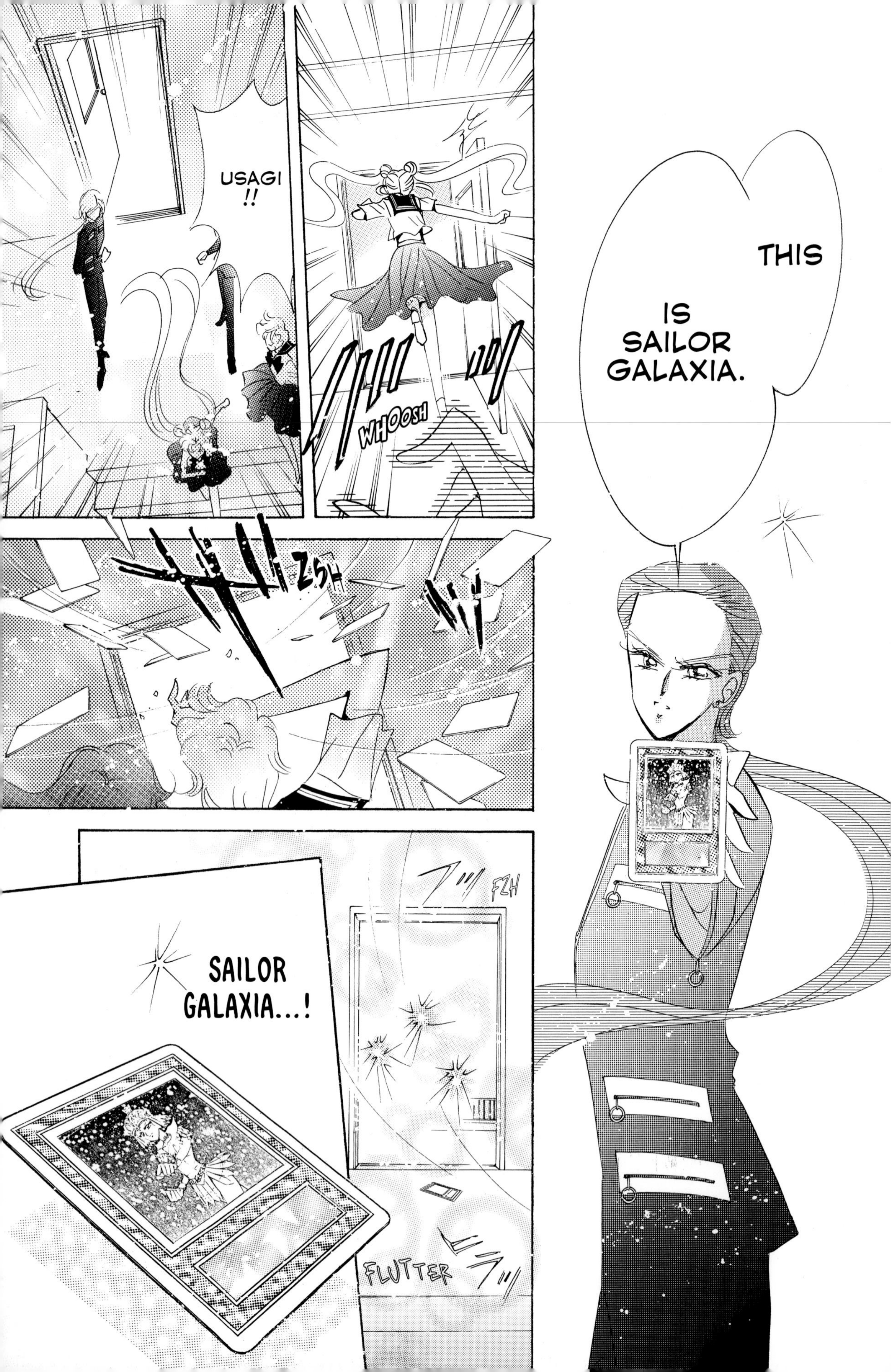
THIS IS SAILOR GALAXIA.
WHOOSH
USAGI !!
ZSH
FZH
SAILOR GALAXIA...!
FLUTTER

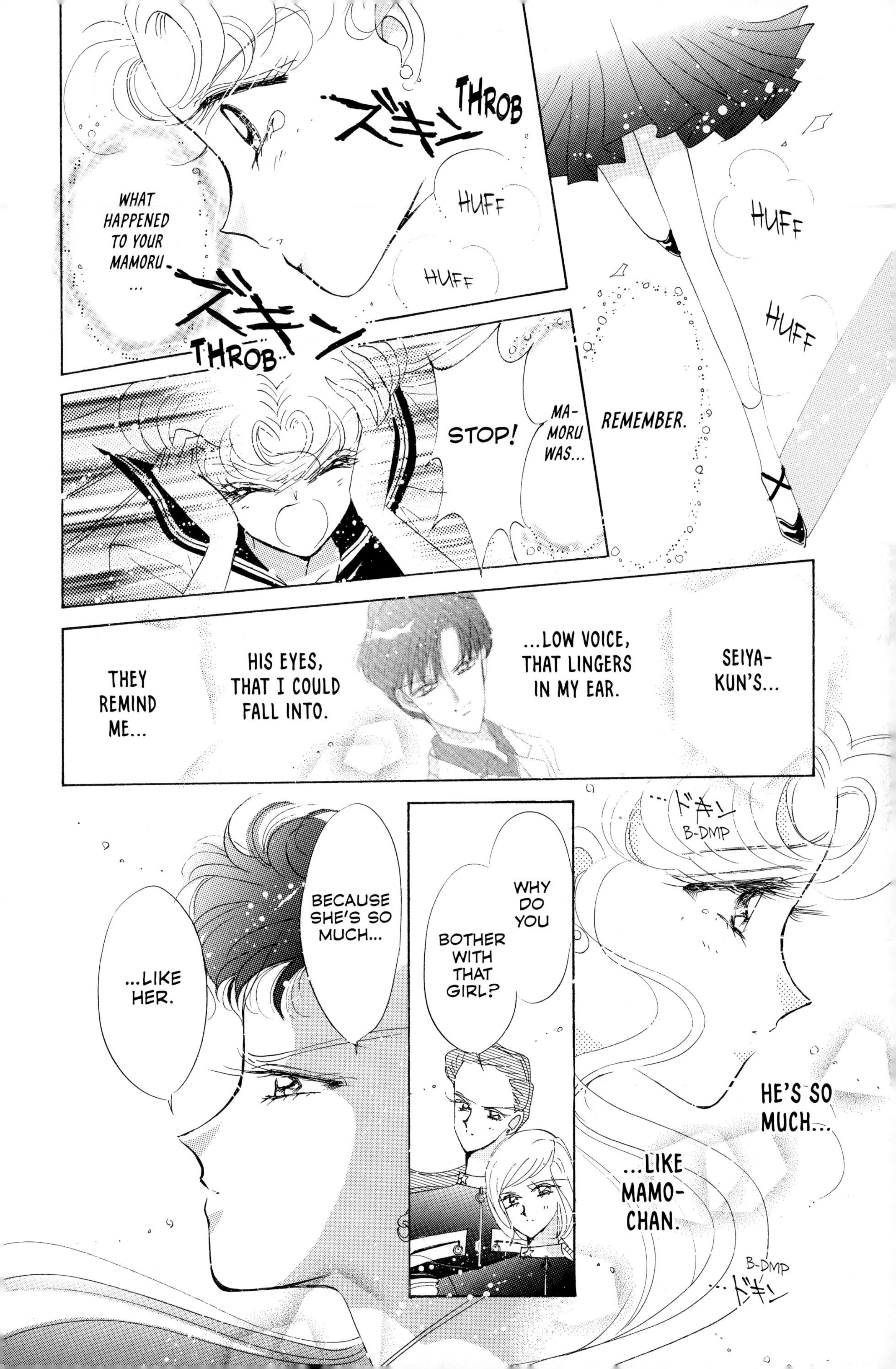
HUFF
HUFF
ズキン
THROB
WHAT HAPPENED TO YOUR MAMORU...
HUFF
HUFF
ズキン
THROB
REMEMBER.
MA-MORU WAS...
STOP!
SEIYA-KUN'S...
...LOW VOICE, THAT LINGERS IN MY EAR.
HIS EYES, THAT I COULD FALL INTO.
THEY REMIND ME...
...ドキン
B-DMP
HE'S SO MUCH...
...LIKE MAMO-CHAN.
B-DMP
...ドキン
WHY DO YOU BOTHER WITH THAT GIRL?
BECAUSE SHE'S SO MUCH...
...LIKE HER.

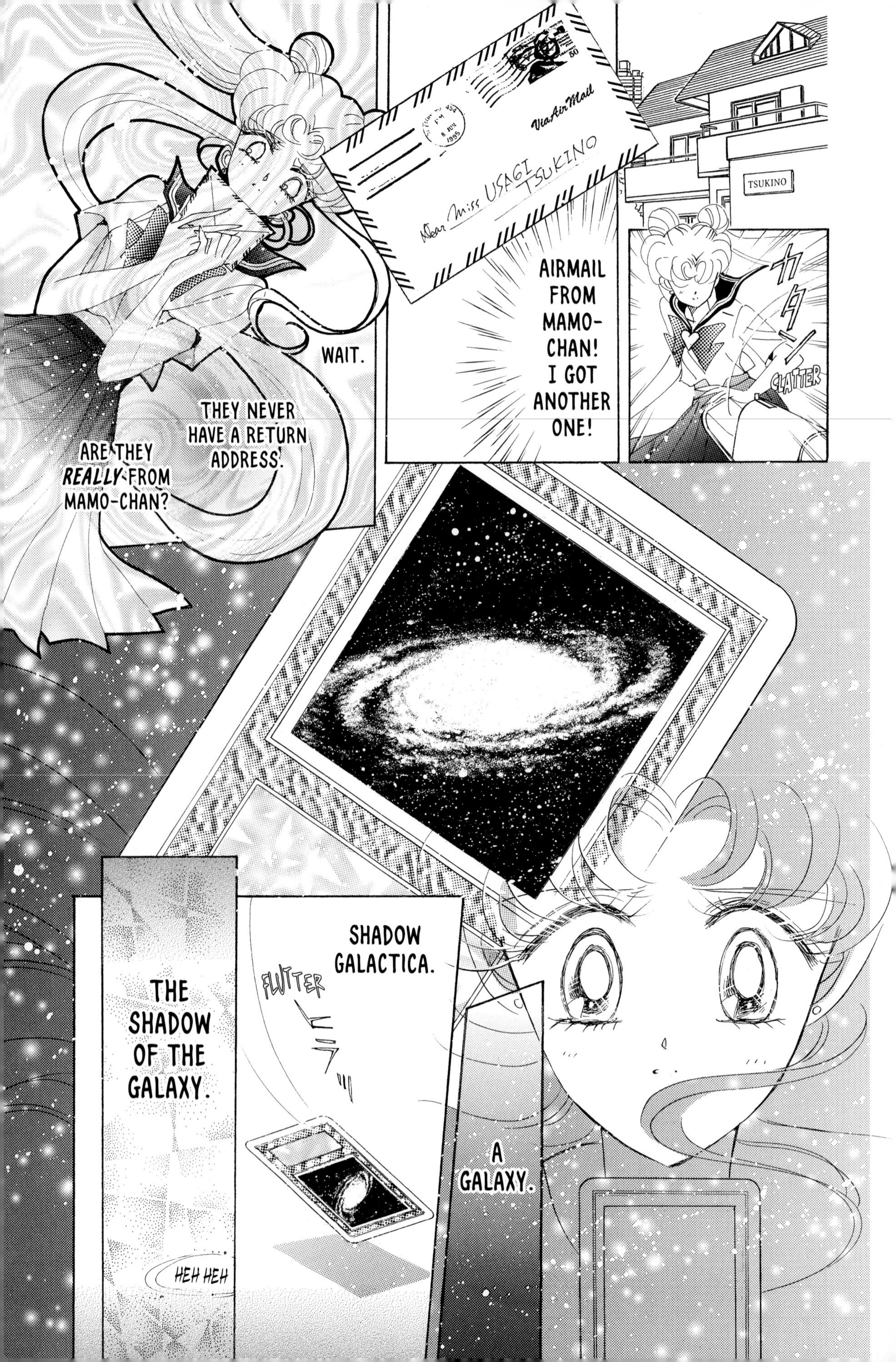

TSUKINO
CLATTER
Via Air Mail
Dear Miss USAGI TSUKINO
AIRMAIL FROM MAMO-CHAN! I GOT ANOTHER ONE!
WAIT.
THEY NEVER HAVE A RETURN ADDRESS.
ARE THEY *REALLY* FROM MAMO-CHAN?
A GALAXY.
SHADOW GALACTICA.
FLUTTER
THE SHADOW OF THE GALAXY.
HEH HEH

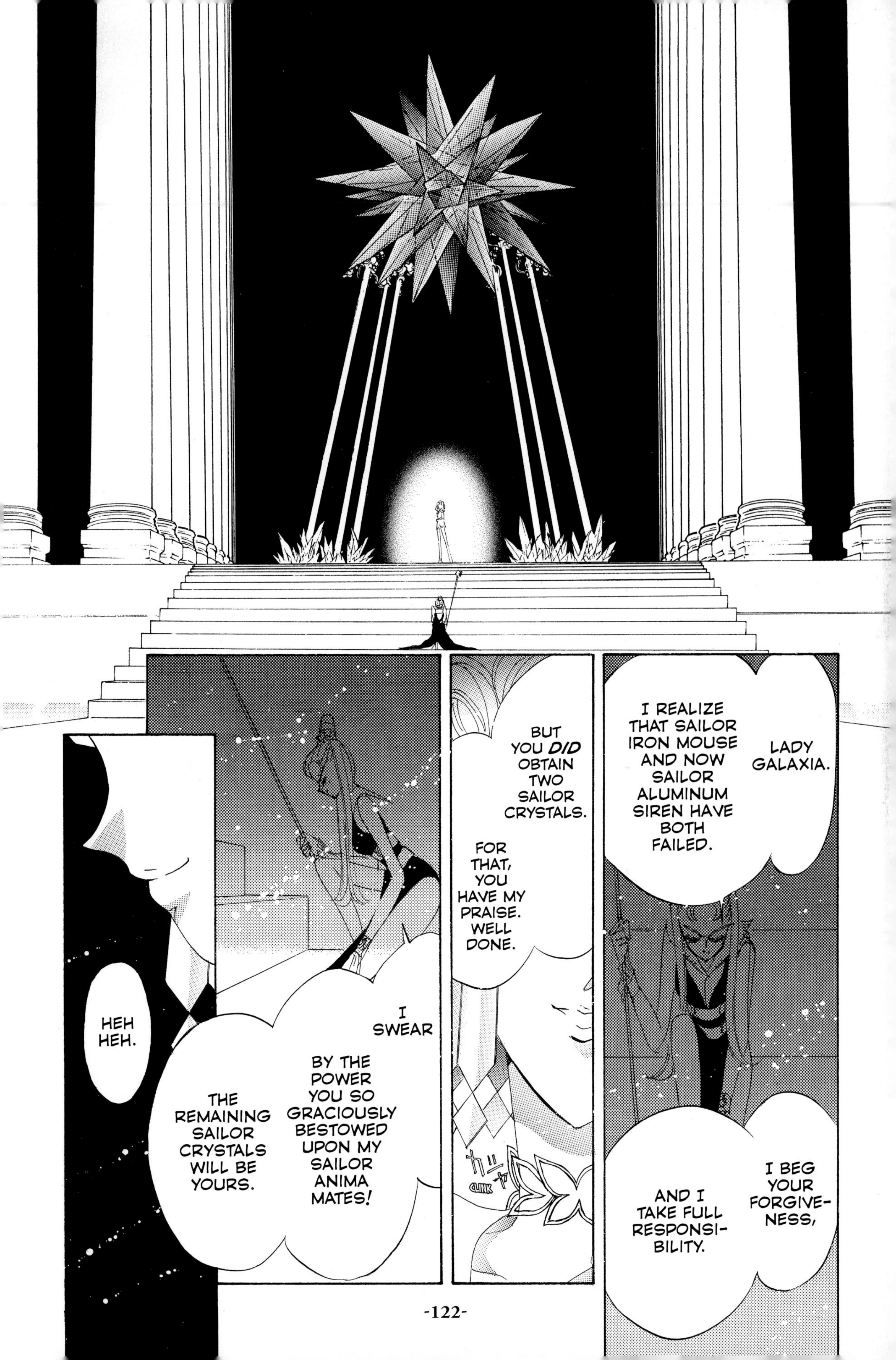
LADY GALAXIA.
I REALIZE THAT SAILOR IRON MOUSE AND NOW SAILOR ALUMINUM SIREN HAVE BOTH FAILED.
I BEG YOUR FORGIVENESS,
AND I TAKE FULL RESPONSIBILITY.
BUT YOU *DID* OBTAIN TWO SAILOR CRYSTALS.
FOR THAT, YOU HAVE MY PRAISE. WELL DONE.
カシャ
CLINK
I SWEAR
BY THE POWER YOU SO GRACIOUSLY BESTOWED UPON MY SAILOR ANIMA MATES!
THE REMAINING SAILOR CRYSTALS WILL BE YOURS.
HEH HEH.

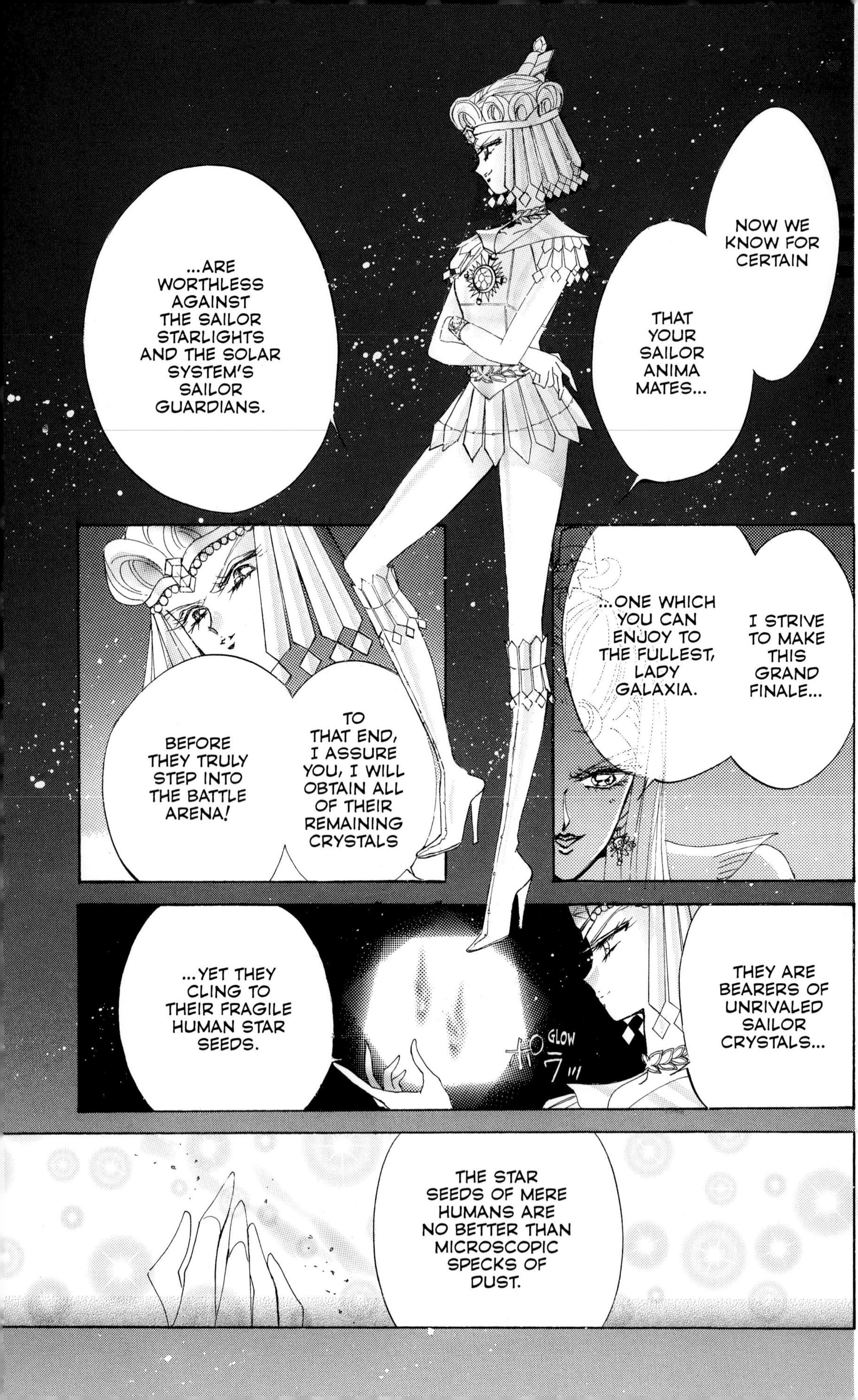
NOW WE KNOW FOR CERTAIN
THAT YOUR SAILOR ANIMA MATES...
...ARE WORTHLESS AGAINST THE SAILOR STARLIGHTS AND THE SOLAR SYSTEM'S SAILOR GUARDIANS.
I STRIVE TO MAKE THIS GRAND FINALE...
...ONE WHICH YOU CAN ENJOY TO THE FULLEST, LADY GALAXIA.
TO THAT END, I ASSURE YOU, I WILL OBTAIN ALL OF THEIR REMAINING CRYSTALS
BEFORE THEY TRULY STEP INTO THE BATTLE ARENA!
THEY ARE BEARERS OF UNRIVALED SAILOR CRYSTALS...
GLOW
...YET THEY CLING TO THEIR FRAGILE HUMAN STAR SEEDS.
THE STAR SEEDS OF MERE HUMANS ARE NO BETTER THAN MICROSCOPIC SPECKS OF DUST.

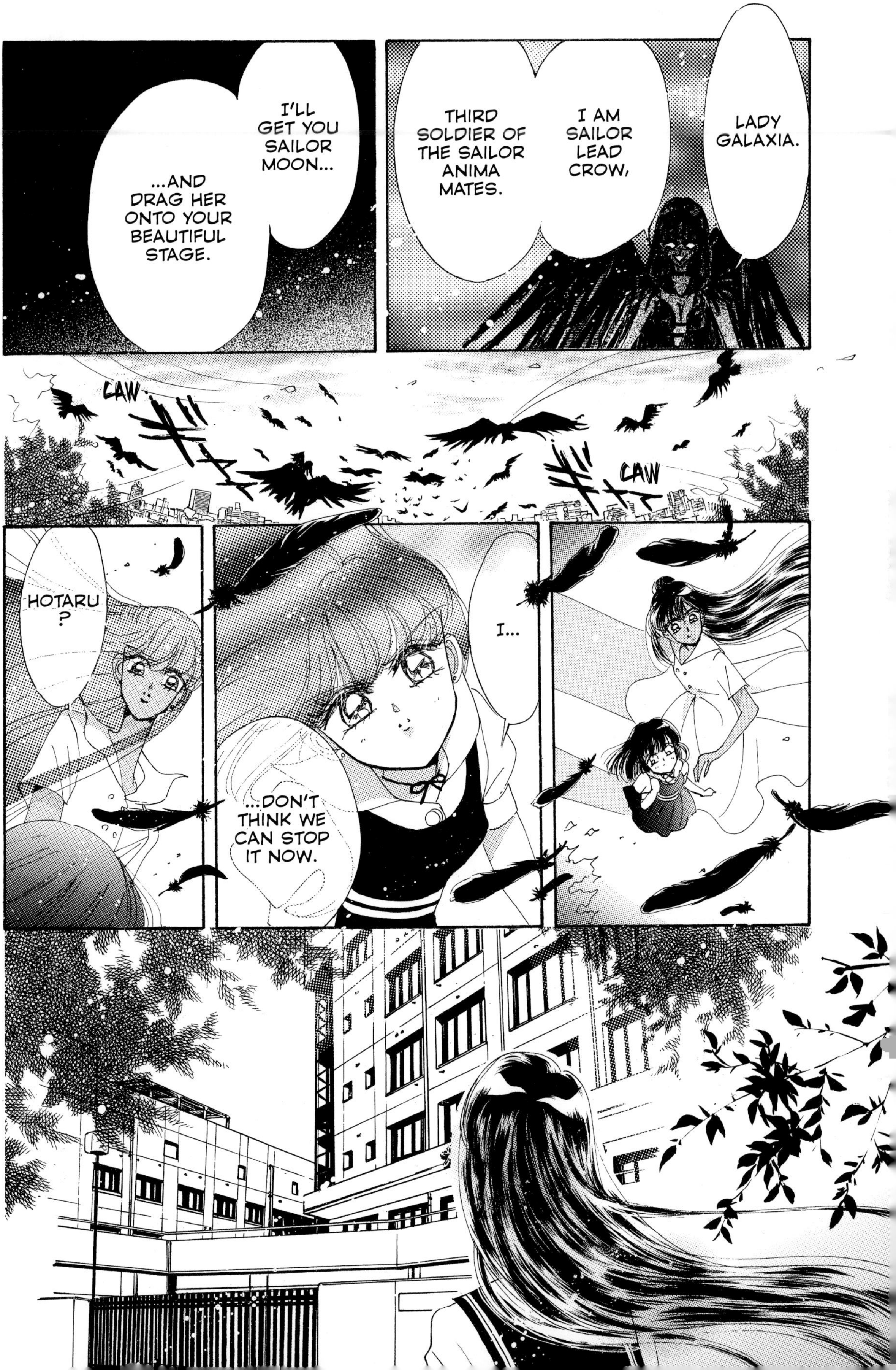
LADY GALAXIA.
I AM SAILOR LEAD CROW,
THIRD SOLDIER OF THE SAILOR ANIMA MATES.
I'LL GET YOU SAILOR MOON...
...AND DRAG HER ONTO YOUR BEAUTIFUL STAGE.
CAW
CAW
I...
...DON'T THINK WE CAN STOP IT NOW.
HOTARU?

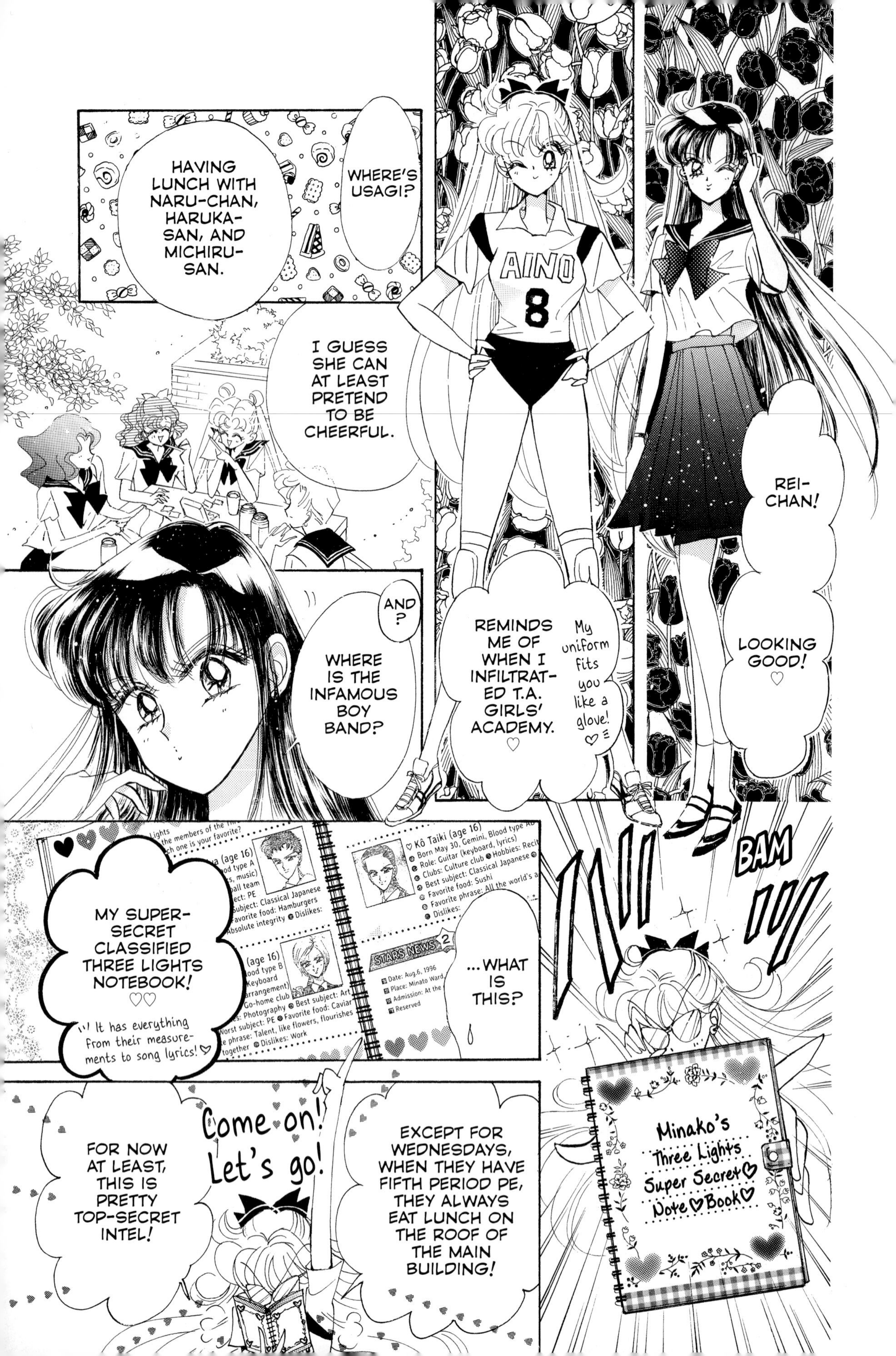

REI-CHAN!
LOOKING GOOD! ♡
REMINDS ME OF WHEN I INFILTRATED T.A. GIRLS' ACADEMY. ♡
My uniform fits you like a glove! ♡
WHERE'S USAGI?
HAVING LUNCH WITH NARU-CHAN, HARUKA-SAN, AND MICHIRU-SAN.
I GUESS SHE CAN AT LEAST PRETEND TO BE CHEERFUL.
AND?
WHERE IS THE INFAMOUS BOY BAND?
BAM
Minako's Three Lights Super Secret♡ Note♡Book♡
...WHAT IS THIS?
MY SUPER-SECRET CLASSIFIED THREE LIGHTS NOTEBOOK! ♡♡
It has everything from their measurements to song lyrics! ♡
EXCEPT FOR WEDNESDAYS, WHEN THEY HAVE FIFTH PERIOD PE, THEY ALWAYS EAT LUNCH ON THE ROOF OF THE MAIN BUILDING!
Come on! Let's go!
FOR NOW AT LEAST, THIS IS PRETTY TOP-SECRET INTEL!

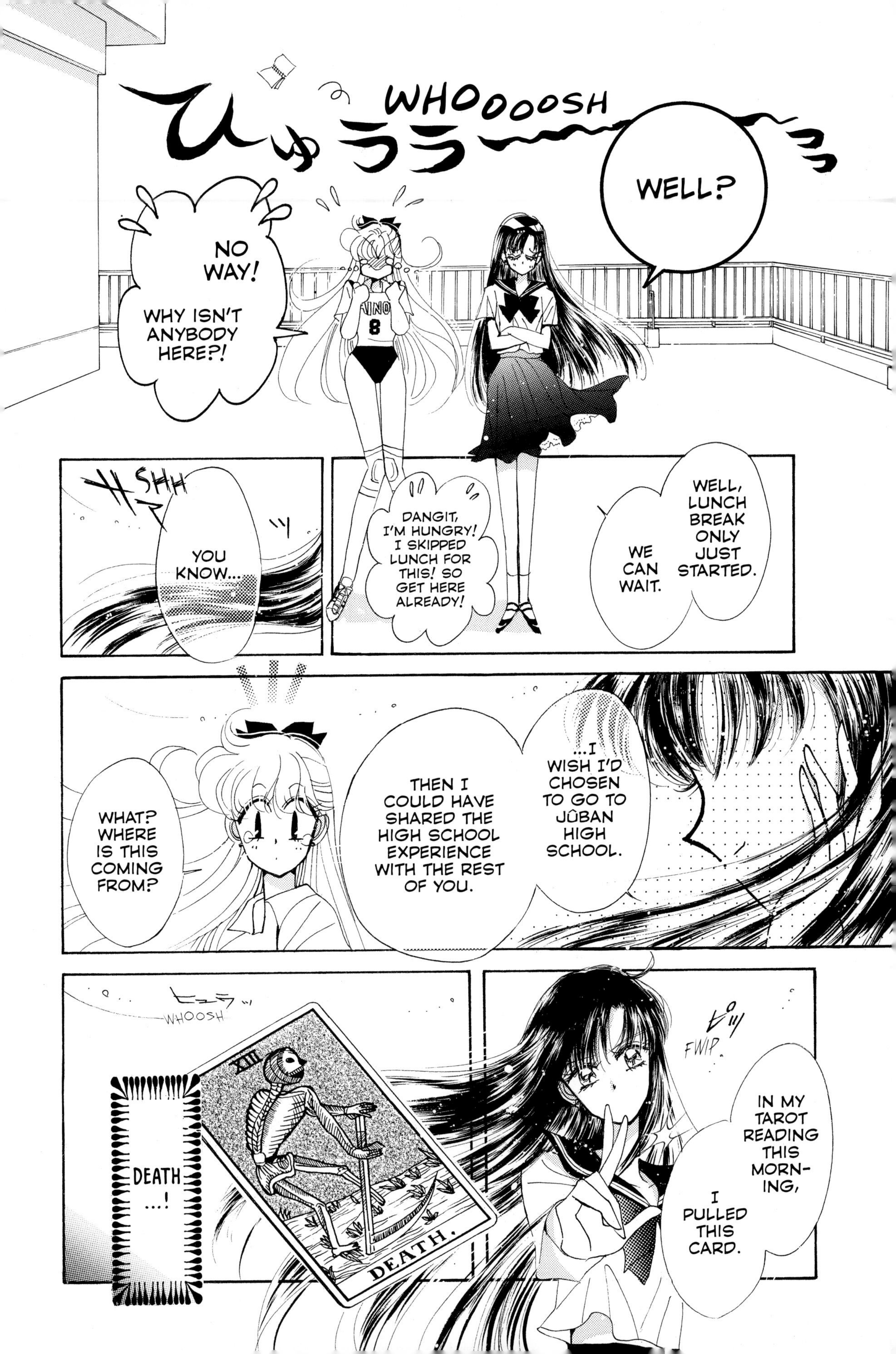
ひゅララ
WHOOOOOSH
WELL?
NO WAY!
WHY ISN'T ANYBODY HERE?!
WELL, LUNCH BREAK ONLY JUST STARTED.
WE CAN WAIT.
DANGIT, I'M HUNGRY! I SKIPPED LUNCH FOR THIS! SO GET HERE ALREADY!
SHH
YOU KNOW...
...I WISH I'D CHOSEN TO GO TO JÛBAN HIGH SCHOOL.
THEN I COULD HAVE SHARED THE HIGH SCHOOL EXPERIENCE WITH THE REST OF YOU.
WHAT? WHERE IS THIS COMING FROM?
FWIP
IN MY TAROT READING THIS MORNING,
I PULLED THIS CARD.
WHOOSH
XIII
DEATH.
DEATH ...!

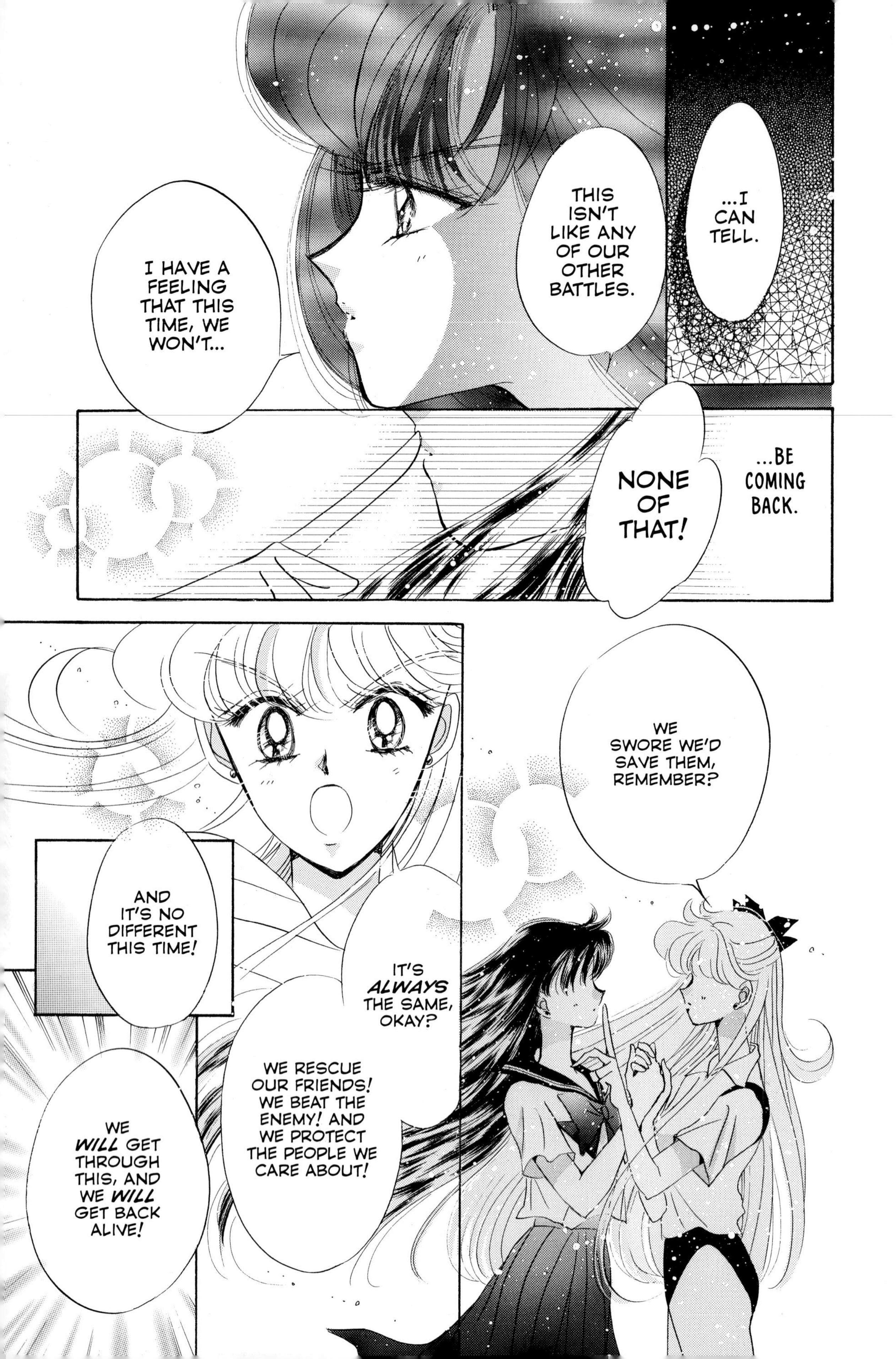
...I CAN TELL.
THIS ISN'T LIKE ANY OF OUR OTHER BATTLES.
I HAVE A FEELING THAT THIS TIME, WE WON'T...
...BE COMING BACK.
NONE OF THAT!
WE SWORE WE'D SAVE THEM, REMEMBER?
AND IT'S NO DIFFERENT THIS TIME!
IT'S *ALWAYS* THE SAME, OKAY?
WE RESCUE OUR FRIENDS! WE BEAT THE ENEMY! AND WE PROTECT THE PEOPLE WE CARE ABOUT!
WE *WILL* GET THROUGH THIS, AND WE *WILL* GET BACK ALIVE!

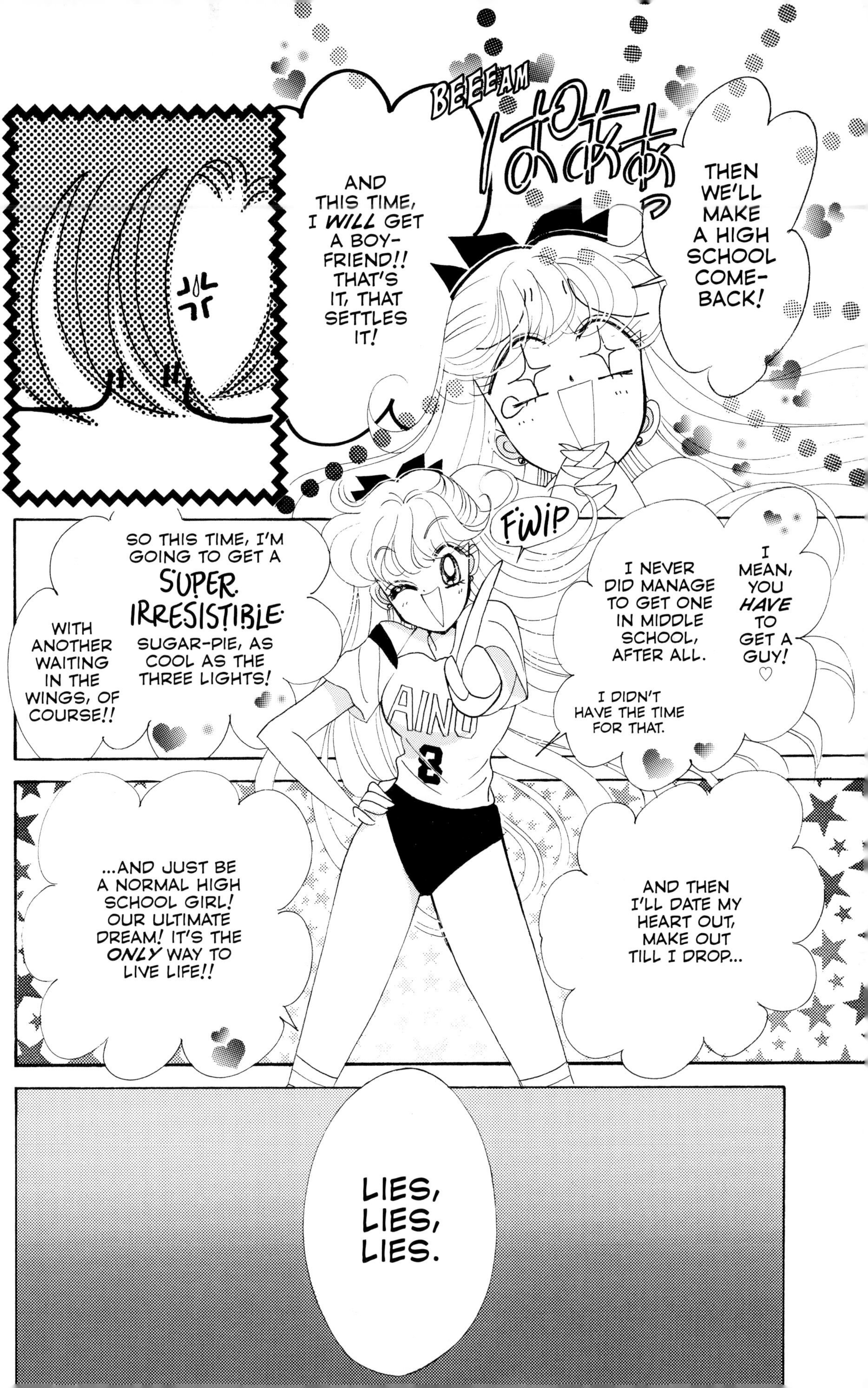
BEEEAM
THEN WE'LL MAKE A HIGH SCHOOL COME-BACK!
AND THIS TIME, I WILL GET A BOY-FRIEND!! THAT'S IT, THAT SETTLES IT!
I MEAN, YOU HAVE TO GET A GUY! ♡
I NEVER DID MANAGE TO GET ONE IN MIDDLE SCHOOL, AFTER ALL.
I DIDN'T HAVE THE TIME FOR THAT.
FWIP
SO THIS TIME, I'M GOING TO GET A SUPER IRRESISTIBLE SUGAR-PIE, AS COOL AS THE THREE LIGHTS!
WITH ANOTHER WAITING IN THE WINGS, OF COURSE!!
AND THEN I'LL DATE MY HEART OUT, MAKE OUT TILL I DROP...
...AND JUST BE A NORMAL HIGH SCHOOL GIRL! OUR ULTIMATE DREAM! IT'S THE ONLY WAY TO LIVE LIFE!!
LIES, LIES, LIES.

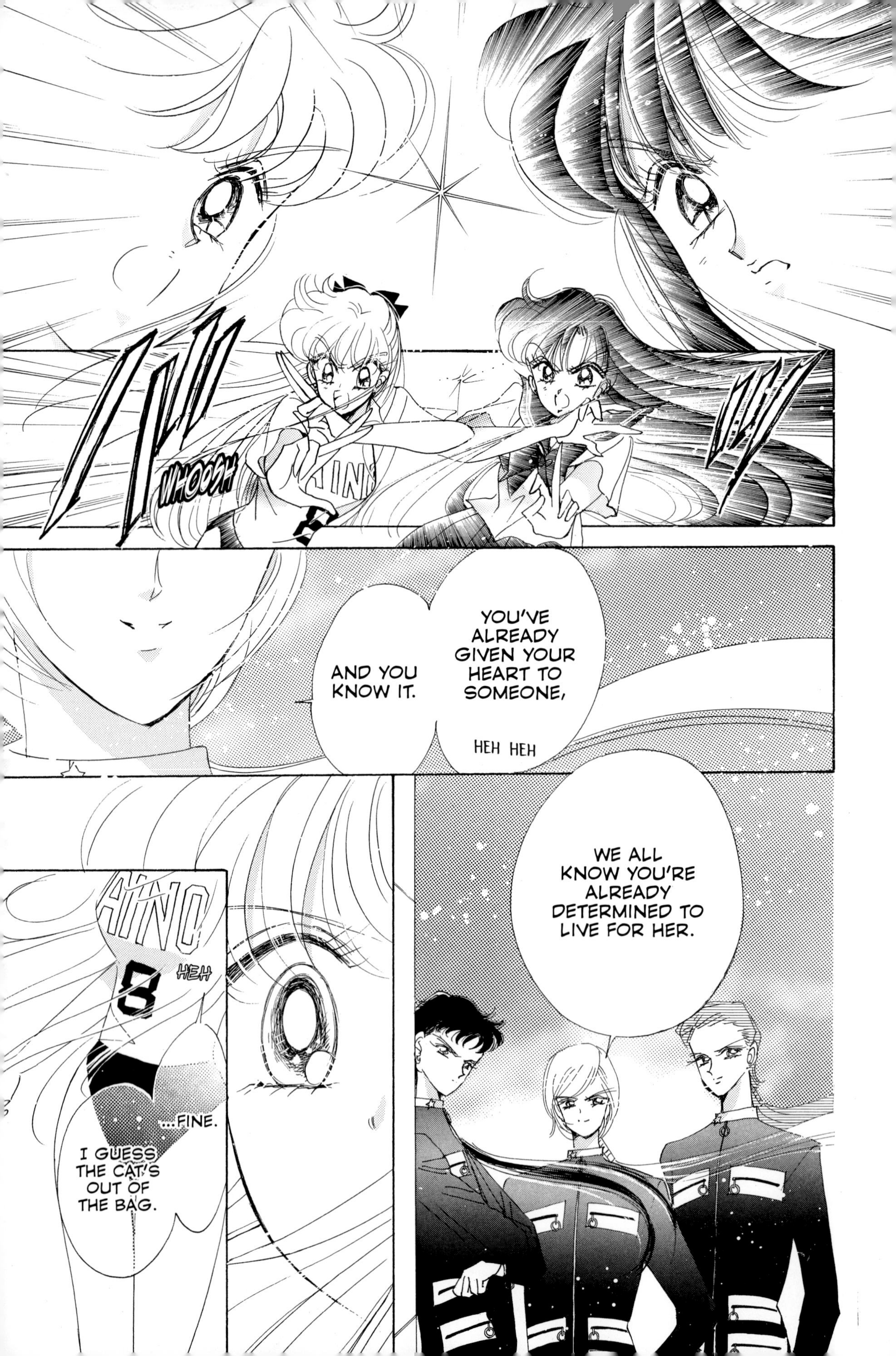
WHOOSH
YOU'VE ALREADY GIVEN YOUR HEART TO SOMEONE,
HEH HEH
AND YOU KNOW IT.
WE ALL KNOW YOU'RE ALREADY DETERMINED TO LIVE FOR HER.
AINO
8
HEH
...FINE.
I GUESS THE CAT'S OUT OF THE BAG.

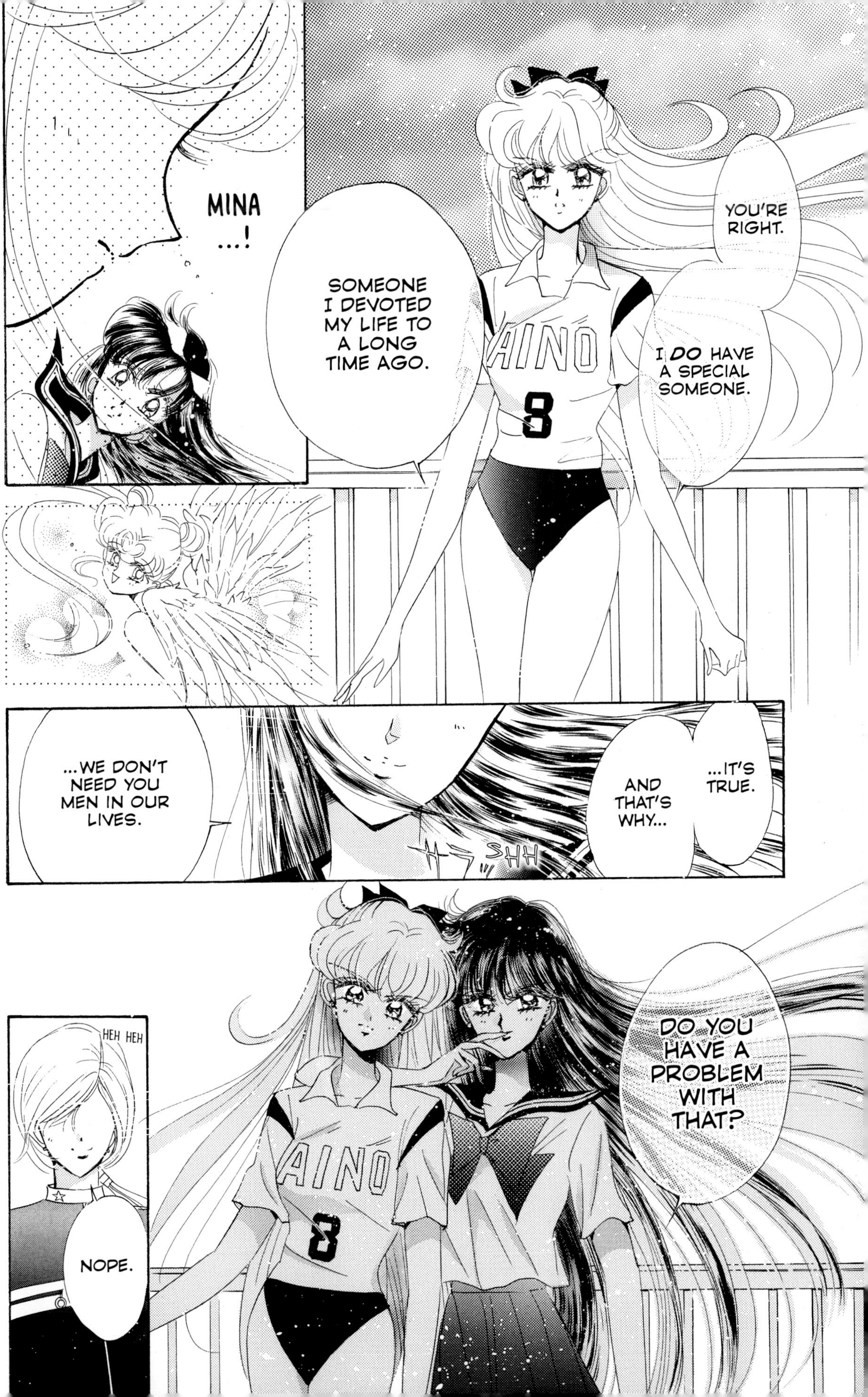
YOU'RE RIGHT.
I DO HAVE A SPECIAL SOMEONE.
SOMEONE I DEVOTED MY LIFE TO A LONG TIME AGO.
MINA ...!
...IT'S TRUE.
AND THAT'S WHY...
SHH
...WE DON'T NEED YOU MEN IN OUR LIVES.
DO YOU HAVE A PROBLEM WITH THAT?
HEH HEH
NOPE.

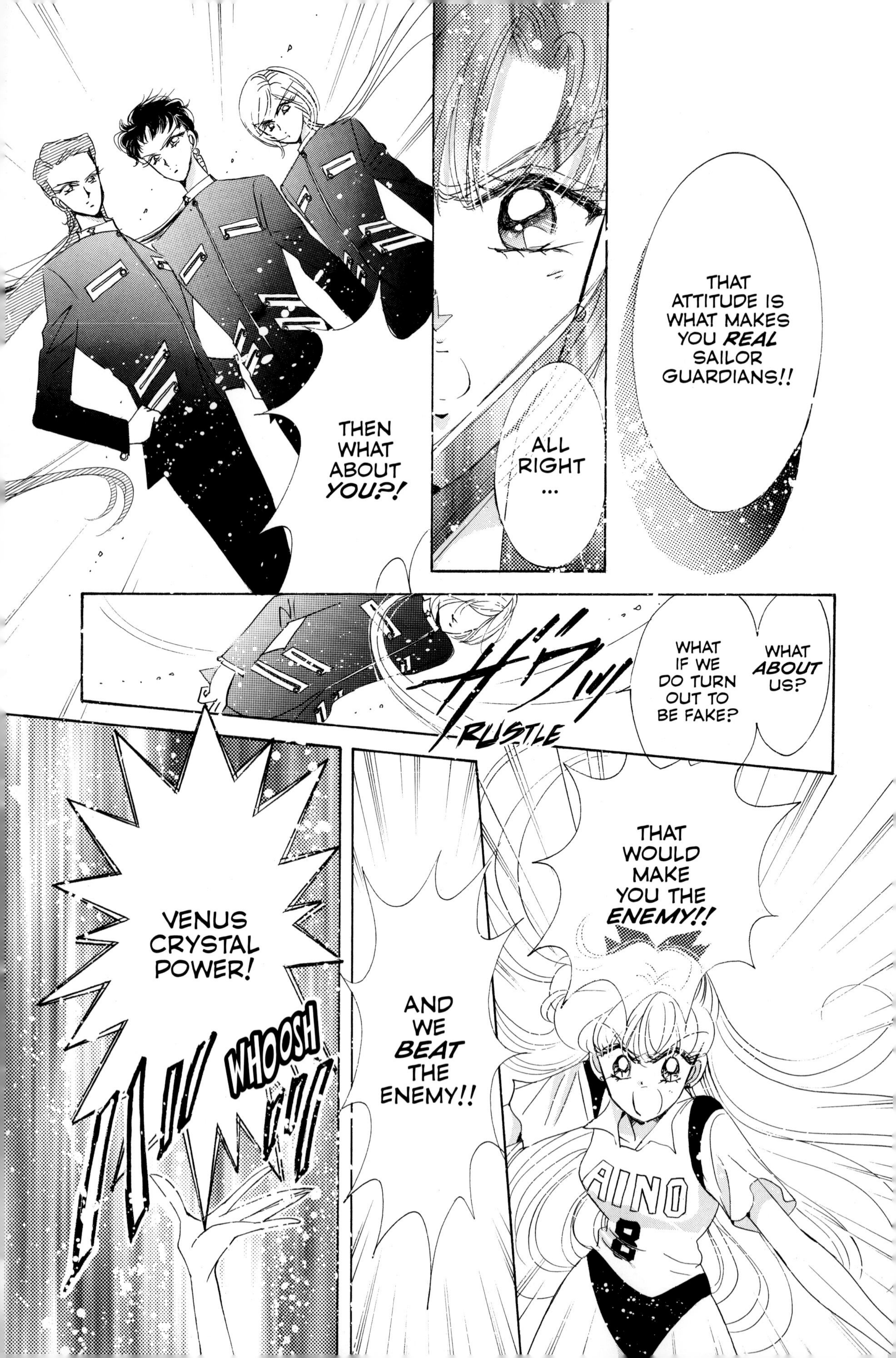
THAT ATTITUDE IS WHAT MAKES YOU *REAL* SAILOR GUARDIANS!!
ALL RIGHT ...
THEN WHAT ABOUT *YOU?!*
WHAT *ABOUT* US?
WHAT IF WE DO TURN OUT TO BE FAKE?
RUSTLE
THAT WOULD MAKE YOU THE *ENEMY!!*
AINO
8
AND WE *BEAT* THE ENEMY!!
VENUS CRYSTAL POWER!
WHOOSH

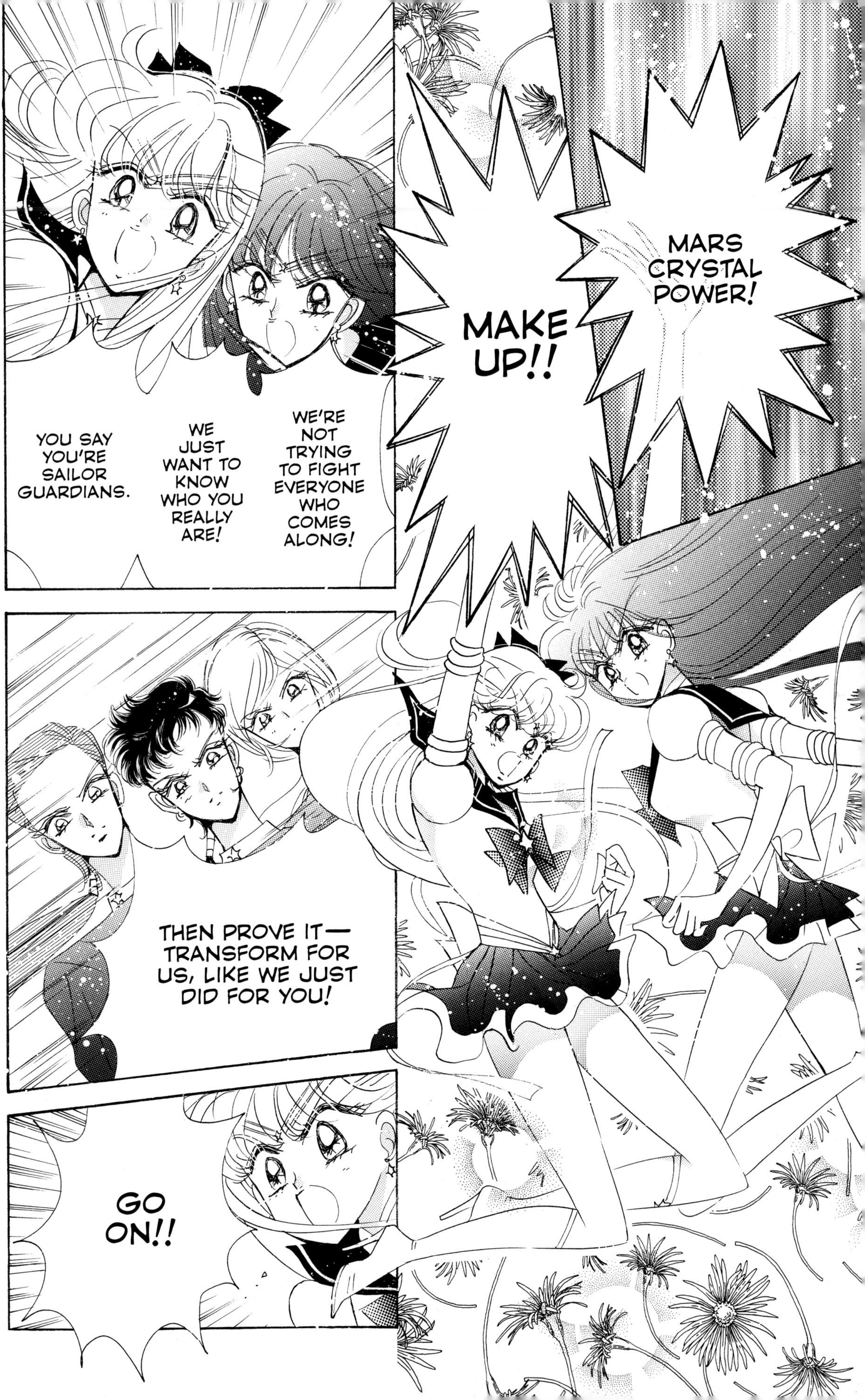
MARS CRYSTAL POWER!
MAKE UP!!
WE'RE NOT TRYING TO FIGHT EVERYONE WHO COMES ALONG!
WE JUST WANT TO KNOW WHO YOU REALLY ARE!
YOU SAY YOU'RE SAILOR GUARDIANS.
THEN PROVE IT—TRANSFORM FOR US, LIKE WE JUST DID FOR YOU!
GO ON!!

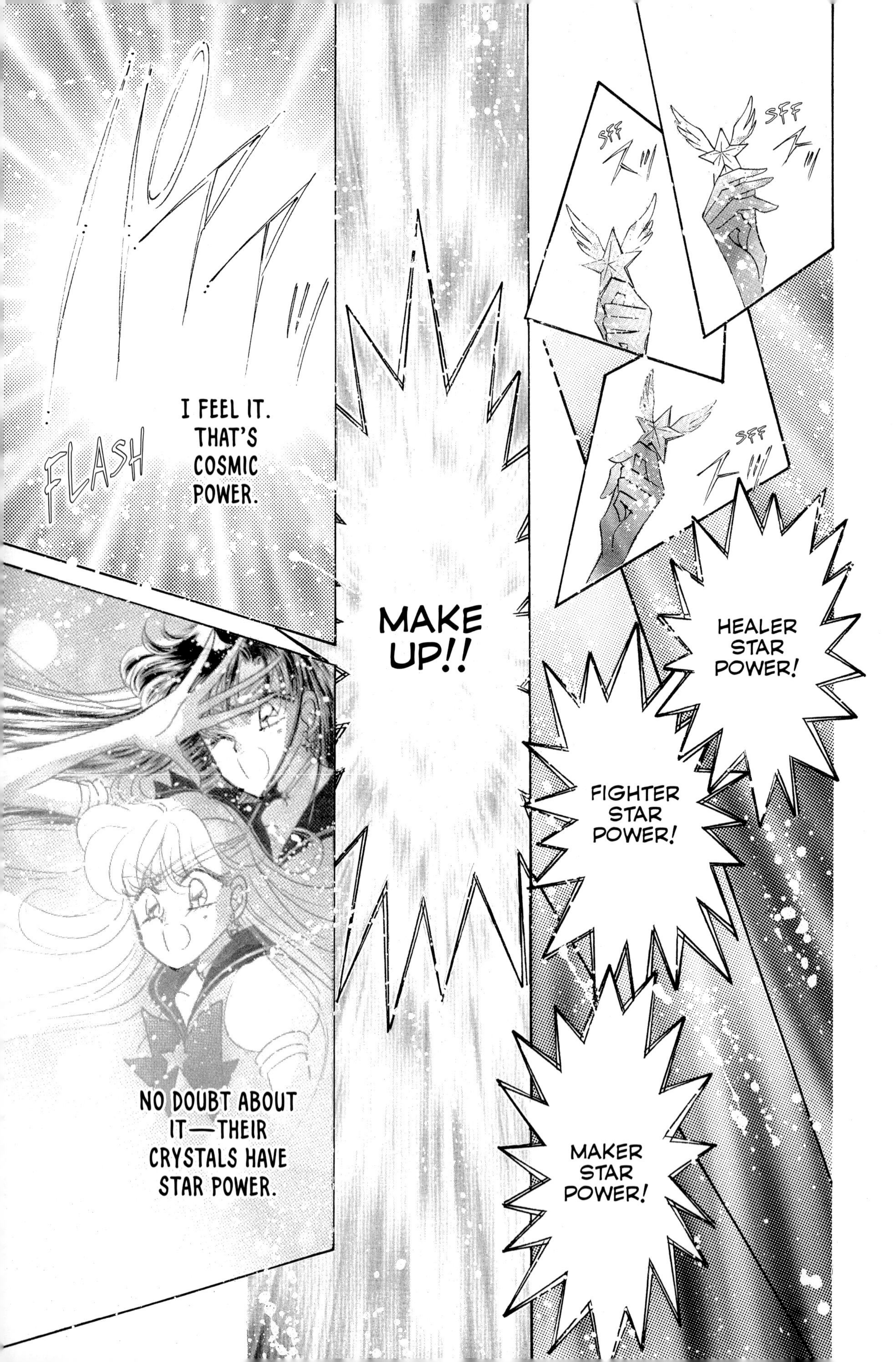
SFF
SFF
SFF
HEALER STAR POWER!
FIGHTER STAR POWER!
MAKER STAR POWER!
MAKE UP!!
I FEEL IT. THAT'S COSMIC POWER.
FLASH
NO DOUBT ABOUT IT—THEIR CRYSTALS HAVE STAR POWER.

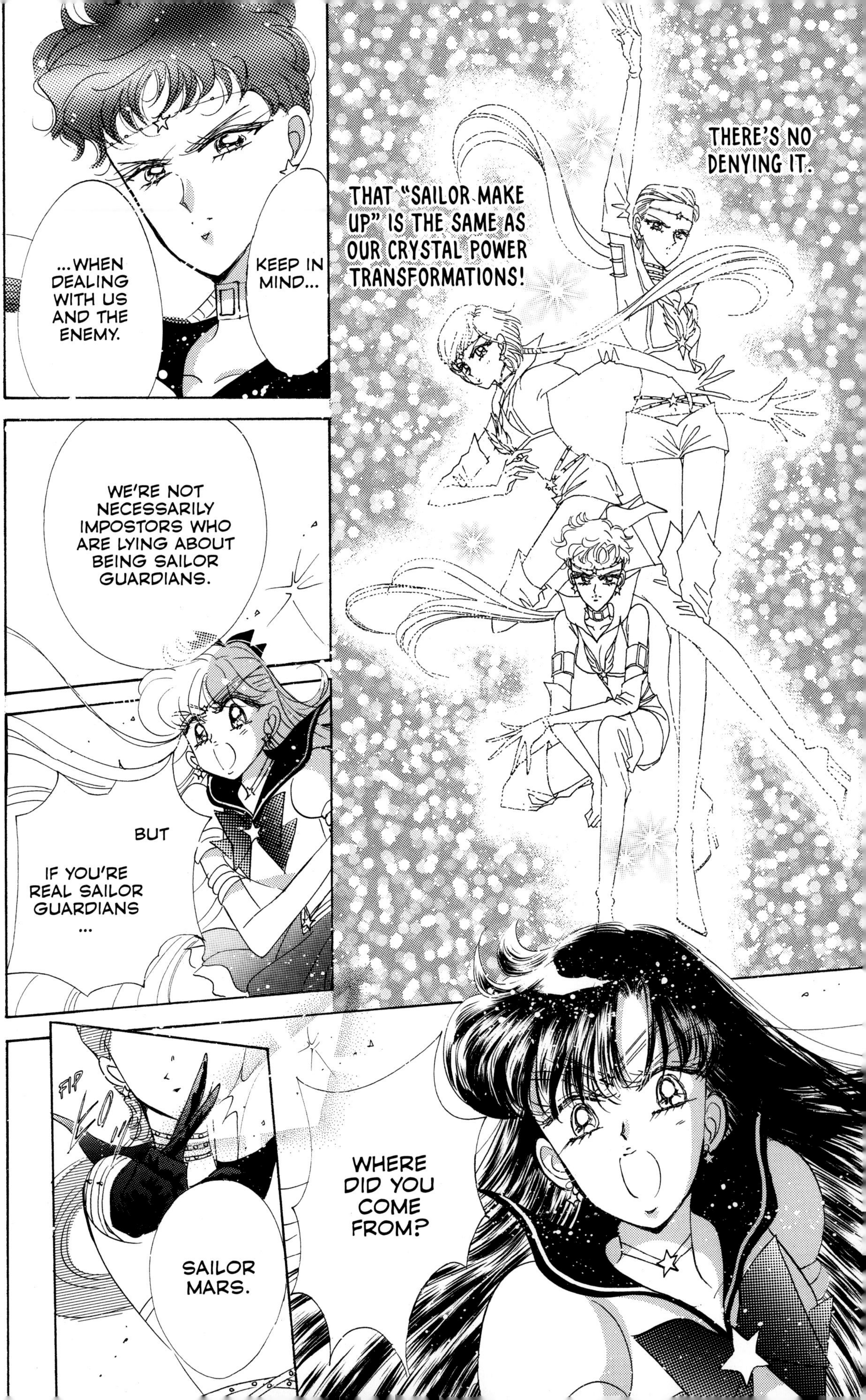
THERE'S NO DENYING IT.
THAT "SAILOR MAKE UP" IS THE SAME AS OUR CRYSTAL POWER TRANSFORMATIONS!
KEEP IN MIND...
...WHEN DEALING WITH US AND THE ENEMY.
WE'RE NOT NECESSARILY IMPOSTORS WHO ARE LYING ABOUT BEING SAILOR GUARDIANS.
BUT
IF YOU'RE REAL SAILOR GUARDIANS ...
WHERE DID YOU COME FROM?
FLIP
SAILOR MARS.

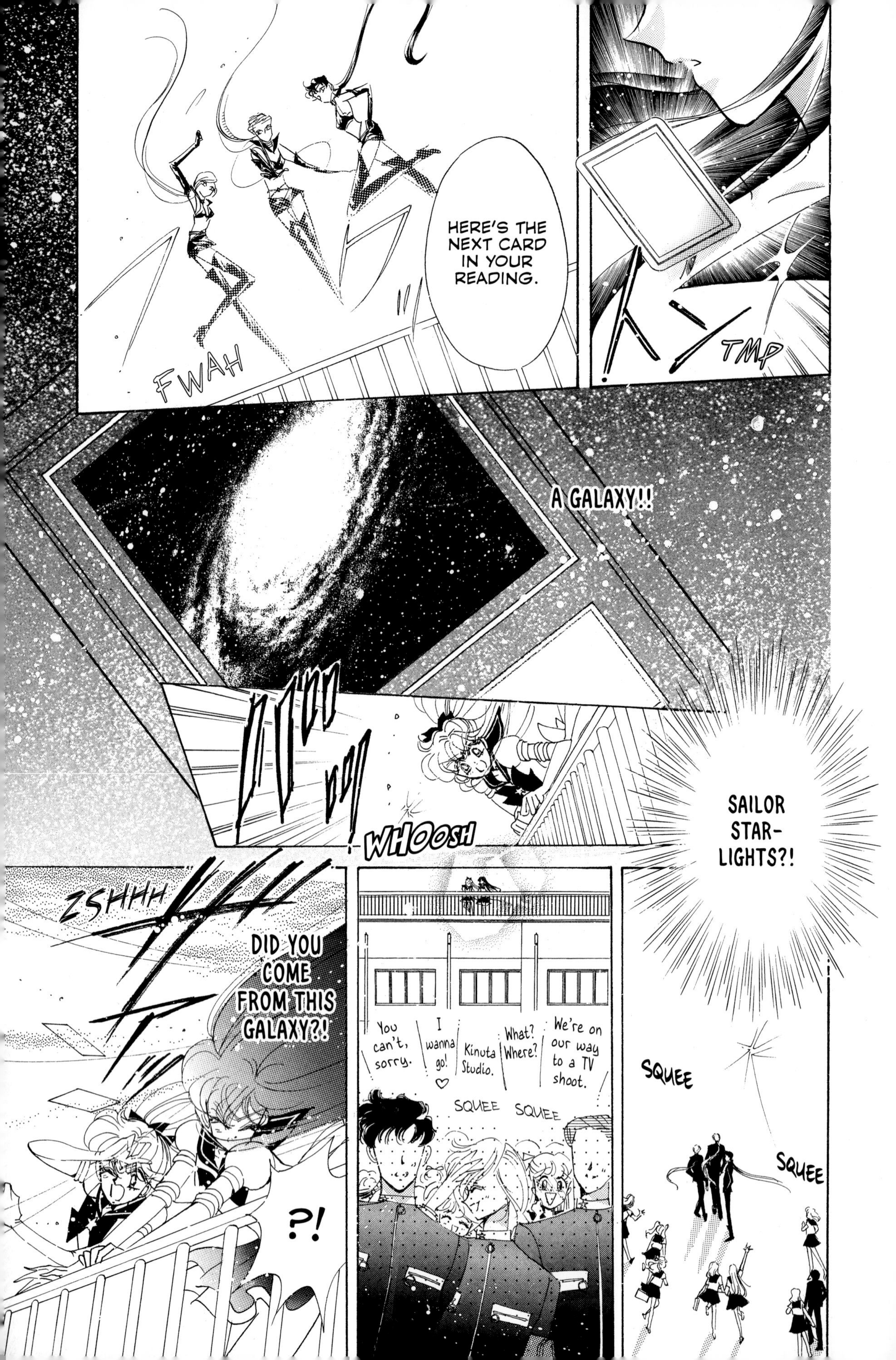
TMP
HERE'S THE NEXT CARD IN YOUR READING.
FWAH
A GALAXY!!
SAILOR STAR-LIGHTS?!
WHOOSH
SQUEE
SQUEE
We're on our way to a TV shoot.
What? Where?
Kinuta Studio.
I wanna go! ♡
You can't, sorry.
SQUEE SQUEE
ZSHHH
DID YOU COME FROM THIS GALAXY?!
?!

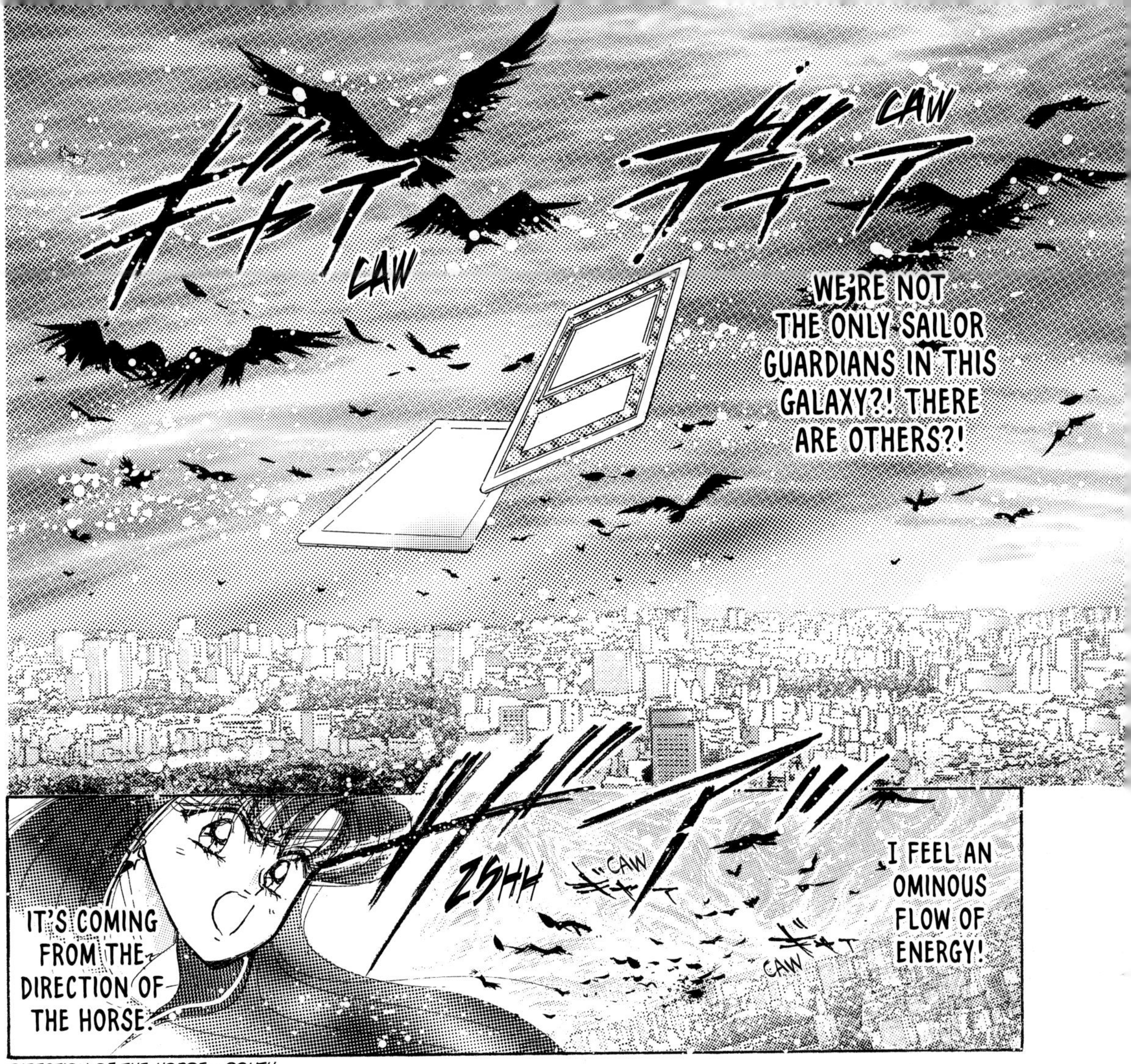
CAW
CAW
WE'RE NOT THE ONLY SAILOR GUARDIANS IN THIS GALAXY?! THERE ARE OTHERS?!
I FEEL AN OMINOUS FLOW OF ENERGY!
CAW
CAW
ZSHH
IT'S COMING FROM THE DIRECTION OF THE HORSE.

DIRECTION OF THE HORSE = SOUTH

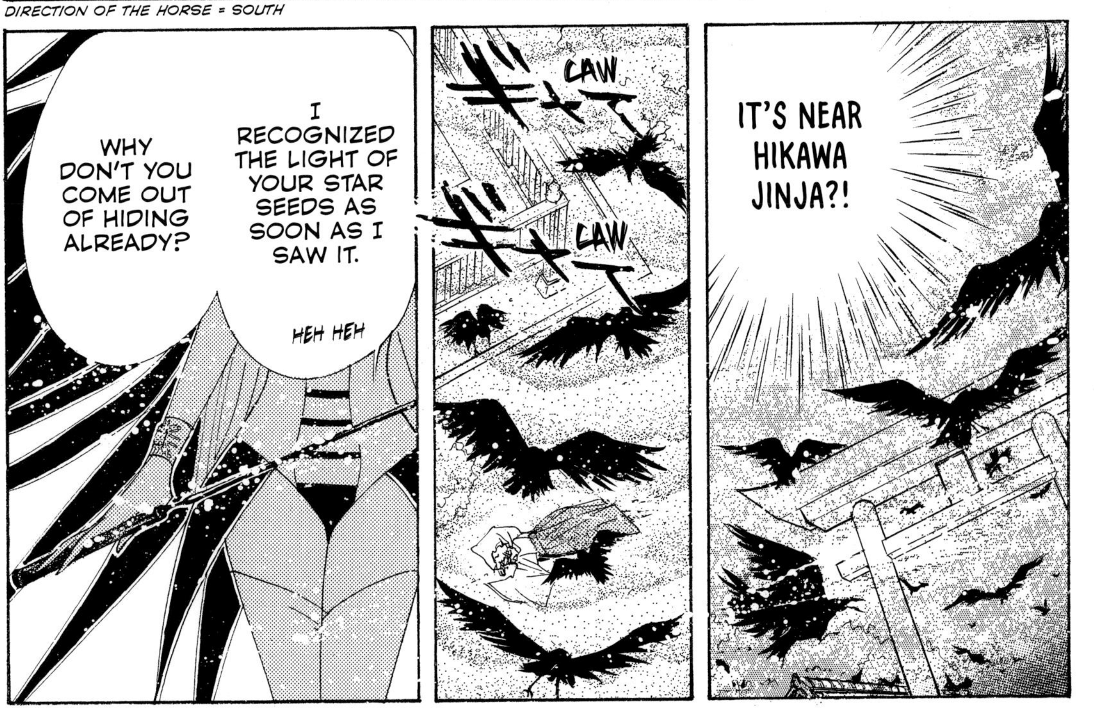
IT'S NEAR HIKAWA JINJA?!
CAW
CAW
I RECOGNIZED THE LIGHT OF YOUR STAR SEEDS AS SOON AS I SAW IT.
WHY DON'T YOU COME OUT OF HIDING ALREADY?
HEH HEH

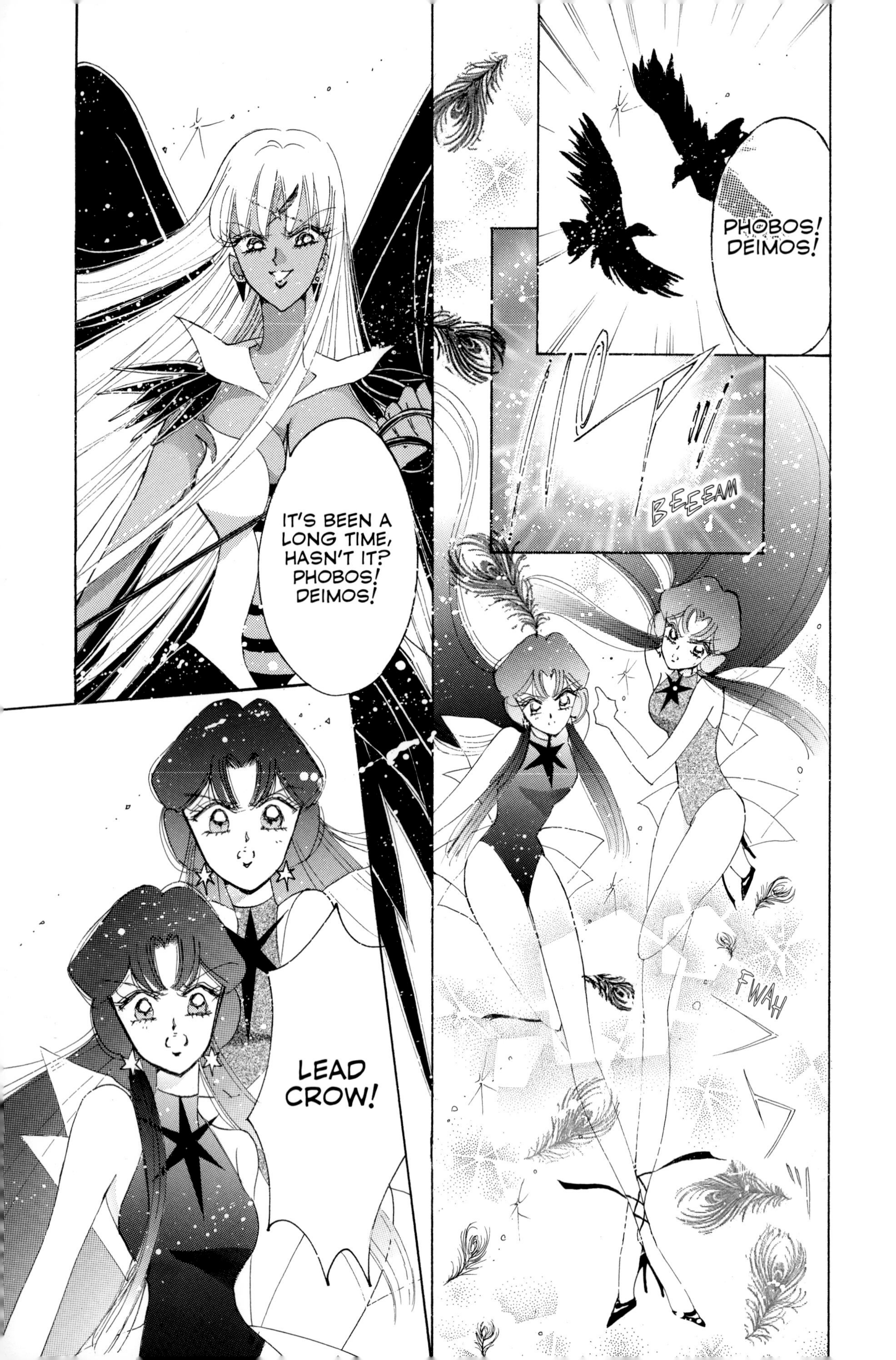
PHOBOS! DEIMOS!
BEEEAM
FWAH
IT'S BEEN A LONG TIME, HASN'T IT? PHOBOS! DEIMOS!
LEAD CROW!

Pretty Guardian

Sailor Moon

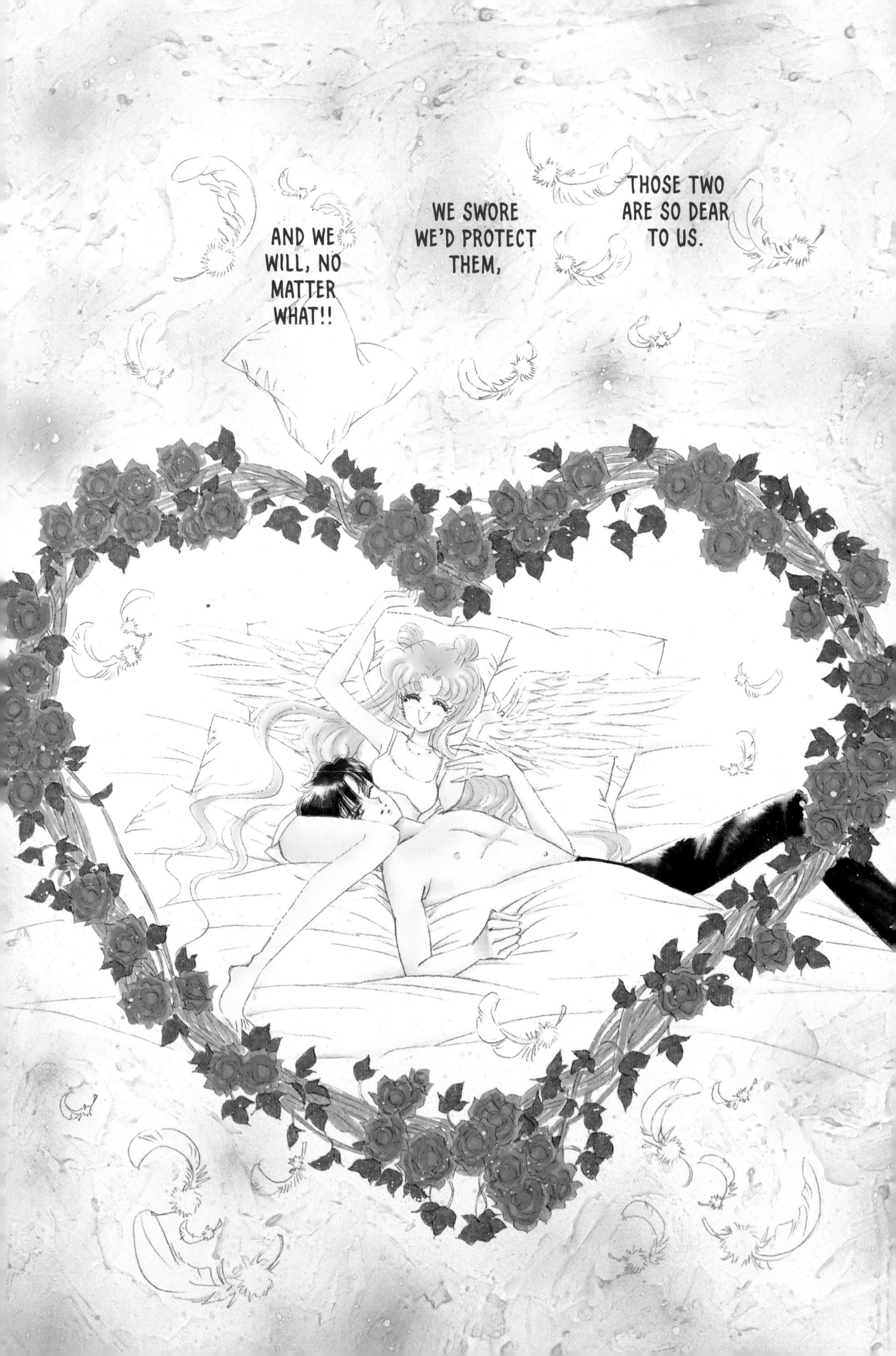
THOSE TWO ARE SO DEAR TO US.
WE SWORE WE'D PROTECT THEM,
AND WE WILL, NO MATTER WHAT!!

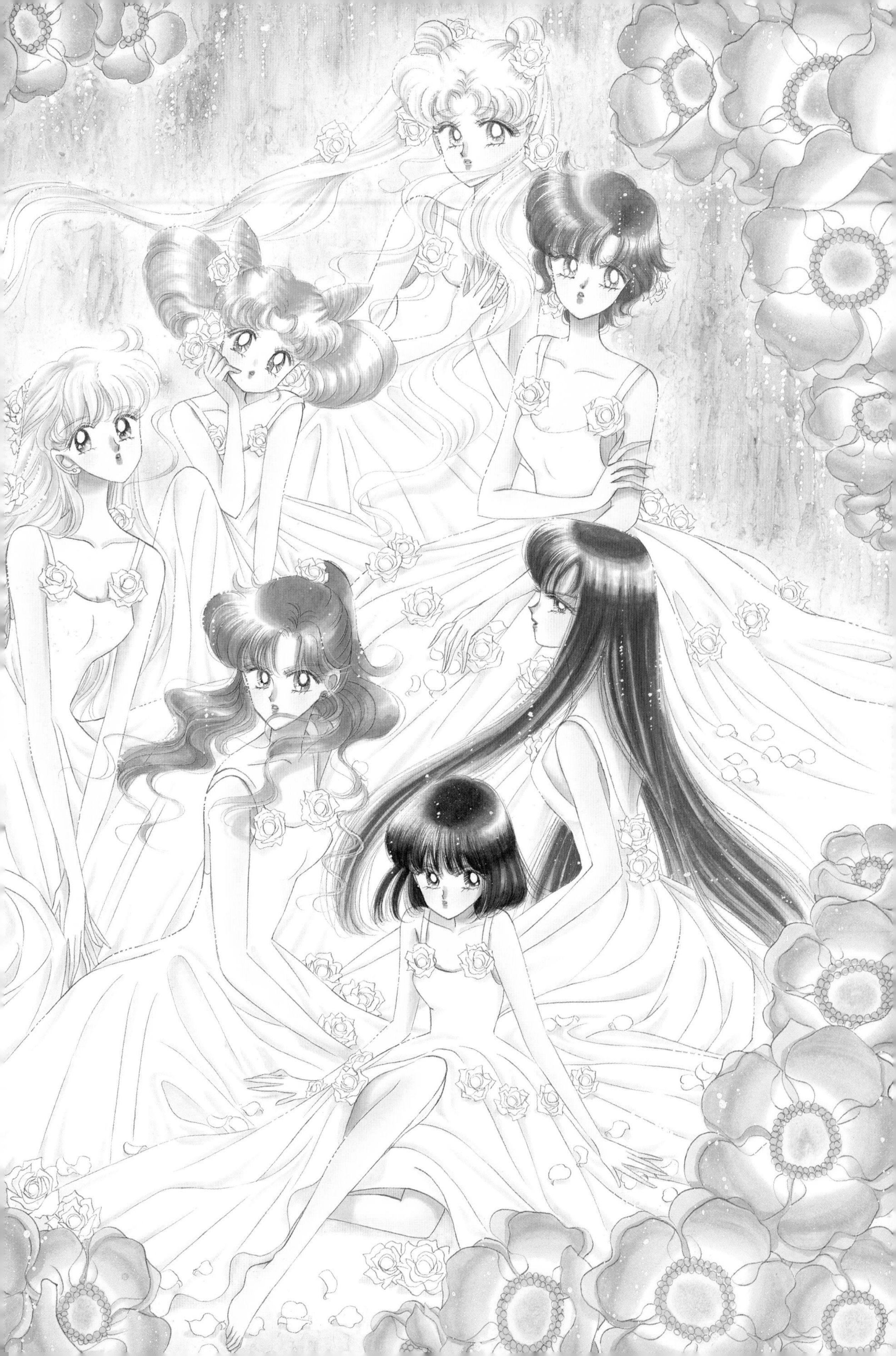

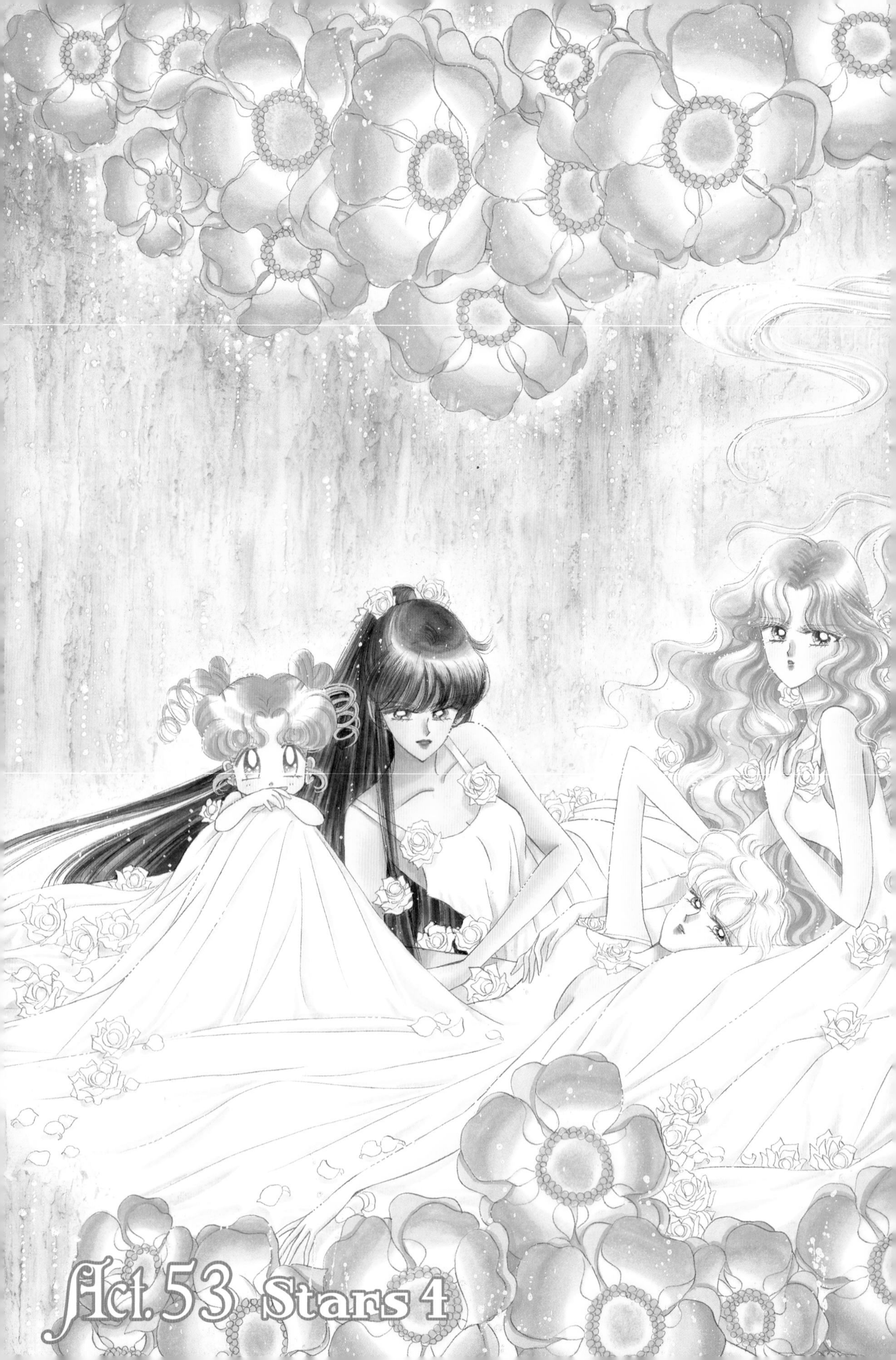
Act.53 Stars 4

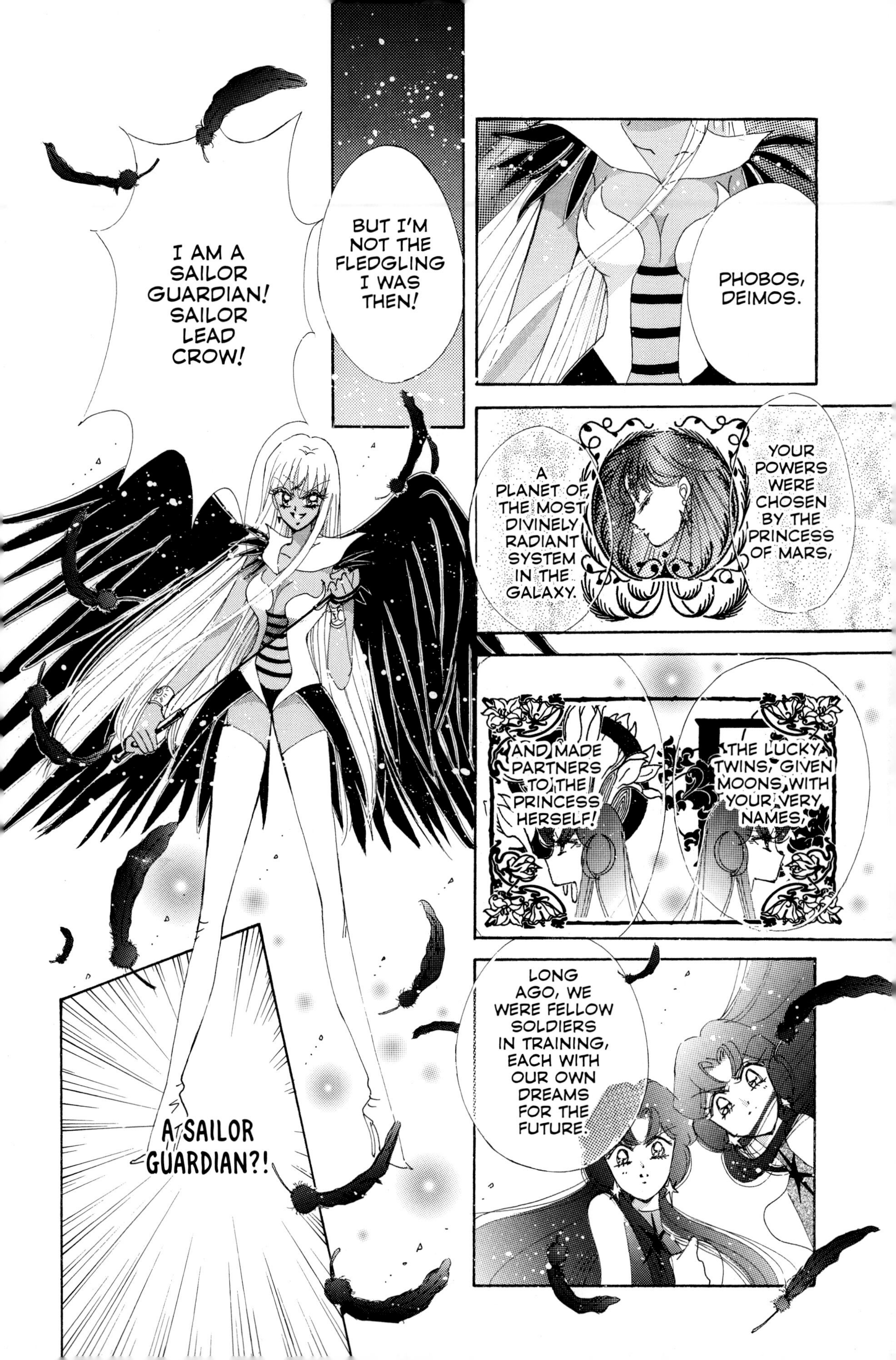
PHOBOS, DEIMOS.
YOUR POWERS WERE CHOSEN BY THE PRINCESS OF MARS,
A PLANET OF THE MOST DIVINELY RADIANT SYSTEM IN THE GALAXY.
THE LUCKY TWINS, GIVEN MOONS WITH YOUR VERY NAMES,
AND MADE PARTNERS TO THE PRINCESS HERSELF!
LONG AGO, WE WERE FELLOW SOLDIERS IN TRAINING, EACH WITH OUR OWN DREAMS FOR THE FUTURE.
BUT I'M NOT THE FLEDGLING I WAS THEN!
I AM A SAILOR GUARDIAN! SAILOR LEAD CROW!
A SAILOR GUARDIAN?!

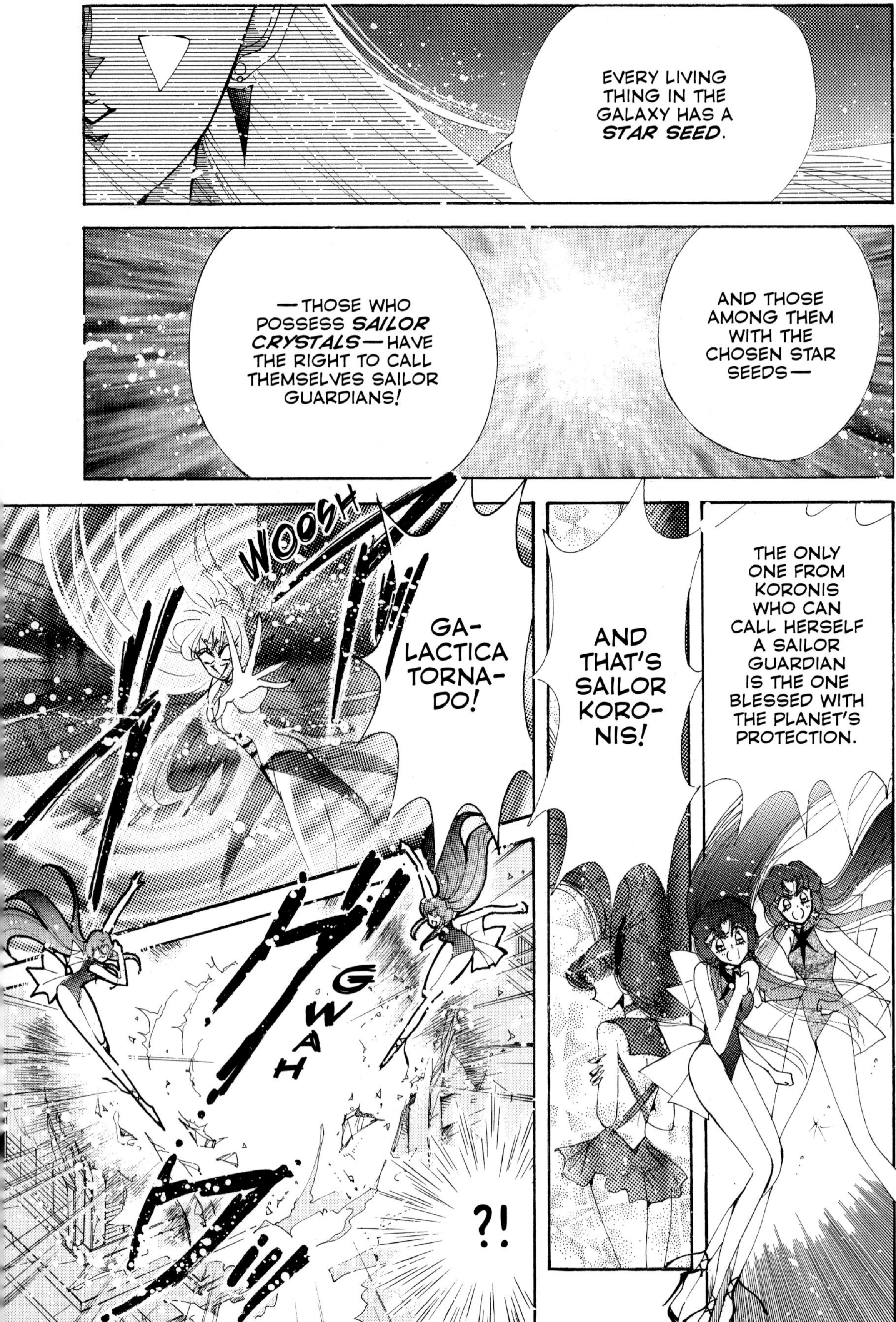
EVERY LIVING THING IN THE GALAXY HAS A ***STAR SEED***.
AND THOSE AMONG THEM WITH THE CHOSEN STAR SEEDS—
—THOSE WHO POSSESS ***SAILOR CRYSTALS***—HAVE THE RIGHT TO CALL THEMSELVES SAILOR GUARDIANS!
THE ONLY ONE FROM KORONIS WHO CAN CALL HERSELF A SAILOR GUARDIAN IS THE ONE BLESSED WITH THE PLANET'S PROTECTION.
AND THAT'S SAILOR KORO-NIS!
GA-LACTICA TORNA-DO!
WOOSH
GWAH
?!

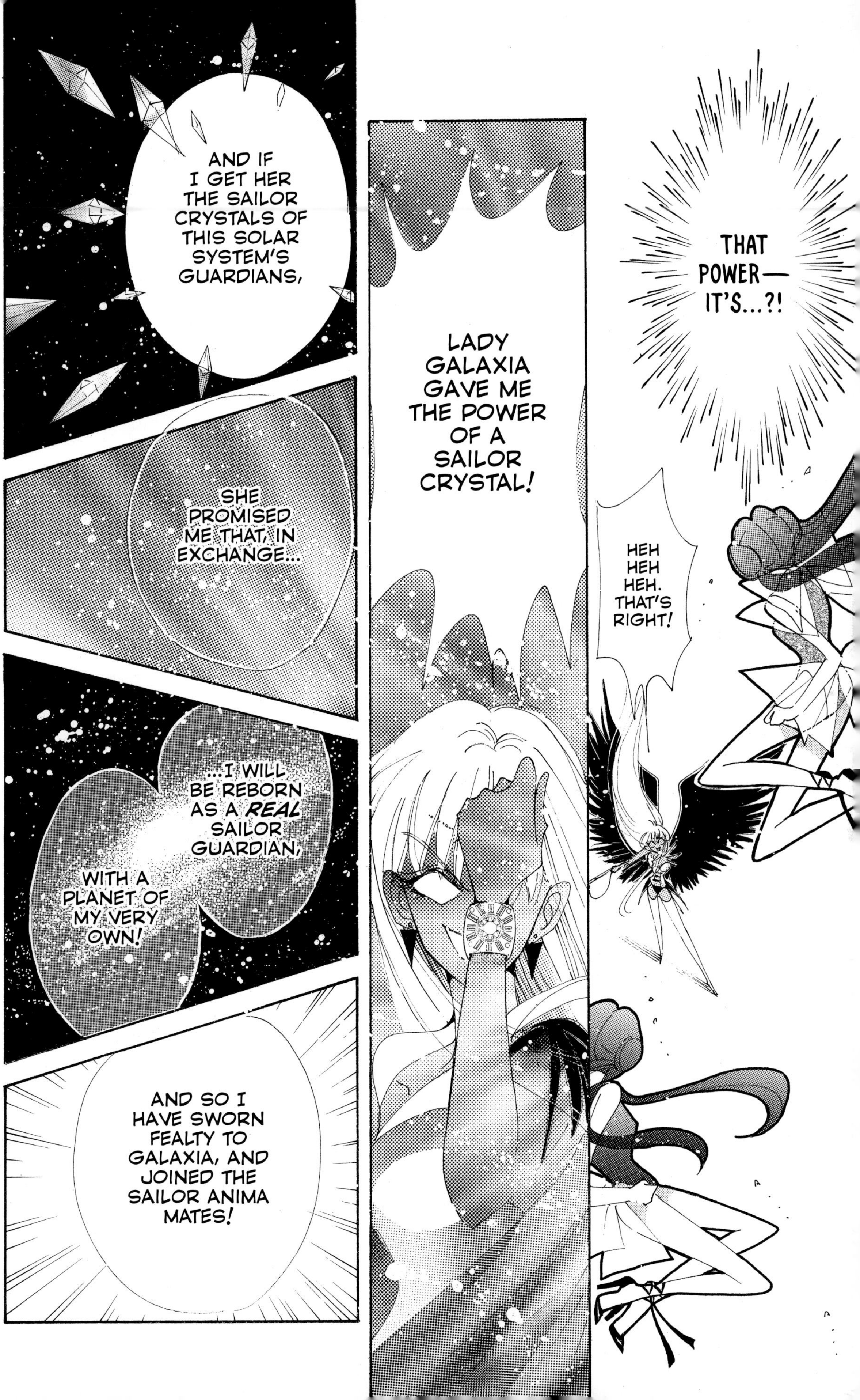
THAT POWER—IT'S...?!
HEH HEH HEH. THAT'S RIGHT!
LADY GALAXIA GAVE ME THE POWER OF A SAILOR CRYSTAL!
AND IF I GET HER THE SAILOR CRYSTALS OF THIS SOLAR SYSTEM'S GUARDIANS,
SHE PROMISED ME THAT, IN EXCHANGE...
...I WILL BE REBORN AS A *REAL* SAILOR GUARDIAN,
WITH A PLANET OF MY VERY OWN!
AND SO I HAVE SWORN FEALTY TO GALAXIA, AND JOINED THE SAILOR ANIMA MATES!

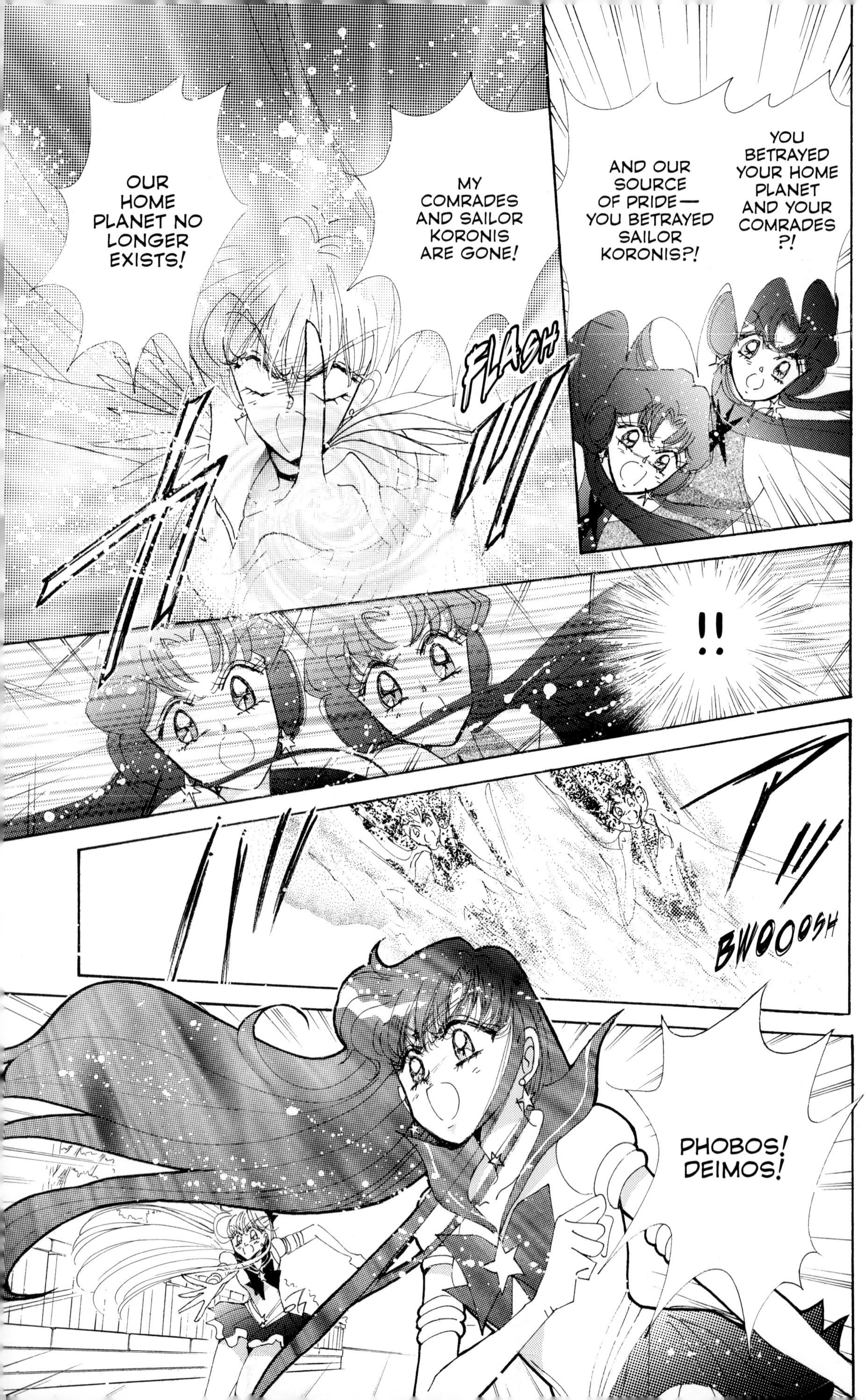
YOU BETRAYED YOUR HOME PLANET AND YOUR COMRADES?!
AND OUR SOURCE OF PRIDE— YOU BETRAYED SAILOR KORONIS?!
MY COMRADES AND SAILOR KORONIS ARE GONE!
OUR HOME PLANET NO LONGER EXISTS!
FLASH
!!
BWOOOSH
PHOBOS! DEIMOS!

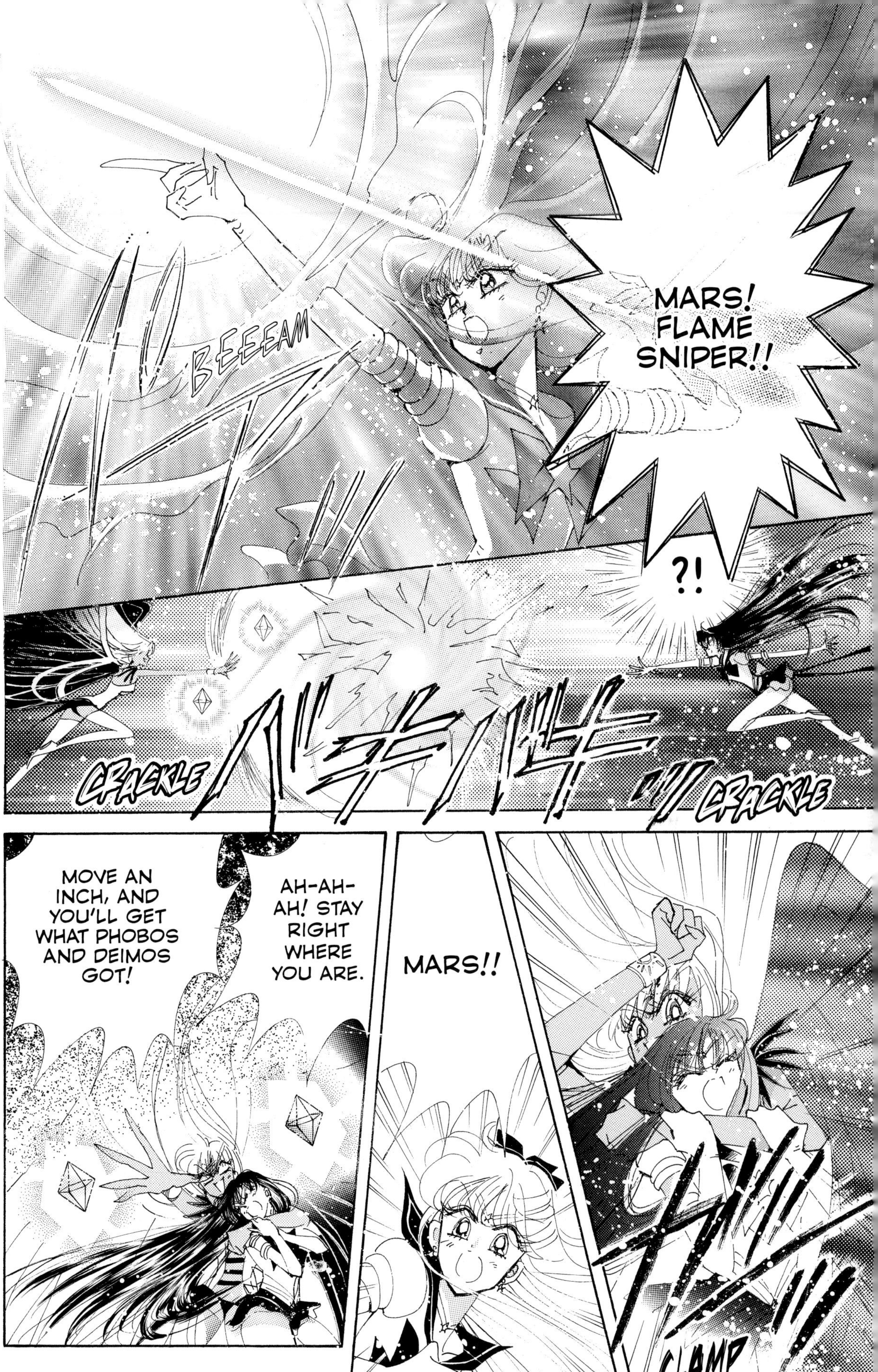
MARS! FLAME SNIPER!!
BEEEEAM
?!
CRACKLE
CRACKLE
CLAMP
MARS!!
AH-AH-AH! STAY RIGHT WHERE YOU ARE.
MOVE AN INCH, AND YOU'LL GET WHAT PHOBOS AND DEIMOS GOT!

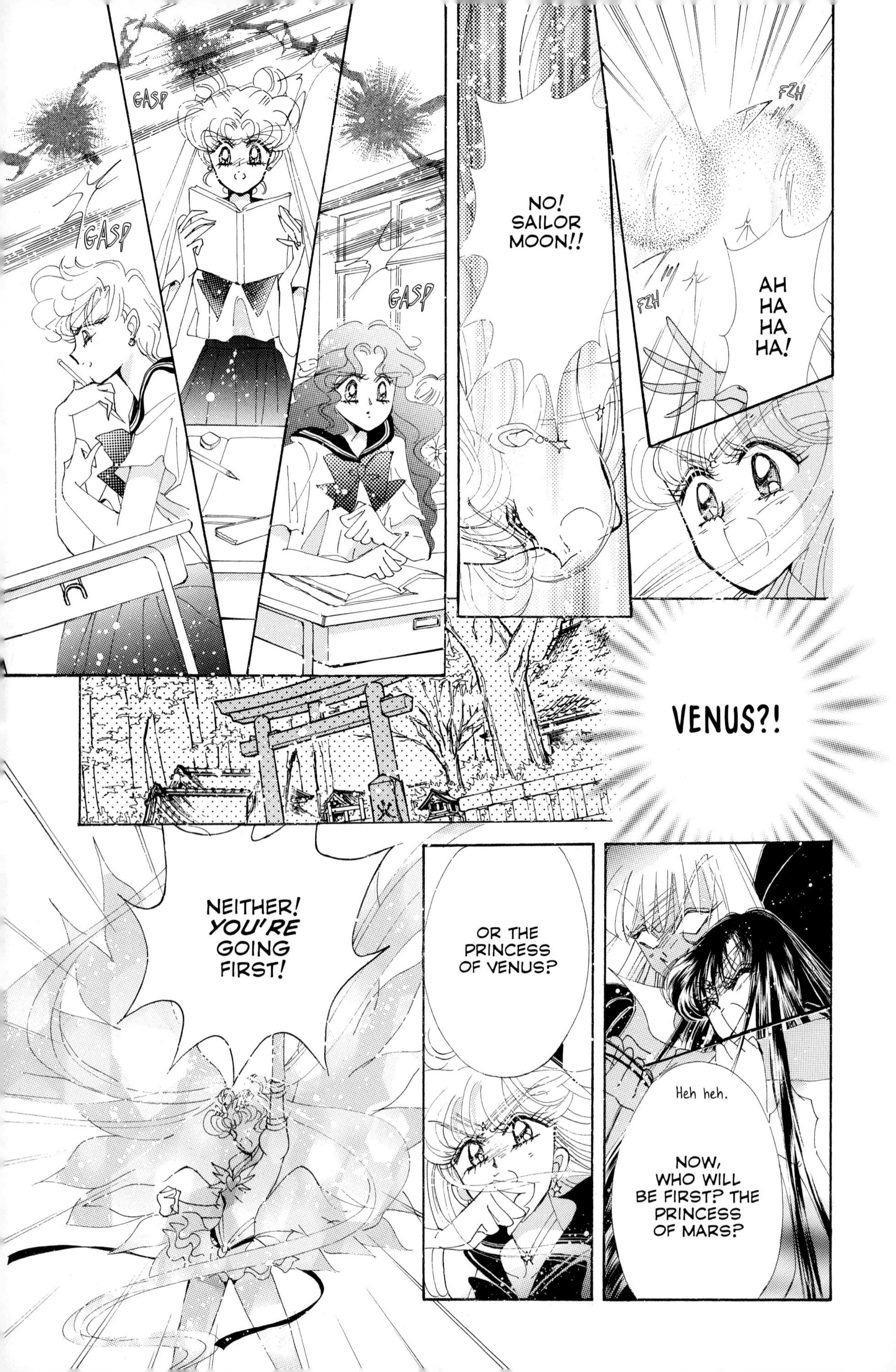

FZH
AH HA HA HA!
FZH
NO! SAILOR MOON!!
GASP
GASP
GASP
VENUS?!
Heh heh.
NOW, WHO WILL BE FIRST? THE PRINCESS OF MARS?
OR THE PRINCESS OF VENUS?
NEITHER! *YOU'RE* GOING FIRST!

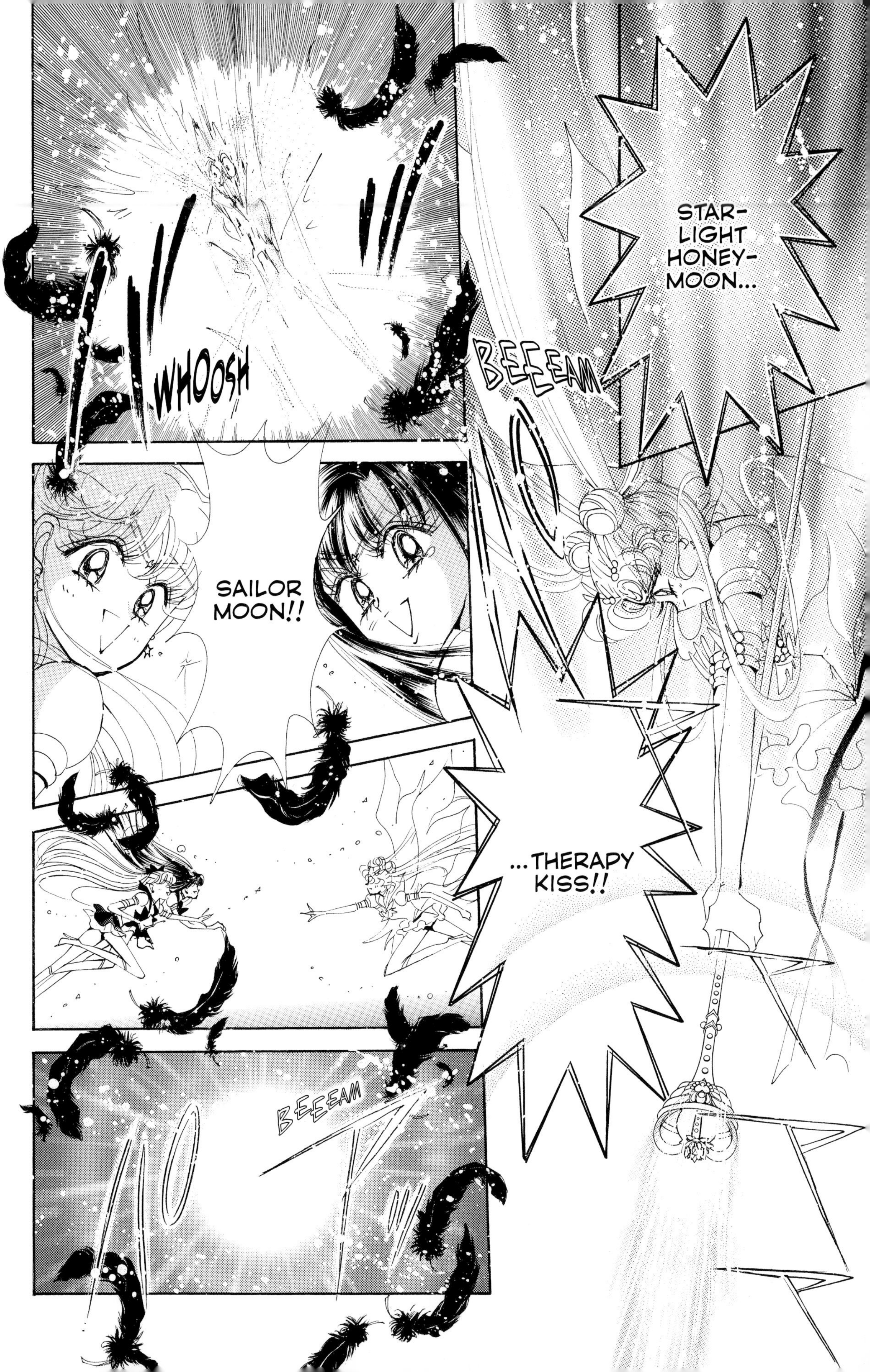
STAR-LIGHT HONEY-MOON...
BEEEAM
...THERAPY KISS!!
WHOOSH
SAILOR MOON!!
BEEEAM

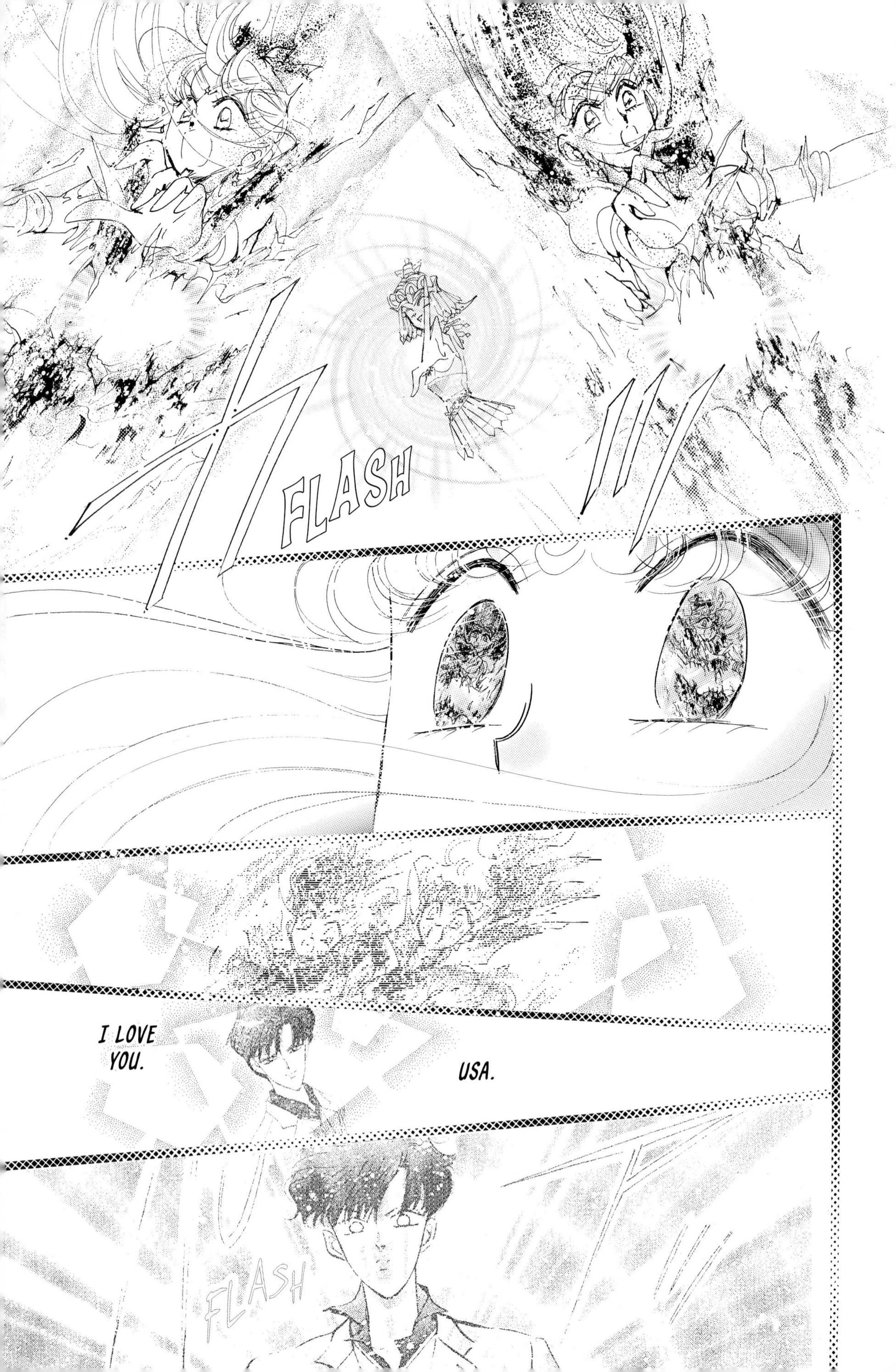
FLASH
I LOVE YOU.
USA.
FLASH

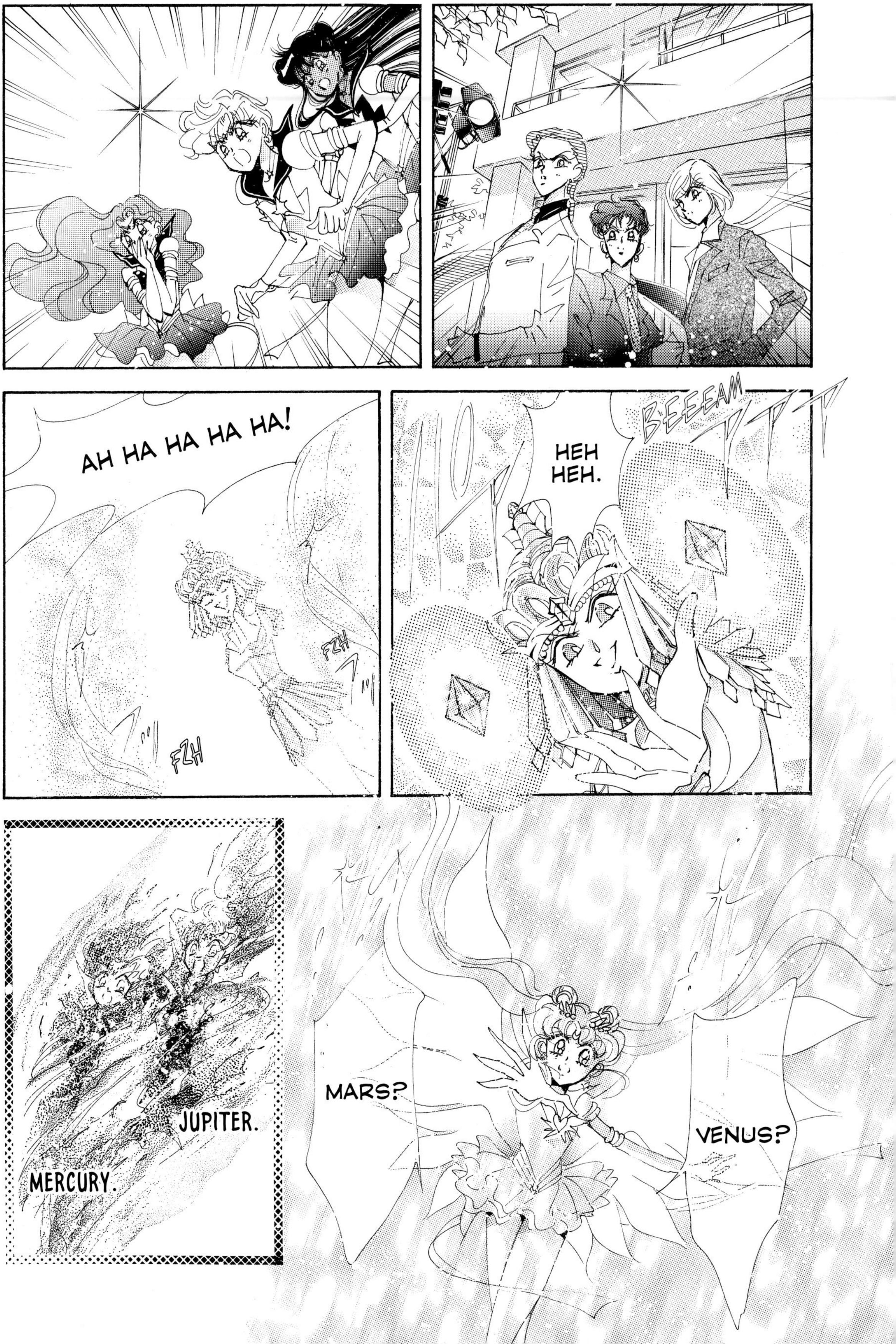
BEEEAM
HEH HEH.
AH HA HA HA HA!
FZH
FZH
VENUS?
MARS?
JUPITER.
MERCURY.

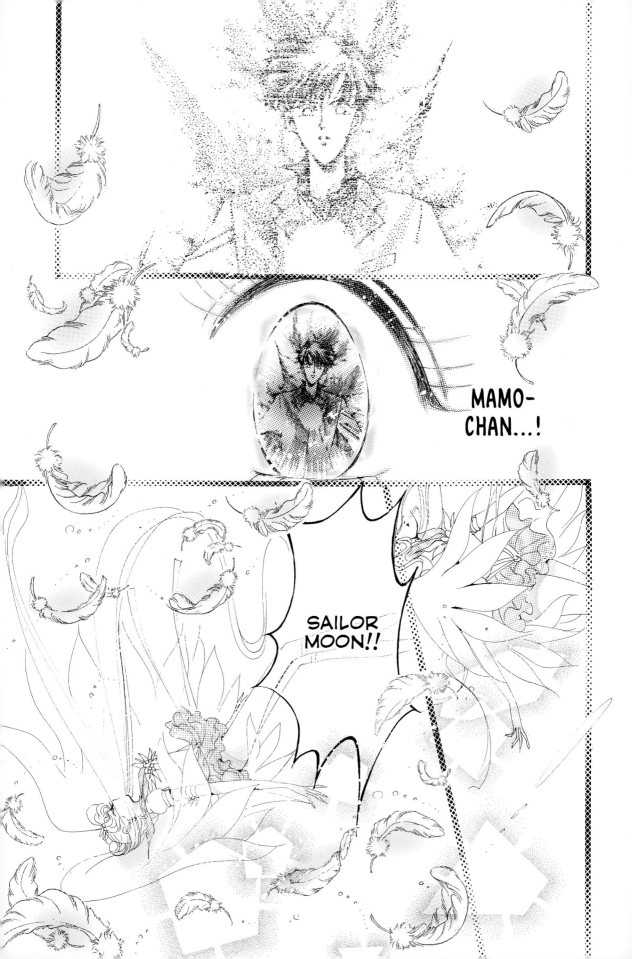

MAMO-CHAN...!

SAILOR MOON!!

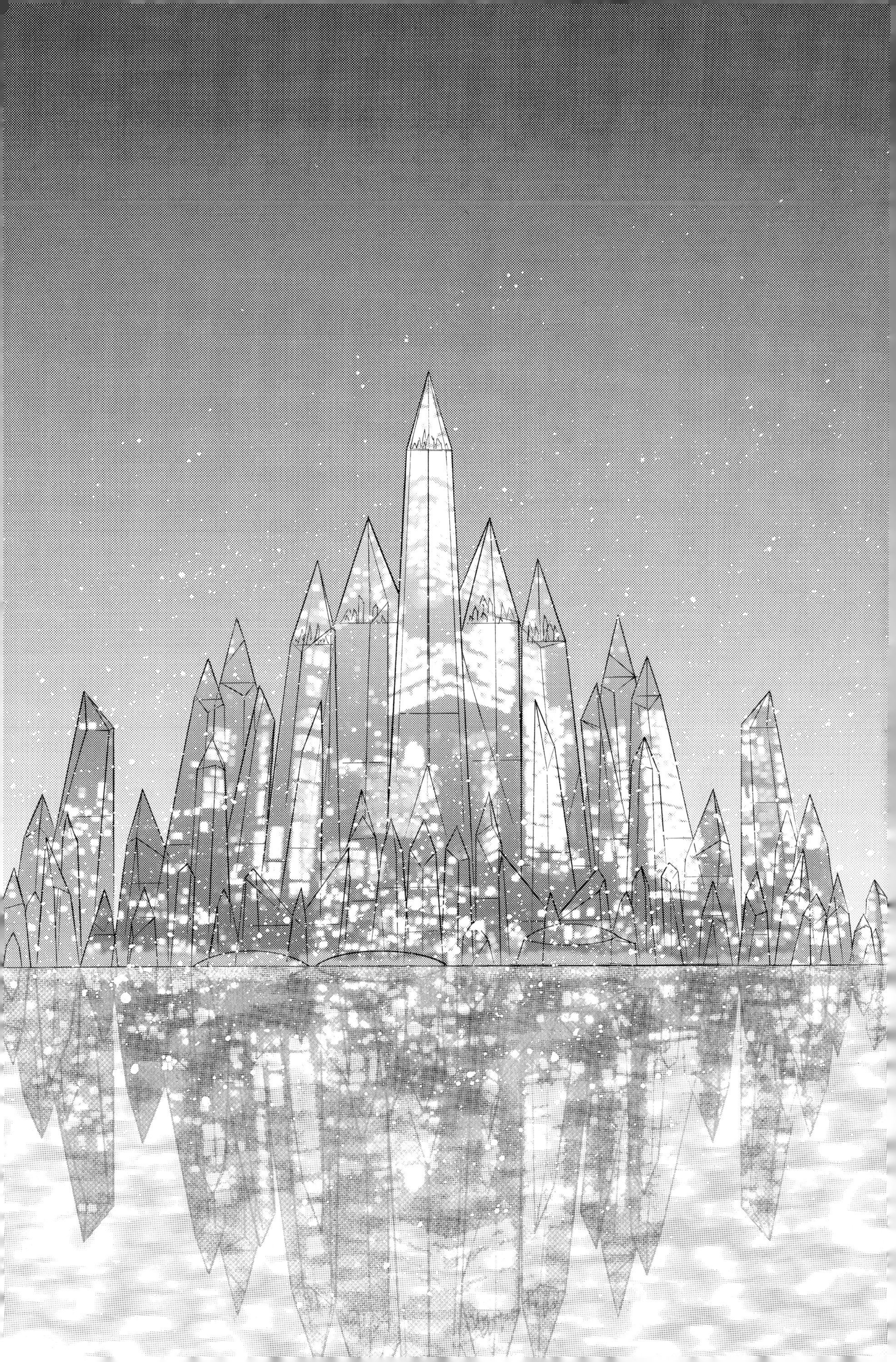

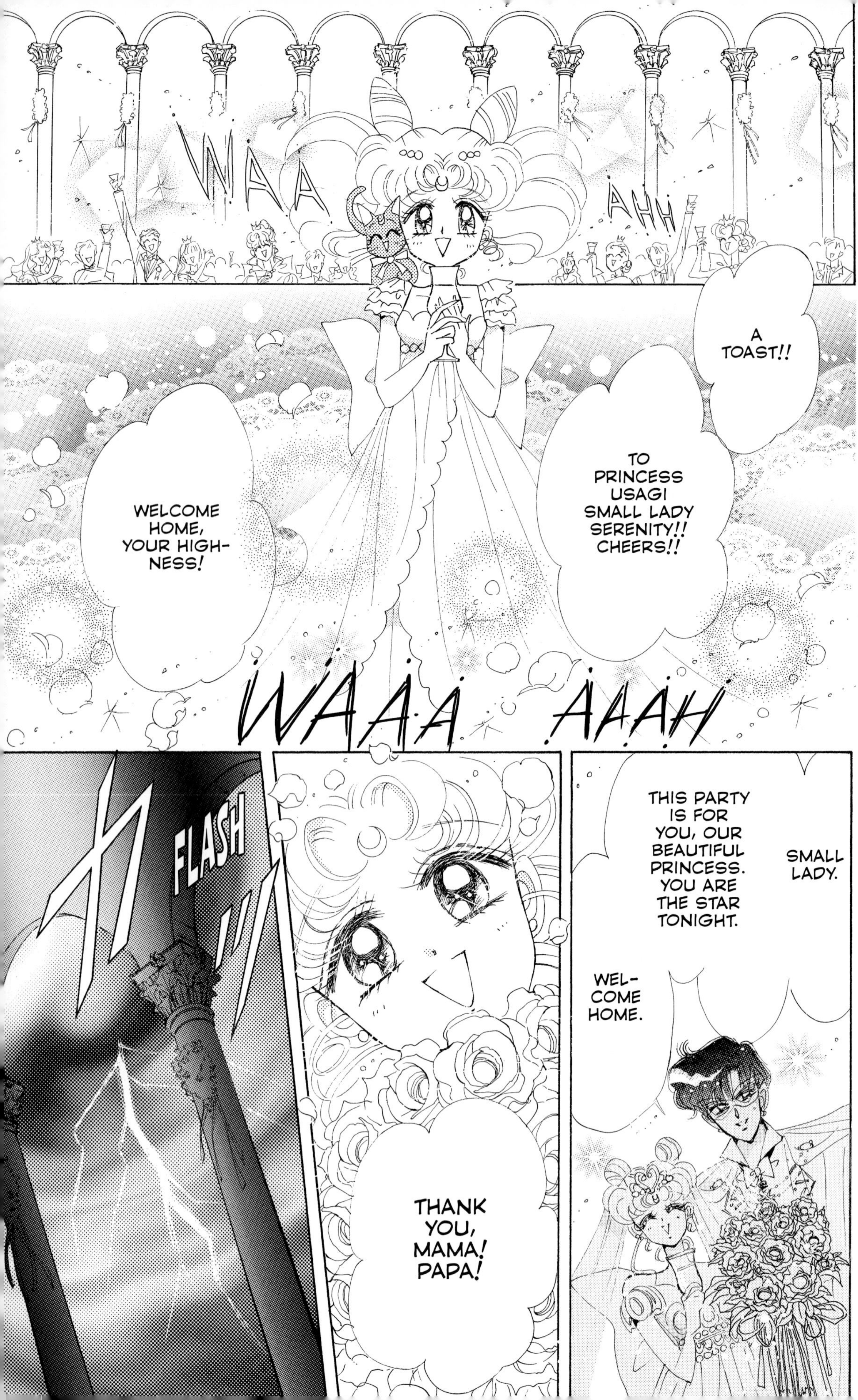
WAAA AHH
A TOAST!!
TO PRINCESS USAGI SMALL LADY SERENITY!! CHEERS!!
WELCOME HOME, YOUR HIGH-NESS!
WAAA AAAH
SMALL LADY.
THIS PARTY IS FOR YOU, OUR BEAUTIFUL PRINCESS. YOU ARE THE STAR TONIGHT.
WEL-COME HOME.
THANK YOU, MAMA! PAPA!
FLASH

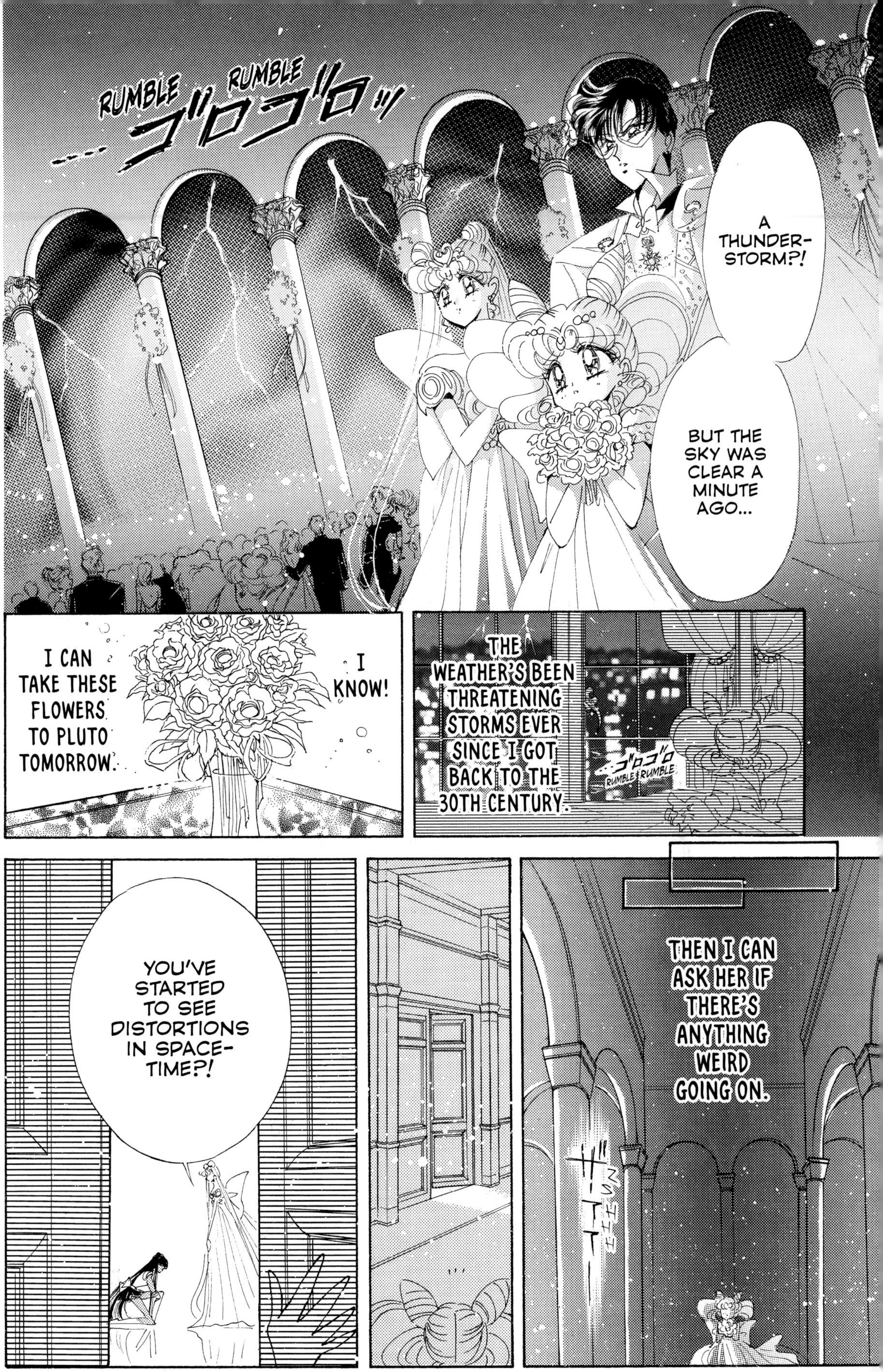

RUMBLE RUMBLE
ゴロゴロッ
A THUNDER-STORM?!
BUT THE SKY WAS CLEAR A MINUTE AGO...
THE WEATHER'S BEEN THREATENING STORMS EVER SINCE I GOT BACK TO THE 30TH CENTURY.
ゴロゴロ RUMBLE RUMBLE
I KNOW!
I CAN TAKE THESE FLOWERS TO PLUTO TOMORROW.
THEN I CAN ASK HER IF THERE'S ANYTHING WEIRD GOING ON.
...
YOU'VE STARTED TO SEE DISTORTIONS IN SPACE-TIME?!

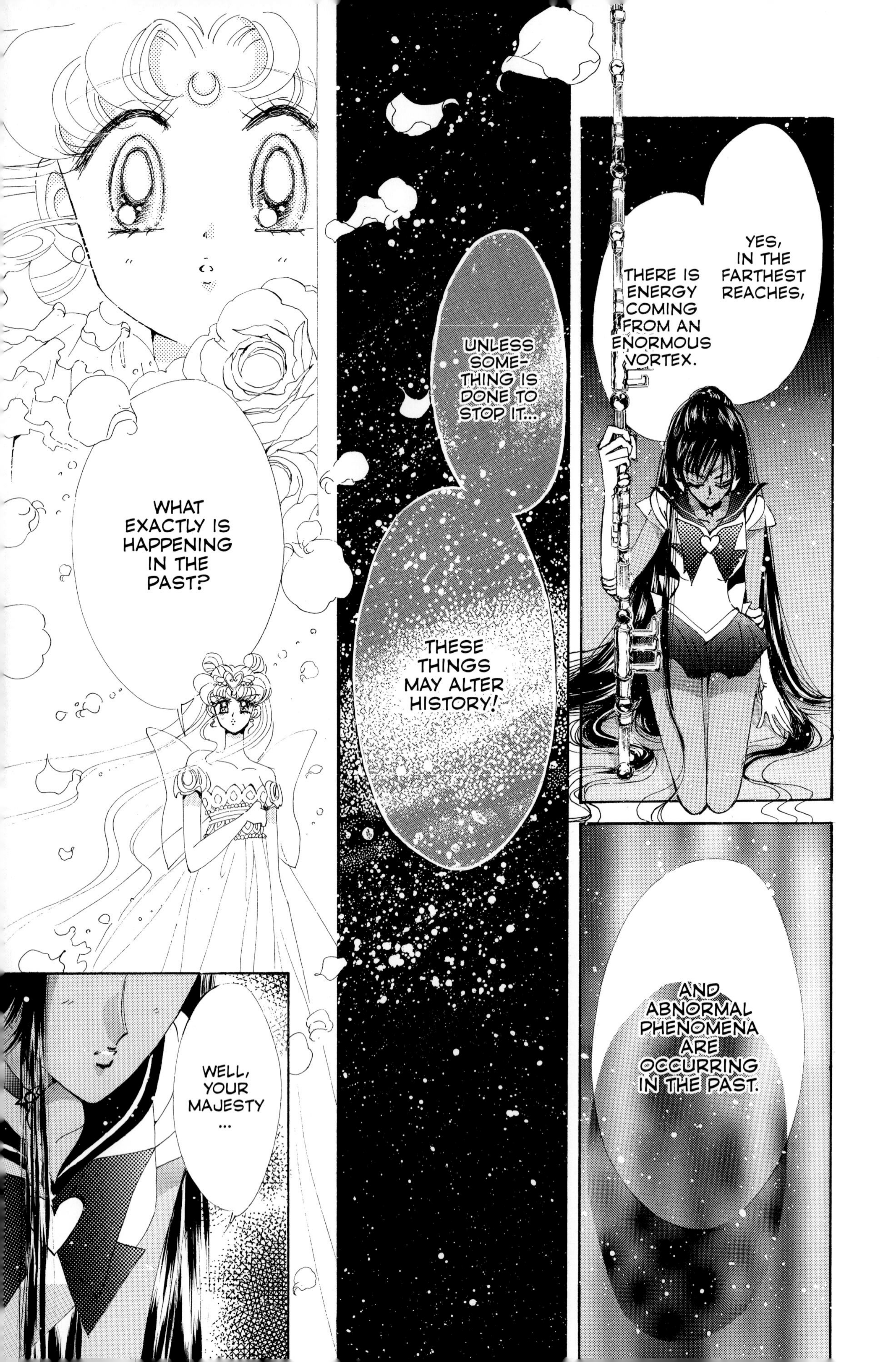
YES, IN THE FARTHEST REACHES,
THERE IS ENERGY COMING FROM AN ENORMOUS VORTEX.
AND ABNORMAL PHENOMENA ARE OCCURRING IN THE PAST.
UNLESS SOME-THING IS DONE TO STOP IT...
THESE THINGS MAY ALTER HISTORY!
WHAT EXACTLY IS HAPPENING IN THE PAST?
WELL, YOUR MAJESTY ...

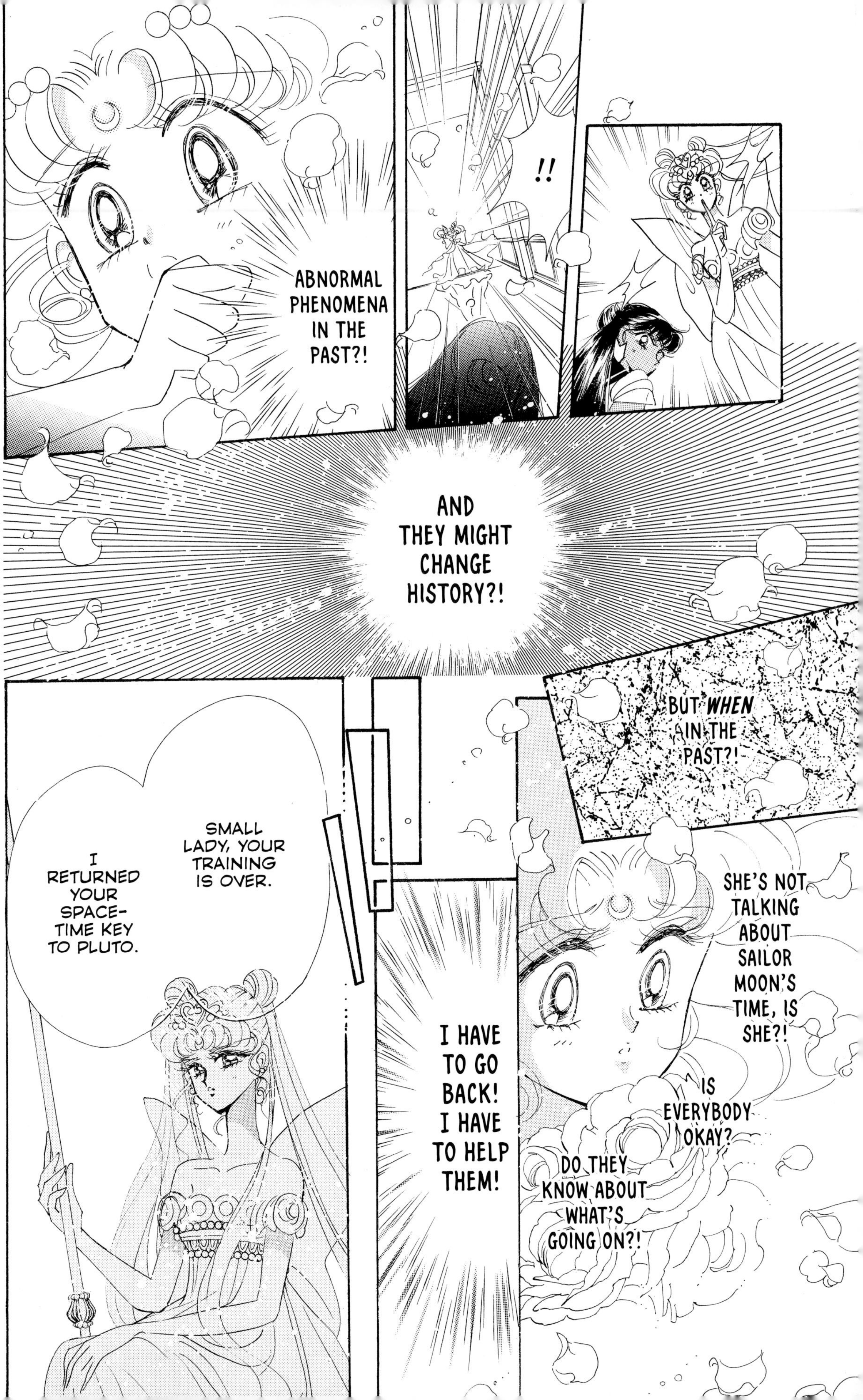
!!
ABNORMAL PHENOMENA IN THE PAST?!
AND THEY MIGHT CHANGE HISTORY?!
BUT WHEN IN THE PAST?!
SHE'S NOT TALKING ABOUT SAILOR MOON'S TIME, IS SHE?!
IS EVERYBODY OKAY?
DO THEY KNOW ABOUT WHAT'S GOING ON?!
I HAVE TO GO BACK! I HAVE TO HELP THEM!
SMALL LADY, YOUR TRAINING IS OVER.
I RETURNED YOUR SPACE-TIME KEY TO PLUTO.

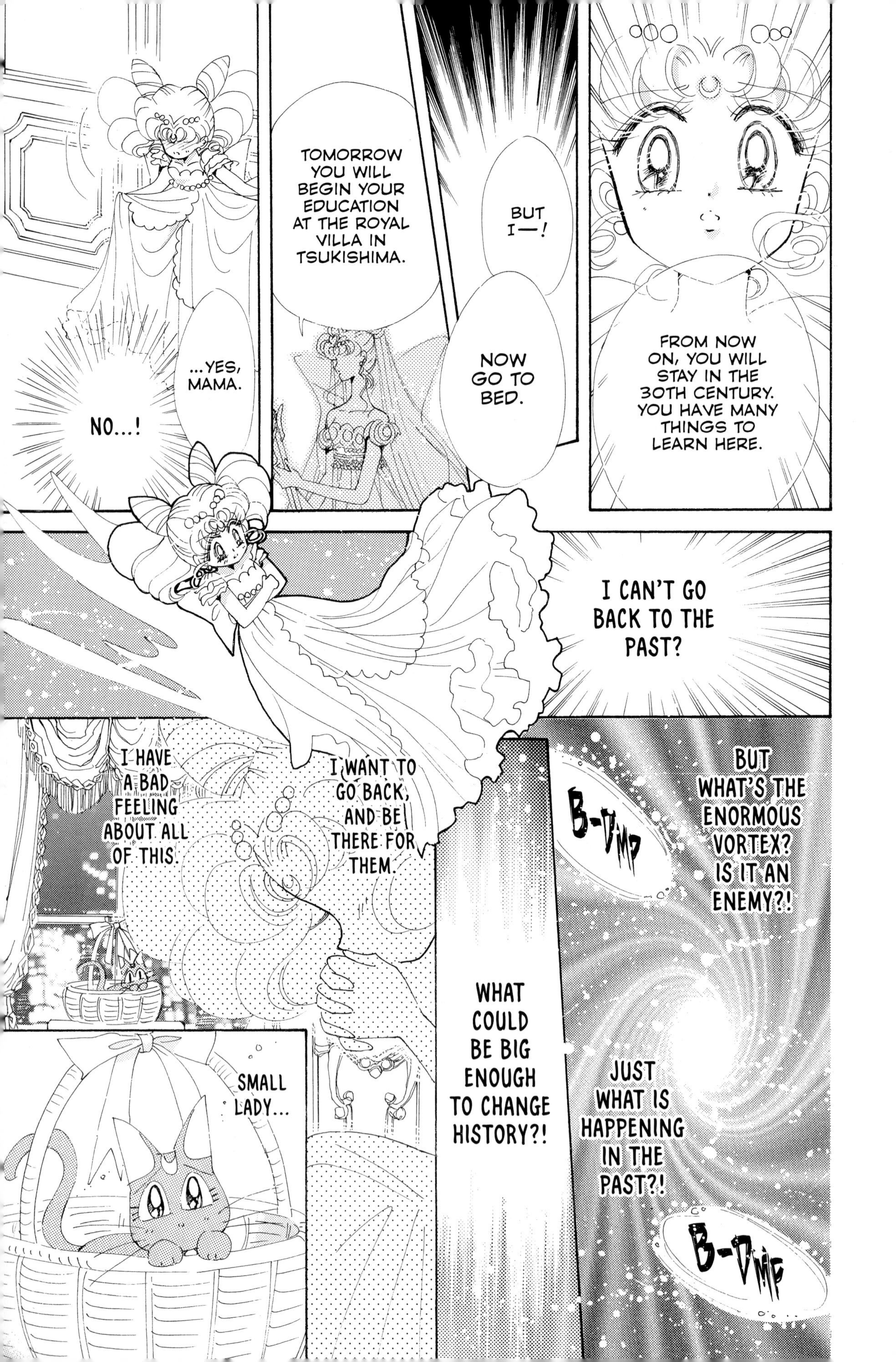
FROM NOW ON, YOU WILL STAY IN THE 30TH CENTURY. YOU HAVE MANY THINGS TO LEARN HERE.
BUT I—!
NOW GO TO BED.
TOMORROW YOU WILL BEGIN YOUR EDUCATION AT THE ROYAL VILLA IN TSUKISHIMA.
...YES, MAMA.
NO...!
I CAN'T GO BACK TO THE PAST?
BUT WHAT'S THE ENORMOUS VORTEX? IS IT AN ENEMY?!
B-DMP
JUST WHAT IS HAPPENING IN THE PAST?!
B-DMP
WHAT COULD BE BIG ENOUGH TO CHANGE HISTORY?!
I WANT TO GO BACK, AND BE THERE FOR THEM.
I HAVE A BAD FEELING ABOUT ALL OF THIS.
SMALL LADY...

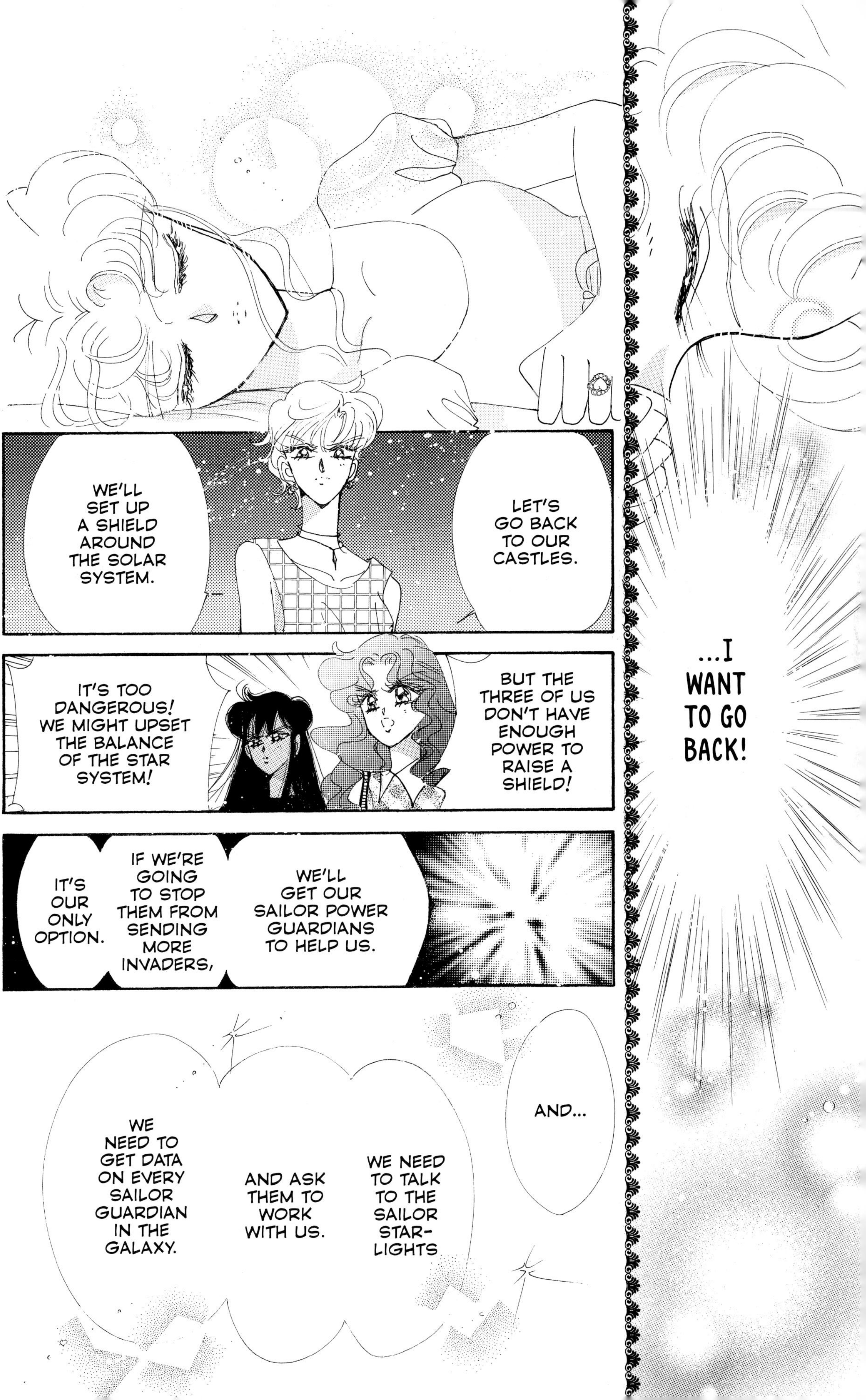
...I WANT TO GO BACK!
LET'S GO BACK TO OUR CASTLES.
WE'LL SET UP A SHIELD AROUND THE SOLAR SYSTEM.
BUT THE THREE OF US DON'T HAVE ENOUGH POWER TO RAISE A SHIELD!
IT'S TOO DANGEROUS! WE MIGHT UPSET THE BALANCE OF THE STAR SYSTEM!
WE'LL GET OUR SAILOR POWER GUARDIANS TO HELP US.
IF WE'RE GOING TO STOP THEM FROM SENDING MORE INVADERS,
IT'S OUR ONLY OPTION.
AND...
WE NEED TO TALK TO THE SAILOR STAR-LIGHTS
AND ASK THEM TO WORK WITH US.
WE NEED TO GET DATA ON EVERY SAILOR GUARDIAN IN THE GALAXY.

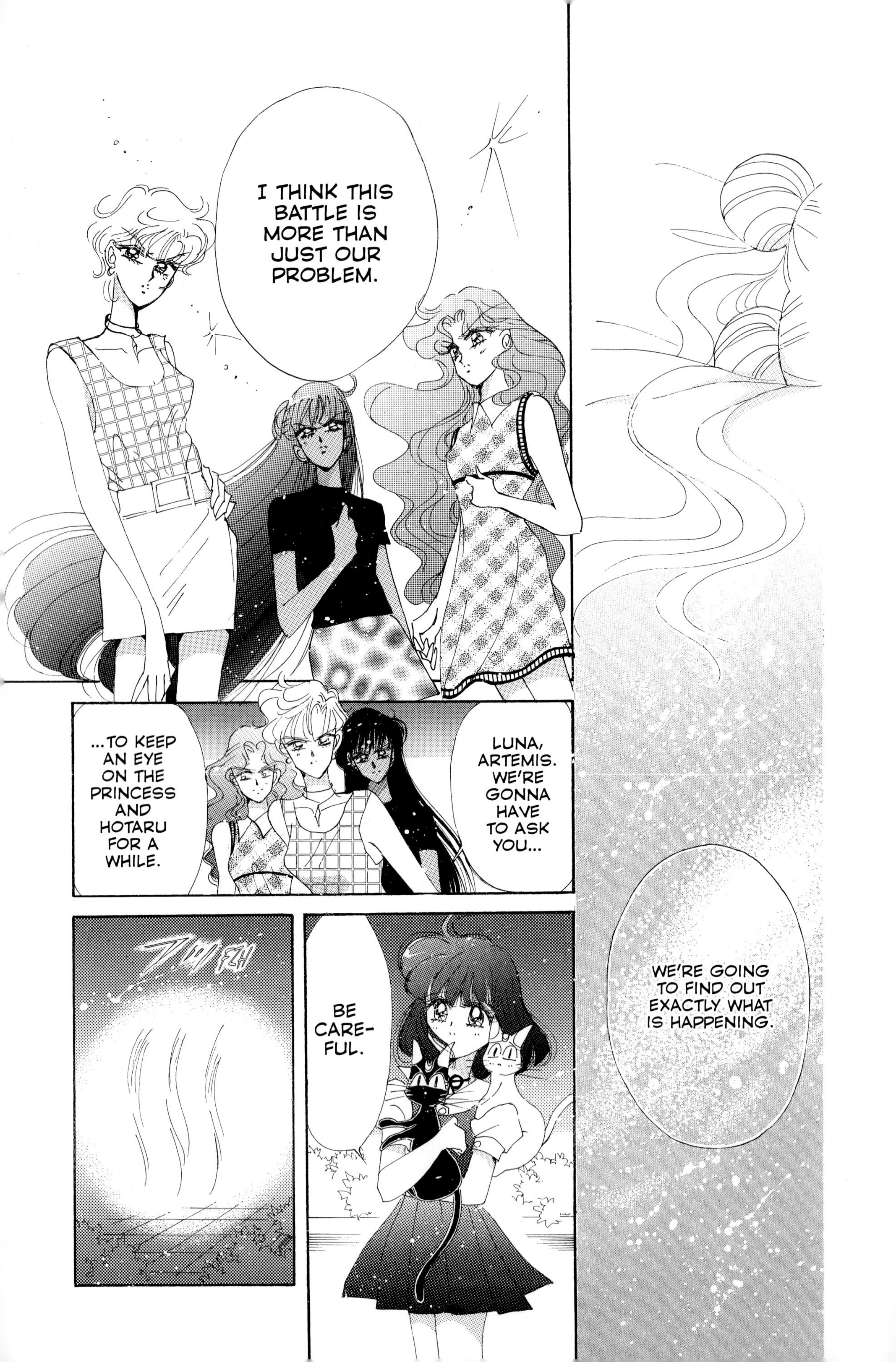
WE'RE GOING TO FIND OUT EXACTLY WHAT IS HAPPENING.
I THINK THIS BATTLE IS MORE THAN JUST OUR PROBLEM.
LUNA, ARTEMIS. WE'RE GONNA HAVE TO ASK YOU...
...TO KEEP AN EYE ON THE PRINCESS AND HOTARU FOR A WHILE.
BE CARE-FUL.
FZH

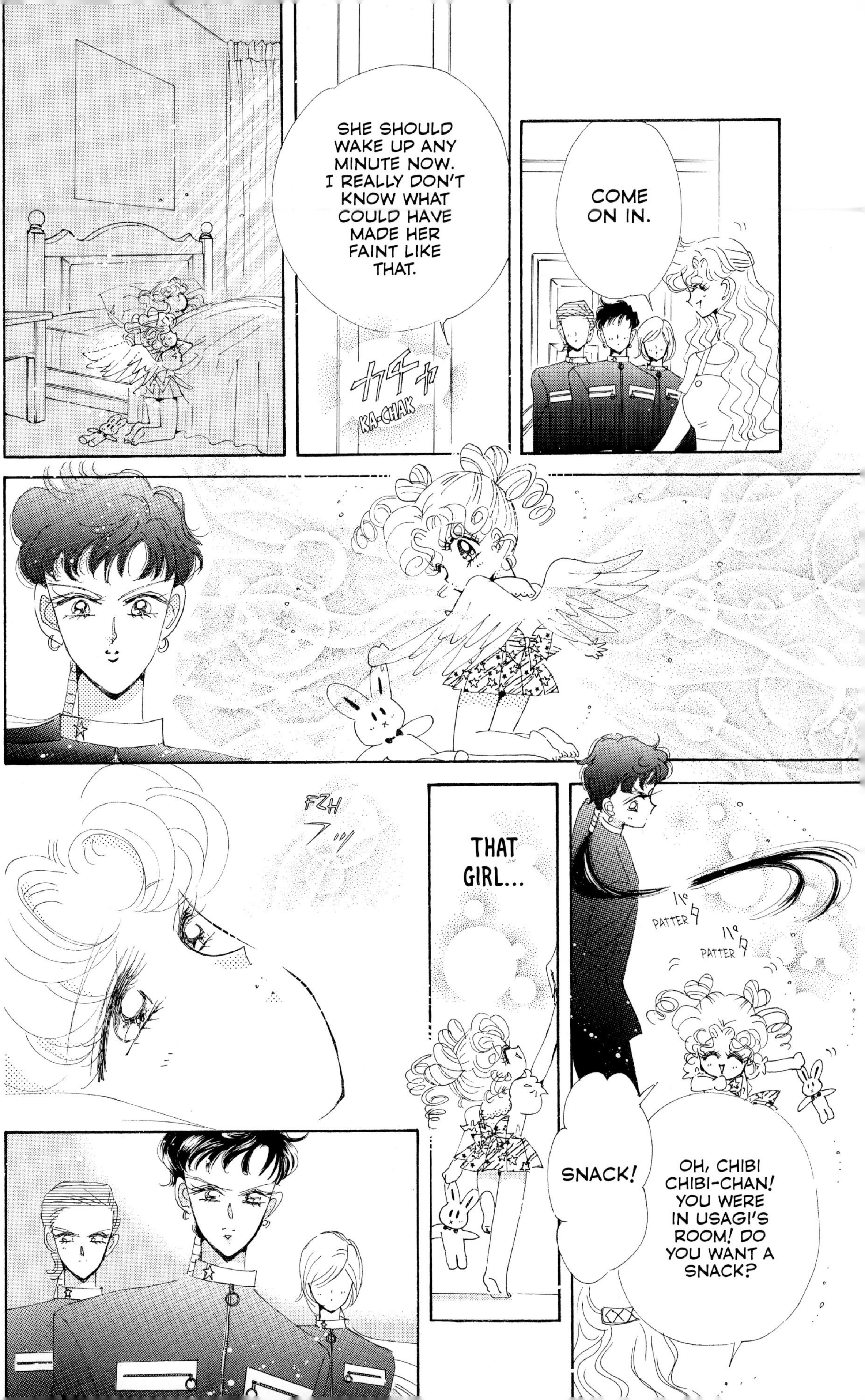
COME ON IN.
SHE SHOULD WAKE UP ANY MINUTE NOW. I REALLY DON'T KNOW WHAT COULD HAVE MADE HER FAINT LIKE THAT.
カチャ
KA-CHAK
パタ
PATTER
パタ
PATTER
OH, CHIBI CHIBI-CHAN! YOU WERE IN USAGI'S ROOM! DO YOU WANT A SNACK?
SNACK!
THAT GIRL...
フッ
FZH

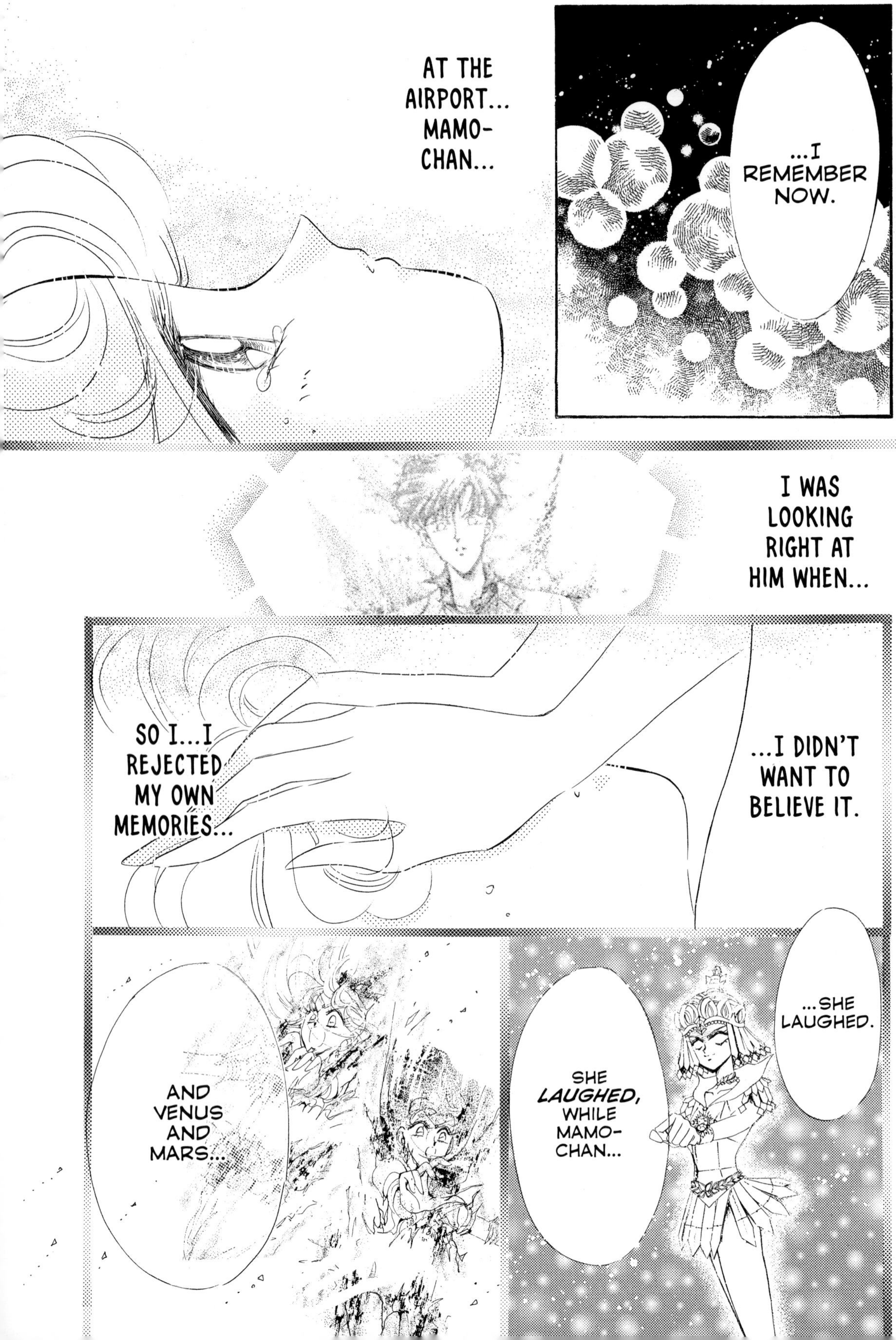
...I REMEMBER NOW.
AT THE AIRPORT... MAMO-CHAN...
I WAS LOOKING RIGHT AT HIM WHEN...
...I DIDN'T WANT TO BELIEVE IT.
SO I...I REJECTED MY OWN MEMORIES...
...SHE LAUGHED.
SHE *LAUGHED,* WHILE MAMO-CHAN...
AND VENUS AND MARS...

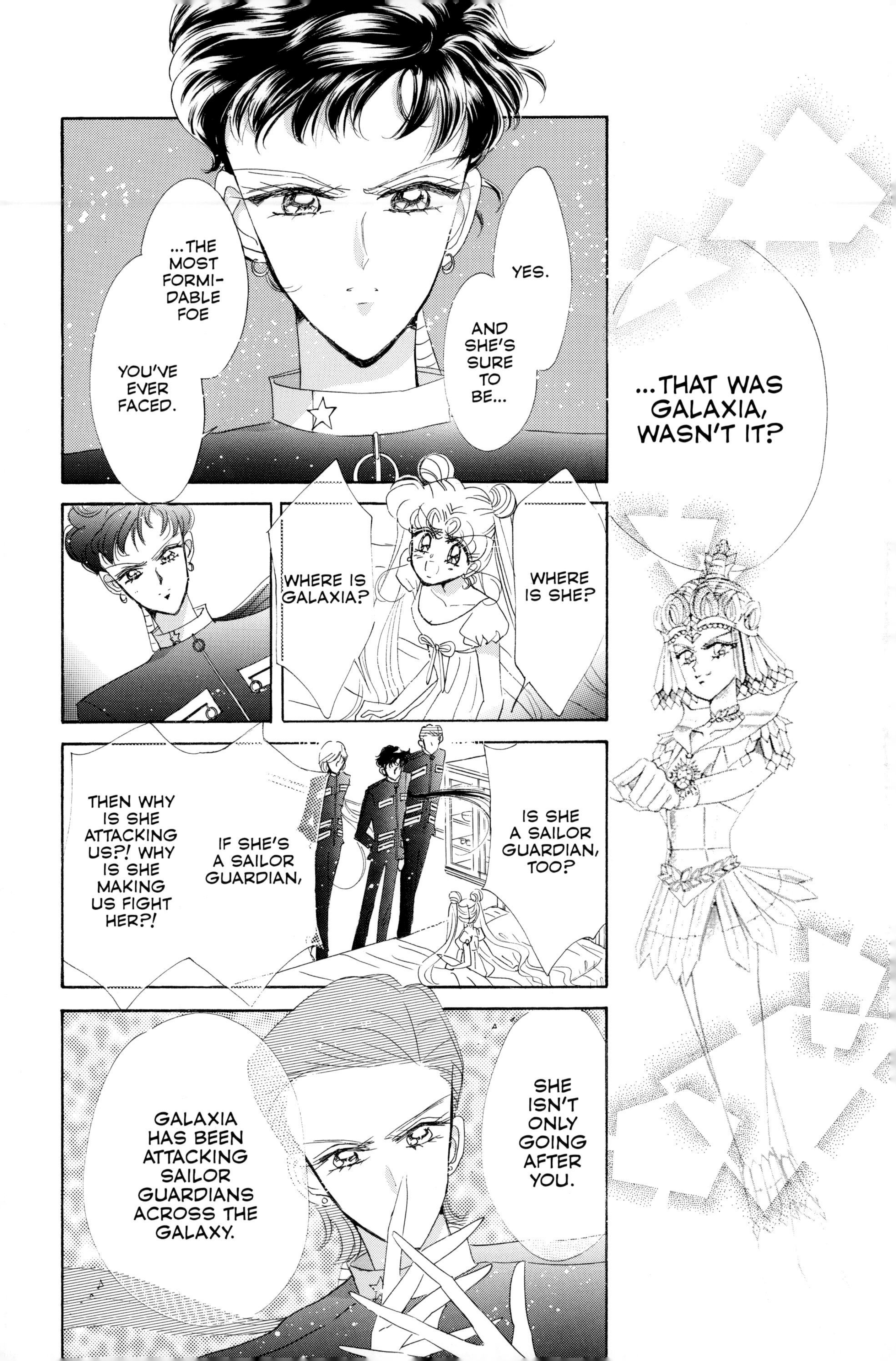
...THAT WAS GALAXIA, WASN'T IT?
YES.
AND SHE'S SURE TO BE...
...THE MOST FORMIDABLE FOE YOU'VE EVER FACED.
WHERE IS SHE?
WHERE IS GALAXIA?
IS SHE A SAILOR GUARDIAN, TOO?
IF SHE'S A SAILOR GUARDIAN,
THEN WHY IS SHE ATTACKING US?! WHY IS SHE MAKING US FIGHT HER?!
SHE ISN'T ONLY GOING AFTER YOU.
GALAXIA HAS BEEN ATTACKING SAILOR GUARDIANS ACROSS THE GALAXY.

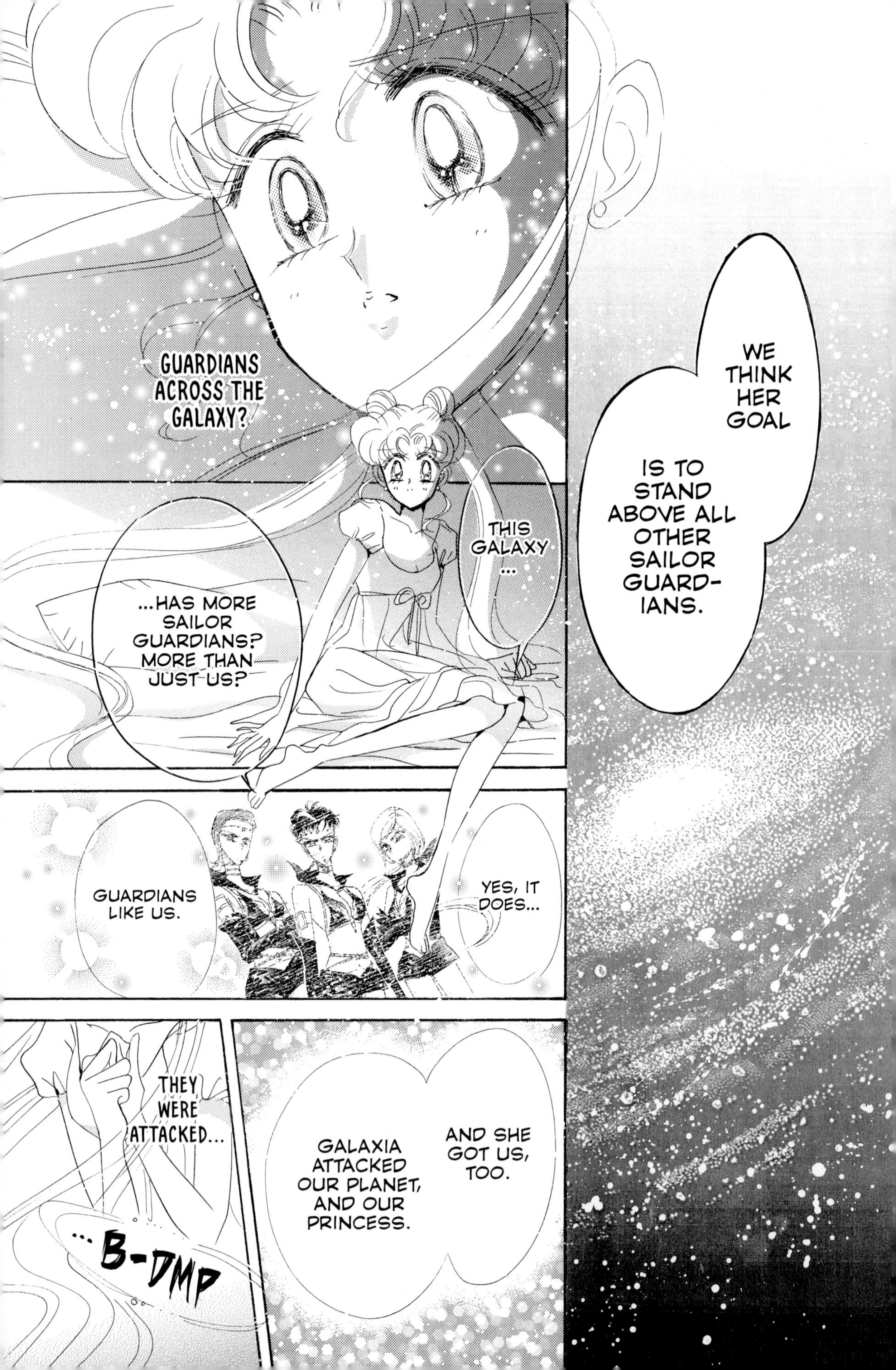

WE THINK HER GOAL
IS TO STAND ABOVE ALL OTHER SAILOR GUARD-IANS.
GUARDIANS ACROSS THE GALAXY?
THIS GALAXY...
...HAS MORE SAILOR GUARDIANS? MORE THAN JUST US?
YES, IT DOES...
GUARDIANS LIKE US.
GALAXIA ATTACKED OUR PLANET, AND OUR PRINCESS.
AND SHE GOT US, TOO.
THEY WERE ATTACKED...
...B-DMP

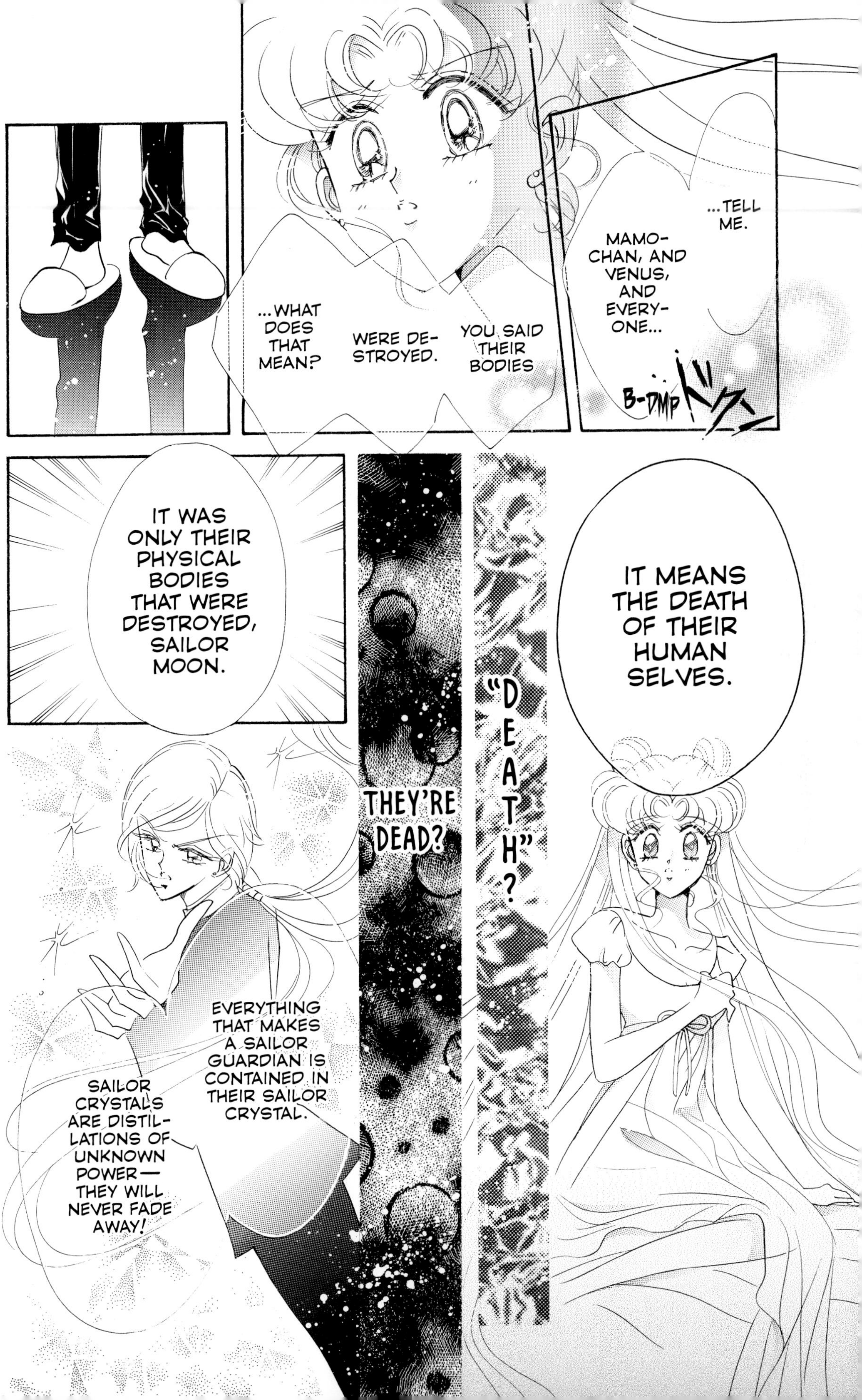
...TELL ME.
MAMO-CHAN, AND VENUS, AND EVERY-ONE...
B-DMP
YOU SAID THEIR BODIES
WERE DE-STROYED.
...WHAT DOES THAT MEAN?
IT MEANS THE DEATH OF THEIR HUMAN SELVES.
"DEATH"?
THEY'RE DEAD?
IT WAS ONLY THEIR PHYSICAL BODIES THAT WERE DESTROYED, SAILOR MOON.
EVERYTHING THAT MAKES A SAILOR GUARDIAN IS CONTAINED IN THEIR SAILOR CRYSTAL.
SAILOR CRYSTALS ARE DISTIL-LATIONS OF UNKNOWN POWER— THEY WILL NEVER FADE AWAY!

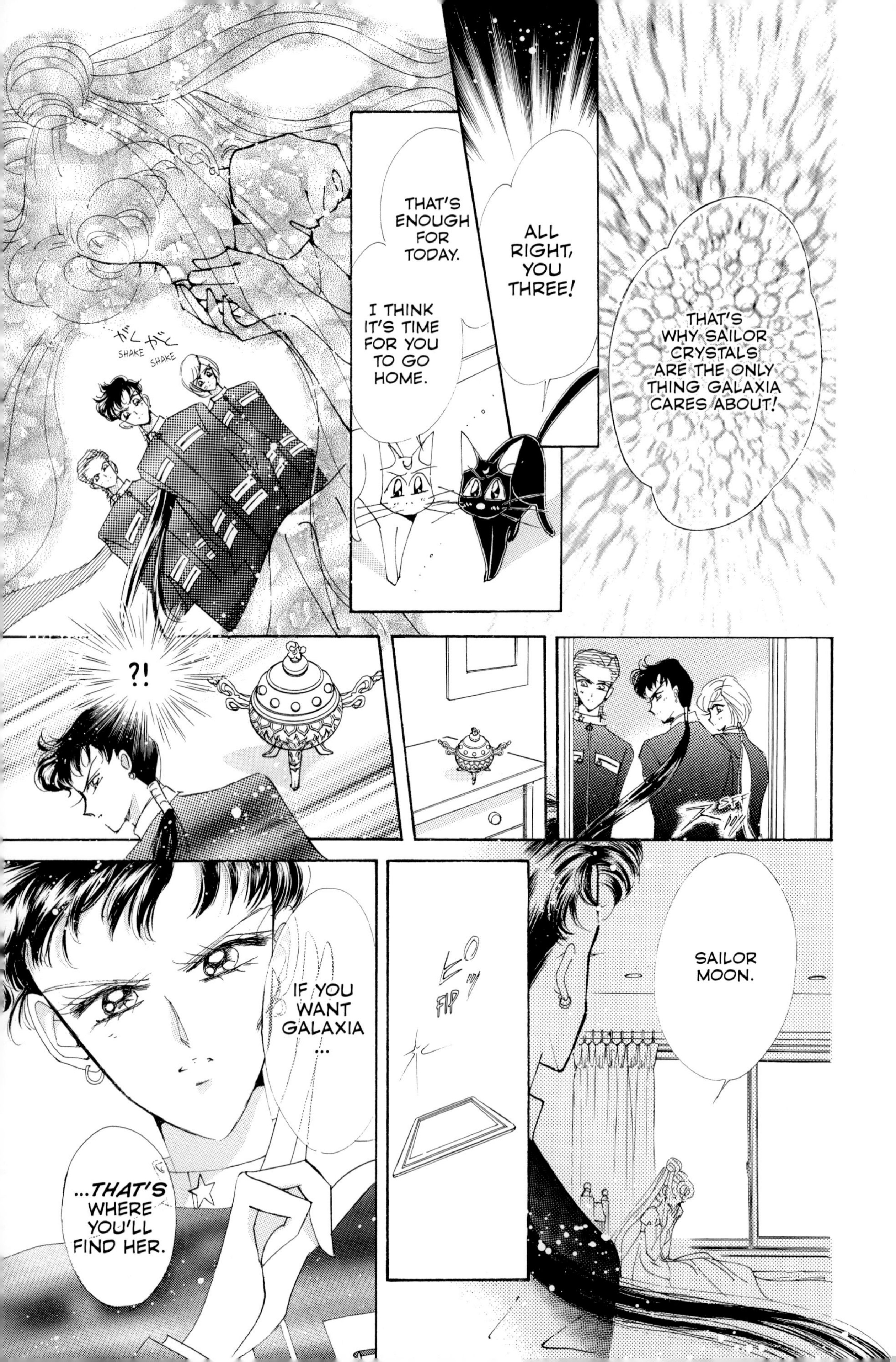

THAT'S WHY SAILOR CRYSTALS ARE THE ONLY THING GALAXIA CARES ABOUT!
ALL RIGHT, YOU THREE!
THAT'S ENOUGH FOR TODAY.
I THINK IT'S TIME FOR YOU TO GO HOME.
SHAKE SHAKE
?!
SAILOR MOON.
FIP
IF YOU WANT GALAXIA...
...THAT'S WHERE YOU'LL FIND HER.

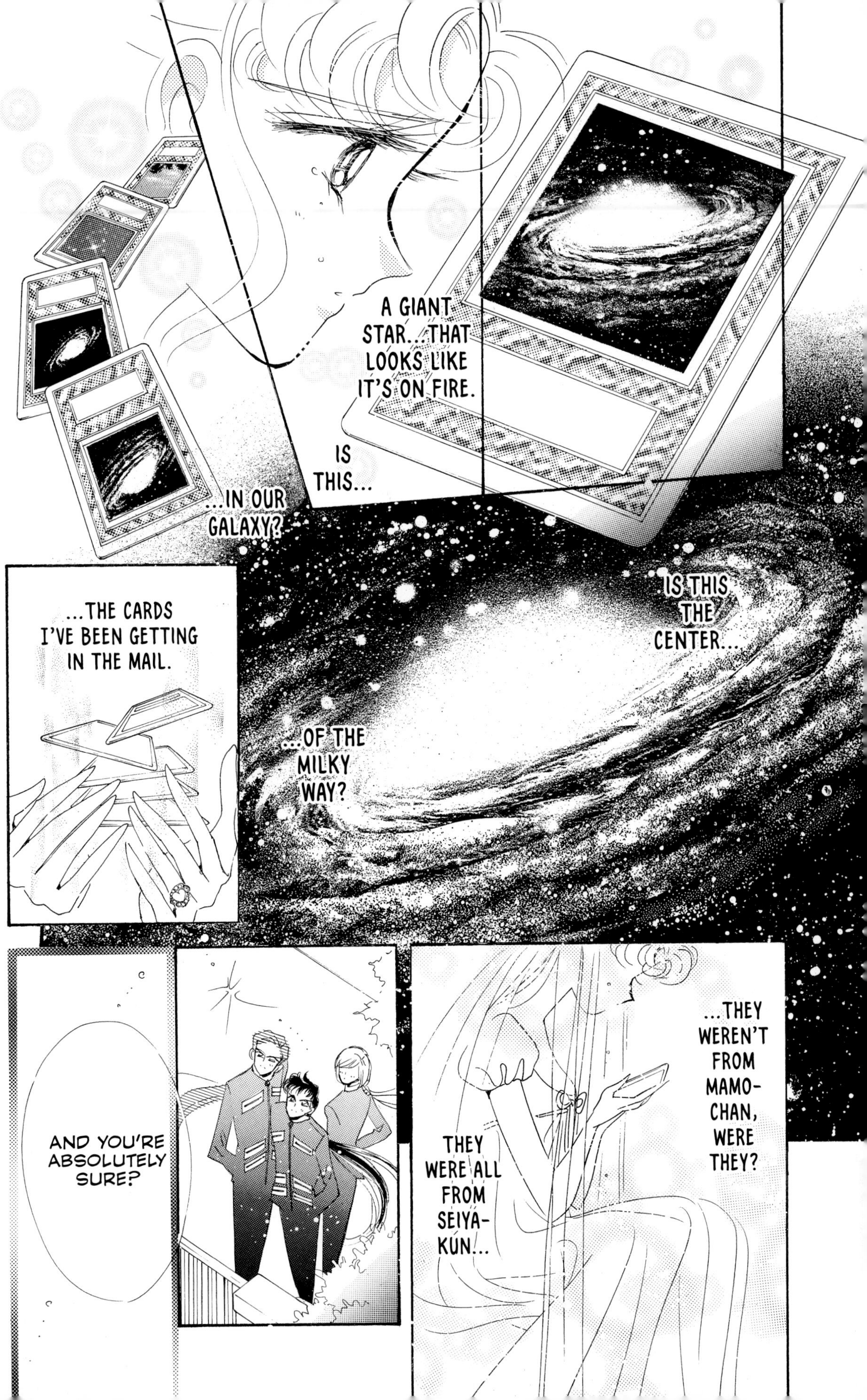
A GIANT STAR... THAT LOOKS LIKE IT'S ON FIRE.
IS THIS...
...IN OUR GALAXY?
IS THIS THE CENTER...
...OF THE MILKY WAY?
...THE CARDS I'VE BEEN GETTING IN THE MAIL.
...THEY WEREN'T FROM MAMO-CHAN, WERE THEY?
THEY WERE ALL FROM SEIYA-KUN...
AND YOU'RE ABSOLUTELY SURE?

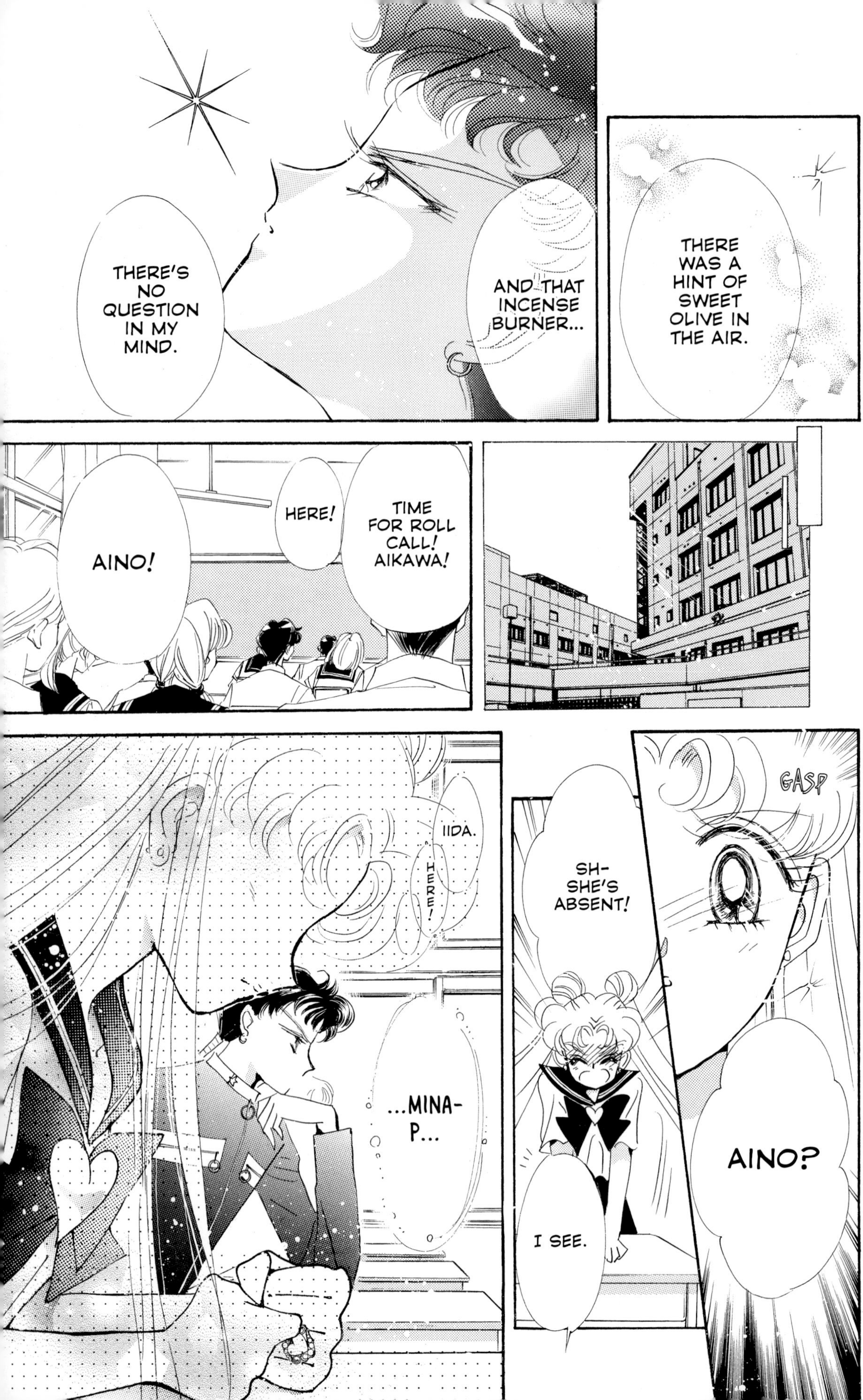
THERE WAS A HINT OF SWEET OLIVE IN THE AIR.
AND THAT INCENSE BURNER...
THERE'S NO QUESTION IN MY MIND.
TIME FOR ROLL CALL! AIKAWA!
HERE!
AINO!
GASP
AINO?
SH-SHE'S ABSENT!
I SEE.
IIDA.
HERE!
...MINA-P...

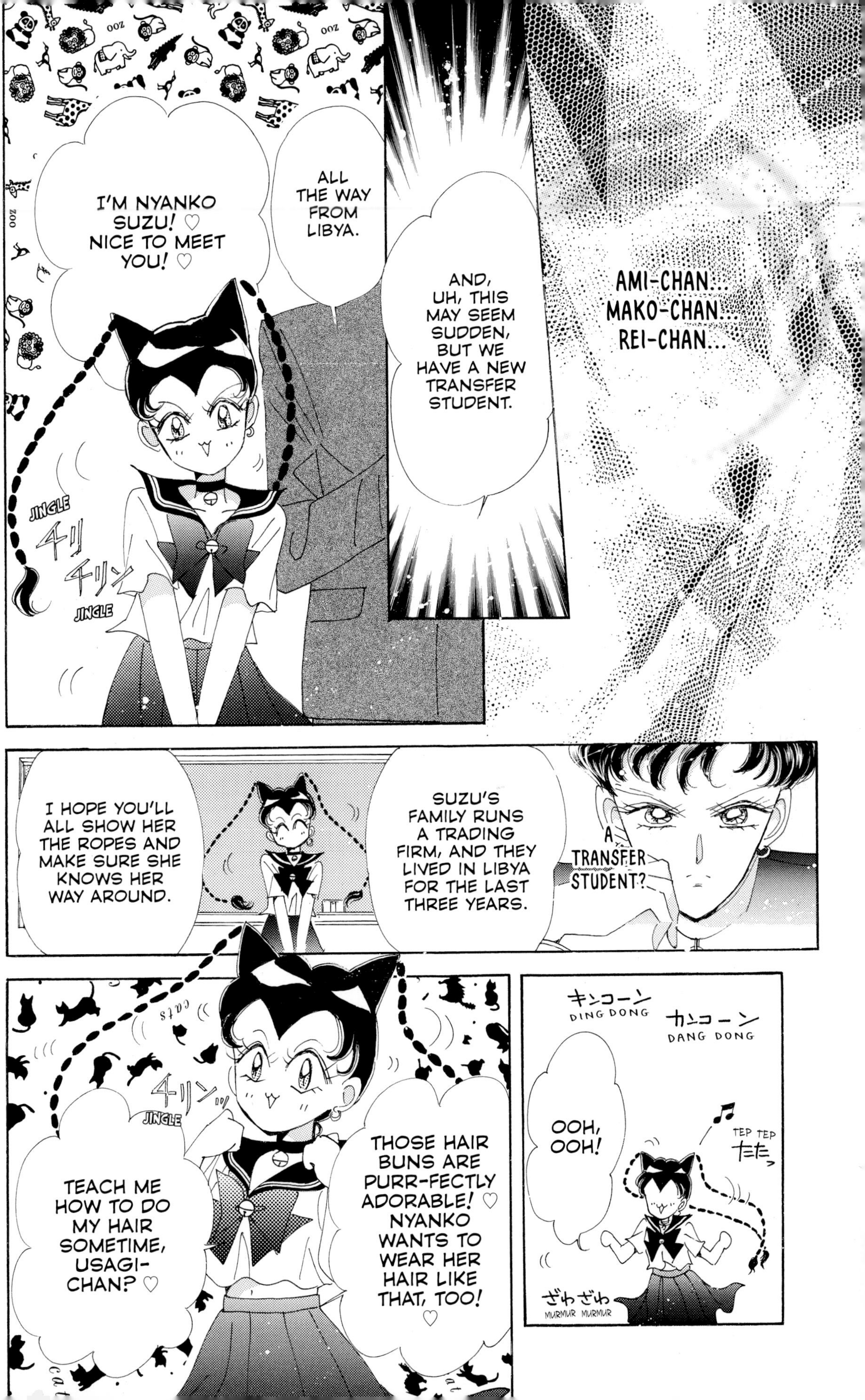
AMI-CHAN... MAKO-CHAN... REI-CHAN...
AND, UH, THIS MAY SEEM SUDDEN, BUT WE HAVE A NEW TRANSFER STUDENT.
ALL THE WAY FROM LIBYA.
I'M NYANKO SUZU! ♡ NICE TO MEET YOU! ♡
チリ JINGLE
チリン JINGLE
A TRANSFER STUDENT?
SUZU'S FAMILY RUNS A TRADING FIRM, AND THEY LIVED IN LIBYA FOR THE LAST THREE YEARS.
I HOPE YOU'LL ALL SHOW HER THE ROPES AND MAKE SURE SHE KNOWS HER WAY AROUND.
キンコーン DING DONG
カンコーン DANG DONG
OOH, OOH!
たたっ TEP TEP
ざわざわ MURMUR MURMUR
THOSE HAIR BUNS ARE PURR-FECTLY ADORABLE! ♡ NYANKO WANTS TO WEAR HER HAIR LIKE THAT, TOO! ♡
チリンッ JINGLE
TEACH ME HOW TO DO MY HAIR SOMETIME, USAGI-CHAN? ♡

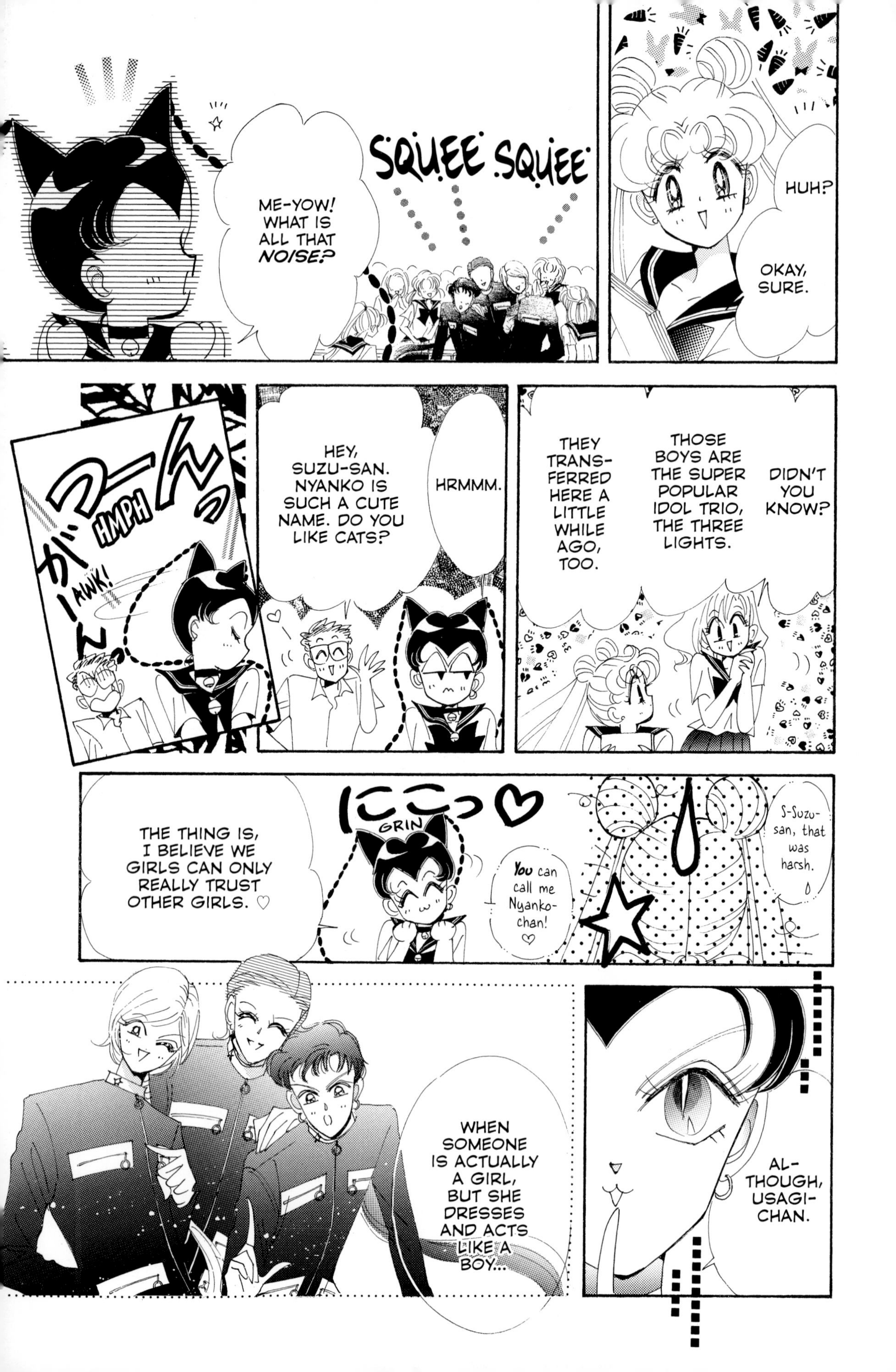
HUH?
OKAY, SURE.
SQUEE SQUEE
ME-YOW! WHAT IS ALL THAT NOISE?
DIDN'T YOU KNOW?
THOSE BOYS ARE THE SUPER POPULAR IDOL TRIO, THE THREE LIGHTS.
THEY TRANS-FERRED HERE A LITTLE WHILE AGO, TOO.
HRMMM.
HEY, SUZU-SAN. NYANKO IS SUCH A CUTE NAME. DO YOU LIKE CATS?
つーんっ
HMPH
がーん
AWK!
S-Suzu-san, that was harsh.
にこっ
GRIN
You can call me Nyanko-chan! ♡
THE THING IS, I BELIEVE WE GIRLS CAN ONLY REALLY TRUST OTHER GIRLS. ♡
AL-THOUGH, USAGI-CHAN.
WHEN SOMEONE IS ACTUALLY A GIRL, BUT SHE DRESSES AND ACTS LIKE A BOY...

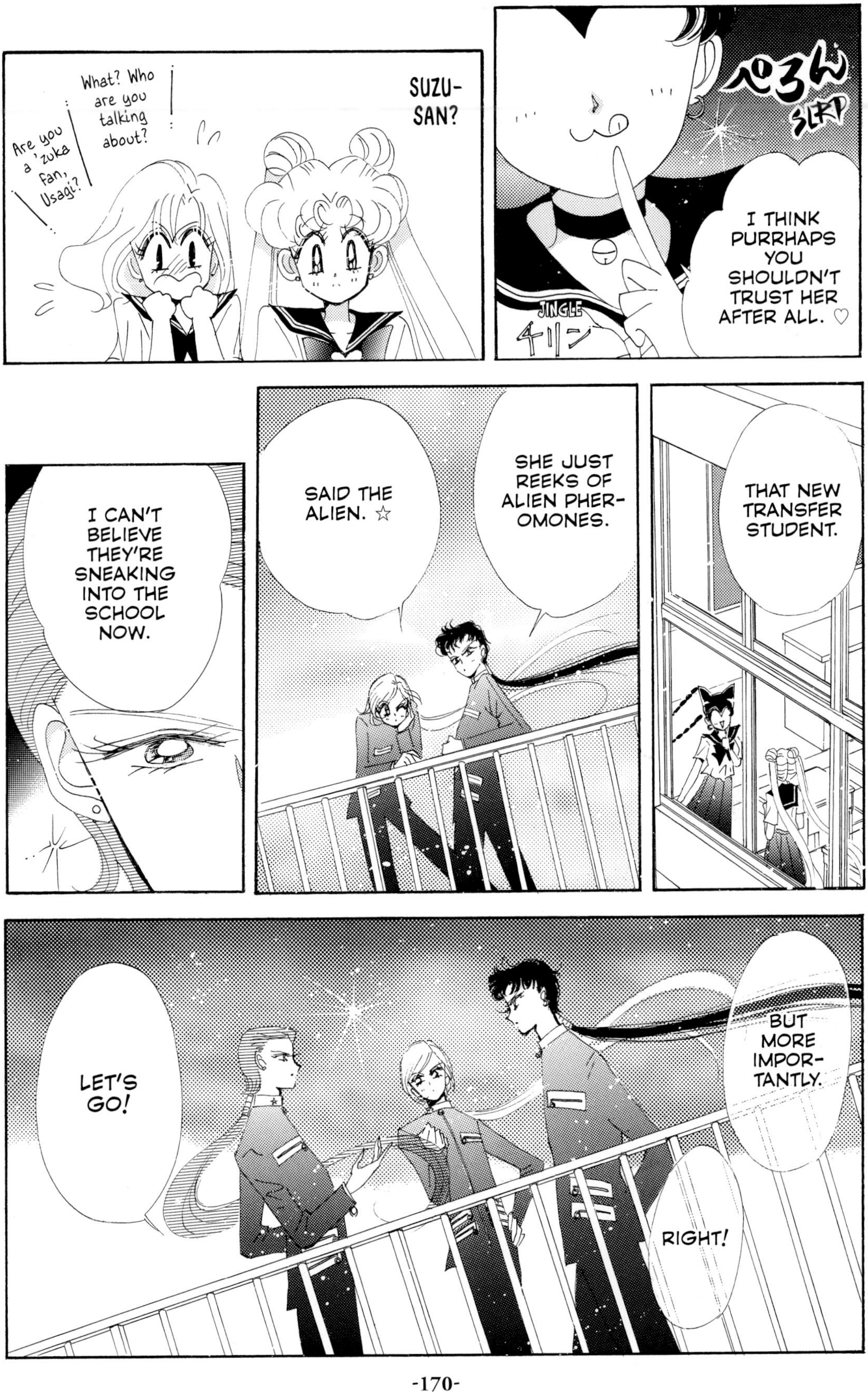
ぺろん
SLRP
I THINK PURRHAPS YOU SHOULDN'T TRUST HER AFTER ALL. ♡
JINGLE
チリン
SUZU-SAN?
What? Who are you talking about?
Are you a 'zuka fan, Usagi?
THAT NEW TRANSFER STUDENT.
SHE JUST REEKS OF ALIEN PHEROMONES.
SAID THE ALIEN. ☆
I CAN'T BELIEVE THEY'RE SNEAKING INTO THE SCHOOL NOW.
BUT MORE IMPORTANTLY.
RIGHT!
LET'S GO!

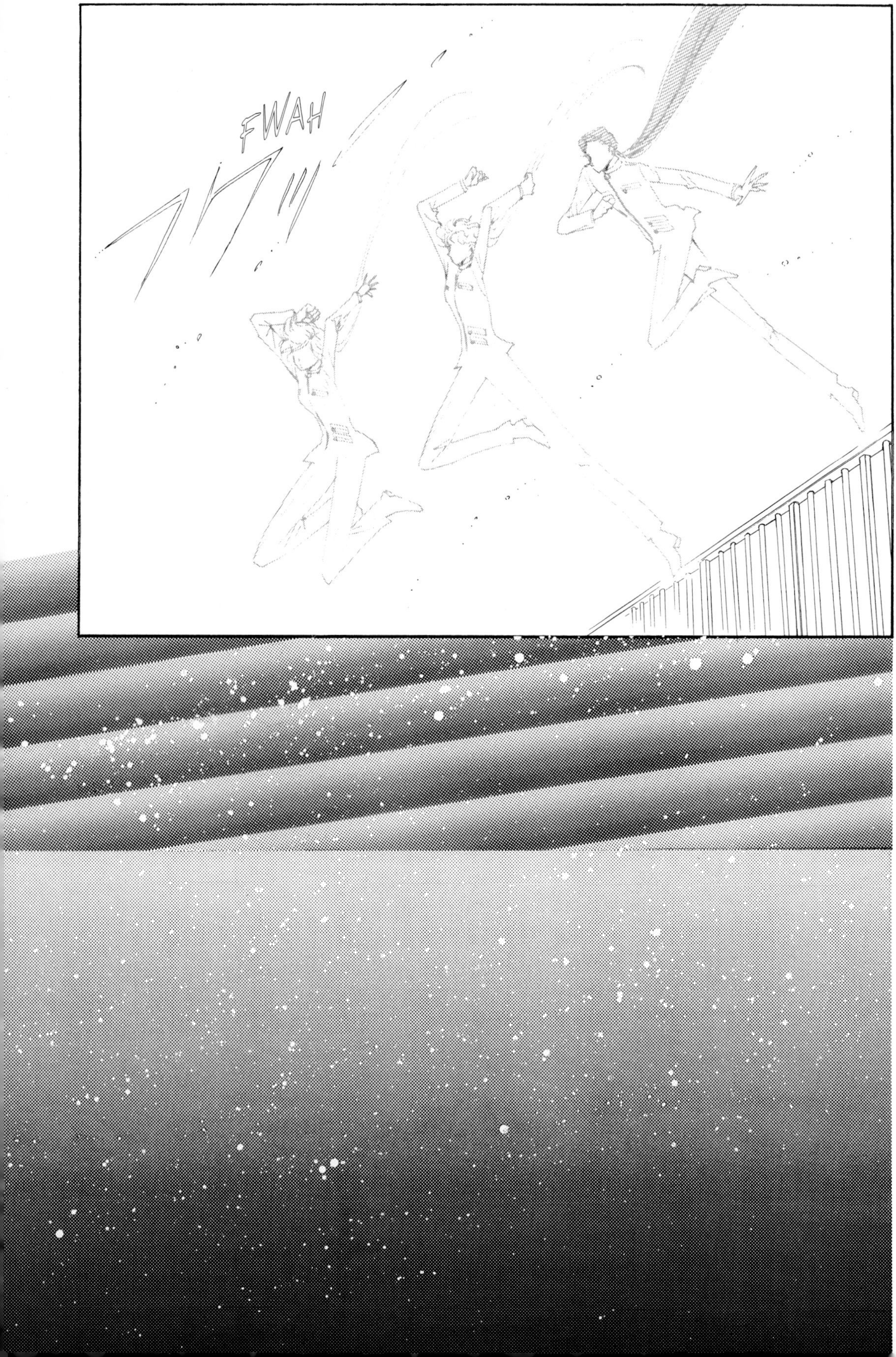
FWAH
フワッ!!

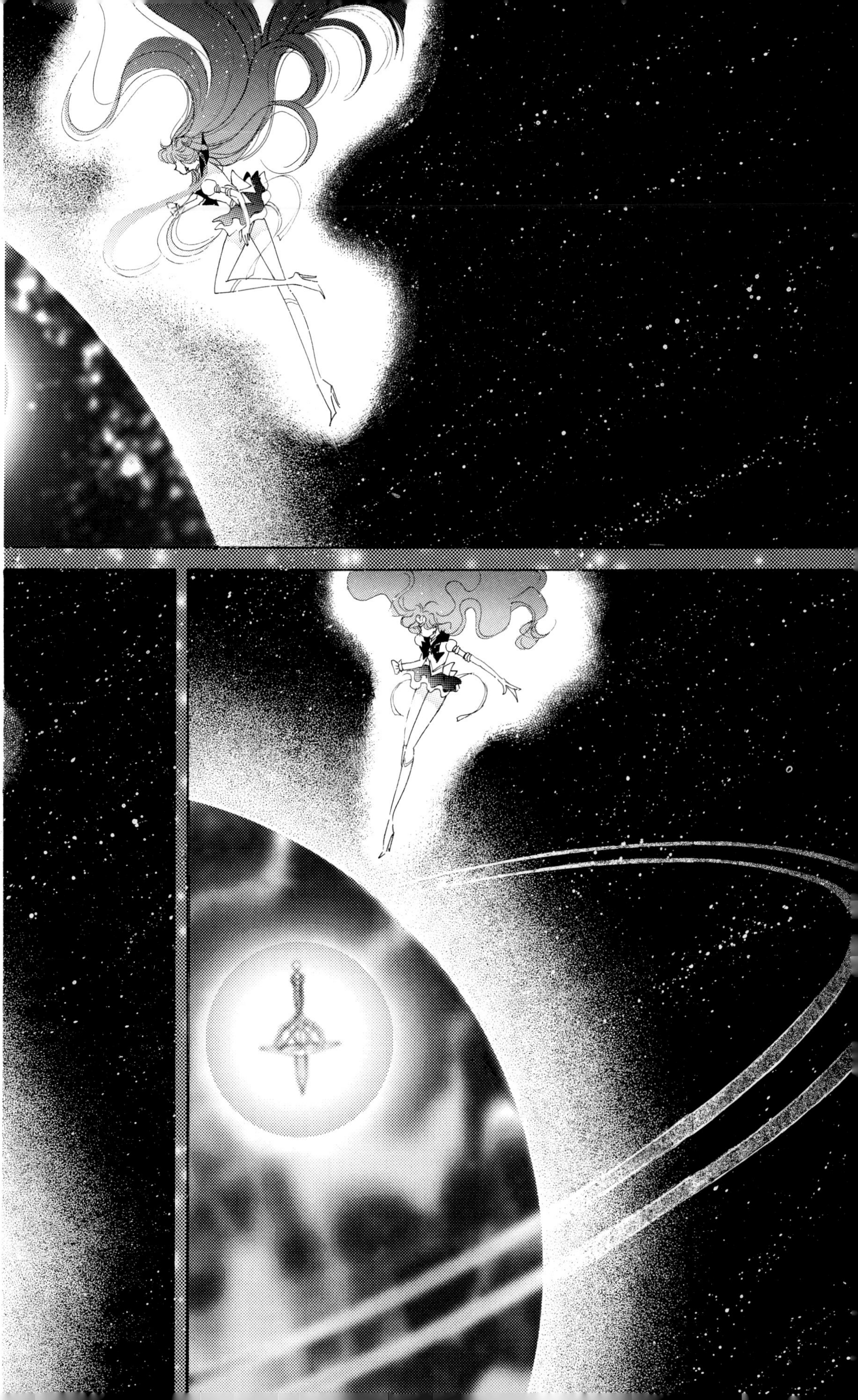

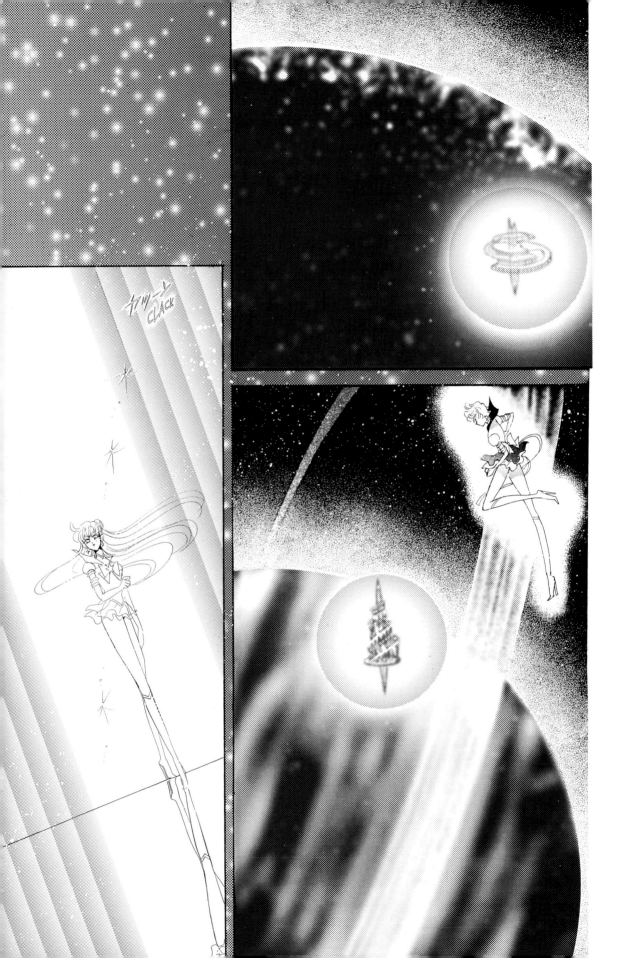

クラック
CLACK

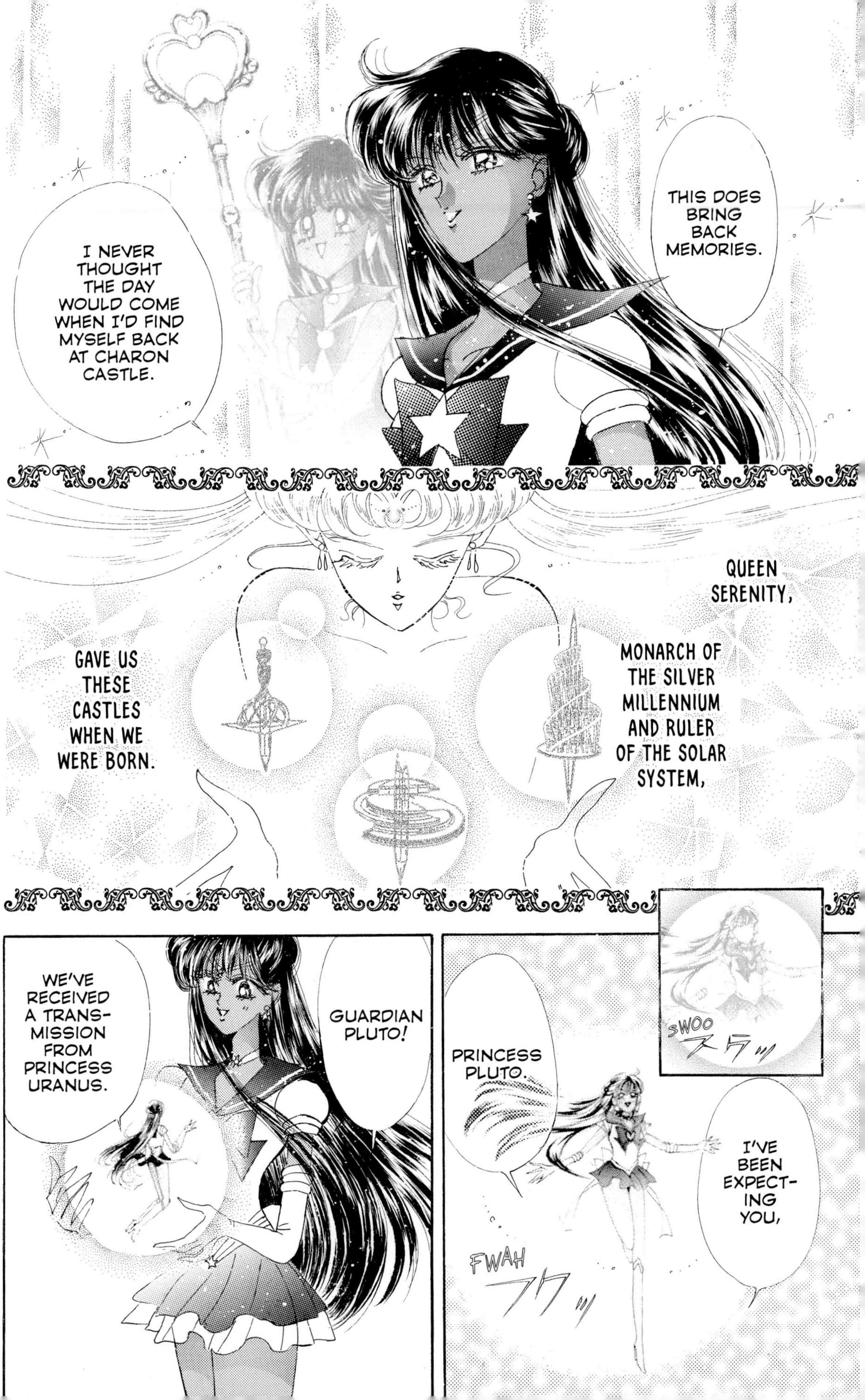
THIS DOES BRING BACK MEMORIES.
I NEVER THOUGHT THE DAY WOULD COME WHEN I'D FIND MYSELF BACK AT CHARON CASTLE.
QUEEN SERENITY,
MONARCH OF THE SILVER MILLENNIUM AND RULER OF THE SOLAR SYSTEM,
GAVE US THESE CASTLES WHEN WE WERE BORN.
SWOO スラッ
PRINCESS PLUTO.
I'VE BEEN EXPECTING YOU,
FWAH フワッ
GUARDIAN PLUTO!
WE'VE RECEIVED A TRANSMISSION FROM PRINCESS URANUS.

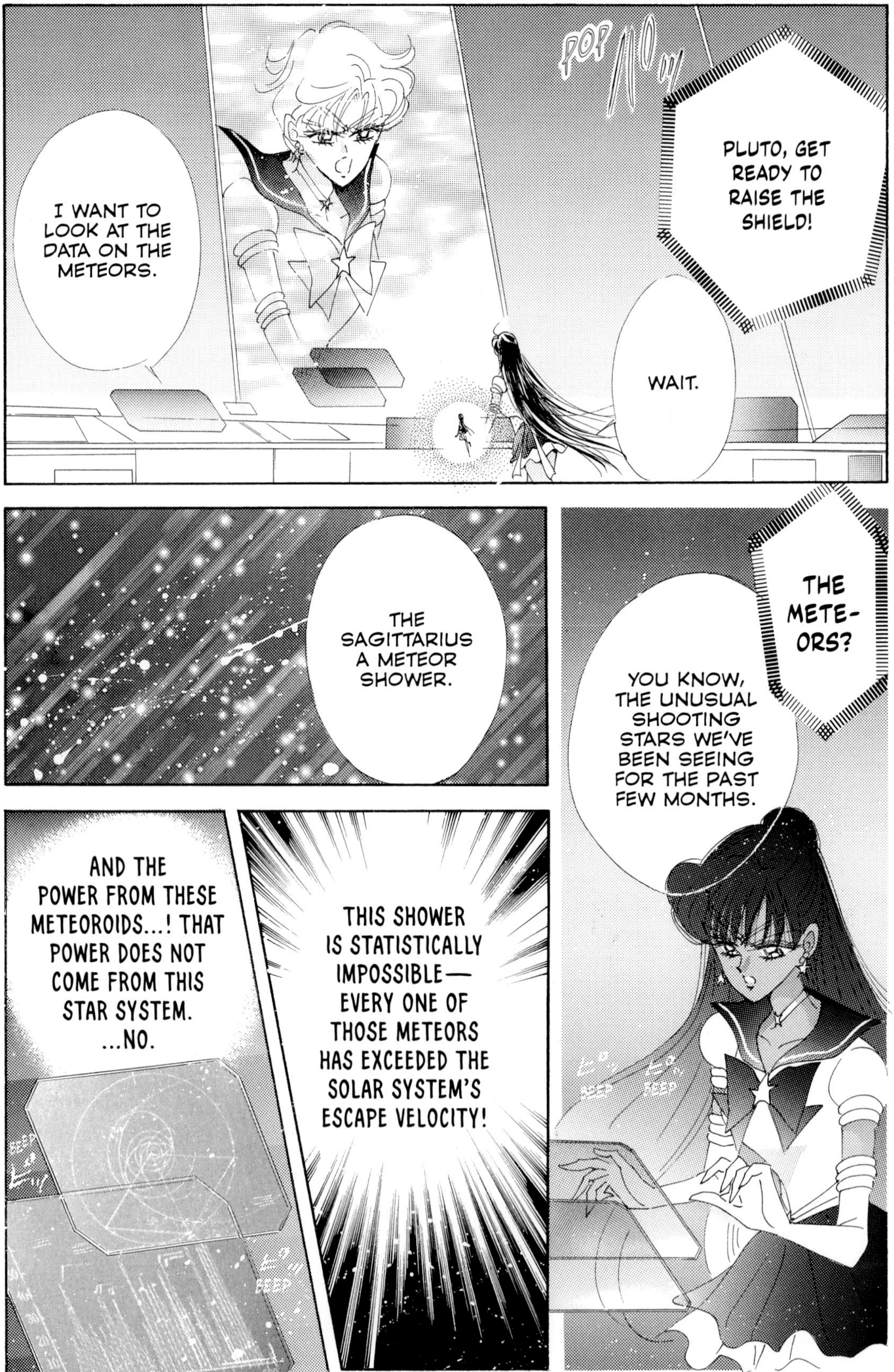

POP
PLUTO, GET READY TO RAISE THE SHIELD!
WAIT.
I WANT TO LOOK AT THE DATA ON THE METEORS.
THE METEORS?
YOU KNOW, THE UNUSUAL SHOOTING STARS WE'VE BEEN SEEING FOR THE PAST FEW MONTHS.
BEEP
BEEP
THE SAGITTARIUS A METEOR SHOWER.
THIS SHOWER IS STATISTICALLY IMPOSSIBLE—EVERY ONE OF THOSE METEORS HAS EXCEEDED THE SOLAR SYSTEM'S ESCAPE VELOCITY!
AND THE POWER FROM THESE METEOROIDS...! THAT POWER DOES NOT COME FROM THIS STAR SYSTEM. ...NO.
BEEP
BEEP

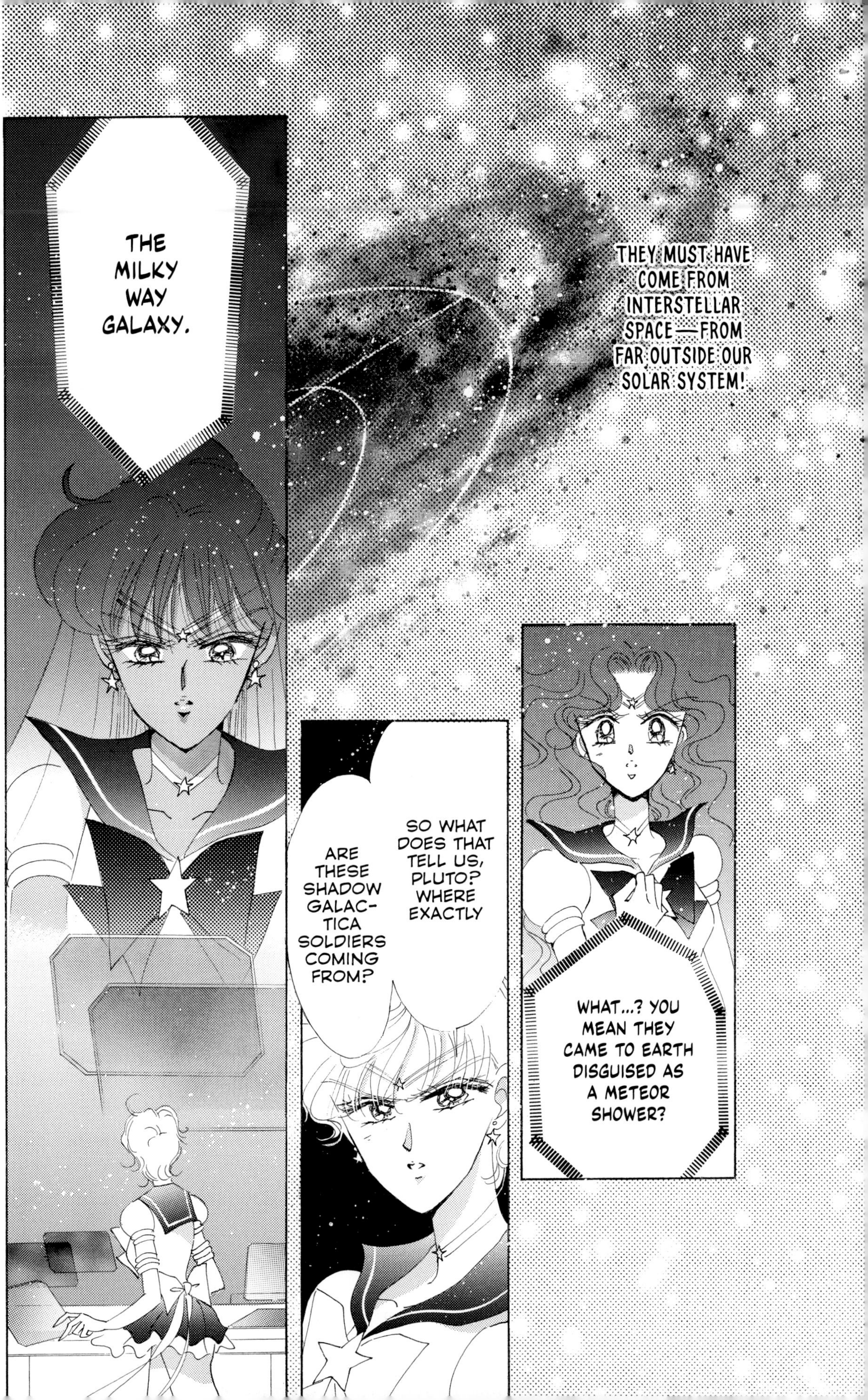
THEY MUST HAVE COME FROM INTERSTELLAR SPACE—FROM FAR OUTSIDE OUR SOLAR SYSTEM!
WHAT...? YOU MEAN THEY CAME TO EARTH DISGUISED AS A METEOR SHOWER?
SO WHAT DOES THAT TELL US, PLUTO? WHERE EXACTLY
ARE THESE SHADOW GALACTICA SOLDIERS COMING FROM?
THE MILKY WAY GALAXY.

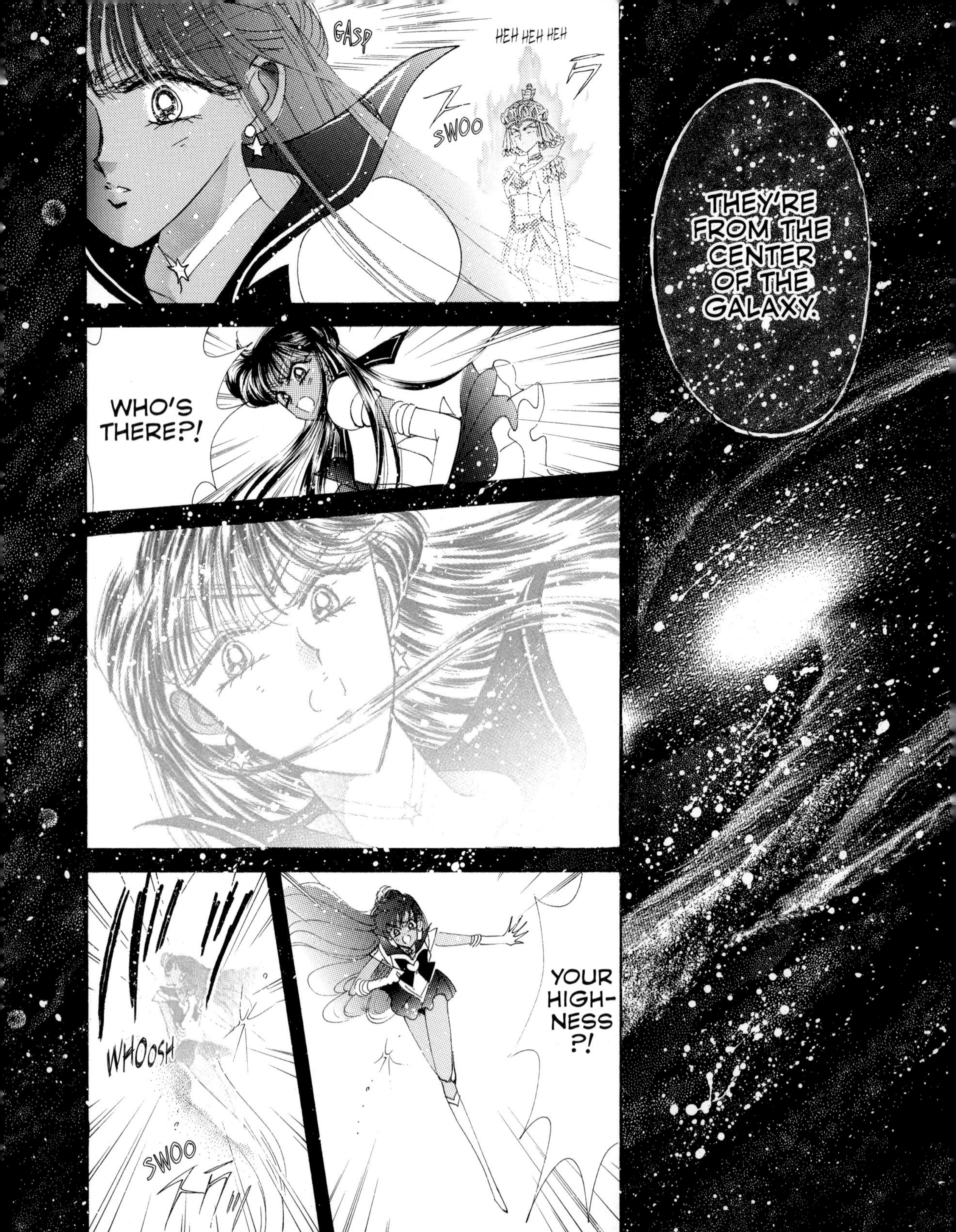
THEY'RE FROM THE CENTER OF THE GALAXY.
HEH HEH HEH
GASP
SWOO
WHO'S THERE?!
YOUR HIGH-NESS?!
WHOOSH
SWOO

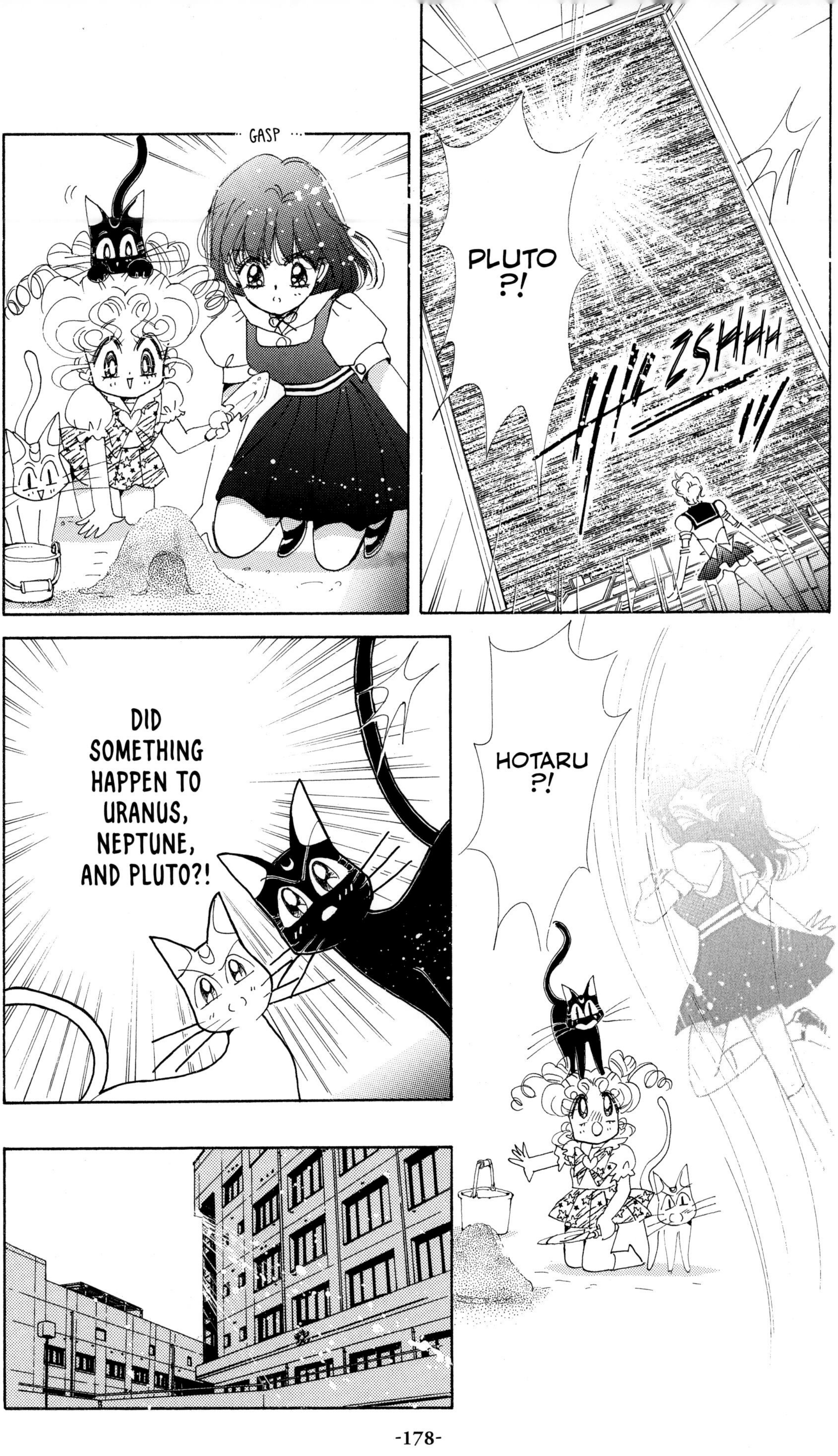
PLUTO ?!
ZSHHH
GASP
HOTARU ?!
DID SOMETHING HAPPEN TO URANUS, NEPTUNE, AND PLUTO?!

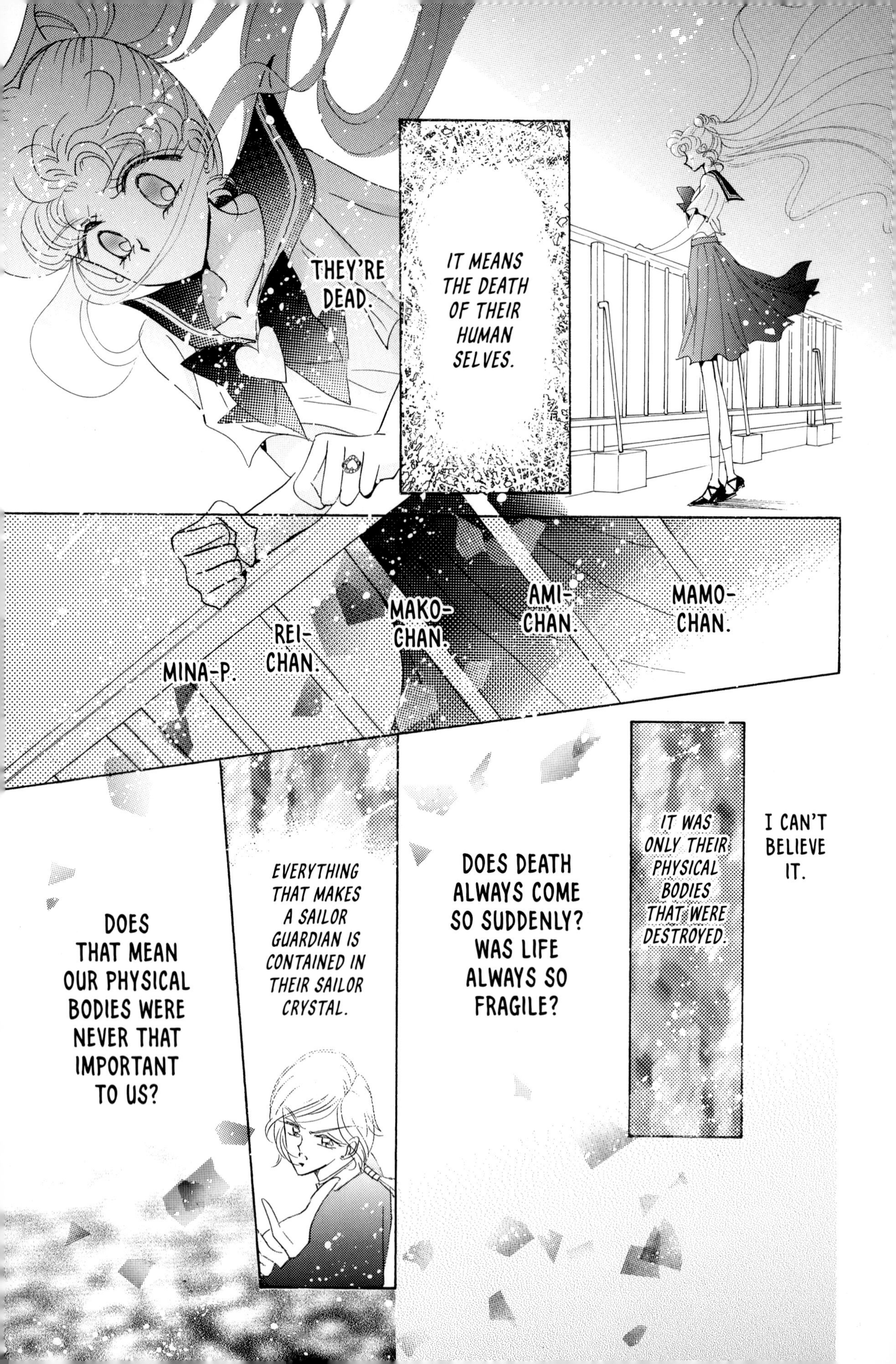
IT MEANS THE DEATH OF THEIR HUMAN SELVES.
THEY'RE DEAD.
MAMO-CHAN.
AMI-CHAN.
MAKO-CHAN.
REI-CHAN.
MINA-P.
I CAN'T BELIEVE IT.
IT WAS ONLY THEIR PHYSICAL BODIES THAT WERE DESTROYED.
DOES DEATH ALWAYS COME SO SUDDENLY? WAS LIFE ALWAYS SO FRAGILE?
EVERYTHING THAT MAKES A SAILOR GUARDIAN IS CONTAINED IN THEIR SAILOR CRYSTAL.
DOES THAT MEAN OUR PHYSICAL BODIES WERE NEVER THAT IMPORTANT TO US?

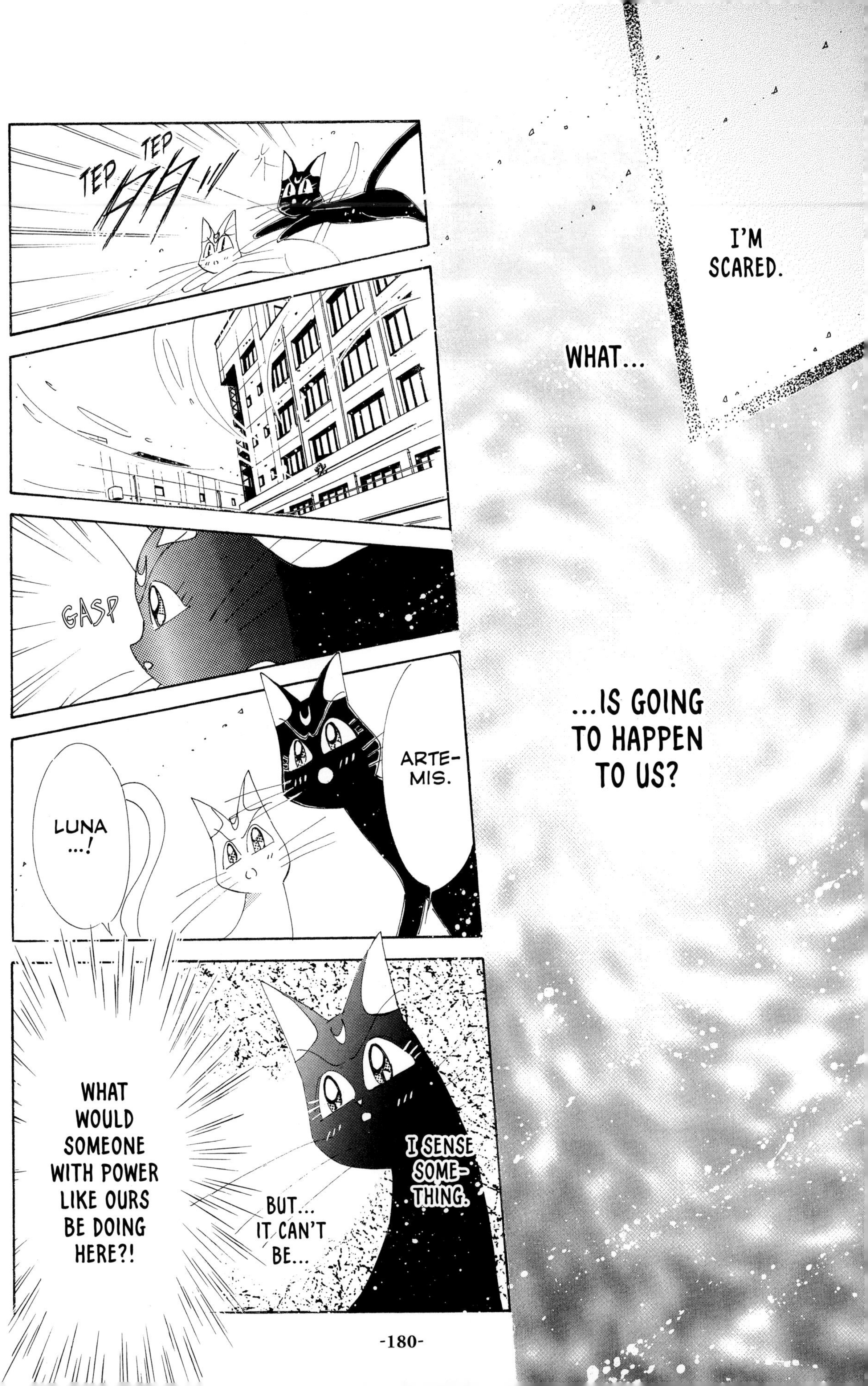
I'M SCARED.
WHAT...
...IS GOING TO HAPPEN TO US?
TEP TEP TEP
GASP
ARTE-MIS.
LUNA ...!
I SENSE SOME-THING.
BUT... IT CAN'T BE...
WHAT WOULD SOMEONE WITH POWER LIKE OURS BE DOING HERE?!

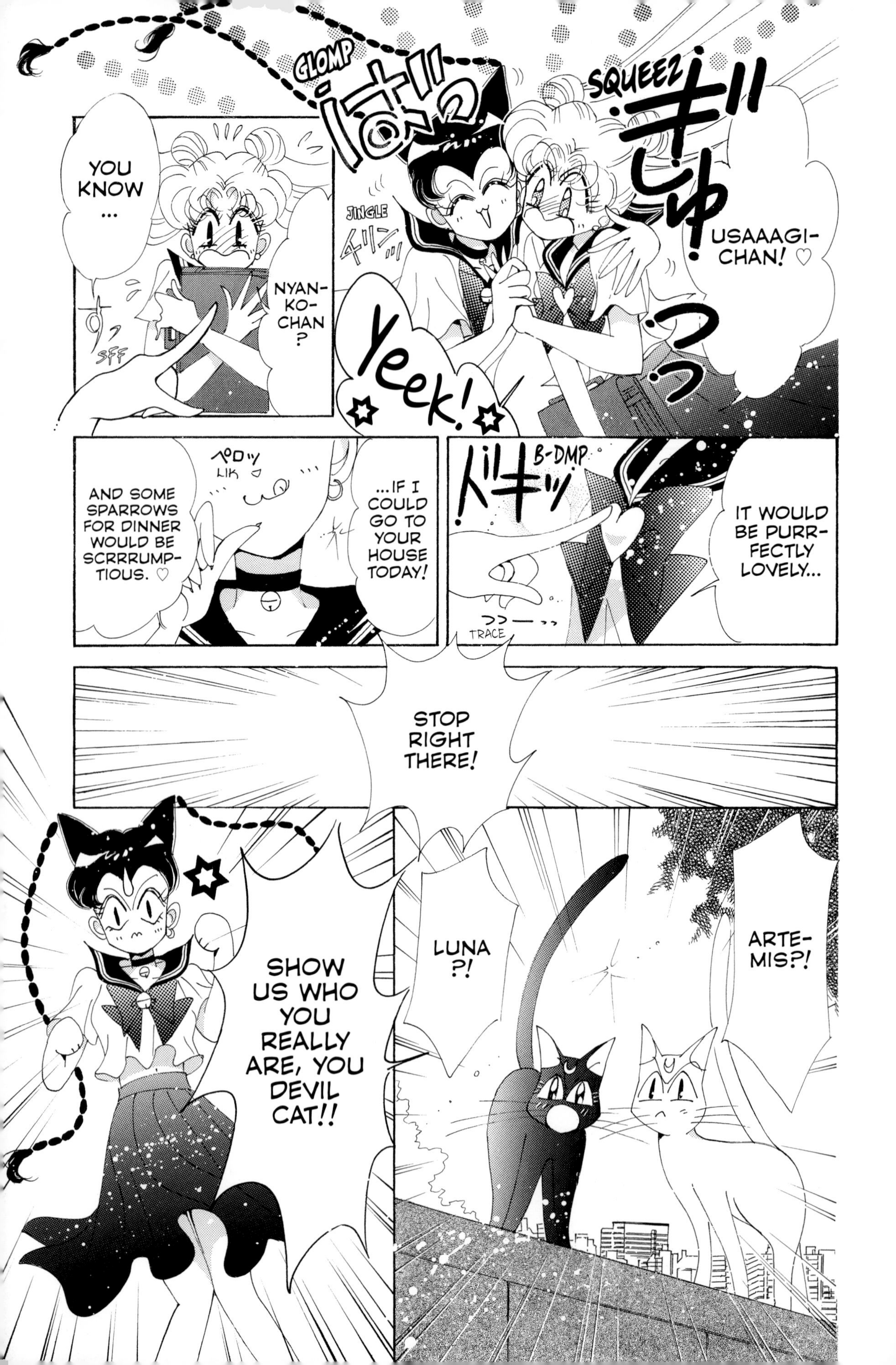
SQUEEZ
USAAAGI-CHAN! ♡
GLOMP
JINGLE
Yeek!
NYAN-KO-CHAN?
YOU KNOW...
SFF
IT WOULD BE PURR-FECTLY LOVELY...
ドキッ
B-DMP
TRACE
...IF I COULD GO TO YOUR HOUSE TODAY!
ペロッ
LIK
AND SOME SPARROWS FOR DINNER WOULD BE SCRRRUMP-TIOUS. ♡
STOP RIGHT THERE!
ARTE-MIS?!
LUNA?!
SHOW US WHO YOU REALLY ARE, YOU DEVIL CAT!!

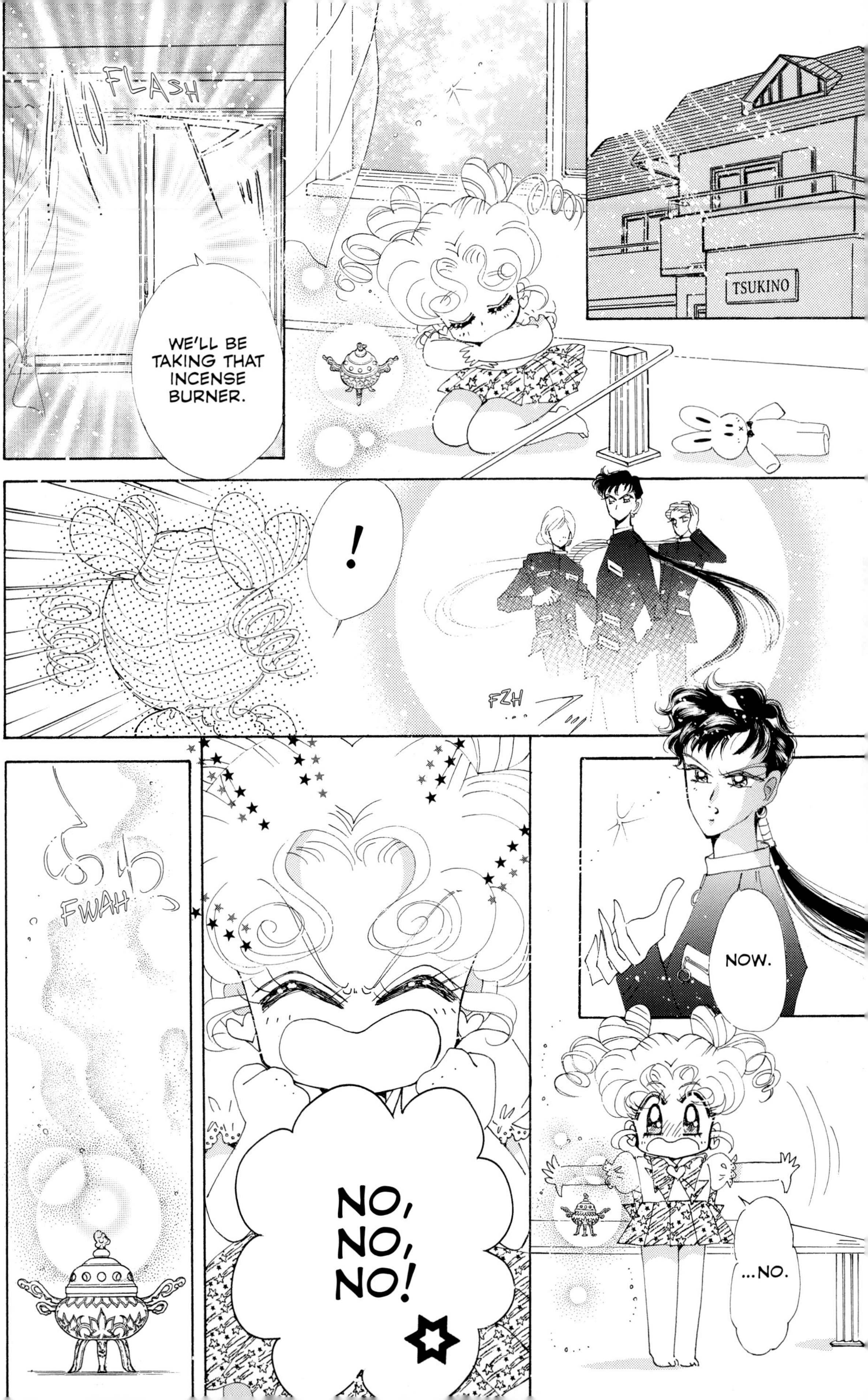
TSUKINO
FLASH
WE'LL BE TAKING THAT INCENSE BURNER.
FZH
!
NOW.
...NO.
NO, NO, NO!
FWAH

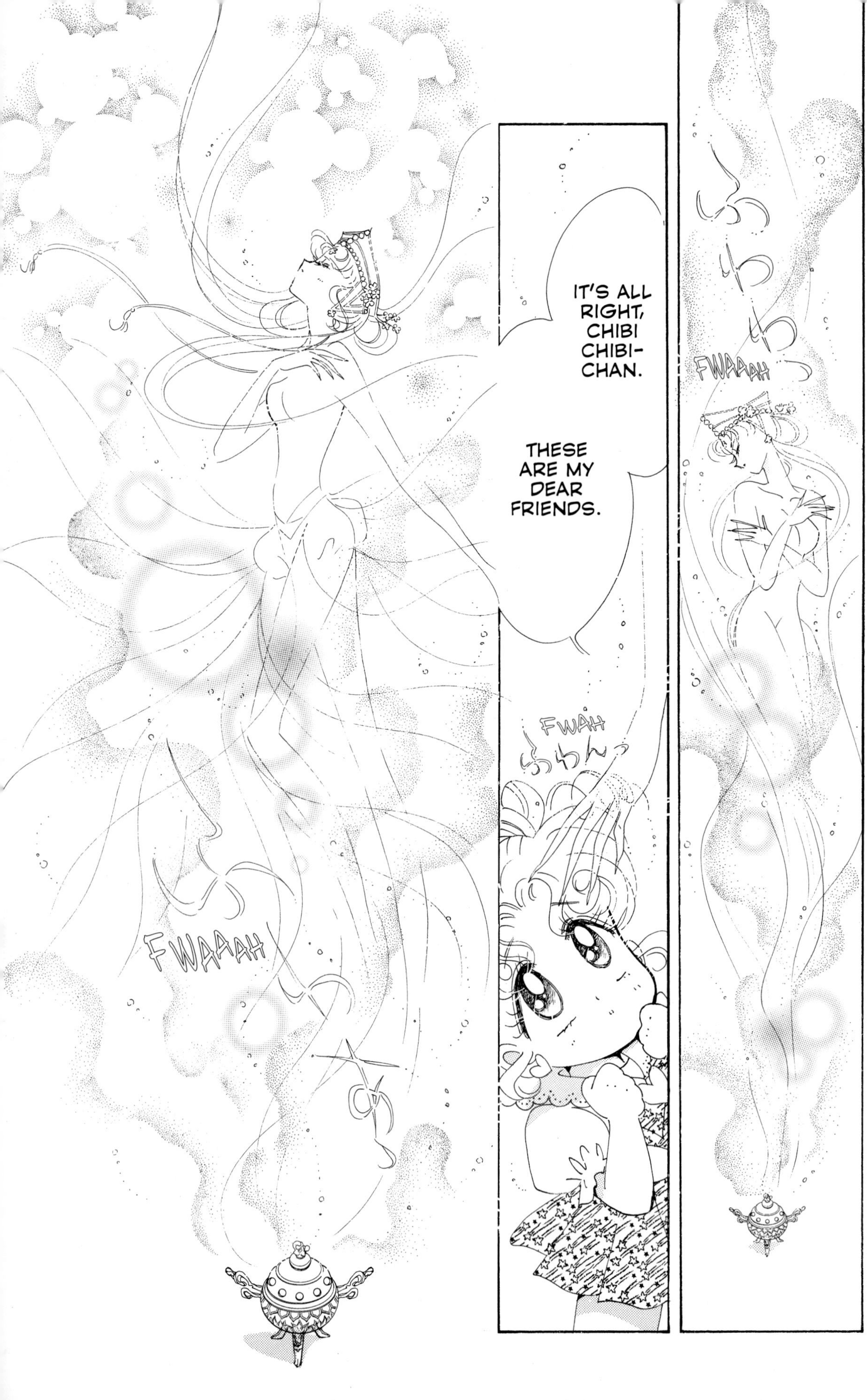
FWAAAH
IT'S ALL RIGHT, CHIBI CHIBI-CHAN.
THESE ARE MY DEAR FRIENDS.
FWAH
FWAAAH

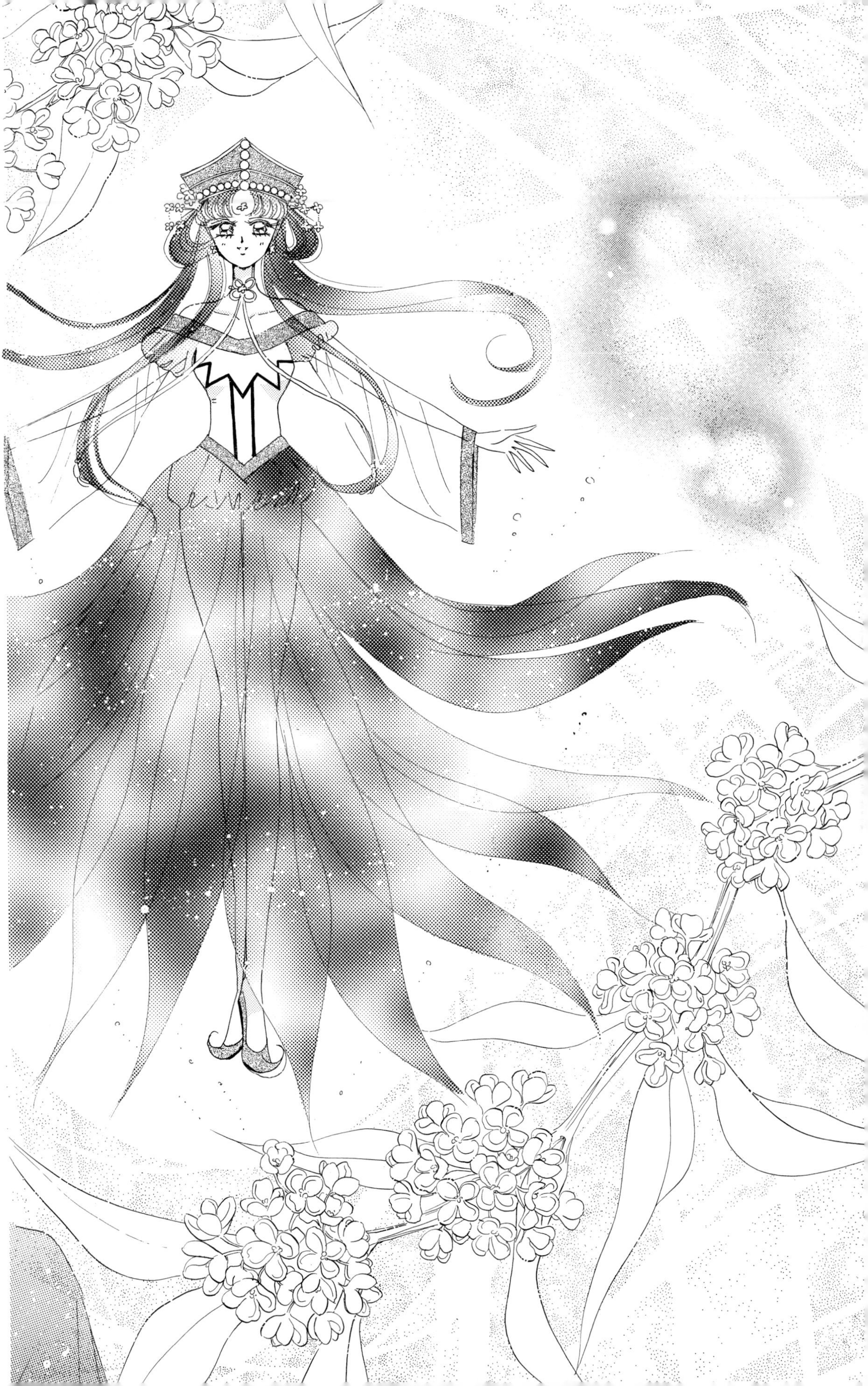

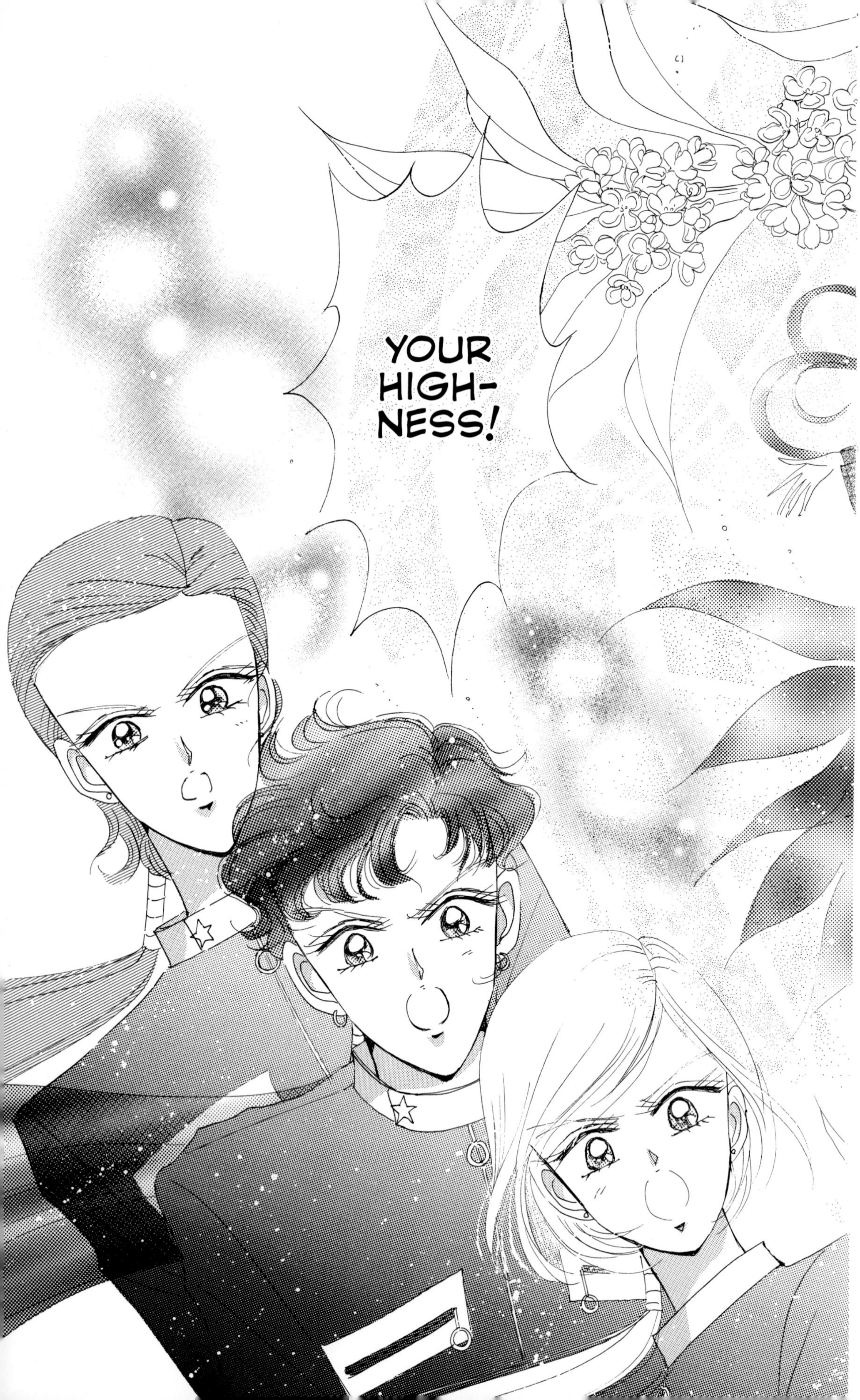
YOUR HIGH-NESS!

Pretty Guardian

Sailor Moon

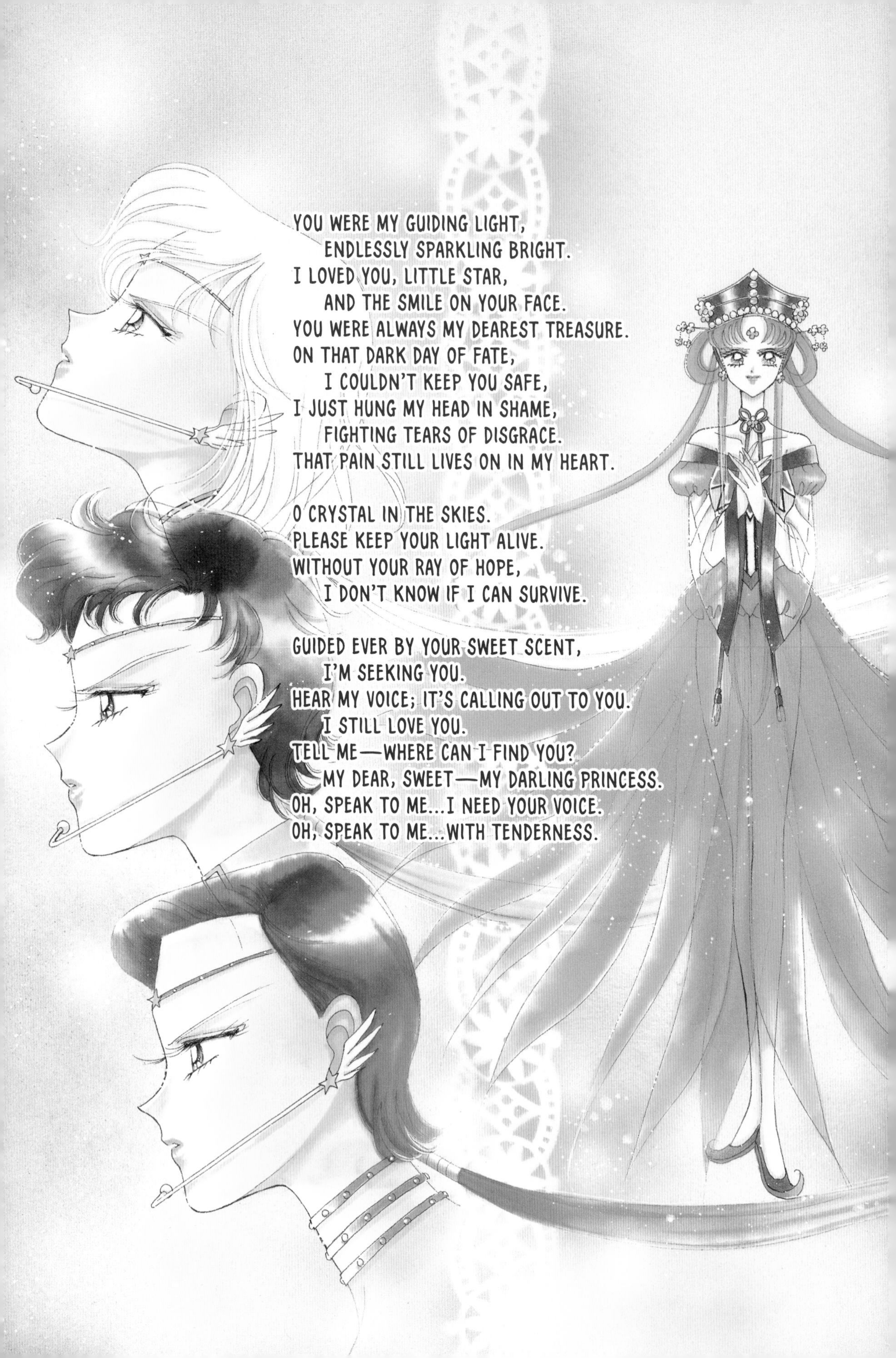
YOU WERE MY GUIDING LIGHT,
ENDLESSLY SPARKLING BRIGHT.
I LOVED YOU, LITTLE STAR,
AND THE SMILE ON YOUR FACE.
YOU WERE ALWAYS MY DEAREST TREASURE.
ON THAT DARK DAY OF FATE,
I COULDN'T KEEP YOU SAFE,
I JUST HUNG MY HEAD IN SHAME,
FIGHTING TEARS OF DISGRACE.
THAT PAIN STILL LIVES ON IN MY HEART.
O CRYSTAL IN THE SKIES.
PLEASE KEEP YOUR LIGHT ALIVE.
WITHOUT YOUR RAY OF HOPE,
I DON'T KNOW IF I CAN SURVIVE.
GUIDED EVER BY YOUR SWEET SCENT,
I'M SEEKING YOU.
HEAR MY VOICE; IT'S CALLING OUT TO YOU.
I STILL LOVE YOU.
TELL ME—WHERE CAN I FIND YOU?
MY DEAR, SWEET—MY DARLING PRINCESS.
OH, SPEAK TO ME...I NEED YOUR VOICE.
OH, SPEAK TO ME...WITH TENDERNESS.

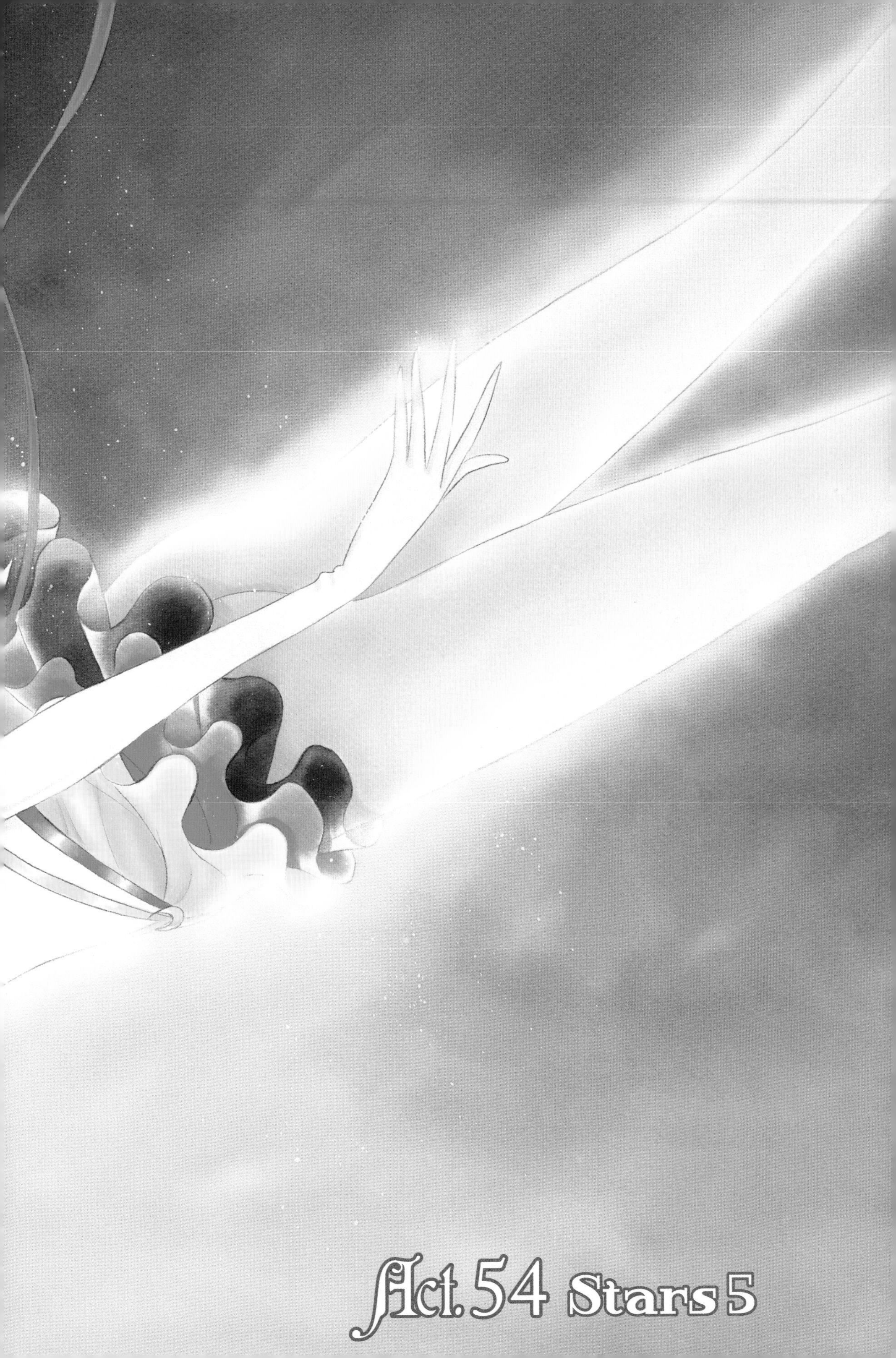

Act.54 Stars 5

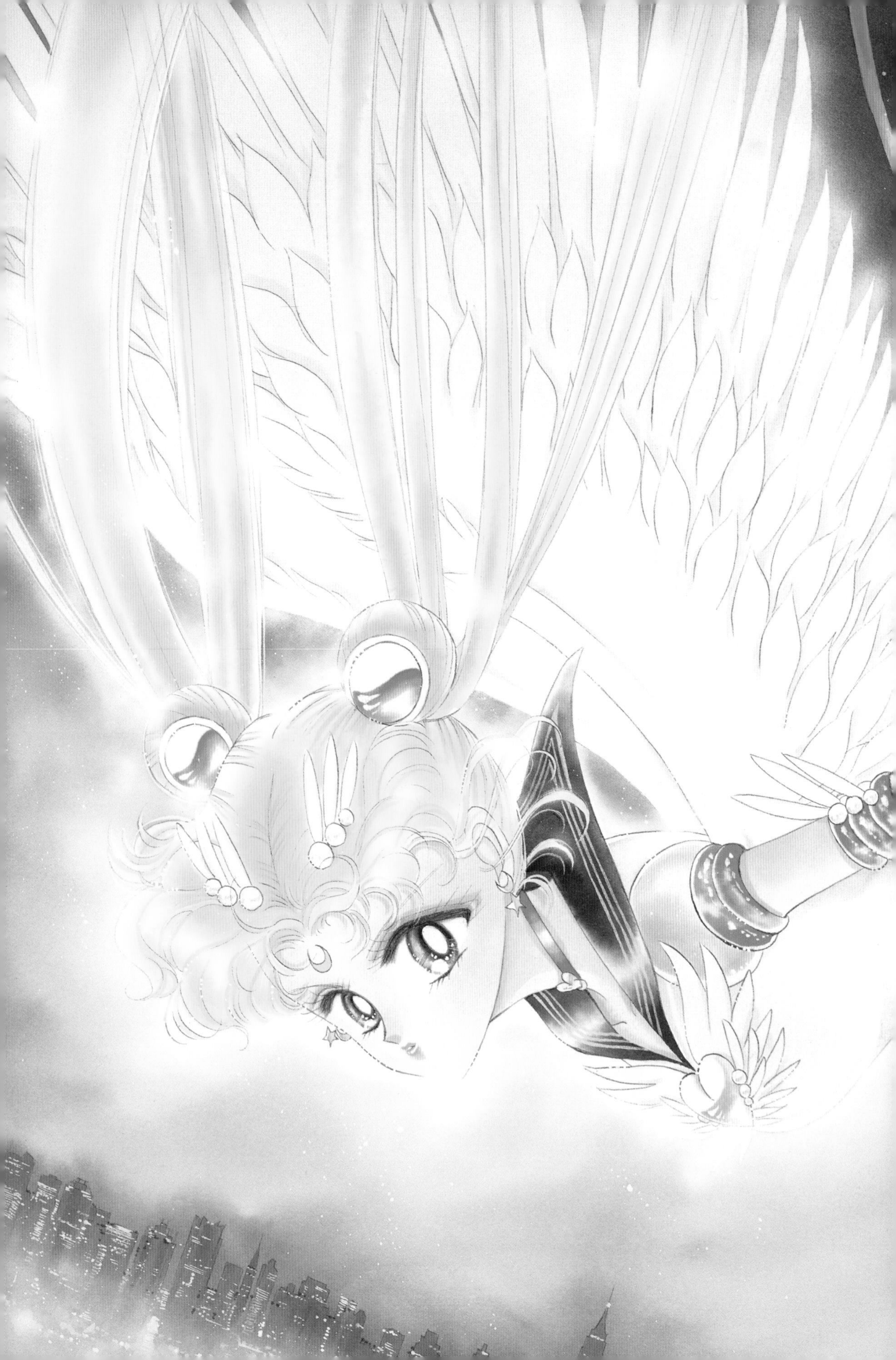

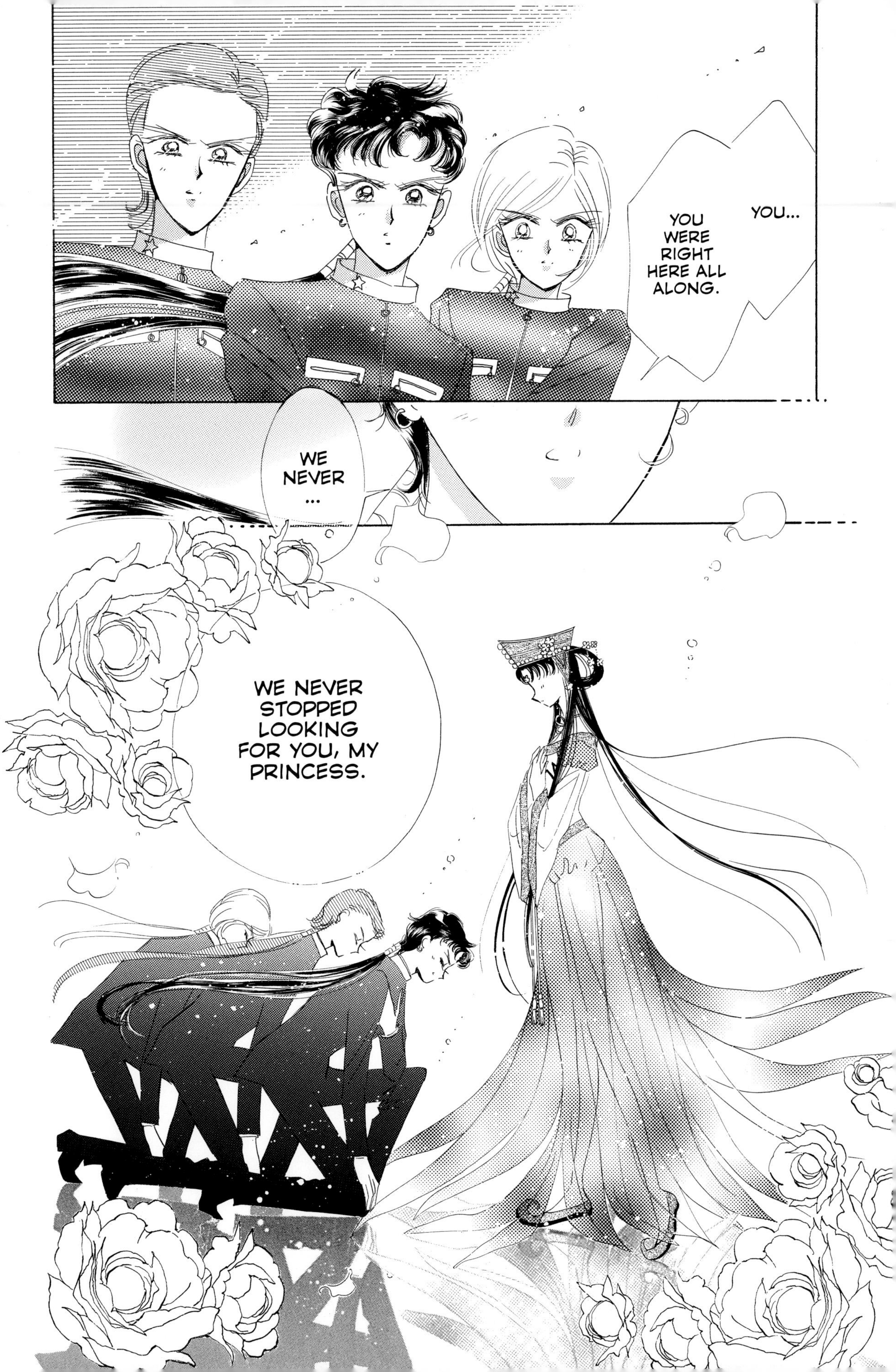
YOU...
YOU WERE RIGHT HERE ALL ALONG.
WE NEVER ...
WE NEVER STOPPED LOOKING FOR YOU, MY PRINCESS.

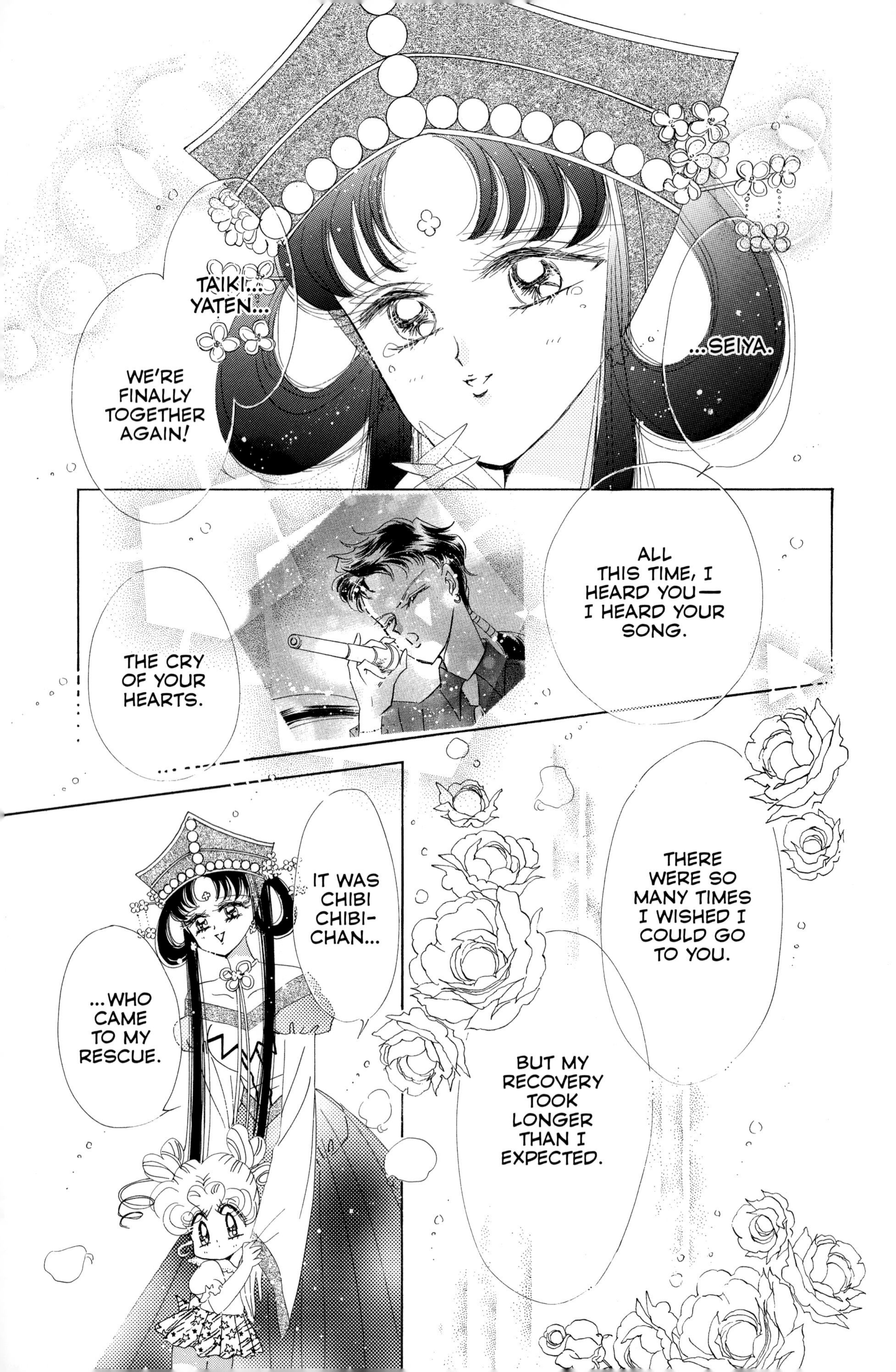
TAIKI... YATEN...
...SEIYA.
WE'RE FINALLY TOGETHER AGAIN!
ALL THIS TIME, I HEARD YOU— I HEARD YOUR SONG.
THE CRY OF YOUR HEARTS.
THERE WERE SO MANY TIMES I WISHED I COULD GO TO YOU.
BUT MY RECOVERY TOOK LONGER THAN I EXPECTED.
IT WAS CHIBI CHIBI-CHAN...
...WHO CAME TO MY RESCUE.

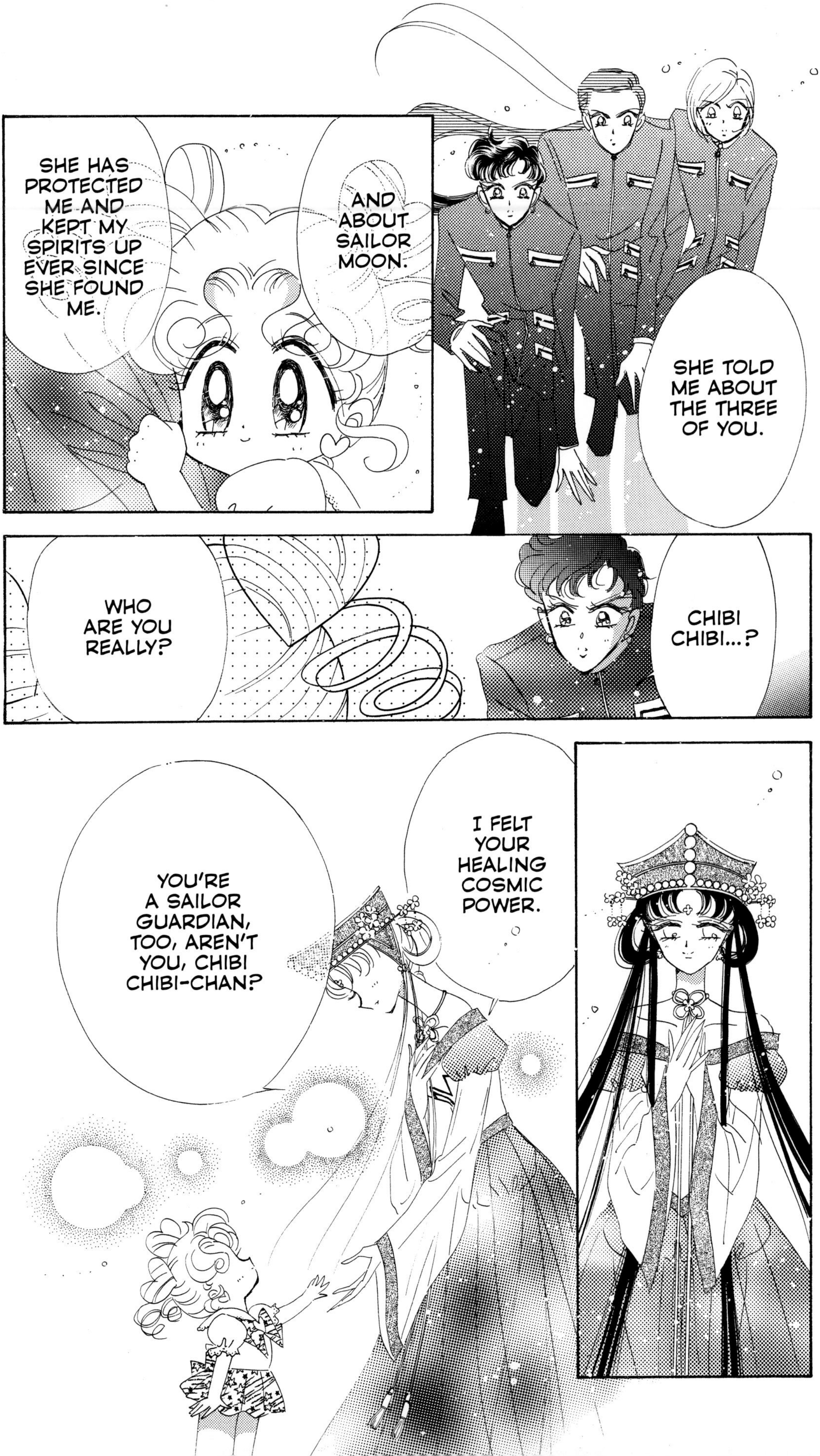
SHE TOLD ME ABOUT THE THREE OF YOU.
AND ABOUT SAILOR MOON.
SHE HAS PROTECTED ME AND KEPT MY SPIRITS UP EVER SINCE SHE FOUND ME.
CHIBI CHIBI...?
WHO ARE YOU REALLY?
I FELT YOUR HEALING COSMIC POWER.
YOU'RE A SAILOR GUARDIAN, TOO, AREN'T YOU, CHIBI CHIBI-CHAN?

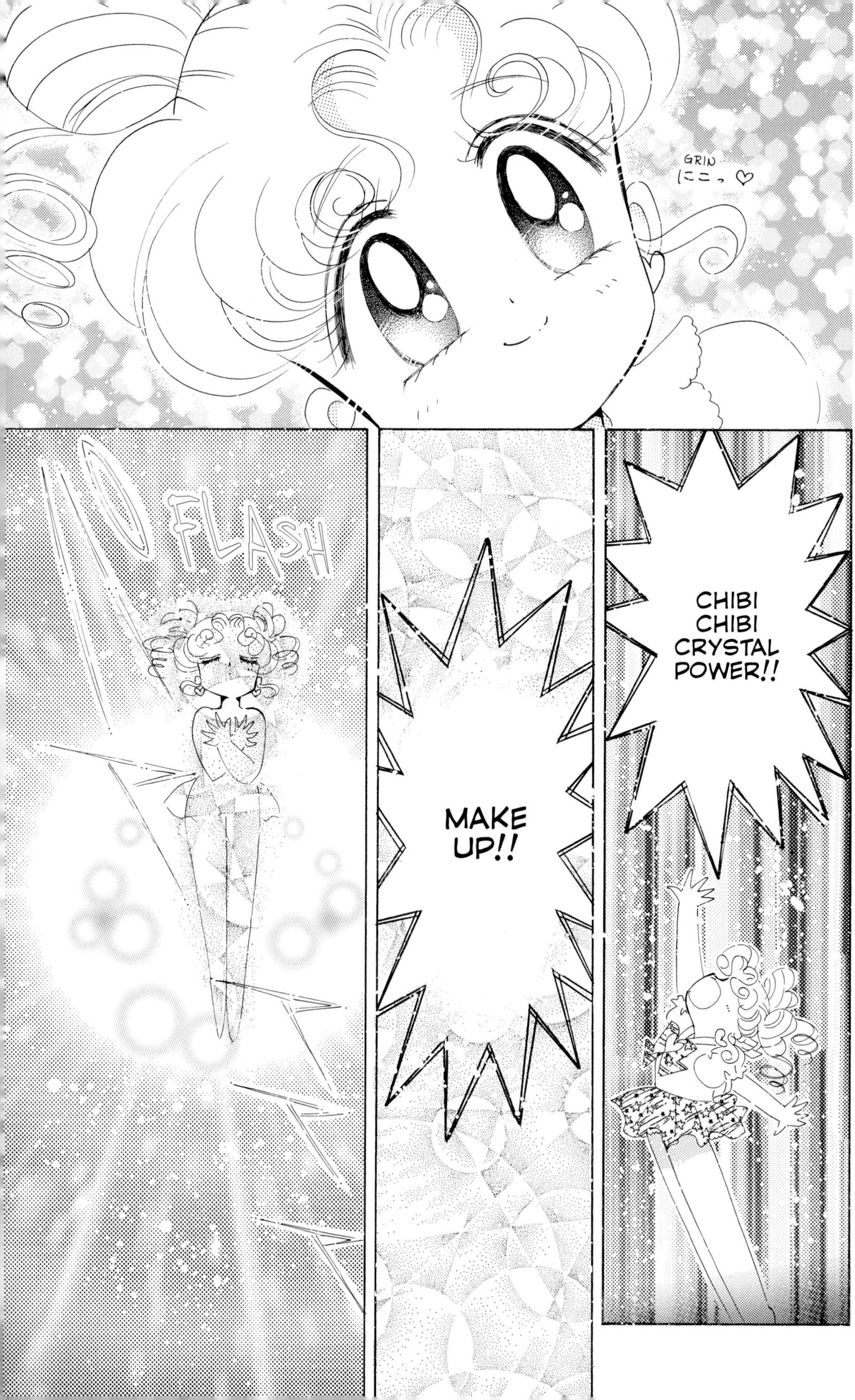
GRIN
にこっ♡
CHIBI CHIBI CRYSTAL POWER!!
MAKE UP!!
FLASH

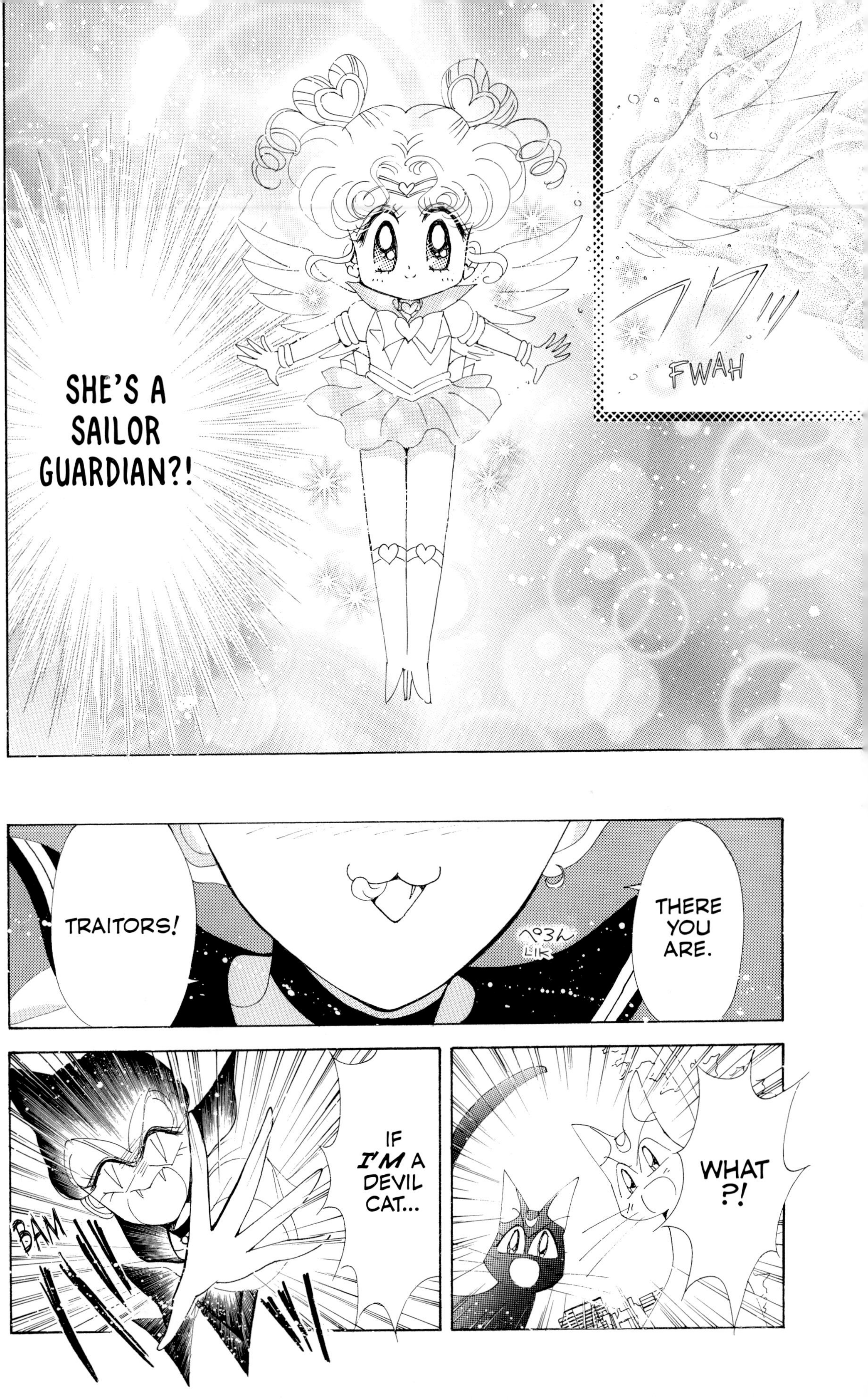
FWAH
SHE'S A SAILOR GUARDIAN?!
THERE YOU ARE.
LIK
TRAITORS!
WHAT?!
IF I'M A DEVIL CAT...
BAM

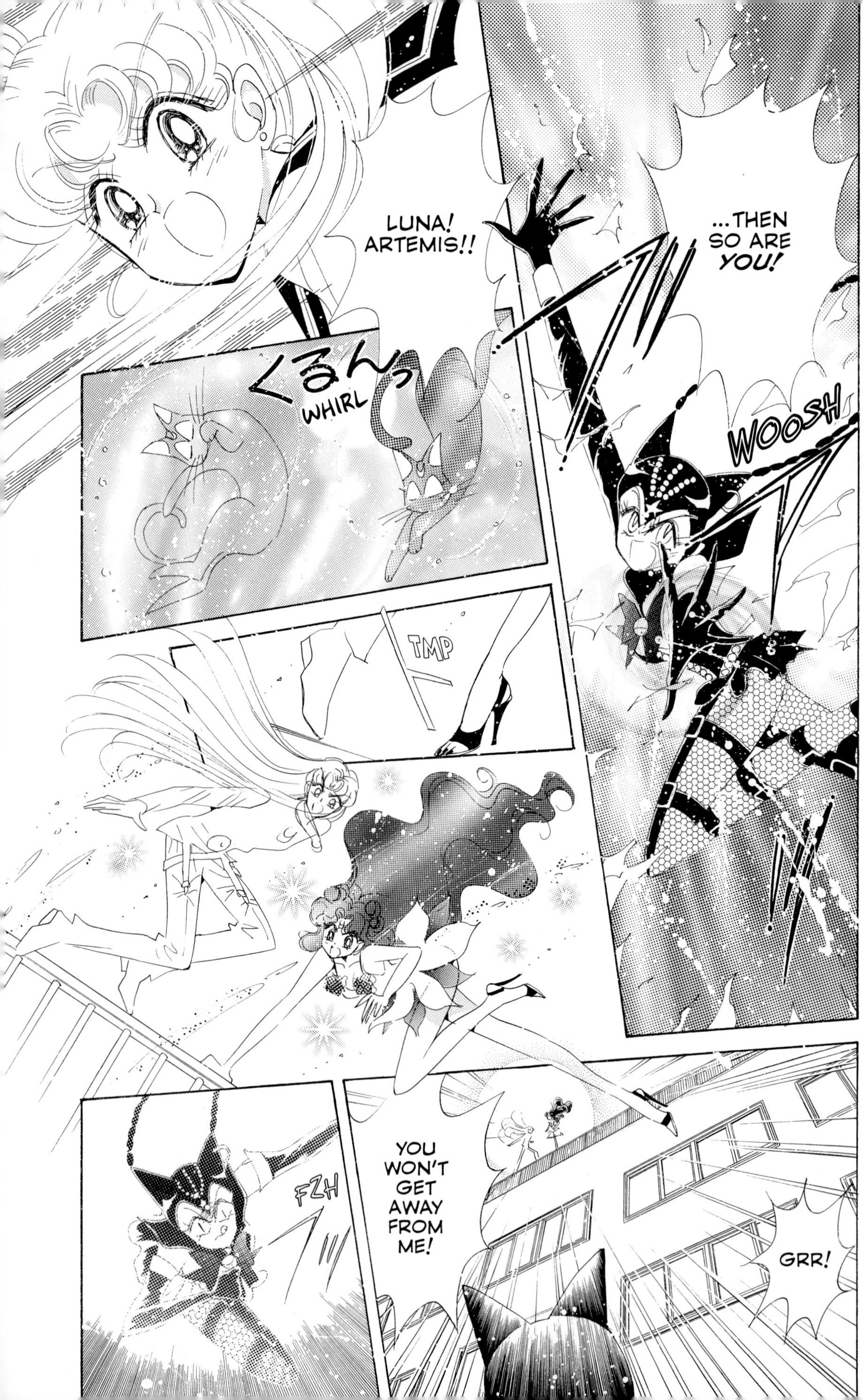
...THEN SO ARE YOU!
WOOSH
LUNA! ARTEMIS!!
くるんっ
WHIRL
TMP
GRR!
YOU WON'T GET AWAY FROM ME!
FZH

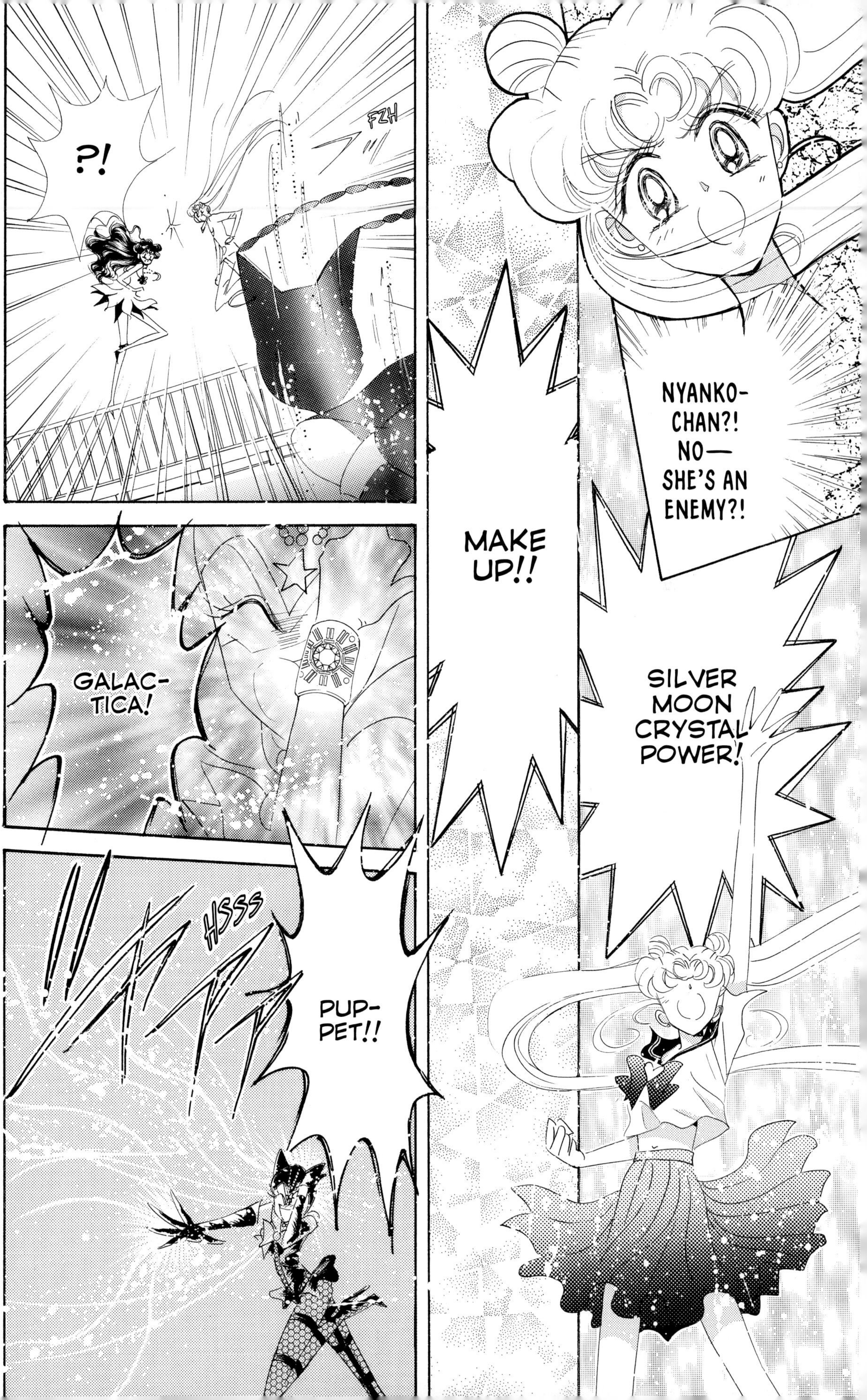
NYANKO-CHAN?! NO—SHE'S AN ENEMY?!
SILVER MOON CRYSTAL POWER!
MAKE UP!!
FZH
?!
GALAC-TICA!
HSSS
PUP-PET!!

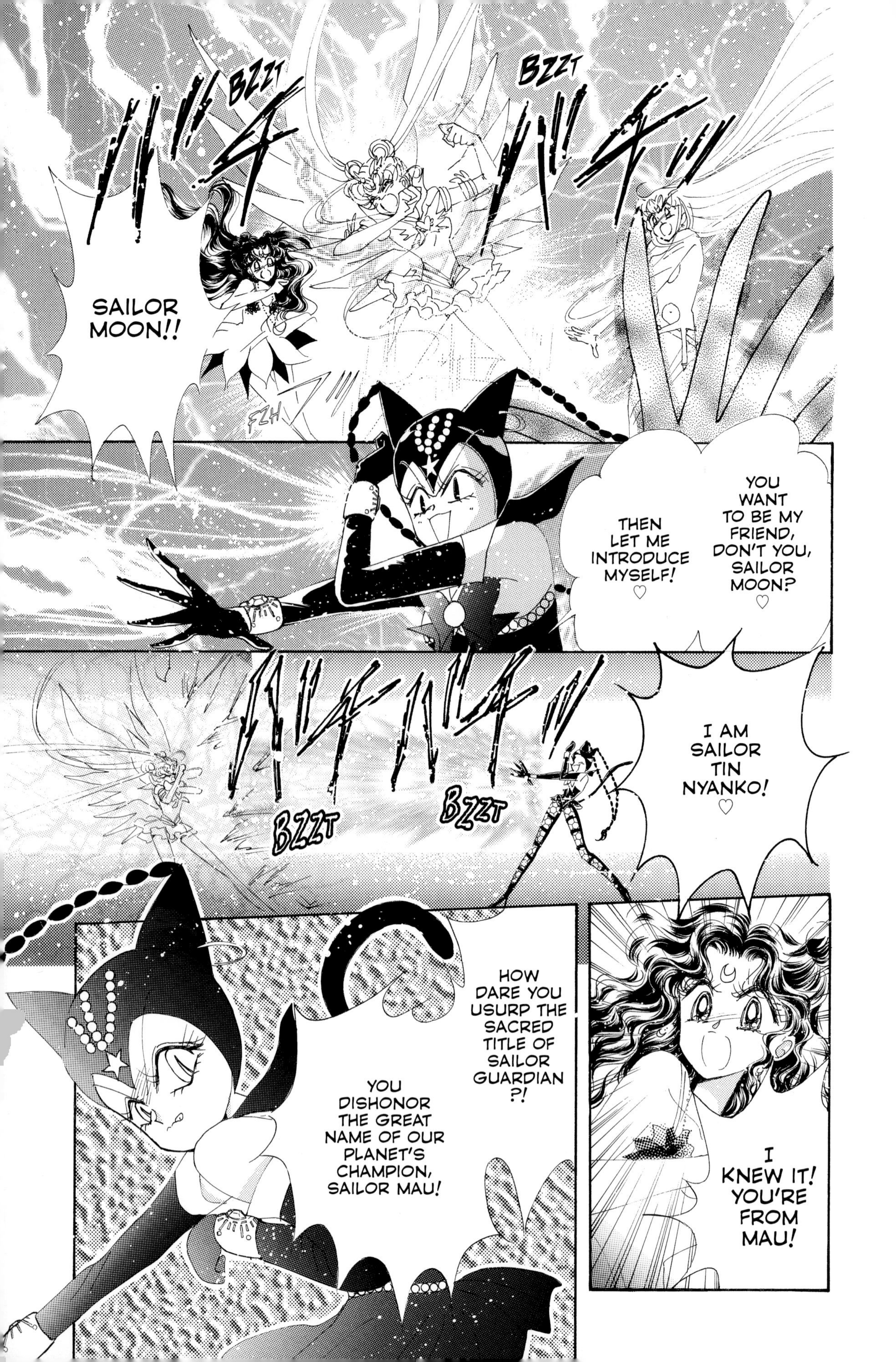
BZZT
BZZT
SAILOR MOON!!
FZH
YOU WANT TO BE MY FRIEND, DON'T YOU, SAILOR MOON? ♡
THEN LET ME INTRODUCE MYSELF! ♡
I AM SAILOR TIN NYANKO! ♡
BZZT
BZZT
I KNEW IT! YOU'RE FROM MAU!
HOW DARE YOU USURP THE SACRED TITLE OF SAILOR GUARDIAN?!
YOU DISHONOR THE GREAT NAME OF OUR PLANET'S CHAMPION, SAILOR MAU!

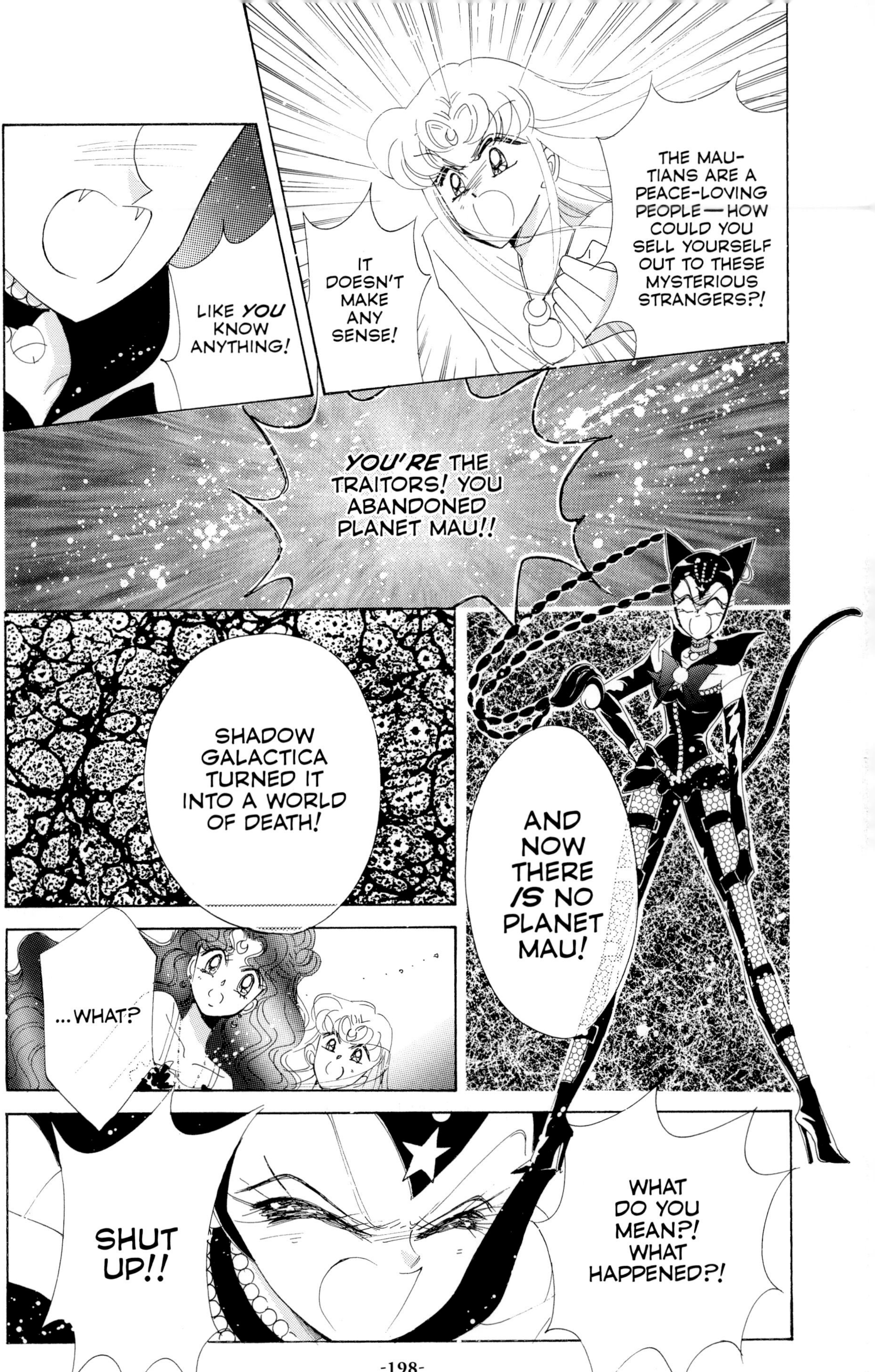
THE MAU-TIANS ARE A PEACE-LOVING PEOPLE—HOW COULD YOU SELL YOURSELF OUT TO THESE MYSTERIOUS STRANGERS?!
IT DOESN'T MAKE ANY SENSE!
LIKE *YOU* KNOW ANYTHING!
YOU'RE THE TRAITORS! YOU ABANDONED PLANET MAU!!
SHADOW GALACTICA TURNED IT INTO A WORLD OF DEATH!
AND NOW THERE *IS* NO PLANET MAU!
...WHAT?
WHAT DO YOU MEAN?! WHAT HAPPENED?!
SHUT UP!!

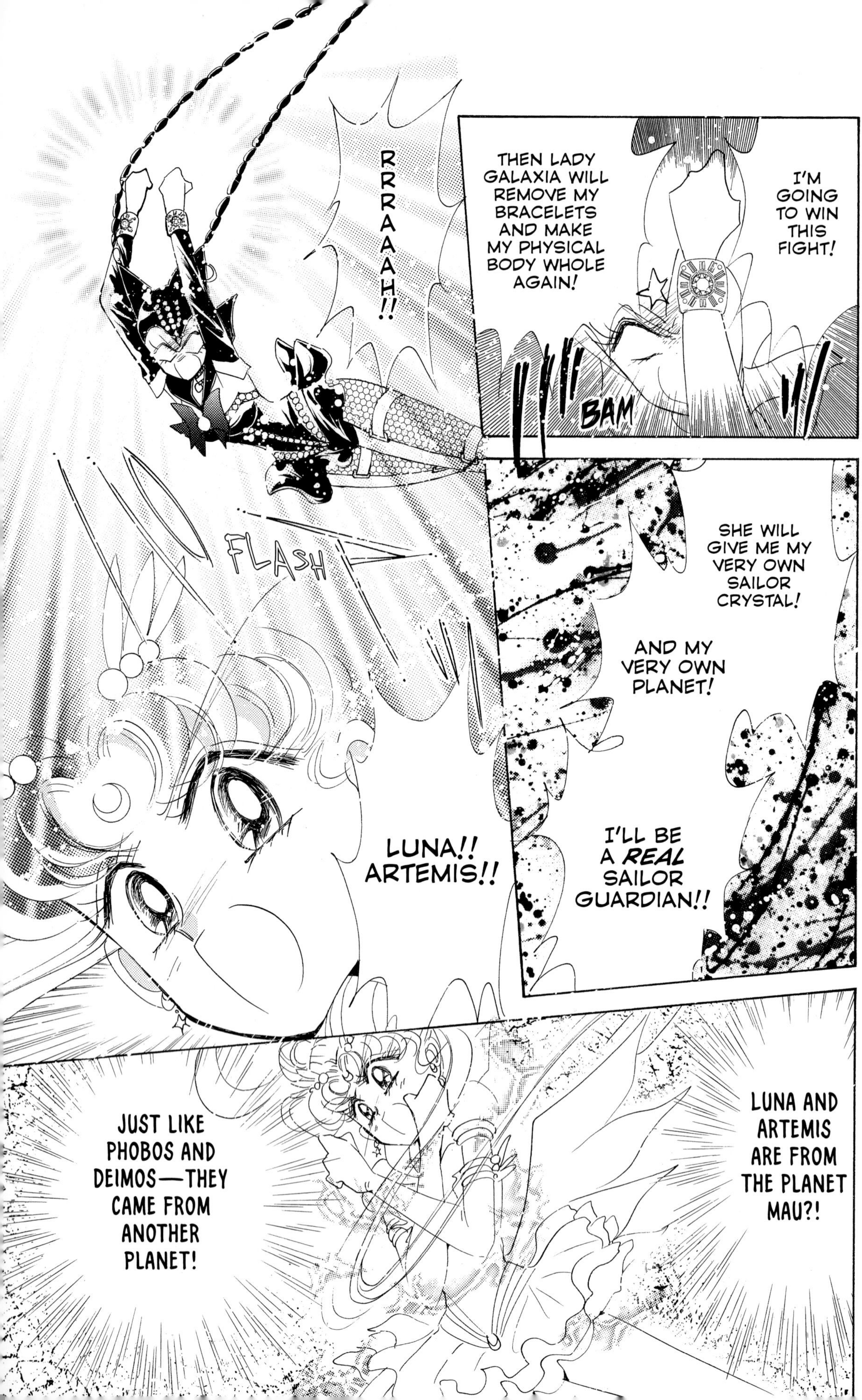
I'M GOING TO WIN THIS FIGHT!
THEN LADY GALAXIA WILL REMOVE MY BRACELETS AND MAKE MY PHYSICAL BODY WHOLE AGAIN!
BAM
SHE WILL GIVE ME MY VERY OWN SAILOR CRYSTAL!
AND MY VERY OWN PLANET!
I'LL BE A *REAL* SAILOR GUARDIAN!!
RRRAAAAH!!
FLASH
LUNA!! ARTEMIS!!
LUNA AND ARTEMIS ARE FROM THE PLANET MAU?!
JUST LIKE PHOBOS AND DEIMOS—THEY CAME FROM ANOTHER PLANET!

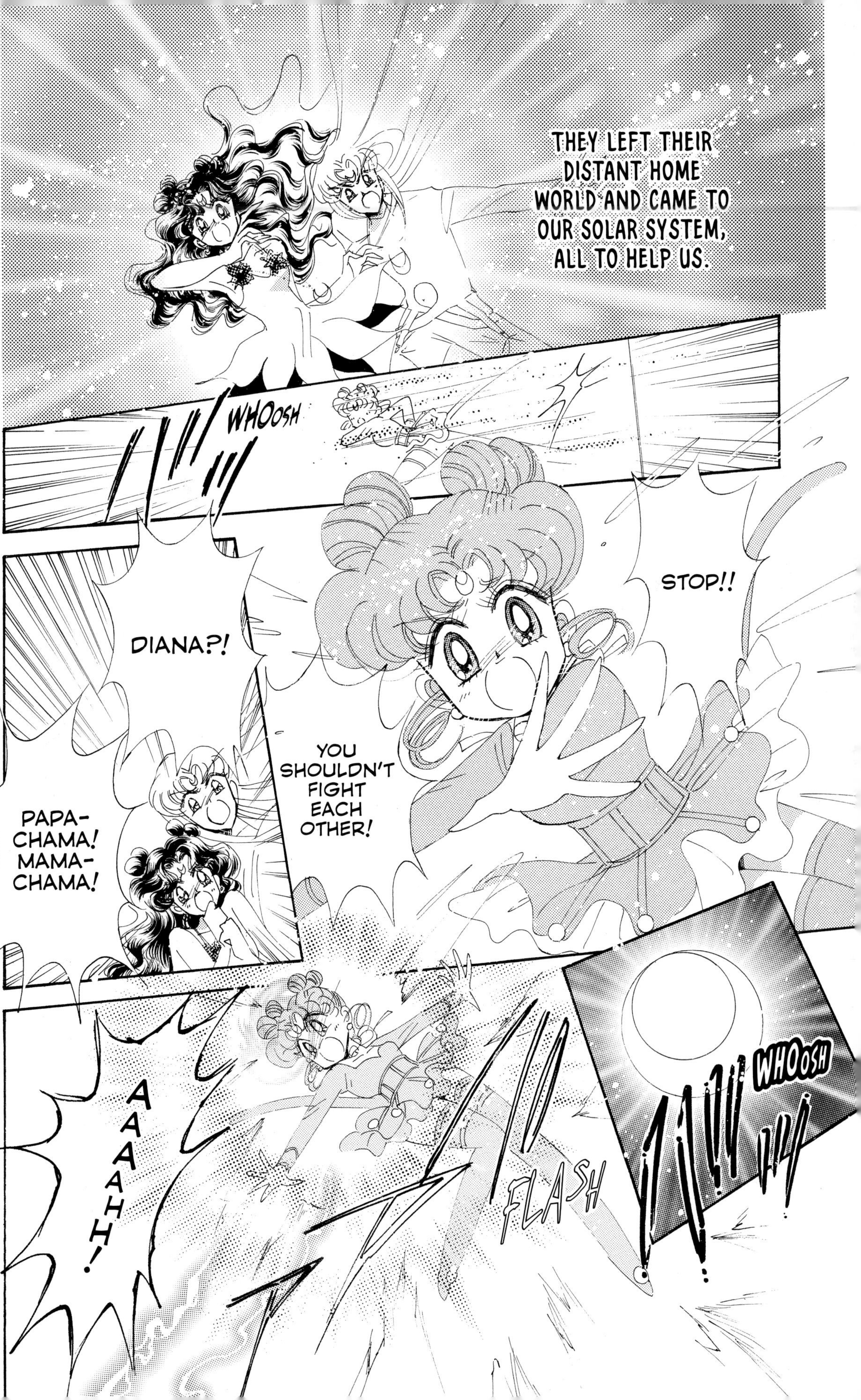
THEY LEFT THEIR DISTANT HOME WORLD AND CAME TO OUR SOLAR SYSTEM, ALL TO HELP US.
WHOOSH
STOP!!
YOU SHOULDN'T FIGHT EACH OTHER!
DIANA?!
PAPA-CHAMA! MAMA-CHAMA!
WHOOSH
FLASH
AAAAHH!

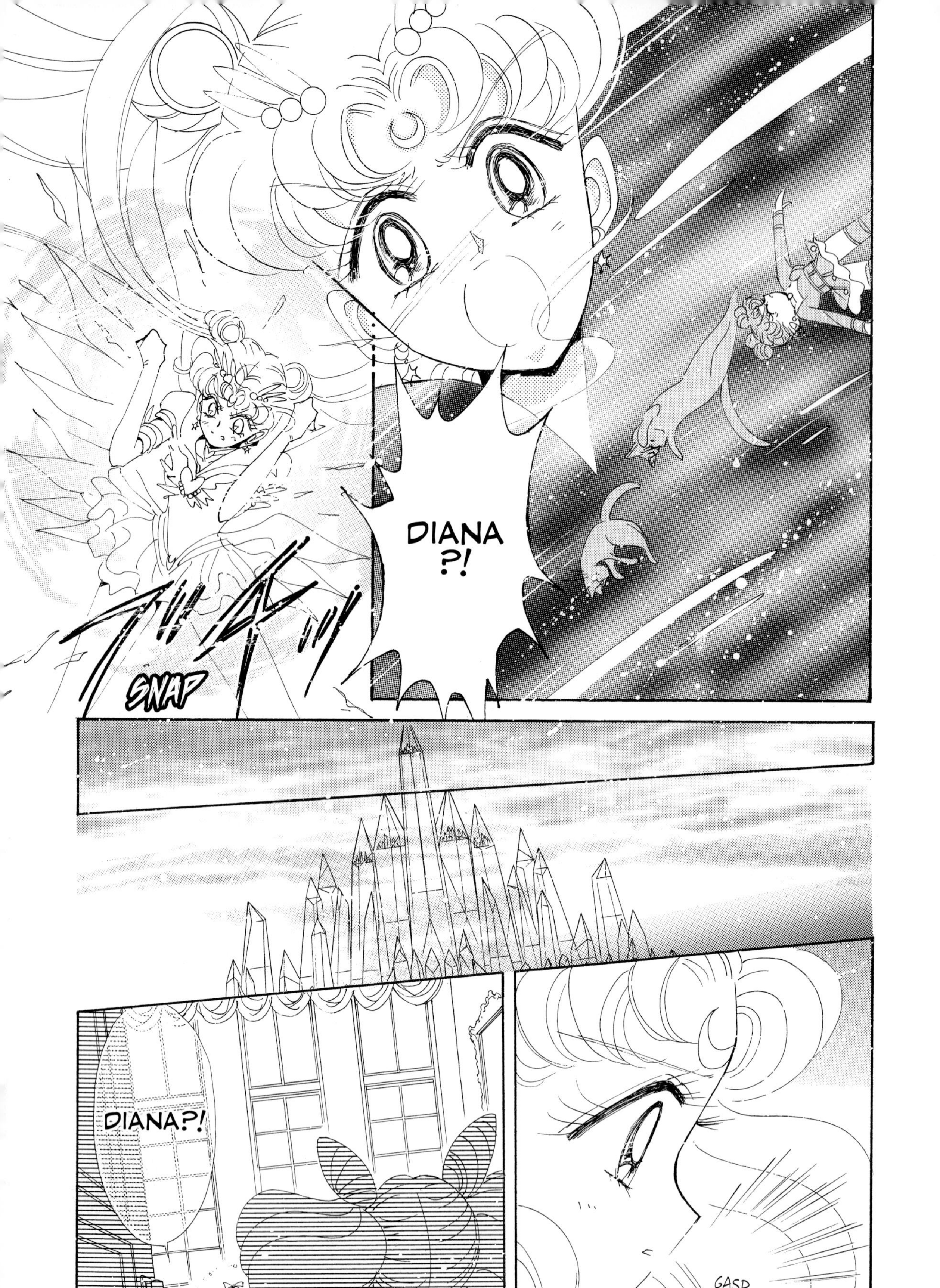
DIANA ?!
SNAP
...
GASP
DIANA?!

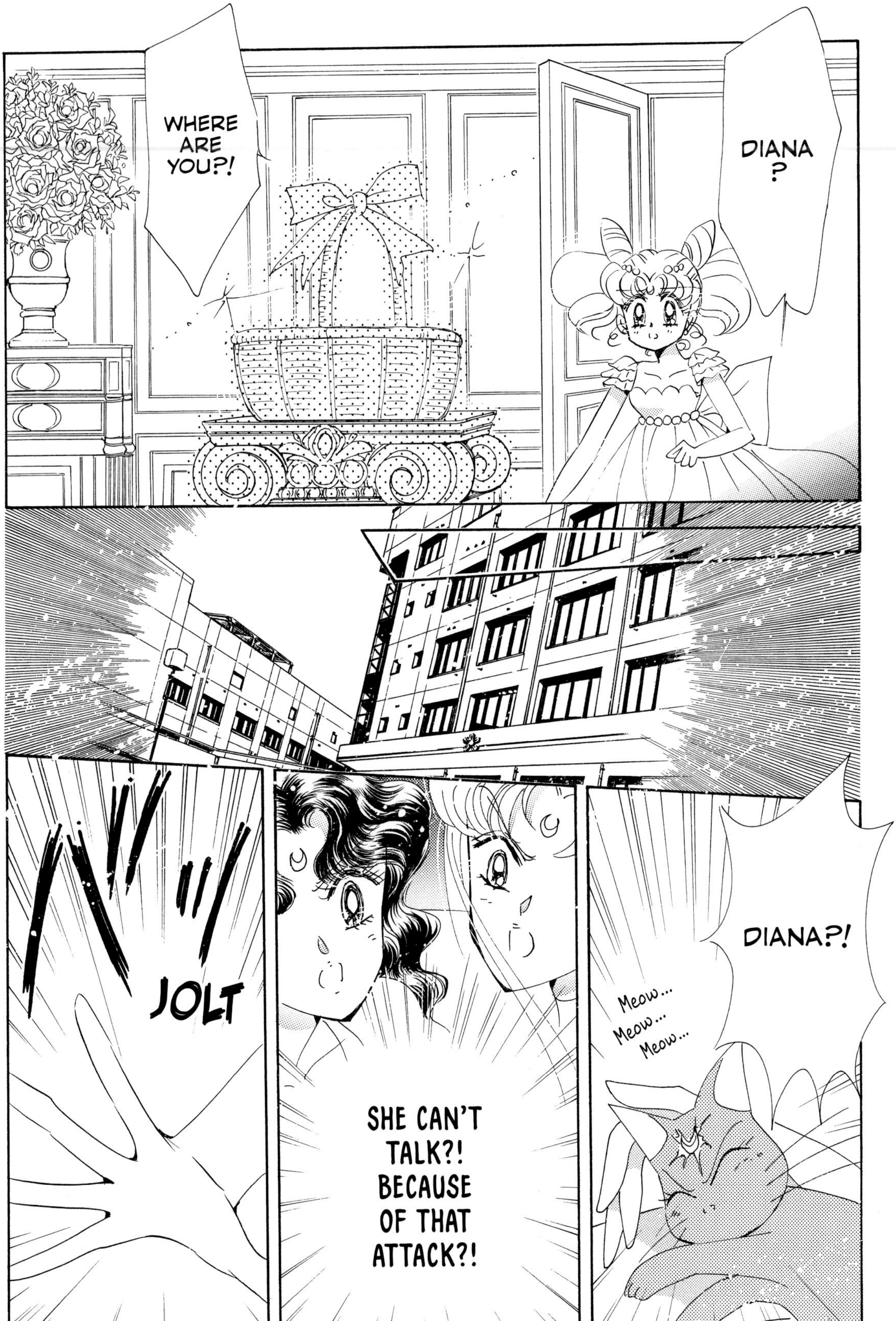
DIANA ?
WHERE ARE YOU?!
DIANA?!
Meow... Meow... Meow...
SHE CAN'T TALK?! BECAUSE OF THAT ATTACK?!
JOLT

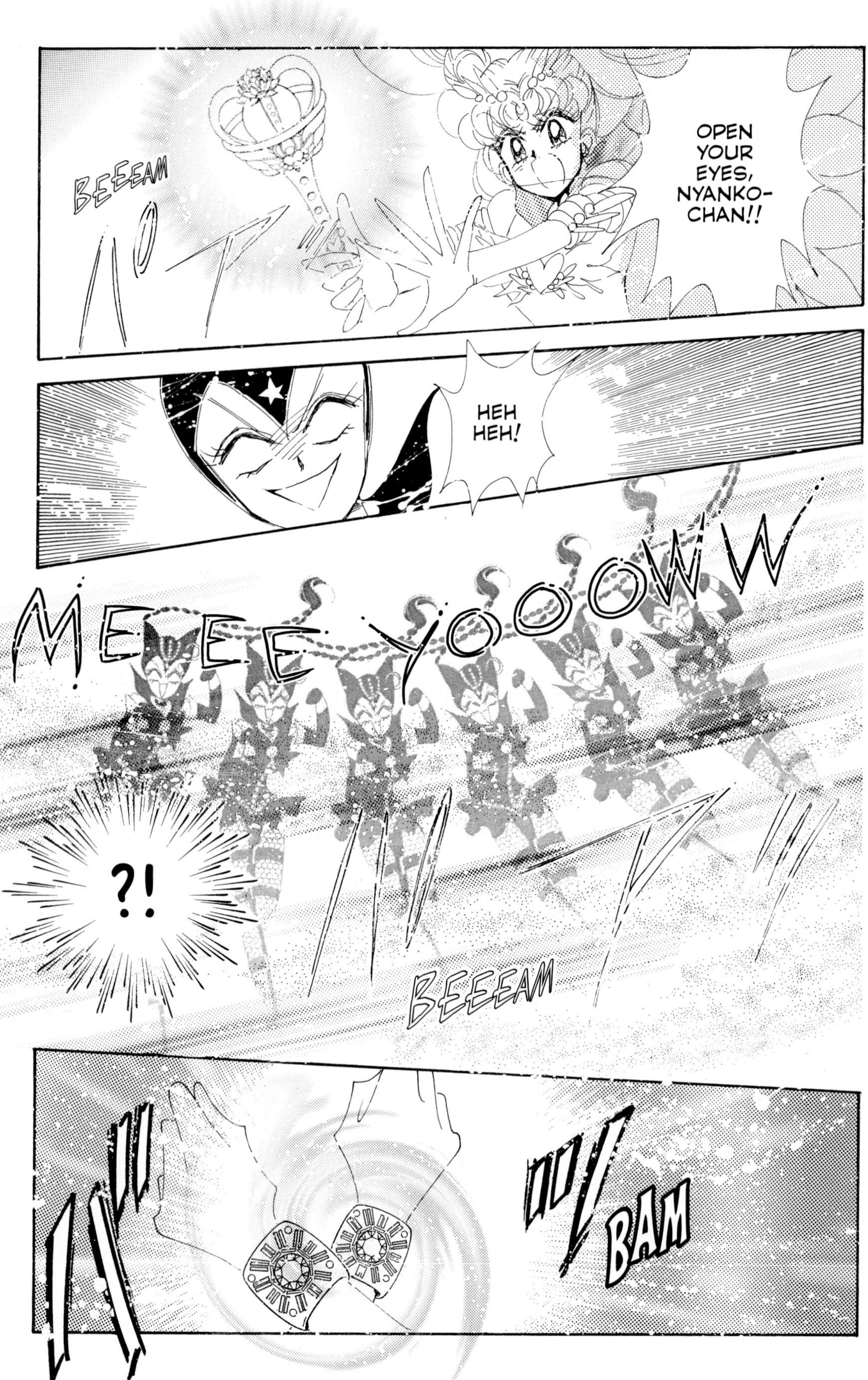
OPEN YOUR EYES, NYANKO-CHAN!!
BEEEAM
HEH HEH!
MEEEYOOOWW
?!
BEEEAM
BAM

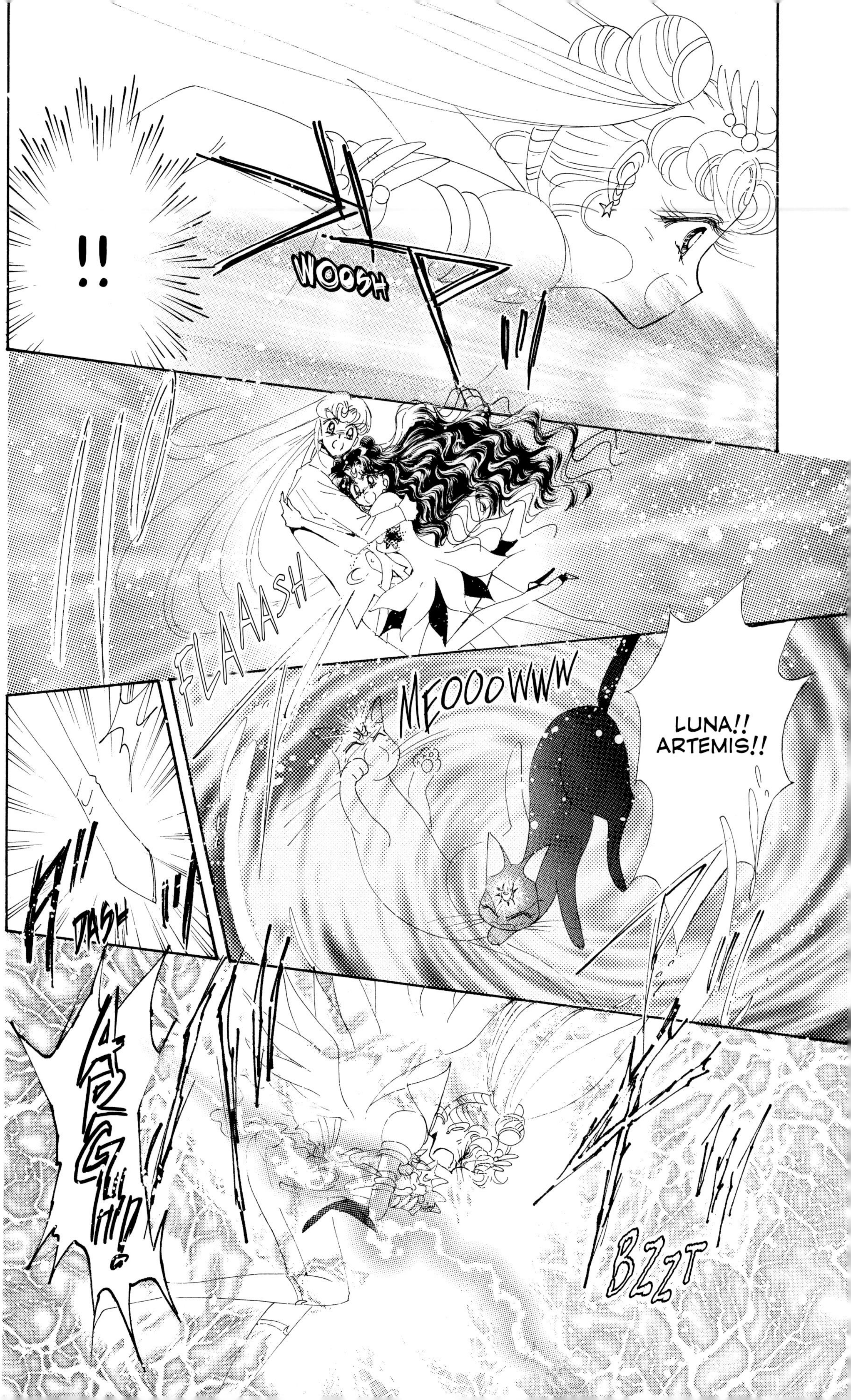
WOOSH
!!
FLAAASH
LUNA!! ARTEMIS!!
MEOOOWWW
DASH
BZZT

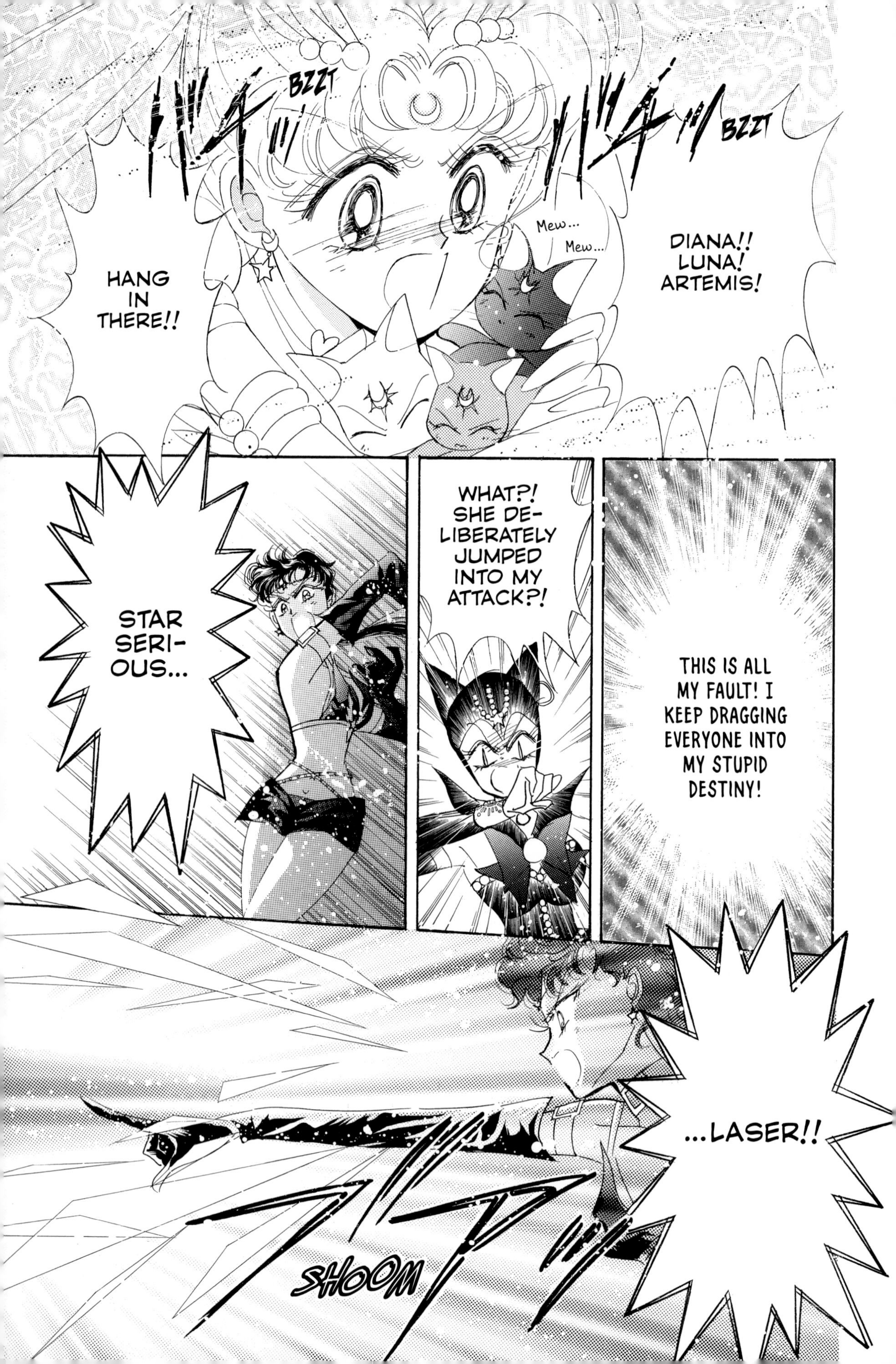
BZZT
Mew...
Mew...
DIANA!! LUNA! ARTEMIS!
BZZT
HANG IN THERE!!
THIS IS ALL MY FAULT! I KEEP DRAGGING EVERYONE INTO MY STUPID DESTINY!
WHAT?! SHE DE-LIBERATELY JUMPED INTO MY ATTACK?!
STAR SERI-OUS...
...LASER!!
SHOOM

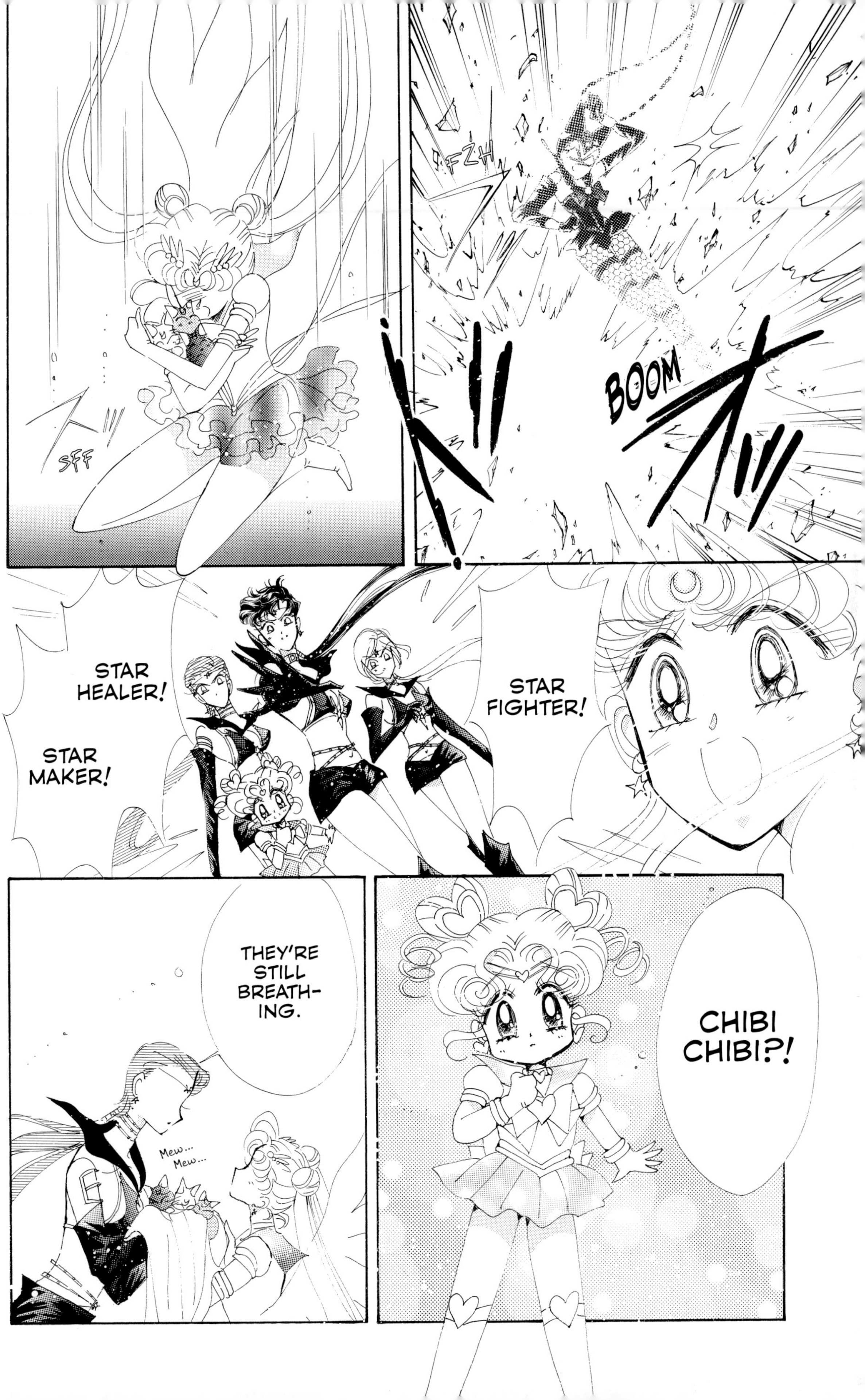
FZH
BOOM
SFF
STAR FIGHTER!
STAR HEALER!
STAR MAKER!
CHIBI CHIBI?!
THEY'RE STILL BREATH-ING.
Mew... Mew...

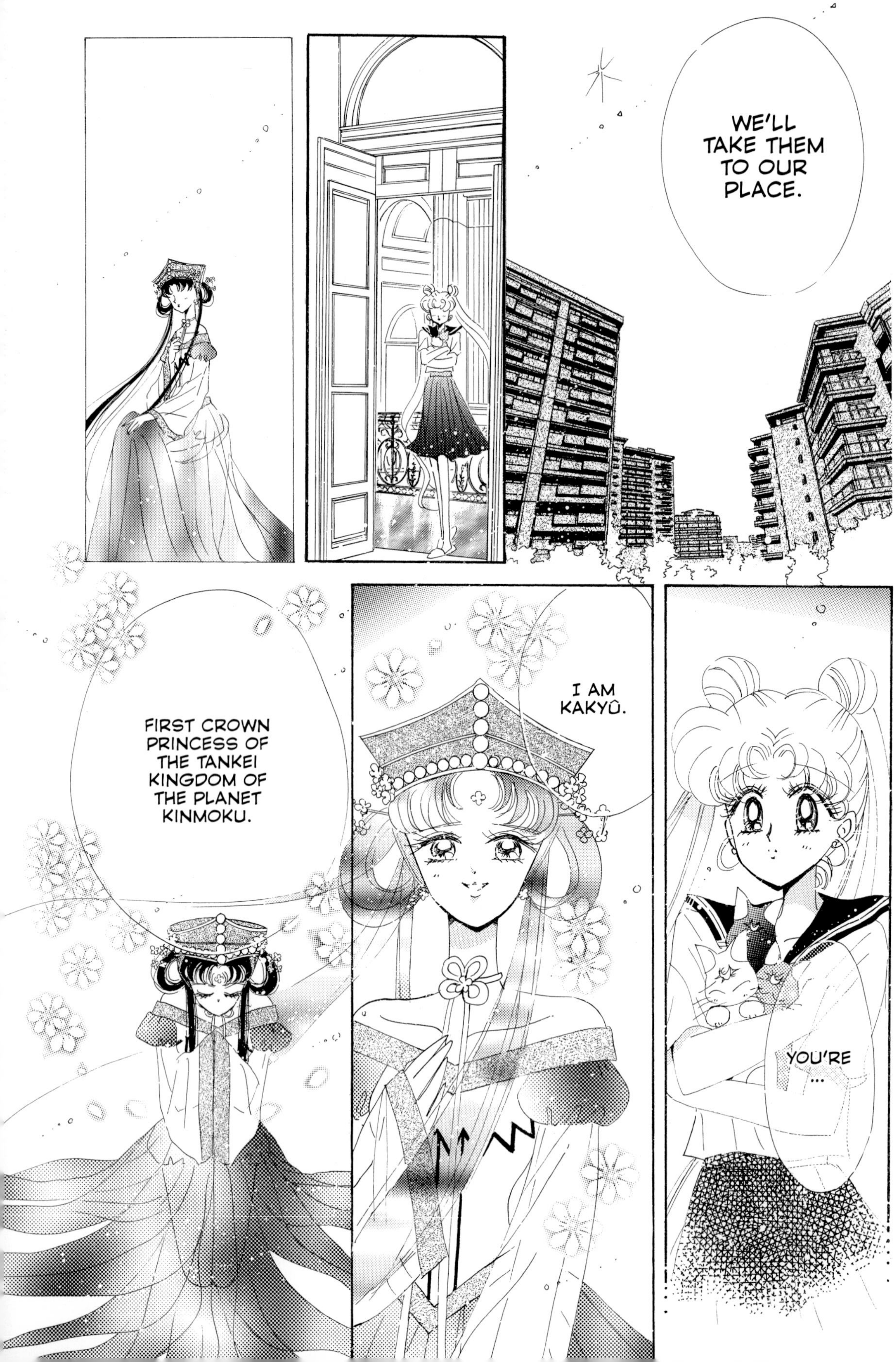
WE'LL TAKE THEM TO OUR PLACE.
YOU'RE ...
I AM KAKYÛ.
FIRST CROWN PRINCESS OF THE TANKEI KINGDOM OF THE PLANET KINMOKU.

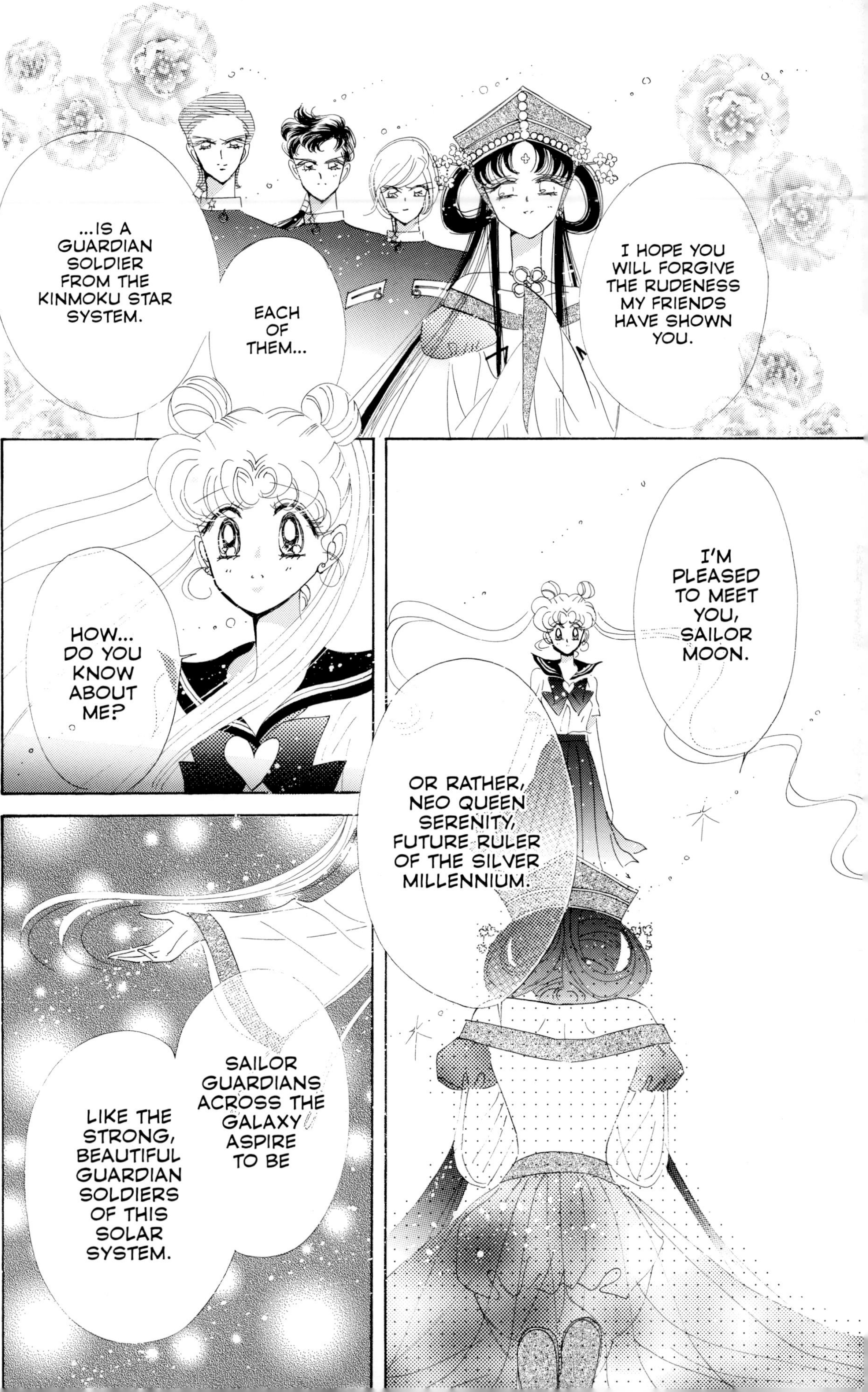
I HOPE YOU WILL FORGIVE THE RUDENESS MY FRIENDS HAVE SHOWN YOU.
EACH OF THEM...
...IS A GUARDIAN SOLDIER FROM THE KINMOKU STAR SYSTEM.
I'M PLEASED TO MEET YOU, SAILOR MOON.
OR RATHER, NEO QUEEN SERENITY, FUTURE RULER OF THE SILVER MILLENNIUM.
HOW... DO YOU KNOW ABOUT ME?
SAILOR GUARDIANS ACROSS THE GALAXY ASPIRE TO BE
LIKE THE STRONG, BEAUTIFUL GUARDIAN SOLDIERS OF THIS SOLAR SYSTEM.

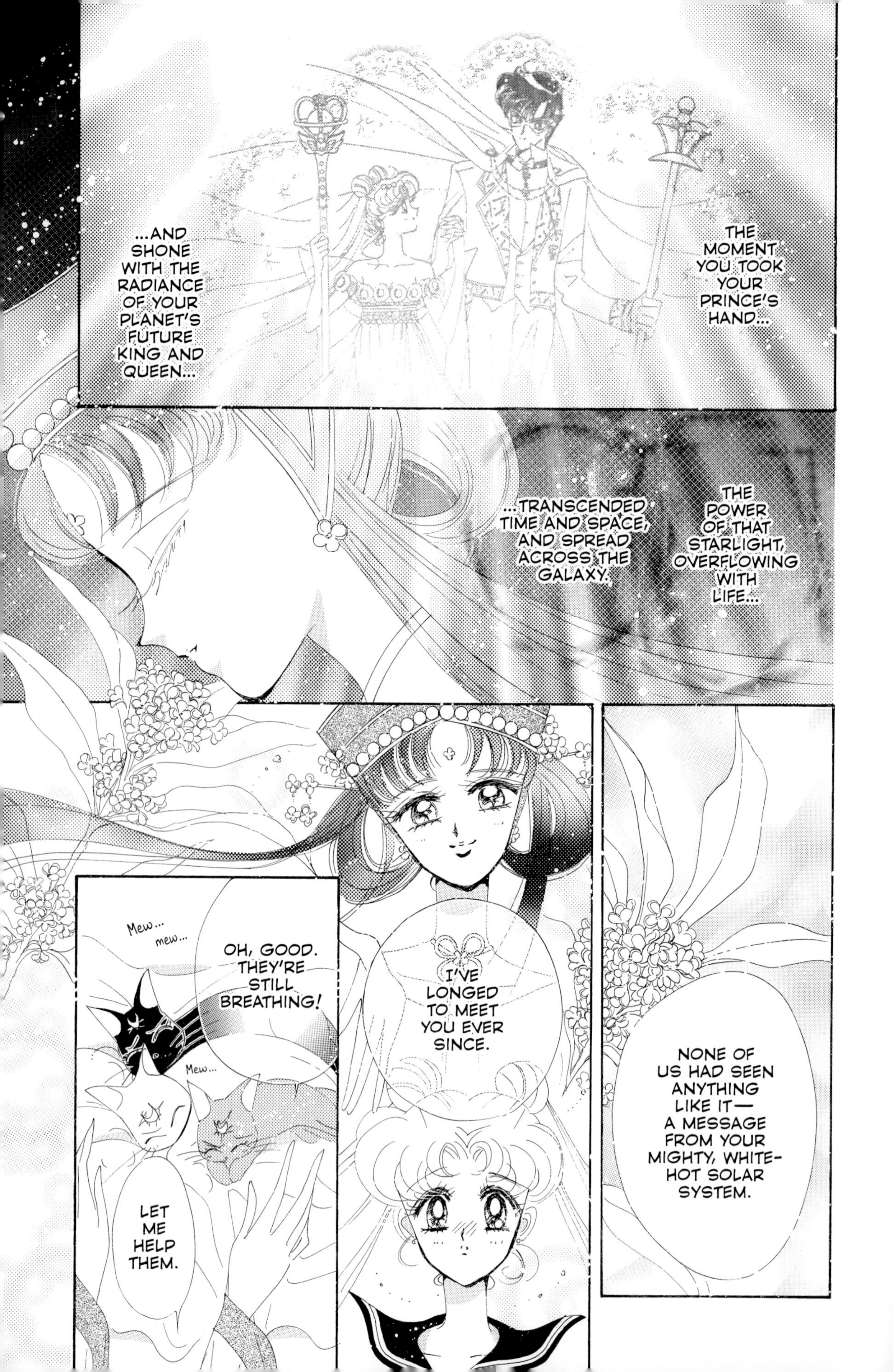
THE MOMENT YOU TOOK YOUR PRINCE'S HAND...
...AND SHONE WITH THE RADIANCE OF YOUR PLANET'S FUTURE KING AND QUEEN...
THE POWER OF THAT STARLIGHT, OVERFLOWING WITH LIFE...
...TRANSCENDED TIME AND SPACE, AND SPREAD ACROSS THE GALAXY.
NONE OF US HAD SEEN ANYTHING LIKE IT— A MESSAGE FROM YOUR MIGHTY, WHITE-HOT SOLAR SYSTEM.
I'VE LONGED TO MEET YOU EVER SINCE.
Mew... mew...
OH, GOOD. THEY'RE STILL BREATHING!
Mew...
LET ME HELP THEM.

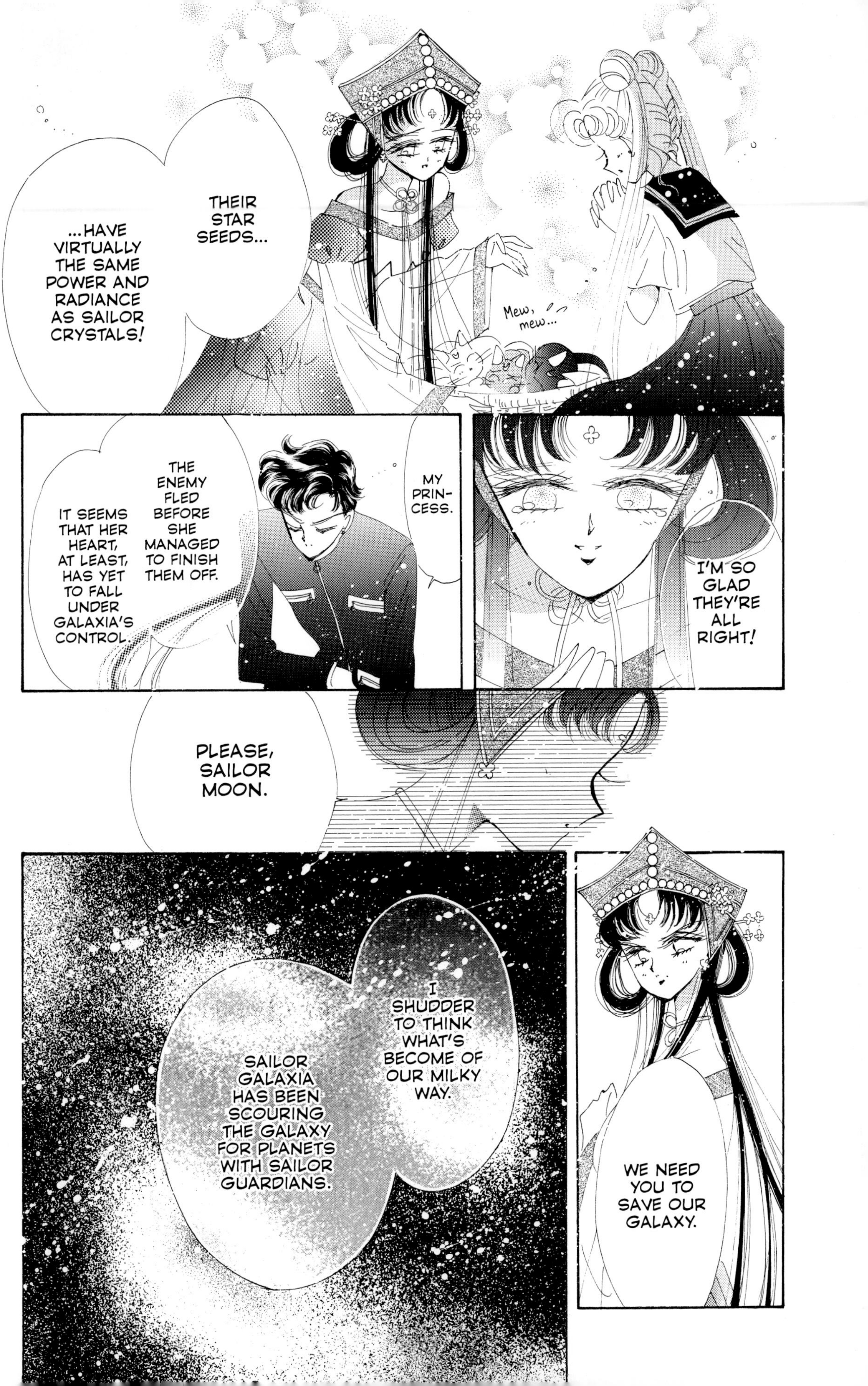
THEIR STAR SEEDS...
...HAVE VIRTUALLY THE SAME POWER AND RADIANCE AS SAILOR CRYSTALS!
Mew, mew...
I'M SO GLAD THEY'RE ALL RIGHT!
MY PRINCESS.
THE ENEMY FLED BEFORE SHE MANAGED TO FINISH THEM OFF.
IT SEEMS THAT HER HEART, AT LEAST, HAS YET TO FALL UNDER GALAXIA'S CONTROL.
PLEASE, SAILOR MOON.
WE NEED YOU TO SAVE OUR GALAXY.
I SHUDDER TO THINK WHAT'S BECOME OF OUR MILKY WAY.
SAILOR GALAXIA HAS BEEN SCOURING THE GALAXY FOR PLANETS WITH SAILOR GUARDIANS.

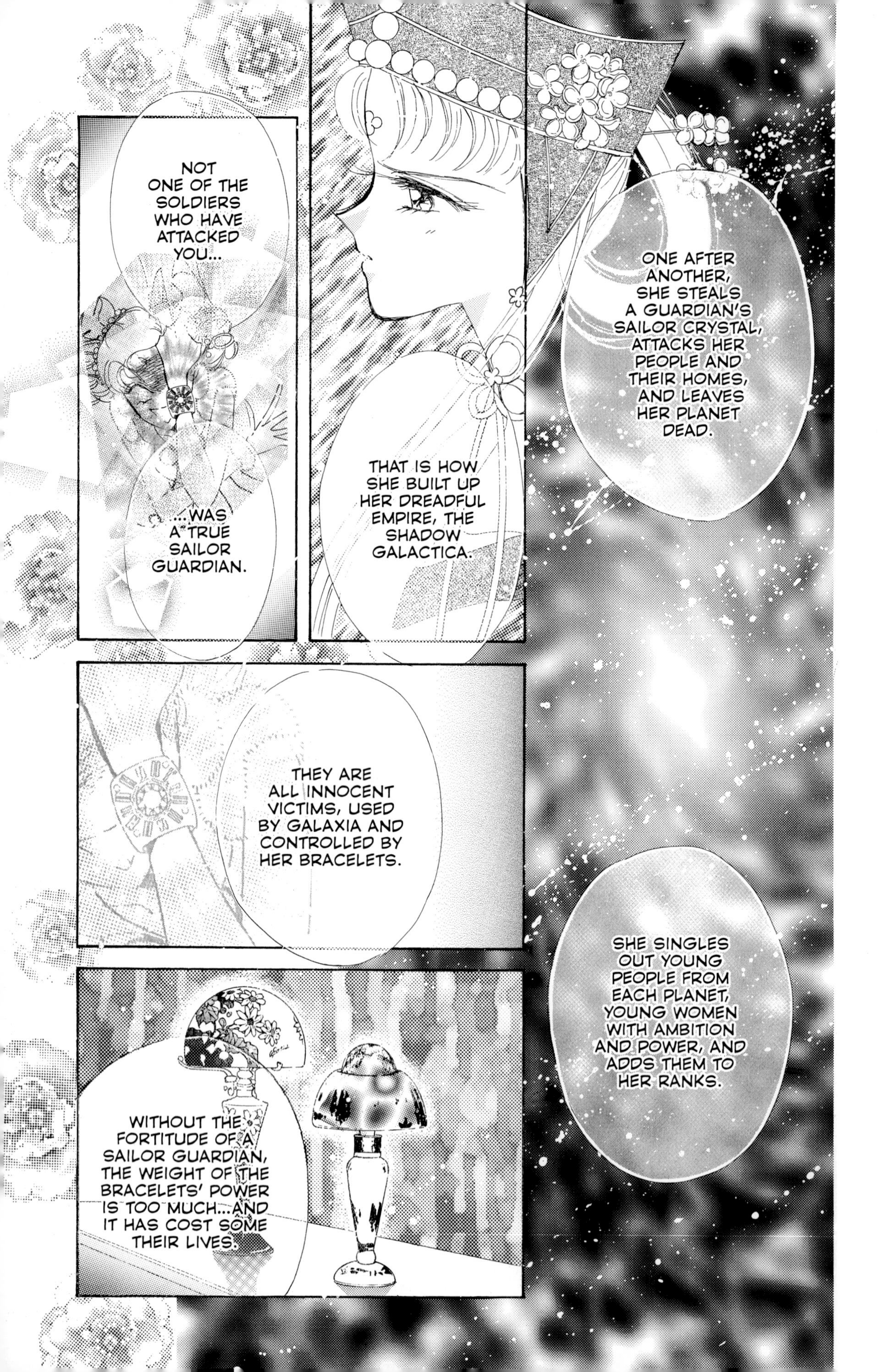
ONE AFTER ANOTHER, SHE STEALS A GUARDIAN'S SAILOR CRYSTAL, ATTACKS HER PEOPLE AND THEIR HOMES, AND LEAVES HER PLANET DEAD.
SHE SINGLES OUT YOUNG PEOPLE FROM EACH PLANET, YOUNG WOMEN WITH AMBITION AND POWER, AND ADDS THEM TO HER RANKS.
THAT IS HOW SHE BUILT UP HER DREADFUL EMPIRE, THE SHADOW GALACTICA.
NOT ONE OF THE SOLDIERS WHO HAVE ATTACKED YOU...
...WAS A TRUE SAILOR GUARDIAN.
THEY ARE ALL INNOCENT VICTIMS, USED BY GALAXIA AND CONTROLLED BY HER BRACELETS.
WITHOUT THE FORTITUDE OF A SAILOR GUARDIAN, THE WEIGHT OF THE BRACELETS' POWER IS TOO MUCH...AND IT HAS COST SOME THEIR LIVES.

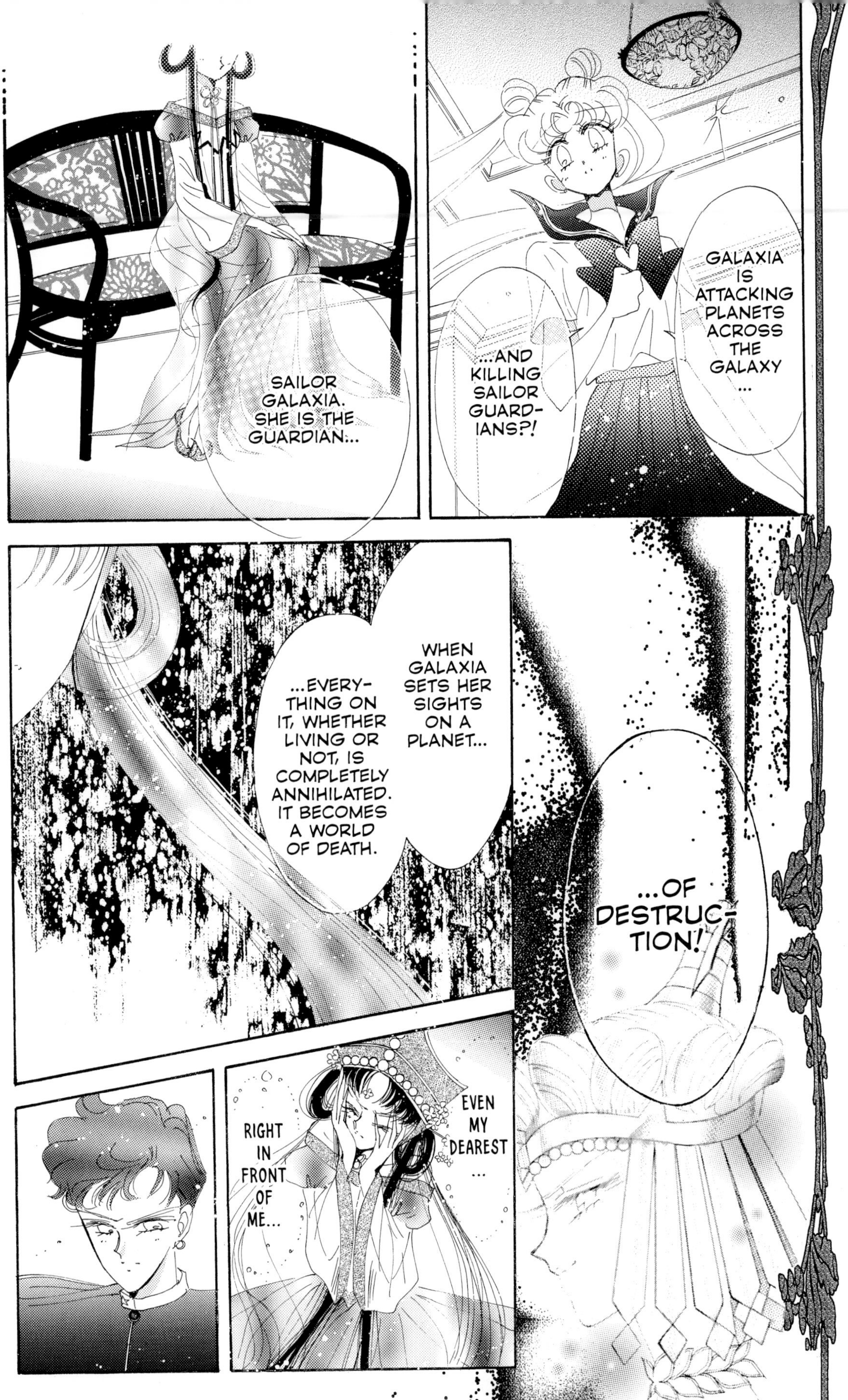
GALAXIA IS ATTACKING PLANETS ACROSS THE GALAXY ...
...AND KILLING SAILOR GUARD-IANS?!
SAILOR GALAXIA. SHE IS THE GUARDIAN...
...OF DESTRUC-TION!
WHEN GALAXIA SETS HER SIGHTS ON A PLANET...
...EVERY-THING ON IT, WHETHER LIVING OR NOT, IS COMPLETELY ANNIHILATED. IT BECOMES A WORLD OF DEATH.
EVEN MY DEAREST ...
RIGHT IN FRONT OF ME...

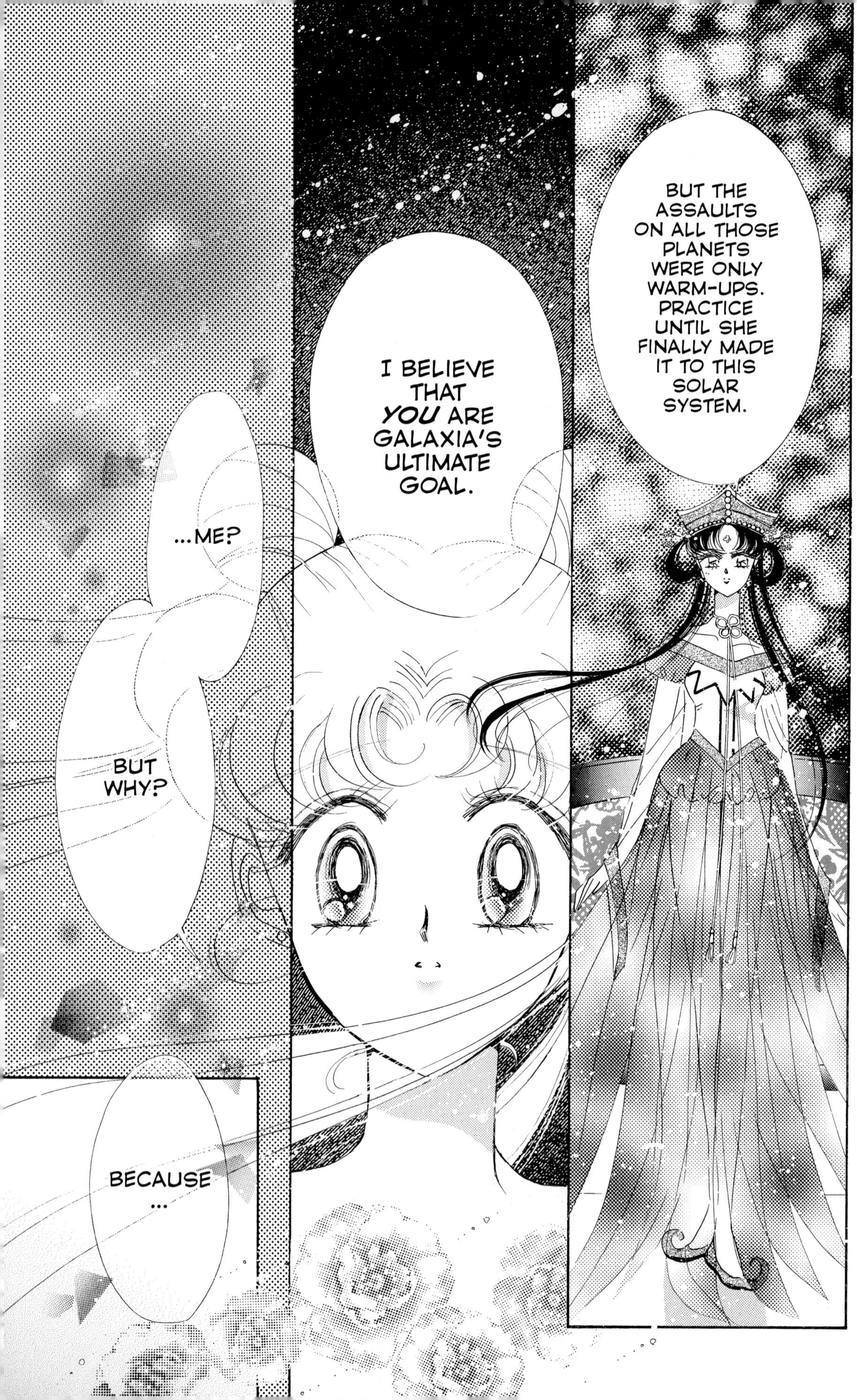
BUT THE ASSAULTS ON ALL THOSE PLANETS WERE ONLY WARM-UPS. PRACTICE UNTIL SHE FINALLY MADE IT TO THIS SOLAR SYSTEM.
I BELIEVE THAT *YOU* ARE GALAXIA'S ULTIMATE GOAL.
...ME?
BUT WHY?
BECAUSE ...

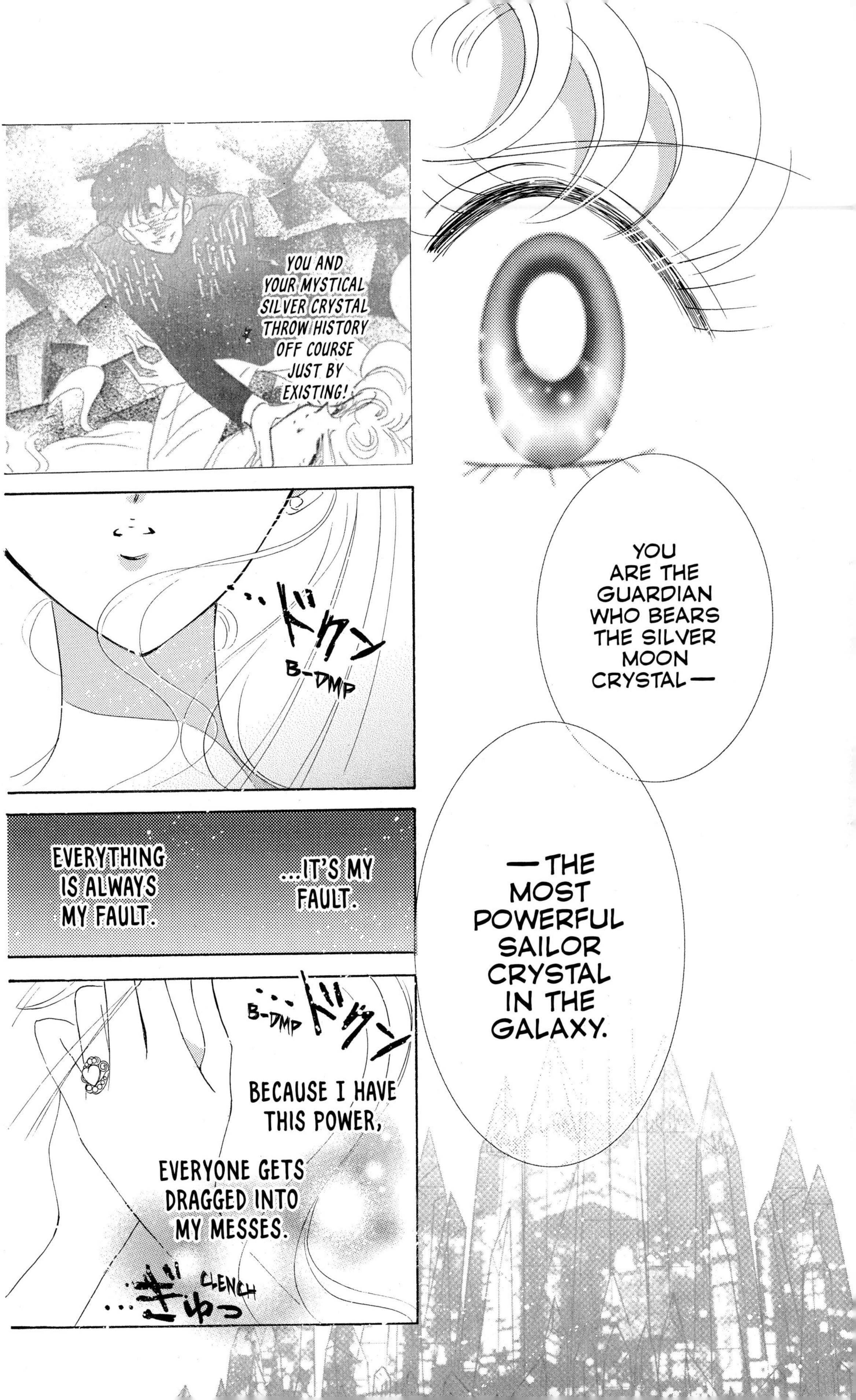
YOU ARE THE GUARDIAN WHO BEARS THE SILVER MOON CRYSTAL—
—THE MOST POWERFUL SAILOR CRYSTAL IN THE GALAXY.
YOU AND YOUR MYSTICAL SILVER CRYSTAL THROW HISTORY OFF COURSE JUST BY EXISTING!
...ドクン
B-DMP
...IT'S MY FAULT.
EVERYTHING IS ALWAYS MY FAULT.
...ドクン
B-DMP
BECAUSE I HAVE THIS POWER,
EVERYONE GETS DRAGGED INTO MY MESSES.
...ぎゅっ
CLENCH

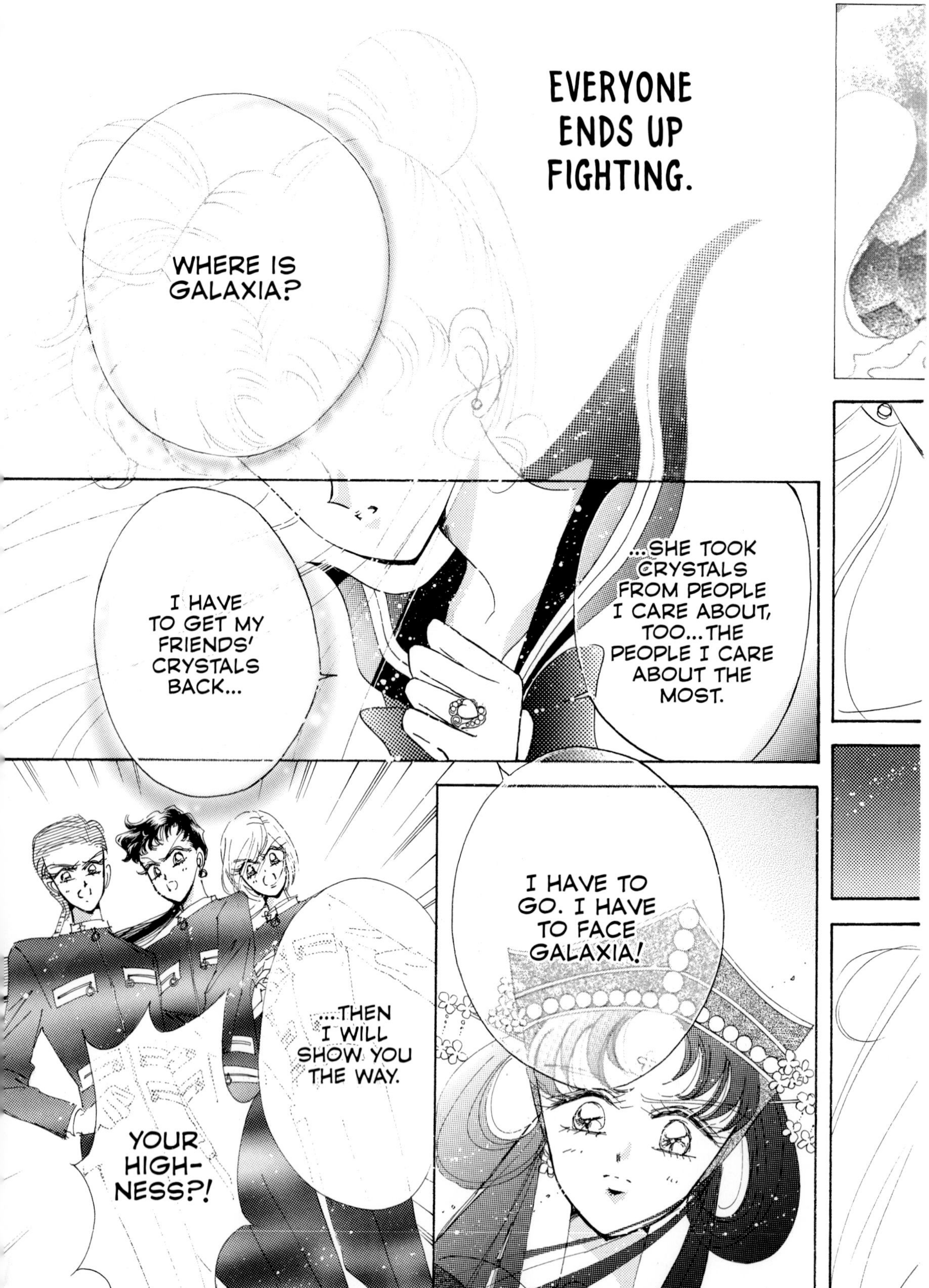
EVERYONE ENDS UP FIGHTING.
WHERE IS GALAXIA?
...SHE TOOK CRYSTALS FROM PEOPLE I CARE ABOUT, TOO...THE PEOPLE I CARE ABOUT THE MOST.
I HAVE TO GET MY FRIENDS' CRYSTALS BACK...
I HAVE TO GO. I HAVE TO FACE GALAXIA!
...THEN I WILL SHOW YOU THE WAY.
YOUR HIGHNESS?!

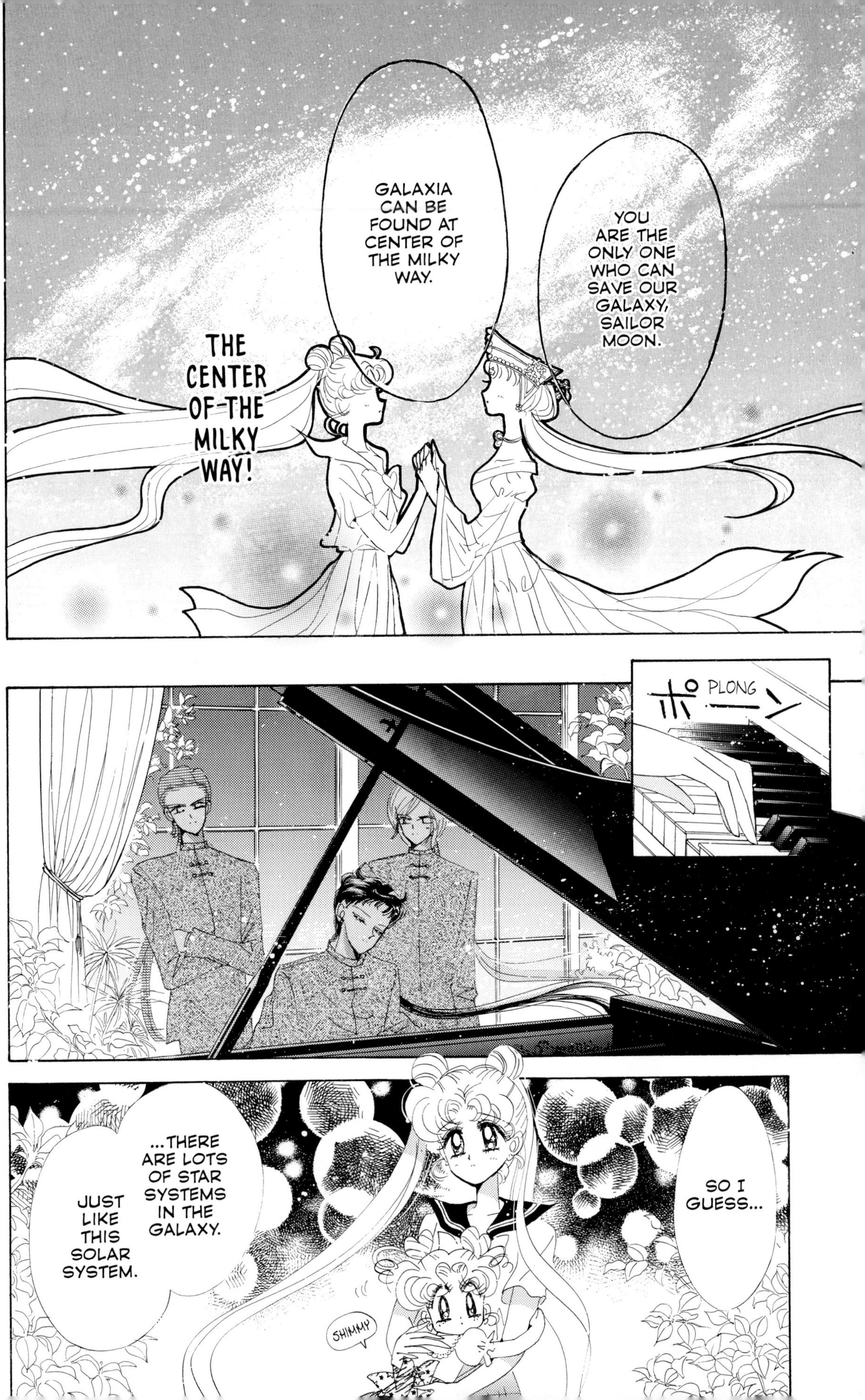
YOU ARE THE ONLY ONE WHO CAN SAVE OUR GALAXY, SAILOR MOON.
GALAXIA CAN BE FOUND AT CENTER OF THE MILKY WAY.
THE CENTER OF THE MILKY WAY!
ポーン
PLONG
SO I GUESS...
...THERE ARE LOTS OF STAR SYSTEMS IN THE GALAXY.
JUST LIKE THIS SOLAR SYSTEM.
SHIMMY

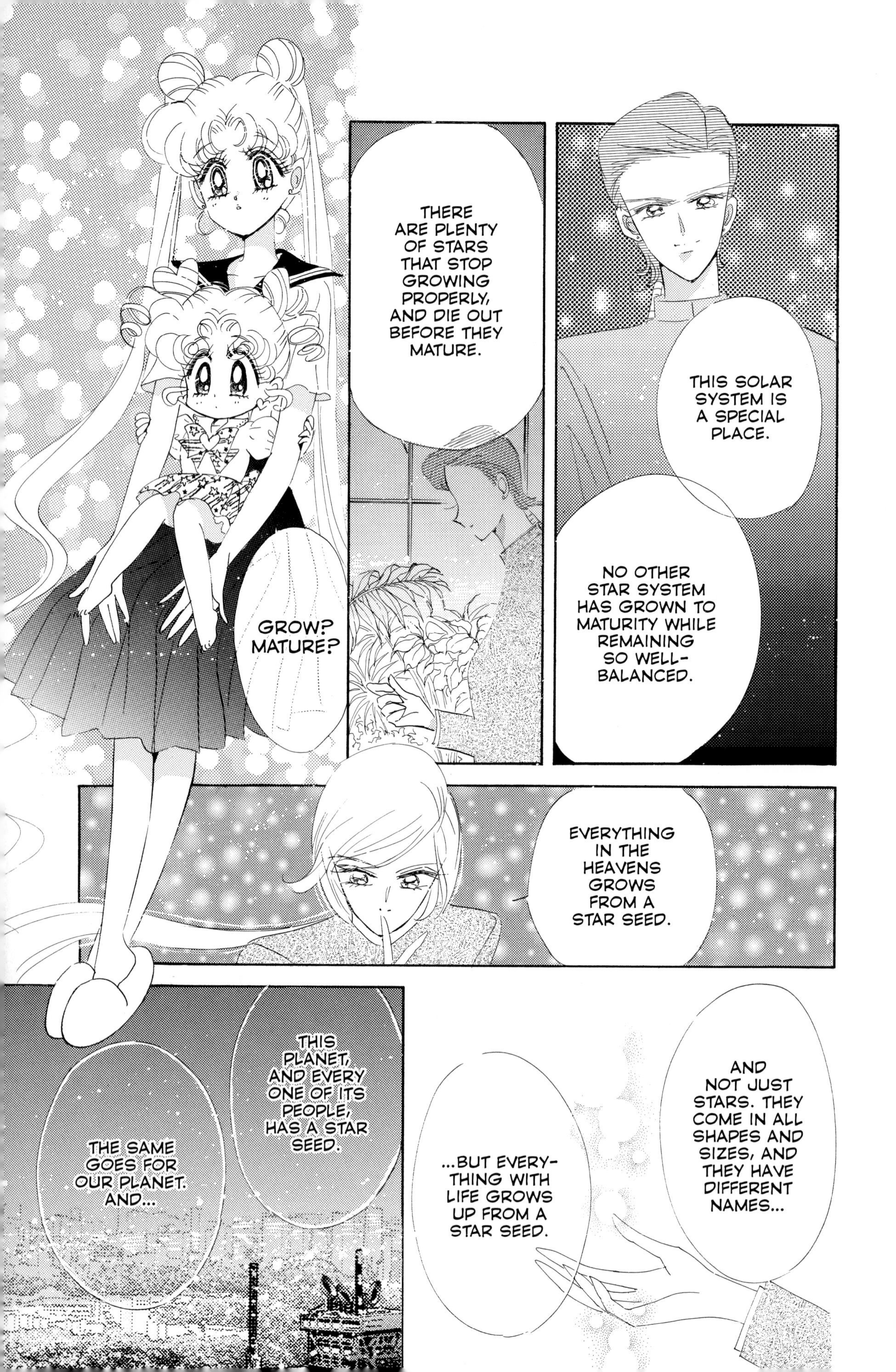
THIS SOLAR SYSTEM IS A SPECIAL PLACE.
NO OTHER STAR SYSTEM HAS GROWN TO MATURITY WHILE REMAINING SO WELL-BALANCED.
THERE ARE PLENTY OF STARS THAT STOP GROWING PROPERLY, AND DIE OUT BEFORE THEY MATURE.
EVERYTHING IN THE HEAVENS GROWS FROM A STAR SEED.
GROW? MATURE?
AND NOT JUST STARS. THEY COME IN ALL SHAPES AND SIZES, AND THEY HAVE DIFFERENT NAMES...
...BUT EVERYTHING WITH LIFE GROWS UP FROM A STAR SEED.
THIS PLANET, AND EVERY ONE OF ITS PEOPLE, HAS A STAR SEED.
THE SAME GOES FOR OUR PLANET. AND...

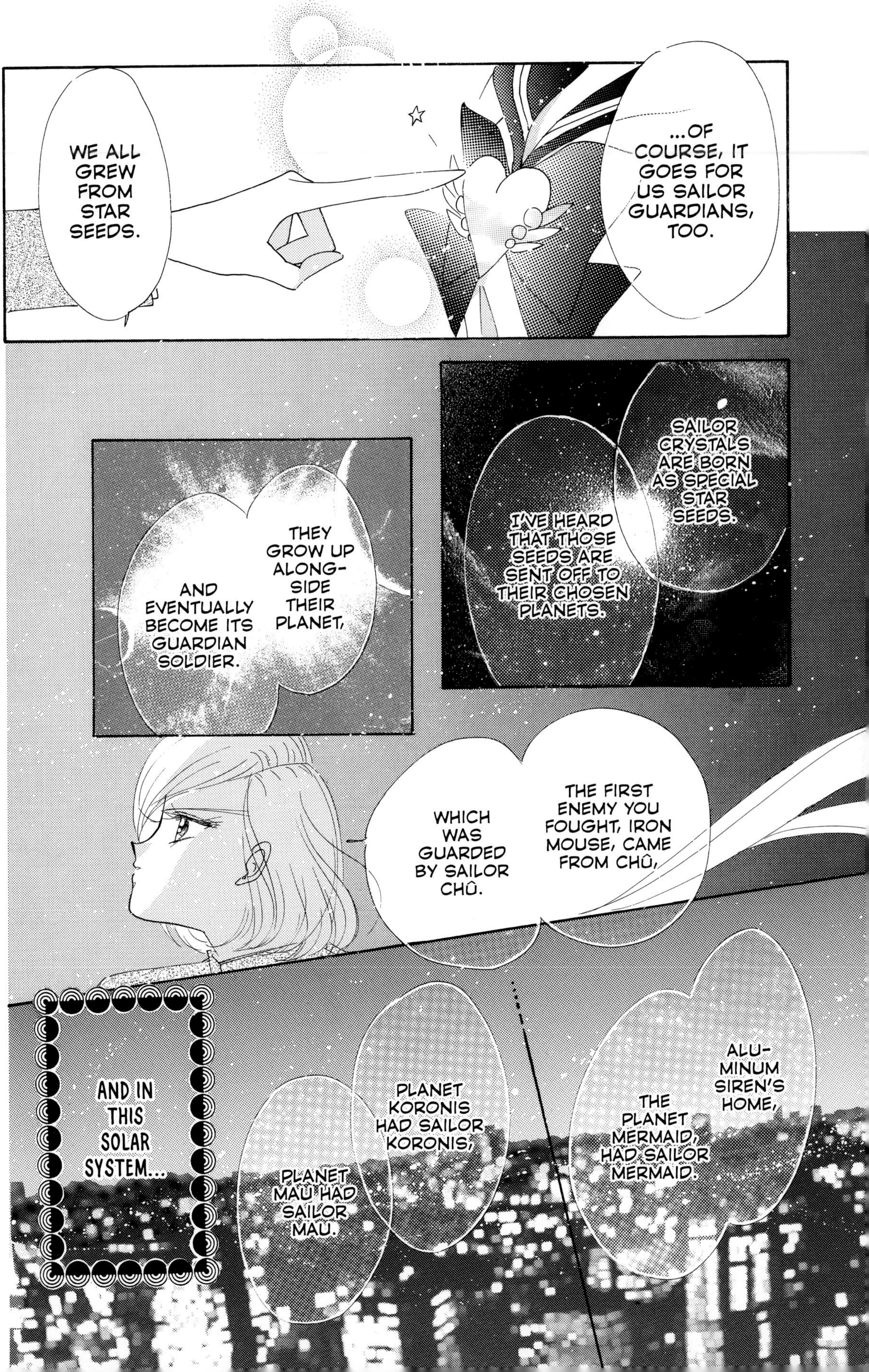
...OF COURSE, IT GOES FOR US SAILOR GUARDIANS, TOO.
WE ALL GREW FROM STAR SEEDS.
SAILOR CRYSTALS ARE BORN AS SPECIAL STAR SEEDS.
I'VE HEARD THAT THOSE SEEDS ARE SENT OFF TO THEIR CHOSEN PLANETS.
THEY GROW UP ALONG-SIDE THEIR PLANET,
AND EVENTUALLY BECOME ITS GUARDIAN SOLDIER.
THE FIRST ENEMY YOU FOUGHT, IRON MOUSE, CAME FROM CHÛ,
WHICH WAS GUARDED BY SAILOR CHÛ.
ALU-MINUM SIREN'S HOME,
THE PLANET MERMAID, HAD SAILOR MERMAID.
PLANET KORONIS HAD SAILOR KORONIS,
PLANET MAU HAD SAILOR MAU.
AND IN THIS SOLAR SYSTEM...

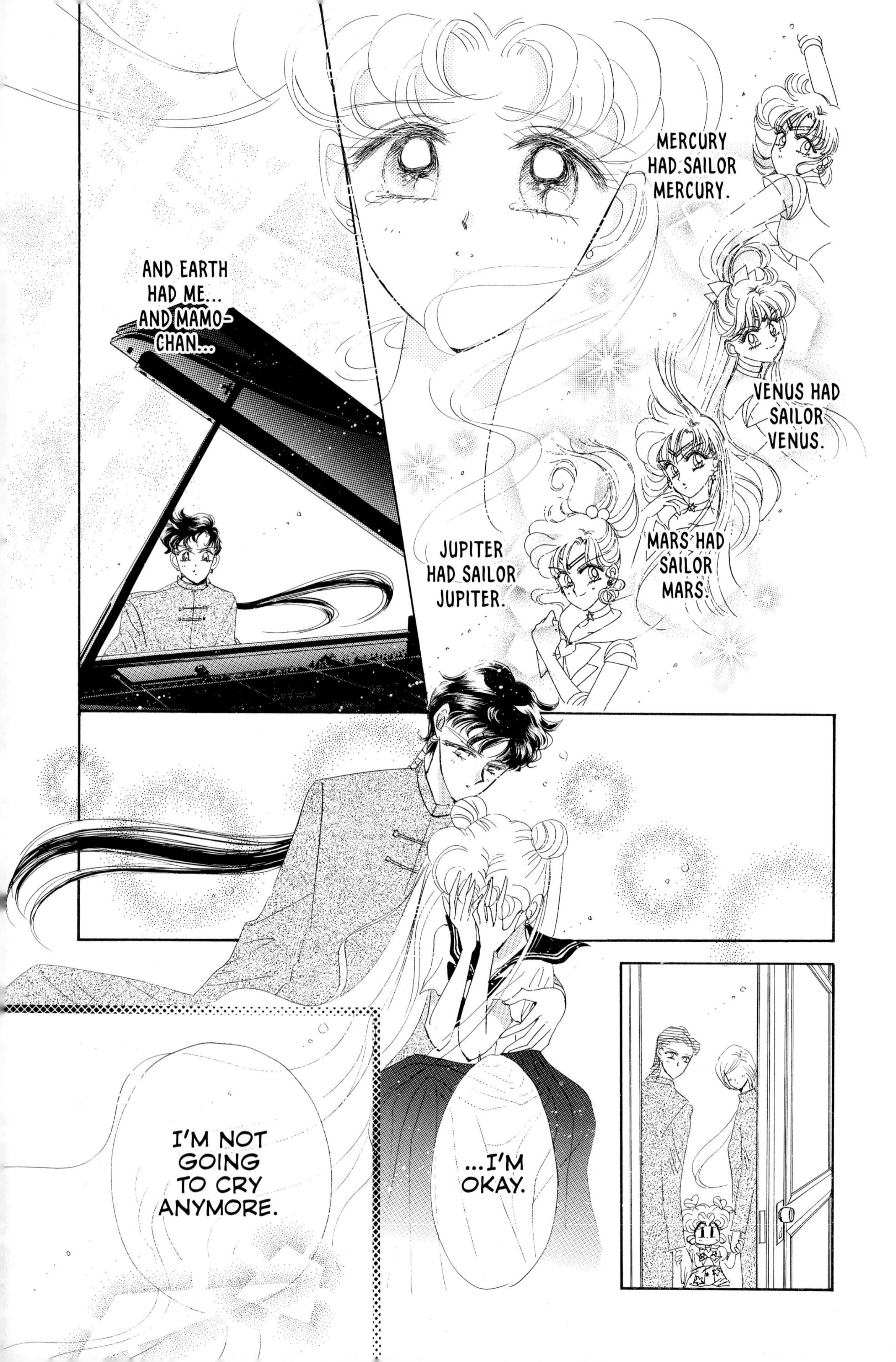
MERCURY HAD SAILOR MERCURY.
VENUS HAD SAILOR VENUS.
MARS HAD SAILOR MARS.
JUPITER HAD SAILOR JUPITER.
AND EARTH HAD ME... AND MAMO-CHAN...
...I'M OKAY.
I'M NOT GOING TO CRY ANYMORE.

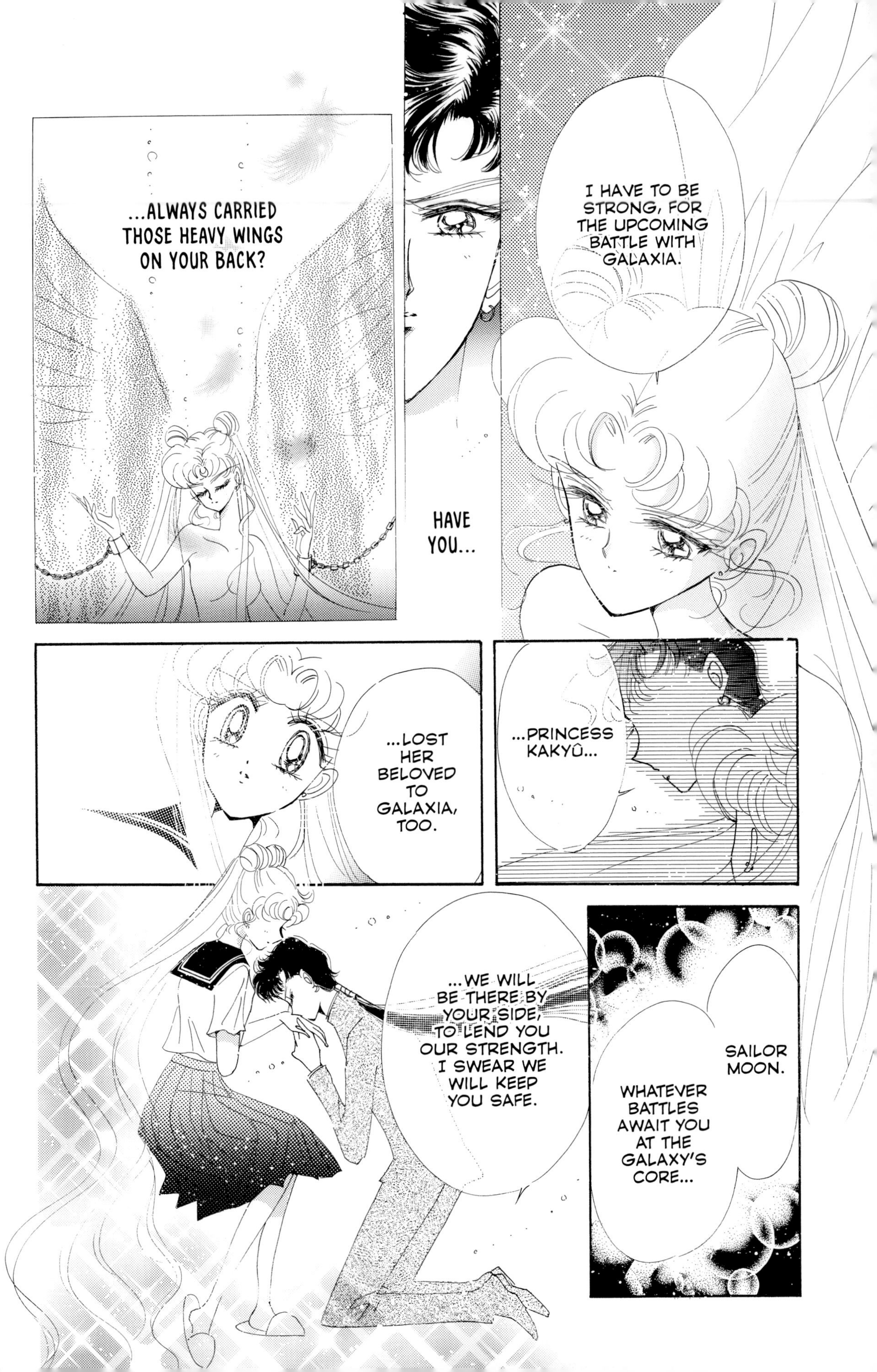
I HAVE TO BE STRONG, FOR THE UPCOMING BATTLE WITH GALAXIA.
HAVE YOU...
...ALWAYS CARRIED THOSE HEAVY WINGS ON YOUR BACK?
...PRINCESS KAKYÛ...
...LOST HER BELOVED TO GALAXIA, TOO.
SAILOR MOON.
WHATEVER BATTLES AWAIT YOU AT THE GALAXY'S CORE...
...WE WILL BE THERE BY YOUR SIDE, TO LEND YOU OUR STRENGTH. I SWEAR WE WILL KEEP YOU SAFE.

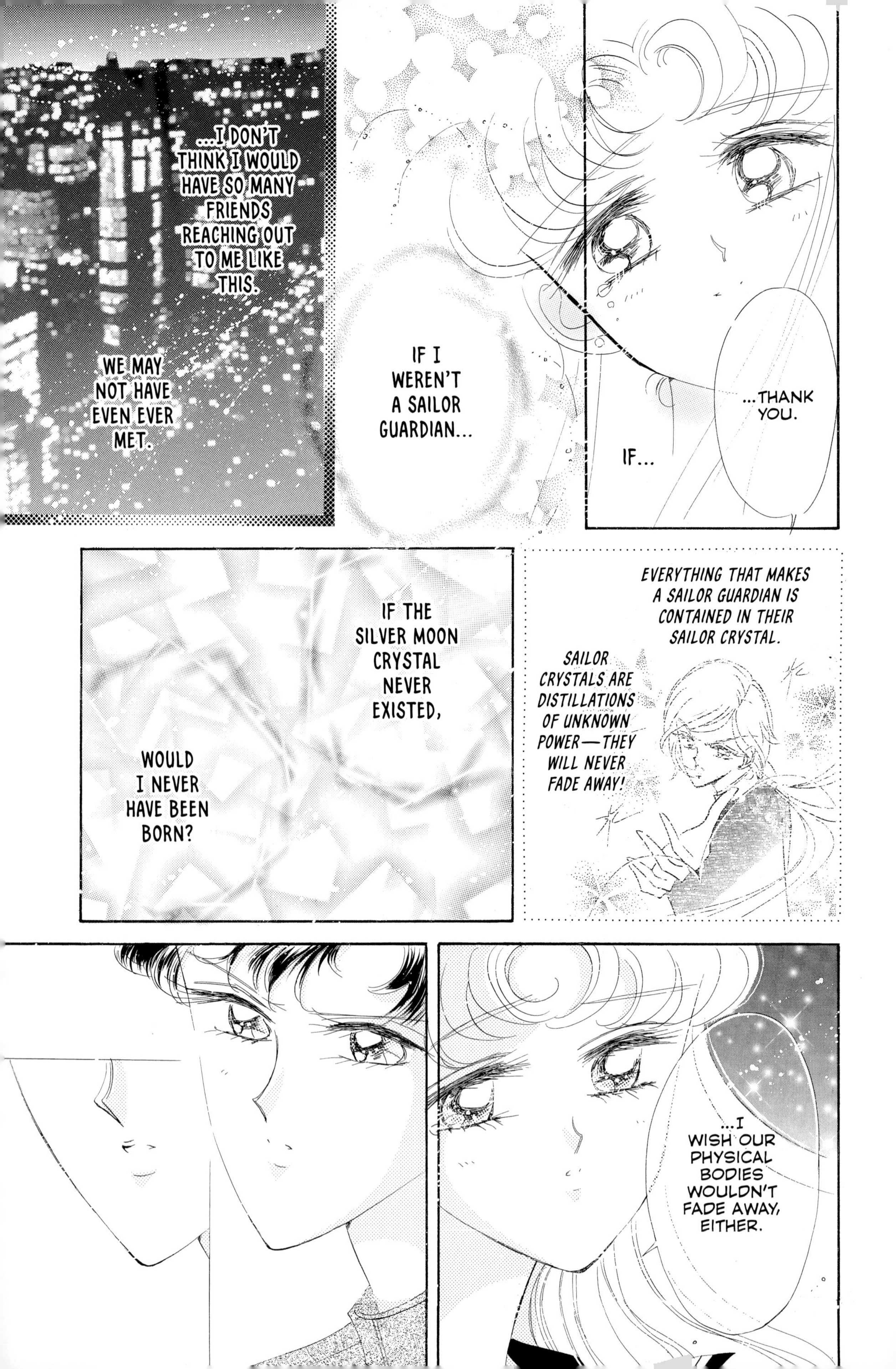
...THANK YOU.
IF...
IF I WEREN'T A SAILOR GUARDIAN...
...I DON'T THINK I WOULD HAVE SO MANY FRIENDS REACHING OUT TO ME LIKE THIS.
WE MAY NOT HAVE EVEN EVER MET.
EVERYTHING THAT MAKES A SAILOR GUARDIAN IS CONTAINED IN THEIR SAILOR CRYSTAL.
SAILOR CRYSTALS ARE DISTILLATIONS OF UNKNOWN POWER—THEY WILL NEVER FADE AWAY!
IF THE SILVER MOON CRYSTAL NEVER EXISTED,
WOULD I NEVER HAVE BEEN BORN?
...I WISH OUR PHYSICAL BODIES WOULDN'T FADE AWAY, EITHER.

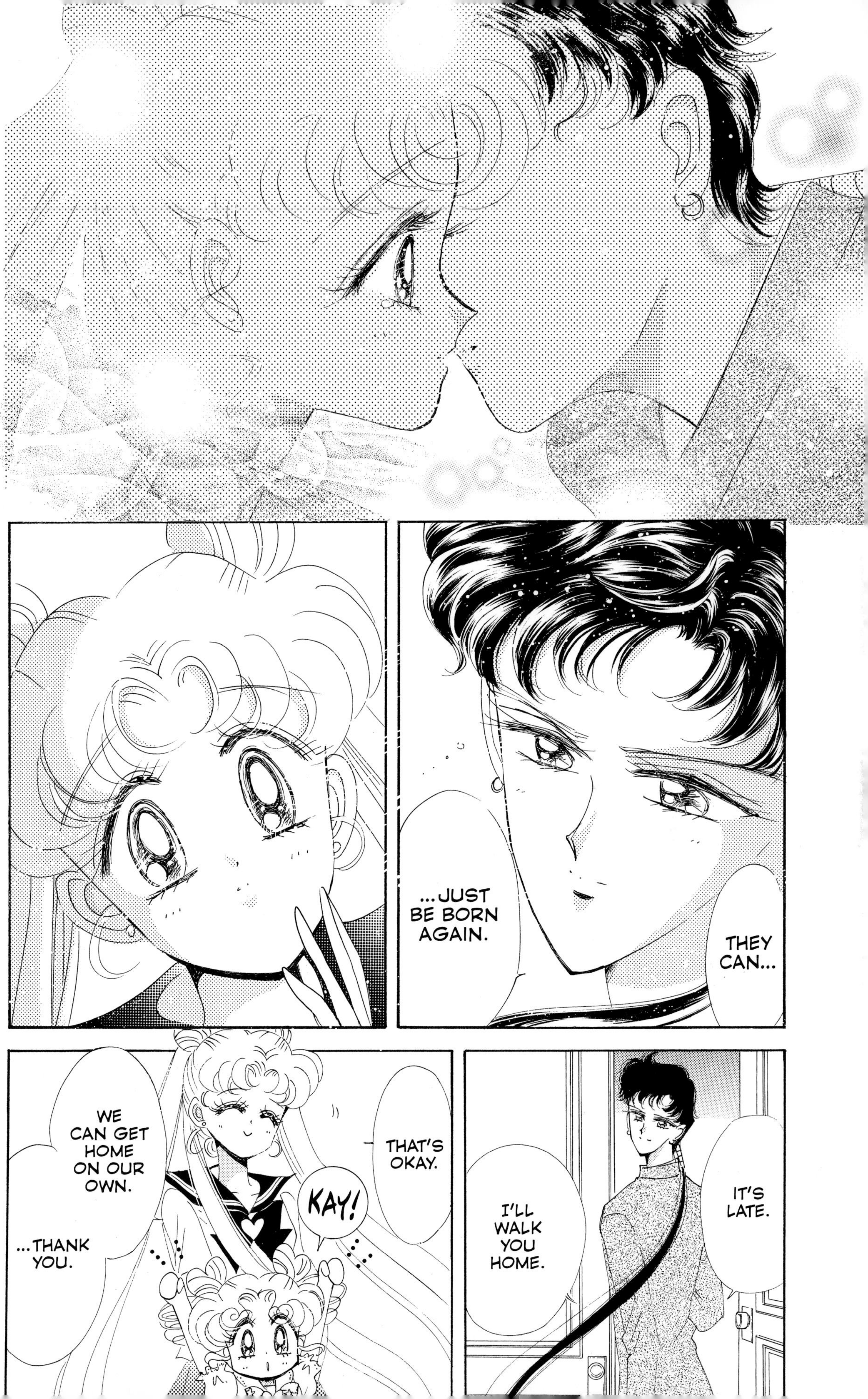
THEY CAN...
...JUST BE BORN AGAIN.
IT'S LATE.
I'LL WALK YOU HOME.
THAT'S OKAY.
WE CAN GET HOME ON OUR OWN.
KAY!
...THANK YOU.

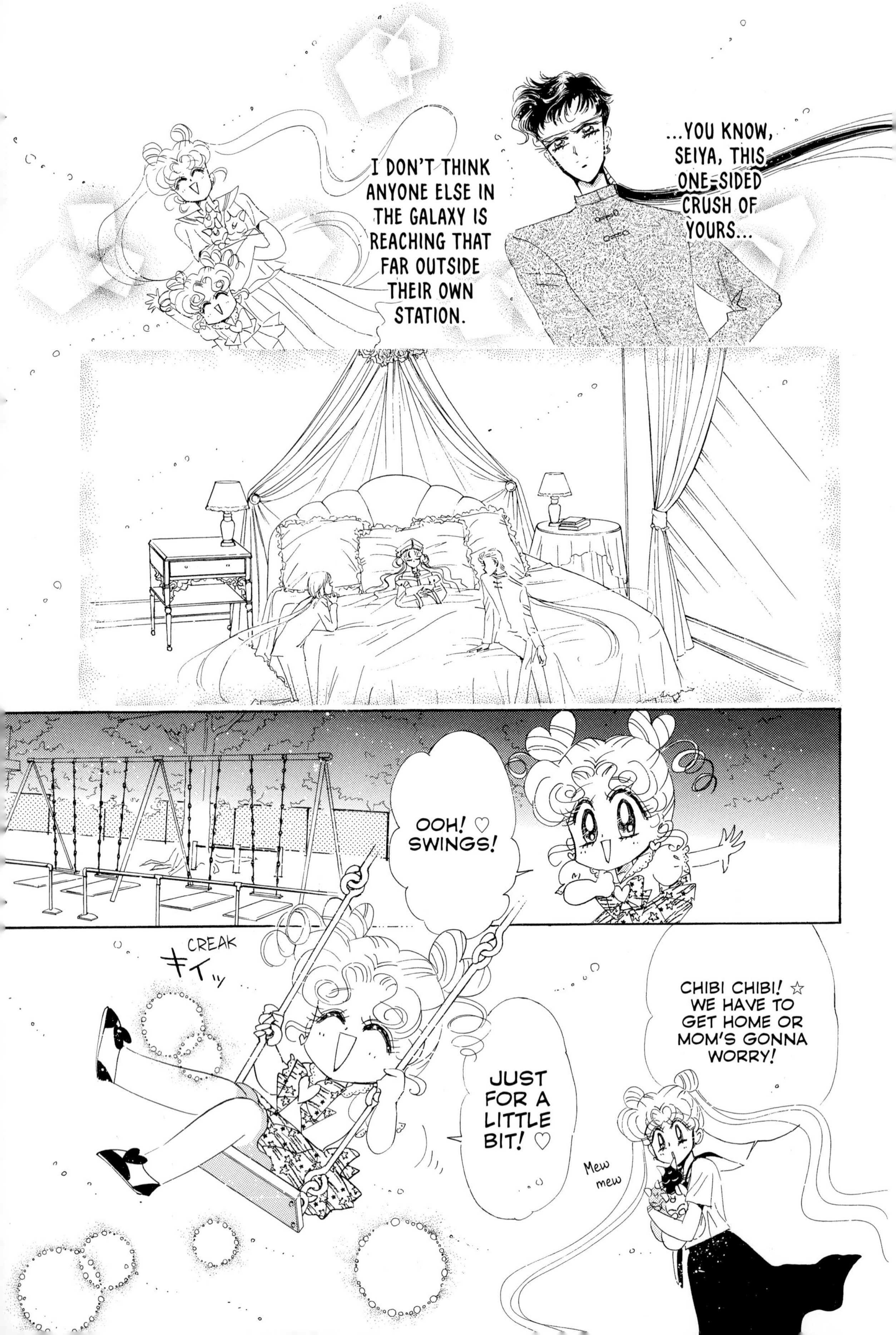
...YOU KNOW, SEIYA, THIS ONE-SIDED CRUSH OF YOURS...
I DON'T THINK ANYONE ELSE IN THE GALAXY IS REACHING THAT FAR OUTSIDE THEIR OWN STATION.
OOH! ♡ SWINGS!
CHIBI CHIBI! ☆ WE HAVE TO GET HOME OR MOM'S GONNA WORRY!
Mew mew
JUST FOR A LITTLE BIT! ♡
CREAK
キイッ

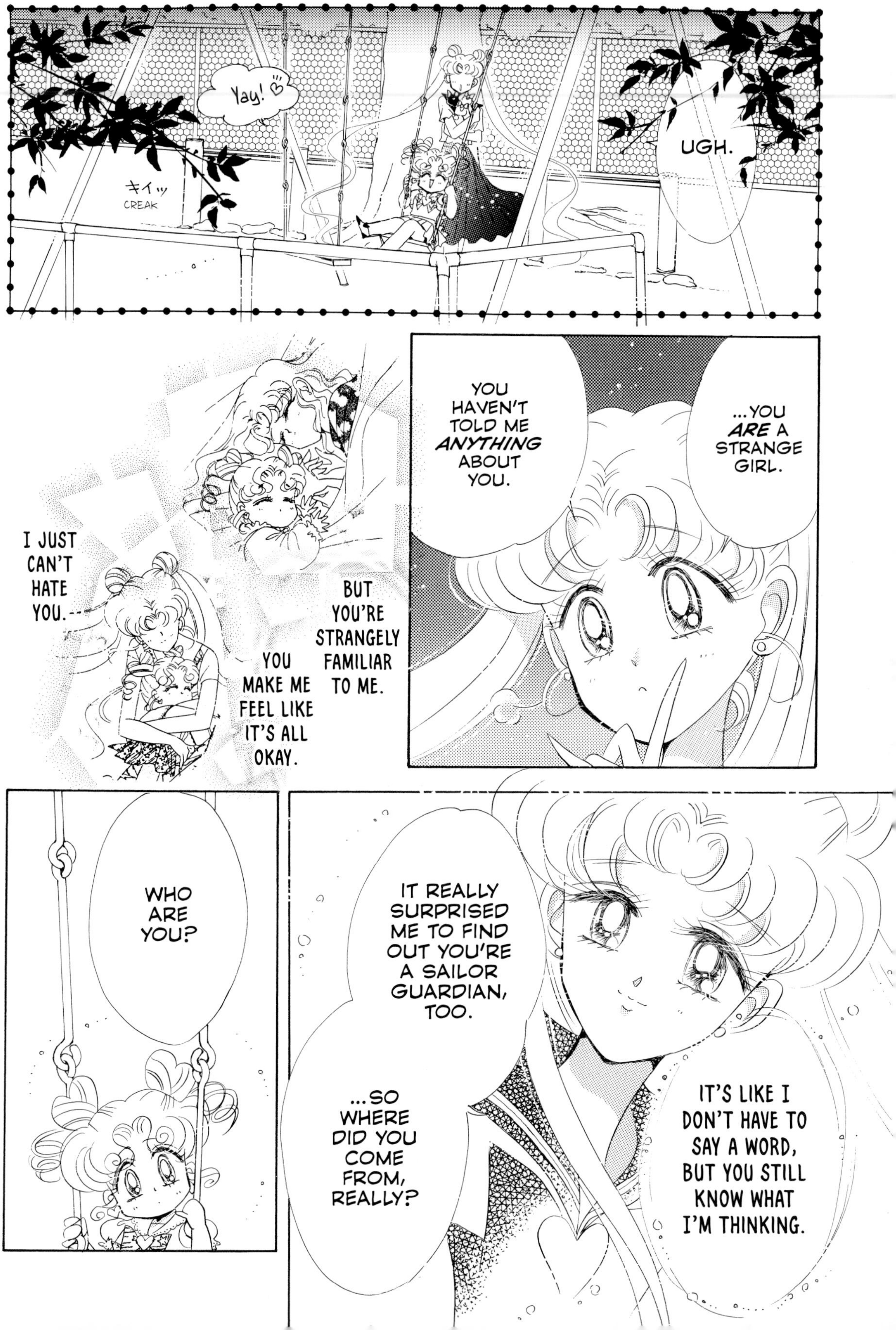
Yay!
UGH.
キイッ
CREAK
...YOU ARE A STRANGE GIRL.
YOU HAVEN'T TOLD ME ANYTHING ABOUT YOU.
BUT YOU'RE STRANGELY FAMILIAR TO ME.
YOU MAKE ME FEEL LIKE IT'S ALL OKAY.
I JUST CAN'T HATE YOU.
IT'S LIKE I DON'T HAVE TO SAY A WORD, BUT YOU STILL KNOW WHAT I'M THINKING.
IT REALLY SURPRISED ME TO FIND OUT YOU'RE A SAILOR GUARDIAN, TOO.
...SO WHERE DID YOU COME FROM, REALLY?
WHO ARE YOU?

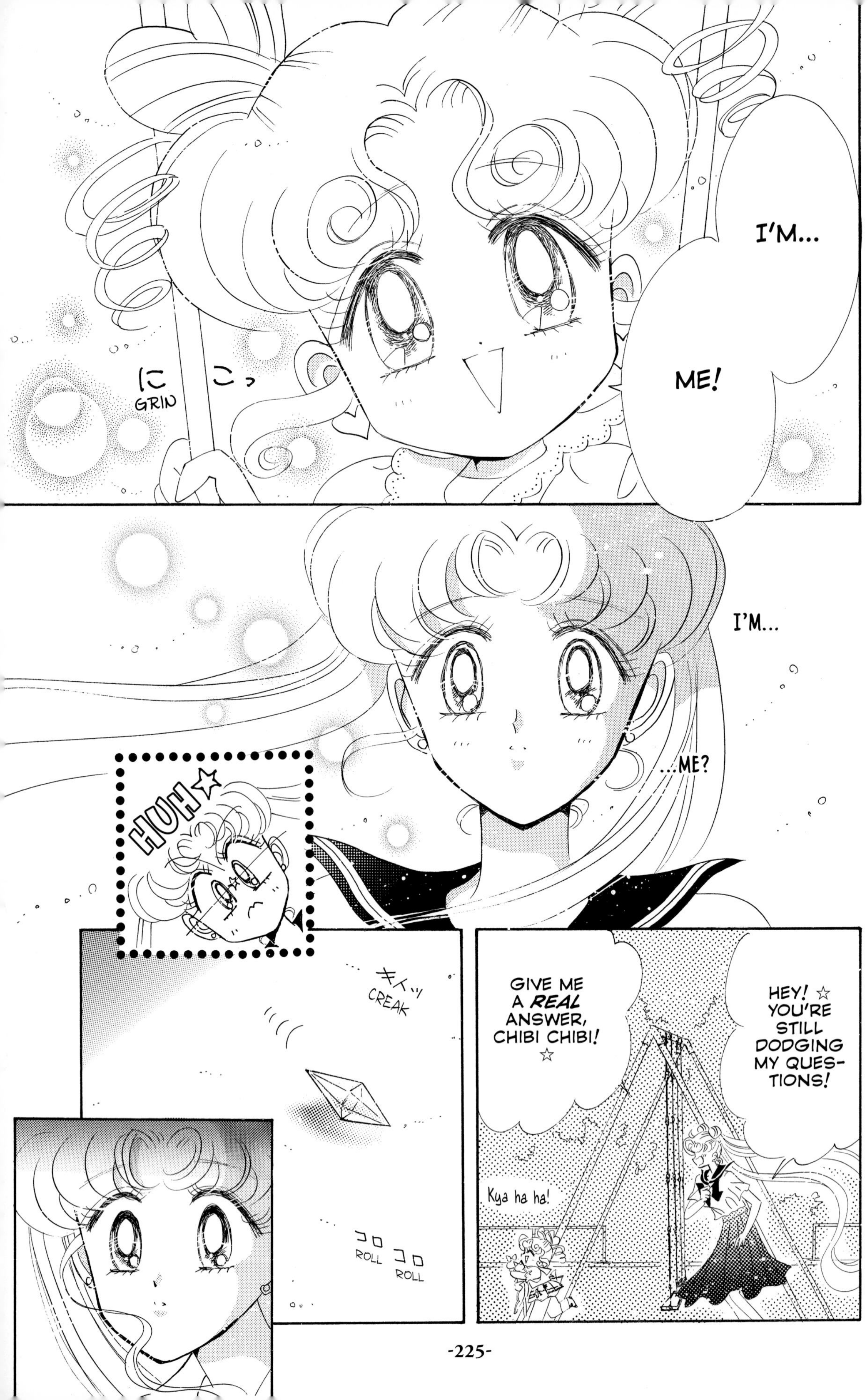
I'M...
ME!
にこっ
GRIN
I'M...
...ME?
HUH☆
HEY! ☆ YOU'RE STILL DODGING MY QUES-TIONS!
GIVE ME A **REAL** ANSWER, CHIBI CHIBI! ☆
Kya ha ha!
キイッ
CREAK
コロ
ROLL
コロ
ROLL

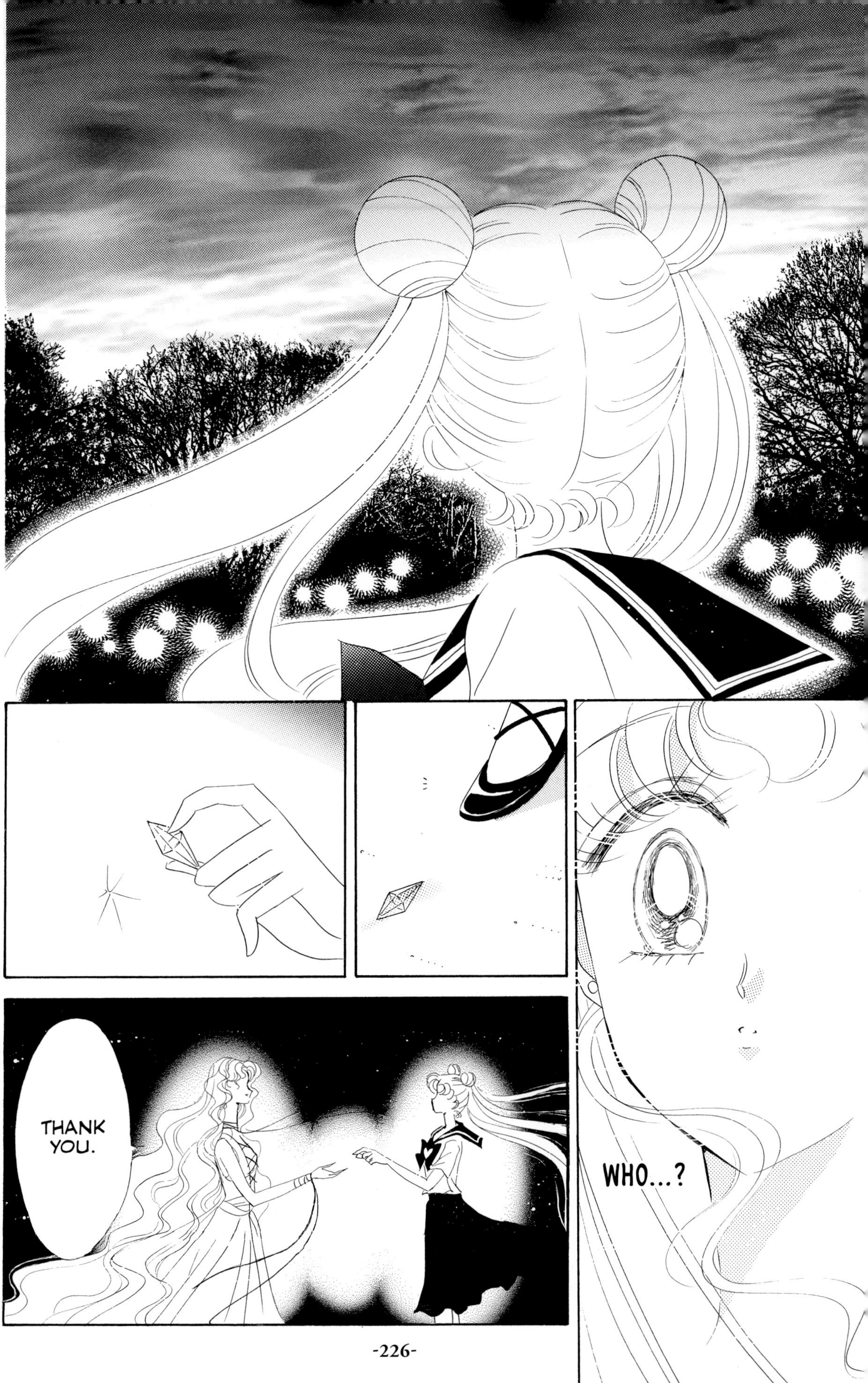
WHO...?
THANK YOU.

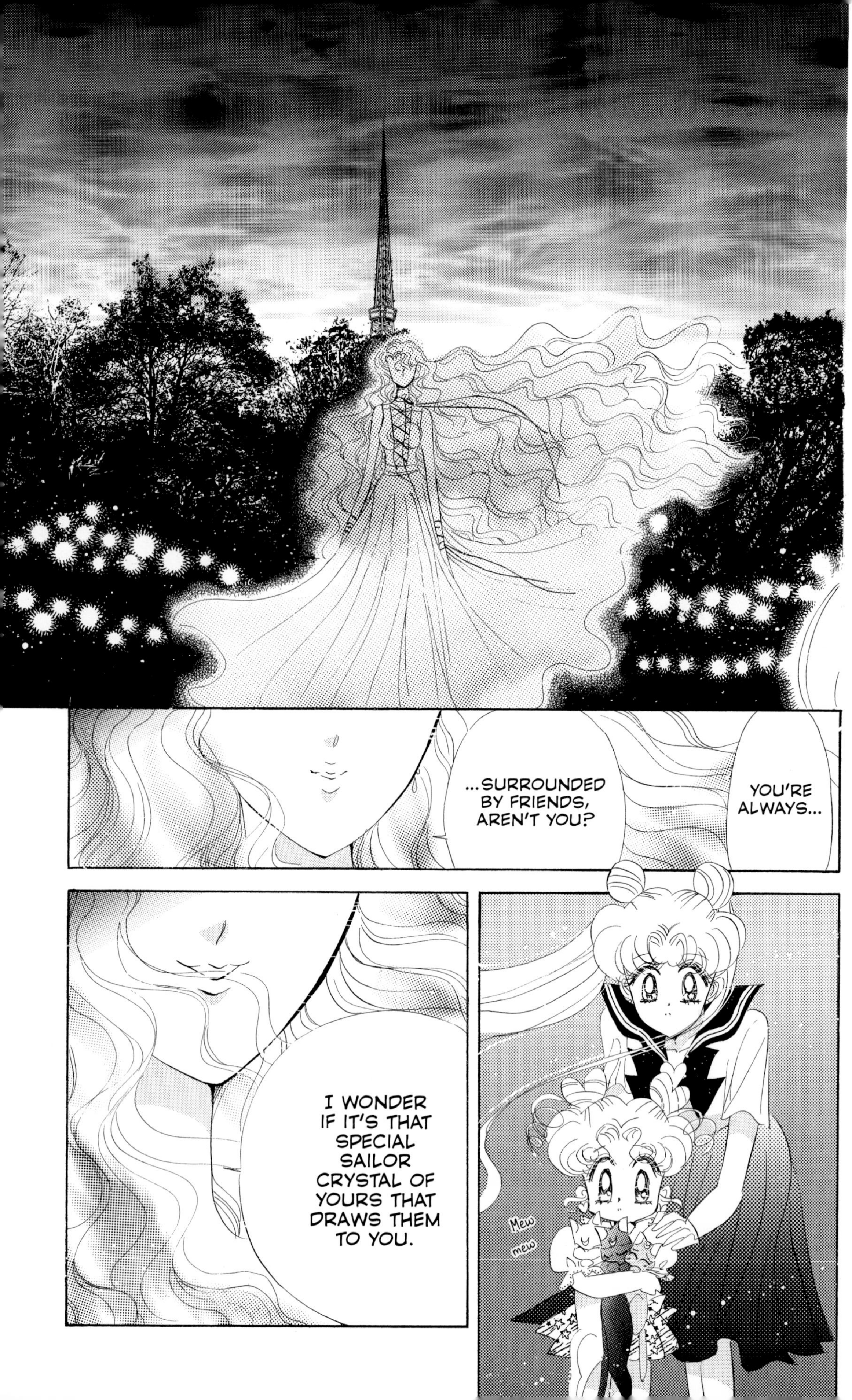
YOU'RE ALWAYS...
...SURROUNDED BY FRIENDS, AREN'T YOU?
Mew mew
I WONDER IF IT'S THAT SPECIAL SAILOR CRYSTAL OF YOURS THAT DRAWS THEM TO YOU.

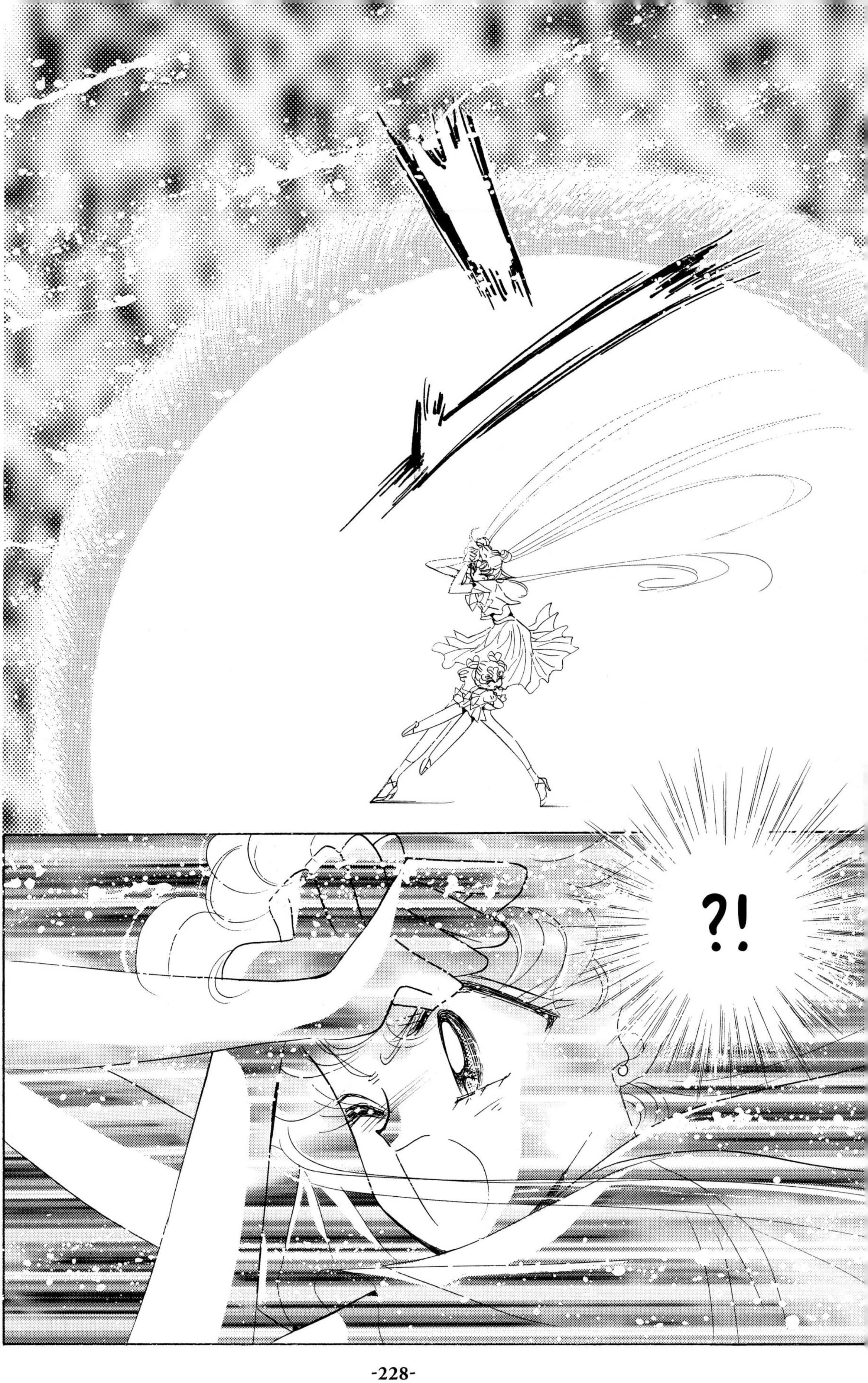
?!

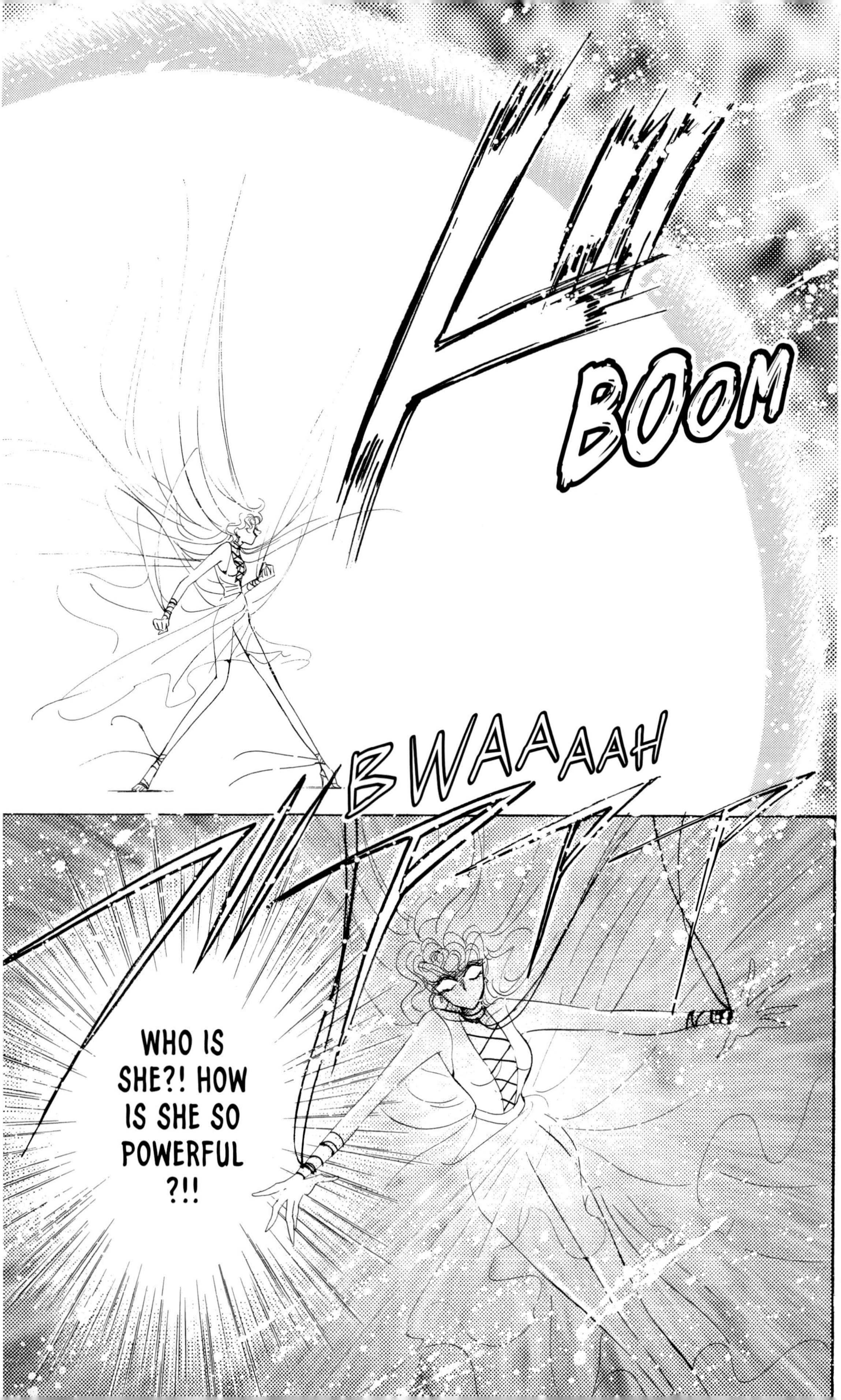
BOOM
BWAAAAAH
WHO IS SHE?! HOW IS SHE SO POWERFUL ?!!

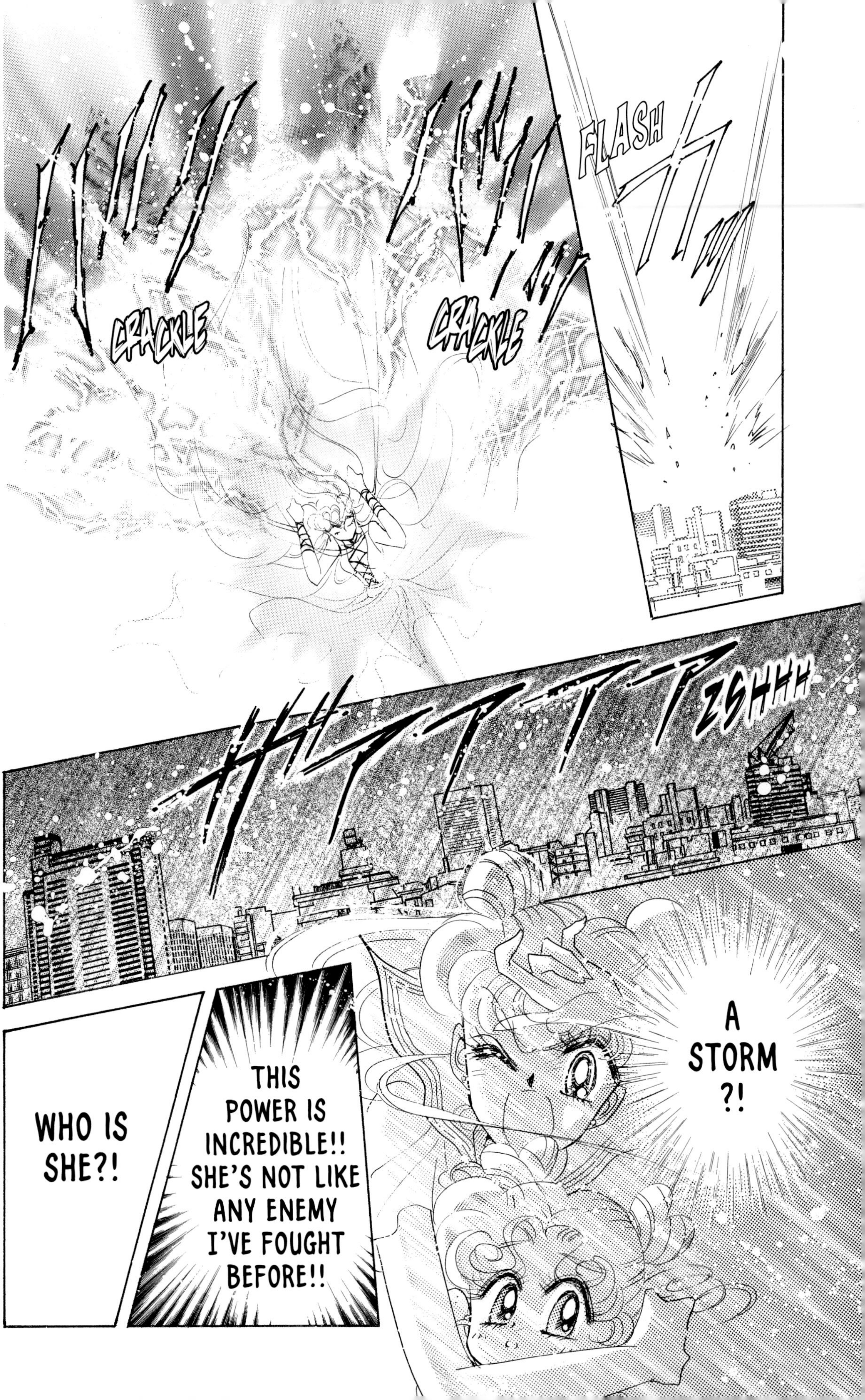
FLASH
CRACKLE
CRACKLE
ZSHHH
A STORM?!
THIS POWER IS INCREDIBLE!! SHE'S NOT LIKE ANY ENEMY I'VE FOUGHT BEFORE!!
WHO IS SHE?!

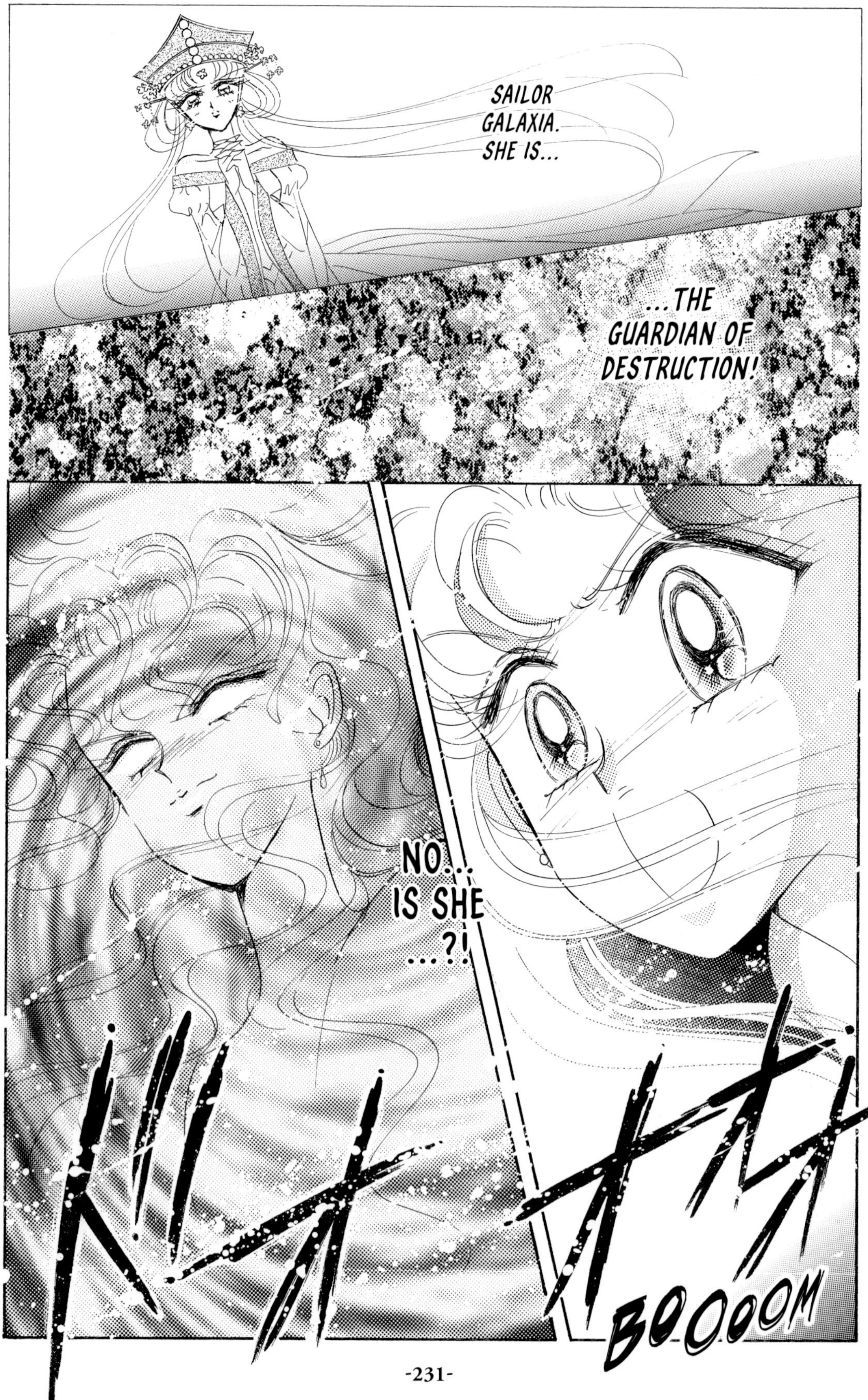

SAILOR GALAXIA. SHE IS...
...THE GUARDIAN OF DESTRUCTION!
NO... IS SHE ...?!
BOOOOM

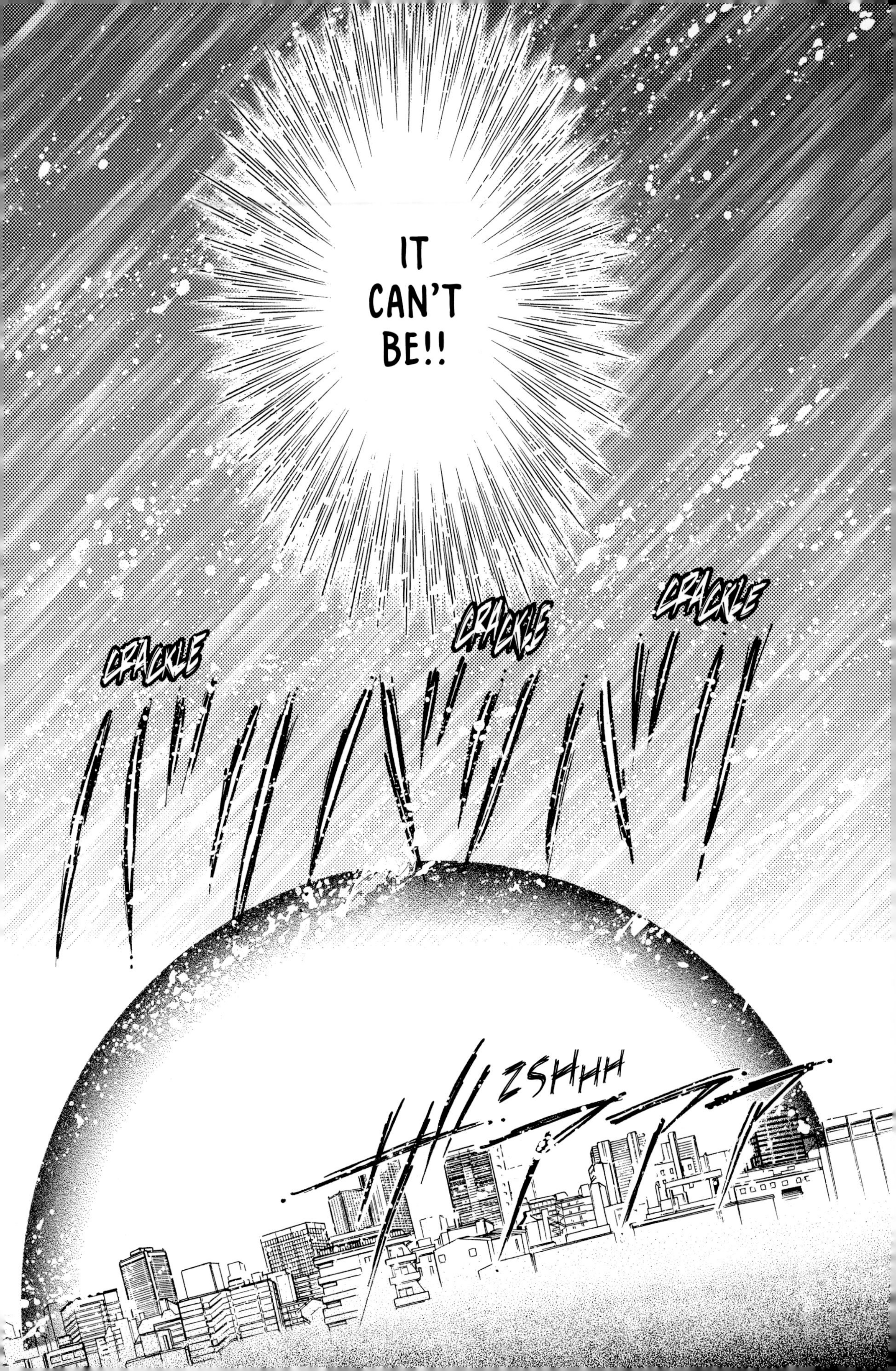
IT CAN'T BE!!
CRACKLE
CRACKLE
CRACKLE
ZSHHH

Act.55 Stars 6

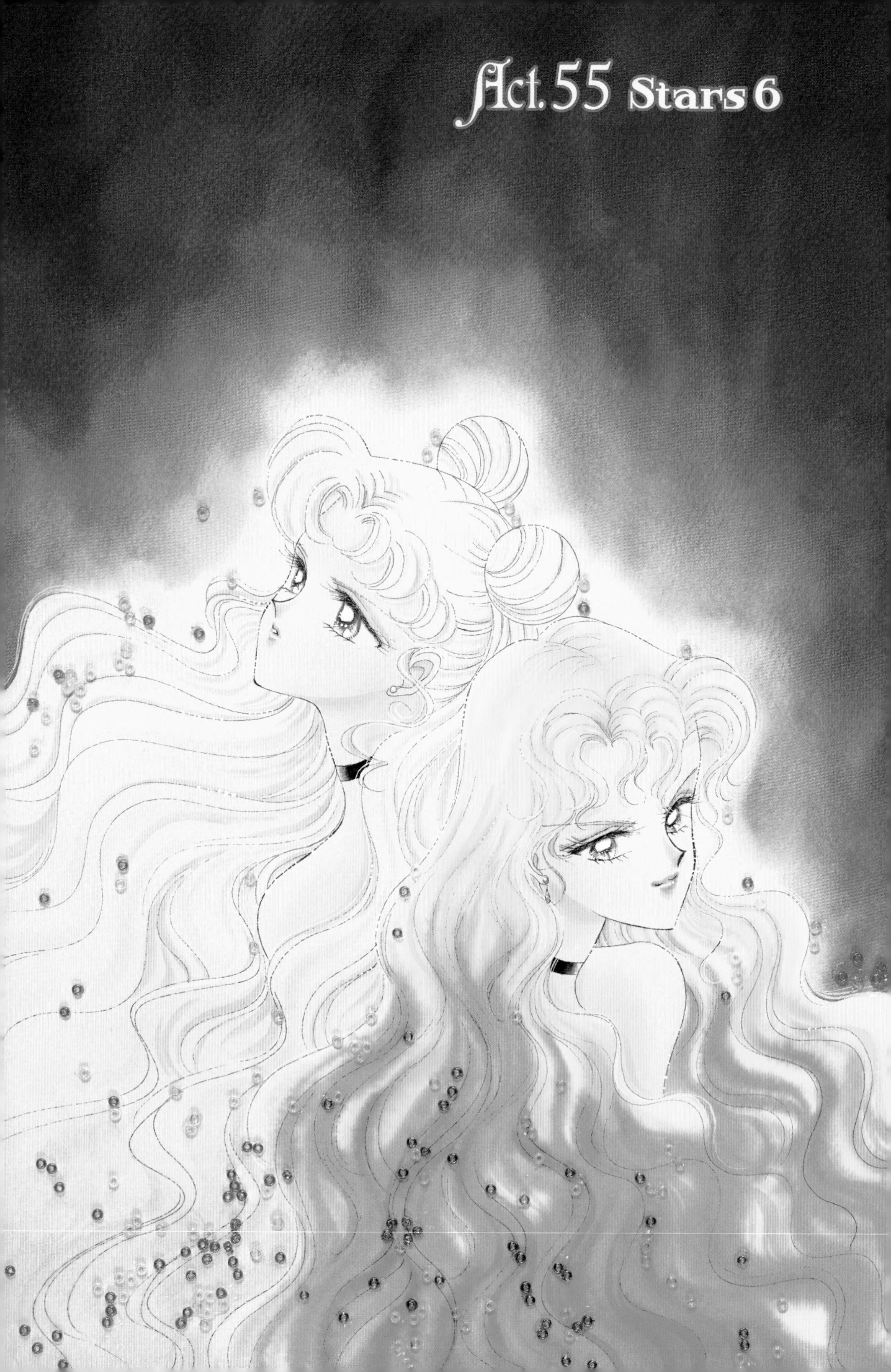

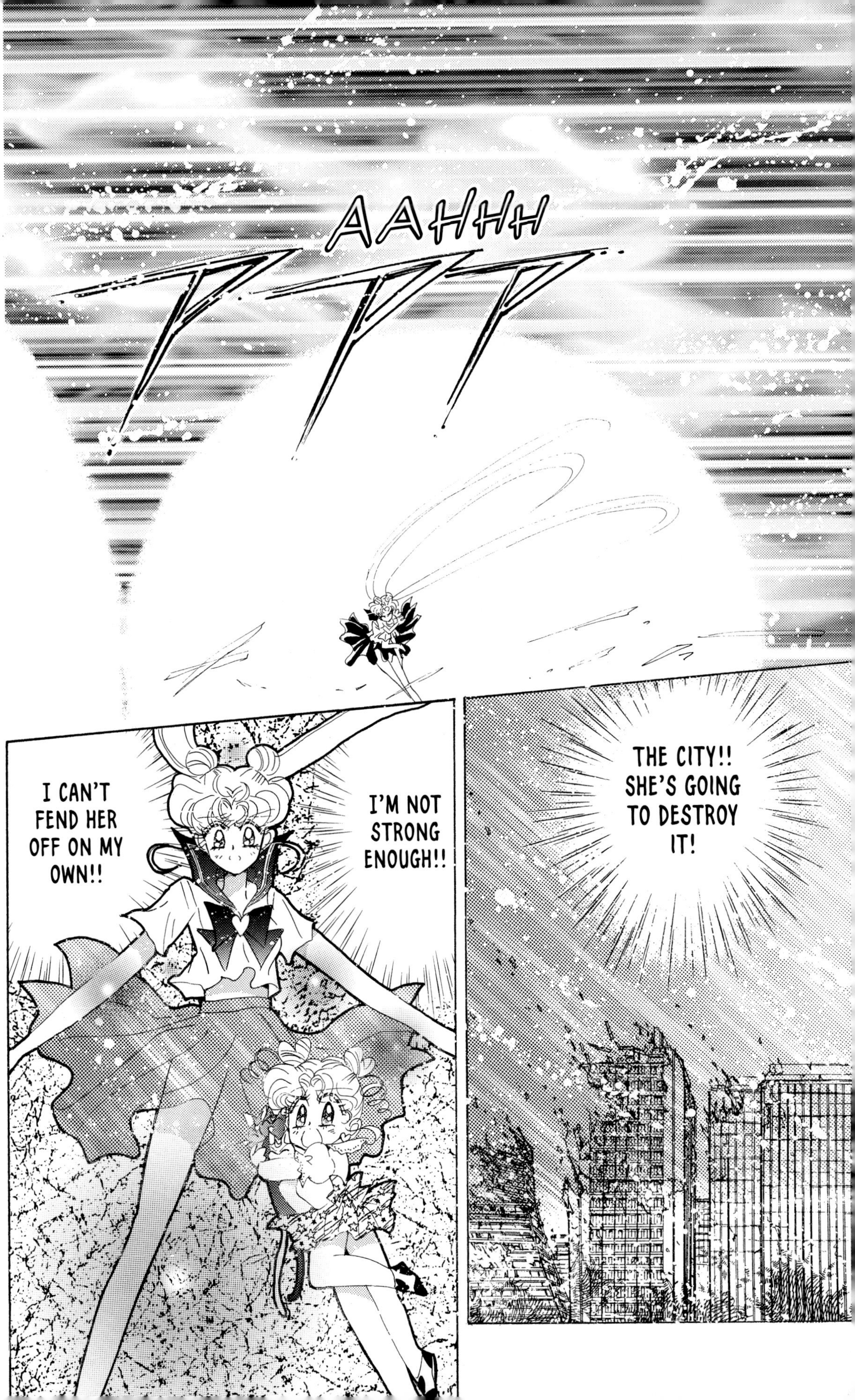
AAHHH
THE CITY!! SHE'S GOING TO DESTROY IT!
I'M NOT STRONG ENOUGH!!
I CAN'T FEND HER OFF ON MY OWN!!

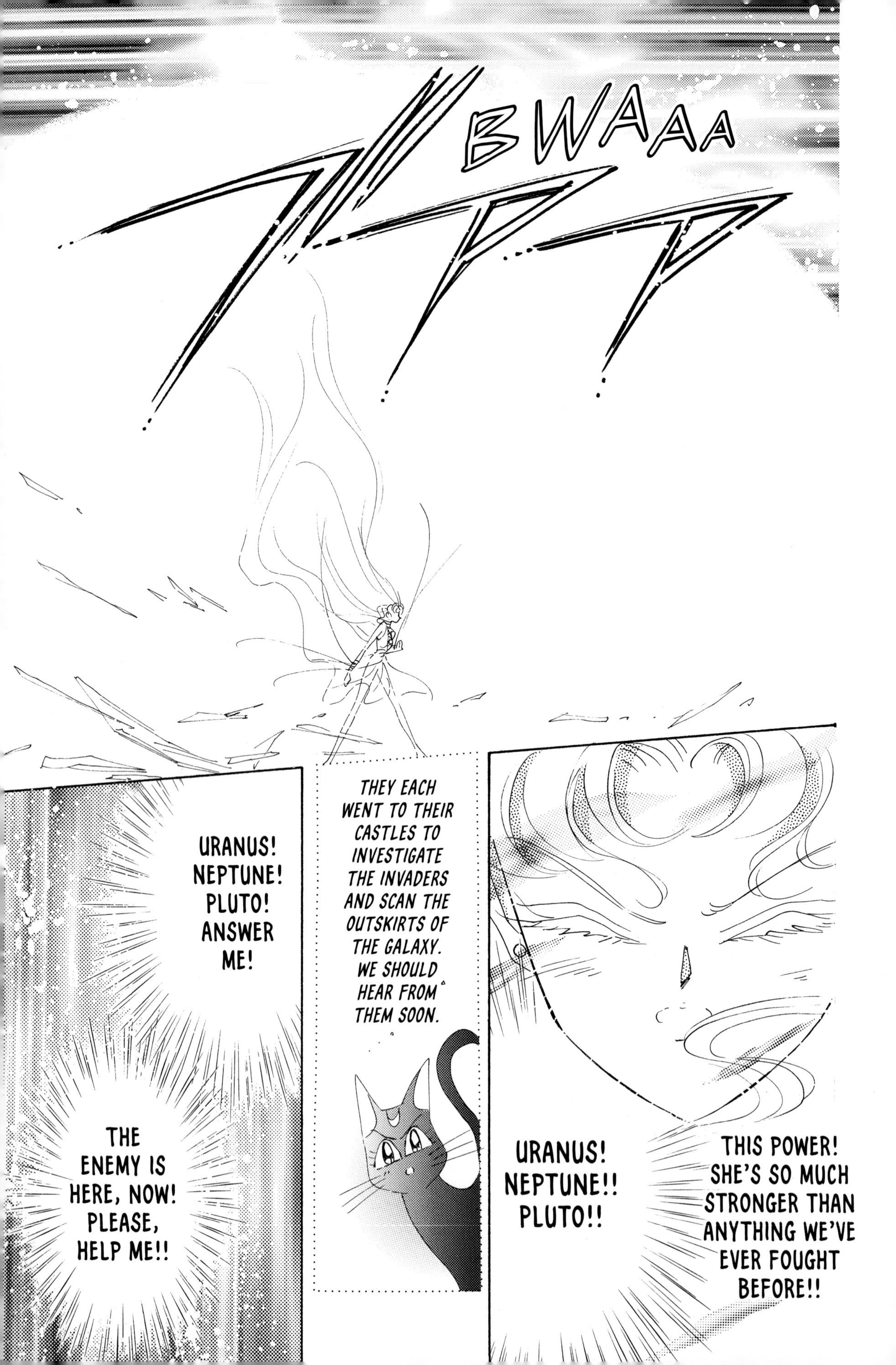
BWAAA
THIS POWER! SHE'S SO MUCH STRONGER THAN ANYTHING WE'VE EVER FOUGHT BEFORE!!
URANUS! NEPTUNE!! PLUTO!!
THEY EACH WENT TO THEIR CASTLES TO INVESTIGATE THE INVADERS AND SCAN THE OUTSKIRTS OF THE GALAXY. WE SHOULD HEAR FROM THEM SOON.
URANUS! NEPTUNE! PLUTO! ANSWER ME!
THE ENEMY IS HERE, NOW! PLEASE, HELP ME!!

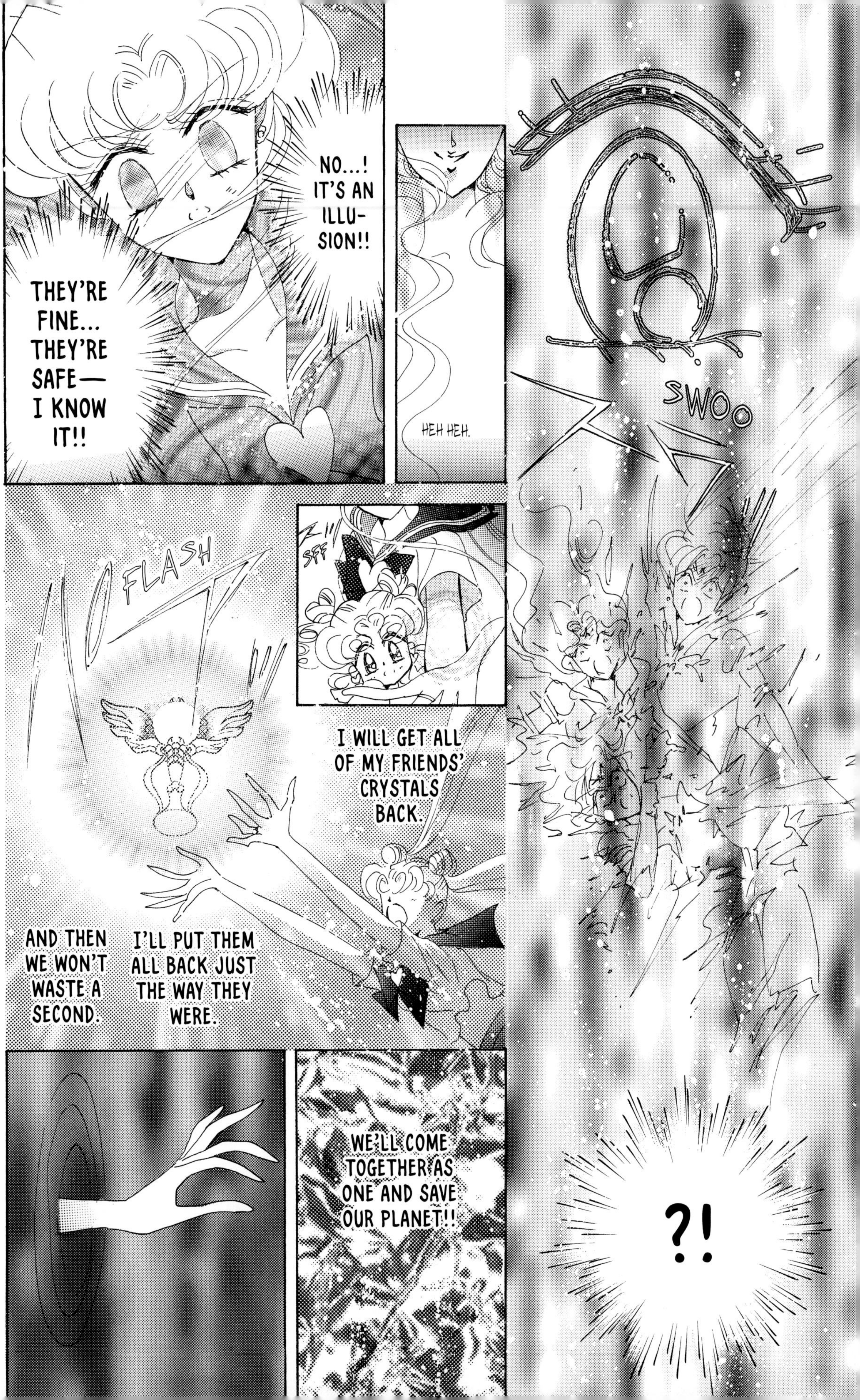
SWOO
?!
HEH HEH.
NO...! IT'S AN ILLUSION!!
THEY'RE FINE... THEY'RE SAFE— I KNOW IT!!
SFF
FLASH
I WILL GET ALL OF MY FRIENDS' CRYSTALS BACK.
I'LL PUT THEM ALL BACK JUST THE WAY THEY WERE.
AND THEN WE WON'T WASTE A SECOND.
WE'LL COME TOGETHER AS ONE AND SAVE OUR PLANET!!

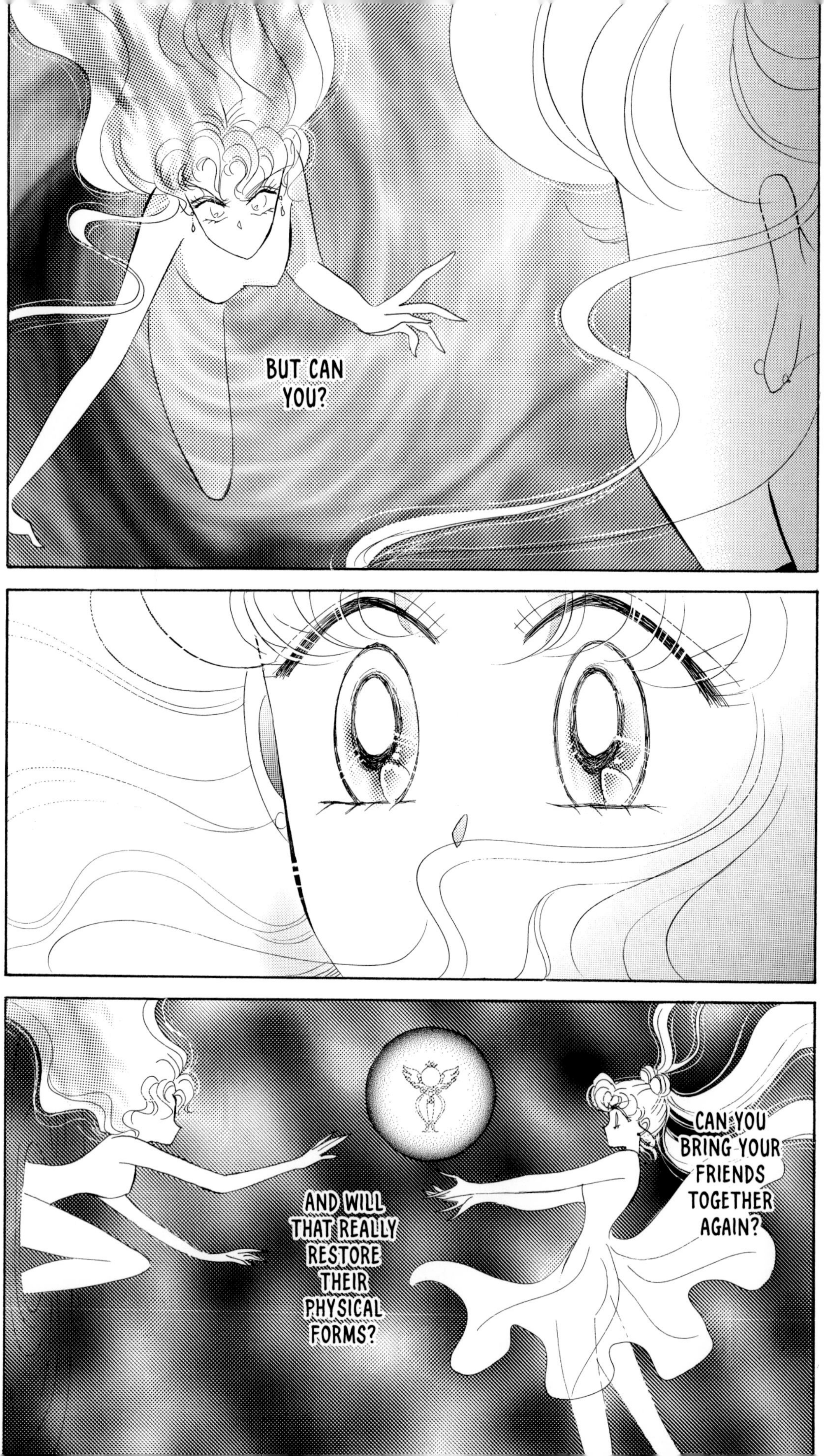
BUT CAN YOU?
CAN YOU BRING YOUR FRIENDS TOGETHER AGAIN?
AND WILL THAT REALLY RESTORE THEIR PHYSICAL FORMS?

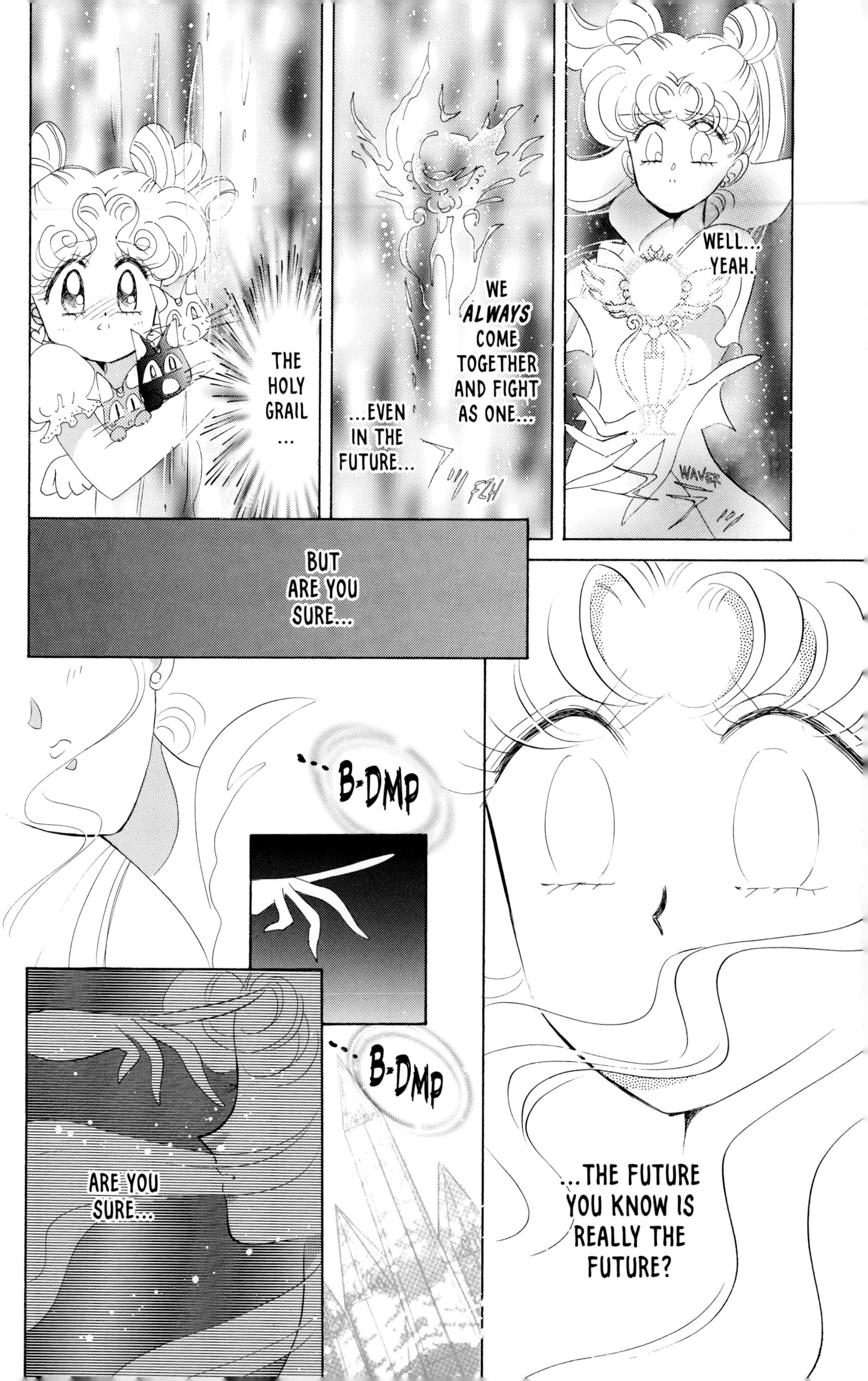

WELL... YEAH.
WAVER
WE ALWAYS COME TOGETHER AND FIGHT AS ONE...
...EVEN IN THE FUTURE...
FZH
THE HOLY GRAIL ...
...THE FUTURE YOU KNOW IS REALLY THE FUTURE?
BUT ARE YOU SURE...
B-DMP
B-DMP
ARE YOU SURE...

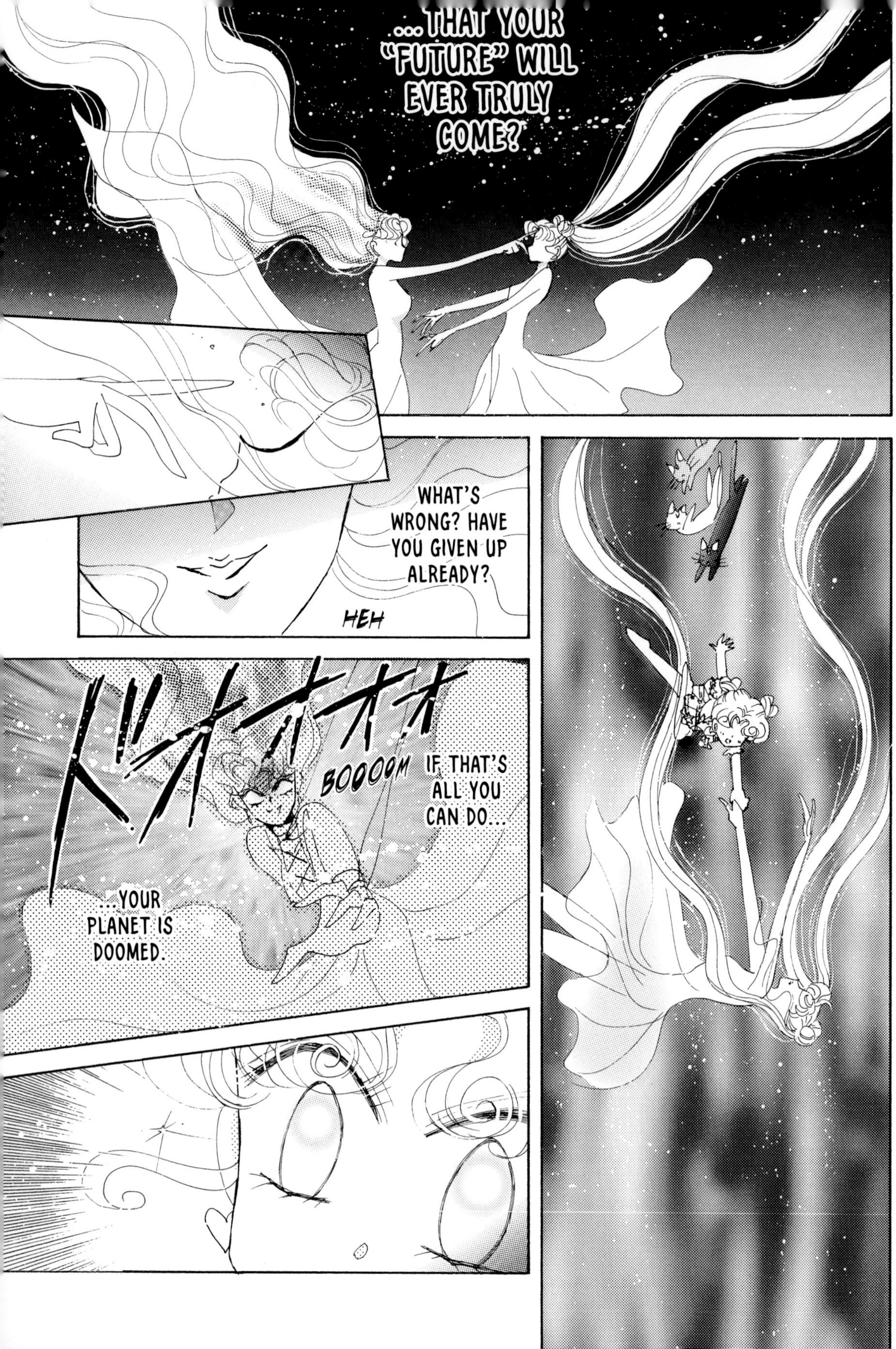
...THAT YOUR "FUTURE" WILL EVER TRULY COME?
WHAT'S WRONG? HAVE YOU GIVEN UP ALREADY?
HEH
BOOOOM
IF THAT'S ALL YOU CAN DO...
...YOUR PLANET IS DOOMED.

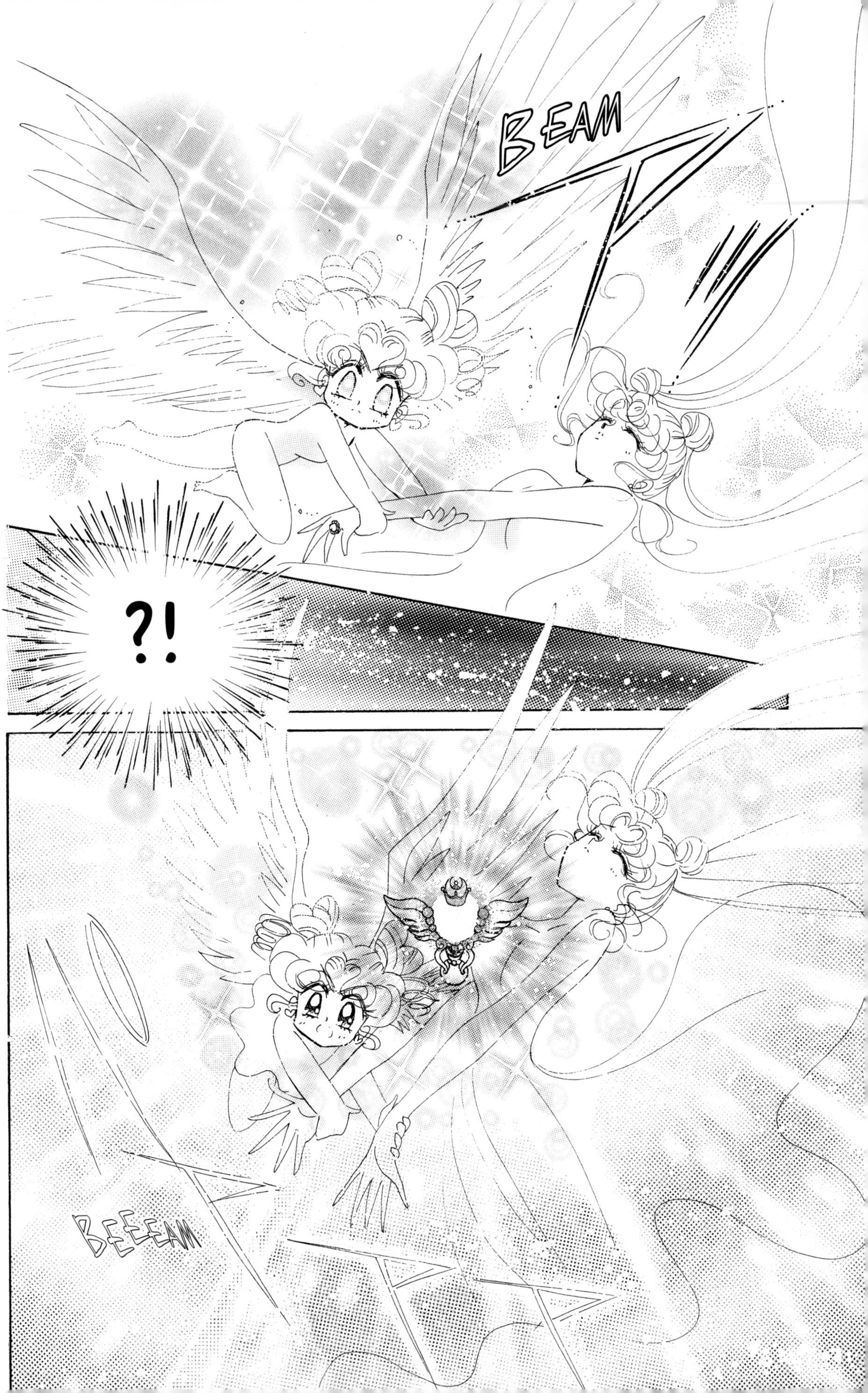
BEAM
?!
BEEEAM

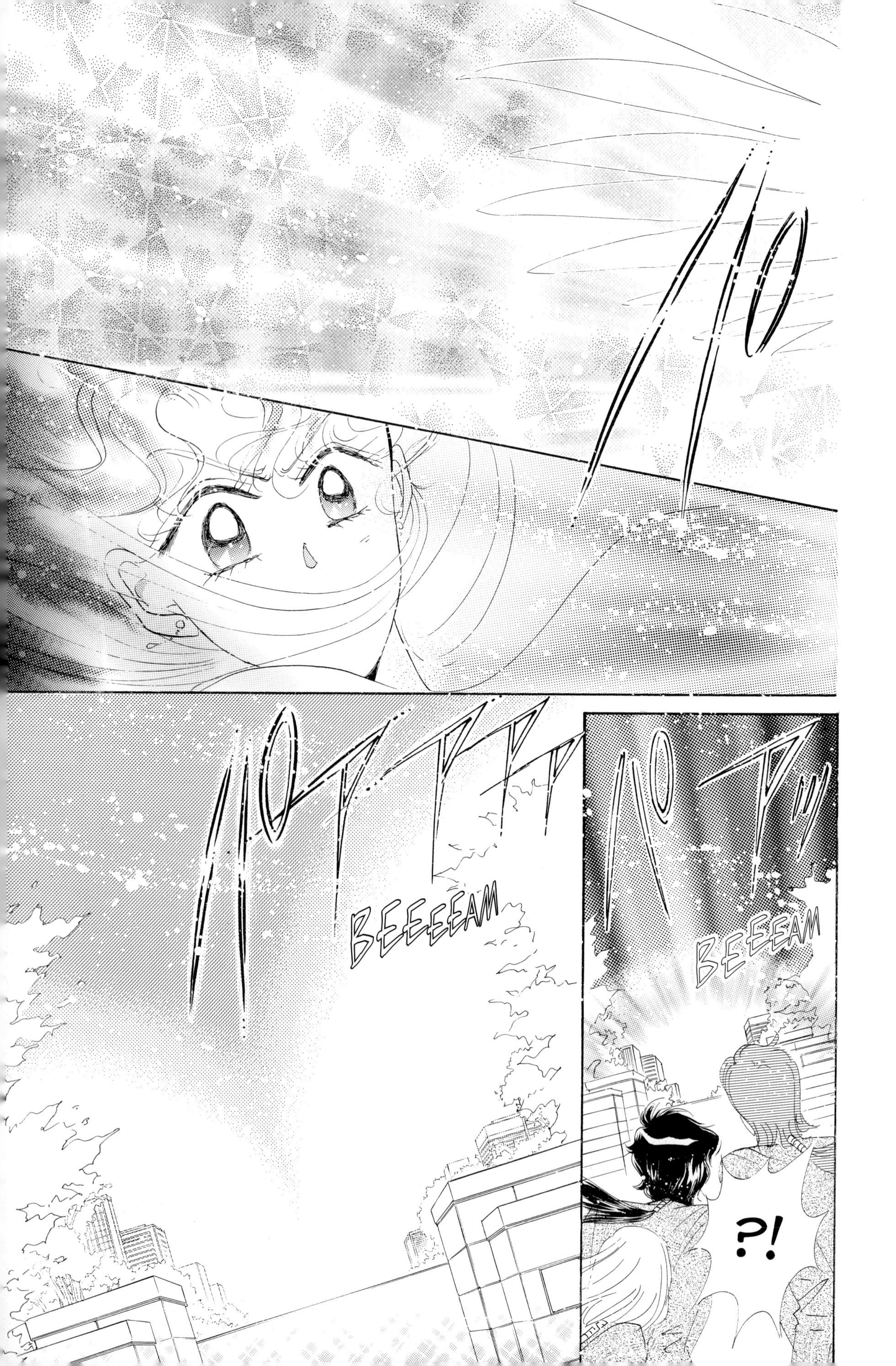
パ
パアッ
BEEEAM
?!
パアアアッ
BEEEEAM

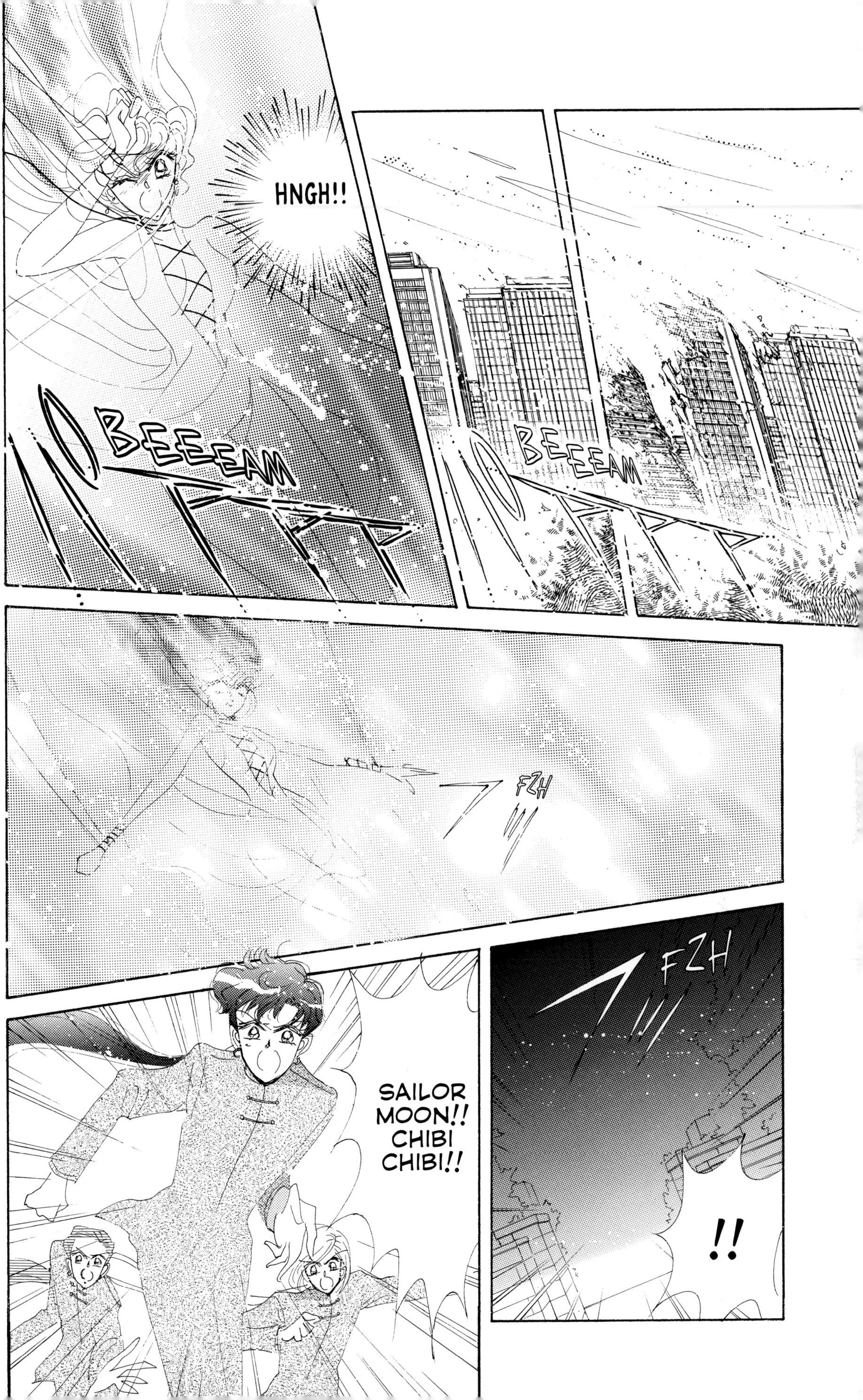
BEEEAM
HNGH!!
BEEEAM
FZH
FZH
!!
SAILOR MOON!! CHIBI CHIBI!!

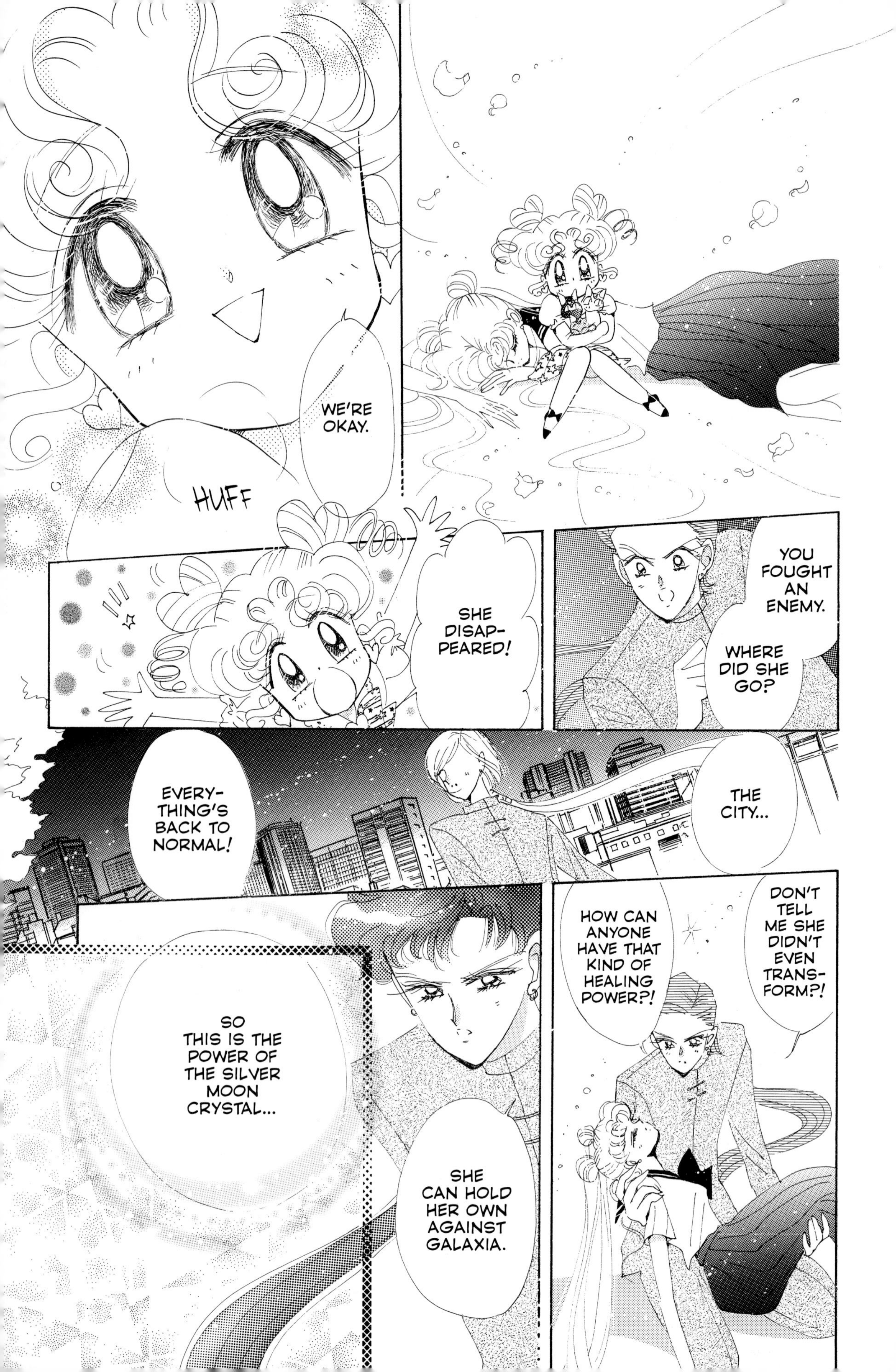

WE'RE OKAY.
HUFF
YOU FOUGHT AN ENEMY.
WHERE DID SHE GO?
!!!
SHE DISAPPEARED!
THE CITY...
EVERYTHING'S BACK TO NORMAL!
DON'T TELL ME SHE DIDN'T EVEN TRANSFORM?!
HOW CAN ANYONE HAVE THAT KIND OF HEALING POWER?!
SO THIS IS THE POWER OF THE SILVER MOON CRYSTAL...
SHE CAN HOLD HER OWN AGAINST GALAXIA.

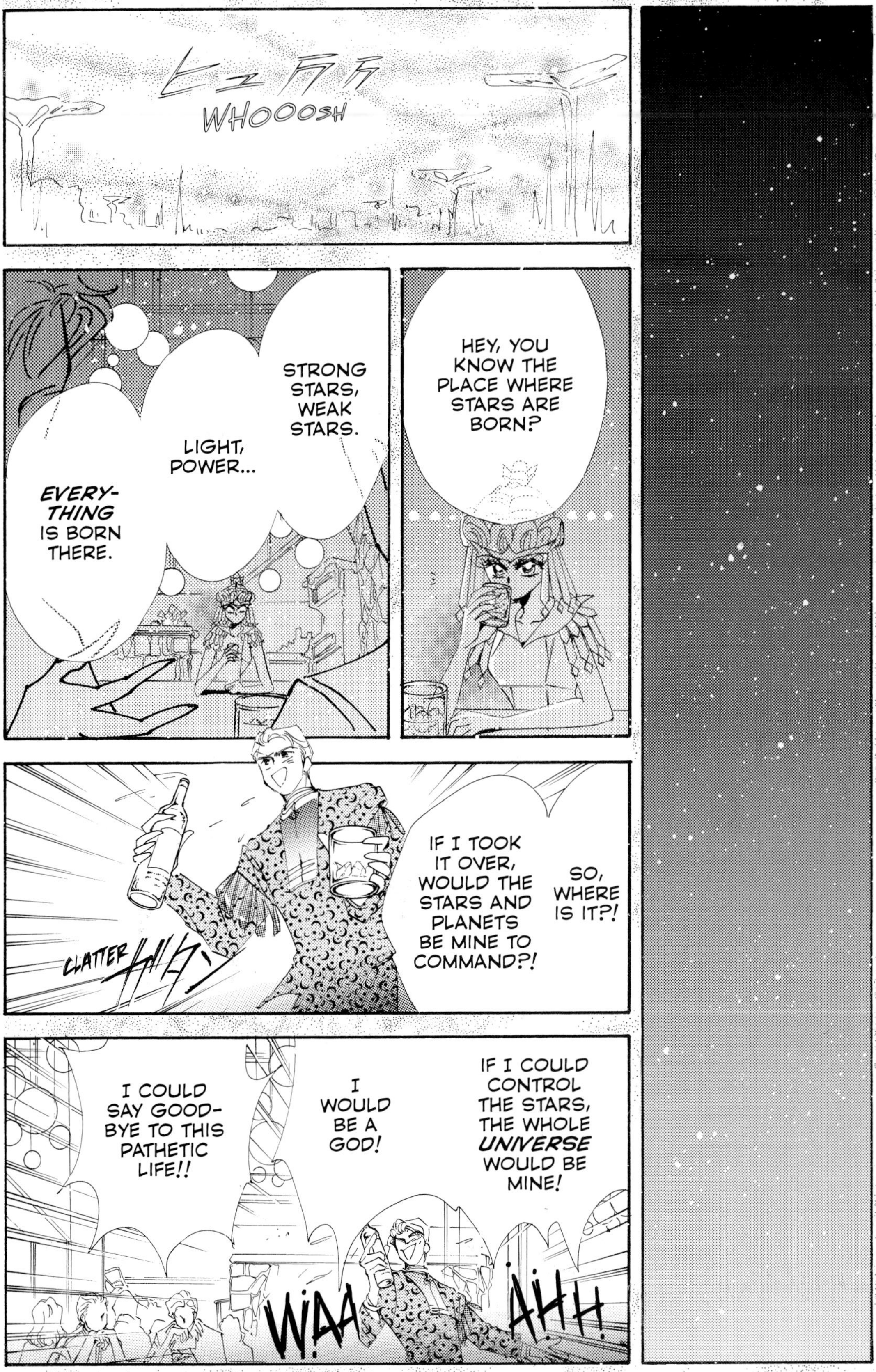
WHOOOSH
HEY, YOU KNOW THE PLACE WHERE STARS ARE BORN?
STRONG STARS, WEAK STARS.
LIGHT, POWER...
EVERYTHING IS BORN THERE.
SO, WHERE IS IT?!
IF I TOOK IT OVER, WOULD THE STARS AND PLANETS BE MINE TO COMMAND?!
CLATTER
IF I COULD CONTROL THE STARS, THE WHOLE *UNIVERSE* WOULD BE MINE!
I WOULD BE A GOD!
I COULD SAY GOOD-BYE TO THIS PATHETIC LIFE!!
WAA
AHH

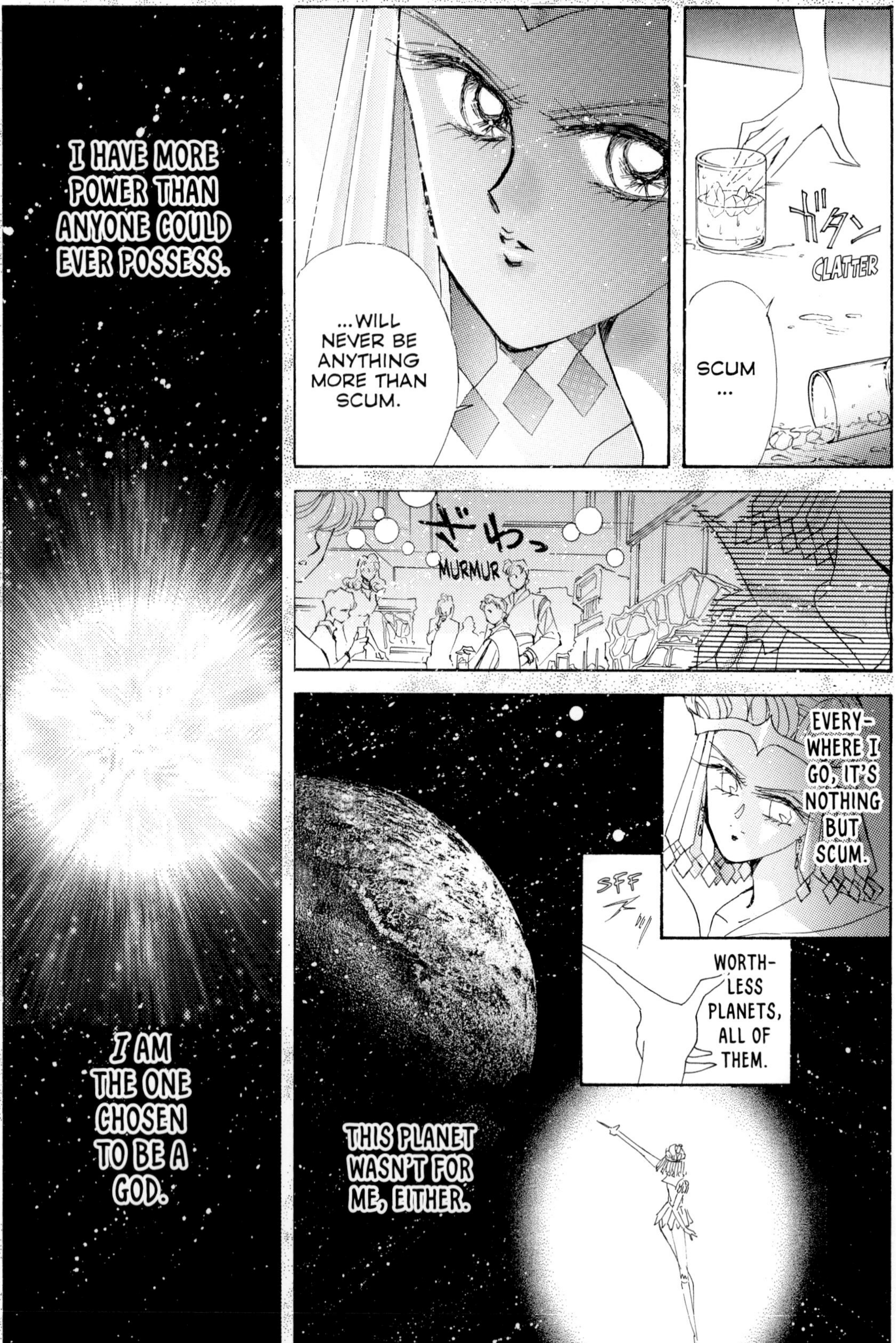
ガタン
CLATTER
SCUM ...
...WILL NEVER BE ANYTHING MORE THAN SCUM.
ざわっ
MURMUR
EVERY-WHERE I GO, IT'S NOTHING BUT SCUM.
SFF
WORTH-LESS PLANETS, ALL OF THEM.
THIS PLANET WASN'T FOR ME, EITHER.
I HAVE MORE POWER THAN ANYONE COULD EVER POSSESS.
I AM THE ONE CHOSEN TO BE A GOD.

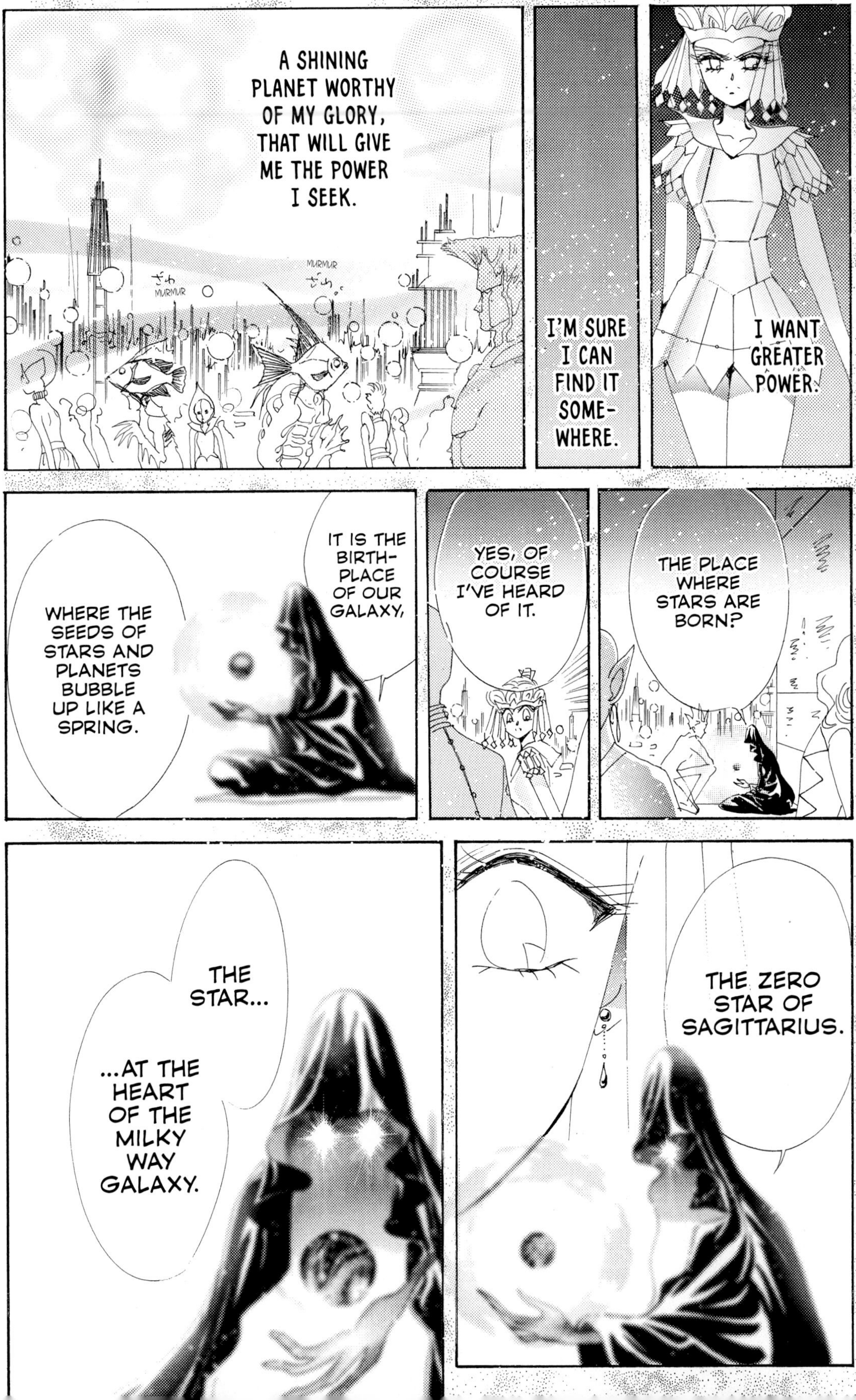
I WANT GREATER POWER.
I'M SURE I CAN FIND IT SOMEWHERE.
A SHINING PLANET WORTHY OF MY GLORY, THAT WILL GIVE ME THE POWER I SEEK.
MURMUR
MURMUR
THE PLACE WHERE STARS ARE BORN?
YES, OF COURSE I'VE HEARD OF IT.
IT IS THE BIRTHPLACE OF OUR GALAXY,
WHERE THE SEEDS OF STARS AND PLANETS BUBBLE UP LIKE A SPRING.
THE ZERO STAR OF SAGITTARIUS.
THE STAR...
...AT THE HEART OF THE MILKY WAY GALAXY.

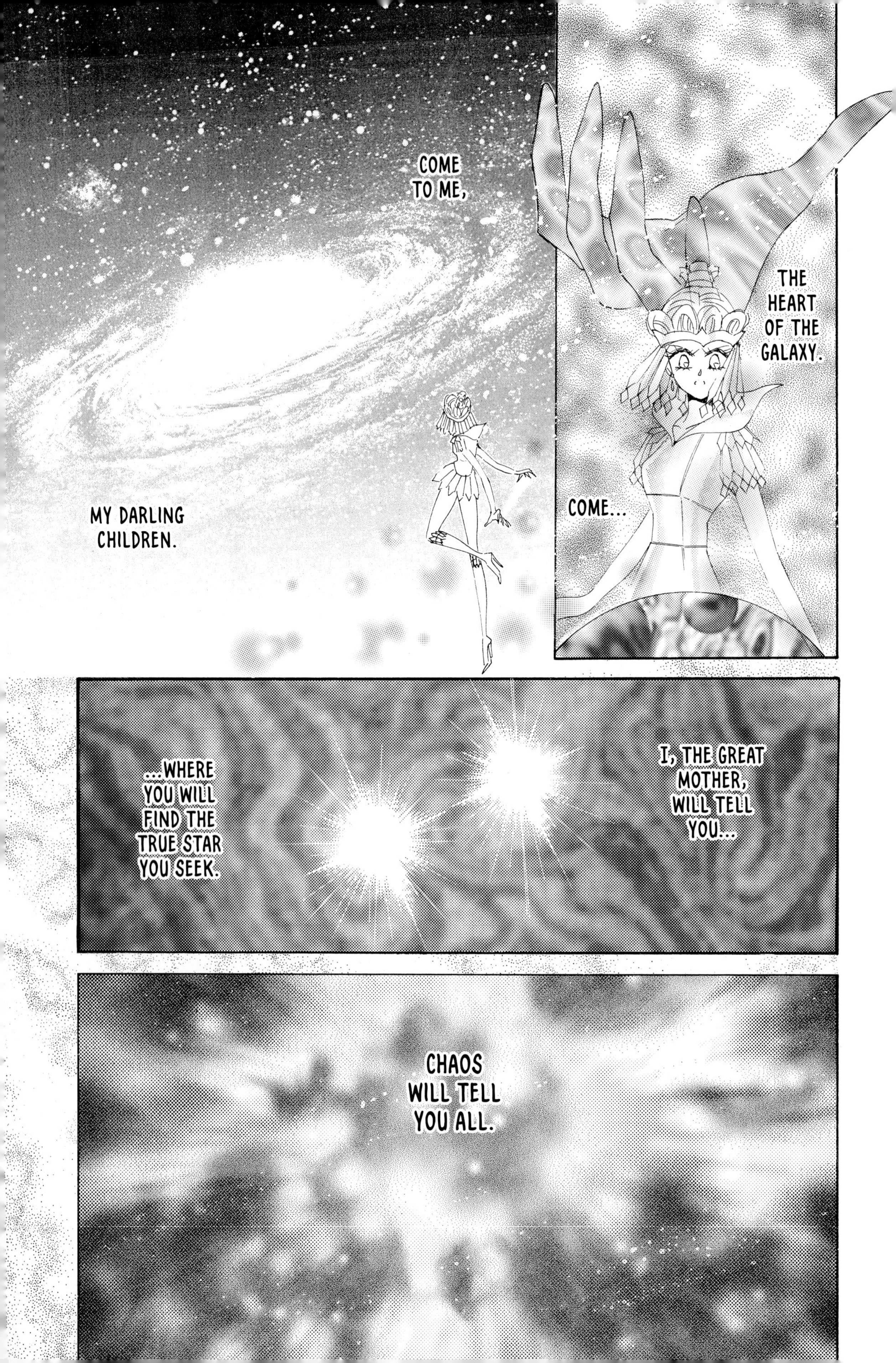
THE HEART OF THE GALAXY.
COME...
COME TO ME,
MY DARLING CHILDREN.
I, THE GREAT MOTHER, WILL TELL YOU...
...WHERE YOU WILL FIND THE TRUE STAR YOU SEEK.
CHAOS WILL TELL YOU ALL.

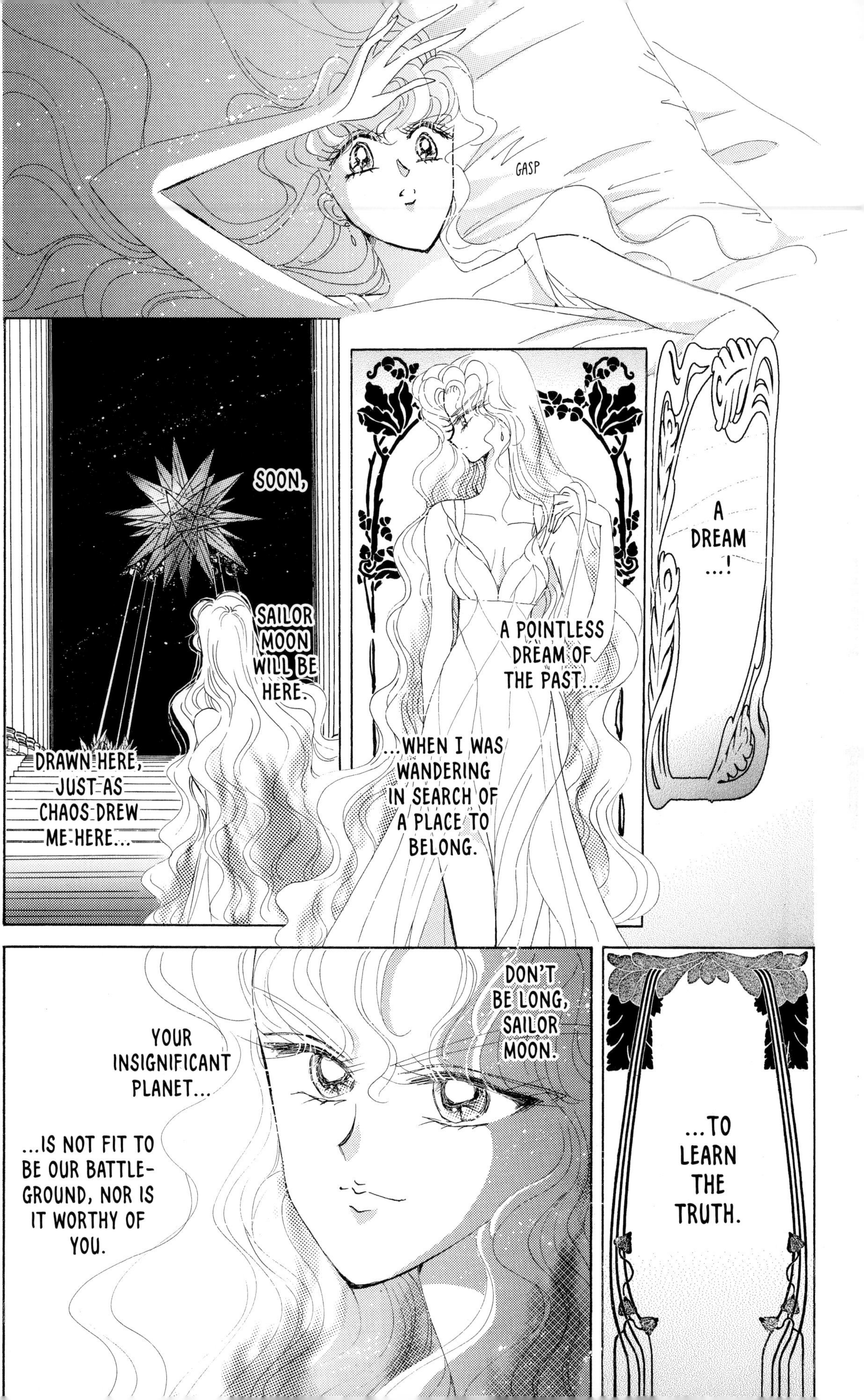
GASP
A DREAM ...!
A POINTLESS DREAM OF THE PAST...
...WHEN I WAS WANDERING IN SEARCH OF A PLACE TO BELONG.
SOON,
SAILOR MOON WILL BE HERE.
DRAWN HERE, JUST AS CHAOS DREW ME HERE...
...TO LEARN THE TRUTH.
DON'T BE LONG, SAILOR MOON.
YOUR INSIGNIFICANT PLANET...
...IS NOT FIT TO BE OUR BATTLE-GROUND, NOR IS IT WORTHY OF YOU.

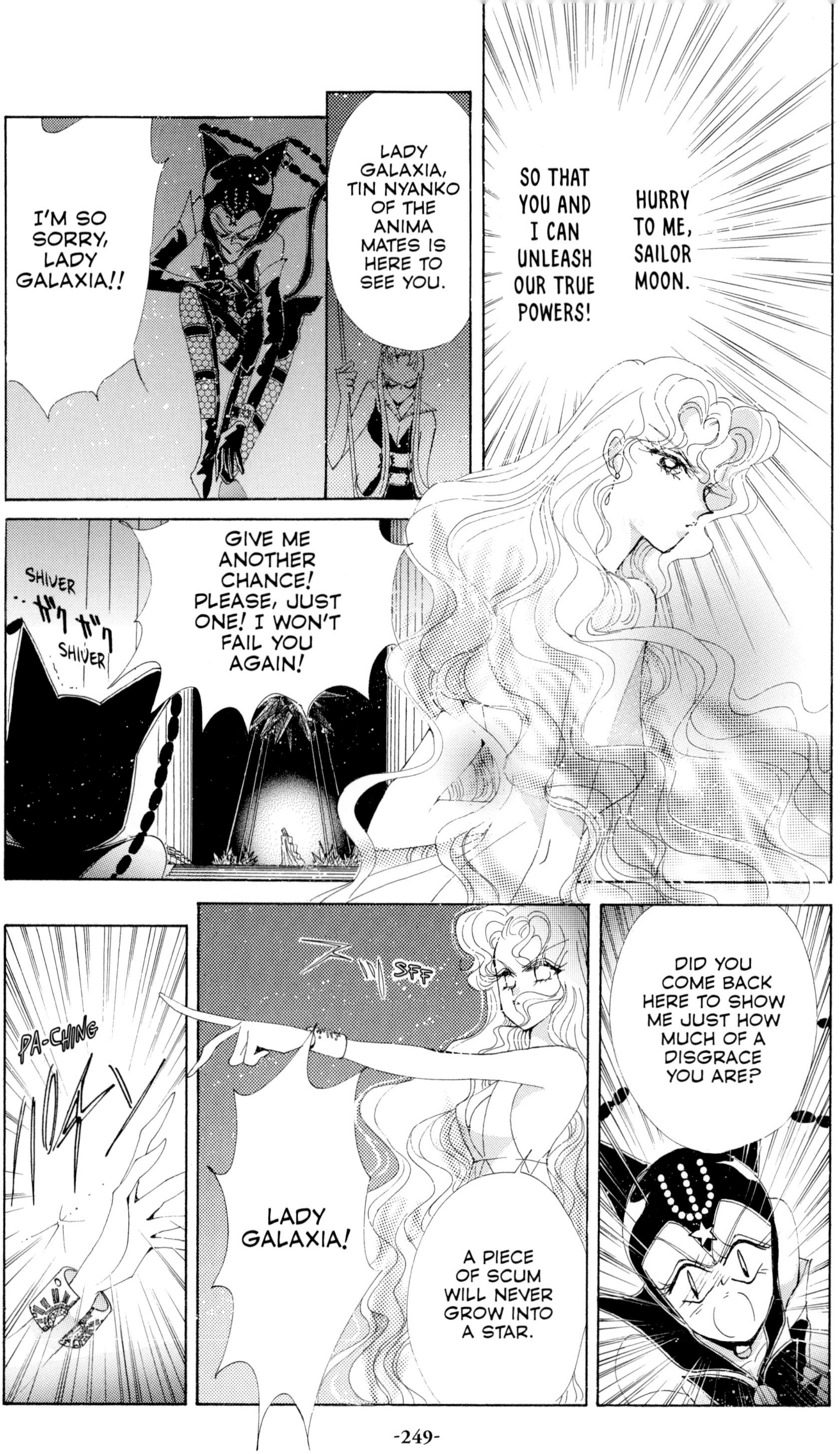
HURRY TO ME, SAILOR MOON.
SO THAT YOU AND I CAN UNLEASH OUR TRUE POWERS!
LADY GALAXIA, TIN NYANKO OF THE ANIMA MATES IS HERE TO SEE YOU.
I'M SO SORRY, LADY GALAXIA!!
SHIVER
SHIVER
GIVE ME ANOTHER CHANCE! PLEASE, JUST ONE! I WON'T FAIL YOU AGAIN!
DID YOU COME BACK HERE TO SHOW ME JUST HOW MUCH OF A DISGRACE YOU ARE?
SFF
A PIECE OF SCUM WILL NEVER GROW INTO A STAR.
LADY GALAXIA!
PA-CHING

WHERE...

...AM I?

CLANG

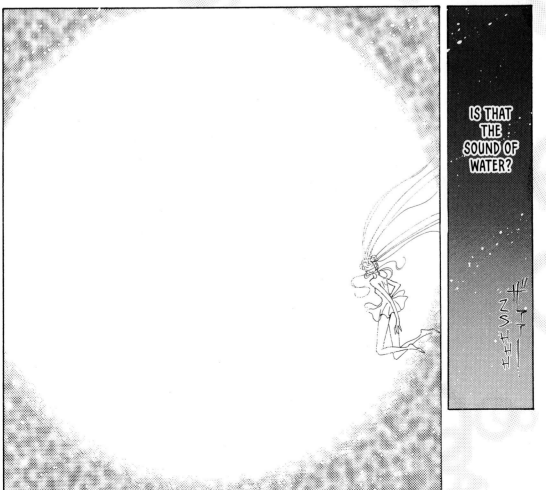

IS THAT THE SOUND OF WATER?

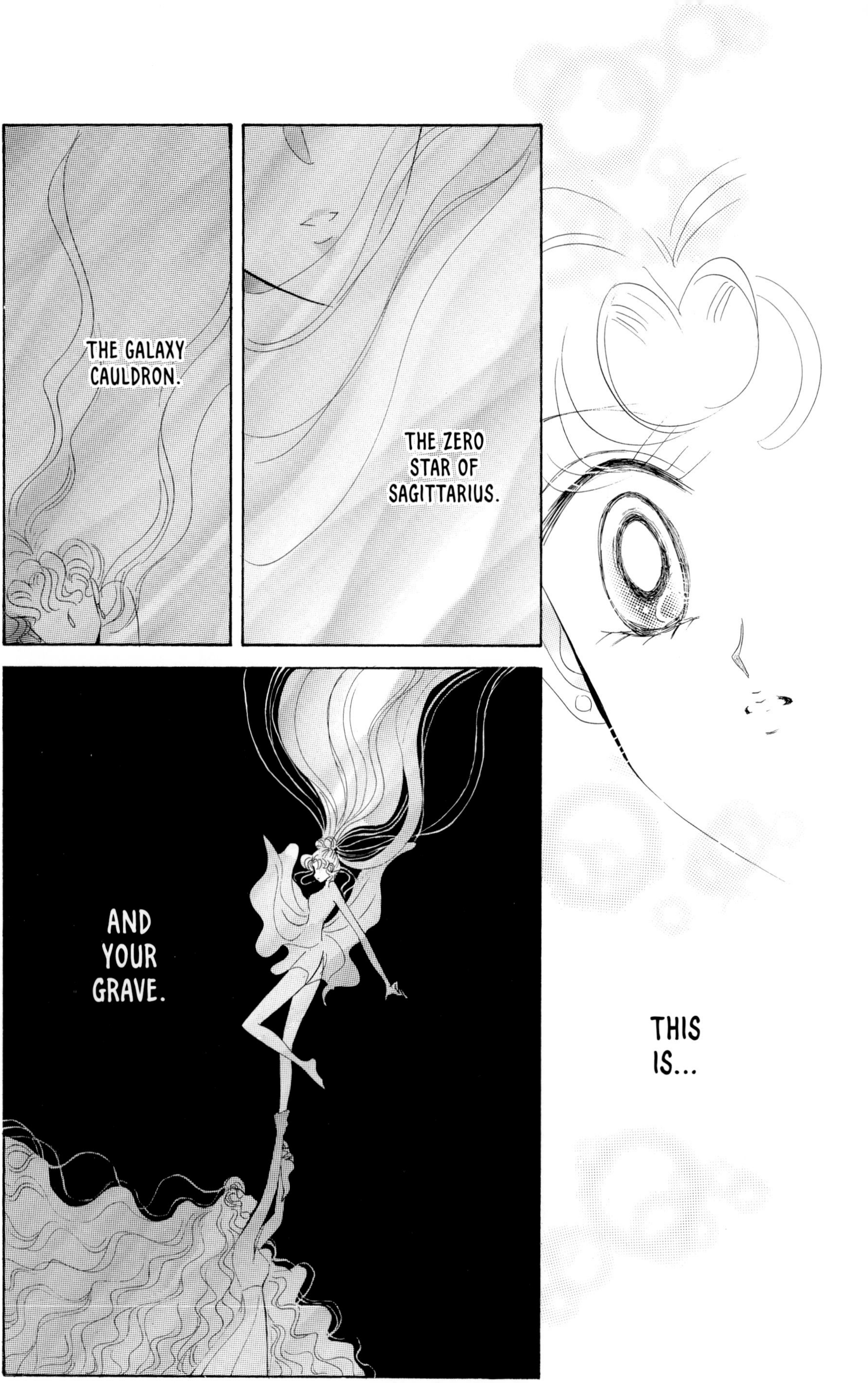
THIS IS...
THE ZERO STAR OF SAGITTARIUS.
THE GALAXY CAULDRON.
AND YOUR GRAVE.

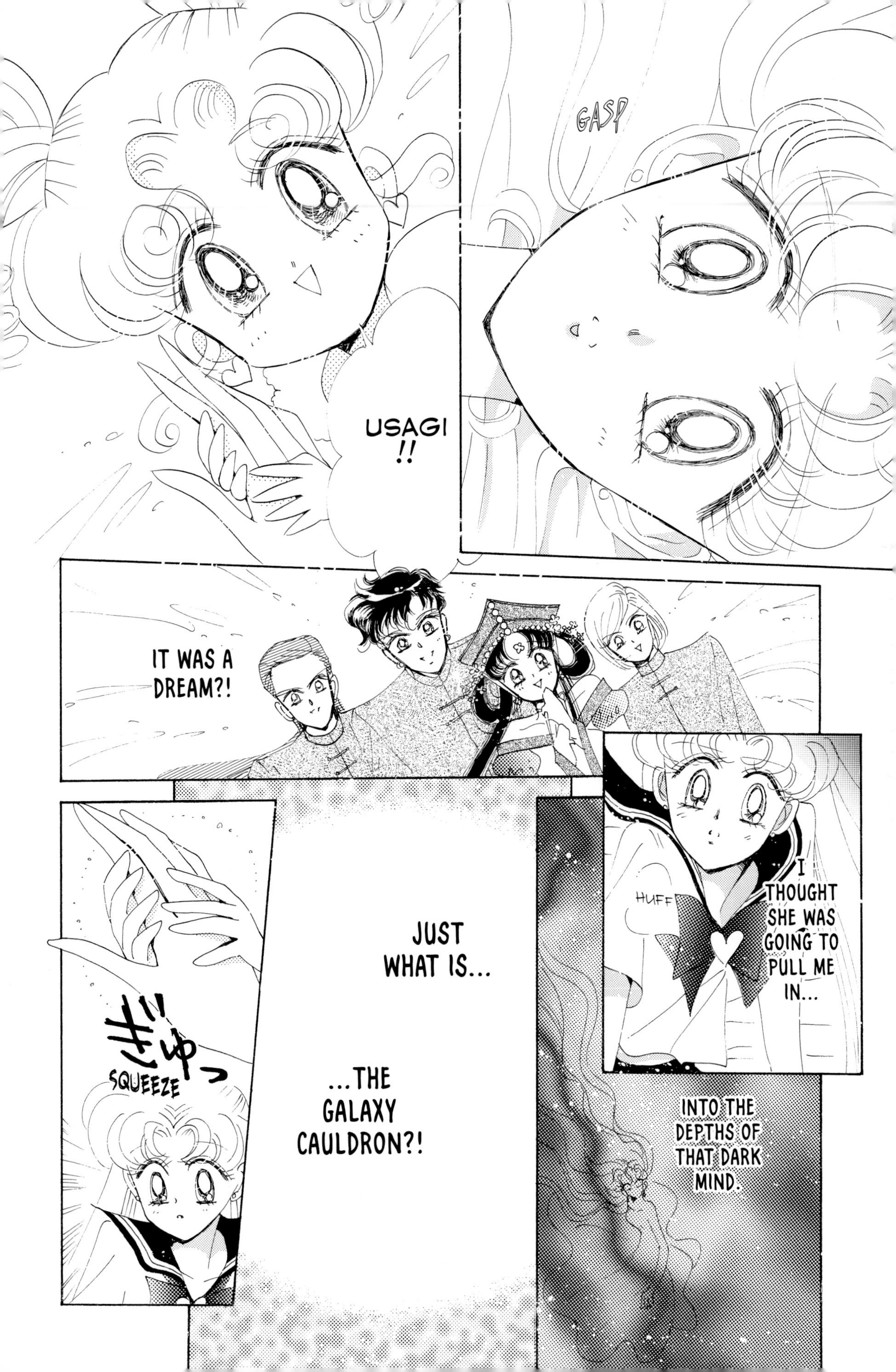
GASP
USAGI !!
IT WAS A DREAM?!
HUFF
I THOUGHT SHE WAS GOING TO PULL ME IN...
INTO THE DEPTHS OF THAT DARK MIND.
JUST WHAT IS...
...THE GALAXY CAULDRON?!
ぎゅっ
SQUEEZE

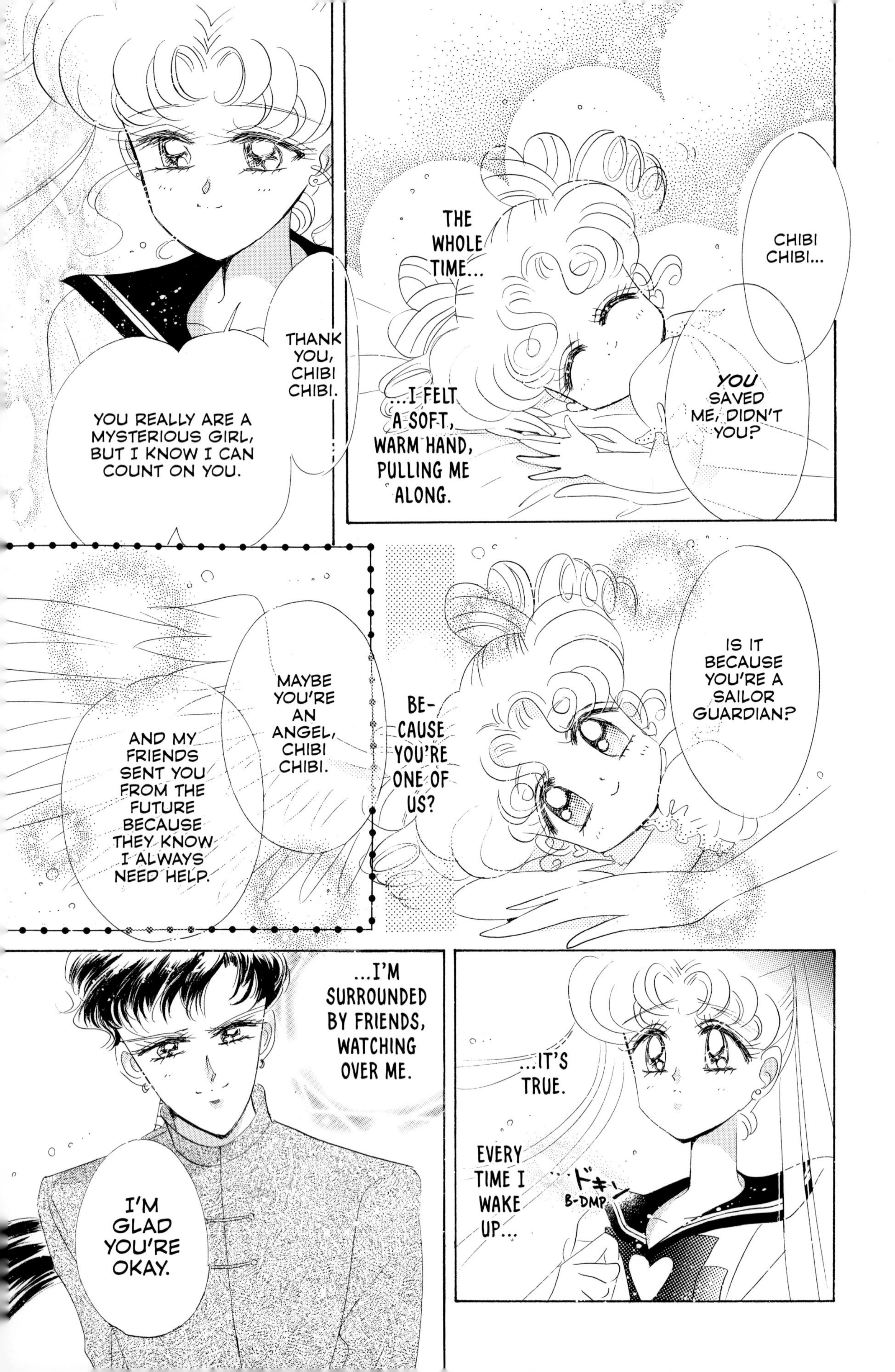
CHIBI CHIBI...
YOU SAVED ME, DIDN'T YOU?
THE WHOLE TIME...
...I FELT A SOFT, WARM HAND, PULLING ME ALONG.
THANK YOU, CHIBI CHIBI.
YOU REALLY ARE A MYSTERIOUS GIRL, BUT I KNOW I CAN COUNT ON YOU.
IS IT BECAUSE YOU'RE A SAILOR GUARDIAN?
BE-CAUSE YOU'RE ONE OF US?
MAYBE YOU'RE AN ANGEL, CHIBI CHIBI.
AND MY FRIENDS SENT YOU FROM THE FUTURE BECAUSE THEY KNOW I ALWAYS NEED HELP.
...IT'S TRUE.
EVERY TIME I WAKE UP...
ドキ
B-DMP
...I'M SURROUNDED BY FRIENDS, WATCHING OVER ME.
I'M GLAD YOU'RE OKAY.

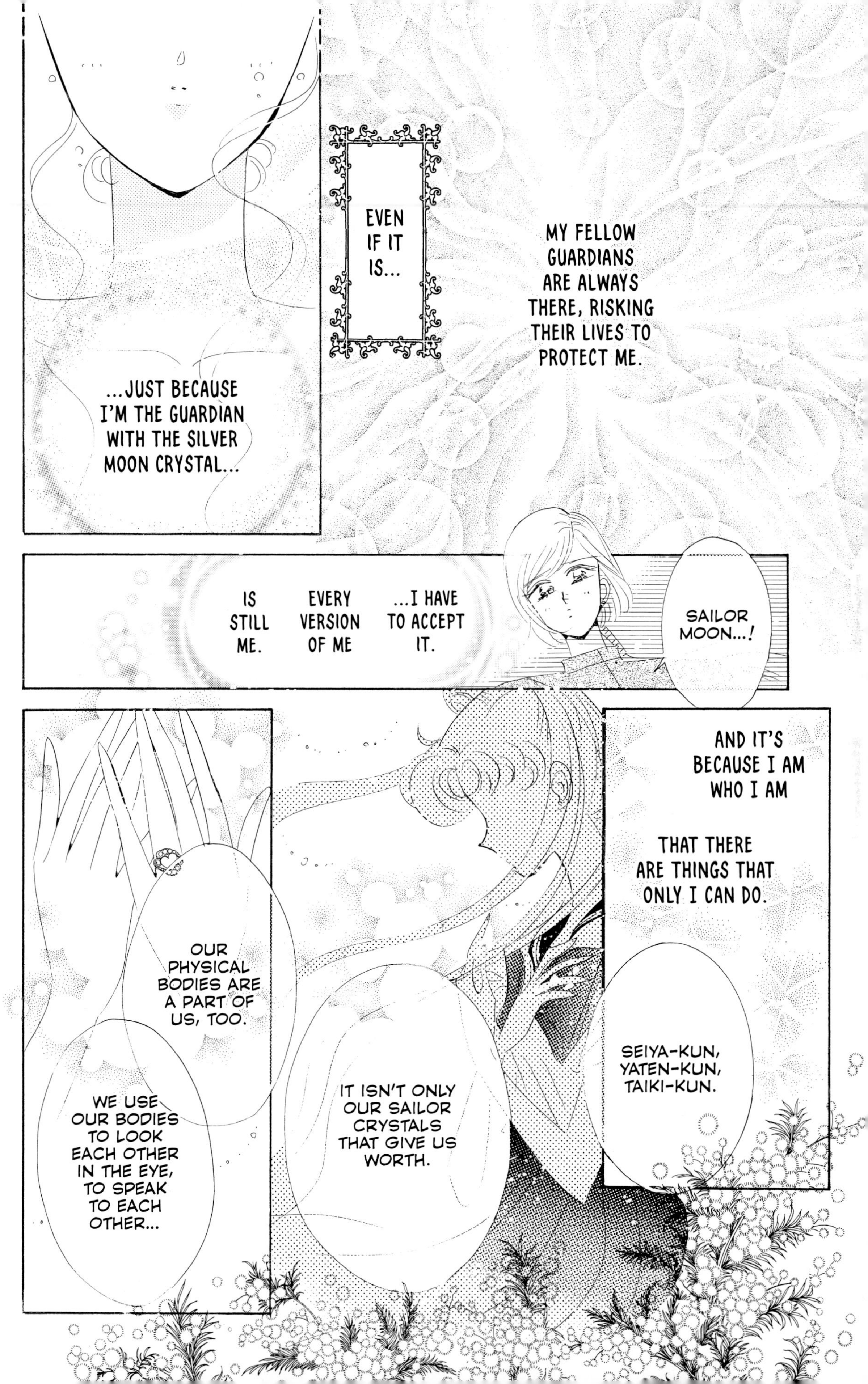
MY FELLOW GUARDIANS ARE ALWAYS THERE, RISKING THEIR LIVES TO PROTECT ME.
EVEN IF IT IS...
...JUST BECAUSE I'M THE GUARDIAN WITH THE SILVER MOON CRYSTAL...
SAILOR MOON...!
...I HAVE TO ACCEPT IT.
EVERY VERSION OF ME
IS STILL ME.
AND IT'S BECAUSE I AM WHO I AM
THAT THERE ARE THINGS THAT ONLY I CAN DO.
SEIYA-KUN, YATEN-KUN, TAIKI-KUN.
IT ISN'T ONLY OUR SAILOR CRYSTALS THAT GIVE US WORTH.
OUR PHYSICAL BODIES ARE A PART OF US, TOO.
WE USE OUR BODIES TO LOOK EACH OTHER IN THE EYE, TO SPEAK TO EACH OTHER...

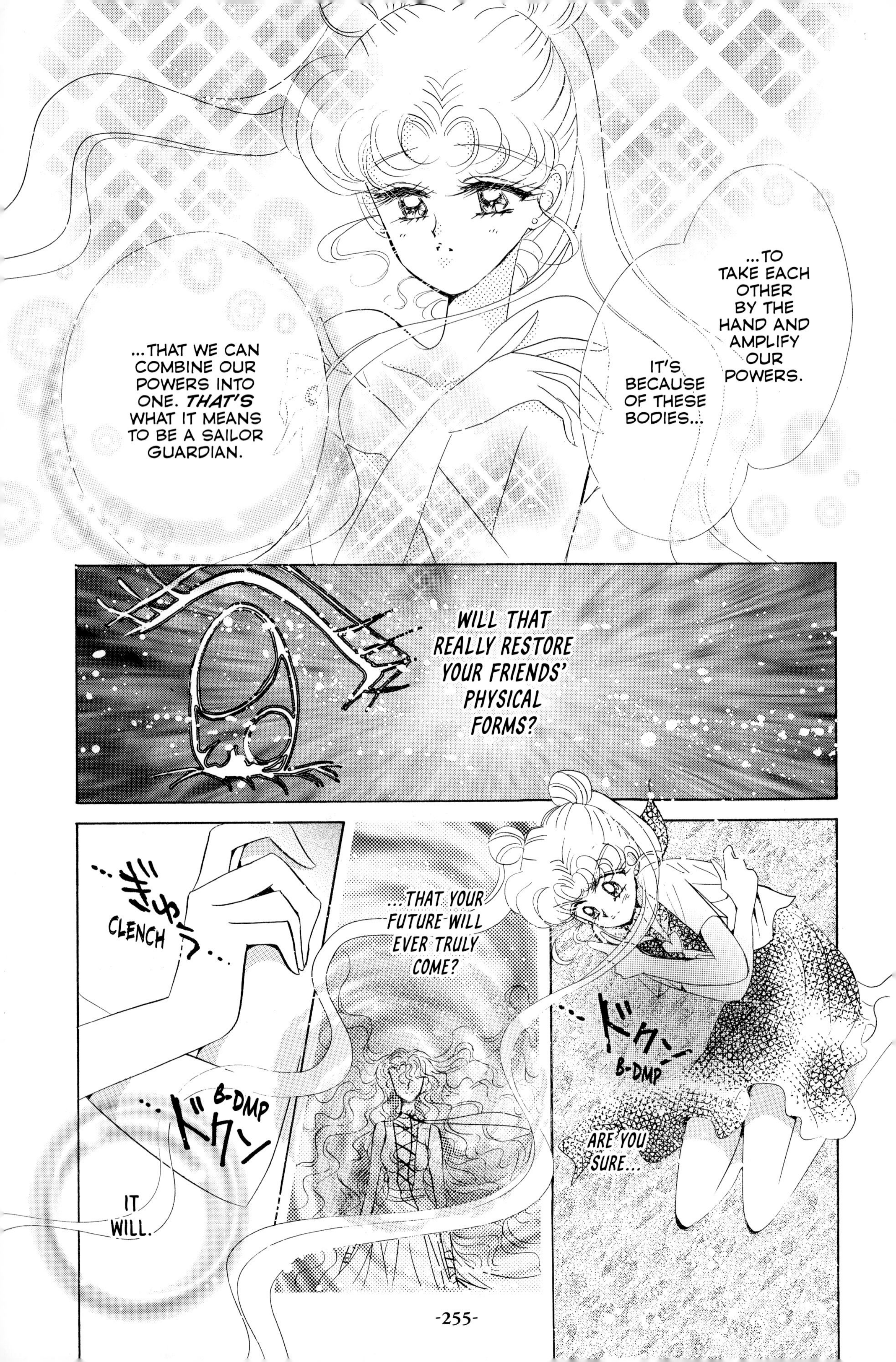
IT'S BECAUSE OF THESE BODIES...
...TO TAKE EACH OTHER BY THE HAND AND AMPLIFY OUR POWERS.
...THAT WE CAN COMBINE OUR POWERS INTO ONE. *THAT'S* WHAT IT MEANS TO BE A SAILOR GUARDIAN.
WILL THAT REALLY RESTORE YOUR FRIENDS' PHYSICAL FORMS?
ARE YOU SURE...
...THAT YOUR FUTURE WILL EVER TRULY COME?
...ドクン B-DMP
...ぎゅっ... CLENCH
...ドクン B-DMP
IT WILL.

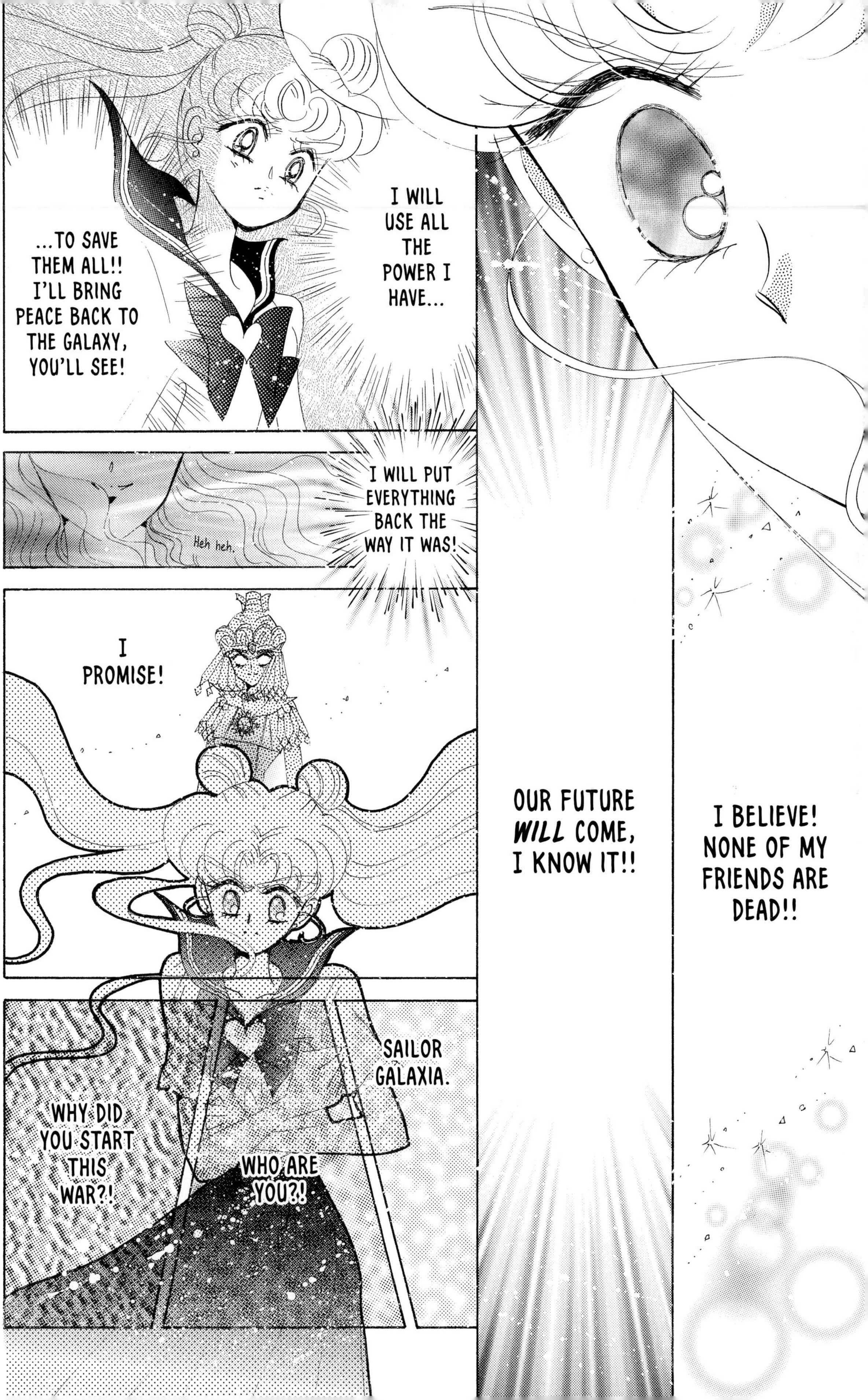
I BELIEVE! NONE OF MY FRIENDS ARE DEAD!!
OUR FUTURE *WILL* COME, I KNOW IT!!
I WILL USE ALL THE POWER I HAVE...
...TO SAVE THEM ALL!! I'LL BRING PEACE BACK TO THE GALAXY, YOU'LL SEE!
I WILL PUT EVERYTHING BACK THE WAY IT WAS!
Heh heh.
I PROMISE!
SAILOR GALAXIA.
WHO ARE YOU?!
WHY DID YOU START THIS WAR?!

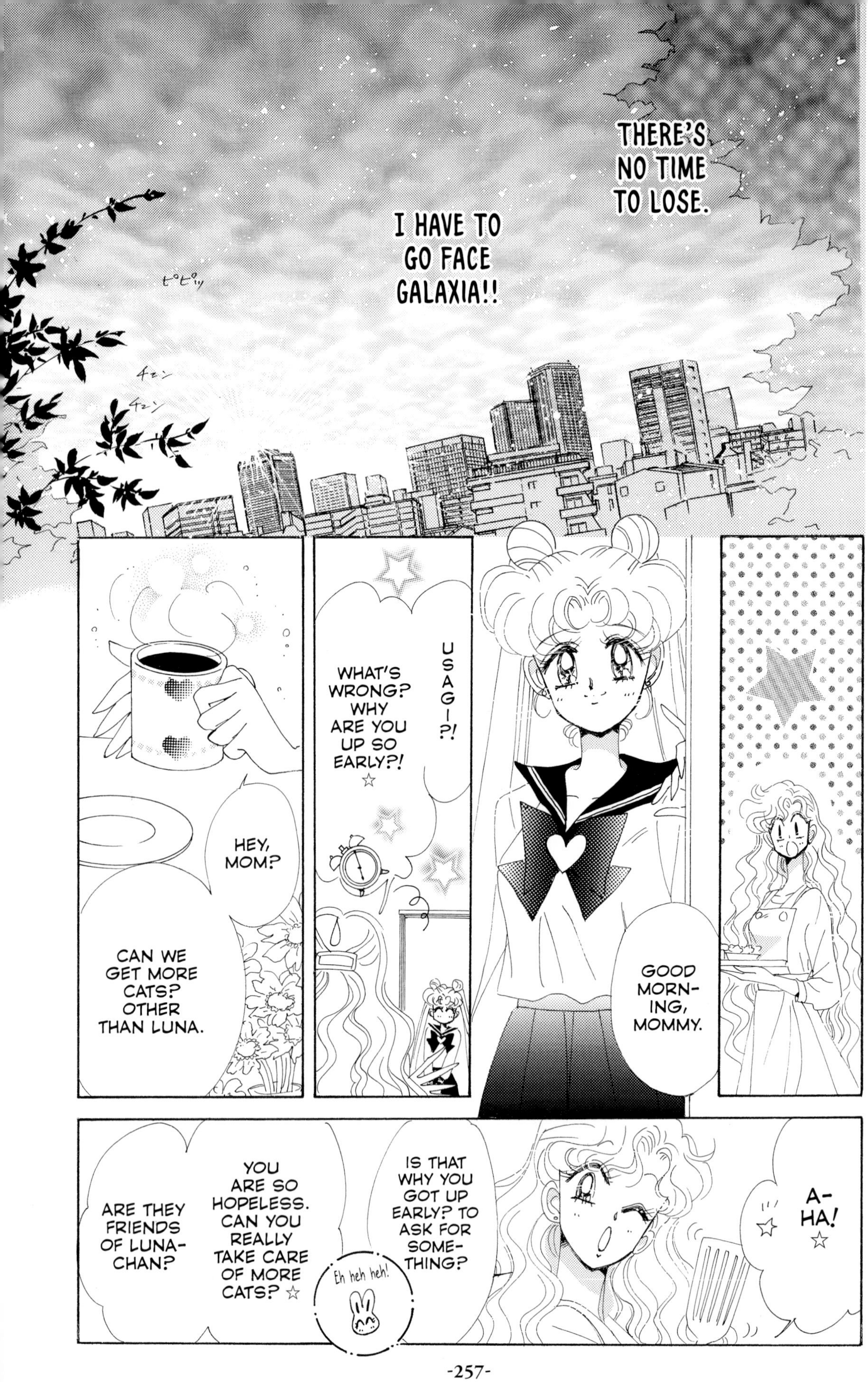
THERE'S NO TIME TO LOSE.
I HAVE TO GO FACE GALAXIA!!
ピピッ
チュン
チュン
GOOD MORNING, MOMMY.
USAGI?!
WHAT'S WRONG? WHY ARE YOU UP SO EARLY?! ☆
HEY, MOM?
CAN WE GET MORE CATS? OTHER THAN LUNA.
A-HA! ☆
IS THAT WHY YOU GOT UP EARLY? TO ASK FOR SOMETHING?
Eh heh heh!
YOU ARE SO HOPELESS. CAN YOU REALLY TAKE CARE OF MORE CATS? ☆
ARE THEY FRIENDS OF LUNA-CHAN?

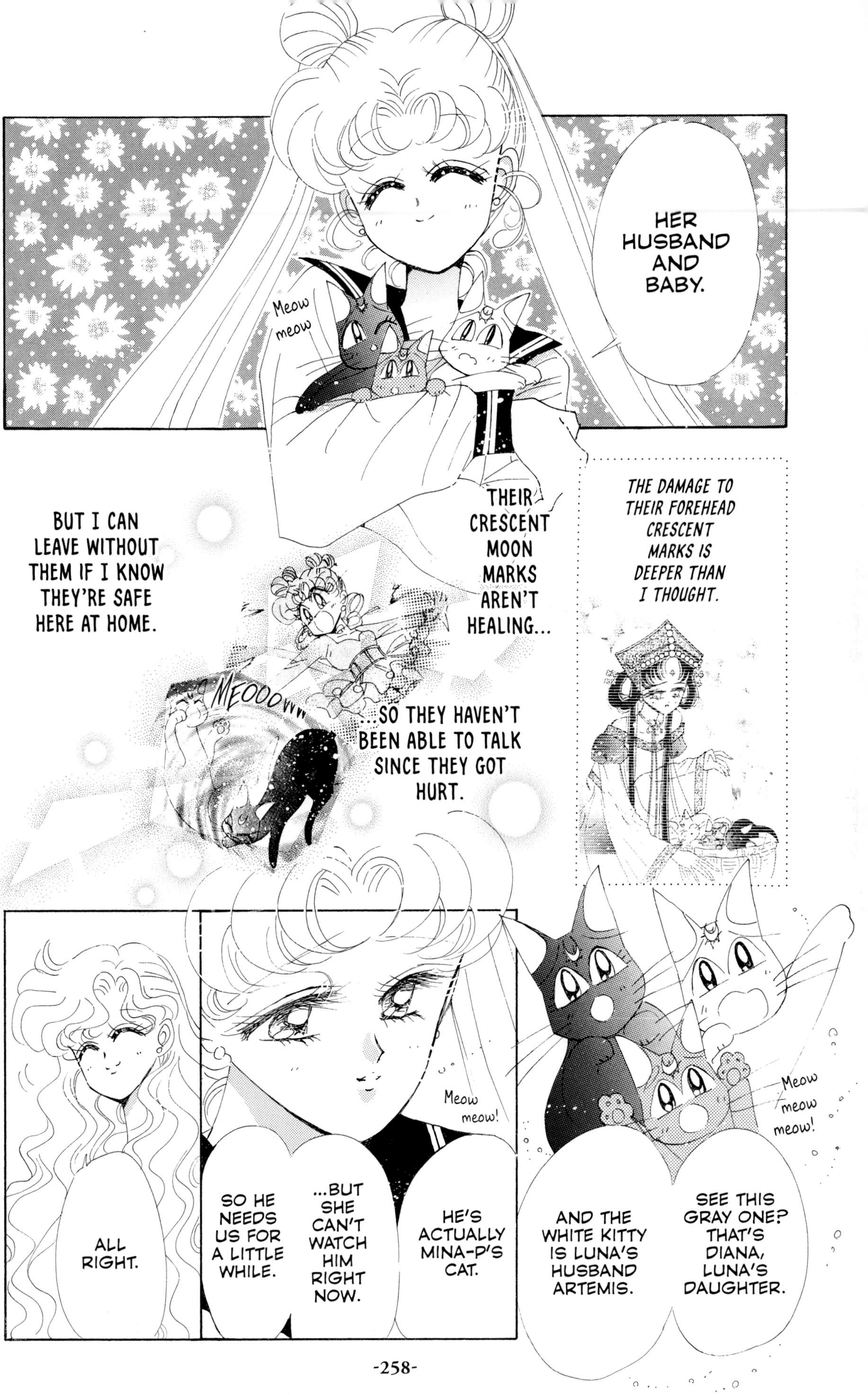
HER HUSBAND AND BABY.
Meow meow
THE DAMAGE TO THEIR FOREHEAD CRESCENT MARKS IS DEEPER THAN I THOUGHT.
THEIR CRESCENT MOON MARKS AREN'T HEALING...
...SO THEY HAVEN'T BEEN ABLE TO TALK SINCE THEY GOT HURT.
MEOOOWWW
BUT I CAN LEAVE WITHOUT THEM IF I KNOW THEY'RE SAFE HERE AT HOME.
Meow meow meow!
SEE THIS GRAY ONE? THAT'S DIANA, LUNA'S DAUGHTER.
AND THE WHITE KITTY IS LUNA'S HUSBAND ARTEMIS.
Meow meow!
HE'S ACTUALLY MINA-P'S CAT.
...BUT SHE CAN'T WATCH HIM RIGHT NOW.
SO HE NEEDS US FOR A LITTLE WHILE.
ALL RIGHT.

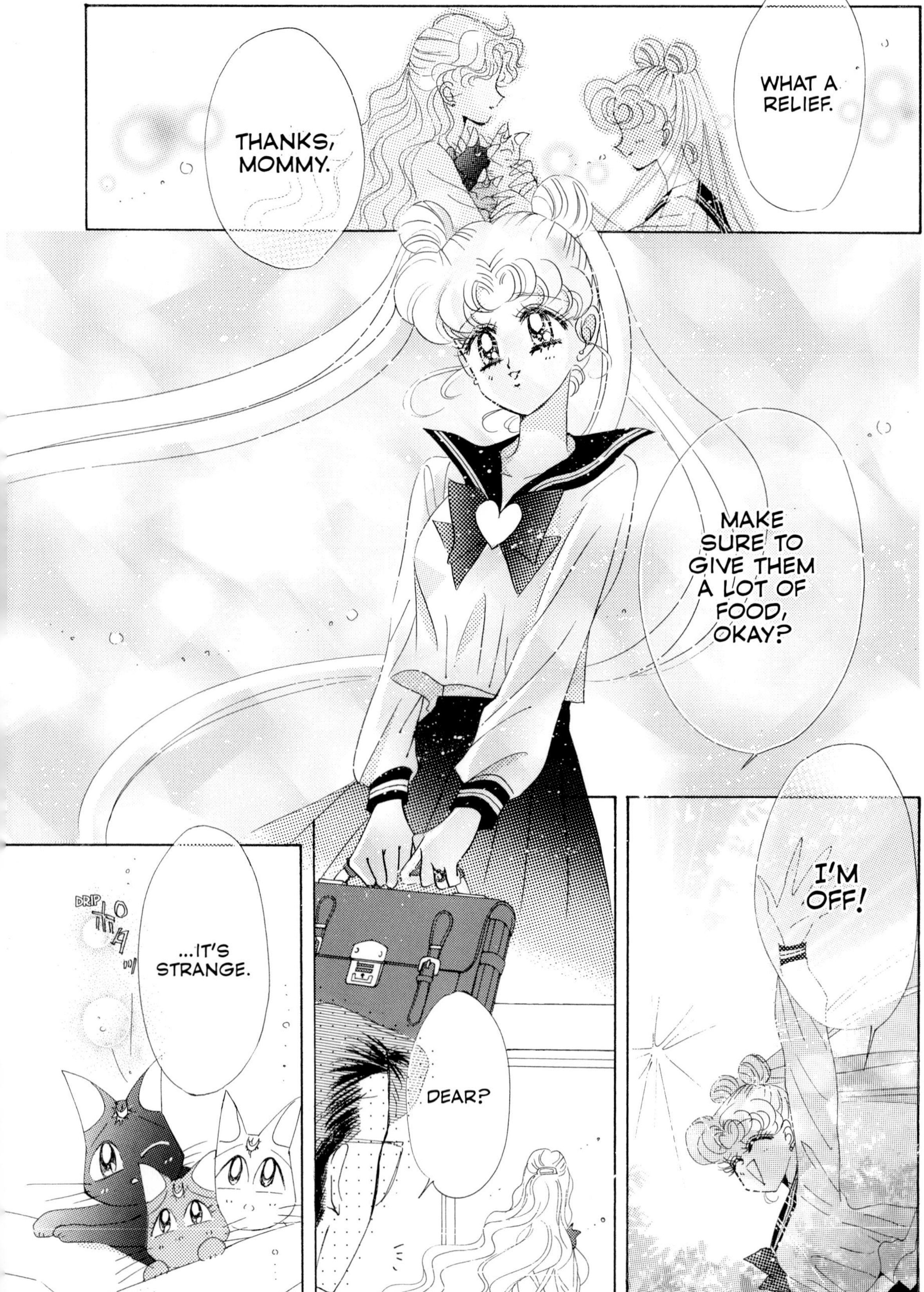
WHAT A RELIEF.
THANKS, MOMMY.
MAKE SURE TO GIVE THEM A LOT OF FOOD, OKAY?
I'M OFF!
DEAR?
...IT'S STRANGE.
DRIP

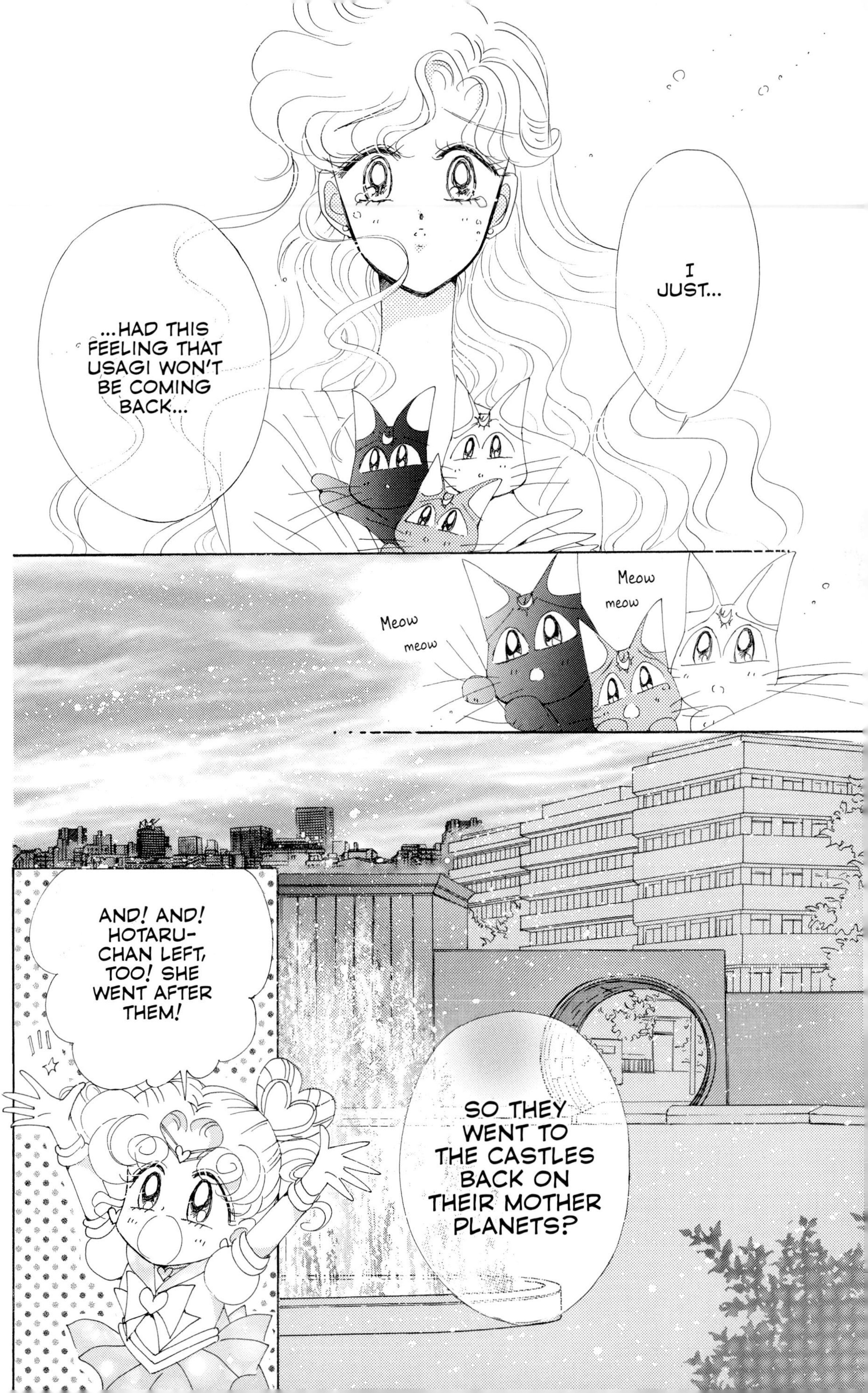
I JUST...
...HAD THIS FEELING THAT USAGI WON'T BE COMING BACK...
Meow meow
Meow meow
SO THEY WENT TO THE CASTLES BACK ON THEIR MOTHER PLANETS?
AND! AND! HOTARU-CHAN LEFT, TOO! SHE WENT AFTER THEM!

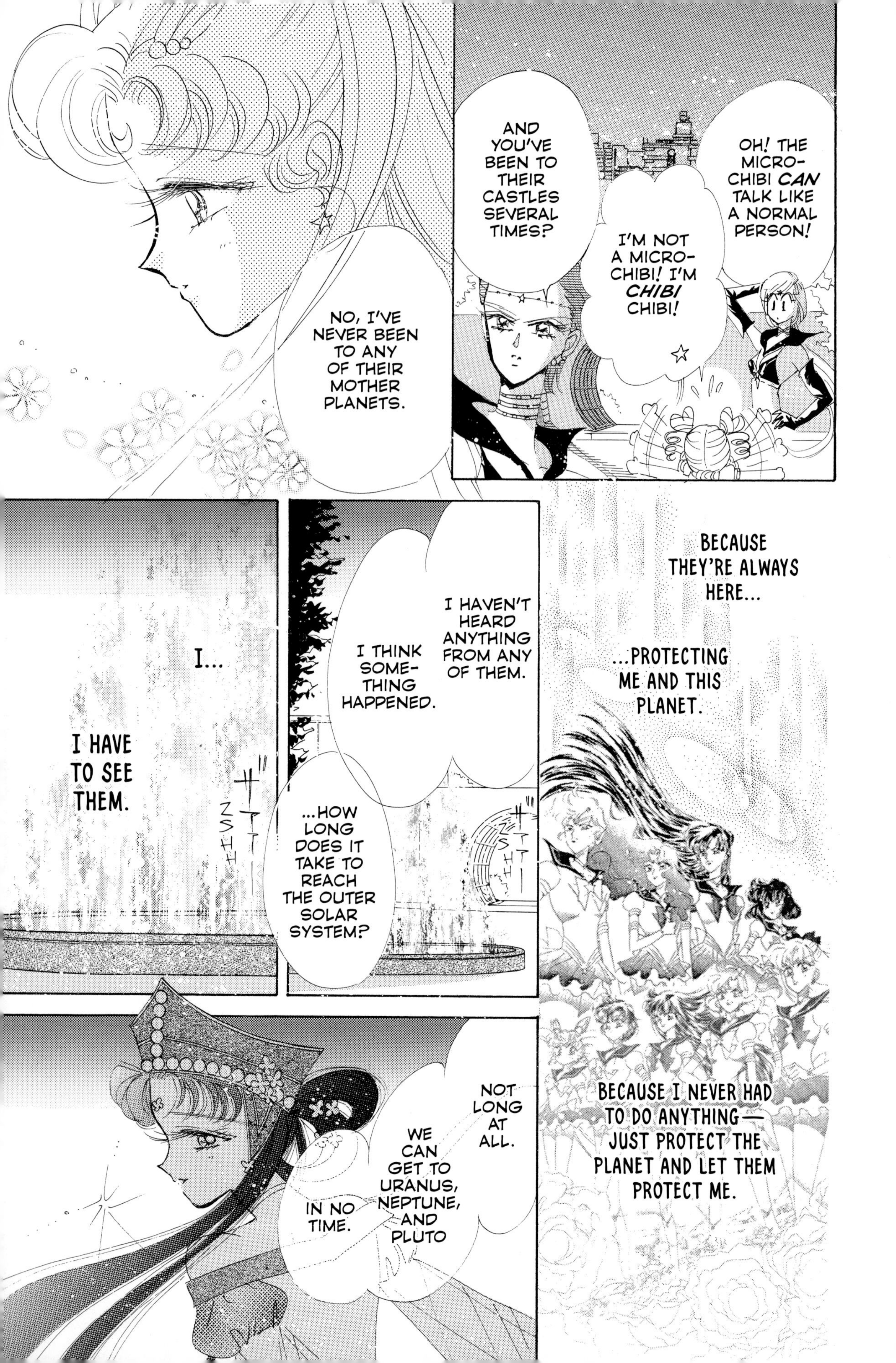
OH! THE MICRO-CHIBI CAN TALK LIKE A NORMAL PERSON!
I'M NOT A MICRO-CHIBI! I'M CHIBI CHIBI!
AND YOU'VE BEEN TO THEIR CASTLES SEVERAL TIMES?
NO, I'VE NEVER BEEN TO ANY OF THEIR MOTHER PLANETS.
BECAUSE THEY'RE ALWAYS HERE...
...PROTECTING ME AND THIS PLANET.
BECAUSE I NEVER HAD TO DO ANYTHING— JUST PROTECT THE PLANET AND LET THEM PROTECT ME.
I HAVEN'T HEARD ANYTHING FROM ANY OF THEM.
I THINK SOMETHING HAPPENED.
...HOW LONG DOES IT TAKE TO REACH THE OUTER SOLAR SYSTEM?
SHHH
I...
I HAVE TO SEE THEM.
SHHH
NOT LONG AT ALL.
WE CAN GET TO URANUS, NEPTUNE, AND PLUTO
IN NO TIME.

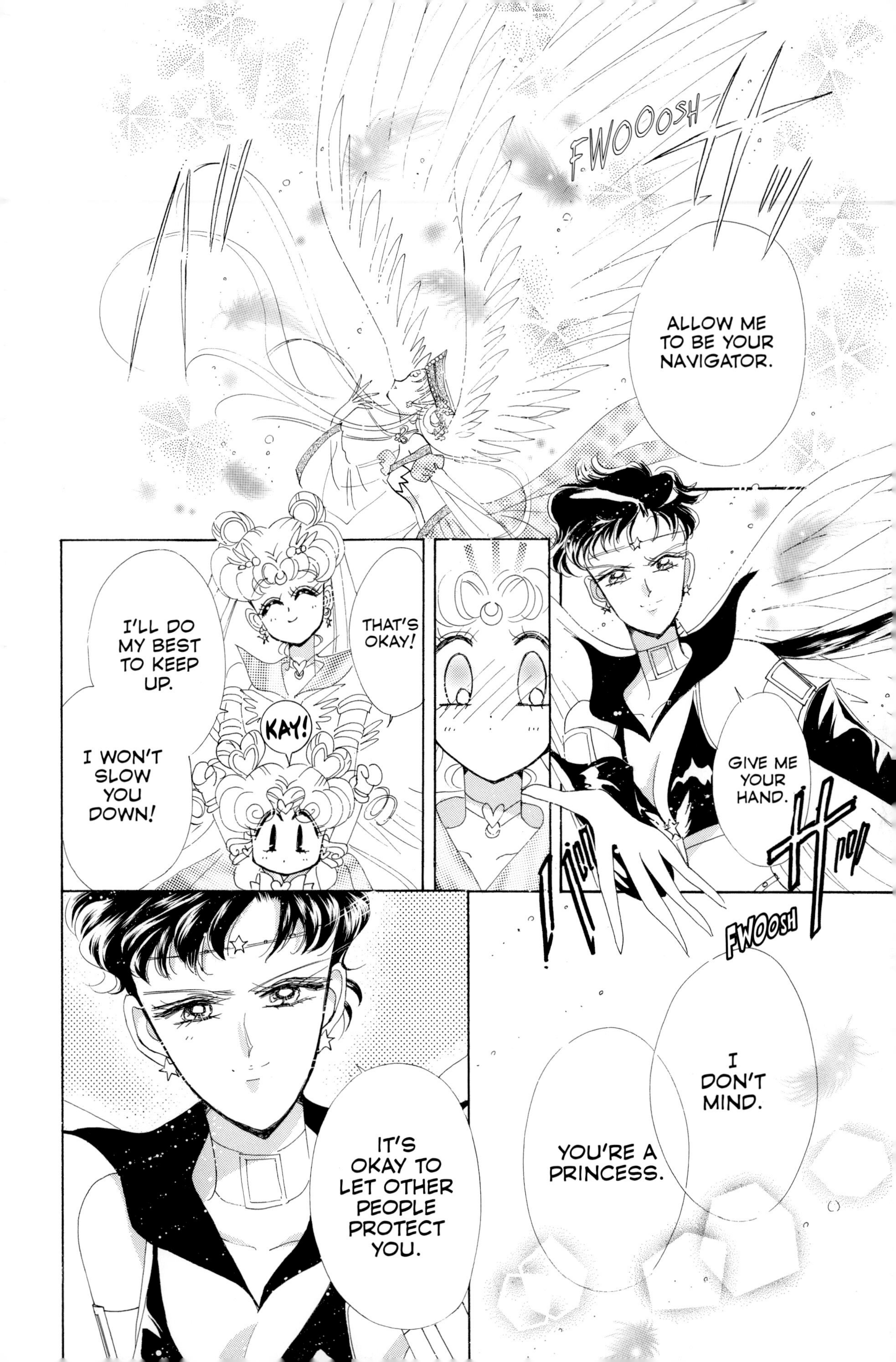
FWOOOSH
ALLOW ME TO BE YOUR NAVIGATOR.
GIVE ME YOUR HAND.
FWOOSH
THAT'S OKAY!
I'LL DO MY BEST TO KEEP UP.
KAY!
I WON'T SLOW YOU DOWN!
I DON'T MIND.
YOU'RE A PRINCESS.
IT'S OKAY TO LET OTHER PEOPLE PROTECT YOU.

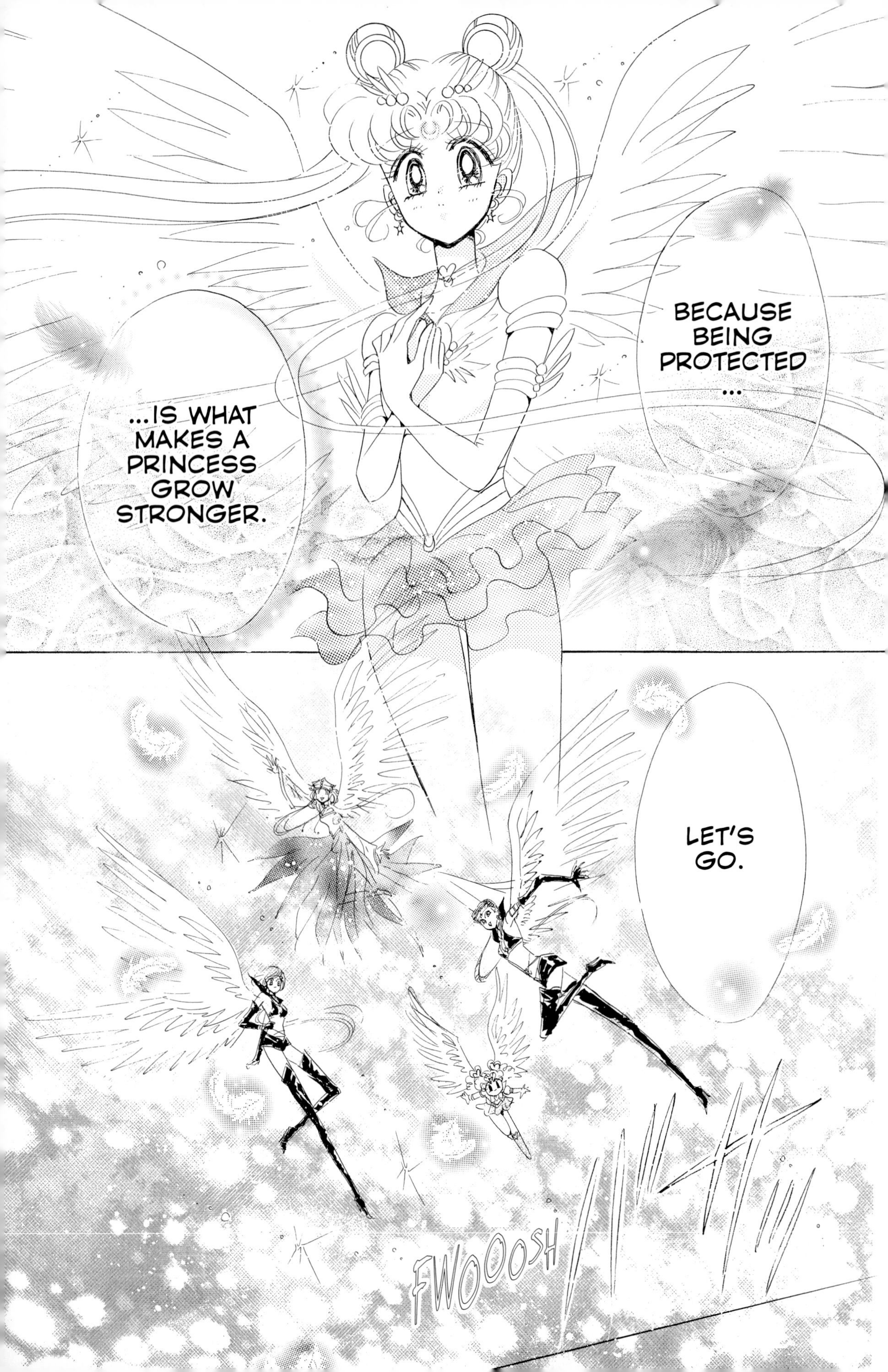
BECAUSE BEING PROTECTED ...
...IS WHAT MAKES A PRINCESS GROW STRONGER.
LET'S GO.
FWOOOSH

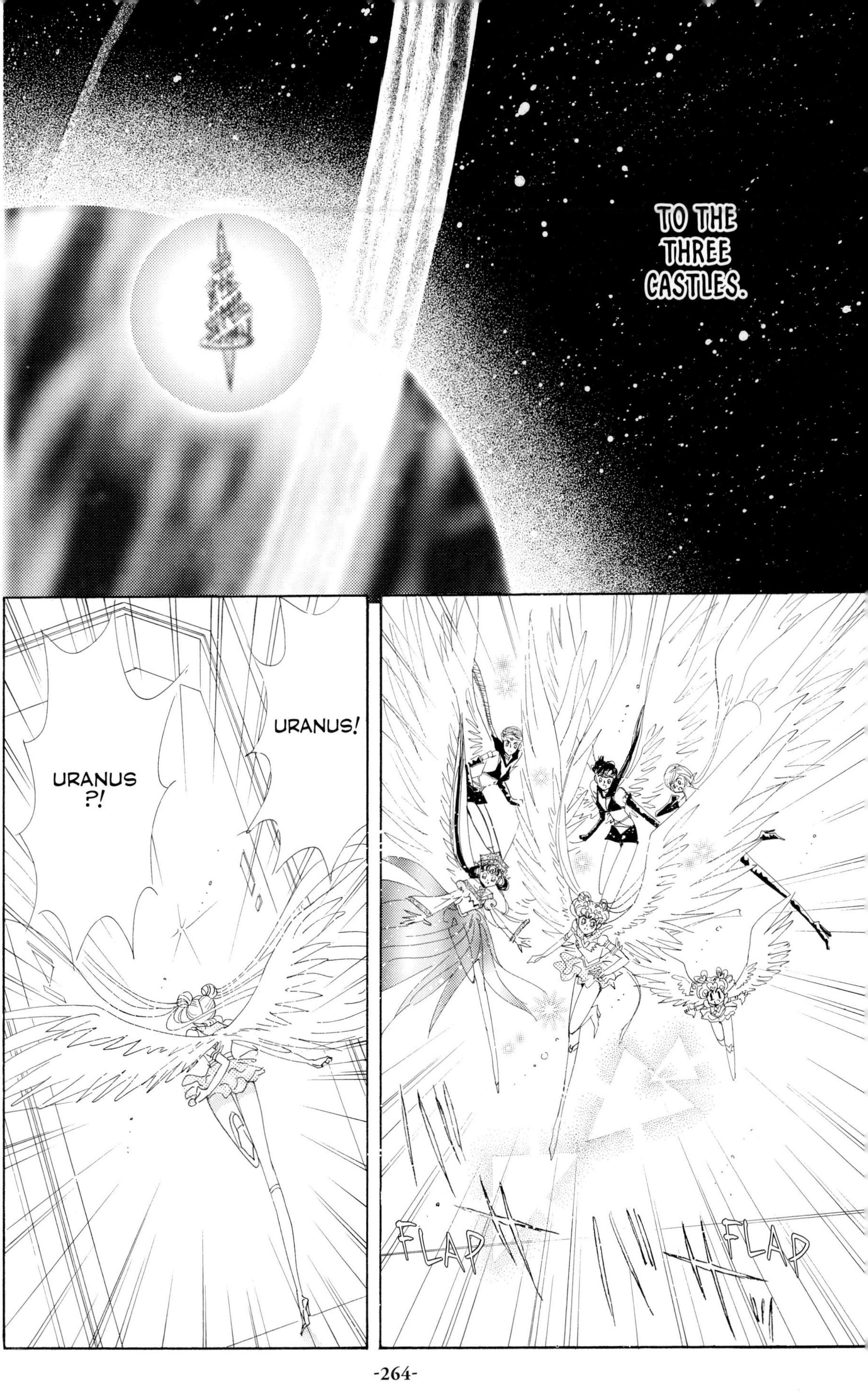
TO THE THREE CASTLES.
FLAP
FLAP
URANUS!
URANUS ?!

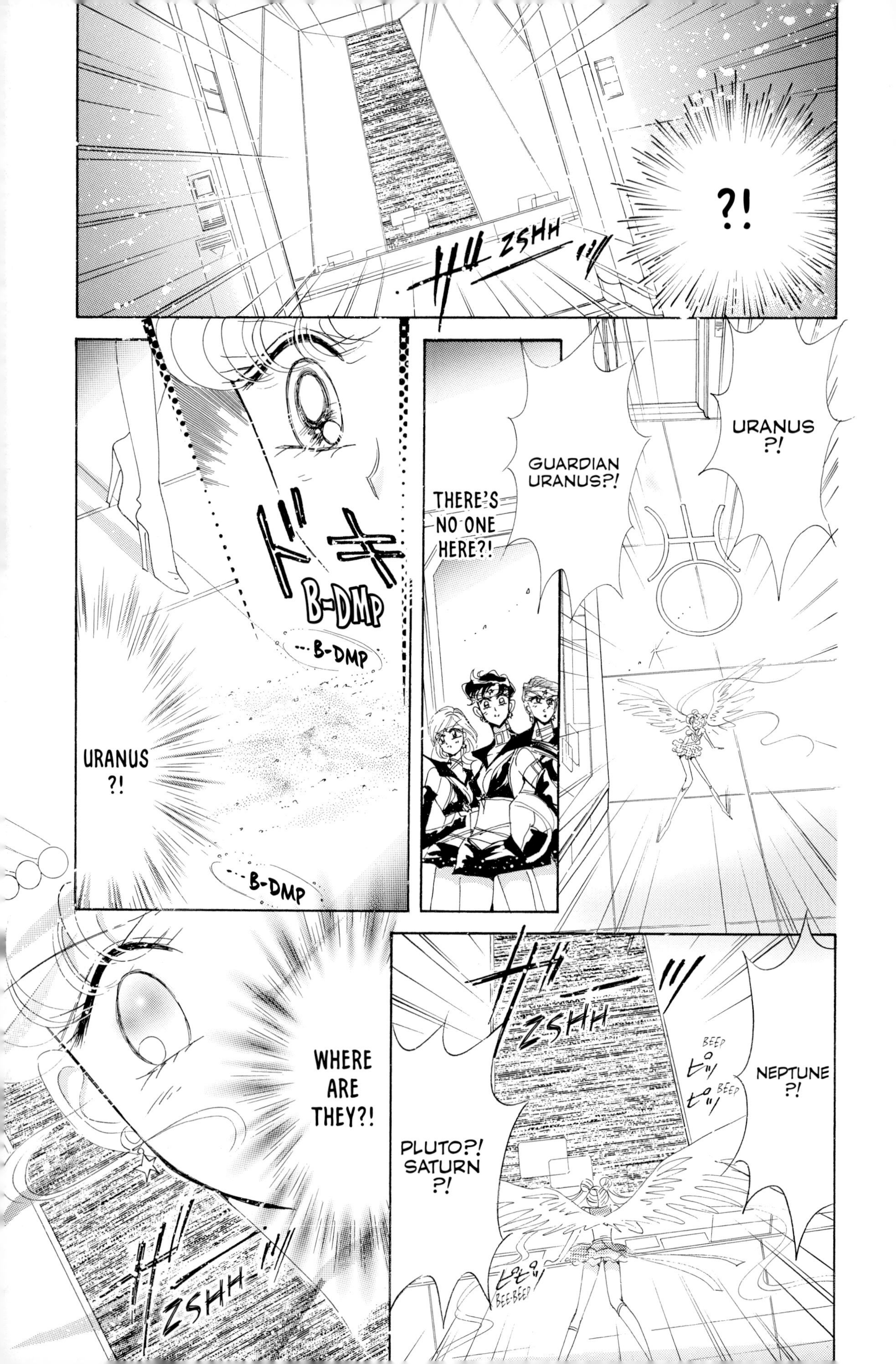
?!
ZSHH
URANUS ?!
GUARDIAN URANUS?!
THERE'S NO ONE HERE?!
ドキ
B-DMP
...B-DMP
URANUS ?!
...B-DMP
ZSHH
NEPTUNE ?!
BEEP
BEEP
PLUTO?! SATURN ?!
BEE-BEEP
WHERE ARE THEY?!
ZSHH

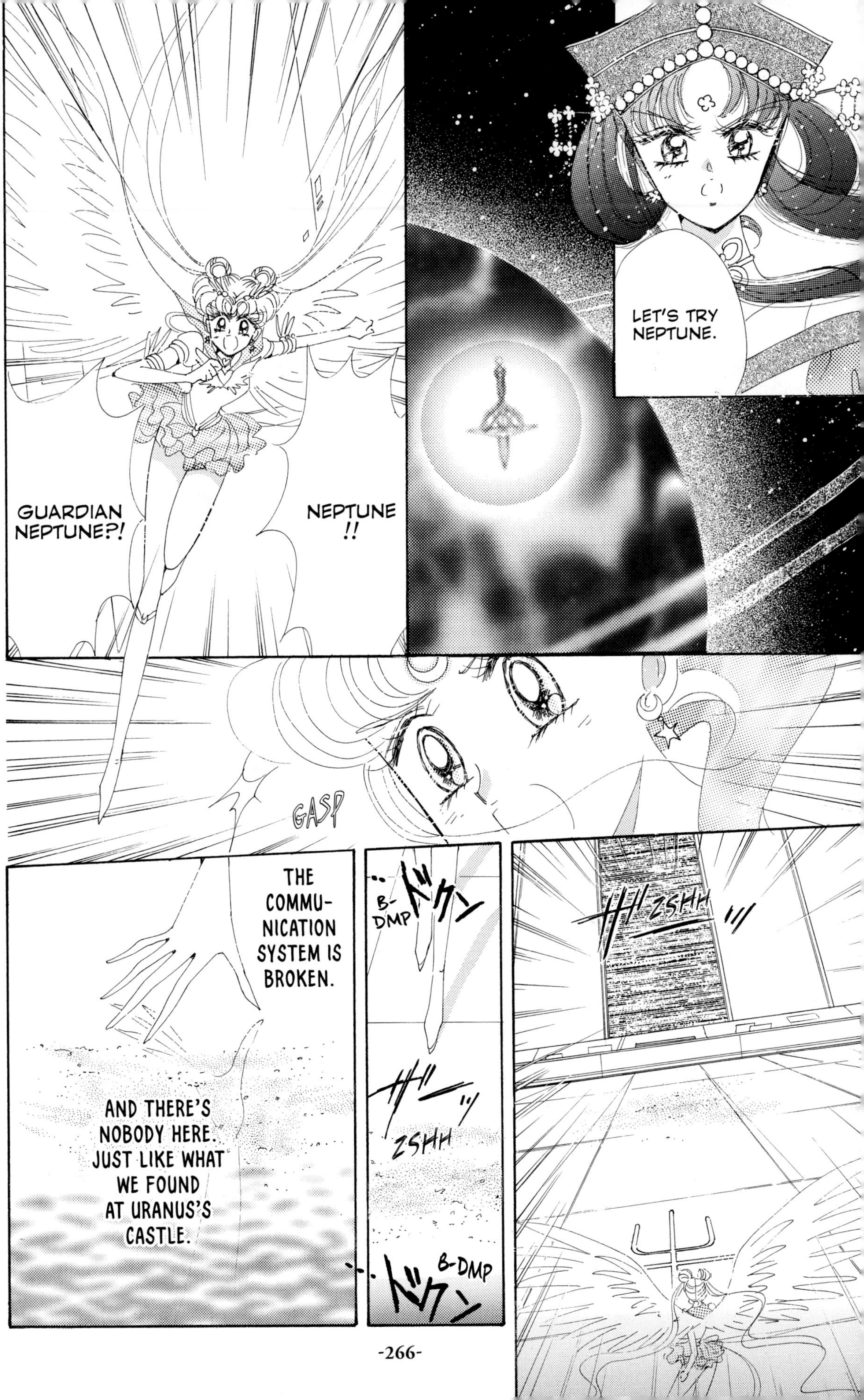
LET'S TRY NEPTUNE.
NEPTUNE !!
GUARDIAN NEPTUNE?!
GASP
ZSHH
B-DMP
ZSHH
B-DMP
THE COMMUNICATION SYSTEM IS BROKEN.
AND THERE'S NOBODY HERE. JUST LIKE WHAT WE FOUND AT URANUS'S CASTLE.

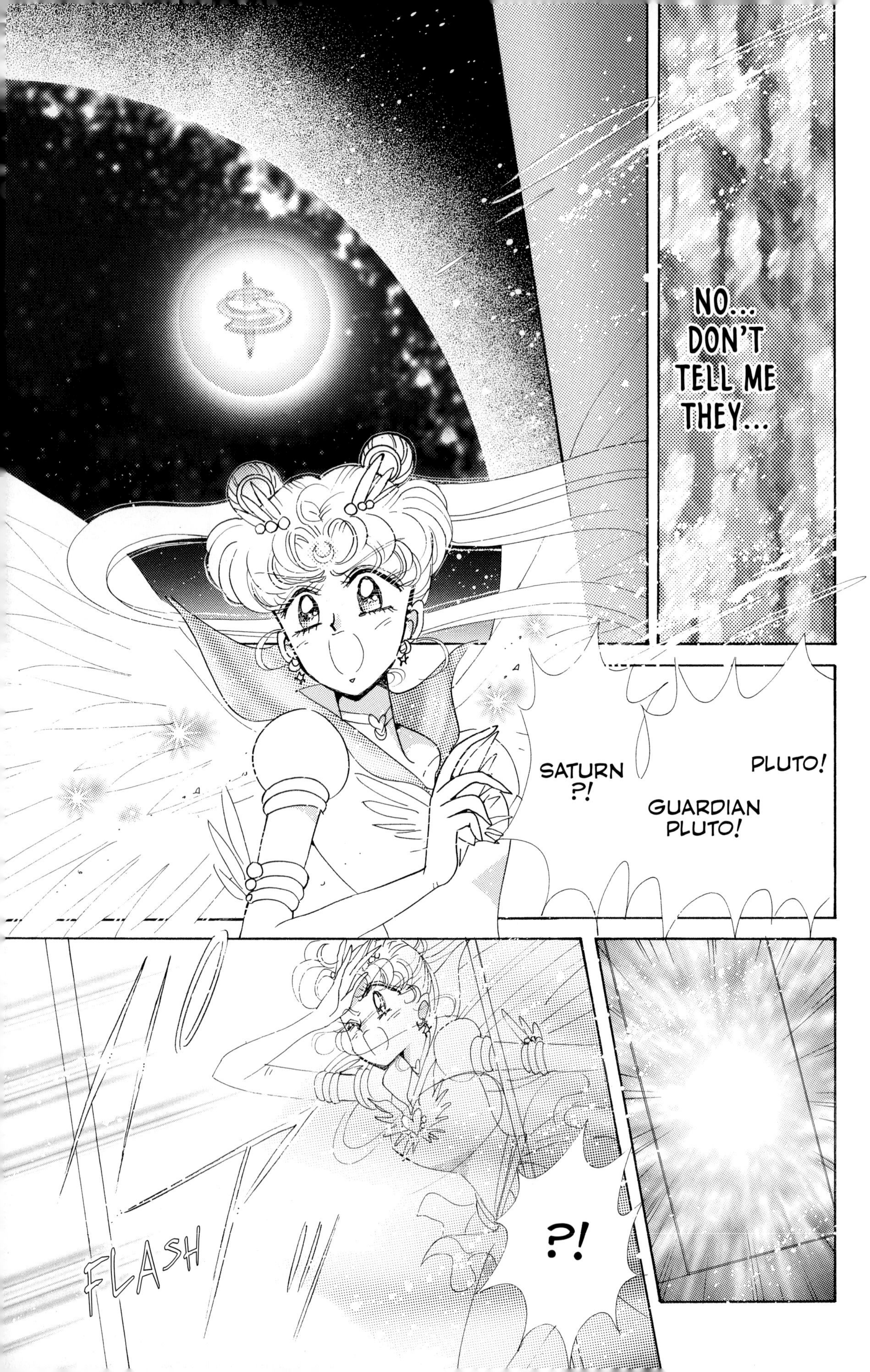
NO... DON'T TELL ME THEY...
PLUTO!
SATURN ?!
GUARDIAN PLUTO!
?!
FLASH

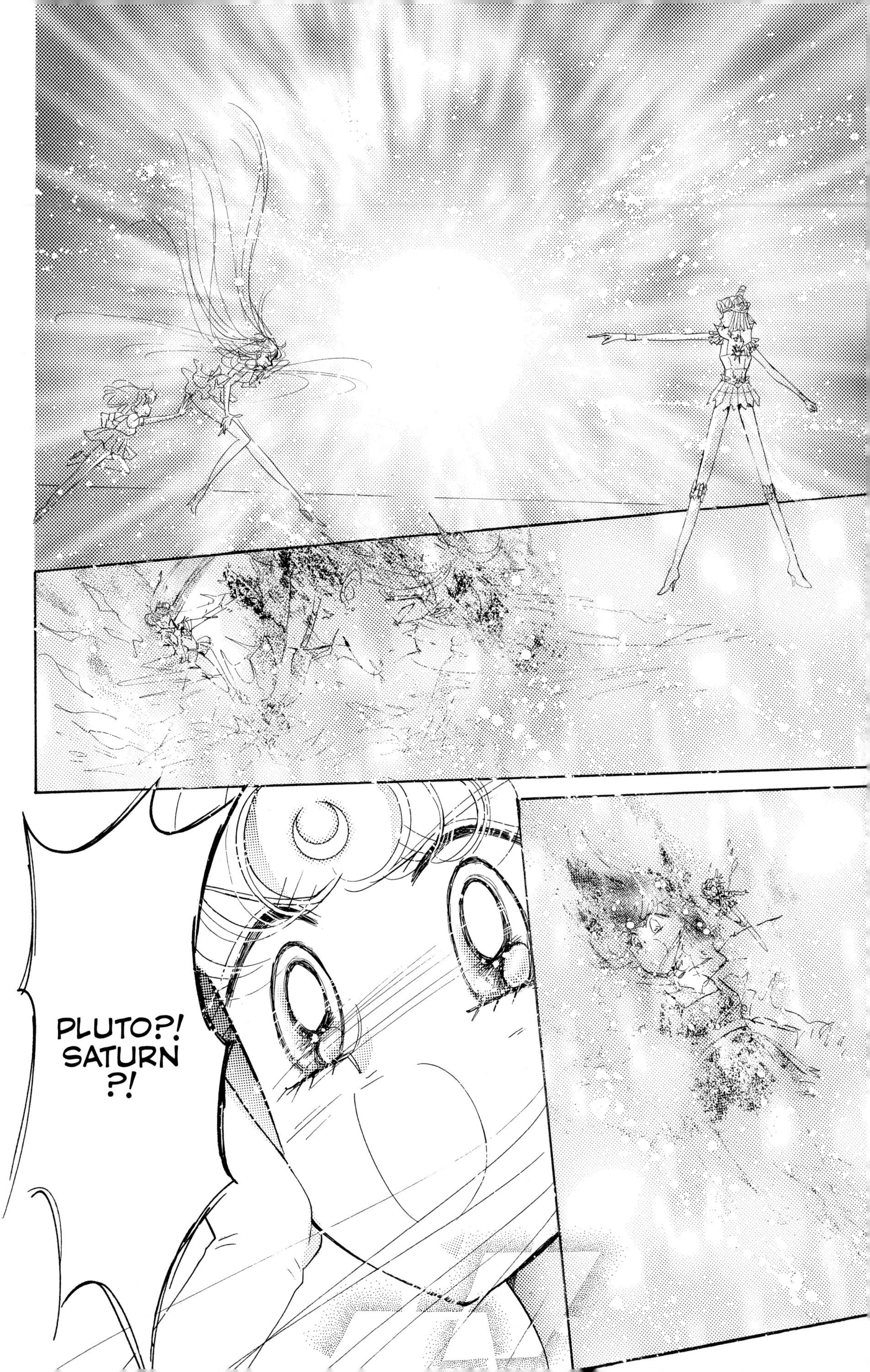
PLUTO?! SATURN?!

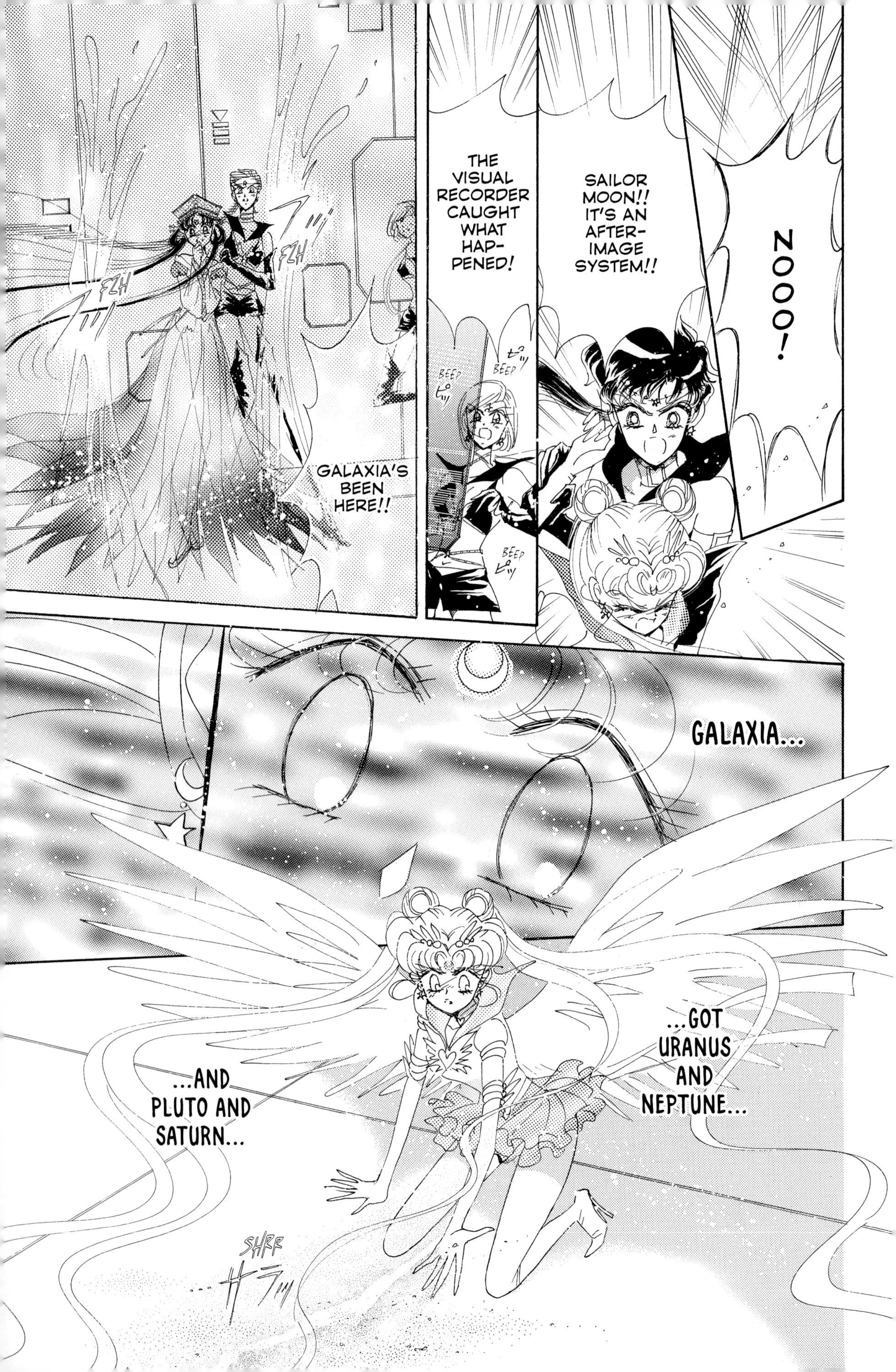
NOOOO!
SAILOR MOON!! IT'S AN AFTER-IMAGE SYSTEM!!
BEEP
BEEP
BEEP
THE VISUAL RECORDER CAUGHT WHAT HAP-PENED!
FZH
FZH
GALAXIA'S BEEN HERE!!
GALAXIA...
...GOT URANUS AND NEPTUNE...
...AND PLUTO AND SATURN...
SHRR

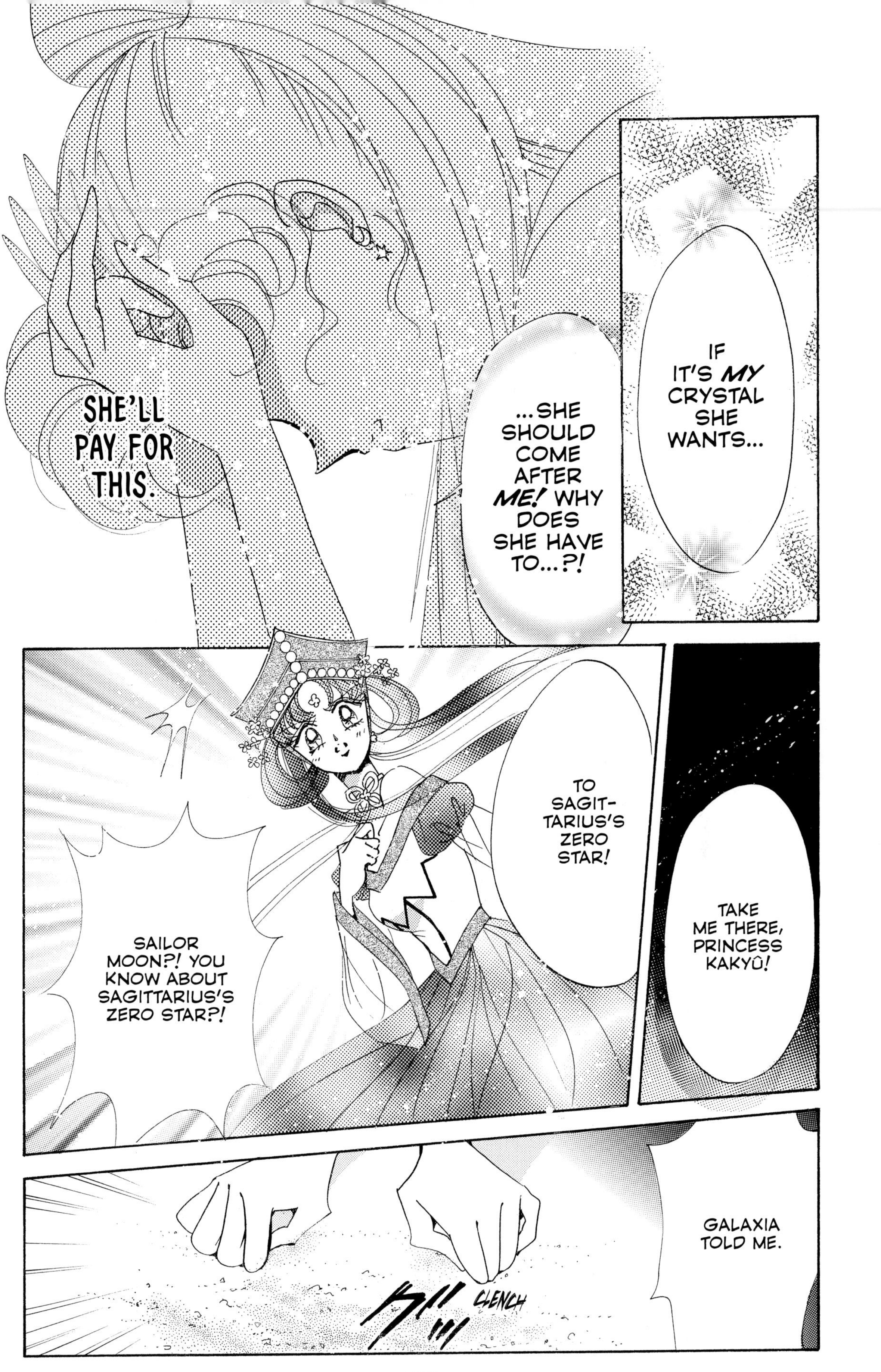
IF IT'S *MY* CRYSTAL SHE WANTS...
...SHE SHOULD COME AFTER *ME!* WHY DOES SHE HAVE TO...?!
SHE'LL PAY FOR THIS.
TAKE ME THERE, PRINCESS KAKYÛ!
TO SAGITTARIUS'S ZERO STAR!
SAILOR MOON?! YOU KNOW ABOUT SAGITTARIUS'S ZERO STAR?!
GALAXIA TOLD ME.
CLENCH

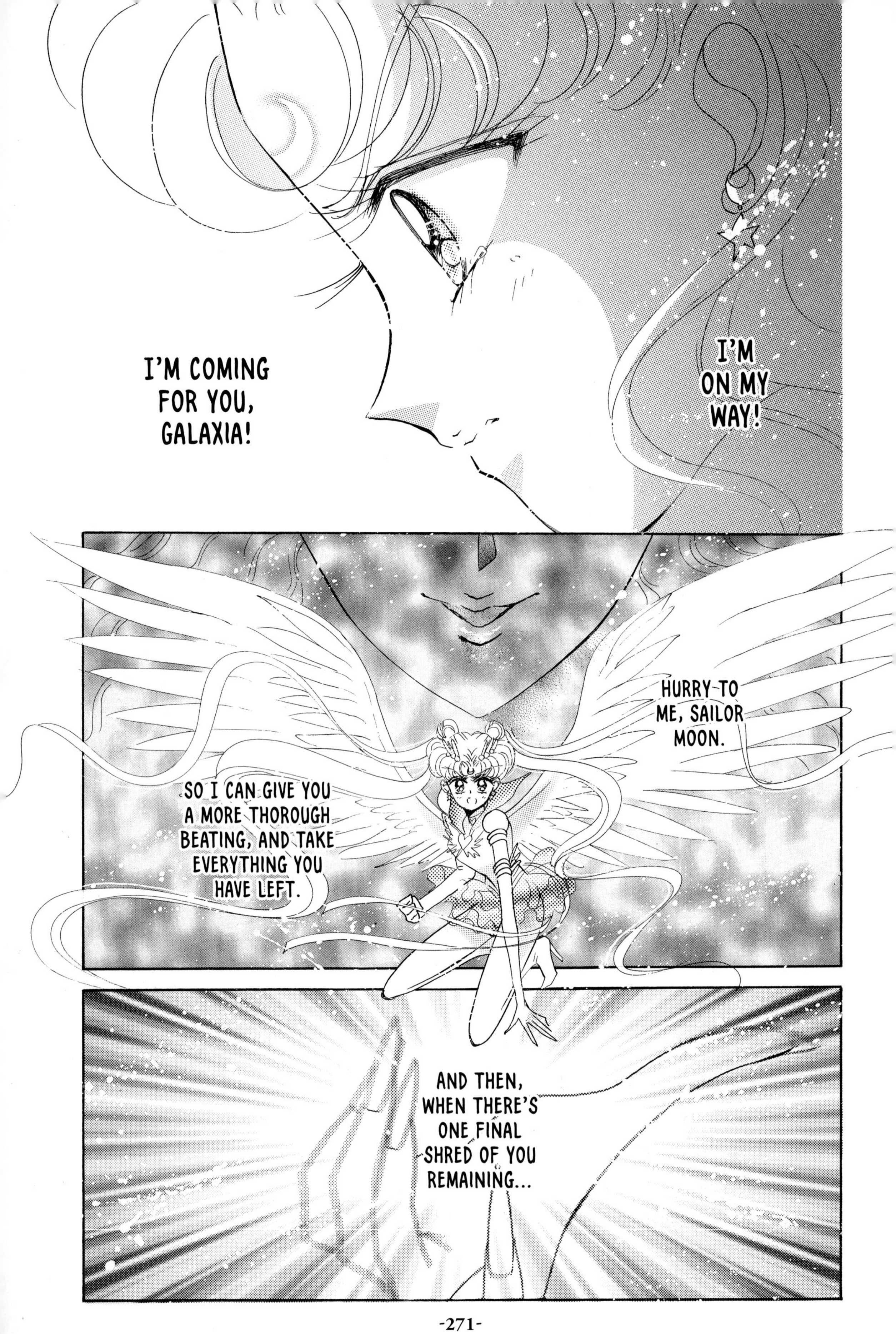

I'M ON MY WAY!
I'M COMING FOR YOU, GALAXIA!
HURRY TO ME, SAILOR MOON.
SO I CAN GIVE YOU A MORE THOROUGH BEATING, AND TAKE EVERYTHING YOU HAVE LEFT.
AND THEN, WHEN THERE'S ONE FINAL SHRED OF YOU REMAINING...

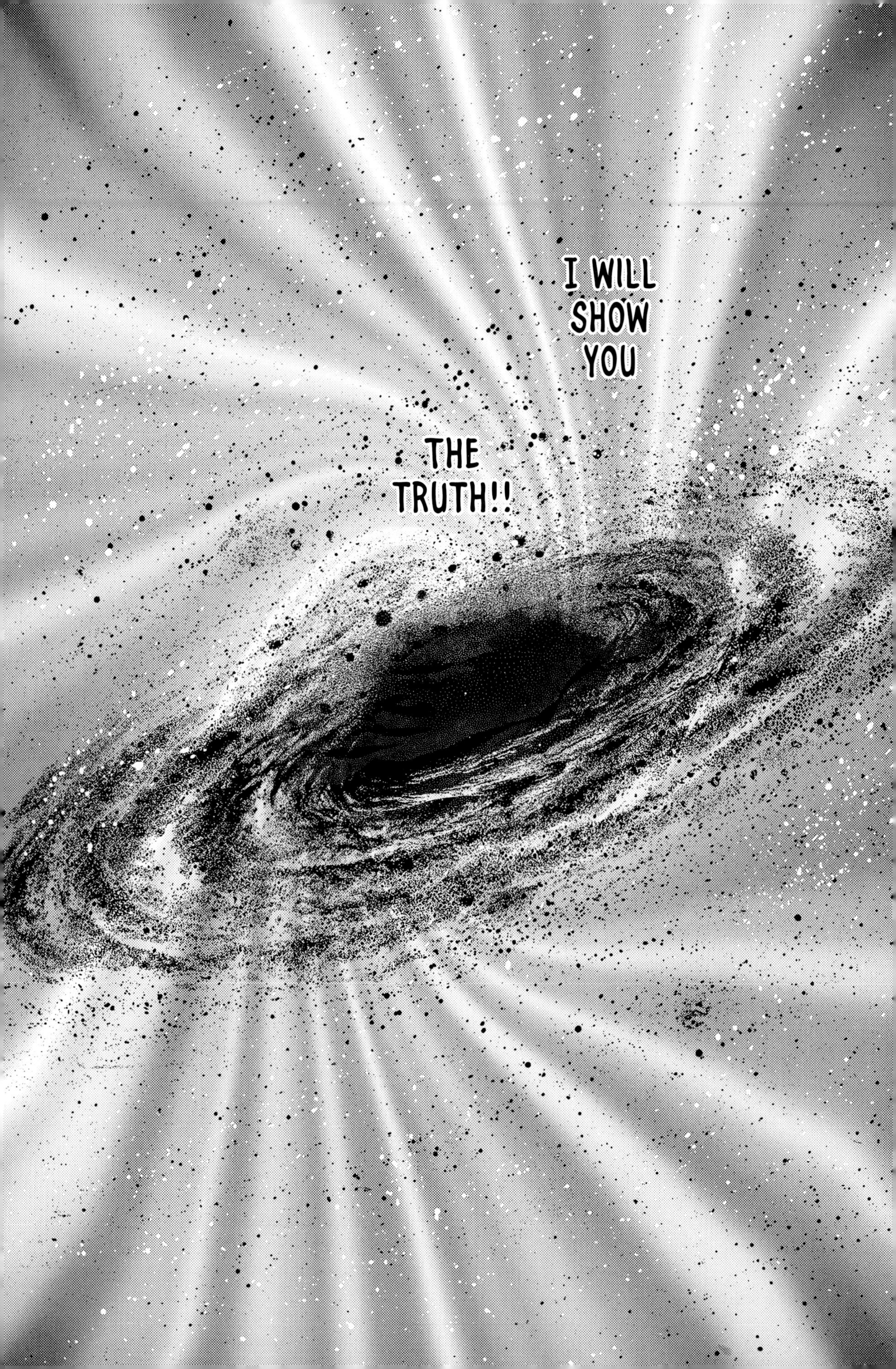
I WILL SHOW YOU
THE TRUTH!!

Pretty Guardian

Sailor Moon

Translation Notes

The Three Lights, page 17

The members of everyone's favorite boy band each have names that call to mind star-quality images. Yaten means "night sky," Taiki means "atmosphere," and Seiya means "field of stars." Each of the three has the given name Kô, which is likely the inspiration for their group's name, as it means "light."

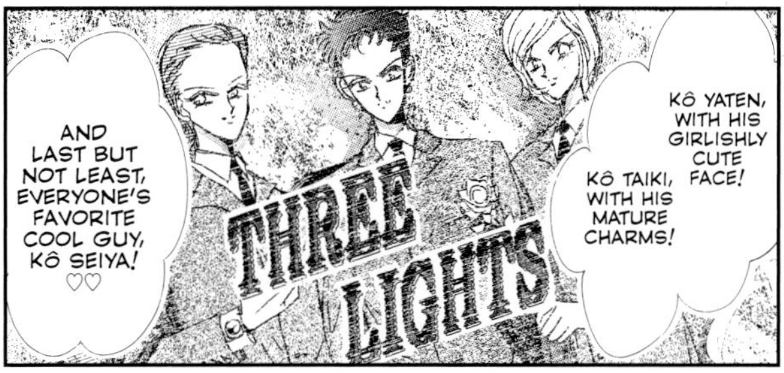
KÔ YATEN, WITH HIS GIRLISHLY CUTE FACE!
KÔ TAIKI, WITH HIS MATURE CHARMS!
THREE LIGHTS
AND LAST BUT NOT LEAST, EVERYONE'S FAVORITE COOL GUY, KÔ SEIYA! ♡♡

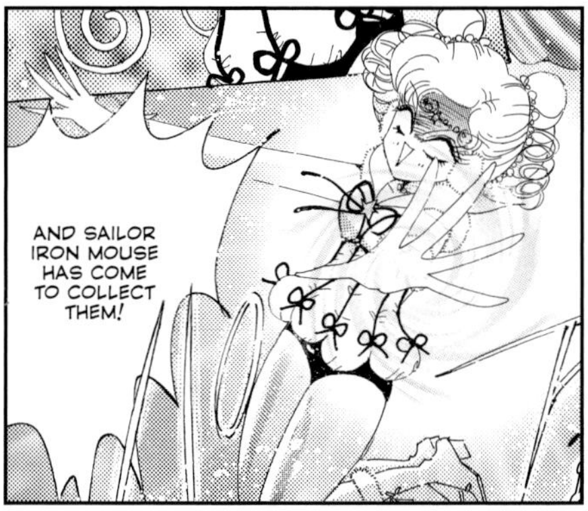
AND SAILOR IRON MOUSE HAS COME TO COLLECT THEM!

Sailor Iron Mouse, page 42

Iron is one of the seven metals known to the classical world, and in classical alchemy, each metal was associated with a planet. This may be why each of the Sailor Anima Mates is named after a metal.

There is also, in Japanese folklore, a legend of a supernatural creature called Tesso, which literally translates to "iron mouse." Tesso was the vengeful spirit of a Buddhist priest who transformed into a giant mouse/rat and summoned an army of rodents to attack a rival Buddhist temple.

Galactica Crunch, page 48

Though widely disproven by now, there was once a theory that posited that the universe would end in the opposite of a Big Bang—a Big Crunch. According to this theory, eventually the density of matter would cause gravity to overcome the expansion of the universe, and everything would fall back in on itself in a big crunch. This may be where Sailor Iron Mouse got the inspiration for her attack name.

Dinner time, page 57

Harvard in Massachusetts is 14 hours behind Jûban in Tokyo during standard time. If Usagi is getting out of bed at 7:30 on a Monday morning, it would be 5:30 Sunday evening at Harvard.

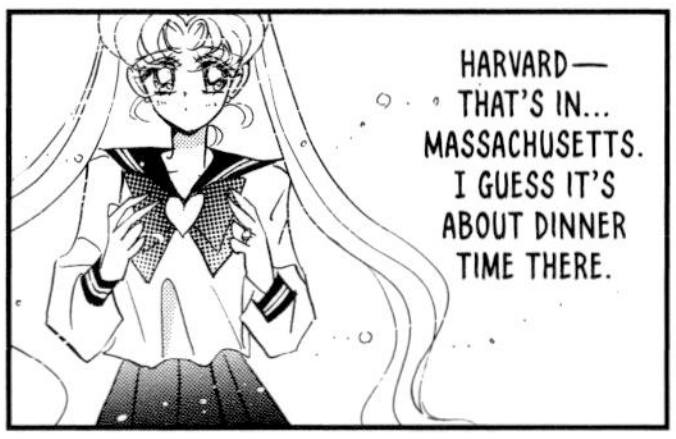
HARVARD— THAT'S IN... MASSACHUSETTS. I GUESS IT'S ABOUT DINNER TIME THERE.

Airmail, page 69

After the advent of aviation, letters could be carried to more distant locales *par avion*, or "by airplane." This was called "sending a letter by airmail," and was the most common way to communicate with someone in a far-off country, due in large part to the expense involved in making long-distance telephone calls. The recipient a letter sent in this manner would know that it had traveled by plane by the distinctive red and blue slanted marks bordering the envelope. This is what causes Usagi to believe that the letter came from America despite the lack of a return address.

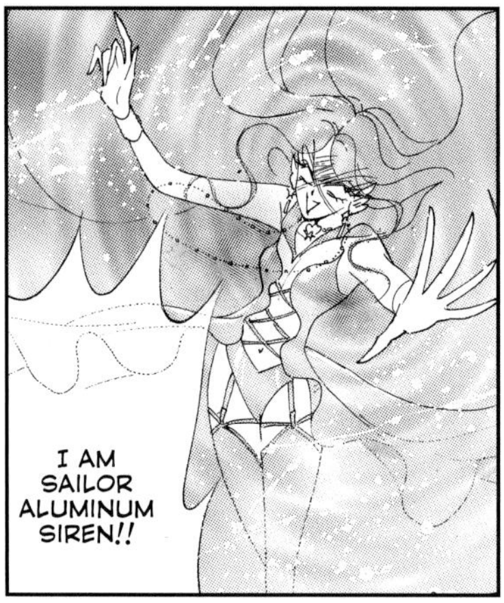
I AM SAILOR ALUMINUM SIREN!!

Sailor Aluminum Siren and Galactica Tsunami, page 87
The translators would like to assure our readers that, normally, when the Japanese speak of the lightweight silver metal, the word used is "aluminium," though they abbreviate it to "alumi." However, this Sailor Soldier pronounces her name with no I between the N and the U, using the same spelling as Humphry Davy, the chemist who gave the metal its name. She also bases her pronunciation of "Siren" on the original word (from Greek), and so technically it sounds closer to say-rain than SIGH-ren.
Sailor Aluminum Siren is also the only one of the Sailor Anima Mates in this volume who does not share her name with one of the seven planetary metals of alchemy. However, aluminum *is* associated with space, in that all human-made space vehicles have included aluminum in their construction since Earth's first human-made satellite in 1957.
The name Galactic Tsunami may have been inspired by a phenomenon sometimes called a "cosmic tsunami," which refers to the shockwaves produced when galaxies collide, and also perhaps for her heritage as coming from the (presumably water-related) planet Mermaid.

The Sagittarius A meteor shower, page 108

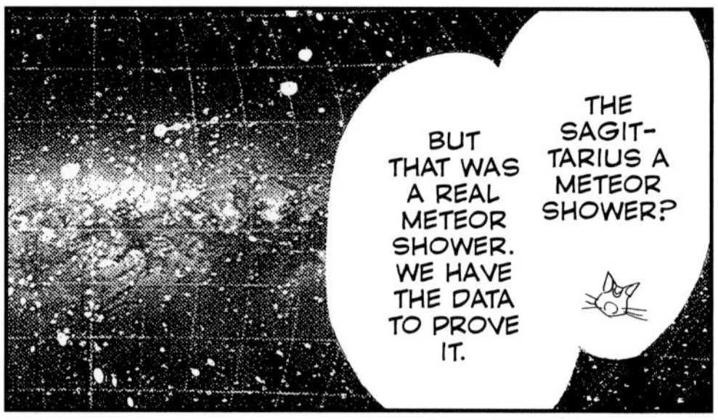
THE SAGIT-TARIUS A METEOR SHOWER?
BUT THAT WAS A REAL METEOR SHOWER. WE HAVE THE DATA TO PROVE IT.

Meteor showers are named after their radiant—the place in the sky from which they seem to radiate. Often this means they are named after a constellation. The Sagittariids meteor shower takes place in June every year, and that may be the real meteor shower that Artemis is referring to. But this time, the shower radiates from a very specific part of the large constellation: Sagittarius A. Not to be confused with Alpha Sagittarii (the alpha star of the Sagittarius constellation, designated with the lower case Greek letter α), Sagittarius A is a complex heavenly object found at the center of our Milky Way Galaxy. It consists of three components: the supernova remnant Sagittarius A East, the cosmic "Minispiral" Sagittarius A West, and Sagittarius A* (pronounced "A-star"), the supermassive black hole that is the gravitational center of the galaxy. It should be noted that the Roman letter A and the Greek letter Alpha look the same when capitalized, so while the pronunciation provided for the star in the original Japanese text is "alpha," the written character representing the whole word is A, which can be a capital alpha or a capital A.

Direction of the Horse, page 136

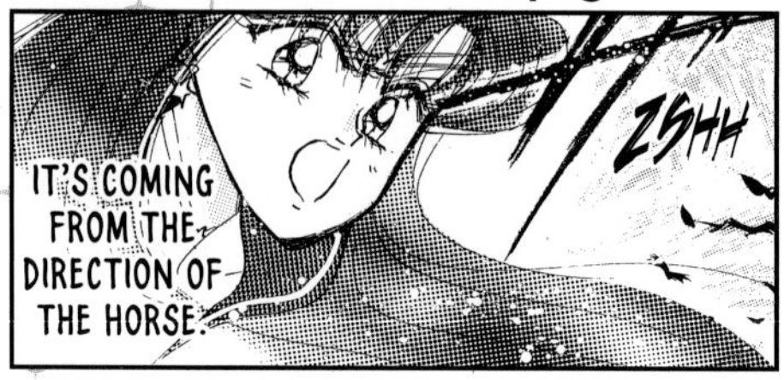
ZSHH
IT'S COMING FROM THE DIRECTION OF THE HORSE!

The twelve signs of the lunar zodiac are not only applied to years and hours of the day, but to directions as well. It starts with the Rat in the north and goes clockwise. The Horse is the seventh sign of the zodiac, which puts it in the south. In other words, Rei was using a mystical way of saying, "Ominous energy at six o'clock!"

Sailor Koronis, page 143
The name Koronis may be derived from the Greek *korone*, meaning "crow," or the Greek koronis, meaning "curved one." Either way, it appears in Greek mythology in relation to crows more than once. Most notably, a lover of Apollo named Coronis was unfaithful to him, and it was a crow that gave Apollo news of her affair. She is often associated with the constellation Corvus, the crow.

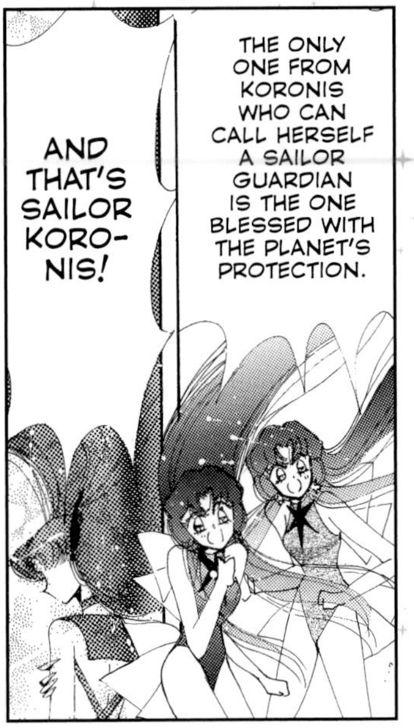
THE ONLY ONE FROM KORONIS WHO CAN CALL HERSELF A SAILOR GUARDIAN IS THE ONE BLESSED WITH THE PLANET'S PROTECTION.
AND THAT'S SAILOR KORO-NIS!

Galactica Tornado, page 143
The name for this attack may have been inspired by space tornadoes, which are the giant solar windstorms that are believed to be the cause of the aurora borealis phenomenon. It may also refer to cosmic tornadoes farther out in space that are caused by Herbig-Haro objects, which form when stars shoot ionized gas out into space, and that gas barrels into clouds of space gas and dust. As the HH object charges through space, it leaves a trail that looks much like a tornado.

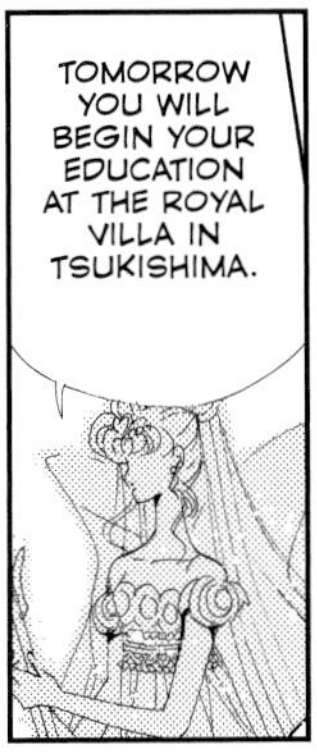
TOMORROW YOU WILL BEGIN YOUR EDUCATION AT THE ROYAL VILLA IN TSUKISHIMA.

Tsukishima, page 157
Literally meaning "moon island," Tsukishima is a real island in Tokyo that was built using reclaimed land. But this is a thousand years in the future, so it is unclear if this is a reference to the actual Tsukishima (which would now be a part of Crystal Tokyo), or if it is a new Moon Island named in honor of the Queen's lunar heritage.

Nyanko Suzu, page 168
Nyanko is an unusual name, even in Japanese—or at least, it is for a person. While it's not uncommon for a girl's name to end in -ko, *nyan* means "meow," and is therefore generally reserved for animals that make that noise. A literal translation of the name would be "meow child"... in other words, "kitty." *Suzu* means "bell," as in the bells Nyanko wears on her choker and uniform bow, or the bells attached to cat collars to prevent them from sneaking up on birds or people. With a different *kanji* character, the word *suzu* refers to one of the planetary metals: tin.

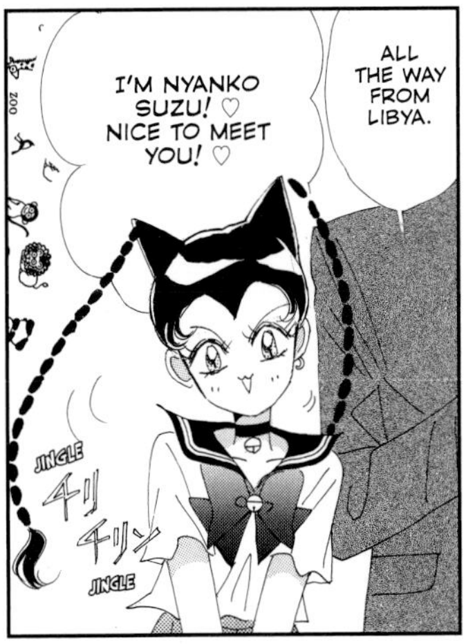
ALL THE WAY FROM LIBYA.
I'M NYANKO SUZU! ♡ NICE TO MEET YOU! ♡
JINGLE
JINGLE

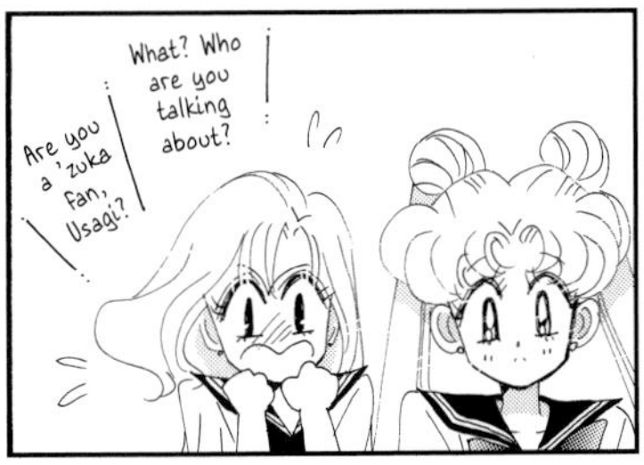
What? Who are you talking about?
Are you a 'zuka fan, Usagi?

A 'zuka fan, page 170
Short for the Takarazuka Revue, which is a theatre troupe of all women who put on big, elaborate stage shows. Because the troupe is all female, even the male roles are played by women. Usagi's friend doesn't know which girls at school might be dressing as boys, or which boys might actually be girls, so the Takarazuka Revue is the first thing she thinks of when Nyanko brings it up.

Sparrows for dinner, page 181

In Japan, there are two dishes called *suzume-yaki*, or "grilled sparrow." One is a local delicacy of Chiba Prefecture, and is actually a kebab of crucian carp, a fish native to that region. It may have gotten its name from its resemblance to the other *suzume-yaki*, which actually is a kebab of grilled sparrow, and can be purchased in the Fushimi Inari area of Kyoto.

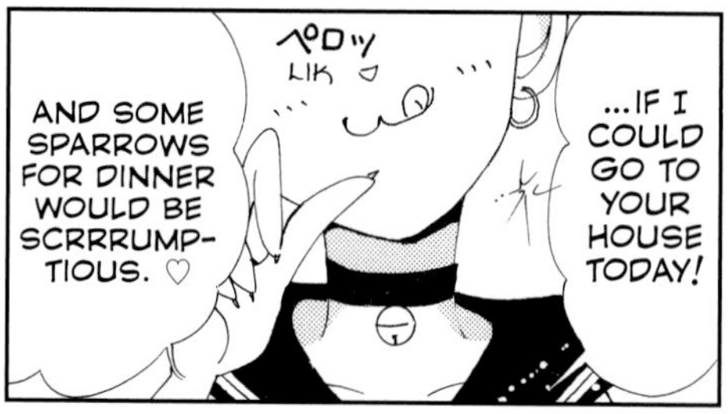
...IF I COULD GO TO YOUR HOUSE TODAY!
AND SOME SPARROWS FOR DINNER WOULD BE SCRRRUMPTIOUS. ♡

Galactica Puppet, page 196

The name of this attack may have been inspired by a science fiction novel from the 1950s called *The Cosmic Puppets*, about humans who get caught in the crossfires of a supernatural war between demigods. One of the characters in the book has control over cats.

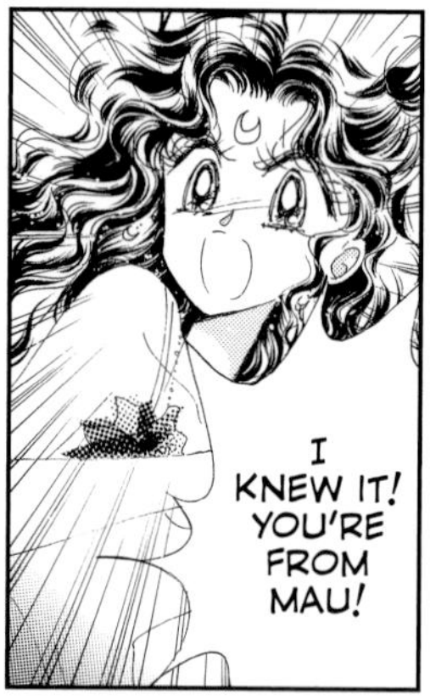
I KNEW IT! YOU'RE FROM MAU!

The Planet Mau, page 197

Mau means "cat" in the language of Egypt, where cats were highly honored for killing venomous snakes and scorpions. There were two feline Egyptian goddesses, both of whom were seen as protectors.

Princess Kakyû, page 207

The word *kakyû* literally means fireball, and is not only a ball of fire, but the name for extraordinarily bright shooting stars. She hails from the Tankei Kingdom of *Kinmoku-sei*, both of which have names related to the sweet olive blossom, or sweet osmanthus—the pale orange blossoms seen on Kakyû's headdress. The Japanese name for the flower is *kinmokusei*, and since *sei* can also mean "star" or "planet," the Planet (or Star) Kinmoku—*kinmoku-sei* in Japanese—turns into a pun. Tankei is the Japanese pronunciation of the Chinese word for the tree on which these blossoms grow. Chinese legend has it that there is a sweet olive tree growing on the moon. In the language of flowers, the sweet olive blossom means "humility" or "noble one."

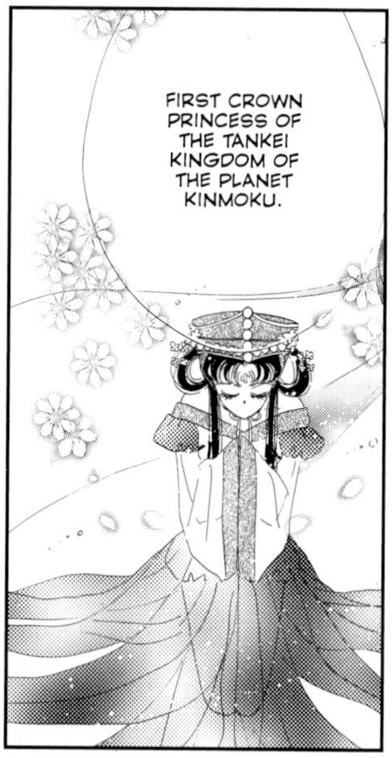
FIRST CROWN PRINCESS OF THE TANKEI KINGDOM OF THE PLANET KINMOKU.

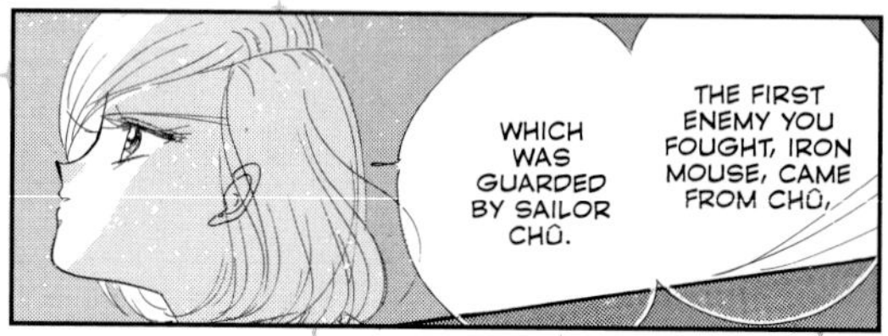
THE FIRST ENEMY YOU FOUGHT, IRON MOUSE, CAME FROM CHÛ,
WHICH WAS GUARDED BY SAILOR CHÛ.

Sailor Chû, page 218

Chû is the Japanese word for the sound mice make, or "squeak."

A Kodansha Comics Trade Paperback Original
Sailor Moon Eternal Edition volume 9 copyright © 2014 Naoko Takeuchi
English translation copyright © 2020 Naoko Takeuchi
First published in Japan in 2014 by Kodansha Ltd., Tokyo.

Published in the United States by Kodansha Comics, an imprint of
Kodansha USA Publishing, LLC, New York.

Publication rights for this English edition arranged through
Kodansha Ltd, Tokyo.

ISBN 978-1-63236-596-5

Printed in China.

www.kodanshacomics.com

9 8 7 6 5 4 3 2 1

Translation: Alethea Nibley & Athena Nibley
Lettering: Lys Blakeslee
Editing: Lauren Scanlan
Kodansha Comics edition cover design by Phil Balsman